# BY FRANZ PICK

BLACK MARKET YEARBOOKS, 1951-1955 (Pick Publishing, New York)
COMMON STOCKS VS. GOLD (Pick Publishing, New York)
GOLD - HOW AND WHERE TO BUY AND HOLD IT (Pick Publishing, New York)
THE NUMBERED ACCOUNT (Pick Publishing, New York)
PICK'S CURRENCY YEARBOOKS, *An Annual Publication since 1955* (Pick Publishing, New York)
PICK'S WORLD CURRENCY REPORTS, *A Monthly Publication since 1945* (Pick Publishing, New York)
SILVER - HOW AND WHERE TO BUY AND HOLD IT (Pick Publishing, New York)
UNITED STATES DOLLAR - ANALYSIS OF CRITICAL DEPRECIATION (Pick Publishing, New York)
UNITED STATES DOLLAR - DEFLATE OR DEVALUE (Pick Publishing, New York)
UNITED STATES DOLLAR - REQUIEM FOR A DEAD HALF (Pick Publishing, New York)

*In Collaboration with Richard Lewinsohn:*

LA BOURSE (Payot, Paris)
SINN UND UNSINN DER BOERSE (S. Fischer Verlag, Berlin)

# BY RENÉ SÉDILLOT

ABC DE L'ECONOMIE (Hachette, Paris)
ABC DE L'INFLATION (Plon, Paris)
D'ACHILLE A ASTERIX, 25 PASTICHES D'HISTOIRE (Flammarion, Paris)
COMMENT LIRE UN JOURNAL ECONOMIQUE ET FINANCIER (avec Jacques Gascuel) (Dunod, Paris)
LE DRAME DES MONNAIES (Sirey, Paris)
LE FISC, OU L'ECOLE DES CONTRIBUABLES (Amiot-Dumont, Paris)
DU FRANC BONAPARTE AU FRANC DE GAULE (Calmann-Lévy, Paris)
LE FRANC ENCHAINE (Sirey, Paris)
LE FRANC, HISTOIRE D'UNE MONNAIE (Sirey, Paris)
LA GRANDE AVENTURE DES CORSES (Fayard, Paris)
HISTOIRE DES COLONISATIONS (Fayard, Paris)
HISTOIRE DES MARCHANDS ET DES MARCHES (Fayard, Paris)
L'HISTOIRE N'A PAS DE SENS (Fayard, Paris)
LA MAISON DE WENDEL (Riss, Paris)
PARIS (Fayard, Paris)
PERSPECTIVES DE L'ECONOMIE CONTEMPORAINE (Radar, Genève)
PEUGEOT (Plon, Paris)
LES SECRETS DU MARCHE DE L'OR (Sirey, Paris)
SURVOL DE L'HISTOIRE DE L'EUROPE (Fayard, Paris)
SURVOL DE L'HISTOIRE DE FRANCE (Fayard, Paris)
SURVOL DE L'HISTOIRE DU MONDE (Fayard, Paris)
TOUTES LES MONNAIES DU MONDE (Sirey, Paris)
LA VICTOIRE DE L'OR (André Martel, Paris)

# ALL
# THE MONIES
# OF
# THE WORLD

*A CHRONICLE OF CURRENCY VALUES*

## FRANZ PICK-RENÉ SÉDILLOT

*Published by*

PICK PUBLISHING CORPORATION • NEW YORK, N.Y. 10006

Library of Congress Catalog Card Number: 72-154984

*Printed in the United States of America by*
CROWN ADVERTISING PROCESS, INC., *New York, N. Y.*

# ACKNOWLEDGMENTS

René Sédillot's book, *Toutes les Monnaies du Monde,* was translated from the original French by

## CAROL J. GOLDEN

\* \* \*

Currency analysis, research and editing were conducted by the capable staff of Pick's World Currency Report:

## PHILIP P. COWITT, RONALD M. GREENEY, GEORGE T. STEVE

\* \* \*

The typing and retyping of the thousands of pages of constantly reworked manuscript was dutifully performed by a sometimes panicky Rosella T. Warner, assisted by Gloria Condorelli. Administrative procedures were efficiently handled by Helen Emmert.

Roy Blumenthal, President of the public relations firm, Roy Blumenthal International Associates, Inc., guided the publisher in presentation and promotion of this volume.

# FOREWORD TO THE FIRST EDITION

A brilliant economist was recently explaining to me, with the help of profound technical terminology, some very attractive theories. I was awed by the manner this man of principle reasoned, expounded and concluded until the moment when, impelled by I do not know what demon, I questioned him on a point of history. To my surprise he knew almost nothing about it. Was he ignoring the lessons of the past? I do not think so. He had not had the means or the opportunity of studying the matter. He was satisfied with assumptions in the light of recent experiments he had witnessed in his own little corner of our planet. He boldly elaborated his theorems on the basis of his own hypotheses.

This case is not unique. How many plans have thus been constructed in the dark of night? And how many definitive works have been written without the benefit of basic knowledge?

On the subject of currency, everyone, from ministers to housewives, has his own little pet ideas these days. Each one proposes and disposes. But who really knows the science of monetary facts?

I have on my desk a project submitted by an astute correspondent with a view to the creation of a "dualistic currency". The gist of it is to restore a unit of account parallel to current money. The author obviously does not have the slightest inkling that for eight or nine centuries all of Europe lived under this system. Undoubtedly, in a few hundred years from now, an expert of the same caliber will certainly reinvent the gold standard.

It is not because I feel contempt for such systems that I concentrated on simply gathering facts. It is more in view of supplying a base for the construction of doctrines. Moreover, it is because of personal preference for concrete certainties.

History in its crude state will be found in this chronicle. It is perhaps the only history that owes nothing to literature - an almost arithmetical history, condensed to a confrontation of dates and figures.

Monetary history does not lie. One can always split hairs about a battle or a discovery. Who won? Who discovered? No mistake can be made on the meaning of a devaluation; figures are pitiless.

I am aware that history is not a recapitulation of events, even if they are expressed mathematically. It must be interpreted, in other words understood, meaning that causes and effects must be linked. Monetary history is not exempt from this rule. But, in its domain, comments are often superfluous.

Political actions generate monetary facts: wars, revolutions and bad management precipitate the destiny of currencies. Monetary actions, in turn, give birth to political facts: major inflations, for instance, foster dictatorships. The comparison of a given social and political history and its simultaneous monetary history is sufficient to understand causes and effects.

Monetary events are interrelated: any exchange control implies a depreciation which, sooner or later, becomes a devaluation; any accelerating inflation inevitably erodes the value of a currency. It is only necessary to place the phenomena side by side according to their exact chronological succession to grasp their continuity.

This is why this chronicle was intended to be as dry as a catalogue. It would have been an easy matter to delve at length on the fate of every currency and every nation. It seemed preferable to me to avoid any idle chatter, and I intentionally adopted a telegraphic style whose very clipped manner is eloquent. I hope I will be believed when I state that I did not succumb to laziness of the pen when I resorted to an excessive dearth of words.

## CURRENCIES FROM A TO Z

My ambition would have been to gather into this volume the history of all currencies, from the dawn of the monetary age to the present time. But the history of three thousand years is already too prolific with respect to currencies. So, in order not to be accused of having erected a fragile monument for the sole use of rare erudites, I was obliged to touch only lightly on local and accidental issues: feudal or obsidional coins, those of Greek cities or of minor German princedoms, currencies of trust or of necessity. I have instead stressed mintings or printings of sovereign states. Even within this framework, I have the feeling my work is incomplete, and I would be surprised if it were not inaccurate in a few instances. How can one surely eliminate errors in such a wide grouping? I only hope that I have made few mistakes, and that they are not unforgivable.

The sources for this work were, in fact, as numerous as the currencies and the countries mentioned in it. They include all the classics on numismatics, monetary economics and the principal historical indices. I did not ignore Diderot's Encyclopaedia (Encyclopaedia of Commerce), the old currency almanacs, or contemporary dictionaries. Regarding our century, I am greatly indebted to the reports and publications of the League of Nations, the Bank for International Settlements and the International Monetary Fund (see bibliography).

\*   \*   \*

This chronicle has the same drawback inherent to dictionaries, in that it could never be read from A to Z. I expect those who refer to it are interested only in parts of particular benefit to themselves. Businessmen, bankers and exporters will be concerned with the latest definition of currencies. Sociologists will look for their original definition, historians for lines of descent; numismatists will be concerned with metallic coins, philatelists with divisional units and economists with fiduciary circulation. The object of a dictionary or chronicle is to present facts suitable for a variety of purposes.

There may be some inquisitive enough to enjoy learning about the origins of seashell money, of the various forms of the Ecu (5 Franc silver piece) and of the most recent exchange of banknotes in totalitarian countries. Honest men in our century have learned about monetary affairs - often at their own expense. They only need to know that the catastrophes, which have victimized them and which they believe are unique, have recurred throughout the ages and in each and every country.

How will they find out? - By leafing through the pages of this book and discovering how currencies are born, how they live and how they die.

# HOW ARE CURRENCIES BORN?

They come into existence at the very moment groups of human beings, who have become aware of the advantages to be derived from trading, progress beyond the elementary technique of barter and resort to an intermediate tool capable of measuring and representing values. In the 20th Century, we have witnessed the fall of proud civilizations which were doomed to revert to the barter age (i.e. clearing systems), after having failed to preserve a currency worthy of the name. Let us not, therefore, have contempt for the primitive societies who, by trial and error, invented money.

What money? Pastoral people naturally turned to animal currency. Cattle played a widely known role with the Indo-Europeans (see the origin of the name of the Rupee under *Rupee India;* see *India,* see *Rome*). Seafarers considered using fish as currency (see *Iceland*). This is what the Indian tribes of Canada resorted to (see *Wampum*) as well as the natives of Melanesia (see *Diwarra*). This explains the stupendous circulation on half the planet, from the archipelagoes of the Pacific to the Atlantic shores of the African continent, of a small porcelain-like shell, right up to the present time in certain instances (see *Cowrie*).

Agricultural currencies, more perishable and commonplace, were less successful. Certain peoples of Asia chose tea for that purpose (see *Tibet*) or rice (see *Korea*). Others selected a bitter almond from the Persian deserts (see *Badam*). The Aztecs resorted to cocoa beans (see *Mexico*). It so happened that Guinean negroes developed a passion for white cotton fabric with blue stripes which, by fulfilling a monetary function, received the name of Guineas (see *French Guinea*). It is also well-known that wheat and rye become monetary standards every time so-called civilized currencies begin to founder.

Mineral currencies were the most practical, because they were the most durable. Records show that certain tribes used millstones for money (see *Caroline Islands*). Other tribes in the Sahara or in Ethiopia still use salt bricks (see *Kantou, Amolés*). Let us not, therefore, consider them as relics or remnants of an absolutely defunct past. Further tampering with paper currency could, tomorrow, resurrect even more barbaric currency practices.

With metals, however, man advanced on the road to monetary practicality. Base metals were a definite improvement over common stones. Sparta and China used iron (see *Greece, China*); Sumatra and India used tin (see *Cache, Cheda, Bazarucco*); Argentina used tinplate (see *Peso Argentina*). Siam used lead (see *Rengui*). After Rome (see *As*), the whole world used bronze and copper, then nickel for divisionary coins. Platinum, a precious metal minted into coins, became an instrument of payments in Russia (see *Ruble*).

It is unnecessary to recall the triumph of silver and gold. These metals were predestined for their monetary mission, and everyone is aware of the recent and peculiar obsession of the yellow world for the white metal and that of the white world for the yellow metal.

Under what shape did metallic currencies spread? The plainest was the ingot, which persisted in Japan (see *Oban*). In primitive times, Sweden issued large copper plaques (see *Platmynt*); ancient Egypt used metal rods (see *Deben*). African blacks used bracelets (see *Manilla*). Greece made use of nails (see *Obol*), and wire threads were used in the Middle East (see *Larin*). Lydia and Ionia taught the Western World the method of stamping disc-shaped coins (see *Stater*). China sometimes preferred more exotic shapes resembling shoes (see *Sycee*), knives or the fruit of the elm tree (see *China*). Pre-Colombian America resorted to gold dust stuffed into bird bones (see *Mexico*), and the Sudan measured gold dust against the weight of carobtree seeds or grains of wheat (see *Miscal*).

Then came the age of fiduciary currency. It can be metallic if base metals or poor quality alloys are given excessive value - a thing which has often been done. It can be of an infinite variety of raw materials, from the moment a fixed value is decreed for any commodity. Carthage is said to have had leather currencies whose nominal value exceeded their real value (see *Carthage*).

China used squares of buckskin before our era (see *P'i Pi*), then silk fabrics, and finally paper (see *Pao Ch'ao, Kiao tze, Yen Ch'ao, Sseu Ch'ao ...*) more or less representing tea, salt or silk. Persia played its part in the advent of paper money. Venice introduced it in Europe (see *Venice*). France eyed paper money with distrust and preferred to try it out in its overseas trading posts (see *Canada, Mauritius*) before experimenting with it directly (see *Livre Tournois*).

# HOW DO CURRENCIES LIVE?

How do currencies live? Well or badly, long or briefly, depending on the solvency of princes or issuing states. Progressive erosion is the rule. Longevity is the exception. Like men and nations, no currency is eternal.

Certain currencies manage to survive through the centuries, not by remaining intact, but because of a slow rhythm of depreciation (see *Pound, Rupee India ...*). In France, a solid coin such as the Ecu and a unit of account such as the Livre Tournois held fast for over half a millenium.

The constant debasement of a given currency must be followed through the turmoil of the centuries to understand the life of the money. Admirably solid at the outset, it fritters away after every war, every revolution, every crisis. Ultimately, it weighs nothing at all, except if measured on high precision scales. Look up the Sou and its offspring, the Maravedi of Spain, which were made of gold, the Liard and the Denier which were made of silver and which now are nothing but ghosts.

But currencies manage to survive and to perpetuate themselves by propagating one another in such fashion that it becomes hard to tell if one is dealing with a particular currency or a family of currencies, with a mother unit or with a great granddaughter. They transmit their own substance either through recasting or by simple embossing (see *Resellado, Brazil, Jafimske...*). They bequeath their patronymic names to each other, the same way a title of nobility is handed down. In modern Greece, the Drachma is obviously only remotely related to the one of ancient Greece (see *Drachma*), even though in 1944, the Drachma succeeded its precursor after an exchange of 50 billion old units for one new one.

It sometimes happens that the genealogy of a currency family tolerates liberties of sorts with first names, which become part of a permanent name. Thus the Rentenmark succeeded the Mark before passing on the torch to the Reichsmark, then to the Deutsche Mark and, eventually, even to the East Mark. Who can remember their ancestors ranging from the Hamburg Mark to the old Cologne Mark, which represented half a pound of silver?

It sometimes happens that a name transforms itself in time or space with a change of language. The Roman Denarius became the Carolingian Denier, which gave birth to the Denier Tournois and the Denier Parisis - without even mentioning countless feudal Deniers, the Denaro and the Spanish Dinero. In northern countries, it was supplanted by the Penny, Pfennig, Penning, Penni, Fennigy ... In the Orient, it made an impact on the Arabian Dinar, on the Persian Dinar and even reached right up to the present Dinars of Yugoslavia, Iraq and Jordan (see all these names).

Likewise, the silver coin struck in the Bohemian city of Joachimsthal and which was named Joachimsthaler, or Thaler for short (see *Thaler*), was worthy of a remarkable fate in the monetary language - not only in the Old World with Dalers, Daalders, Doleras, Talars, Talaris, Talleros ..., but also, and especially so, in the New World, where the Thaler underwent a metamorphosis into the Dollar. Gathering new momentum, it sprang across the Pacific, giving its name to the Chinese Dollar, the Hong Kong Dollar and the Straits Settlements Dollar.

This time, the loyalty shown toward the name was duplicated by the loyalty to the very type of currency itself. Just as the multiples of the Drachma had conquered the Mediterranean at the dawn of the monetary era, or in the same manner the Roman Denarius had spread and had been copied in barbarian Europe, certain types of currencies have lastingly attracted people in modern times. One of the most successful coins was the 22 to 27 gram silver coin which met with considerable acceptance to a degree. Certain countries like Indochina, for example, refused for a long time to accept any other means of payment.

This type of coin was born in Spain right after the discovery of America, which looked promising as a source of the white metal. It first received the name of Duro (see *Duro*). The Thaler, a heavier money, was gradually debased to a weight close to that of the Duro (see *Thaler*). The Spanish and the German coins, both produced under the Holy Roman Empire of Charles V, were destined to radiate all over the world.

*xi*

The Maria Theresia Thaler of Central Europe (Austria) conquered the Arab and African worlds which, from the Persian Gulf to Nigeria (see *Maria Theresia Thaler*), remained until the 20th Century stubbornly loyal to the coinage bearing the effigy of an unknown empress.

Transplanted to Mexico, the Spanish coin (see *Mexican Piaster*) gave birth to all the Pesos of Latin America, all the Dollars of North America and of the Pacific shores and even to coins of Madagascar.

It is certainly not by accident that when the French Ecu was changed to silver (see *Ecu*), it more or less aligned itself with that of the reigning coin, and that its descendant, the French 5 Franc piece of Germinal which contained an almost equal amount of silver, became widely accepted not only within the framework of the Latin Monetary Union (see *Union Latine*) but also in the Caribbean (see *Gourde*) and in South America (see *Peso Argentina, Peso Colombia, Bolívar...*).

The astonishing circulation of this type of coin from the 16th to the 19th Century is only one example of the expansion of certain reputable currencies. As a general rule, the prestige of coins is equal to that of the states that mint them. In other words, the eminence of a nation, when established on the political level, also extends to literature, the arts, science, economics and, consequently, to the currency.

The age of Greek supremacy witnessed the triumph of Greek coinage from Aegina and Athens and later from Corinth and Rhodes. The Roman era consecrated the victory of Roman coinage, which was perpetuated by the Carolingian Denier on one hand and by the Byzantine Sou (Bezant) on the other.

In barbarian times, the Mediterranean became the last stronghold for gold. The Arabs copied the Bezant, called it the Dinar and spread it in Spain, where it became the Maravedi.

With the Crusades, gold reemerged in Sicily (Augustalis), in Florence (Florin, Fiorino or Guilder), in Venice (Zecchino), in Genoa (Genovino) and in Paris (Denier à l'Ecu). It was then that France, which had become one of the first ranking western nations, minted the Gros of Saint Louis, the heaviest of all silver coins, which supplanted the Denier and set a pattern for the whole of Europe.

The age of the Italian Republics during the artistic momentum of the Quattrocento saw the flourishing of the old Venetian Zecchino or Ducat, which swarmed all over the Near East, in barbaric nations, in Hungary, in the Holy Roman Empire and the Low Countries, and the spread of the Florentine Fiorino, Florin or Guilder, "which made fortunes" in Central Europe.

The Spanish age, as is well known, bequeathed a successful silver coin to the world. It also left as a legacy a gold coin, commonly called the Pistole (see *Pistole*), which served as a model for the French Louis.

The French era, in turn, glorified the Louis and laid the foundation for the worship of the Franc which, in the 19th Century, became the model for approximately fifteen young monetary units ranging from the Lev to the Lira, the Leu to the Peseta and later, for almost all the Pesos of Latin America, the

Russian Imperial, the Austrian Gulden, the Perper of Montenegro and even included the Persian Toman (see all *Francs*).

The British era was that of the Pound (see *Pound* ), and it is difficult to tell whether it was British grandeur which made the Pound, or if the greatness of the Pound made England. Both grandeurs buttressed each other. The gold standard, born in London by chance and through practical experience, drew all currencies into the wake of the British unit. Numerous countries based their currencies in relation to the Pound Sterling or guaranteed them by Sterling cash balances, e.g. currencies of the Dominions and of the Empire, Egyptian Pounds, Scandinavian Crowns, Portuguese Escudos... A number of Latin American Pesos deserted the Franc for the Pound, when they switched to the gold standard. Later, with the advent of exchange controls, the Sterling ·Area was more precisely defined. But, nevertheless, certain newly independent countries preferred to remain within the Area, such as India, Burma, Ireland, Jordan, Iraq and Iceland.

The American era is that of the Dollar (see *Dollar*). Having attained world supremacy, the United States made the Dollar the number one currency. It is in terms of Dollars that the system, born of the Bretton Woods Agreement, defined all exchange rates. It is on a rate equivalent to the Dollar that the European Payments Union defined its unit of account (see *EPU Unit of Account*). In the general collapse of foreign exchange values, the Dollar assumed the role of a life preserver at the very moment when American credits were propping up drowning economies and budgets.

Challenging the mighty Dollar, the Ruble tried to masquerade as a financial success by pretending, in the first place, to be a real currency. The satellite countries of the Soviet Union in Europe and in Asia, ranging from the Zloty to the Lev, Leu, Forint, Koruna and Tughrik, defined their currencies in Rubles. To show its contempt for the Dollar, the Ruble Bloc sang praises of the virtue of gold.

Among all these blue-blooded monetary families born of glory or of might, thousands of other monies - intruders born in obscurity - have wormed their way into the currency records during the course of the centuries. To list them all within this framework is tantamount to the sketching of an outline of a "History of Currencies" and a "Monetary Geography", an offshoot of human geography, for which the basic elements will be found in this work.

# THE PROLIFERATION OF CURRENCIES

Is the number of different currencies actually decreasing? Taking into consideration the countless number of currencies in circulation in feudal times, and that in recent centuries Germany and Italy had as many currencies as there were kingdoms, principalities or republics, it seemed that the trend, which was headed for a long time toward disintegration, had reversed itself and was leaning toward integration, and that progress realized on the road to political unification also implied monetary simplification.

This synopsis really is far too elementary. The truth is that the world goes through cycles of fragmentation and consolidation, each of which, in turn, multiplies or diminishes the number of currencies. There is reason to believe that the present trend leans more toward political and monetary separation. Monetary nationalism scores a double triumph by erecting higher frontiers and by multiplying them.

The very concept of monetary frontiers is a modern idea. More exactly, although countries had thought for a long time of isolating their currencies, they have really managed to do so only recently. In ancient times, such as the Feudal age and the era of monarchies, all currencies, de facto and often de jure, circulated everywhere. Greek, Persian and Roman coins circulated well beyond the limits of the cities or the nations, which had minted them. The English Esterlin (see *Esterlin*) was accepted all over the Continent, which struck imitations and flooded England with them. Saint Louis paid his ransom in Bezants. The ancient trade fairs of the old province of Champagne were the favorite rendezvous of all contemporary currencies. Even during the centuries of triumphant mercantilism, payments were made in Austria with French Ecus, in France with Spanish Pistoles, in Spain with British Guineas, in England with Venetian Zecchini and in Venice with Turkish Piastres.

In the *Miser and the Ape,* La Fontaine, the renowned French fabulist, illustrates quite well the geographic variety to be found in a hoarder's strongbox:

... He picked up a Doubloon,
A Jacobus, a Ducaton
Then a Rose Noble. ...

Where does this internationalism of currencies still exist today? Perhaps in the small shops of the rue Es-Siaghine in Tangiers and probably nowhere else. Every currency lives in solitary confinement and remains snugly sheltered at home. Former British Dominions have demonetized the Pound Sterling. Cuba has rejected the Dollar. If, by chance, certain coins are still currently in use far from their birthplace, they have, however, ceased to be legal tender in their own country. For example, the Sovereign which still circulates in Saudi Arabia, or the Maria Theresia Thaler, to which the Ethiopians have remained attached for so long.

Modern foreign exchange controls have pushed monetary nationalism to unprecedented heights, which has not only hindered the flow of monetary metals, but also that of paper money.

If borders are less penetrable than in bygone days, they have, nevertheless, considerably increased in number. Political partition has resulted in monetary separation. In the 18th Century, only four currencies existed on the American Continents. In the middle of the 20th Century, their number had increased to twenty-four, not counting the Caribbean Area. Central America alone, which had but a single Peso in 1830, now has the Quetzal in Guatemala, the Colón in El Salvador, the Lempira in Honduras, the Dollar of British Honduras, the Córdoba in Nicaragua, the Colón in Costa Rica and the Balboa in Panama. One currency split into seven different ones. Nonetheless, the New World sanctimoniously pretends to give lessons about unity to the Old World.

# HOW DO CURRENCIES DIE?

How do currencies die? Some fade away rapidly or are promptly wiped out following financial calamities (see *Mandat*), or else they follow the fate of shaky nations (see *Lat, Litas, Kuna, Carbovanez*) or, perhaps, their career lasts only as long as that of the prince they publicize (see *Carolus, Fredericks d'Or, Guillaume d'Or...*). Some of these promotional currencies have survived their creators, either because the ruler they extolled was of great renown, or because several successive sovereigns bore the same first name such as, for instance, the Louis.

Sooner or later, all monies die of wear and tear as a result of clipping or reduction in weight, or of debasement, depreciation and devaluation. As they become more and more devoid of substance, ruined currencies perpetuate their existence through their multiples. The Milreis replaced 1,000 Reis, and the Bilpengoe tried to substitute for a billion Pengoe. In anticipation of such events, there are strong currencies ready to take over weaker units. The Conto was worth 1,000 Escudos. The Greek Talent was equal to 6,000 Drachmae or 36,000 Obols. In Java, the Bahar was good for 100 million Candareens. In India, the Nil replaced one hundred billion Rupees...

Primitive peoples figured multiples of coins by stringing them together, by gathering them in pouches or rolls. In Indochina, a bundle of Sapèques stood for 600 perforated pieces. In China, a Tiao of Cash represented 10 rolls of 100 coins. In Java, 200 Caixas on a length of straw constituted a Sata, and 5 Satas became a Sapèque. In Angola, the Macuta was the equivalent of 2,000 Cowries.

These stratagems did not save currencies doomed by the passage of time. Some coins were flattened to the point where they were as thin as a sheet of paper (see *Bracteate*), or actually chopped up into strips, just as it was done to the 5 Franc coin in Madagascar (see *Madagascar*), or cut up into bits of all sizes and shapes as in the West Indies (see *Moco, Guiotin*) or in Russia (see *Jaftmske*). Some were punctured, and the hole then plugged with inferior metal (see *Moeda*).

More often and more surely as well, inflation gnaws into currencies and hastens their passage from life to death. Slow inflation in France, for instance, eventually wiped out all the submultiples of the Franc (see *Centime, Sou*). Galloping inflation, on the other hand, precipitates disasters (see *Assignat, Mark, Krone Austria, Ruble, Drachma, Pengoe*).

With a little perseverance it could, no doubt, be feasible to establish the general rules governing the degradation of currencies in relationship to political institutions and to geographical locations. Changes of regime produce widespread catastrophes. Democracies wear out currencies faster than monarchies. Money erodes more rapidly in warm climates than in northern latitudes.

The remains of dead currencies are the fortunes and misfortunes that they engendered and sometimes their names which remain engraved in the memories of mankind. The Liard and the Maille have become firmly rooted in proverbs and in a few expressions. The Fels of the Berbers and the Picaillon of Turin are now French slang expressions. The name of the deceased currency may lose all monetary meaning, when it becomes part of everyday speech. For example, the French word *mitraille* evolved from the Flemish *myte,* and the word gazette was derived from the Venetian coin Gazzetta, one of which paid for the first newspaper ever published. Even such bits of trivia will be found in this chronicle and, perhaps, a monetary philosophy revealed by the course of history will emerge by reading between the lines - the inevitability of deterioration.

Periods of monetary peace will appear to be short and rare. Currency disasters will be found to be plentiful, even during centuries reputed for their stability. Does this mean that there should be no faith in peace or in health? That would indeed be heartbreaking, and everything should be tried to make sure that currencies last as long as possible. But, since it is also useless to ignore war and disease, it would also be wise not to have blind faith in eternal peace or eternal health.

"It will come to a bad end" repeated Jacques Bainville's parrot in *Jaco et Lori.*

In the case of currencies, alas, it always ends badly.

René Sédillot
Paris, 1954

*xvi*

# FOREWORD TO THE SECOND EDITION

Nobody but my good friend, René Sédillot, could have written a better foreword to this volume. Due to our many years of cooperation in financial and monetary reporting, I asked and received approval for my organization to update and thus enlarge his unique volume, *Toutes les Monnaies du Monde, Dictionnaire des Changes,* published in Paris in 1954. We agreed to its presentation in English, which necessitated substantial reclassification of countries and names of units because of their different spellings. Therefore, countries and currencies are listed alphabetically, country headings being bold italic [*BELGIUM*] and currencies bold Roman [RUBLE]. When the name of the currency is used by more than one country, the name comes before the country [PESO ARGENTINA]. Otherwise, the original system of analysis of monetary changes has been scrupulously maintained. The only commentary besides the historic development of practically uninterrupted expropriation of currency owners was the addition of historic lows of the monetary units in the black market.

René Sédillot's masterly research covered the period from the origin of money until the end of 1953. My job began with the start of 1954 and extended over seventeen years of currency ruination which, unfortunately, did not cease when my colleagues and I terminated our chronicle on December 31, 1970.

It seems unbelievable that during these 17 years of world monetary survey which was added to the basic work of Mr. Sédillot, not less than 418 full or partial devaluations were decreed by some 108 governments. Certain currencies underwent numerous devaluations, Chile's unit being cut over 100 times and Brazil's at least 50. In other countries, such as Indonesia, not even an estimate of the number of these fraudulent state bankruptcies has been possible. Very little publicity has been given to these events which destroyed billions, if not trillions, of asset values without any kind of compensation for their cheated owners. The tombstones in the currency cemetery read as follows for the period of January 1, 1954 to December 31, 1970:

Afghanistan, Albania, Algeria, Argentina, Barbados, Bermuda, Bolivia, Brazil, British Honduras, Bulgaria, Cambodia, Cameroon, Canada, Central African Republic, Ceylon, Chad, Chile, Mainland China, Colombia, Comoro Islands, Congo-Brazzaville, Congo-Kinshasa, Costa Rica, Cyprus, Czechoslovakia, Dahomey, Denmark, Ecuador, Egypt, Falkland Islands, Fiji Islands, Finland, France, French Guiana, French Polynesia, Gabon, Gambia, Germany East, Ghana, Gibraltar, Guadeloupe, Guinea, Guyana, Hong Kong, Hungary, Iceland, India, Indonesia, Iran, Ireland, Israel, Ivory Coast, Jamaica, Korea South, Korea North, Laos, Lebanon, Macao, Malagasy Republic, Malawi, Mali, Malta, Martinique, Mauritania, Mauritius, Mexico, Monaco, Morocco, Nepal, New Caledonia, New Zealand, Nicaragua, Niger, Outer Mongolia, Pakistan, Paraguay, Peru, Philippines, Poland, Réunion, Romania, Rwanda, Saint Pierre et Miquelon, Saudi Arabia, Seychelles, Senegal, Sierra Leone, South Yemen, Spain, Sudan, Syria, Taiwan, Thailand, Togo,

Trinidad and Tobago, Tunisia, Turkey, Upper Volta, U.S.S.R., U.K., Uruguay, Venezuela, Viet Nam North, Viet Nam South, Wallis et Futuna, West Irian, Yugoslavia.

In addition to the units which were devalued, 80 currencies hit historic lows of value in worldwide free or black markets during the period covered. This dubious distinction could be applied to the monies of:

Afghanistan, Albania, Algeria, Angola, Argentina, Bolivia, Brazil, Bulgaria, Burma, Cambodia, Ceylon, CFA Area, CFP Area, Chile, Mainland China, Colombia, Congo-Kinshasa, Cuba, Czechoslovakia, Denmark, Dominican Republic, Ecuador, Egypt, El Salvador, Ethiopia, France, Ghana, Greece, Guatemala, Guinea, Haiti, Hong Kong, Hungary, Iceland, India, Indonesia, Iraq, Ireland, Israel, Japan, Jordan, Kenya, Korea North, Korea South, Laos, Libya, Malawi, Mali, Mexico, Morocco, Mozambique, New Zealand, Pakistan, Paraguay, Peru, Philippines, Poland, Portugal, Rhodesia, Romania, Ruanda-Urundi, Saudi Arabia, South Africa, Spain, Sudan, Surinam, Taiwan, Tanzania, Thailand, Tunisia, Turkey, Uganda, U.S.S.R., United Kingdom, Uruguay, Venezuela, Viet Nam South, West Irian, Yugoslavia, Zambia.

In contrast to this rather large grouping, only three countries proceeded with an increase in the value of their currencies in terms of gold during the report period. They were Canada, West Germany and the Netherlands. The Bahamas, Fiji and Hong Kong made technical upward adjustments of their units. However, all these so-called "upvaluations" were practically wiped out by the sharp increase of the cost of living in these countries.

At the beginning of 1971 when this extensive study went to press, a major monetary revolution was brewing. The United States Minidollar, still the globe's key reserve unit, had reached the inevitable destiny of every mismanaged currency. Preparation of a census of all individual monetary assets abroad (IRS Form 4683-U.S. Information Return on Foreign Bank, Securities and Other Financial Accounts), a major step to foreign exchange control and to gigantic black markets which automatically accompany such a system, will affect the entire world of paper money and lead to more expropriation of all those who obeyed currency legislation everywhere.

In concluding this foreword, I go back to the last sentence of René Sédillot's "avant-propos" of the 1954 edition and repeat it here in its original version:

"Pour les monnaies, ça finit toujours mal."

Franz Pick
New York, 1971

*xviii*

# ABBASI

**I.** - Unit of account and silver coin of **Persia**. From 17th to 19th Century Abbasi was worth ¹⁄₅₀ Toman or ¹⁄₅ Kran or Hor and was equivalent of 2 Mahmudis, 4 Shahis, 10 Bisti, 40 Kazbegi, or 200 Dinars.

Origin of name - From Persian Shah, Abbas I (1587-1629).

Variations of name - Bassi, Abagi, Abaze, Abbajer, Abassis.

**II.** - Silver coin in **Georgia**. Valued at 2 Usalton, 4 Chaouri or 40 Carbequi. Minted by decree on October 21, 1802, until 1833 in Russian-annexed Georgia. It was then called Abaze. Equivalent to 20 Kopeks.

**III.** - Submultiple (¹⁄₃) of **Afghanistan** Rupee, corresponding to 20 Pice. - See *Rupee Afghanistan*.

# ABU DHABI

**1892** (March) - Sheikdom entered into "Exclusive Agreement" with Great Britain becoming part of Trucial States protectorate. - See *Trucial States*.

Principal currency in circulation was Indian Rupee. - See *Rupee India*.

**1958** - Oil discovery transformed economy of Abu Dhabi.

**1959** (April 28th) - Special Persian Gulf Rupee replaced Indian Rupee. - See *Rupee Persian Gulf*.

**1966** (June 5th) - Following devaluation of Indian Rupee, Abu Dhabi adopted Bahrain Dinar as its currency. - See *Dinar Bahrain*.

**1969** (October 22nd) - Abu Dhabi became provisional capital of newly formed Federation of Arab Emirates. - See *Federation of Arab Emirates*.

# ABUKASH

Name given to Dutch Daalder by the **Arabs** and **Egyptians** during 17th Century in **Smyrna, Constantinople** and the **Levant**.

Origin of name - From Turkish *aslain*, Arabic *abuquelp* (from imprint of lion on coin).

Variations of name - Abukesb, Abukesh, Abou-kelb.

# ABYSSINIA

See *Ethiopia*.

## ACKEY

Silver coin minted in 1796 and 1818 by British African Company for circulation on **Gold Coast**. Divided into 8 silver Takoe and worth 20 grains of gold dust.


## *ADEN*

Arabic monies (see *Arabia*), followed around 1886 by introduction of monetary system of British India. - See *Rupee India*.

**1951** (October 1st) - Legal tender status given to East African Shilling of 100 Cents. - See *Shilling East Africa*. Continued circulation of the Maria Theresia Thaler.

**1963** (January 18th) - Joined 14 other emirates, protectorates, sultanates and sheikdoms to make up Federation of South Arabia.

**1965** - East African Shilling replaced by South Arabian Dinar at par. - See *Dinar South Arabia*.

**1967** (November 30th) - Southern Yemen People's Republic proclaimed. - See *Southern Yemen*.


## AFGHANI

Monetary unit of **Afghanistan** created in 1927. Divided into 2 Kran or 100 Puli or Pouli.

Multiple - Amani, a gold coin of 20 Afghanis.

Bank of issue - Da Afghanistan Bank.

Predecessors - See *Afghanistan, Rupee Afghanistan*.

**1927** - The Afghani replaced Afghanistan Rupee at par. Minted as silver coin of 100 grams of 900 fine silver. Circulated along with foreign gold coins and Persian silver coinage.

**1936** - Stabilization in relation to Indian Rupee:
      1 Indian Rupee = 3.65 Afghanis

**1947** - Official parity: 1 U.S. Dollar = 13.44 Afghanis

**1948** (December 23rd) - 1 U.S. Dollar = 14.17 Afghanis

**1949** (October 1st) - 1 U.S. Dollar = 16.80 Afghanis

**1952** (February) - Multiple rate system created:
      1 U.S. Dollar = 16.80 Afghanis (basic rate)
      1 U.S. Dollar = 21.00 Afghanis (second category for imports)

**1954** (March 19th) - 1 U.S. Dollar = 30.00 Afghanis (third category for imports)

**1956** (October 24th) - Three above official rates revised. Multiple rate system still in existence:
      1 U.S. Dollar = 20.00 Afghanis (first category)
      1 U.S. Dollar = 28.00 Afghanis (second category)

Various other rates created, periodically adjusted and applicable to imports and exports.

Also, officially acknowledged fluctuating free market rate existed.

**1961** - Three fluctuating free market rates in existence:
Bank of Afghanistan Rate
Pashtany Commercial Bank Rate
Bazaar Rate

**1963** (March 22nd) - Comprehensive reform of exchange rate system. Official parity registered with International Monetary Fund:
1 Afghani = 19.7482 milligrams of fine gold
1 U.S. Dollar = 45.00 Afghanis
1 U.S. Dollar = 32.00 Afghanis (official rate minus 28.29%
tax for cotton exports)
1 U.S. Dollar = 34.00 Afghanis (official rate minus 24.44%
tax for wool exports)
1 U.S. Dollar = 38.00 Afghanis (official rate minus 15.56%
tax for karakul exports)

Multiple rate system constantly revised by changing export taxes and shifting categories.

**1965** (June 17th) - Da Afghanistan Bank began to keep its fluctuating rate within 2 Afghanis either side of Bazaar rate.

**1968** (May 5th) - Export taxes replaced by various subsidies, except in the case of walnuts.

**1970** (December) - Value of Afghani on the Bazaar deteriorated to record low of 86.50 per U.S. Dollar.


## AFGHANISTAN

**19th Century** - Circulation of Persian, Indian and Russian monies.

**1890** - Attempt at establishing a mint for coining of national money.

**1907** - British occupation. Monetary system: combination of Indian and Persian with Afghanistan Rupee or Rupee of Kabul (Kabuli Rupee) as currency unit. Divided into 2 Kran, 3 Abbasis, or 60 Pice. - See *Rupee Afghanistan.*

**1921** - Independence.

**1927** - Adoption of a national currency. - See *Afghani.*


## AGNEL

**I.** - Gold money of **France** from 14th to 15th Century, also called Mouton.

Origin of name - From design of Easter lamb on coin.

Plural - Agneaux.

**1311** (January 27th) - Philip the Fair minted gold Denier called Agnel, copied from Ecu of Saint Louis. It contained 4.19 grams fine gold, but had exchange rate of 20 Sous Tournois.

**1313** (June) - Exchange rate of Agnel reduced to 15 Sous.

**1316** (January 15th) - Exchange rate of Agnel lowered to 12 Sous 6 Deniers.

**1317** - Exchange rate raised to 18 Sous.

**1319** (July) - Exchange rate increased to 18 Sous 9 Deniers.

**1319** (December) - Exchange rate raised again to 20 Sous.

**1322** (October) - Exchange rate reduced to 12 Sous 9 Deniers.

**1325** - Exchange rate raised to 21 Sous.

**1343** - Minting of Agnel with same weight and exchange rate as the Denier à l'Ecu of Saint Louis.

**1354** (October 31st) - Minting of Mouton of 4.70 grams fine gold, having exchange rate of 15 Sous.

**1357** (March 12th) - Exchange rate raised to 30 Sous.

**1358** (January 23rd) - Exchange rate increased to 37 Sous 6 Deniers.

**1417** (May 10th) - Minting of Agnel/Mouton of 2.44 grams fine gold, having exchange rate of 20 Sous.

**1417** (October 21st) - Fineness of coinage reduced to 2.30 grams fine gold.

**1419** - Exchange rate reduced to 16 Sous 8 Deniers.

**1423** (March 10th) - Charles VII minted Mouton of 2.02 grams fine gold and having exchange rate of 17 Sous 6 Deniers.

**II.** - Gold coin imitation of the French Agnel or Mouton minted in a number of European states: **Savoy** (14th Century), **Flanders** (14th Century) and **Holland** (14th Century).


## AGORA

Submultiple (¹/₁₀₀) of **Israel** Pound since January 1, 1960. - See *Pound Israel.*
Plural - *Agorot.*


## AIDAN

In **Liege,** in **Maestricht** and in **Westphalia,** unit of account during 18th Century. Also called Liard or Oord (Ortje). - See *Oord.*


## AKCHEH

**I.** - Silver/copper coin in **Turkey,** introduced in 1328. Akcheh, or little Asper, worth ¹/₃ or ¹/₄ Para.
Variation of name - Akce.

**17th Century** - With introduction of Qurush, it was divided into 50 Akcheh. Relationship between two coins constantly changed.

**II.** - In currency of **Tunis,** Akcheh similar to Asper, or ¼ Kharub.

## AKSA

Monetary unit of **Tuva** in 1936. Divided into 100 Kopeks and equal to Ruble. - See *Tuva.*

## *ALASKA*

**Primitive money** - Strings of shells in form of teeth.

**19th Century** - Russian monies.

**20th Century** - Monetary system of United States. - See *Dollar.*

## *ALBANIA*

Greek, Roman, Byzantine, Venetian, Hungarian and Turkish monies.

**14th Century** - Issue of a Gros copied from Grosso of Venice.

**17th Century** - Venice issued Liretti and Soldi of silver, and Gazzetta of copper.

**18th Century** - Minting of silver Galeazzo, valued at 3 Lire.

**Before 1912** - Turkish monies: use of Piastre (or Qurush) of 40 Para. - See *Piastre Turkey.*

**1912 to 1925** - No unified monetary system. Composite circulation of Napoléons, Francs, Austrian Kronen, Lire and Drachmae.

**1925** (July 5th) - Adoption of an independent monetary system:
　　　　1 Albanian Franc = 1 Franc Germinal
　　　　1 Albanian Franc = 290.3225 milligrams of fine gold
　- See *Franc Albania.*

**1938** - Italian occupation:
　　　　1 Albanian Franc = 6.25 Lire

**1943** - German occupation. Issue of Reichskreditkassenscheine, denominated in Reichsmarks.

**1946** (November) - Lek, heretofore a submultiple of Albanian Franc, became monetary unit of Albania. - See *Lek.*

## ALBERTIN

Gold coinage in **Brabant, Tournai, Flanders** during government of Albert (beginning of 17th Century). Weight: 5.10 grams of gold 900 fine, or 4.6 grams fine gold.

## ALBUS

Unit of account and silver/copper coinage in various states of **Rhineland.**

Origin of name - Latin *Albus* (white). - See also *Blanc, Blanco, Witten, Hvid.*

**15th Century -** Minted by various German states.

**16th Century -** Albus minted by Four Electors of the Rhine. Exchange rate: 1/28 Guilder (Gulden).

**18th Century -** Albus was unit of account: Cologne (1/78 Thaler, or 12 Heller), Trier (1/54 Thaler), Upper Palatinate (1/30 Guilder, or 6 Pfenning), Hesse-Kassel (1/32 Reichsthaler, or 12 Heller).
It was a silver/copper coin in Cologne and Trier (sometimes called Petermaenger). In Cologne, 4 Albus coin called Blaffert or Plappart.

## ALEXANDER

**Bulgarian** gold coin of 20 Leva: 6.4516 grams 900 fine, or 5.80 grams fine gold. Equal to French 20 Franc coin (Napoléon).

Origin of name - From Alexander I of Battenberg, first Prince of Bulgaria from·1879 to 1886.

## ALFONSINO

In **Naples** and **Sicily,** silver coin minted by Alfonso I (1416-1458) called Dinheiro Alfonsino, with exchange rate of 1/9 Soldo.
Minted in gold by same king and called Alfonsino d'Oro.
Minted in silver by Alfonso V (Alfonsin or Grosso).

## ALFONSO

**Spanish** gold piece in the late 19th and early 20th Century: 8.065 grams 900 fine, equal to 25 Pesetas.

Variations of name - Alfonsino, Alphonse.

## *ALGERIA*

Monies of Carthage, Rome, the Vandals, Byzantines, Arabs, Moors, Spaniards, Turks, people of Barbary.

**17th Century -** For Oran, minting of copper coins in Maravedis (1618 and 1691). Mixed circulation of Spanish, Portuguese, French, Turkish and local coins, as well as Maria Theresia Thalers.

**18th Century** - In Kingdom of Tlemcen, gold coinage: Rubie (35 Aspers), Median (50 Aspers), Zian or Dian (100 Aspers).

**End of 18th Century** - Unit of account: Asper had multiples of Muzuna (29 Aspers), Saime or Double (50 Aspers), Pataca (8 Muzunas or 232 Aspers).
Specie money (as valued in Aspers): Pataca Gourda (696), Muzuna (29), Kharub (14), Sequin (1,972), Zecchino (2,320).
General circulation of Portuguese and Spanish specie monies.

**19th Century** - Before French conquest, local minting of Budschu (with multiples and submultiples). - See *Budschu.*
After French conquest, introduction of French monetary system.

**1851** (August 4th) - Privilege of banknote issue given to Banque de l'Algérie.

**1878** - Opening of an account by French Treasury with Banque de l'Algérie, thus permitting linking of Algerian currency to currency of Metropolitan France.

**1906** - In Southern Territories (Sahara), withdrawal from circulation of foreign coinage (Maria Theresia Thaler, Duros,. . .), often chipped or punctured by Nomads.

**1920** (August 8th) - Legal tender status for currency of Metropolitan France, including all divisionary coinage. - See *Franc Algeria.*

**1962** (December 31st) - Banque Centrale d'Algérie replaced Banque de l'Algérie as Central Bank.

**1964** (April 1st) - Algerian Dinar replaced Algerian Franc. - See *Dinar Algeria.*


## ALTILIK

**19th Century** - Silver/copper coinage in **Turkey,** largest of Metalliks: 12.90 grams 440 or 446 fine.

**1828** - Exchange rate 6 Piastres.

**20th Century** - Exchange rate of worn coins 5 Piastres.


## ALTYN

**I.** - Originally, unit of account in **Russia.**

Variations of name - Allin, Altinnik, Altininck.

**1655** - Russian copper coin worth 3 Kopeks. Exchange rate at par with silver specie. Rapidly depreciated to ¼ of initial value in 1662, to ⅕ in 1663).

**1663** - Withdrawn from circulation.

**1704-1721** - Minted in silver 700 fine. Valued at 3 Kopeks or 6 Dengi. Word "Altyn" remained unit of account.

**II.** - In **Turkey,** gold coin (called Altun) minted in 1478 in Constantinople, having same weight as Venetian Zecchino (3.49 grams).

Variations of name - Zekin (for Zecchino), Flury (for Florin), Ashrafi (in Egypt), Sultani (Barbary States), Funduk (beginning in 17th Century). - See *Funduk.*

# AMANI

I. - Gold coin of **Afghanistan** equal to 15 silver Kabuli Rupees, then 20 Afghanis.
II. - Silver coin of **Afghanistan** equal to 1 Kabuli Rupee.
Variation of name - Amania.

# AMERICAN SAMOA

**1899** - Treaty of Berlin gave United States authority over Samoan Islands now known as American Samoa. Use of American monetary system. - See *Dollar.*

# AMINDIVI ISLANDS

**19th Century** - British control. Introduction of monetary system of India. - See *Rupee India.*

# AMLIRA

Name (Allied Military Lira) given to banknotes denominated in Lire, issued by Allies in 1943 for occupied **Italy.**

# AMOLES

**17th and 18th Centuries** - Tablets of rock salt mined from Lafta Mountain and divided into smaller pieces according to need. Later, a salt bar from 20 to 25 centimeters in length, weighing about 700 grams. Extracted from former lake bed at Alalé-Bad, located south of Massaua. Served as divisionary money in **Ethiopia,** or as a submultiple of Talari. - See *Talari.*
Exchange rate between Amolés and Talari varied according to distance from place of extraction to place of usage:
　　　In Addis Ababa: 1 Talari = 5 to 6 Amolés
　　　In Harar: 1 Talari = 7 to 8 Amolés
Variations of name - Emolé, Annelet.

# ANCONA

Monies of Rome (see *Rome*), later Carolingian monetary system, then monetary systems of Papal States. - See *Papal States.*
**18th Century** - Scudo served as unit of account divided into 10 Paoli, 20 Soldi, 30 Bolognini, 100 Baiocco, or 240 Denari.

**19th Century** - Italian monetary system. - See *Italy*.

## ANDAMAN AND NICOBAR ISLANDS

**1858 and 1869** - British occupation. Subsequent introduction of Indian monetary system. - See *Rupee India*.

## ANDORRA

Mixed monetary system. - See *Peseta* and *Franc*.

## ANGE D'OR

**I. - French** gold coin minted by Philip VI in 1341 (6.30 grams fine gold) and in 1342 (5.70 grams fine gold).

Origin of name - From crowned angel on the obverse.

**II. -** Money used in the **Netherlands.**

**14th Century -** Gold coin in Flanders (minted 1387 equal to 60 Groten) and Brabant.

**15th Century -** Gold coin in Hainaut and Brabant (minted 1420). Also called Haies d'Or.

## ANGEL

Early gold coinage in **England.**

Origin of name - Coin pictured Archangel Michael slaying dragon.

**1465 -** Under Edward IV, minting of gold Angel, weighing 5.5 grams. Exchange rate: 6 Shillings 8 Pence. The ½ Angel called Angelet.

**1526** (October 30th) - Henry VIII raised exchange rate of Angel to 7 Shillings 6 Pence.

**1544** (May 16th) - Exchange rate raised to 8 Shillings.

**1552 -** Exchange rate raised to 10 Shillings.

**1604 -** Weight reduced to 4.6 grams.

**1619 -** Weight reduced to 4 grams.

## ANGELOT

**I. - French** gold coin (2.33 grams fine), issued by English in Paris during reign of Henry VI. Exchange rate: 15 Sous.

Origin of name - See *Angel*.

**II.** - In **England,** gold coin (called Angelet) struck by Edward IV in 1465 and equal to ½ Angel. Also minted by Edward V in 1483, by Richard III in 1484 and by Henry VIII in 1489.

## ANGOLA

Early unit of account - See *Macuta.*

Early unit of payment - Cowrie shells called Zembi, coming from Maldive Islands. - See *Cowrie.*

1 Macuta = 2,000 Cowries

**17th and 18th Centuries** - Introduction of Portuguese monetary system. Copper coins of 10 and 20 Reis (1693-1699, 1752-1757).

**1762** - Minting of coins denominated in Macutas: 2 to 12 Macutas in silver; 1 Macuta ' and its submultiples in copper.

1 Macuta = 50 Reis

**1814** - Minting of copper coins of 1 and 2 Macutas. - See *Macuta.*

**19th Century** - Portuguese monetary system. - See *Escudo Portugal.*

**1926** (September) - Monetary unit: Angolar of 100 Centavos linked to Escudo. - See *Angolar.*

New coin of 5 Centavos retained name Macuta.

**1958** (December 31st) - Angolar replaced. - See *Escudo Angola.*

## ANGOLAR

Early monetary unit of **Angola.** Divided into 100 Centavos.

Bank of issue - Banco de Angola established in 1926.

Predecessor - See *Angola.*

Plural - Angolares.

**1926** (September) - Creation of Angolar.

**1928** (July 1st) - Exchange of money denominated in Angolan Escudos for money denominated in Angolares at rate of:

80 Angolares = 100 Angolan Escudos

Angolar fixed at par with Escudo of Metropolitan Portugal:

1 Angolar = 1 Escudo

1 U.S. Dollar = 28.95 Angolares

**1958** (December 31st) - All banknotes bearing name Angolar withdrawn from circulation and ceased to be legal tender. Angolar replaced by Angolan Escudo at par with Portuguese Escudo. - See *Escudo Angola.*

# ANGSTER

Minor coinage of silver/copper or plain copper in some **Swiss** Cantons. Appeared as early as 15th Century.

**18th Century -** Equivalent of 2 Deniers, or ½ Rappe, ⅙ Shilling (in Lucerne), or 2 Heller (in Zurich).
Unit of account in Zurich: ¼ Kreuzer or 1/240 Guilder (Gulden).

## *ANGUILLA*

See *Leeward Islands*.

## ANNA

**I. -** In **Mogul Empire** and in **Bengal,** subdivided into 2 Poni, 8 Burrie, 40 Gunda, 160 Cowries.
**II. -** Submultiple (1/16) of **Indian** Rupee in form of a copper coin and nickel coins from ½ to 8 Anna until 1955. Afterwards, 4 and 8 Anna coins continued to circulate with value of 25 and 50 Cents.
Present day subdivisions: 4 Pice, 12 Pie.
**III. -** Submultiple (1/16) of **Pakistan** Rupee.
**IV. -** Submultiple (1/16) of **Burmese** Rupee, divided into 12 Pie.

## *ANNAM*

See *Indochina*.

## *ANTIGUA*

See *Leeward Islands*.

## *ARABIA*

**Before Christian Era -** Biblical monies: Siglos, Shekel.
**Before Mohammedan Era -** Byzantine gold Sou, Persian silver Drachma.
**7th Century -** Circulation of gold Dinars patterned after Bezant of Byzantium, silver Dirhem derived from Drachma, and copper Falus. - See *Dinar, Dirhem, Fels.*
**Arab expansion -** Koranic Law fixed and regulated medium of exchange as well as its

usage during Mohammed's time (c. 570-632): Dinar, Dirhem.

**1517** - Turkish conquest. - See *Turkey.*

**18th Century** - Unit of account: Piastre, divided into 80 Kabirs (or Kabukt, or Caveer). Specie money: Turkish, Egyptian, Spanish, Venetian types. Minting of silver/copper Comassir.

In Basra and around coastal area of Persian Gulf, system of account dervied from Persia: Toman equal to 100 Mahmudis, 1,000 Danims, or 10,000 Falus. Minting of copper Danims.

In Goumron (southern region of Persian Gulf), controlled by Persia until 1800: Toman equal to 100 Mahmudis or Abbasis.

**19th Century** - Turkish specie monies (see *Turkey*). Circulation of Maria Theresia Thaler which Turkish Government unsuccessfully tried to forbid.

**1913-1918** - Decline of Turkish influence. - See *Iraq, Jordan, Yemen, Muscat and Oman, Kuwait, Aden, Bahrain* and *Saudi Arabia.*


# AREB

Unit of account in States of **Grand Mogul,** especially in Amadabath.
Equal to 1/4 Crore, 25 Lakhs, or 2,500,000 Rupees.


# ARGENTEUS

Silver money of **Roman Empire,** created in 214 A.D. by Caracalla under name *Argenteus Antoninianus.*
Weight: 5.45 grams (heavier than Denarius of 3.89 grams, which became *Argenteus Minutulus).*

1 Argenteus Antoninianus = 1 1/4 Denarii = 5 Sestertii

Progressive debasement of metal content, with coinage fineness rapidly falling below 500.

**280** - Under Probus, Argenteus Minutulus fell to nearly 3 grams, with a metal fineness of less than 50.

**290** - Constantine's monetary reform. Weight of Argenteus Minutulus raised to 3.41 grams. Maintained at slightly less weight (about 3 grams) until 360 A.D.


# *ARGENTINA*

**16th - 18th Century** - Circulation of silver Spanish and Mexican Piasters.

**18th Century** - Unit of account: Piaster or Peso worth 8 Reales or 272 Maravedis. Specie money in gold (Doubloon) and silver (Piaster).

**1813** - Argentina retained Spanish monetary system by continuing circulation of Peso over and into new Republic. - See *Peso Argentina.*

# ARGENTINO

Gold coin of **Argentina,** worth 5 Pesos. Weight: 8.0645 grams 900 fine, or 7.26 grams fine gold (late 19th Century, early 20th Century). - See *Peso Argentina.*

# ARIARY

Early silver money of **Madagascar,** imitating Mexican Piaster (27 grams). Worth 2 Loso, 4 Kirobo, 8 Sikaju, 12 Roavoamena, 48 Ilavoamena, 72 Eranambatry, 96 Varifitoventy, 144 Varidimoventy.

# *ARMENIA*

Persian, Greek, Roman, Byzantine monies.

**12th Century** - Christian kingdom copied Venetian Grosso under name of Tahegan. Minting of a ½ submultiple (Tram) and copper coins.

**14th Century** - Minting of gold Tenar.

**15th - 20th Century** - See *Turkey.*

**1920** (November 29th) - Armenia proclaimed a Soviet Socialist Republic. - See *Russia* and *Ruble.*

# ARTIG

Silver money minted at the beginning of 16th Century in **Livonia** by Archbishops of Riga. It was similar to Obol and was a fractional part of a Schilling.

Plural - Artiger.

# ARTILUCCO

Silver money minted in **Ragusa** in 1627, worth 3 Grossetti.

Origin of name - Turkish *altiluk* (six-fold).

Variation of name - Artiluk.

# AS

Bronze bar, then bronze coinage used in **Rome,** in central Italy, then throughout Roman world.

Multiples - Quadrussis (4 Asses), Quincussis (5 Asses).

Submultiples - Semis (½), Triens (⅓), Quadrans (¼), Sextans (⅙), Oncia (1/12).

Origin of name - From Greek *eis* (single); Sanskrit *ayas* (total).
Variations of name - Aes, Assis.
Plural - Asses.

**6th Century B.C.** - Usage of large bronze bars (copper alloyed with lead and tin), having theoretical weight of 327 grams (1 Roman Livre/Pound).

**5th Century B.C.** - Rome legally substituted payments in bronze (pecunia) for payments in cattle (pecus): an ox was worth 100 Asses, a sheep 10 Asses.

**4th Century B.C.** - Adoption of lenticular-shaped coin. Everywhere, As was clipped on basis of Roman Livre/Pound (*As Libralis*) with weight ranging according to region (from 290 grams to 100 grams). Usual weight in Rome: 273 grams.

**3rd Century B.C.** - Debasement of As during wars against Pyrrhus and Carthage: from 164 grams in 286 B.C. to 82 grams in 280 B.C., 55 in 264 B.C., and to 27 in 217 B.C. (still less in Roman Spain). Subdivision of As: Libelle.

**2nd Century B.C.** - As weighed 23 grams, as its decline continued.

**89 B.C.** - Weight of As reduced to 11.5 grams, while value of silver Denarius increased from 10 to 16 Asses, that of Sestertius from 2.5 to 4 Asses. Bronze ceased to be used for coinage.

**49 B.C.** - Resumption of minting bronze coinage.

**1st Century A.D.** - Imperial As weighed 7.5 grams. Thereafter, it was minted in copper.

**180** - Submultiples of As no longer minted.

**217** - End of As coining. Rare mintings of its multiples (Dripondius worth 2 Asses; Sestertius worth 4 Asses).


## ASCENSION ISLAND

Use of British monies. - See *England* and *Pound.*


## ASHRAFI

**I.** - **Arabic** money. Replaced Dinar in Asia prior to 18th and 19th Centuries.

**II.** - Name given in **Egypt** to Altun, gold Turkish money.

**III.** - In **Persia**, gold coin weighing 3.4 grams, roughly similar to contemporary Venetian Zecchino and similar European gold pieces (Ducats). First issued under Safawid Dynasty (1502-1736) and disappeared with coinage of Karim Khan (1750-1779).

Variations of name - Ashrefi, Scherif, Sherify, Scherefi.

**IV.** - In **India (Hydersbad)**, name given to gold Mohur. - See *Mohur.*

**V.** - In **Nepal**, name used for gold Mohar. - See *Mohar.*

**VI.** - In **Abyssinia**, small silver coin struck by Emirs of El Harar.

**19th Century** - Unit of account equal to ⅓ Talari.

## ASLANI

Name given to Dutch Daalder in **Ottoman Empire.**
Cf. *Abukash.*

## ASPER

Coinage of Middle East.

Origin of name - From Greek *aspron,* meaning new money.

I. - Unit of account and specie money in **Turkey** until 19th Century. Minted in copper in Trebizond in 13th Century and Rhodes in 14th Century. Worth 1/20 Sequin (Zecchino) or 8 Carats.
Unit of account Asper represented 1/120.000 Juik, 1/60.000 Beutel, 1/120 Piastre, 1/10 Timmin, 1/3 Para, or 4 Mangir.
In Smyrna, British and Swedes made Grand Asper equal to 1/80 Piastre. As specie money, Asper was small silver coin.
Lesser Asper, or Akcheh, was silver/copper coin.

II. - Unit of account in various countries under Turkish control or influence in 18th Century.
   - In **Syria** and **Greece,** Asper represented 1/80 Piastre.
   - In **Cyprus,** Asper represented 1/100 Mina.
   - In **Tripoli** and **Tunis,** Asper equalled 1/52 Piastre (in Tripoli, 1/4 Grimellin; in Tunis, 12 Burbes).
   - In **Algiers,** Asper equalled 1/696 Pataca Gourda, 1/232 Pataca Chica, 1/29 Muzunas, 1/50 Saime.
   - In **Egypt,** Asper represented 1/75.000 Beutel, 1/99 Piastre, 1/3 Medino (or Para), or 2 Forlis, 2 2/3 Burbes.

III. - Unit of account on **Greek Islands** under sphere of influence of Republic of Venice in 18th Century; worth 1/100 Reale, or 1/10 Lira. Also called Soldo.

IV. - In **Georgia** during 18th Century, Asper or Carbequi, a copper money, was worth 1/10 Chaouri, 1/20 Usalton, 1/40 Abbasi, 1/105 Piastre.

## ASSIGNAT

Paper money issued in **France** from 1789 to 1796 and denominated in Livres or Francs.

Origin of name - The word *assignat,* from 16th Century on, meant settling of an annuity; from *signum* (sign).

Predecessor - See *Livre Tournois.*

**1789** (December 19th-21st) - Decree creating a special Treasury authorized to issue Assignats as counterpart to sale of royal domains.

**1790** (April 16th-17th) - Legal tender status conferred on Assignats.

**1790** (September 12th) - Contracts stipulated in specie money to be fulfilled by Assignats. Issues of paper money increased.

**1791** (June 21st) - Embargo on export of precious metals.

**1793** (April 11th) - Forbidding of payments in specie money as well as specie money clauses in contracts.

**1793** (November 13th) - Seizure of hidden precious metals.

**1795** (February) - Return to free circulation of specie money. Rise in price of gold.

**1795** (November 26th and December 23rd) - Issue of Assignats limited to 40 billion.

**1796** (February 19th) - Destruction of Assignat printing plates.

**1796** (March 18th) - Exchange of Assignats for Mandats at 30 for 1. - See *Mandat.*


## ASSIGNATZIA

Paper money issued in **Russia** from 1769 to 1843.

Predecessor - See *Ruble.*

**1768** (December 29th) - Catherine II authorized two imperial banks (in St. Petersburg and Moscow) to issue paper money exchangeable for metallic money. This paper was called Banco Ruble, or Assignatzia (Assignat).

**1774** (January 10th) - Ceiling for issues fixed at 20 million Rubles.

**1786** (June 26th) - Merger of two issuing banks into Bank of Assignatzia. Lifting of ceiling on banknote issues. Inflation and depreciation.

**1812** - Introduction of counterfeit Assignatzia by French troops. Decline of Assignatzia to less than 20 silver Kopeks per paper Ruble.

**1818** - Repudiation of 223 million Ruble Assignatzia with 595 million remaining in circulation.

**1839** (July 1st) - Consolidation of depreciated paper at rate of 1 silver Ruble = 3.50 Ruble Assignatzia.

**1843** (June 1st) - Withdrawal of Assignatzia from circulation. Replaced by credit notes on basis of 1 Ruble (credit note) = 3.50 Ruble Assignatzia.
See *Ruble.*


## AT

Submultiple ($^1/_{100}$) of Kip, monetary unit of **Laos.**


## ATT

**I.** - Submultiple ($^1/_{64}$ then $^1/_{100}$) of **Siamese** Tical. Minted in bronze at end of 19th Century.

**II.** - In early coinage of **Cambodia,** $^1/_{400}$ Tical.

## AUGUST D'OR

Gold coin of **Saxony** during 18th Century (6 grams of fine gold). Exchange rate: 5 Thaler.

Origin of name - From Elector of Saxony.

Multiple and submultiple - Double August, Half August.

## AUGUSTALIS

Gold money minted in **Sicily** by Frederick II from 1197-1220. Valued at 1¼ gold Gulden.

Weight: 5.235 grams 857 fine, or 4.49 grams fine gold. Minting of gold ½ Augustalis.

Origin of name - As Emperor of Holy Roman Empire, Frederick II took name of Augustus.

**13th Century** - Under Charles of Anjou, Augustalis was called gold Reale.

## AUKSINAS

Monetary unit of **Lithuania** from 1917-1922, equal to Mark. Divided into 100 Statiku.

## AUREUS

Basic gold coinage of monetary system of **Rome** and Roman world. First named Nummus Aureus (gold money) or Denarius Aureus (gold Denier) from which was derived Arabic word Dinar. Commonly called Aureus and eventually Solidus Aureus (solid gold money). Shortened to Solidus from which were derived the Sol, Sou.

Plural - Aurei.

**End of 3rd Century B.C.** - Minting of gold coins by Rome, weighing 1/30 Roman Livre/Pound, or 10.91 grams, and worth 25 silver Denarii, or 250 bronze Asses. Stability lasted for a century and a half.
Subsequent debasements:

| *Year* | *Under* | *Grams of Gold* |
|---|---|---|
| 81 B.C. - | Sulla | 10.91 |
| 50 B.C. - | Pompeius | 9.09 |
| 46 B.C. - | Caesar | 8.18 |
| 15 B.C. - | Augustus | 7.80 |
| 60 A.D. - | Nero | 7.27 |
| 214 A.D. - | Caracalla | 6.55 |
| 292 A.D. - | Diocletian | 5.45 |
| 312 A.D. - | Constantine | 4.54 |
| 367 A.D. - | Valentinian | 3.89 |

**214 A.D.** - Aureus was named Aureus Antoninianus by Caracalla.

**312 A.D.** - Reform of Constantine. Aureus became Solidus. - See *Solidus.*

## AUSTRALIA

**18th Century** - Minting by merchants of copper Token denominated as a Penny.

**19th Century** - British monies. - See *Pound.*

**1909** - Adoption of Australian Pound as monetary unit. - See *Pound Australia.*

**1966** (February 14th) - New monetary unit and decimalization. - See *Dollar Australia.*

## AUSTRIA

Roman monies, then monies of Carolingian monetary system.

See *Rome* and *Holy Roman Empire.*

**11th Century** - Minting of silver Deniers.

**12th to 14th Century** - Variations of Pfennig, which were soon disassociated from prototype: Heller, Kreuzer. - See *Heller* and *Kreuzer.* In 1359, end of annual recoining of Pfennig.

**14th Century** - Minting of a gold Gulden imitating Florentine Guilder. - See *Guilder.* Beginning of system of accounting in Gulden of 60 Kreuzer.

**15th Century** - Minting of silver Gros.

**1519** - On south slope of Harz Mountains, Counts of Schlick Family, owners of silver mines in Joachimsthal, minted famous silver coins called Joachimsthaler, shortened to Thaler. - See *Thaler.*

**1693** - Austria abided by decisions of Conference of Leipzig. - See *Holy Roman Empire.*

**18th Century** - Unit of account: Gulden of 60 Kreuzer or 240 Pfennig.
Specie monies:
   In gold - Ducat, Sovereign
   In silver - Reichsthaler, Guilder
   In silver/copper - multiples of Kreuzer
   In copper - Kreuzer, Groschel, Pfennig

**1753** - Agreement between Austria and Bavaria sanctioning Gulden as general monetary unit and unifying their coinage.
Coins in common:
      In gold - Ducat
      In silver - Thaler, Kopfstück, Groschen
Coins circulating only in Austria: Pultura (½ Groschen), Groeschel, Zweier.
- See *Gulden* until 18th Century.

**1761** - Issue of bonds, at first interest-bearing and pegged at an arbitrary price, then without interest and at freely quoted prices.

**1792-1811** - For Banco Zettel, see *Gulden Austria.*

**1857** (January 24th) - Vienna Agreement linked Germanic Monetary Union to silver standard. Thaler fixed at 1.50 Austrian Gulden divided into 100 Kreuzer.
Specie money:
      In gold - Krone (without fixed value)
      In silver - Thaler
Monies circulating only in Austria (Landsmünzen):
      In gold - Ducat and Quadruple Ducat
      In silver - Gulden
      In copper - Kreuzer

**1867** - Austria ceased to be part of Germanic Monetary Union. - See *Gulden Austria.*

**1870** (March 9th) - Imperial decree authorized minting of coins patterned after those of Latin Monetary Union. Gold coins of 4 and 8 Gulden (corresponding to 10 and 20 Francs) issued until 1892.

**1892** (August 2nd) - Introduction of a common Austro-Hungarian monetary system with adoption of gold standard.
New monetary unit: Krone of 100 Heller. - See *Krone Austria.*

**1918-1920** - In successor states, creation or introduction of new monies: Czechoslovak Koruna, Hungarian Korona, Yugoslav Dinar, Italian Lira, Romanian Leu.

**1923** (December) - After collapse of Austrian Krone, creation of Schilling, divided into 100 Groschen. - See *Schilling Austria.*


# AVO

Submultiple (½00) of Pataca, monetary unit of **Macao** and **Timor.**
Plural - Avos.


# *AZORES*

Monetary system of Portugal. - See *Portugal.*

## AZTECA

**Mexican** 20 Peso gold coin containing 16.666 grams 900 fine, or 15 grams fine gold. First minted in 1916.

## BADAM

**I.** - Bitter almond growing on bushes on rock formations in deserts of Lar Province in Persia and in Carmania (Asia Minor). Imported to **India** and used as minor money until 18th Century in Kingdom of Gujarat and in Mogul Empire. From 40 to 68 Badams equal to a Pacha (or Pecha), copper coin subdivision of Rupee. Variations of name - Padens, Padan, Baden.

**II.** - Unit of account in **Mogul** States: $1/100$ Nil, 100 Crore, 10,000 Lakhs or 1 million Rupees.

## BAGARONE

In **Bologna, Ferrara, Modena, Parma,** copper money, worth $1/4$ Quattrino in 15th and 16th Centuries.
Variation of name - Bogherone.

## BAGATTINO

**Venetian** copper money, equivalent to $1/2$ Soldo. Minted as early as 1477 in Duchy of Reggio.
Origin of name - From *bagata* (trifle).
Variation of name - Bagattin.

## BAHAMA ISLANDS

**Before 19th Century** - See *British West Indies.*

**19th Century** - Pound Sterling notes were legal tender, and local government currency, Bahama Pound notes, began circulating at par with Sterling. - See *Pound Bahama Islands.*
British gold, silver and copper coins circulated.

**Early 20th Century** - American gold and silver certificates of U.S. $5.00 and upward entered circulation. American and Canadian coins in use.

**1934** - American and British gold coins withdrawn from circulation.

**1936** (November 1st) - British Treasury notes ceased to be legal tender. British silver coins no longer legal tender for transactions greater than 40 Shillings.

## BAHAR

Early unit of account in **Java.** Divided into 10 Uta, 100 Catties, 1,000 Laxsan, 10,000 Peccoes, 250,000 Tayell, 500,000 Sata, 2,500,000 Mas, 10 million Cash, or 100 million Candareens.

Variation of name - Baar.

## BAHRAIN

**1862** - Islands became British protectorate by treaty. General money in circulation, see *Rupee India* and *Pound.*

**1959** - Persian Gulf Rupee replaced Indian Rupee. - See *Rupee Persian Gulf.*

**1965** (October) - Bahrain Dinar introduced to replace Gulf Rupee. - See *Dinar Bahrain.*

**1969** (October 22nd) - Bahrain became part of newly formed Federation of Arab Emirates. - See *Federation of Arab Emirates.*

## BAHT

Monetary unit of **Thailand** (Siam) since 1928, divided into 100 Satang. Sometimes called by its former name, Tical.

Bank of issue - By State until 1941, by Central Bank of Thailand since April 1942.

Predecessors - See *Thailand* and *Tical.*

**1928** (April 15th) - Adoption of gold standard with substitution of Baht for Tical on basis of:

    1 Baht = 1 Tical

    1 Baht = 665.67 milligrams of fine gold

    1 Baht = 1/11 Pound Sterling

Minting of a gold coin of 10 Bahts, called Dos. Minting of silver Baht.

**1932** (May 11th) - Abandonment of gold standard and currency depreciation. Rejoined Sterling Area at rate of:

    1 Baht = 1/11 Pound Sterling

**1939** (September 7th) - Foreign exchange controls.

**1942** (February) - New definition of currency:

    1 Baht = 326.39 milligrams of fine gold

**1942** (April 22nd) - Linking of currency to Yen with 37% devaluation:

    1 Baht = 1 Yen

**1946** (May 1st) - Devaluation:

    1 Baht = 1/40 Pound Sterling = 6 Pence

**1947** - System of multiple exchange rates:

    1 U.S. Dollar = 10.00 Bahts (official rate for government imports and purchases of petroleum products)

    1 U.S. Dollar = 20.00 Bahts (fluctuating free rate for most other imports and exports, except rice, tin and rubber, and for capital transfers)

**1949** (September 26th) - After devaluation of Pound Sterling, 20% devaluation of official rate:

    1 U.S. Dollar = 12.50 Bahts

Fluctuating free rate below 20.00 Bahts per U.S. Dollar.

**1952** (December 31st) - No par value. Official rates were 12.45/12.55 Bahts per U.S. Dollar for government receipts and payments, rice exports and student remittances. There were multiple rates for both exchange receipts and payments. Fluctuating free market rate for some exports and imports and most invisibles and capital 16.51/16.69 Bahts per U.S. Dollar).

**1953** (November 13th) - Further restrictions on imports introduced. Fluctuating free market rate 21.05/21.16 Bahts per U.S. Dollar.

**1954** (June 15th) - Bank of Thailand announced it was prepared to purchase U.S. Dollars and Sterling at free market rates.

**1955** (July 13th) - Exchange Equalization Fund established to prevent undue fluctuations in free market.

**1956** (January 1st) - Official rates of 12.45/12.55 Bahts per U.S. Dollar no longer used except for outstanding commitments.
All authorized transactions took place at freely fluctuating market rate of approximately 20.80 Bahts per U.S. Dollar.

**1963** (October 20th) - Initial par value established with International Monetary Fund:
1 Baht = 42.7245 milligrams of fine gold
1 U.S. Dollar = 20.80 Bahts
Rate applied to all exports, imports and financial transactions.


## BAIOCCO

**Italian** money, also called Baïoque, Bayoque, or Bajoccho.
Plural - Baiocci.

**I. -** In **Papal States** (Rome), unit of account used until 1866 worth 1/160 Ducat of Camera, 1/100 Roman Scudo, 1/30 Testone, 1/20 Papetto, 1/10 Paolo (or Guilo), 5 Quattrini, or 10 Mezzi Quattrini. Minted in copper.

**II. -** In **Ancona,** unit of account worth 1/100 Scudo, 1/10 Paolo, 1/5 Soldo, or 24 Denari.

**III. -** In **Bologna,** unit of account also called Bolognino, equal to Soldo or 1/20 Lira, 6 Quattrini, or 12 Denari. Minted in copper and in silver.

**IV. -** In **Lucca,** unit of account also called Bolognino, worth 1/10 Lira, 2 Soldi, or 24 Denari.


## BAIOCCONE

In **Papal States,** name given to copper coin valued at 5 Baiocci.


## BAIOCHELLA

Money used in **Italy** until 19th Century before unification. Also called Baioquelle.
Origin of name - Diminutive of Baiocco.

**I. -** In **Papal States** (Rome), coin made of silver/copper, worth 2 Baiocco.

**II.** - In **Bologna,** coin made of silver/copper, also called Murajolo, Muragliola, worth 2 Soldi.

## BAIZA

**I.** - Coin of copper and cupro-nickel used in **Musat and Oman** (Arabia). Equal to 1/64 Rupee, and 1/230 Maria Theresia Thaler. - See *Besa.*
**II.** - Submultiple (1/1000) of the Rial Saidi, monetary unit of **Oman** since May 1970.

## BAJOIRE

Silver coin of Canton of **Geneva** during 18th Century and until 1850. Exchange rate: 3 Livres 15 Sols.
Origin of name - Name given to coins or medals with two heads face to face. Form of *baisoir,* derived from *baiser.*

## BALBOA

Monetary unit of **Panama,** divided into 10 Centesimos. Also called *Panamanian Dollar.*
Origin of name - From Vasco Nuñez de Balboa, Spanish explorer, who discovered the Pacific in 1513.
Bank of issue - None, as the Balboa only circulates as silver coin (1 Balboa) or as divisionary coinage.
Predecessors - Before Panamanian Independence (1904), the Colombian monetary system based on the silver standard. - See *Spanish America, Colombia* and *Panama.*
**1904** (June 27th) - Adoption of U.S. Dollar standard:
      1 Balboa = 1,504.6 milligrams of fine gold
      1 U.S. Dollar = 1 Balboa
**1934** (February) - Alignment to devalued U.S. Dollar:
      1 Balboa = 888.67 milligrams of fine gold
      1 U.S. Dollar = 1 Balboa
**1946** (December 18th) - Parity registered with International Monetary Fund.

## BANCO

Name formerly given to bank money, representing fixed weight of gold or silver on deposit in a bank, and protected from alterations in value.
Origin of name - From Italian *banco.*
Applications - Florin-Banco of Bank of Amsterdam (1609); Mark-Banco of Bank of

Hamburg. Such bank money (units of account) commanded a premium over corresponding metallic money.
Name incorrectly given to Paper Ruble until 19th Century. Banco-Ruble, which was confused with Assignatzia, had depreciated greatly in relation to silver Ruble. - See *Assignatzia.*

## BANIU

Submultiple (1/100) of the Kuna, monetary unit of **Croatia.** - See *Kuna.*

## BANU

Submultiple (1/100) of the Leu, monetary unit of **Romania.** - See *Leu.*
Plural - Bani.

## *BARBADOS*

**Until 19th Century** - See *British West Indies.*
**Early 19th Century** - Use of Spanish Piasters that were countermarked or fragmented.
**1822** - Silver coins representing submultiples of U.S. Dollar.
**1834** - Copper coins of 3 Pence and 3 Half Pence.
**20th Century** - Use of Dollar of British West Indies. - See *Dollar British West Indies.*
Issued by Barclays Bank, Royal Bank, Canadian Bank and by Treasury.
Simultaneous circulation of government currency notes from British Guiana and Trinidad, and British gold, silver and bronze coins.
Certain American coins accepted.
**1951** (August 1st) - Local banknotes and government currency replaced by issue of unified currency of British Caribbean. - See *Dollar British West Indies.*
**1955** (October 1st) - New subsidiary coins based on British West Indies Dollar came into circulation.
**1965** (October 6th) - East Caribbean Dollar replaced British West Indies Dollar at par. - See *Dollar East Caribbean.*
**1966** (November 30th) - Barbados became independent state within Commonwealth.

## BARBUDA

**Portuguese** silver/copper coin issued by Fernando (1367-1383). Valued at 3 Dinheiros. Variation of name - Barbue.

## *BASUTOLAND*

Former British Protectorate with monetary system of South Africa. - See *South Africa*.
**1966** (October 4th) - Changed name and became independent member of Commonwealth. - See *Lesotho*.

## BATZ

Early money of various **German** and **Swiss** States.
Origin of name - From Betz, for *Bär* (bear); the bear being the symbol of Berne.
Plural - Batzen.
**I.** - In the **German** States, at end of 15th Century, Batz worth 1/15 Thaler or 4 Kreuzer.
**18th Century** - Batz equalled 4 Kreuzer. It was unit of account in Upper Palatinate
(1/15 Guilder or 2 Albus), silver money in Württemberg (coins of 9 and 3 Batzen),
silver/copper money in Trier (coins of 6 and 3 Batzen).
**II.** - In **Swiss** Cantons, silver/copper money. Appeared in Berne in 1490 (exchange rate
equal to 4 Kreuzer or 24 Heller).
**18th Century** - Unit of account as well as silver/copper or copper coin.
- In Basel, Bon Batz (in old French: le Bon Bat) represented 1/15 Guilder, 1/27
Thaler, or 4 Kreuzer, 10 Rappen, or 20 Pfennig.
- In Berne, Lucerne and Freiburg, "short" Batz, or Swiss Batz, was only equal to
9 Rappen.
- In Berne, 1/10 Livre, 1/25 Crown.
- In Saint Gall, 1/15 Guilder.
- In Zurich, 2.5 Schillings (minted in 1749).
- In Neuchatel, 1/15 Guilder, or 4 Kreuzer.
**1798** - Swiss Republic minted coins of 1, 5, 10 and 40 Batzen.
**1799** (March 17th) - Batz of 10 Rappen became 1/10 Swiss Franc, monetary unit of
Swiss Republic.
Minting of silver coins of 5, 10 and 20 Batzen, of silver/copper coins of 1 Batz.
**1806** - Neuchatel minted silver/copper Batz.
**19th Century** - Name Batz used for a long time to designate Swiss coin of 10 Centimes.

## *BAVARIA*

See *Holy Roman Empire*.
**10th Century** - Minting of Deniers (Pfennig) and silver Obols (Halbling).
**13th Century** - Regensburg minted special Denier: Regensburger.
**14th Century** - Bavaria imitated Heller of Halle. - See *Heller*.
**1506** - Minting of first gold Florin (Gulden).
**18th Century** - Unit of account: Florin (Gulden) of 60 Kreuzer or 240 Pfennig.
Black money (Schwarze Münze) for calculation of taxes and fines; Livre (Pfund)

of 41 Schillings, 164 Groschen, 494 Regensburger, 1,230 Pfennig, or 2,460 Heller.

Relationship between two systems: 1 Livre = 5.85 Gulden.

Specie money:

> In gold - Carl, Maximilian d'Or, Dukaten, Gulden
>
> In silver - Reichsthaler, Gulden
>
> In silver/copper - Kreuzer and its multiples
>
> In copper - Pfennig, Heller

**1753** - Agreement with Austria for unification of various monies.

Coins in common:

> In gold - Dukaten
>
> In silver - Thaler, Kopfstück, Groschen

**1837** (August 5th) - Agreement with Württemburg, Hesse-Darmstadt and Frankfurt-/Main defining silver Gulden as being 9.55 grams.

**1857** (January 24th) - German Monetary Agreement: 1 Gulden of Southern States = $4/7$ Thaler = $6/7$ Austrian Guilder.

**1871** (December 4th) - Monetary unification of Germany: 10 Marks replaced 5.50 Gulden. - See *Germany*.


# BAZARUCCO

In Goa **(Portuguese India),** unit of account and copper or tin coin used in 18th Century. A Bazarucco of good alloy equalled $1/300$ Pardao, $1/75$ Good Tanga, $1/60$ Bad Tanga. A Bazarucco of poor alloy equalled $1/360$ Pardao, $1/90$ Good Tanga, $1/72$ Bad Tanga, $1/180$ Bad Vintem.

Variation of name - Basaruco.

**End of 18th Century** - Tin Bazarucco was money used in minor trade.


# BAZZO

See *Batz*.


# *BECHUANALAND*

Former British Protectorate with monetary system of South Africa. - See *South Africa*.

**1966** (September 30th) - Changed name and became independent member of Commonwealth. - See *Botswana*.

## BEKAH

A coin equal to a ½ Shekel, under monetary system of the **Hebrews** during reign of Simon Maccabaeus (143-135 B.C.).

## BEKOMARK

See *Mark German Federal Republic.*

## BELGA

Former unit of account in **Belgium** used for foreign exchange transactions from 1926 to 1945. Divided into 5 Belgian Francs or 500 Centimes.

Origin of name - Same root as Belgium.

Predecessor - See *Franc Belgium.*

**1926** (October 25th) - Royal edict creating Belga:
        1 Belga = 5 Belgian Francs
        1 Belga = 209.211 milligrams of fine gold

**1935** (March 31st) - Devaluation of 28%:
        1 Belga = 150.632 milligrams of fine gold

**1940** (May) - German occupation:
        1 Belga = 0.50 Reichsmark

**1940** (July) - 1 Belga = 0.40 Reichsmark.

**1945** (December) - Belga abolished. - See *Franc Belgium.*

## BELGIAN CONGO

Former Belgian Protectorate. Monetary unit: Congo Franc. - See *Franc Congo.*

**1960** (June 30th) - Became independent nation. - See *Congo Democratic Republic.*

## BELGIUM

Roman, Carolingian, Austrian monies. - See *Netherlands.*

**18th Century -** In Brabant, unit of account: Livre (Pondt Vlaam) of 2.5 Rixdales or Patacons, 6 Gulden or Guilders, 20 Schelling or Escalins, 120 Stuyver or Sols, 240 Groten or Gros, 1,920 Penning or Deniers, 5,760 Mijten.
Specie money in Brabant:
        In gold - Sovereign or Severin, Austrian Ducat
        In silver - Ducaton, Crown (Croon)
        In silver/copper - Escalin (Schelling), Plaquette
        In copper - Ort,Duyte

In Liege and Westphalia, unit of account: Patacon or Ecu of 4 Gulden or Guilders, 8 Escalins, 80 Stuyver or Sols, 320 Oord or Liards or Aidans, 1,280 Penning or Deniers.

Specie money in Liege:
> In gold - Ducat, Gulden
> In silver - Patacon, Escalin (Schelling), Blamüser (1/2 Escalin)

**1832** (June 5th) - After independence, creation of independent monetary system copied after Franc. - See *Franc Belgium.*

**1926 - 1945** - Adoption of new monetary unit, Belga of 5 Belgian Francs. - See *Belga.*

**1945** (December) - Belga abolished - See *Franc Belgium.*

## BENGAL

Primitive monetary unit - See *Cowrie.*

Later monetary unit - Rupee (see *Rupee India*) and its submultiples (see *Cawne, Anna, Poni, Burrie, Gunda* and *Cowrie*).

## BER

Name given to Talari or Maria Theresia Thaler in **Ethiopia.** - See *Maria Theresia Thaler.*

Origin of name - Amharic word for silver.

Variation of name - Bep.

## BERGAMO

Monies of **Rome** (see *Rome*), then Carolingian monetary system.

**15th Century** - Venetian monies. - See *Venice.*

**18th Century** - Units of account: Scudo, divided in 7 Lire, 140 Soldi, or 1,680 Denari; Ducato, divided into 24 Grossi, 288 Piccioli, or 1,488 Denari.

**19th Century** - Monies of Lombardy (see *Milan*), and after unification, Italian monies (see *Italy*).

## BERLIN

Predecessor - See *Germany.*

**1948** - Before monetary reform, Reichsmark and military Mark.

In Western Sectors, circulation of Ostmark (see *Mark German Democratic Republic*) and of German Mark or Deutsche Mark (see *Mark German Federal Republic* ) issued by Bank Deutscher Länder and by Berliner Landeszentralbank.

In Russian Sector, Ostmark only legal tender. No transferability from Berlin to Western Occupation Zones.

**1949** (May 20th) - Deutsche Mark became only legal tender in Western Sectors. Rates of exchange in Western Sectors fixed each day (4.50 Ostmark for 1 Deutsche Mark in June 1949). At border of Russian Sector, official rate of exchange:

1 Ostmark = 1.25 Deutsche Mark

**After 1949** - See *Mark German Democratic Republic* and *Mark German Federal Republic.*

## BERMUDA

**17th Century** - Brass coins of 1 Shilling, of 6, 3 and 2 Pence (often called Hog Money) minted especially for Sommer Islands.

**19th Century** - Bermuda Pound entered circulation based on British monetary system. Bermuda Government issued local currency notes in 1 Pound denominations. - See *Pound Bermuda.*

British 1 Pound and 10 Shilling banknotes circulated beside gold and silver coinage of Great Britain. U.S. Dollar banknotes in circulation used mainly for remittances to United States. Treasury Chest Office drafts formed principal medium of exchange between Bermuda and trading partners.

**20th Century** - Increased tourism resulted in free circulation of American and Canadian banknotes. Local hotels kept their accounts in U.S. Dollars.

**1965** (February 3rd) - Silver Bermuda Crown entered into circulation (22.6213 grams 500 fine):

1 Bermuda Crown = 5 Shillings

**1970** (February 6th) - Decimalization and creation of new monetary unit to replace Bermuda Pound. - See *Dollar Bermuda.*

American and Canadian banknotes continued to circulate freely.

## BESA

**I.** - Submultiple ($^1/_{100}$) of Talari and small copper coin in **Ethiopia.** - See *Talari.*

Variations of name - Beiza, Baiza. - See *Baiza.*

Plural - Bese.

**II.** - Small copper coin struck in Rome by royal decree of January 28, 1909, for **Italian Somaliland.** Represented $^1/_{100}$ silver Rupee. Multiples of 2 and 4 Bese.

## BESHLIK

**I.** - Silver coin in **Turkey.** Minted in 18th and 19th Centuries: in 1828, 28 grams 175 or 225 fine, then 6.013 grams 830 fine. Value: 5 Paras, then 4¾ Piastres.

Worn coins in early 20th Century (Metallik series) had exchange rate of only 2.5 Piastres.

**II.** - Copper coin in **Egypt** in 19th Century worth 5 Medini.

## BEUTEL

**I.** - Unit of account, gold and silver money in early **Turkey.**

Origin of name - All gold or silver which came into Treasury of the Serail were locked in leather purses (beutel).

Variation of name - Bourse.

**18th and 19th Centuries** - Beutel in silver, called Keser, equalled ½ Juik, or 500 Piastres, 6,000 Timmin, 20,000 Paras, 50,000 Mina, or 60,000 Aspers.

**1811** - Minting of gold Beutel called Kitze (36.08 grams 916 fine) having exchange rate of 30,000 Piastres.

**II.** - **Egyptian** unit of account in 18th and 19th Centuries equal to 25,000 Paras (Medini), or 75,000 Aspers.

**20th Century** - Beutel equal to 500 Piastres.

## BEZANT

**I.** - Gold coin of **Byzantine Empire,** a continuation of Roman Aureus and Solidus.

Origin of name - Latin *Byzantinus, Byzantium, Besantum.*

Variations of name - Solidus Byzantius, Gold Byzantine Sou, Besant, Byzantin.

Submultiples in gold - ½ Sou (Semissis or Semision), ⅓ Sou (Triens, Tremissis, Trimisium or Kokhos).

**312 A.D.** - Monetary reform of Constantine. Aureus became Solidus of 4.54 grams of gold. - See *Aureus* and *Solidus.*

**4th Century** - After split in Roman Empire, coin continued to be minted in pure gold by Eastern Emperors and became Bezant. Outside Eastern Empire, Bezant benefited from its Roman prestige at a time when gold practically disappeared.

**11th Century** - Made thinner and smaller, Bezant became concave.

**12th Century** - It became custom in France to present 13 of these coins at Holy Mass of the Kings. Henry II had them minted especially for this ceremony.

**13th Century** - Ransom demanded for Saint Louis (Louis IX): 1 million Bezants that the historian Joinville valued at 500,000 Livres Tournois (1 Bezant for 10 Sous Tournois, or 4.13 grams fine gold).
Palaeologus Dynasty minted Bezant at 375 fine.

**14th Century** - In Rhodes, 6.66 Bezants equaled 1 Sequin, and 1 Bezant was worth 1.5 Gigliati, 3 Aspers, 24 Carats, or 48 Deniers.

**15th Century** - End of Eastern Empire and minting of Bezants.

**II.** - Imitated by **Arabs,** Bezant became Saracen Bezant which was identical with Dinar of the Caliphs. - See *Dinar.*

Bezant of Byzantium and Saracen Bezant became principal monetary instruments during Crusades. Crusaders minted them despite excommunication by Innocent IV. On coat of arms of a Knight, Bezant indicated that he had been to Holy Land.

**III.** - In **Cyprus,** during 12th and 13th Centuries, the Lusignan family minted some concave gold Bezants copied after those of Byzantium with fineness of 917, called white Bezants. They circulated (into 14th Century) as equivalent to 2 silver Gros.

## BHUTAN

**19th and 20th Centuries** - General circulation of metallic coinage of India. - See *India.* Bhutanese tendency to hoard coins with precious metal content created periodic money shortages.

**1967** - Minting in India of Half Rupee nickel coin for circulation in Bhutan. Commonly called Tikchung. - See *Tikchung.*
Simultaneous circulation of Indian Rupees and cupro-nickel Bhutanese Rupee coins at par with Indian Rupees.

## BIA

Former unit of account in **Thailand** (Siam) equal to 200 Cowries, a shell from the Maldive Islands, which served as money. - See *Cowrie.*
1 Tical = 8 Fuang = 32 Pais = 6,400 Bias

## BIAFRA

Predecessor - See *Nigeria.*

**1967** (May) - Secessionist state established. Monetary unit unchanged. - See *Pound Nigeria.*

**1968** (January 10th) - New currency created. - See *Pound Biafra.*

**1970** (January 9th) - Surrender of Biafra, and reincorporation into Nigeria.

## BICHE

Monetary unit used in Calicut on coast of Malabar, in **India.** Coins minted in copper in 18th Century at Pondicherry (1, 1/2 and 1/4 Biche), for district of Mahé. Corresponded to Pice and was 1/15 Fanam as coin and as unit of account. In Cannanore, on northern coast of Malabar, equivalent to 1/16 Fanam as unit of account.

Variation of name - Bise.

## BIGATUS

Silver **Roman** money, minted in Spain towards end of 3rd Century B.C. and scattered throughout Gaul. Weight: 3.89 grams (like classic Denier).

Origin of name - From Latin *bigatus,* meaning a two horse chariot (bis-jugum, yoke). Coin marked with 2 horse chariot. Earlier Quadrigatus marked with 4 horse chariot.

Plural - Bigati.

**2nd Century B.C.** - Classic silver Denarius (3.89 grams, like Bigatus) succeeded Bigatus.

## *BISMARCK ARCHIPELAGO*

**Primitive money** - Diwarra, a worked and ornamented shell. - See *Diwarra.*

**19th Century** - German monies.

**1920** - Australian money.

**1942-1944** - Military Yen (Gumpyo). Japanese monetary system.

**1945** - Reintroduction of Australian money. - See *Pound Australia.*

## BISSONA

Silver coin minted in **Milan** by Louis XII at beginning of the 16th Century. Valued at 3 Soldi.

## BISTI

**I.** - Copper coin of **Persia** under Shah Abbas I (1587-1629). Equal to ¼ Kazbegi. One Shahi was equivalent of 2.5 Bisti.

**II.** - In **Georgia,** coin circulating in 13th Century.

Submultiple - ½ Bisti or Nim-Bisti.

## BIT

**I.** - Central portion of Spanish Peso or Colonato, cut out and counterstamped for use in British Colonies, especially in **British West Indies,** during 18th and 19th Centuries. Equivalent to 7½ Pence.

**II.** - In **Danish Antilles,** silver/copper coin used in 18th Century, equal to 1 Real or ⅛ Piaster (or Riksdaler).

**19th Century** - Bit corresponded to ⅟₅₀₀ Daler, ⅟₁₀₀ Franc, or ⅕ Cent. Until 1916, Bit was submultiple of Franc (⅟₁₀₀).

**III.** - In **Guyana** during 20th Century, Bit remained as name given to silver coin of 4 Pence minted locally at 1.88 grams 500 fine.


# BLAFFERT

**I.** - Silver/copper money minted after 15th Century in various **Swiss** States (Berne, Lucerne, Zurich, Saint Gall). Exchange rate: 15 Heller, 3 Kreutzer or 6 Rappen.

**18th Century** - Unit of account and silver/copper money in Canton of Basel. Equal to 1/25 Guilder, 6 Rappen or 12 Pfennig.

**II.** - Early coin of **Germany** worth from 2 Pfennig to 4 Albus.

**16th Century** - Gradually replaced by Batzen. - See *Batz.*

**III.** - Silver/copper **Danish** coin, worth 2 Penning in monetary system of 1513.

Variations of name - Blaffart, Plappart, Plappert.


# BLAMUSER

**I.** - Silver coinage in areas of **Liege, Maestricht** and **Westphalia,** having exchange rate during 18th Century of 1/2 Schelling (Escalin).

Variation of name - Blamuyser.

**II.** - Unit of account in **Munster,** equal to 1/8 Thaler, or to 42 Pfennig, in 18th Century.

Variation of name - Blamuse.


# BLANC

Name given in **France** to various silver coins. - Cf. *Albus, Witten.*

Variation of name - Blanque.

**I.** - Denier Blanc with Fleur de Lis. - See *Fleur de Lis.*

**II.** - Blanc à la Couronne. - See *Crown.*

**III.** - Blanc aux Ecus: Coin minted in France by British occupation forces (Henry VI) in 1422; 3.26 grams of which 1.63 were silver. Exchange rate: 10 Deniers.

**IV.** - Petit Blanc or 1/2 Blanc: Coin minted in France by the British occupation forces (Henry VI) in 1423; 1.63 grams of which 0.68 were silver. Exchange rate: 5 Deniers. It then became copper coin, worth 5 Deniers.

**17th Century** - Minting of coins of 3 Blancs (15 Deniers) and of 6 Blancs (30 Deniers).

**18th Century** - Unit of account for 5 Deniers: 3 Blancs for 15 Deniers; 6 Blancs for 30 Deniers.

**V.** - Gros Blanc. - See *Gros.*

**VI.** - Various coins created by Charles VII in 1431:
Blanc aux Rondeaux (3.06 grams of which 1.53 were silver; exchange rate: 15 Deniers)
Blanc Dentillé (3.06 grams of which 1.02 were silver; exchange rate: 10 Deniers)

Blanc des Gens d'Armes (3.06 grams of which 1.27 were silver; then lowered to 1.02 silver; exchange rate: 10 Deniers).

**VII.** - From Louis XI to Francis I, minting of Grand Blanc having 12 Deniers as its exchange rate. Replaced by Douzain.

**VIII.** - For **Friesland,** see *Witten.* For **Denmark** and **Norway,** see *Hvid.* For **Spain,** see *Blanco.*

## BLANCO

**Spanish** silver coin, then silver/copper, from 17th to 18th Century.

Origin of name - From Spanish *blanco* (white). Cf. *Blanc, Witten.*

Predecessor  - See *Spain.*

**1252** - Minting of Blanco of 4.79 grams silver, worth 15 Deniers (see *Denario*).

**1258** - Minting of Blanco Burgales, worth 2 Denarios or 1/90 gold Maravedi.

**1471** (April 10th) - Blanco weighed less than 1.12 grams. Value: 1/2 Maravedi.

**1497** (June 13th) - General demonetization. Blanco became silver/copper coin (0.85 grams copper, 0.35 grams silver) worth 1/2 Maravedi.

**1552** (May 23rd) - Amount of silver in Blanco reduced to 0.27 grams.

**1566** (December 14th) - Amount of silver reduced to 0.20 grams.

## BLANQUILLO

Unit of account as well as a silver coin in **Morocco** during early 18th Century. Equal to 1/48 gold Ducat, or 8, 20, or 24 copper Falus.

Origin of name - Diminutive of Blanca, from its white appearance.

## BODULARI

Silver/copper, then copper coin of **Maldive Islands.** First minted in 1913. Multiple of Lari:

  1 Bodulari = 4.00 Laree

Plural - Bodularee.

## BOGACHE

Submultiple (1/40) of Imaldi, former monetary unit of **Yemen.** Divided into 2 Halalas. Minted in silver and in copper.

## BOHEMIA

**10th Century** - Minting of silver Denier (Pfennig), derived from Carolingian Denier.

**11th Century** - Debasement of Denier.

**13th Century** - Small units of Denier became Bracteates.

**1300** - Monetary reform of Wenceslas II. Creation of Gros of Prague, patterned after French Gros. Circulated throughout Central Europe.

**14th Century** - Minting of gold coins (Guilder, Royal, Chaise) and of silver Heller.

**15th Century** - The Jagellon family minted gold Ducats. Gros of Prague minted in Joachimsthal.

**16th Century** - Bohemia taken over by Hapsburgs. Austrian monies. - See *Austria*.

**18th Century** - Accounting units in Prague were either kept in Guilders (Gulden) of 60 Kreuzer or 240 Pfennig, or in Schock Groschen (Kopy-Grossuw-Czeskich) of 60 Groschen, the Schock Groschen being worth 3 Gulden.
Specie monies: Hungarian, Austrian and Dutch Ducats, Sovereigns of Brabant, Reichsthaler, Groschen.

**20th Century** - See *Czechoslovakia*.

## BOKCHA

Copper coin used in **Ethiopia** in late 19th Century as minor coinage.
Variations of name - Bogsha, Bugsha.

## BOLIVAR

Originally, name sometimes given to the Venezolano, first national money of **Venezuela**. Since 1887, monetary unit of Venezuela. Divided into 2 Reales or 100 Centimes.

Origin of name - From Simon Bolívar, liberator of South America.

Bank of issue - Six national banks (private); Bank of Venezuela, Bank of Caracas, Venezolano Credit Bank, Mercantile and Agricultural Bank, Bank of Maracaibo, Commerical Bank of Maracaibo. Banco Central de Venezuela assumed Central Bank functions in 1940.

Predecessors - See *Venezuela* and *Venezolano*.

**19th Century** - Unit of account, the Bolívar was worth ⅕ Venezolano.

**1871** (May 11th) - Monetary law providing for minting of Bolívar gold coins linked to the gold coin of 100 Francs (32.258 grams 900 fine) worth 20 Venezolanos.

**1880** - Issue of postage stamps on which word Venezolano replaced word Bolívar (of 100 Centimos).

**1887** (June 2nd) - Creation of a money defined in gold, the Bolívar, equal to Franc and Peseta: 1 Bolívar = 290.322 milligrams of fine gold = 1 Franc Germinal.
Minting of gold coins (multiples of Bolívar: 100, 25, 20, 10 ) on this monetary base.

The Bolívar was minted in form of a 5 gram silver coin 835 fine (equal to Franc).

**1910** - Effective establishment of gold standard.

**1914** (August) - Restrictions on export of gold.

**1923** - Restoration of gold parity.

**1930** - Prohibition of gold exports. Depreciation (maximum: 30%), then currency appreciation.

**1934** (August) - De facto adherence to U.S. Dollar Area on basis of:
1 U.S. Dollar = 3.915 Bolívares
Foreign exchange controls.

**1936** (December 1st) - Export premiums.

**1937** (April 27th) - Partial revaluation:
1 U.S. Dollar = 3.18 Bolívares

**1940** (August 15th) - Banco Central de Venezuela assumed banknote issuing authority.

**1941** (July 23rd) - New official exchange rate:
1 U.S. Dollar = 3.35 Bolívares.
Adoption of multiple exchange rates:
Buying: 3.05 and 3.09 (petroleum), 3.32 (general exports),
4.25 (cocoa), 4.25 and 4.80 (coffee)
Selling: 3.09 (government imports), 3.35 (essential imports),
3.42 and 4.00 (other imports)

**1942** (May 10th) - Unification of selling rate to importers at 3.35 per U.S. Dollar.

**1947** (April 18th) - Parity registered with International Monetary Fund:
1 Bolívar = 265.275 milligrams of fine gold
1 U.S. Dollar = 3.35 Bolívares

**1948** - Multiple exchange rates, from 3.09 Bolívares per U.S. Dollar (gasoline imports) to 4.80 (coffee exports).

**1959** (January 31st) - Partial devaluation. Rate for government imports changed to 1 U.S. Dollar = 3.335 Bolívares.

**1960** (November 8th) - Complete revision of multiple rate structure. Freely fluctuating market rate applied to certain invisibles, export proceeds and capital transactions. Official market rate applied to most other transactions. Development of significant black market.

**1961** (March 17th) - Exchange system modified. Official market became controlled market.
Rate set at 3.33/3.35 Bolívares per U.S. Dollar.

**1961** (April 1st) - Official free market established and Exchange Stabilization Fund set up for Central Bank's foreign exchange operations.

**1961** (April 17th) - Further shuffling of transactions eligible for various exchange markets.

**1961** (May) - Bolívar on black market reached record low of 4.98 per U.S. Dollar.

**1961** (December 30th) - Official free market exchange rate 4.565/4.58 Bolívares. Fluctuating free market rate approximately 4.578 Bolívares per U.S. Dollar.

**1962** (April 2nd) - Major portion of payments (i.e., 80% of imports, and virtually all capital repatriation and servicing) transferred from controlled market to official free market. Certain receipts also transferred.

**1964** (January 18th) - Major reform of exchange system. Official free market abolished. Rates of 4.40 and 4.50 Bolívares per U.S. Dollar applied to almost all transactions. Par value unchanged and applicable only to imports of some foodstuffs, basic raw materials, biological products and agricultural machinery.

## BOLIVIA

**16th Century** - Introduction of Mexican and Peruvian Piasters.

**1650** - Opening of a monetary mint in Potosi. Minting of Piasters (Pesos).

**1825** - Bolivia, independent from Peru, retained Spanish monetary system with Peso of 8 Reales.

**1863** (June 23rd) - Monetary reform, with adoption of decimal system. Monetary unit was Peso or Boliviano of 100 Centavos, similar to silver coin of 5 Francs and equal to 25 grams 900 fine, or 22.50 grams fine silver.
Gold monies (Onza, Doubloon, Escudo) were minted only in small quantities and their values varied according to the price of gold.

- See *Boliviano*.

## BOLIVIANO

Former monetary unit of **Bolivia** divided into 100 Centavos.

Bank of issue - Until December 31, 1913 by Banco de la Nacion, Banco Nacional and Mercantile Bank. From 1914 to 1932, monopoly on banknote issue held by Banco de la Nacion. Since 1932, monopoly held by Banco Central de Bolivia (Central Bank of Bolivia).

Predecessor - See *Bolivia*.

**1863** (June 23rd) - Silver standard, linked to French 5 Franc coin: 1 Peso or Boliviano = 25 grams of silver 900 fine, or 22.5 grams fine silver.
Gold coins (Onzo, Doubloon, Escudo) were rare and their value varied according to price of gold.

**1908** (December 31st) - Adoption of gold standard:
1 Boliviano = 585.79 milligrams of fine gold
1 Pound Sterling = 12.50 Bolivianos

**1914** (October 24th) - Suspension of gold standard.

**1928** (July 11th) - Stabilization Law with devaluation of 6.2%:
1 Boliviano = 549.17 milligrams of fine gold
1 Pound Sterling = 13.50 Bolivianos

**1931** (September 25th) - Abandonment of gold standard, and de facto adherence to Sterling Area. Boliviano linked to price of tin in London.

**1931** (October 3rd) - Foreign exchange controls. Introduction of multiple exchange rates.

**1932** (May) - Official exchange rate:
1 Pound Sterling = 17 Bolivianos

**1933** (February 20th) - Official exchange rate:
1 Pound Sterling = 20 Bolivianos

**1936** (April 1st) - After conclusion of peace with Paraguay:
1 Pound Sterling = 50 Bolivianos

**1936** (June 14th) - Revaluation of reserves of Central Bank on basis of 1 Pound Sterling = 80 Bolivianos.

**1937** (July 29th) - Exchange rate fixed by exchange control authorities: 1 Pound Sterling = 100 Bolivianos. Free rate of exchange of commercial banks: 1 Pound Sterling = 120 Bolivianos.

**1938** (January) - Official rate of exchange for all transactions: 1 Pound Sterling = 100 Bolivianos.

**1938** (June 20th) - Buying rate of foreign exchange from exporters:
1 Pound Sterling = 82 Bolivianos
Selling rate of foreign exchange to importers:
1 Pound Sterling = 141 Bolivianos

**1939** (September 5th) - 1 Pound Sterling = 120/160 Bolivianos.

**1940** - Link to U.S. Dollar:
1 U.S. Dollar = 40 Bolivianos (essential imports)
1 U.S. Dollar = 55 Bolivianos (other imports)

**1941** (June 21st) - Official rate of exchange: 1 U.S. Dollar = 46 Bolivianos.

**1943** (February 12th) - 1 U.S. Dollar = 42 Bolivianos.

**1946** (December 18th) - Parity registered with International Monetary Fund:
1 Boliviano = 21.1588 milligrams of fine gold
1 U.S. Dollar = 42 Bolivianos

**1947** (October 20th) - Three exchange rates in force:
1 U.S. Dollar = 42.00/43.42 Bolivianos (official rate for export proceeds, essential imports)
1 U.S. Dollar = 55.50/56.05 Bolivianos (special rate for mineral exports, nonessential imports)
1 U.S. Dollar = 64.06 (1947 average) Bolivianos (free rate for luxury imports, noncommercial transactions)

**1948** (April) - Exchange tax of 1 Boliviano per U.S. Dollar on all sales of foreign exchange (except government imports and noncommercial transactions).

**1950** (February 27th) - Four exchange rates, not including rates with taxes:
1 U.S. Dollar = 42.00 Bolivianos (official rate for part of receipts from agricultural or mining exports)
1 U.S. Dollar = 42.42 Bolivianos (essential imports)
1 U.S. Dollar = 60.00 Bolivianos (special rate for tin exports, part of receipts from other exports)
1 U.S. Dollar = 100.00 Bolivianos (free rate for part of receipts from imports, nonessential imports, non-

commercial transactions)

**1950** (April 8th) - Elimination of special rate and devaluation:

    1 Boliviano = 14.8112 milligrams of fine gold

    1 U.S. Dollar = 60.00/60.60 Bolivianos (official buying and selling rate for export proceeds and import receipts)

    1 U.S. Dollar = 100.00 Bolivianos (free rate for all other commercial and noncommercial transactions)

Exchange taxes introduced in April 1948 still existed.

**1951** - Multiple rates as high as 190.00 Bolivianos per U.S. Dollar.

**1952** (August 19th) - Central Bank initially quoted free market rate for invisibles and nonregistered capital at 67.00 Bolivianos per U.S. Dollar, later raised to 245.00 Bolivianos.

**1953** (May 14th) - Devaluation registered with International Monetary Fund. De facto elimination of multiple rates:

    1 Boliviano = 4.67722 milligrams of fine gold

    1 U.S. Dollar = 190.00 Bolivianos (official)

    1 U.S. Dollar = 900.00 Bolivianos (fluctuating free market)

Exports of Bolivian Mining Corporation based on official rate minus tax of 35 Bolivianos.

**1954** (August 12th) - Tax of 200 Bolivianos added to official rate for student allocations abroad.

**1954** (December) - Fluctuating free market rate deteriorated to 1,808 Bolivianos per U.S. Dollar.

**1955** (March-December) - Fluctuating free market rate further deteriorated to 3,000 - 5,000 Bolivianos per U.S. Dollar. Gold coins issued by government and freely available and exportable. De facto reintroduction of multiple rates based on premiums of 320-1,310 Bolivianos per U.S. Dollar.

**1956** (February) - Link to U.S. Dollar Area.

**1956** (March-October) - Heavy inflation. Fluctuating free rate rose to 12,500 Bolivianos per U.S. Dollar.

**1956** (December 15th) - Inoperative official rate of 190 Bolivianos and multiple rate system replaced by fluctuating rate initially set at 7,745 Bolivianos per U.S. Dollar. Subsequently depreciated.

**1959** (January) - Free rate stabilized at 11,885 Bolivianos per U.S. Dollar.

**1963** (January 1st) - Boliviano replaced. - See *Peso Bolivia.*


## *BOLOGNA*

Roman monies (see *Rome*), then Carolingian monetary system.

**16th Century** - Monetary system of Papal States (see *Papal States*).

**18th Century** - Unit of account: Lira of 20 Soldi, 240 Denari, 2 Paoli or 120 Quattrini; Scudo of 85 Soldi.

Specie money: Petrone or Testone, Giustino, Paolo or Giulio, Maiorchino, Baiocco or Bolognino, Bagarone.

**1860** - Italian monetary system. - See *Italy.*

## BOLOGNINO

Silver and copper coins as well as unit of account in various **Italian** States.
- In **Bologna,** general name given to Soldo (Sol), unit of account worth $\frac{1}{20}$ Lira, or 6 Quattrini, 12 Denari, as well as a silver coin in 12th to 14th Century worth $\frac{1}{2}$ Grosso.

**16th Century** - Copper coin under Papal rule.
- In **Ancona,** Bolognino was unit of account worth $\frac{1}{80}$ Scudo, $\frac{1}{8}$ Paolo, $\frac{1}{4}$ Soldo, or 1.25 Baiocci, 3 Denari.
- In **Modena,** name for Soldo which was unit of account worth $\frac{1}{100}$ Ducato, $\frac{1}{20}$ Lira, or 12 Denari, as well as silver coin in 13th Century.

**17th and 18th Centuries** - Copper coins.
- In **Ferrara,** silver/copper coin in 13th Century; $\frac{1}{2}$ Bolognino called Ferrarino.
- In **Lucca,** copper coin in 18th Century.
- In **Lucca,** unit of account, also called Baiocco, worth $\frac{1}{10}$ Lira, or 2 Soldi, 24 Denari.

## BONK

In **Netherlands East Indies** (1796-1818), pieces of copper rod worth from $\frac{1}{2}$ to 8 Stuyvers, depending on the stamping.

## BONNET

Gold money of **Scotland** minted in 1539 and 1540 and weighing 5.83 grams.
Origin of name - From bonnet instead of crown decorating king's head.

## BORJOOKE

Glass beads of different colors used as minor specie money in **Ethiopia.** Valued at $\frac{1}{30}$ Para. 32,430 Borjookes equalled 1 Wakea.

## *BORNEO*

Primitive monies - Human skulls, dog's teeth.

In British North Borneo, adoption of Malayan Dollar (see *Dollar Malaya*) on December 31, 1952.
For rest of Borneo, see *Indonesia*.


## BOTDRAGER

Silver money of the **Netherlands**. Also called Helmeted Lion.
Origin of name - From pot carrier, because helmet on lion's head resembled an inverted pot.
Minted in Flanders in 1364 for 2 Grooten; in 1384 by Philip the Bold; in 15th Century silver plaque of 2 Grooten.
Minted in Holland under William V (1346-1389).


## *BOTSWANA*

Independent Republic (1966) formerly called Bechuanaland. Monetary system of South Africa. - See *South Africa*.


## BOUACHERA

**Tunisian** gold coin minted during 19th Century and withdrawn in 1891. Worth 10 Tunisian Piastres: 1.916 grams 900 fine. Equal to 1/10 Boumia, 1/5 Boukhamsin, 1/2.5 Boukoufa, or 2 Boukhama.


## BOUKHAMA

**Tunisian** gold coin minted during 19th Century and withdrawn in 1891. Worth 5 Tunisian Piastres: 0.94 grams 900 fine. Equal to 1/20 Boumia, 1/10 Boukhamsin, 1/5 Boukoufa, 1/2 Bouachera.
Variation of name - Boukhamsa.


## BOUKHAMSIN

**Tunisian** gold coin minted during 19th Century and withdrawn in 1891. Worth 50 Tunisian Piastres: 9.76 grams 900 fine. Equal to 1/2 Boumia, or 2 Boukoufa, 5 Bouachera, 10 Boukhama.

## BOUKOUFA

**Tunisian** gold coin minted during 19th Century and withdrawn in 1891. Worth 25 Tunisian Piastres: 4.855 grams 900 fine. Equal to ¼ Boumia, ½ Boukhamsin, 2.5 Bouachera, or 5 Boukhama.

## BOUMIA

**Tunisian** gold coin minted during 19th Century and withdrawn in 1891. Worth 100 Tunisian Piastres: 19.492 grams 900 fine. Equal to 2 Boukhamsin, 4 Boukoufa, 10 Bouachera or 20 Boukhama.

## BOURGEOIS

Minor coinage of silver/copper minted in **France** under Philip the Fair; also called Bourgeoise.

**1311** (January 27th) - Creation of simple or single Bourgeois, worth 1 Denier Parisis (0.31 grams of silver), and of heavy or double Bourgeois worth 2 Deniers Parisis.

## BOURSE

See *Beutel.*

## BOUTHLATA

**Tunisian** silver coin minted during 19th Century and withdrawn in 1891. Worth 2 Francs.

## BRACTEATE

From 12th to 14th Century, minted on one side of a very thin silver blank coin, thus depressed on one side and raised on the other. From 18th Century on, name given to silver Deniers (sometimes to copper ones), in Northern and Central Europe.

Origin of name - From Latin *Bractea,* metal leaf.

Plural - Bracteaten.

**12th Century -** In Saxony and in eastern sections of Swabia and Franconia, Deniers (Pfennige), made lighter and thinner, were no longer minted except on a single side of a silver leaf. Bracteaten were scattered across Norway, Sweden and Poland.

**13th Century -** Bracteaten appeared in Switzerland (in Basel, first round ones, then square), Bohemia, Hungary, Prussia (Teutonic Order).

**14th Century** - Continued circulation of Bracteaten in Basel, Berne and Saxony. Minting of Bracteaten in Bremen. Danish Pennig degenerated into Bracteate.

**15th Century** - Minting of copper Bracteaten in Riga (Latvia).

**16th Century** - Disappearance of Bracteaten in Berne.


## BRANDENBURG

See *Holy Roman Empire,* then *Prussia.*


## BRAZIL

**1645** - The Dutch West India Company minted square gold coins of 3, 6, and 12 Guilders; then in 1654, square silver coins of 10, 12 and 40 Stuyver.

**1679** - Use of Spanish monies counter-marked "640 Reis".

**1694** - First mint in Brazil. Introduction of Portuguese monetary system, with Real (plural Reis) as unit of account. - See *Real.*
Gold coinage: Moeda (of 4,000, 2,000 and 1,000 Reis); silver coinage: Patacao (320 Reis), Double Patacao (640 Reis), Vintem (20 Reis) and its multiples.

**1729** - Minting of copper coins. Rate of exchange of copper Portuguese monies in terms of Reis double rate prevailing in Portugal.

**1758-1774** - Minting of special silver coins for mining regions: mining Moedas (75 to 600 Reis).

**19th Century** - Use of gold Oitava. - See *Oitava.*

**1807** - To alleviate scarcity of silver money, introduction of Spanish Piasters, counter-marked in 1808 and exchangeable for 960 Reis. Raising of exchange rate of local money by 1/15, after affixing of a counter-mark.

**1846** (September 11th) - Adoption of Milreis as legal monetary unit. - See *Milreis.*

**1942** (November 1st) - Milreis became Cruzeiro. - See *Cruzeiro.*


## BRIQUET

Silver money issued in **Netherlands** by Charles the Bold, according to decree of October 27, 1474; equal to 2 Groten. Coin worth 1 Groot called Half Briquet.

Variation of name - In Dutch, *Vuurijzer.*


## BRITISH ANTILLES

See *British West Indies.*

## BRITISH EAST AFRICA

Consisted of British Protectorates of Kenya, Tanganyika, Uganda and Zanzibar. - See *individual protectorates.*

## BRITISH GUIANA

**1620** - Settled by Dutch West India Company. Dutch monetary system. Accounts kept in Stuyver and Duiten. Payments made in counter-marked Spanish Piasters.

**18th Century** - British silver and bronze coins and coins of French Antilles circulated.

**1814** - Ceded to Great Britain.

**1935** - Introduction of British West Indies Dollar. Circulated as government treasury notes. Continued circulation of British silver and copper coins and some silver Bits (a four penny local coin). - See *Dollar British West Indies.*

**1951** - Became a member of British Caribbean Currency Board.

**1962** - British Guiana withdrew from British Caribbean Currency Board.

**1965** (October 15th) - Bank of Guyana established as Central Bank.

**1965** (November 15th) - New monetary unit, Guyana Dollar, introduced to replace West Indies Dollar. - See *Dollar Guyana.*

**1966** (May 26th) - British Guiana changed name and became independent. - See *Guyana.*

## BRITISH HONDURAS

**18th Century** - Spanish and Mexican money. - See *Honduras.*

**19th Century** - British gold and silver coins and U.S. gold coins circulated.

**1885** - Locally minted bronze cent entered circulation.

**1894** (October) - Government notes were issued on a par with U.S. Dollar. - See *Dollar British Honduras.*
U.S. gold coins were standard of currency. British Sovereigns and Half Sovereigns were legal tender. Nickel-bronze five cent piece entered circulation.

## BRITISH SOLOMON ISLANDS

**1893-1900** - British Protectorate status established. Subsequent introduction of British monetary system. - See *Pound.*

**1920** - Use of monetary system of Australia. - See *Pound Australia.* British coins remained legal tender.

## BRITISH SOMALILAND

Former British Protectorate. Early 20th Century, Indian Rupee was basis of currency. Government of India notes circulated. - See *Rupee India.*

**1940** - East African Shilling circulated beside the Indian Rupee. - See *Shilling East Africa.*

**1951** - East African Shilling became sole legal tender.

**1960** (July 1st) - Newly independent British Somaliland became a part of Somalia. - See *Somalia.*

## BRITISH VIRGIN ISLANDS

**Before 1956** - Part of Leeward Islands group. - See *Leeward Islands.*

**1956** - Became separate British Colony. U.S. currency in circulation (abundant). British Caribbean Currency Board and British notes were also legal tender, but had virtually no use. - See *Dollar.*

## BRITISH WEST AFRICA

Consisted of British Protectorates of Nigeria, Gambia, Gold Coast, and Sierra Leone. - See *individual protectorates.*

## BRITISH WEST INDIES

Consists of Bahama Islands, Barbados, Jamaica with Cayman and Turks Islands, Leeward Islands, Trinidad and Tobago, and Windward Islands.

**Before 18th Century** - Spanish coins predominant, some English, Dutch, and French coins in circulation.

**18th Century** - Unit of account in Leeward Islands was Livre of 20 Sols or 240 Deniers, worth one-third less than the Livre Tournois:

      100 Livres Tournois = 133.33 Livres

Different unit of account used in Jamaica. - See *Jamaica.*

Specie monies: English coins and banknotes (rare). Portuguese monies predominant (see *Joe*). Some counter-marked Spanish Piasters in use.

**1730** - Introduction of silver coins of 6 and 12 Sols, then of 2 Sols (Marqués, then Tampés), minted in the French Antilles and given a local marking.

Coins of 3 Sols, counter-marked and introduced into British West Indies, had exchange rate of 1/6 Bit, a British Colonial unit worth 7 1/2 Pence.

**1788** - Copper Penny minted for circulation in British West Indies.

Note: For exceptions see individual Colonies.

**19th Century** - New monetary systems. - See *Bahama Islands, Barbados, Jamaica, Leeward Islands, Trindidad and Tobago,* and *Windward Islands.*

## *BRUNEI*

**1888** - Brunei became a British Protectorate. Currency in circulation, see *Piaster Mexico.*

**1903** (June 25th) - Currency in circulation, see *Dollar Straits Settlements.*

**1946** (April 1st) - Currency in circulation, see *Dollar Malaya.*

**1967** (June 12th) - Brunei issued a new currency. - See *Dollar Brunei.*

## BU

Small rectangular gold piece in early **Japan.** First issued in 1599. Equal to ¼ Ryo, standard unit of value. Divided into four parts, each one called a Shu. Also minted in silver in 1830.

Suffix gin means silver, kin means gold.

Cf. *Ichi Bu gin, Ichi Bu ban, Shu gin, Shu kin.*

## BUDSCHU

Unit of account and former silver coin of **Algeria** until French conquest. Divided into 24 Muzunas.

Variation of name - Boudjou.

Multiples and submultiples - 2 Budschu (Zudi Budschu), 1 (Rial Budschu), ¼ (Rebja or Rebia Budschu), ⅛ (Temin Budschu); all minted locally.

## BUGSHA

Submultiple (¹⁄₄₀) of Yemen Riyal, monetary unit of **Yemen Arab Republic.** Minted in silver and in copper.

Variations of name - Buqsha, Bugshah.

Predecessor - See *Bogache.*

## *BULGARIA*

First Greek, then Byzantine monies.

**13th Century** - Independent Bulgaria minted Gros in silver copying Grosso of Venice, and copper coins patterned after Byzantium.

**15th - 19th Century** - See *Turkey.*

**1880** - Adoption of an autonomous monetary unit, the Lev of 100 Stotinki. - See *Lev.*

## BURBE

Unit of account as well as a copper money in various countries under control or influence of **Turkey** from 17th to 19th Century.

Variations of name - Burbat, Burbas, Borbe, Bourbe.
 - In Egypt, Burbe was worth 1/264 Piastre, or 1/8 Para (or Medino).
 - In Tunis, Burbe was worth 1/624 Piastre, or 1/12 Asper.
 - In Tunis and Algiers, Burbe was divisionary copper coin.

## *BURMA*

Predecessor - See *India.*

**18th Century** - In Kingdom of Pegu, accounting based on Ticals of 16 Toques.
Specie money: Ganza (alloy of tin and copper).
Circulation of Mexican Piasters (each Piaster worth about 1.6 Ticals).

**19th Century** - Indian money circulated.

**1937** (April 1st) - Political separation of Burma from India. Banknotes of Reserve Bank of India maintained same exchange rate in Burma, but with overprint "Legal tender in Burma only". Convertible into silver Rupees.

**1939** (April 1st) - Indian Rupee and divisionary coins of India ceased to be legal tender in Burma. - See *Rupee Burma.*

**1942** - Circulation of Japanese military currency, called Gumpyo. Denominated in Burmese Rupees.

**1952** (February 1st) - Introduction and substitution of Kyat for Burmese Rupee at same parity. - See *Kyat.*

## BURRIE

In ancient **Mogul Empire** and **Bengal,** unit of account worth 1/4 Poni, 1/8 Anna, 1/64 Cawne and 1/128 Rupee. - See *Rupee India.*

Submultiples - Burrie was divided into 5 Gunda, or 20 Cowries.

## *BURUNDI*

Formerly a part of Ruanda-Urundi. - See *Ruanda-Urundi.*

**1962** (July 1st) - Burundi became independent state.

**1964** (May 19th) - Banque du Royaume du Burundi established as Central Bank. Issued new currency to replace Ruanda-Burundi Franc. - See *Franc Burundi.*

**1964** (September 30th) - Monetary and customs union with Rwanda dissolved.

**1966** (November 28th) - Burundi declared a Republic. Central Bank changed name to Banque de la République du Burundi (Bank of the Republic of Burundi).

## BUTUT

Proposed (1971) submultiple ($^1/100$) of Dalasy, monetary unit of **Gambia.** - See *Dalasy.*

## *BYZANTIUM*

**4th Century** - With split in the Roman Empire, Eastern Empire inherited Roman monetary system.

Gold coins - Solidus, commonly called Bezant. - See *Bezant.*

Silver coins - Miliarensis of 2 Siliquae. - See *Miliarensis, Siliqua.*

Copper coins - Follis of 20 Nummia. - See *Follis.*

Relationship of the coins:

1 Solidus = 12 Miliarensis = 288 Follis = 5,760 Nummia

**End of 5th Century** - Same coins, Siliqua having become the Keration.

Relationship of the coins:

1 Bezant = 12 Miliarensis = 24 Keratia = 180 to 210 Follis
= 5,760 to 6,720 Nummia

**10th Century** - After Basil I:

1 Bezant = 12 Miliarensis = 24 Keratia = 144 Follis = 288 Obols

Relationsip maintained until the fall of Constantinople.

## CACHE

Copper coin and submultiple in **India.**

Variation of name - Kas.

**I.** - In **India** (Southern States: Moslem monetary system), submultiple of Hun or Pagoda ($1/3.360$), Fanam ($1/320$) and Faluce ($1/20$). In Travancore, submultiple of Rupee ($1/512$), Fanam ($1/64$) and Chackram ($1/16$).

**II.** - In **French India,** early division of French Rupee.

**18th Century** - Copper money used in Pondicherry. 60 Cache needed for 1 Fanam, 420 for 1 silver Rupee, and 1,440 for 1 gold Pagoda.

**19th Century** - 96 Cache were equal to 1 French Rupee, 12 to 1 Fanam, and 4 to 1 Duddu.

**1871** (June 2nd) - Decree demonetizing copper Cache. Remained unit of account in Pondicherry (1 Cache = 2 Pie).

## CAGLIARESE

Small copper piece in **Sardinia,** first struck in 16th Century and in use until 19th Century. Usually computed at 2 Denari.

Origin of name - From Cagliari, capital of the island.

## CAIXA

**I.** - Money made of lead and copper slag, punctured with square hole in the middle. Manufactured in China and used in **Java** (since 1590) and in neighboring islands. 200 Caixa strung on a straw cord formed a Sata, which, when used as unit of account, was worth $1/2$ Tayell. - See *Sata.*

5 Sata, or 1,000 Caixa, made a Sapaku (or Sapèque); 100,000 made 1 Catty.

Variations of name - Kas for Malays, Pitje for Javanese.

**II.** - The Grand Caixa or Old Caixa corresponded to **Chinese** and **Japanese** Cash. - See *Cash.*

## *CAMBODIA*

Predecessor - See *Indochina.*

**1949** (November 8th) - Cambodia recognized as independent associated state within French Union. Currency remained Indochinese Piastre:

> 1 Piastre = 17 French Francs
> 1 U.S. Dollar = 20.59 Piastres

**1951** (December 31st) - Banknote issue turned over to Institut d'Emission Quadripartite, functioning as Central Bank.

**1953** (May 11th) - Devaluation of Piastre:

1 Piastre = 25.391 milligrams of fine gold
1 Piastre = 10 French Francs
1 U.S. Dollar = 35.00 Piastres

**1954** (July 20th) - Geneva Accord partitioned Indochina. - See also *Laos* and *Viet Nam.*

**1954** (December 29th) - Cambodia recognized as independent nation.

**1955** (January 1st) - Banque Nationale du Cambodge (National Bank of Cambodia) established to take over function of Central Bank and note-issuing authority.

**1955** (October 28th) - Cambodian Riel became national currency, and old Piastres removed from circulation. - See *Riel.*


## CAMEROON

Predecessors - See *Cameroon (French)* and *Cameroons (British).*

**1960** (January 1st) - Newly formed Cameroon Republic retained CFA Franc as monetary unit. - See *Franc CFA.*


## CAMEROON (FRENCH) AND CAMEROONS (BRITISH)

Native Money - Knife blades, and iron spears ranging in length from 4 inch minitures (submultiples) to 30 inches. Longest spears were called wife money, 12 spears buying a wife.

**1884** - German occupation. Introduction of German monetary system. - See *Mark.* Circulation of several foreign monies.

**1916** - Allied occupation. Part of Kamerun taken under British mandate, called British Cameroons. Money in circulation same as that of Nigeria. - See *Nigeria.* Remainder of territory under French mandate. - See *Franc.*

**1919** (December 17th) - Banque de l'Afrique Occidentale became note issuing authority in French Cameroon.

**1921** (May) - First issue of Franc notes by Central Bank of French Cameroon.

**1925** (December 31st) - All currencies circulating in French Cameroon, with exceptions of banknotes of Banque de l'Afrique Occidentale and French monies, ceased to be legal tender.

**1939** (September 9th) - Exchange controls introduced in French Cameroon.

**1941** - French Cameroon entered monetary union of French Equatorial Africa. - See *French Equatorial Africa.*

**1945** (December 26th) - Introduction of new monetary unit, CFA Franc, in French Cameroon. - See *Franc CFA.*

**1960** (January 1st) - French Cameroon became independent republic. No change in monetary unit.

**1961** (October 1st) - Southern British Cameroons joined newly formed Cameroon Republic creating Federal Republic of Cameroon. Monetary unit, CFA Franc. - See *Franc CFA.* Northern British Cameroons joined Federation of Nigeria. - See *Pound Nigeria.*

## *CANADA*

**Before colonization** - Use by Indian tribes of a strand of 2 kinds of shells as money, called Wampum. - See *Wampum.* Also use of bearskins as money.

**17th Century** - Moose skins and beaver skins generally used as money by colonists. Gradual introduction of French specie money, limited and controlled to avoid its leaving the Colony or its being hoarded by colonists. Encouragement of barter trade. Payment of civil servants made partly in French specie money and partly in local goods.

Frequent use of foreign coins (Portugese, Spanish, etc.) as result of foreign trade. Regarded as legal tender at favorable exchange rates.

**1654** (July 18th) - Resolution of Council of Quebec giving to French coins unit of accounting value in Livres, 1/5 higher than their value in France. - See *Livre Coloniale.*

**1661** (October 7th) - Premium revised to 1/3.

**1662** (March 20th) - Premium raised to 1/2. French copper coin of 1 Liard circulated in Canada at end of 17th Century under name of Double. Local value: 4 Deniers, as against 2 Deniers in France.

**1665** (November 26th) - Decree of Council-of-State granting to West Indies Company right to issue money.

**1670** (February 19th) - Declaration of Saint-Germain renewing privilege and authorizing minting of coins of 5 and 15 Sols.

**1672** (November 18th) - In order that specie money remained within colonies, decree of Council-of-State giving coins exchange rate higher than their nominal value (15 Sols raised to 20).

**1680** (December 2nd) - By order of Council of Quebec, return to former parity.

**1683** (January 13th) - Decree directing holders of foreign coins to deposit them with Provincial Treasury for weighing and stamping. Coins having correct weight were struck with a fleur-de-lis.

**1685** (June 8th) - In order to alleviate scarcity of means of payment, use of playing cards as money with forced parity (by order of Administrator, Jacques de Meulles).

**1685** (September 5th) - With arrival of funds from France, redemption of playing cards for specie money.

**1686** (February 9th - September 26th) - Second issue of playing card money.

**1714** (May 23rd) - After several issues of same type, on special cards sent from France, inflation (up to 1,600,000 Livres) and depreciation. Reduction to half of prior value of playing cards in circulation.

**1717** - Abolition, in principle, of playing card money which did, in fact, continue to circulate. Linking of exchange rate of specie money to its value in France.

**1721** (March 2nd) - Official reinstatement of playing card money, with ceilings on their issue progressively raised (in 1733, 1741, 1749). Depreciation of paper money.

**1764** - After British victory, renewed inflation: 643,000 Livres Tournois worth of playing card money in circulation.

**1766** - Franco-British agreement for redemption of playing card money. Introduction of British monetary system: Pound Sterling of 20 Shillings or 240 Pence. - See *Pound.*

**Early 19th Century** - No more local minting other than tokens minted by individuals and private banks.

**1853** - Provinces of Canada Currency Act legalized transactions in decimal currency. Gold coin made unlimited legal tender. Adoption of gold standard.

**1870** - Appearance of Canadian Dollar notes. - See *Dollar Canada.*


## *CANARY ISLANDS*

Spanish monetary system. - See *Spain* and *Peseta Spain.*


## CANDAREEN

Monies of the **Far East.**

Variations of name - Candarin, Condorin, Kanderine, Conderie. In Chinese called Fen or Fun.

**I.** - Unit of weight and unit of account in **China** equal to $1/10$ Mace and $1/100$ Tael (Liang). - See *Tael.* Also struck in silver in denominations of 7.2 and 3.6 Candareens.

**II.** - Unit of account in **Japan** in 18th Century equal to $1/10$ Mace and $1/100$ Tael.

**III.** - In **Java,** early lesser unit of account: 100 million Candareens needed for 1 Bahar, 10 million for 1 Uta, 1 million for 1 Catty, 100,000 for 1 Laxsan, 10,000 for 1 Pecco, 400 for 1 Tayell, 200 for 1 Sata, 40 for 1 Mas, 10 for 1 Cash.


## *CAPE VERDE ISLANDS*

**16th-19th Century** - Portuguese settlers made monetary use of cowrie shells imported from Maldive Islands. Simultaneous use of specie money of Portugal. - See *Portugal.*

**1864** - Banco Nacional Ultramarino began issuing Escudo banknotes. - See *Escudo Portugal.*


## CAPELLONE

Silver money worth 5 Soldi in the Duchy of **Modena** during 18th Century.

Origin of name - Italian *capello* (hair), from long hair on portrait.

Variation of name - Cappelono.

# CARAT

Money used in **Rhodes** in 14th Century. Equal to $1/160$ Zecchino (Sequin), $1/24$ Bezant, $1/16$ Gigliato, $1/8$ Asper. Also equivalent of 2 Deniers.

Origin of name - From carat, unit of weight in Venice for trading of metals and unit of fineness for alloys of gold. Italian *carato*, Arabic *girat*, small weights; Greek *keration*, husk or grain from Carob tree.

# CARBEQUI

Copper coin used in **Georgia** in 18th Century. Minted in Tiflis. Also called Asper. Equal to $1/10$ Chaouri or $1/105$ Piastre.

# CARBOVANEZ

Name given to Ruble in **Ukraine** in 1923. From 1942 to 1944, money issued by German Occupation.

Variation of name - Karbovantsiv.

**1941** - German Occupation. Issue of banknotes denominated in Reichsmark by the Reichkreditkassen.

**1942** (March 5th) - Creation of Central Bank of the Ukraine, which from June 1st issued banknotes denominated in Carbovanez and guaranteed by general mortgage on all landed property.

**1942** (July to November) - Exchange of all Ruble money (except banknotes and coins of less than 3 Rubles) for Carbovanez banknotes with partial and temporary blocking. Continued circulation of Reichskreditkassen banknotes at rate of 1 Reichsmark = 10 Carbovanez.

**1944** - Russian Occupation. Substitute of Ruble for Carbovanez. - See *Ruble*.

# CARLINO

**I. -** Unit of account in **Malta** during rule of island by Knights of Malta (1530-1798) and until 19th Century. Also minted in silver as early as 16th Century. Value: $1/2$ Tarin. Its value reduced and in 18th Century, copper Carlini minted.

Origin of name - Italian *Carlino*, from Carlo (Charles d'Anjou, King of Naples).

Variations of name - Carlin, Charlois.

Plural - Carlini.

**Until 1730** - Equal to $1/2$ Tarin, or 2 Cinquini, 10 Grani, 60 Piccioli.

**After 1730** - $1/24$ Scudo, $1/2$ Tarin. Carlino valued at 6 Piccioli or 10 Grani.

**II. -** In **Naples**, gold money minted from 1266 (also called Saluto d'Oro); in 1304, Charles II named it the Carlin Majestic, or Gigliato. Silver coin minted from the 16th Century (19.7 grams of fine silver).

Unit of account until 19th Century; Carlino worth $1/10$ Ducato, $1/2$ Tarin, 4 Cinquini, 19 Grani, 20 Tornesi, 20 Quartini, 60 Piccioli, 120 Cavalli or Denari.
In **Sicily,** unit of account worth $1/60$ Onza, $1/24$ Scudo, $1/12$ Fiorino, $1/2$ Tarin, or 7.5 Ponti, 10 Grani, 60 Piccioli. Silver coin worth 10 Grani.
**III.** - In **Sardinia,** gold money issued in 1755 for 120 Lire.
**IV.** - In Rome **(Papal States),** Carlino, or Grosso papalo, issued in 15th Century for $1/10$ Ducato.

## CAROLIN

**I.** - Gold money of various **German States** (minted with figure of a Prince Karl).
Variation of name - Karolin.
Plural - Caroliner.
**1753** - Agreement of Vienna fixed weight of Carolin at 9.7 grams, of which 7.5 were fine gold. Exchange rate: 11 Florins (Guilders).
Circulated mostly in Bavaria, Franconia (Nürnberg), Württemberg, Upper Palatinate (Heidelberg), Electorate of Cologne.
Multiple and submultiples - Double Carolin, $1/2$ and $1/4$ Carolin.
**II.** - Gold coin minted in **Sweden** by Charles XV, according to the law of July 31, 1868. Patterned after the Napoléon (coin of 10 Francs); 3.22 grams of gold 900 fine, or 2.90 grams of fine gold. Exchange rate: 7 Riksdaler 40 Oere. Also minted in silver by Charles XI and XII.

## CAROLINE ISLANDS

Primitive money - Circular stone discs from 20 centimeters to 1 meter in diameter, popularly called Yap Money. Pieces varies in value most probably according to thickness, diameter of stone. Holes carved in centers of stones to facilitate hanging or carrying.
**19th Century** - Spanish control. Use of Spanish monies for trade transactions.
**1899** - German control. Introduction of German monetary system. - See *Mark.*
**1919** - Japanese control. Monetary system of Japan. - See *Yen.*
**1947** - United States trusteeship. Introduction of United States monetary system. - See *Dollar.*

## CAROLINO

Silver/copper coin of the **Papal States** worth 7.5 Baiocchi.

## CAROLUS

**I.** - **French** money of silver/copper in the 15th and 16th Centuries, also called Karolus.
Origin of name - From Charles VIII, who had the coin minted with the letter K.
  Various mintings, by Charles VII, Louis XI, Francis I, of different degrees of fineness.
  Value: 10 Deniers at time of its repudiation which was decreed by Louis XI. Carolus remained a unit of account to designate sum of 10 Deniers.
  Variations of Carolus in Burgundy, Lorraine and Dauphiné. Imitated in several European states.
**II.** - **English** gold coin minted under Charles I and Charles II. Exchange rate: 23 Shillings.
**III.** - In **Netherlands,** minting of silver Carolus by Charles V in 1542, equal to Thaler. Exchange rate: 1 Guilder or 40 Groten.
**IV.** - Silver coins minted in Southwest **German States** beginning in 1730.

## *CARTHAGE*

For domestic use, primitive money of a paper type: small pieces of leather, prepared in such a way as to render their imitation impossible, and given agreed-upon value. For foreign trade, barter of goods against goods or for raw or unminted gold.
**4th Century B.C.** - First mintings of Spanish silver for commerce with Greeks, and of Mauritanian gold to pay soldiers.
**3rd Century B.C.** - Coins of gold (9.70 grams), of electrum (2/3 gold and 1/3 silver), of silver (Greek model) and of bronze. Paper money continued.
**2nd Century B.C.** - Fall of Carthage. Roman monetary system. - See *Rome.*

## CARZIA

Copper coin of **Cyprus** issued by Prioli family for Nicosia in 16th Century.
Plural - Carzie.

## CASH

Silver, copper or tin money or unit of account in **Orient** and **Far East.**
Variations of name - Cas, Casse, Cassie, Cayas, Caxa, Caixa.
**I.** - In **China,** in 14th Century, 1/1.000 Kuan. Later, 1/10 Candareen, 1/100 Mace, 1/1.111 Tael. Cash identical with Sapèque and Tsien. - See *Sapèque, Tsien.*
  Or 1/16 Candareen, 1/160 Mace, 1/1.600 Tael. - See *Tael.*
**II.** - In **Japan,** copper coin used in 18th Century. Cash were strung 600 to a cord.
**III.** - In Kingdom of Achin in **Sumatra,** unit of account: 25,600 Cash counted for 1 Tayell, 6,400 for 1 Pardaw, 1,300 for 1 Mas, 400 for 1 Koupan.

Appeared in 18th Century in form of tin money.

IV. - In **Java,** early unit of account: 10 million Cash counted for 1 Bahar, 1 million for 1 Uta, 100,000 for 1 Catty, 10,000 for 1 Laxsan, 1,000 for 1 Pecco, 40 for 1 Tayell, 20 for 1 Sata, 4 for 1 Mas. Cash equalled 10 Candareens.

Exchange ratio to Spanish Piaster, introduced by Europeans as unit of account in 18th Century: from 20,000 to 35,000 Cash for 1 Piaster.

## CASTELLANO

Early **Spanish** gold money equivalent in the 15th Century to ½ Dobla Castillana. - See *Doubloon.* Exchange rate in 18th Century: 14 Reales, then raised to 28 Reales.

Demonetized by law of April 15, 1848.

## CATTY

I. - Early unit of account of **Siam.** Corresponded to 20 Tael, 80 Tical, 320 Salung, 640 Fuang, 5,120 Cowries (see *Cowrie*), 1,280 Song Pais, 2,560 Pais, or 5,120 Clam (see *Clam*).

Variations of name - Catti, Kati.

Plural -Catties.

II. - Unit of account in **Java.** Corresponded to 100,000 Caixa, or to ¹⁄₁₀₀ Bahar, ¹⁄₁₀ Uta, 10 Laxsan, 100 Peccoes, 2,500 Tayell, 5,000 Sata, 25,000 Mas, 100,000 Cash, 1 million Candareens.

## CAVALIER

I. - Silver money, created in 1275 at Valenciennes by Marguerite of Constantinople, Countess of **Flanders** and of **Hainaut.** Exchange rate: 2 Esterlins, or 8 Deniers. International prestige of coin gave rise to many imitations: in Orange, Dauphiné, Netherlands, and in Luxembourg.

II. - Various gold monies, with imprint of cavalier: In Milan (14th Century), in Savoy (14th Century), in Brabant (14th Century), in unified Netherlands (15th Century; Gouden Rijder of 45 Gros), in Scotland (15th and 16th Centuries), in Spain (14th and 15th Centuries; issued by Henry II and Jean II: weight, 90 grams with a value of 20 Doblas).

Cf. *Cavallo, Rijder.*

## CAVALLO

Name of various coins in **Italian States** bearing figure of a horse.

Plural - Cavalli.

**I.** - Name given in **Naples** to Denaro, unit of account worth ¹/₁.₂₀₀ Ducato. Then ¹/₁.₀₀₀ of the Ducato after 1818. Minted in pure copper at end of 15th Century. - See *Denaro.*

**II.** - Silver/copper money minted in **Piedmont** in 1616.


## CAVALOTTO

In **Genoa,** early money of silver/copper (3.5 grams, of which 0.7 grams were fine silver). Exchange rate in 18th Century: 6.66 Soldi.

Variations of name - Caboletto, Caballetto, Cavaletto.


## CAWNE

In ancient **Mogul Empire,** in **Bengal,** and in **Maldive Islands,** unit of account worth ¹/₂ Indian Rupee. - See *Rupee India.*

Submultiples - Cawne divided into 8 Annas, 16 Poni, 64 Burrie, 320 Gunda and 1,280 Cowries.


## *CAYMAN ISLANDS*

For money in circulation, see *Dollar Jamaica* and *Dollar Cayman Islands.*


## CEDI

Monetary unit of **Ghana.** Divided into 100 Pesewas.

Origin of name - Akan word, *Sedie,* meaning cowrie. - See *Cowrie.*

Bank of issue - Bank of Ghana.

Predecessors - See *Ghana, Pound Ghana, Pound West Africa.*

**1965** (July 19th) - Devaluation. Ghana Cedi replaced Ghana Pound:
 1 Ghana Cedi = 1,036.78 milligrams of fine gold
 1 Ghana Cedi = 1.17 U.S. Dollars
Just before this action taken, Ghana Pound listed in black market at U.S. $0.90, against official rate of U.S. $2.80. Cedi also listed at U.S. $0.90 in black market. Subsequently dropped to an all-time low of U.S. $0.40 (November).

**1967** (February 17th) - New Cedi replaced Cedi:
 1 New Cedi = 1.20 Cedis
 1 New Cedi = 1,244.14 milligrams of fine gold
 1 New Cedi = 1.40 U.S. Dollars
Move not considered as appreciation or depreciation of Ghana's currency by International Monetary Fund.

**1967** (May 23rd) - Cedi ceased to be legal tender.

**1967** (July 8th) - Devaluation:
1 New Cedi = 870.897 milligrams of fine gold
1 New Cedi = 0.98 U.S. Dollar

## CEITIL

Submultiple (1/16) of **Portuguese** Real. Also earliest copper coin, first issued in 13th Century.

## *CELEBES*

See *Netherlands East Indies.*

## CELLA

Silver money in **Naples** during 15th Century. Various earlier mintings in **Italian** States under name Aquilino.
Origin of name - Italian *Uccello* (bird).

## CELT

Stone hatchet used as some form of money in **Gaul.**

## CENT

Submultiple (1/100) of several monies in 19th and 20th Centuries, generally of **Anglo-Saxon** origin. Also a copper coin.
Cf. *Centu, Sen, Sene, Sent, Seniti, Santi.*
I. - Submultiple of Dollar of Australia, Bahamas, British Honduras, British West Indies, Brunei, Canada, Canton, China, Ethiopia, Fiji Islands, Guyana, Hong Kong, Jamaica, Liberia, Malaysia, New Zealand, North China, Singapore, Taiwan, Trinidad and Tobago, United States.
II. - Submultiple of Guilder of Indonesia, Netherlands, Netherlands Antilles, New Guinea, Surinam.
III. - Submultiple of Leone.
IV. - Submultiple of Rand.
V. - Submultiple of Rupee of Ceylon, East Africa, Indonesia, Maldive Islands, Mauritius, Seychelles.

**VI.** - Submultiple of Shilling of East Africa, then of Shilling of Kenya, Tanzania, Uganda.

## CENTAVO

Submultiple ($^1/_{100}$) of **Spanish, Portuguese** and **Latin American** monies. Also copper coin.

Escudo of Portugal, Portuguese Angola, and Mozambique.

Peso of Argentina, Chile, Colombia, Cuba, Dominican Republic, Ecuador, Mexico, Philippines, Uruguay (until 1859).

Boliviano, Cruzeiro, Sucre, Quetzal, Lempira, Córdoba, Sol, El Salvador Colón, Venezolano.

Plural - Centavos.

## CENTENARIO

**Mexican** gold coins of 50 Pesos, weighing 41.666 grams 900 fine, or 37.5 grams fine gold. Minted from 1921 to 1933 (antiguo) and from 1934 to 1947 (nuevo).

## CENTESIMO

Submultiple ($^1/_{100}$) of **Latin** monies. Also copper coin.

Lira, Vatican Lira, Somalo, Francho.

Balboa, Venezolano, Dominicano.

Somali Shilling.

Peso of Uruguay (since 1859), of Cuba (until 1899), and of Paraguay (from 1870 to 1881).

Escudo of Spain (from 1870 to 1881), Chile.

Italian plural - Centésimi.

Spanish plural - Centésimos.

## CENTIME

**I.** - Submultiple of Franc ($^1/_{100}$), monetary unit of **France.**

**1793** (December 7th) - Law dividing Livre into 100 Centimes.

**1795** (April 7th) - Law making Centime one-hundredth part of Franc, future monetary unit.

**1795** (August 15th) - Official division of Franc into 10 Décimes of 10 Centimes each.

**1796** (October 24th) - Minting of Centime in copper.

**1799** (May 6th) - Francs, Décimes and Centimes became official units of account.

**1852** (May 6th) - Demonetization of copper Centimes. Minting of bronze Centimes (1 gram).

**1914** - Disappearance from circulation of Centime coins.

**1928** (June 25th) - After the Poincaré stabilization, issue of coins of 10 Centimes in nickel/bronze.

**1935** (February 1st) - Demonetization of bronze coins.

**1938** (February 24th) - Decree calling for substitution of zinc for nickel/bronze.

**1940** (November 24th) - Demonetization of Centime.

**1940** (December 21st) - Law ordering minting of coins of 10 Centimes of a zinc base alloy.

**1946** (December 24th) - Demonetization of 10 Centime coins.

**1960** (January) - Reintroduction of Centime coin:
50, 20, 10 Centimes: 20% copper, 20% nickel and 60% aluminum
5, 2, 1, Centime: stainless steel

**II.** - Submultiple ($\frac{1}{100}$) of Franc Albania, Algeria, Belgium, Burundi, CFA, CFP, Congo, Djibouti, Guiana, Guinea, French West Indies, Katanga, Malagasy, Mali, Monaco, Ruanda-Burundi, Rwanda, Switzerland.
Another name for Swiss Centime - Rappen.

**III.** - Submultiple ($\frac{1}{100}$) of other monies: Dinar of Algeria, Gourde of Haiti, Kip of Laos, Piastre of South Viet Nam.
Other names for Laotian Centime - At, Pi.

**IV.** - Submultiple ($\frac{1}{2,000}$) of Lebanese, Syrian, Lebanese-Syrian Pound. Submultiple ($\frac{1}{20}$) of the Lebanese, Syrian, Lebanese-Syrian Piastre.

Plural - Centimes.

## CENTIMO

Submultiple ($\frac{1}{100}$) of **Spanish** monies and monies of **Latin America.** Also copper coin.
Peseta, Costa Rica Colón, Guaraní, Bolívar, Dominican Peso.

Plural - Céntimos.

## *CENTRAL AFRICAN REPUBLIC*

Predecessor - Ubangi-Shari. - See *French Equatorial Africa.*

**1960** (August 15th) - Became independent nation within French community. Money in circulation, see *Franc CFA.*

## *CENTRAL AMERICA*

**Before 1821** - Spanish occupation. Circulation of Spanish and Mexican Piasters - See *Piaster Mexico.*

**1822** - Formed Mexican Empire.

**1823** - Independence and formation of United Provinces, unifying five Republics of Guatemala, Costa Rica, Honduras, Nicaragua and El Salvador.
Use of a Peso derived from Mexican Piaster: 27.064 grams of silver 902 fine, or 24.41 grams fine silver. - See *Peso Central America.*

**1838-1847** - Breakup of United Provinces. - See *Guatemala, Costa Rica, Honduras, Nicaragua, El Salvador.*

## CENTU

Submultiple of Litas (1/100), monetary unit of **Lithuania** from 1922 to 1941. - See *Litas.* Cf. *Cent.*

## *CEYLON*

**Primitive money** - Stylized fish hook, progressively reduced to a bent shaft. Shell money imported from Maldive Islands. - See *Cowrie.*

**16th Century** - Introduction of Portuguese monies.

**17th Century** - Introduction of Dutch monies.

**18th Century** - Mixed circulation of Indian and Dutch money. - See *Rupee India.* Unit of account: Rijksdaalder, divided into 12 Fanams or 48 Stuyver.

**1802** - Ceylon became British Colony.

**1815** - Minting of silver Rijksdaalder and copper Stuyver.

**1827** - Appearance of copper 1/2 Farthings and other British monies, which became predominant.

**1872** - Adoption of Indian Rupee divided into 100 Cents.

**1929** (December 16th) - Autonomous monetary system. - See *Rupee Ceylon.*

## CHACKRAM

In **India,** especially Travancore, submultiple (1/16) of Cash in 18th Century. Minted in bronze and silver.
Variation of name - Chuckram.

## *CHAD*

Predecessor - See *French Equatorial Africa.*

**1960** (August 11th) - Became independent nation within French community. Money in circulation, see *Franc CFA.*

# CHAISE

**I. - French** gold money from 14th to 15th Century.

Variations of name - Denier à la Chaise, Royal à la Chaise, Chaise d'Or.

Origin of name - From imprint showing a seated king.

**1303** (August 15th) - Philip the Fair minted Royal à la Chaise of pure gold (7.09 grams). Exchange rate: 62 Sous 6 Deniers.

**1305** (May 7th) - Exchange rate of Chaise reduced to 41 Sous 3 Deniers.

**1308** (January 18th) - Exchange rate lowered to 25 Sous.

**1313** (June) - Repudiation of Chaise.

**1346** (October 2nd) - Philip VI minted pure gold Chaise (4.70 grams). Rate 20 Sous.

**1347** (February 24th) - Exchange rate raised to 30 Sous.

**Under Charles VI** - Chaise of 6.05 grams fine gold.

**Under Charles VII** - Chaise of 4.10 grams 666 fine, or 2.73 grams fine gold.

**II. -** Gold money of various **Flemish States:**
  - In Luxembourg and Bohemia (minting of Jean the Blind: 1309-1346).
  - In Flanders (14th Century: also called Hardi - 15th Century: also called Clinckaert).
  - In Brabant (14th and 15th Centuries: also called Clinckaert).
  - In Holland (14th and 15th Centuries).

**III. -** Gold coin in **Holy Roman Empire.** Minted in 1328.


# CHALCUS

Submultiple of **Greek** Obol (1/6 Drachma), made up of 4 Dichalcoi or 8 Chalcoi. Chalcus equal to 7 Lepta (singular: Lepton). Minted in copper and periodically reduced in weight.

Origin of name - Greek *chalkos* meaning ore, or Chalcis, city that commanded market for copper.

Plural - Chalcoi.


# CHANDERNAGOR

**Before 18th Century -** See *India.*

**18th - 20th Century -** See *French India* and *Rupee France.*

**1950** (May 2nd) - Return of Chandernagor to India, and substitution of Indian Rupee for French Rupee. - See *Rupee India.*

## CHAOURI

Silver money used in **Georgia** (Tiflis) during 18th Century. Corresponded to ¹/10.5 Piaster, ¼ Abbasi, ½ Usalton, or 10 Aspers (or Carbequi) of copper.

Variations of name - Chaourz, Schauri, Sain.

## CHATEL

Silver coins issued in **France** during 16th Century.

Origin of name - From imprint picturing a chateau.

**1353** (November 9th) - Jean II minted Chatel with imprint of a clover leaf, silver money 750 fine. Fineness progressively debased. Initial exchange rate: 8 Deniers.

**1357** (January 25th) - Minting of Chatel with imprint of the fleur-de-lis (2.19 grams, of which 0.55 grams were fine silver).

## CHEDA

Tin money with round or octagonal shape. In use during 18th Century in **India** (Mogul States).

Valued at about 80 Cowries.

## CHERVONETS

Monetary unit of **Soviet Union** from 1922 to 1935. Divided into 10 Rubles. Since 1935, a multiple (10) of Ruble.

Origin of name - Russian word meaning shining.

Variation of name - Chervonetz.

Bank of issue - State Bank of the R.S.F.S.R. established in 1921. Name changed to State Bank of U.S.S.R. (Gosbank) in 1923.

Predecessor - See *Ruble.*

Plural - Chervontsi.

**1922** (November 27th) - Issue of Chervontsi banknotes in denominations of 1, 2, 3, 5, 10, 25 and 50 denominated in gold, and a 1 Chervonets gold piece:

> 1 Chervonets = 10 Gold Rubles
> 1 Chervonets = 7,742.3436 milligrams of fine gold
> 1 Chervonets = 5.1455 U.S. Dollars

Banknotes to be exchangeable for gold at a later date, but never materialized. Chervontsi circulated along with old Soviet Ruble notes which were still issued by Treasury.

**1924** (February-March) - Unification of monetary system, Chervonets becoming monetary unit.

**1935** (November 14th) - Chervonets devalued 77.15% and replaced by new gold Ruble for purchases of foreign exchange from tourists. - See *Ruble.*


## CHEUN

Submultiple (1/100) of Won, monetary unit of **North Korea.** - See *Won.*
Variations of name - Chon, Chong, Jun, Moun, Mon.


## CHIAO

Submultiple (1/10) of Manchukuo Yuan, former monetary unit of Japanese-occupied **Manchukuo** (Manchuria). Equal to 10 Fen and 100 Li. - See *Yuan Manchukuo.*


## *CHILE*

**17th-19th Century** - Circulation of Spanish, Mexican and Peruvian Piasters. - See *Spanish America.*
**1817** - Independent Chile retained Spanish monetary system with Piaster (or Peso) of 8 Reales. Old coins imprinted with symbol of new republic.
**1834** - Local minting of gold coins.
**1851** (January 9th) - Creation of national money. - See *Peso Chile.*
**1960** (January 1st) - New unit created. - See *Escudo Chile.*


## CHIMFRAM

**Portugese** silver money issued in 15th Century by Alfonso V. Valued at 1/2 Grosso or 3 Espadim of silver/copper.


## *CHINA*

**Primitive monies** - Shells in river areas, animal skins in mountain regions.
**2640 B.C.** - Under Emperor Wan-Ti, major payments made in pearls, gems or gold; minor payments in bronze knives called Tao-Pou. - See *Tao-Pou.* (According to certain writers, first money appeared in 2953 B.C. under reign of Tai Ho).
**2255 B.C.** - First use of silver as a medium of exchange, under Emperor Chuan. Spread of use of silver into outer China, while use of copper prevalent in inner China. These monies took on semblance of jewelry (bracelets and rings).
**1500 B.C.** - Minor payments made with shells, of Cowrie type, use of which persisted until the Tsins (3rd Century A.D.). Cowries imitated in metal from 6th Century B.C.

**1100 B.C.** - In reign of Shang Wang, of Chou Dynasty, minting of first round coins (according to certain sources, only in 606 B.C.).

**220 B.C.** - Monetary reform of Che Hwang Ti excluding precious objects. Adoption of gold money. Weight of copper coins decreased. Casting of Tsien, round punctured copper coins, then of Chia Tsien in form of fruit of elm tree. - See *Tsien.*

**About 170 B.C.** - Under Hiao Wen Ti, prohibition of private minting. Issue of coin weighing 4 Chu or 2.25 grams.

**About 140 B.C.** - Monetary expedients of Wu Ti. Minting of coins made of alloy of silver and tin: round coin (Po Siuan) equal to 3,000 copper coins; square coin equal to 500 copper coins; oval coin equal to 300 copper coins. Issue of squares of white suede or of silk (called P'i Pi or Li Fu) bearing official seal, which had exchange rate of 40,000 copper coins. - See *P'i Pi.*

**40 B.C.** - Monetary confusion under Wang Mang.

**2nd Century A.D.** - Lieou Pei minted large copper coin (3.96 cm. in diameter, and weighing 4.50 grams) with excessive nominal value.

**221** - In Kingdom of Wei (Northern China), copper money withdrawn from circulation, replaced by fabrics and cereal grains.

**3rd Century** - Copper money in disfavor (debasement of small coins, overvalued exchange rate of large ones). Issue of iron money, progressively depreciated.

**6th Century** - Increasing depreciation of iron money. Issue of tin coins. Monetary use of silks, millet, salt (in the South), cinnabar and of rice, and sometimes of gold and silver. Reappearance of copper Tsien. - See *Tsien.*

**621** - T'angs issued Yuan Pao, copper coin of 3.8 grams (weight reduced in the 8th Century) often in bundles of 1,000 coins called Kuan. - See *Yuan Pao.*

**650** - Issue of rectangular paper notes (Pao Ch'ao) worth 10,000 Yuan Pao made of copper.

**758** - Minting of large coins (Kien Yuan chong pao) weighing 5 grams and issued for 10 Yuan Pao.

**759** - Minting of even larger coins (Chong louen tsien) weighing 6 grams, and issued for 50 Yuan Pao. Then lowered to 30 and finally to 3 (in 763).

**804** - Hoarding and disappearance of copper. Monetary use of silk fabrics.

**806** - Holding of more than 50,000 Yuan Pao worth of copper coins forbidden. Issue of checks (Fei tsien or portable Tsien) representing receipt for metal deposited at Treasury.

**811** - Monetary use of silk fabrics and silver bars made obligatory for all payments of more than 10,000 Yuan Pao.

**10th Century** - Because of scarcity of copper, increase in private mintings of lead and iron monies. Payments made in silk goods, gold bars or silver plates: Ting or Sycees. - See *Sycee.*

**924** - Embargo on export of copper Tsien.

**926** - Sale of copper utensils forbidden.

**937** - Manufacture and use of copper utensils forbidden.

**960** - Under Sungs, issue of copper Tsien (Tung Pao and Yuan Pao). In certain provinces lacking copper, issue of iron Tsien, progressively depreciated.

**About 990** - Issue, at first private, of paper banknotes. - See *Kiao tze*. Use of vouchers for tea. - See *Tch'a Yin*.

**1046** - Minting, in Shansi, of large copper and iron coins (K'ing li chong Pao) worth 10, then 2 small Tsien.

**11th Century** - In Shansi, minting of Tsien from a tin alloy. Issue of vouchers for salt. - See *Yen Ch'ao*.

**1154** - In Peking, new issue of paper money. - See *Kiao Ch'ao*.

**1187** - Issue of a money made of copper and silver alloy (Ta Ting T'ong Pao).

**1197** - First minting of silver coins similar to Tsien (Tch'eng An Pao Houo), quickly counterfeited and demonetized in 1200.

**13th Century** - Under Yuan Dynasty, payments made in silver in form of Ting slabs, sometimes in copper in form of Tsien, but usually in banknotes called Sseu Ch'ao, representing raw silk used as monetary cover. - See *Sseu Ch'ao*.

**1308** - New issue of paper money. - See *Yin Ch'ao*.

**1374** - Issue of banknotes of mulberry leaf paper. - See *Pao Ch'ao*.

**16th Century** - Silver bars occupied first place among monetary instruments.

**1575** - Introduction of Mexican Piaster (silver coin 24.4356 grams fine) by Portuguese merchants (via Macao) and Spanish merchants (via Philippines) in exchange for tea, porcelain, silk, etc. Use became widespread. - See *Piaster Mexico*.

**17th and 18th Centuries** - Silver Tael used as unit of account. - See *Tael*. Circulation of copper Sapèques or Tsien. Simultaneous use of Sycees and Mexican Piasters.

**19th Century** - More or less successful introduction of coins copying Mexican Piaster: Bolivian, Chilean, Peruvian Dollars; Saigon Piastre; Japanese Yen; American Trade Dollar. Local imitations: Canton Dollar, Hopei Dollar, Hong Kong Dollar. Puncturing of Mexican Piasters, called Chopped Dollars. Nonpunctured Mexican Piasters called Clean Dollars.

**1800-1840** - Silver drain (over 100 million ounces) from opium imports resulted in severe inflation. Value of copper money diminished in relation to silver.

**1838** - Provincial Treasury of Fukien minted a Dollar similar to Mexican Piaster. - See *Dollar China*.

**After 1850** - Local minting of some gold coins (Taiping, Turkestan, Tibet, Yunnan).

**1852** - Inflation of paper money in Peking by Manchu Dynasty. After bankruptcy, total anarchy in issue of paper money (banknotes of commercial banks and of provinces).

**1902** (September 5th) - Sino-British Treaty by which China created national money.

**1930** (February 1st) - Creation of unit of account for customs. - See *Gold Unit*.

**1930** (May) - Embargo on gold shipments, soon evaded by smuggling.

**1932** (June 11th) - In occupied Manchuria, issue of the Manchukuo Yuan by Japanese. - See *Manchukuo Yuan*.

**1933** (March 8th) - Replacement of Sycees and Taels, and adoption of Chinese Dollar as sole monetary unit.

**1933** (April 5th) - Institution of levy of 2.25% on exports of former monies and silver bars.

**1934** (October 15th) - Levy on silver increased to 7.75% (minted silver) and 10% (bars).

A compensatory duty applied according to price of metal. Creation of Exchange Equalization Fund.

**1935** - Embargo on silver exports.

**After 1935** - New monetary breakup: in Northern China (see *Dollar Northern China*), Southern China (see *Dollar Canton*), Mongolia (see *Yuan Mongolia*).

**1940** - Monetary varieties introduced by Japanese. - See *Yuan Hua-Hsing, Yuan Nanking.*

**1948** (August 19th) - After extreme inflation, creation of new monetary unit. - See *Gold Yuan.*

**1949** (September 21st) - Communist victory. Issue of new monetary unit. - See *Jen Min Piao*. On Taiwan (Formosa), adoption of independent monetary unit. - See *Dollar Taiwan.*

## CHINA (NORTHERN)

In Chinese provinces occupied from 1932 to 1944 by Japanese, issue of local monies. - See *Yuan Manchukuo* and *Dollar Northern China*. For earlier and later money issues see *China.*

## CHO GIN

Silver bar, 640 fine, in form of very elongated ellipse. Cast in **Japan** between 1695 and 1722. Japanese word "gin" means silver.

## CHON

Submultiple (¹/₁₀₀) of Won, monetary unit of **Korea,** then **South Korea.** Also copper coin. - See *Won.*

Variations of name - Cheun, Chong, Jun, Moun, Mon.

## CHRISTIAN D'OR

Gold money of **Denmark,** minted in 1775 by Christian VII, then under reign of Christian VIII (1829-1848). Weight: 6.65 grams of which 6 grams were fine gold. Exchange rate: 4 Riksdaler.

**1848** - Replaced by Fredericks d'Or, sometimes called Pistole.

## CHRISTMAS ISLAND

**1888** - British **Crown Colony.** Use of British monetary system. - See *Pound.*

**1958** (October 1st) - Transferred to Australia. Use of Australian monetary system. - See *Pound Australia.*

## CINQUINA

**I.** - Early unit of account in **Naples:** 1/40 Ducato, 1/8 Tarin, 1/4 Carlino or 2.5 Grani, 5 Tornesi, 7.5 Quartini, 15 Piccioli, 30 Cavalli or Denari. Minted in silver from 16th Century. Valued first at 5 Grani, but then struck in copper at 2½ Grani.

**II.** - On **Malta,** until 1730, Cinquina worth 1/4 Tarin, 1/2 Carlino, or 5 Grani, 30 Piccioli.

Plural - Cinquine.

## CINQUINHO

Silver coin minted in **Portugal** at end of 15th Century and during 16th Century. Exchange rate: 5-10 Reis.

## CISTOPHORUS

Silver money of Kingdom of **Pergamum** in 3rd Century B.C. Originated in Ephesus. Weight: 12.75 grams, equal to about 3 Attic Drachmae or 3 Roman Denarii.

## CLAM

Early unit of account in **Siam,** based on amount of silver equal to weight of 12 grains of rice. Clam equal to 1/2 Pai, 1/4 Song Pai, 1/8 Fuang, 1/16 Salung, 1/64 Tical, 1/256 Tael, 1/5,120 Catty.

## CLINCKAERT

Gold money of **Netherlands** in 15th Century, also called Chaise.

**1418** - In Brabant, minting of a Clinckaert worth 46 Grooten.

**1426** - In Flanders, Philip the Good minted Clinckaert of low fineness.

## COB

Common name for silver/copper coinage in **Haiti.** 1 Cob = 1 Centime or 1/100 Gourde. - See *Piaster Gourde.*

Origin of name - From *cabo de bara,* meaning tip of bar. From 1598 tips of silver bars also used for minting, resulting in coins often misshapen and varying in weight. Expression remained in use for silver/copper coins of poor quality.


## COBAN

I. - Gold bar in elliptical form, used as money in **Japan** from 16th to 19th Century. Equal to 1/10 Oban, or 4 Ichi Bu Ban, or 16 Shu Kin. Used as unit of account under name Ryo. - See *Ryo.*

Variations of name - Koban, Copang, Cobang, Kobang, Copant, Copan.

**1589** - Casting of bars called Coban, weighing 17.8 grams 843 fine.

**1601** - Weight of Coban: 17.81 grams 843 fine.

**1695** - Weight of Coban: 17.78 grams 574 fine.

**1710** - Weight of Coban: 9.34 grams 843 fine.

**1714** - Weight of Coban: 17.78 grams 843 fine.

**1716** - Weight of Coban: 17.78 grams 867 fine.

**1736** - Weight of Coban: 13.05 grams 657 fine.

**1819** - Weight of Coban: 13.09 grams 564 fine.

**1837** - Weight of Coban: 11.21 grams 567 fine.

**1859** - Weight of Coban: 9.00 grams 568 fine.

**1860** - Weight of Coban: 3.30 grams 568 fine.

**1871** - Monetary reform abolished earlier monies. - See *Yen.*

II. - Coban, overstamped with imprint of a lion, introduced in **Dutch East Indies** in 1690, equal to 20 Rijksdaalder.


## COCKIEN

Early unit of account in **Japan.**


## *COLOMBIA*

**17th and 18th Centuries** - Circulation of Spanish and Mexican Piasters. - See *Spanish America.*

**1665** - Mint at Santa Fe de Bogotá struck Piasters.

**1811** - Banknotes pegged at forced parity.

**1819** - Great Colombia, composed of modern Colombia, Panama, Ecuador and Venezuela, retained Spanish monetary system, with Piaster of 8 Reales.

**1837** - After dissolution of Great Colombia, minting of a Peso, similar to Spanish Piaster.

**1847** - Adoption of decimal system. Peso divided into 10 Reales or 100 Centavos. But, due to loyalty to former monetary system, minting of Grenadino of 8 Reales. - See *Grenadino.*

**1871** (June 9th) - Alignment to monetary system inspired by Latin Monetary Union. Colombian Peso linked to 5 Franc coin. - See *Peso Colombia.*


## COLON ARGENTINA

**Argentine** gold coin minted when Argentina adopted gold standard on September 29, 1875: 16.66 grams of gold 900 fine. Exchange rate: 10 heavy Pesos.


## COLON COSTA RICA

Monetary unit of **Costa Rica.** Created in 1896 and divided into 100 Centimos.

Origin of name - From Christopher Columbus (Spanish, *Colón*).

Bank of issue - Four private banks until November 24, 1914, then Banco Internacional de Costa Rica reconstituted as Banco Nacional de Costa Rica in January 1937 and as Banco Central de Costa Rica (Central Bank of Costa Rica) in January 1950.

Predecessors - See *Peso Central America, Peso Costa Rica.*

Plural - Colónes.

**1896** (October 26th) - Adoption of gold standard:
    1 Colón = 700.2 milligrams of fine gold

**1899** - Minting of gold coins of 2, 5, 10 and 20 Colónes (1.55, 3.89, 7.78 and 15.56 grams, respectively, all 900 fine).

**1914** (September 18th) - Suspension of gold standard.

**1914** (November 24th) - Embargo on gold shipments. Depreciation of currency.

**1922** (October 10th) - Creation of Exchange Fund to stabilize Colón at:
    1 Colón = 376.15 milligrams of fine gold
    1 U.S. Dollar = 4.00 Colónes

**1932** (January 16th) - Foreign exchange controls. U.S. Dollar rate raised to 4.50 Colónes.

**1933** - Currency depreciation parallel to that of U.S. Dollar.

**1937** (January) - Rate of exchange fixed by Banco Nacional:
    1 U.S. Dollar = 5.615 Colónes

**1946** (December 18th) - Parity registered with International Monetary Fund:
    1 Colón = 158.267 milligrams of fine gold
    1 U.S. Dollar = 5.615 Colónes

**1948** (October 13th) - Exchange reform. Imports grouped into categories with varying exchange rates.
    1 U.S. Dollar = 5.67 Colónes (official rate for preferential
                and first category imports)
Exchange for imports of 2nd and 3rd categories available either at 5.67 rate plus 20% tax (effective rate 6.80) or at free market rate plus 20% tax.

**1950** (April 1st) - Regrouping of imports into five categories with surcharges ranging from 10% to 100% on official rate, resulting in rates of from 8.63 to 13.73 Colónes per U.S. Dollar. Central Bank authorized to intervene in free market.

**1951** (September 29th) - Surcharges abolished, rate structure simplified:

1 U.S. Dollar = 5.60/5.67 Colónes (official rate for exports, certain invisibles, essential imports and registered capital)

1 U.S. Dollar = 6.98/7.00 Colónes (fluctuating free rate for all other transactions)

**1952** (March 27th) - Banco Central pegged fluctuating free rate at 6.90 Colónes per U.S. Dollar.

**1952** (April 17th) - Free market pegged at 6.75 Colónes.

**1952** (June 21st) - Percentage of proceeds from certain exports allowed access to free market (35% at 5.60 Colónes and 65% at 6.73 Colónes).

**1962** (July 23rd) - Rate in free market reduced to 6.65 Colónes per U.S. Dollar.

**1953** (October) - Minting of coins in stainless steel.

**1956** (March 3rd) - Banco Central created additional mixed rate (1% at 5.60 Colónes and 99% at 6.63 Colónes) for certain exports.

**1952-1961** - Numerous changes made regarding eligibility of specific export commodities for various exchange rates.

**1961** (September 3rd) - Colón devalued and exchange system reformed:

1 Colón = 134.139 milligrams of fine gold

1 U.S. Dollar = 6.625 Colónes

Official and free market rates virtually unified, although legally the latter not abolished.

**1967** (January 2nd) - Free exchange market reactivated with unrestricted access. Free rate fluctuated between 7.00 and 7.35 Colónes per U.S. Dollar for the month. Essential imports entitled to official exchange rates.

Mixed rate (10% at official rate and 90% at free rate) applied to certain transactions.

Free rate to be pegged from time to time by Banco Central.

**1968** (May) - Colón in unofficial dealings fell to low of 9.25 per U.S. Dollar. Subsequent improvement to near the 6.75-7.00 level.

**1969** (December 24th) - Dual exchange market unified through abolition of free exchange market. All transactions conducted at buying and selling rates of 6.62/6.65 Colónes per U.S. Dollar.

## COLON EL SALVADOR

Monetary unit of **Salvador.** Divided into 100 Centavos.

Origin of name - From Christopher Columbus (Spanish, *Colón*).

Bank of issue - Before 1934 by three private banks (Salvadoreno, Occidental, and Agricola Commercial). Since June 1934 by Agricola Commercial, renamed Banco

Central de Reserva de El Salvador (Central Reserve Bank of El Salvador). United States coins and banknotes also legal tender.

Predecessor - See *Peso Salvador.*

Plural - Colónes.

**1919** (September 11th) - Monetary reform with adoption of gold standard:
1 Colón = 1 Peso = 752.3 milligrams of fine gold
1 U.S. Dollar = 2.00 Colónes

**1920** (July 16th) - Monetary law confirming reform.

**1931** (October 8th) - Suspension of gold standard.

**1933** (August) - Foreign exchange controls.

**1933** (October) - Lifting of foreign exchange controls.

**1934** (April) - Stabilization in relation to devalued U.S. Dollar:
1 Colón = 355.468 milligrams of fine gold
1 U.S. Dollar = 2.50 Colónes

**1934** (September) - De jure stabilization on this monetary base.

**1946** (September 18th) - Parity registered with International Monetary Fund.

**1961** (April 11th) - Foreign exchange controls reinstituted, giving rise to black market activity.

**1962** (June) - Colón hit all time low of 3.60 per U.S. Dollar, resulting in premium for the latter of 30%. Gradual improvement followed.


## COMORO ARCHIPELAGO

Consists of Mayotte, Anjouan, Grande Comore and Moheli.

**19th Century** - Circulation of Indian Rupees, silver coins of 10.684 grams fine. - See *Rupee India.*

**1843** - Introduction of Franc on Island of Mayotte, where Rupee continued to circulate. - See *Franc.*

**1889** - Introduction of Franc to other islands of Archipelago, and minting at Paris Mint of special coins of Grande Comore (5 and 10 Centimes in bronze, 5 Francs in silver).

**1912** (July 25th) and **1914** (February 23rd) - Became part of Madagascar and its monetary system. - See *Madagascar.*

**1946** (May 9th) - Broke from Madagascar to form a separate colonial territory. - See *Franc CFA.* Banque de Madagascar and later (1950) Banque de Madagascar et des Comores continued to function as note-issuing authority.


## CONCEPTION

**Portuguese** money, issued as of October 9, 1651, five years after designation of Notre Dame of Conception as Patroness of Kingdom.
In gold - initial exchange rate: 12,000 Reis.

In silver - initial exchange rate: 600 Reis.

# CONDOR

Monies of **South America** bearing imprint of a Condor.

**I.** - Early gold coin of **Chile:** 11.98 grams 916 fine before 1910, and 900 fine after 1910. Value: 10 Pesos before 1885, 20 Pesos after 1885.

**20th Century** - Coins minted of 2, 5 and 10 Condores on base of 2.03 grams of gold 900 fine per Condor.

**1948** - Issue of silver Condor worth 10 Pesos.

**1950** (December 27th) - Law providing for minting of nickel/bronze Condor coins worth 10 Pesos.
Exchange rate for Condor remained linked to 10 Peso banknote at full value.
Half Condor was called Doubloon.

**II.** - Early gold coin of **Colombia:** 15.976 grams 916 fine, or 14.634 grams fine gold. Also 16.185 grams 900 fine, or 16.125 grams 666 fine. Equal to 10 Pesos.
Multiples - 20 Peso coin called Double Condor.
Submultiples - ½ Condor or Doubloon (5 Pesos), ¼ Condor (2.5 Pesos).

**III.** - Early gold coin of **Ecuador.** First defined according to monetary law of May 1, 1884 at 16.129 grams 900 fine, but not minted. After 1898, 8.14 grams 900 fine, or 7.32 grams of fine gold (same weight as Sovereign). Equal to 10 Sucres.

**20th Century** - Name given to gold coins of 8.35 grams 900 fine. Exchange rate of 25 Sucres.

# *CONFEDERATE STATES OF AMERICA*

Formed February 8, 1861 by six Southern States of United States of America, later joined by four other Southern States. For money in circulation, see *Dollar Confederate States.*

**1865** (April 18th) - Civil War ended. Secessionist States rejoined United States of America. - See *Dollar.*

# *CONGO DEMOCRATIC REPUBLIC (Kinshasa)*

Predecessor - See *Belgian Congo.*

**1960** (June 30th) - Became independent nation. Monetary unit unchanged. - See *Franc Congo.*

**1967** (July 22nd) - Creation of new monetary unit to replace Congolese Franc. - See *Zaire.*

## *CONGO PEOPLE'S REPUBLIC* (*Brazzaville)*

Predecessor - Middle Congo. - See *French Equatorial Africa.*

**1960** (August 15th) - Became independent nation of Republic of Congo within French Community.

Money in circulation, see *Franc CFA.*

**1970** (January) - Proclaimed Congo People's Republic. Monetary unit unchanged.

## CONODIS

Small silver/copper money in use in 18th Century in **India** (Coast of Malabar, Kingdom of Cochin, Goa).

## CONTINENTAL DOLLAR

See *Dollar.*

## CONTO

**I.** - Unit of account in **Portugal,** used for long time to designate 1 million Reis.

Origin of name - From Portuguese *conto* (account).

**1931** (June 9th) - Legal definition of Conto: 1 Conto = 1,000 Escudos = 1 million Reis. Conto of Contos worth 1,000 Contos, 1 million Escudos or 1 billion Reis.

**II.** - Copper coin in **Brazil** (1828-1836). As unit of account, equal to 1,000,000 Reis or 1,000 Milreis.

## *COOK ISLANDS*

**1888** - Became British Protectorate. Use of British monetary system. - See *Pound.*

**1901** - Use of monetary system of New Zealand. - See *New Zealand.*

## CORDOBA

Monetary unit of **Nicaragua.** Divided into 100 Centavos.

Bank of issue - Banco Nacional de Nicaragua (March 20, 1912), then from January 1961, Banco Central de Nicaragua (Central Bank of Nicaragua).

Predecessors - See *Nicaragua, Peso Nicaragua.*

**1912** (March 20th) - Creation of gold Córdoba to replace silver Peso:
1 Córdoba = 12.50 Pesos

1 Córdoba = 1,504.6 milligram of fine gold
1 U.S. Dollar = 1 Córdoba

**1931** (November 13th) - Foreign exchange controls.

**1934** (November 23rd) - Devaluation greater than that of U.S. Dollar:
1 Córdoba = 807.88 milligrams of fine gold
1 U.S. Dollar = 1.10 Córdobas

**1937** (August) - 42.10% devaluation:
1 Córdoba = 467.7 milligrams of fine gold
1 U.S. Dollar = 1.90 Córdobas

**1937** (Decemer 24th) - New devaluation:
1 Córdoba = 222.17 milligrams of fine gold
1 U.S. Dollar = 4.00 Córdobas
Purchases and sales of foreign exchange in free market taxed 10%.

**1938** (June) - Official exchange rate raised, de facto devaluation:
1 U.S. Dollar = 5.00/5.04 Córdobas
5% tax on foreign exchange transactions.

**1946** (December 18th) - Parity registered with International Monetary Fund:
1 Córdoba = 177.734 milligrams of fine gold
1 U.S. Dollar = 5.00 Córdobas

**1949** (December 16th) - Free market established for some transactions.

**1950** (October 20th) - New rates of exchange:
1 U.S. Dollar = 5.00 Córdobas (official rate for government transactions and for 20% of exchange proceeds)
1 U.S. Dollar = 6.60 Córdobas (exports)
1 U.S. Dollar = 7.00 Córdobas (essential imports)
1 U.S. Dollar = 8.00 and 10.00 Córdobas (other imports)
Gold price raised from 175 to 231 Córdobas per ounce corresponding to:
1 U.S. Dollar = 6.60 Córdobas
On free market, Dollar quoted from 7.00 to 8.00 Córdobas. Exceeded 8.00 in April 1954.

**1955** (July 1st) - Devaluation and sweeping reform. Prevailing official export rate of 1 U.S. Dollar = 6.60 Córdobas continued to function.
1 Córdoba = 126.953 milligrams of fine gold
1 U.S. Dollar = 7.00/7.05 Córdobas (most exports and all imports)
Other official rates abolished, but semi-official fluctuating free market rate maintained for all other transactions.

**1957** (October 28th) - Proceeds from exports other than coffee and cattle shifted into official buying rate category of 7.00 Córdobas per U.S. Dollar.

**1959** (March 13th) - The 6.60 Córdoba export rate completely phased out. All exports subject to official buying rate.

**1961** (February) - Currency depreciated 25% from official rate in black market.

**1963** (March 1st) - Government unified exchange system by permitting all transactions to be settled at official rate. Semi-Official fluctuating free market abolished.

**1968-1969** - Various surcharges and taxes ranging from 10% - 55% levied on most imports.

## CORNADO

Lesser unit of account and small copper coin in **Spain.** Also silver coin under Alfonso X of Castile (1252-1284).

**14th and 15th Centuries** - Silver/copper coin in Aragon.

**16th Century** - Discontinued as coin in Spain.

**18th Century** - Unit of account in Navarre (½ Maravedi) and Malaga (¼ Maravedi).

## COROA

Coins of **Portugal** in 19th Century.

**1835** (April 24th) - In new monetary system, gold Coroa of 5,000 Reis weighed 9.56 grams 916 fine.
Gold Coroa of 2,000 Reis (3.547 grams 916 fine) called Escudo.

**1837** - Silver Coroa of 1,000 Reis (29.61 grams 916 fine) called Coroa de Prata.

**1882** (June 2nd) - According to monetary reform of 1854, gold Coroa of 10,000 Reis or 10 Milreis weighed 17.735 grams 916 fine.
The 1/10 gold Coroa (1.774 grams 916 fine) worth 1,000 Reis or 1 Milreis. These coins still circulated at beginning of 20th Century.

## CORONA

**I.** - **Spanish** gold coin, created in 1537 by Charles V, also called Escudo. - See *Escudo.*

**II.** - A silver coin of **Naples** issued under Robert of Anjou (1309-1343) and continued by some of his successors.

## CORONADO

Silver/copper coin issued in **Spain** by Sancho IV (1284-1295), equal to 1½ Deniers (or 1/8 Sueldo).

Origin of name - From imprint of crowned king.

## CORONAT

**Polish** silver coin, then of silver/copper, worth ½ Gros. Originated in 15th Century. By 1600, made of almost pure copper.

## CORSICA

Greek, Roman, Byzantine, Papal, Genoese and French monies. Regular use of barter with payment in wheat, barley and olive oil.

**1736** - King Theodore ordered minting of silver Ecus and copper Sous at Orezza.

**1760** - Paoli ordered minting of silver Ecus and copper Sous at Murato.

**1764** - French introduced their currency. Louis equal to 28 Livres 16 Sous, and Ecu equal to 7 Livres 4 Sous. - See *Livre Tournois* and *Franc.*

## CORSINI

Gold coin of **Papal States,** also called gold Scudo or ½ Pistole. Pistole minted by Pope Clement XII (1730-1740). Weight: 3.0 to 3.4 grams of gold 900 fine.

## COSTA RICA

**16th to 19th Century -** Circulation of Spanish and Mexican Piasters.

**1821** - Revolted from Spain.

**1821-1823** - Part of Mexican Empire.

**1823-1838** - Loosely grouped into United Provinces of Central America. - See *Peso Central America.*

**1848** - Independence. Peso of Central America gave rise to Peso of Costa Rica. - See *Peso Costa Rica.* Double Peso called Escudo, ¼ Peso called Peseta.

**1896** - Adoption of Colón of 100 Céntimos. - See *Colón Costa Rica.*

## COTRIM

**Portuguese** silver/copper money issued in 15th Century by Alfonso V. Worth 5 Ceitil.

## COWRIE

White or light yellow shell, from 1 to 2 centimeters long, of porcelain quality (*Cyproea moneta*) used as money since 10th Century and perhaps much earlier in China. - See *China.*

Harvesting of shells after the Spring tides - **Maldive Islands** (Indian Ocean), **Philippines, Tonga Islands** (Polynesia).

Areas of circulation - Coasts of Bengal and Siam, Upper Guinea, Sudan, coasts of Africa. Their value in Africa increased in proportion to their distance from their places of origin (greater from East to West).

Conspicuous use in the Sahara during 11th Century, in 15th Century in Mauritania and Senegal, in 19th Century in Dahomey.

Origin of Name - From Sanskrit Kaparda or Kapardira in land of Maharattes Cauvery.

Variations of name - Cori, Cowry.

Other names for Cowrie - Condaja and Bia (in Siam), Sigueie (in the Philippines), Bouge (in Guinea), Zimbi (in Guinea, Congo, Angola).

On African coasts, Cowrie, imported by Arab and Berber merchants, then by Europeans (especially Portuguese and Dutch), used to buy slaves, gold and ivory. African natives measured Cowries in copper cauldrons. They also used them as necklaces, bracelets and money.

Official monetary status of Cowrie:

**I.** - In **Mogul Empire,** last subdivision of the Indian Rupee: Cowrie represented 1/4 Gunda, 1/20 Burrie, 1/80 Poni, 1/160 Anna, 1/1.280 Cawne, and 1/2.560 Rupee. - See *Rupee India.*

In **Kingdom of Gujarat,** Pacha (Pana?), copper money, subdivision of Rupee, valued from 50 to 60 Cowries. - See *Pacha.*

**II.** - In **Siam** during 18th Century, Cowrie was lesser submultiple of unit of account. 800 Cowries counted for 1 Fuang, 1,600 for 1 Mayon, 6,400 for 1 Tical, 25,000 for 1 Tayell, 512,000 for 1 Catty.

**III.** - In **Angola,** Macuta worth 2,000 Cowries. - See *Macuta.*

**IV.** - In **Uganda** until 1897, Penny worth 50 Cowries.

**V.** - In **Sudan,** French Administration accepted Cowries for payments to government until 1907.

**1899** (April 1st) - Decree of Governor of Dahomey directing special agent of Savalou to accept Cowries stemming from local taxes at rate of 1 bag of 20,000 Cowries for 7 Francs.

**1907**(January 28th) - Decree declaring Cowries unacceptable for payments to the government.


# CRAZIA

Italian name for Kreuzer - See *Kreuzer.*

Variations of name - Crazi, Crassie, Grazia.

Plural - Crazie.

**I.** - Money of Grand Duchy of **Tuscany.**
Unit of account, worth 1/90 gold Scudo, 1/84 Ducato, 1/69 Pezza, 1/24 Testone, 1/12 Lira, 1/8 Paolo (or Giulio). Valued at 5 Quattrini or 20 Denari di Lira. Minted in silver/copper until 1859.
Disappeared from circulation in 1801 at time of French occupation of Tuscany.

**II.** - In **Leghorn,** unit of account equivalent to 1/24 Testone, 1/12 Lira, 1/8 Paolo, or 5 Quattrini, or 20 Denari.

**III.** - In **Trieste,** unit of account equivalent to 1/60 Fiorino (Florin), 1/12 Lira, or 20 Denari. Silver coins from 3 to 20 Crazie.

## CROATIA

Predecessor - See *Yugoslavia.*

**1941** (July) - Independent Croatia created its own money, the Kuna of 100 Banius, linked to the Lira. - See *Kuna.*

## CROIX

Common name given to Vreneli, a **Swiss** coin of 20 Francs with design similar to the Latin Monetary Union and French Napoléon types, and stamped with the Swiss Cross.

## CROIZAT

Common name of silver Genovino, a coin of **Genoa,** stamped with a cross. - See *Genovino.*

Variation of name - Croisat.

## CRORE

Unit of account in ancient **Mogul Empire** and **Bengal,** used as a multiple of Rupee. Valued at 4 Areb, 100 Lakhs, 10 million Rupees, or 25.6 billion Cowries. See *Rupee India* and *India.*

Variations of name - Cruron, Curon, Courons, Crou, Carroa.

Multiples in Surrat - Badam of 100 Crores, Nil of 100 Badam or 10,000 Crores.

## CROWN

Name of several European monies bearing imprint of a crown.

**I.** - In **Great Britain,** gold, then silver coin.

**1526** (November) - Minting by Henry VIII of gold Crowns or ¼ Sovereigns, 3.7 grams 965 fine, or 3.6 grams fine gold, equal to 5 Shillings. Subsequent debasements. Demonetized in 1553 by Mary Tudor.

**1552** - Minting by Edward VI of silver Crowns patterned after Ecu and Thaler on the Continent.

**1554** - Heavier silver Crown minted. Weighed 1 troy ounce (31.10 grams) 922 fine, or 28.7 grams fine silver.

**17th and 18th Centuries** - Discriminatory measures against silver coins. - See *Shilling.*

**End of 18th Century** - Crown weighed 30.2 grams 925 fine, or 28 grams fine silver.

**19th Century** - Crown weighed 28.3 grams 916 fine, or 25.9 grams fine silver.

**20th Century** - Crown weighed 28.3 grams 925 fine, or 26.2 grams fine silver. Fineness reduced to 500 after 1920.

**II.** - In **Berne,** unit of account worth 25 Batzen or 100 Kreuzer.

**III.** - In **France,** name given to various coins:
- Ecu Couronné (crowned), or Ecu à la Couronne, gold coin minted in 1385 by Charles V, then by Charles VII. - See *Ecu.*
- Gros à la Couronne, silver coin minted in 1337 by Philip VI, worth 10 Deniers.
- Couronne d'Or, minted in 1340 by Philip VI (5.35 grams of fine gold).
- Blanca à la Couronne, silver coin minted in 1355 under Jean II, at first 666 fine, then 333 fine (in 1356). Minted in 1357 (3.50 grams, of which 1.46 grams were silver), equal to 12 Deniers. Fineness reduced in 1359 with exchange rate set at 6 Deniers. Value reduced to 4 Deniers in 1360.

**IV.** - In **Netherlands,** gold money, then silver (Crown).

**14th Century** - Gold coin in Holland minted in 1390.

**15th Century** - Gold coin in Hainaut.

**16th Century** - Gold coin of Netherlands within monetary system of Charles V. Minted in 1540, worth 1,728 Myten of Flanders or 2,592 Myten of Brabant.

**18th Century** - Silver coin minted in 1755 of 23.25 grams fine silver. Exchange rate 3 Guilders 5 Sols.

**V.** - For **Austria** and successor states (Hungary, Czechoslovakia), for **Baltic** and **Scandinavian** countries, for **Iceland** and for **Portugal,** see respective countries.


# CRUZADO

**I.** - Early money of **Portugal.**

Origin of name - Latin *crux* (cross), Portuguese *cruz* (cross), *cruzada* (crusade). First Cruzados minted during Crusades, and imprinted with a cross.

Variations of name - Cruzada, Croisade.

Predecessor - See *Portugal.*

**1279-1325** - Under Diniz the Farmer King, minting of Double Cruzado weighing 3.88 grams of gold.

**1438-1481** - Under Alfonso V, minting of gold Cruzado weighing 3.84 grams.

**1499** - Creation, by Manoel I, of gold Portuguez, equal to 10 Cruzados. - See *Portuguez.* Minting of Cruzados of 3.84 grams 989 fine, or 3.80 grams fine gold.

**1538** (November 26th) - Fineness of Cruzado lowered to 943. Weight in fine gold: 3.62 grams.

**1555** (June 10th) - Fineness reduced to 922. Weight in fine gold: 3.54 grams.

**1557-1578** - Cruzado also called Moeda or Moidore.

**1580** (July 14th) - Philip II ordered general demonetization, rescinded August 25th. Raising of rate of Cruzados in terms of units of account (Reis) to 400 Reis, then 500, then to 515. Minting of coins of 4 Cruzados, issued for 2,600 Reis.

**1584** (February 18th) - New Cruzados of 3.11 grams 922 fine, or 2.86 grams fine gold. Rate of exchange: 400 Reis.

**1640** - With return of House of Braganza, minting of silver Cruzados (worth 100 Reis) and of ½ Cruzados. Raising of exchange rate of gold Cruzados to 12,000 Reis.

**1683-1706** - Under Peter II, raising of rate of silver Cruzados, to 400, 480, 500, then 600 Reis. Multiples of Cruzado: gold Lisbonino (10 Cruzados), gold Dobra (50 Cruzados).

**1822** - Minting of last gold Cruzados (0.87 grams of fine gold).

**1854** (July 29th) - Cruzado, silver money valued at 400 Reis, stopped being part of Portuguese monetary system. Adoption of Milreis as monetary unit. - See *Milreis*.

**II.** - From 1500, gold ½ Cruzado appeared in **Portuguese India.**

## CRUZEIRO

Monetary unit of **Brazil** since 1942. Divided into 100 Centavos.

Origin of name - From Portuguese *cruz* (cross).

Bank of issue - By Banco do Brasil, established in 1808, reorganized in 1906. Replaced on April 1, 1965, by Banco Central da República do Brasil (Central Bank of Republic of Brazil) and renamed Banco Central do Brasil (Central Bank of Brazil) on February 28, 1967.

**1926** (November 18th) - Name Cruzeiro gradually began to replace name Milreis.

**1942** (November 1st) - Milreis officially became Cruzeiro. Overprinting of old banknotes:

　　　　1 Cruzeiro = 1 Milreis

Multiple exchange rates:

　　　　1 U.S. Dollar = 16.50 Cruzeiros (official rate for 30% of export proceeds)

　　　　1 U.S. Dollar = 19.47 Cruzeiros (free market rate for balance of export proceeds)

　　　　1 U.S. Dollar = 19.70-20.50 Cruzeiros (special rates including 5% exchange tax for financial transfers)

**1946** (February 28th) - Exchange tax reduced to 3%.

**1946** (July 22nd) - Official exchange rate abolished. Free market rate stabilized and became official rate:

　　　　1 U.S. Dollar = 18.96 Cruzeiros

　　　　1 U.S. Dollar = 19.53 Cruzeiros with tax

**1946** (July 27th) - Abolition of 3% tax. Official buying and selling rate:

　　　　1 U.S. Dollar = 18.38/18.72 Cruzeiros

**1948** (July 14th) - Parity registered with International Monetary Fund:

　　　　1 Cruzeiro = 48.0363 milligrams of fine gold

　　　　1 U.S. Dollar = 18.50 Cruzeiros

Official exchange rate applied to essential imports and exports. Free market rate for nonessential imports and financial transactions.

**1948** - Exchange tax of 5% on most foreign exchange sales, raising U.S. Dollar to 19.66 Cruzeiros. Continuation of free market with depreciating exchange rates.

**1949** (October) - Exchange licensing controls required for almost all exports and imports as well as nontrade payments according to category and priority. Practically all payments abroad subject to 5% exchange tax.

**1952** (January 1st) - Exchange tax raised from 5% to 8%, creating selling rate of 20.2176 Cruzeiros per U.S. Dollar.

**1953** (February 21st) - Free market rate again became official rate, and used for most noncommercial transactions, and for proceeds of fraction of certain exports.

**1953** (October 9th) - New foreign exchange rates: for exporters, buying rate raised with premiums on official rate; for importers, selling rate fixed by auction sales of foreign exchange (U.S. Dollars as well as bilateral clearing currencies) according to categories of merchandise.
Range of auction premiums for hard currencies: 17.00-128.00 Cruzeiros per U.S. Dollar.

**1953** (December) - Controlled free market rate: 52.25/53.25 Cruzeiros per U.S. Dollar.

**1954** (August 16th) - Exporters to surrender 80% of foreign exchange receipts at official exchange rate (18.36 Cruzeiros per U.S. Dollar), increased by 5.00 Cruzeiros (for coffee exports) or 10.00 Cruzeiros (for other exports). Balance sold at free market rate.

**1954** (September) - Surcharge of 15.00 and 18.00 Cruzeiros created for certain payments.

**1954** (November) - Fixed bonus of 13.14 Cruzeiros for coffee exports established for convertible currencies. Various other bonuses for such exports based on other currencies.

**1954** (December) - Controlled free market rate 76.20/77.80 Cruzeiros per U.S. Dollar.
Range of auction premiums for hard currencies: 17.00-186.00 per U.S. Dollar.

**1955** (January) - Exchange tax raised from 8% to 10% and export proceeds regrouped into four categories with two types of export bonuses created: one type applicable to convertible currencies and Pound Sterling; the other to all other currencies.

**1955** (August) - Auction sales of foreign exchange certificates for five import categories now made in U.S. Dollars as well as ACL Dollars (Dollar of Area of Limited Convertibility i.e., multilateral currencies or Pound Sterling, Deutsche Mark, Netherlands Guilder, Belgian Franc and later, Italian Lira and French Franc).
Range of auction premiums for hard currencies until July: 40.25-340.00 Cruzeiros per U.S. Dollar.
Range of auction premiums for U.S. Dollars beginning August: 68.00-324.00 Cruzeiros per U.S. Dollar.
Range of auction premiums for ACL Dollars beginning August: 62.00-407.00 Cruzeiros per U.S. Dollar.

**1955** (December) - Controlled free market rate: 66.80/67.50 Cruzeiros per U.S. Dollar.

**1956** (December) - Controlled free market rate: 63.50/65.50 Cruzeiros per U.S. Dollar.
Range of premiums for U.S. Dollars: 43.00-315.00 Cruzeiros per U.S. Dollar.
Range of premiums for ACL Dollars: 37.00-341.00 Cruzeiros per U.S. Dollar.

**1957** (August 14th) - Five import categories consolidated into two, General and Special. Exchange tax of 10% abolished.

**1957** (December) - Controlled free market rate: 89.50/91.50 Cruzeiros per U.S. Dollar.
Range of premiums for U.S. Dollars: 38.00-368.00 Cruzeiros per U.S. Dollar.
Range of premiums for ACL Dollars: 34.00-362.00 Cruzeiros per U.S. Dollar.

**1958** (June 10th) - Export preceeds regrouped into four categories and bonuses revised ranging from 18.70 to 73.64 Cruzeiros per U.S. Dollar.

**1959** (December) - Controlled free market rate: 142.50/146.50 Cruzeiros per U.S. Dollar.
Range of premiums for U.S. Dollars: 100.00-355.00 Cruzeiros per U.S. Dollar.
Range of premiums for ACL Dollars: 89.00-362.00 Cruzeiros per U.S. Dollar.

**1959** (January) - Exports reclassified into three categories with fixed bonuses ranging from 41.64 to 81.64 Cruzeiros per U.S. Dollar. Other export receipts sold in controlled free market. Exchange auctions for ACL Dollars eliminated and combined with auctions for U.S. Dollars for the two import categories.

**1959** (July 1st) - Export categories regrouped into First and Second Categories. First Category bonus of 57.64 Cruzeiros created effective rate of 76.00 Cruzeiros per U.S. Dollar. Second Category bonus of 81.64 Cruzeiros created effective rate of 120.00 Cruzeiros per U.S. Dollar. Proceeds of exports not included in either Category surrendered at controlled free market rate.

**1959** (December) - Controlled free market rate: 198.00/203.00 Cruzeiros per U.S. Dollar.

**1960** (July 1st) - First Category export bonus increased to 71.64 Cruzeiros creating effective rate of 90.00 Cruzeiros per U.S. Dollar.

**1960** (December) - Controlled free market rate: 199.10/204.10 Cruzeiros per U.S. Dollar.
Range of U.S. Dollar premiums for General Imports: 184.00-225.00 Cruzeiros per U.S. Dollar.
Range of U.S. Dollar premiums for Special Imports: 451.00-629.00 Cruzeiros per U.S. Dollar.

**1961** (March 14th) - Par value of 18.50 Cruzeiros per U.S. Dollar no longer applicable to transactions. Auction of exchange certificates discontinued, with importers to obtain foreign exchange in controlled free market. New exchange rates:
1 U.S. Dollar = 90.00 Cruzeiros (for coffee and cocoa exports)
1 U.S. Dollar = 200.00 Cruzeiros (for preferential imports and financial transfers)

**1961** (May 12th) - Surrender of part of coffee export proceeds with remainder sold in fluctuating free market.

**1961** (May 31st) - Auction of "promessas de liçensa" (import license certificates) introduced for imports via clearing Dollars or convertible U.S. Dollars.

**1961** (July 1st) - Foreign exchange for certain imports obtained in controlled free market.

**1961** (October 4th) - Surrender of 15% of export proceeds of cocoa beans with remainder sold in controlled free market.

**1961** (October 26th) - Controlled free market divided into trade exchange market and "financial" free market. In trade exchange market, export proceeds sold for use only for payments of certain imports. "Financial" free market used for all other foreign exchange dealings.

**1961** (December 29th) - Trade exchange and "financial" free markets combined. Controlled free market rate: 310.00/318.00 Cruzeiros per U.S. Dollar.

Range of U.S. Dollar premiums for General Imports: 210.00-318.50 Cruzeiros per U.S. Dollar.

Range of U.S. Dollar premiums for Special Imports: 638.00-1,045.00 Cruzeiros per U.S. Dollar.

**1962** - Exchange rate structure more complex, with effective rates determined by variety of export bonuses, financing of advance deposits and other taxes on export proceeds. Controlled free market devalued by steps to 460.00/475.00 Cruzeiros per U.S. Dollar.

**1962** (December 31st) 1 U.S. Dollar = 910.70 Cruzeiros (for General Imports).
1 U.S. Dollar = 683.30 Cruzeiros (for Special Imports)

**1963** (April 23rd) - Devaluation of controlled free market rate to 600.00/620.00 Cruzeiros per U.S. Dollar. Increase of exchange surcharges on specified exports, as well as creation of exchange bonus for specified invisibles.

**1964** (February 19th) - Devaluation and creation of new exchange system:
1 U.S. Dollar = 600.00/620.00 Cruzeiros ("special" market
rate for exports of coffee, sugar and petroleum,
and for specified imports)
1 U.S. Dollar = 900.00/950.00 Cruzeiros (official rate for
all other transactions)

**1964** (May 9th) - "Special" market rates abolished. All transactions made at official rate, periodically increased. Effective exchange rates governed by various taxes, financial charges, and assorted advance deposits applicable to export proceeds and imports.

**1964** (December) - Controlled free market rate: 1,825.00/1,850.00 Cruzeiros per U.S. Dollar.

**1964** (December 31st) - Law creating Banco Central da República do Brasil (Central Bank).

**1965** (November 13th) - Devaluation of official rate to 2,200.00/2,220.00 Cruzeiros per U.S. Dollar. Effective exchange rates determined by various contribution quotas and regulations on specified exports, as well as varied financial charges and advance deposits for imports.

**1965** (November 30th) - Black market rate hit historic low of 2,220.00 Cruzeiros per U.S. Dollar.

**1967** (February 9th) - Devaluation of official rate to 2,700.00/2,715.00 Cruzeiros per U.S. Dollar.

**1967** (February 13th) - Monetary reform. Creation of New Cruzeiro replacing old Cruzeiro:
1,000 old Cruzeiros = 1 New Cruzeiro
1 U.S. Dollar = 2,700/2,715 New Cruzeiros (official and
manual market rates)
There was also an official market rate less contribution quotas of 5%-15% for cocoa exports, as well as a specified rate for coffee exports.

**1967** (March 1st) - Reclassification of all imports into General Category.

**1967** (June 8th) - Creation of Exchange Stabilization Fund.

**1968** (January 4th) - Devaluation of official market rate to 3.20/3.22 New Cruzeiros per U.S. Dollar.

**1968** (August 27th) - Devaluation of official market rate to 3.63/3.65 New Cruzeiros per U.S. Dollar. Introduction of system of frequent periodic minidevaluations:

**1968** (September 24th) - 1 U.S. Dollar = 3.675/3.700 New Cruzeiros.

**1968** (November 19th) - 1 U.S. Dollar = 3.745/3.770 New Cruzeiros.

**1968** (December 9th) - 1 U.S. Dollar = 3.805/3.830 New Cruzeiros.

**1969** (February 4th) - 1 U.S. Dollar = 3.905/3.930 New Cruzeiros.

**1969** (March 19th) - 1 U.S. Dollar = 3.975/4.20 New Cruzeiros.

**1969** (May 13th) - 1 U.S. Dollar = 4.025/4.05 New Cruzeiros.

**1969** (July 7th) - 1 U.S. Dollar = 4.075/4.10 New Cruzeiros.

**1969** (August 27th) - 1 U.S. Dollar = 4.125/4.15 New Cruzeiros.

**1969** (October 3rd) - 1 U.S. Dollar = 4.185/4.21 New Cruzeiros.

**1969** (November 14th) - 1 U.S. Dollar = 4.265/4.290 New Cruzeiros.

**1969** (December 18th) - 1 U.S. Dollar = 4.325/4.350 New Cruzeiros.

**1970** (February 4th) - 1 U.S. Dollar = 4.38/4.41 New Cruzeiros.

**1970** (March 3rd) - 1 U.S. Dollar = 4.46/4.49 New Cruzeiros.

**1970** (May 15th) - Term "New" dropped from Cruzeiro.

**1970** (May 18th) - 1 U.S. Dollar = 4.53/4.56 Cruzeiros.

**1970** (July 10th) - 1 U.S. Dollar = 4.59/4.62 Cruzeiros.

**1970** (July 24th) - 1 U.S. Dollar = 4.62/4.65 Cruzeiros.

**1970** (July 31st) - Black market rate of Cruzeiro hit historic low of 5.30 per U.S. Dollar.

**1970** (September 17th) - 1 U.S. Dollar = 4.69/4.72 Cruzeiros.

**1970** (November 3rd) - 1 U.S. Dollar = 4.78/4.81 Cruzeiros.

**1970** (November 18th) - 1 U.S. Dollar = 4.83/4.86 Cruzeiros.

**1970** (December 22nd) - 1 U.S. Dollar = 4.92/4.95 Cruzeiros.


## CUARTILLA

Submultiple of **Mexican** Piaster ($1/32$) and Real ($1/4$) until 1861. Also called Cuartino.
**Prior to 1857** - Minted in copper by some Mexican states.


## CUARTILLO

**I.** - Copper coin minted in **Santo Domingo** by Spaniards from 1814 to 1822.

**II.** - In **Paraguary,** submultiple of Peso ($1/32$), Real ($1/4$) and Medio ($1/2$) until 1870.

**III.** - In **Spain,** silver coin, then copper, worth $1/4$ Real. Minted at end of 15th Century (also called Quartillo). Minted again according to the decree of August 19, 1853.

**IV.** - In **Portugal,** a gold coin called Quartinho. - See *Quartinho.*

# CUARTINO

Copper coin minted in **Venezuela** in 1821 and 1822 by Spaniards. Also silver coin in numerous **Central** and **South American** countries.

# *CUBA*

**16th - 19th Century** - Circulation of Spanish and Mexican silver Piasters.

**Before 1881** - Spanish monetary system based on Peso (until 1859), Peseta (from 1859 to 1864), Escudo (from 1864 to 1868), and Peseta (from 1868 to 1881). - See *Spain.*

**1881** - Adoption of Cuban Peso as monetary unit. - See *Peso Cuba.*

**1899 to 1951** (June 30th) - Simultaneous circulation of American monies. - See *Dollar.*

**1960** (October 18th) - Membership in Dollar Area ceased. Became part of Ruble sphere of influence.

# *CURAÇAO*

See *Netherlands Antilles.*

# CUSTOM GOLD UNIT

**Chinese** customs unit, usually called Gold Unit. - See *Gold Unit.*

# *CYPRUS*

**Primitive unit of account** - Hatchet.

Persian (525 B.C.), Greek (410 B.C.), Ptolomaic (311 B.C.), Roman (58 B.C.), Byzantine, Arab, Genoan, Venetian, Turkish monies.

**12th Century** - Independent Cyprus minted concave silver/copper Deniers.

**12th and 13th Centuries** - Kings of Cyprus minted concave gold coins, copying Bezant, called White Bezants. - See *Bezant.*

**13th and 14th Centuries** - Minting of silver coins, copying Gros of Saint Louis.

**16th Century** - In Cyprus, Venice minted copper Carzia, then silver/copper Soldo.

**18th Century** - Unit of account: Mina equal to 100 Aspers, as in Turkey.

**1878** - British occupation. Concurrent use of Turkish monies (Piastres and Paras) and the British monetary system.

**1917** (September 5th) - Treasury began issuing local banknotes linked to Pound Sterling. - See *Pound Cyprus.*

**1960** (August 16th) - Became independent republic.

## *CYRENAICA*

See *Libya.*

## *CZECHOSLOVAKIA*

Predecessors - See *Austria, Bohemia* and *Hungary.*

**1919** - Prague changed Austrian Krone to Czechoslovak Koruna. - See *Koruna Czechoslovakia.*

**1939** - In Sudetenland, substitution of Reichsmark for Czechoslovak Koruna. In Protectorate of Bohemia-Moravia, simultaneous circulation of two monies. - See *Koruna Czech.* For Slovakia, see *Koruna Slovak.*

**1945** - Èlimination of Reichsmark. - See *Koruna Czechoslovakia.*

# DAALDER

Silver money of **Netherlands,** circulating in 18th Century and equal to 30 Stuyver.
Origin of name - See *Thaler.*
Variations of name - Aslani (Turkish), Abukash (Arabic), Dale (French).


# DABAL

Silver coin of **Nepal.** Submultiple ($^1/_{15}$) of Patla Ashrafi (gold Mohar). Valued at 2 silver
Mohar, 4 Sukas, or 100 Paisa (Pice).
Variation of name - Nepalese Rupee.
**1870** - Gold Mohar of 5.8319 grams 995 fine subdivided into 15 silver Dabals of 171
grains (11.0806 grams 800 fine). Coin circulated beside Indian silver Rupee of 180
grains.
**After WWI** - Indian silver Rupee commanded premium over Dabal.
**1930** - 100 Indian Rupees exchanged for 128 Dabals.
**1945** - Dabal improved in relation to Indian Rupee as result of foreign exchange
restrictions on latter:
     100 Indian Rupees = 65 Dabals
Favorable exchange rate gradually reversed, following reduction in silver content
of Dabal to 333.3 fineness and inflationary issue of Mohar Rupaiya banknotes. -
See *Rupee Nepal.*
**1960** - Rupee banknotes issued by Nepal Rastra Bank gradually replaced silver Dabal
as principal monetary unit throughout Nepal. Subsequent minting of copper coin
called Dabal or Rupee.


# *DAHOMEY*

**Prior to late 19th Century** - Consisted of various tribal kingdoms. Native money:
Cowrie shells. - See *Cowrie.*
**17th to 19th Century** - Some trade with European nations resulted in circulation of
Maria Theresia Thaler. - See *Maria Theresia Thaler.*
**1851** - French established foothold. Wide acceptance of French Franc. - See *Franc.*
**1898** (May 18th) - Official relationship established between French Franc and Maria
Theresia Thaler:
     1 Maria Theresia Thaler = 3.00 French Francs
**1899** (April 1st) - Official exchange rate of Cowries established:
     1 bag of 20,000 Cowries = 7.00 French Francs
**1902** - Became part of French West Africa. - See *French West Africa.*
**1907** (January 28th) - Cowries officially demonetized.
**1945** (December 26th) - Creation and use of CFA Franc. - See *Franc CFA.*
**1960** (August 1st) - Became independent republic. Monetary unit unchanged.

## *DAKAR AND DEPENDENCIES*

See *Senegal.*

## DALASY

Proposed (1971) monetary unit of **Gambia.** Divided into 100 Butut.
1 Dalasy = 4.00 Gambian Shillings = 0.48 U.S. Cents
Variation of name - Dalasi.

## DALER

**I. - Danish** silver money and unit of account.

Origin of name - Scandinavian variation of Thaler. - See *Thaler.*

**1537** - Under Christian III, issue of silver Daler similar to Joachimsthaler. Initial exchange rate: 3 Marks.

**16th and 17th Centuries** - Successive raising of unit of account value of Daler to 4 Marks, then 5 Marks (in 1616) and 6 Marks. Minting of Riksdaler, specie money worth 1.5 Daler.

**18th Century** - Daler sometimes used as unit of account, worth ⅔ Riksdaler, or 4 Marks, 32 Stuyver, 64 Skilling, 28 Fyrk, 192 Hvid, 768 Penning.

**19th Century** - In Danish Antilles (under Christian IX), Daler equal to 100 Cents or 500 Bits.

**II. - Swedish** metal money and unit of account.

**1534** - Appearance of Daler.

**1560** - Under Erik XIV, system of accounting in Dalers divided into 4 Marks, 32 Oere, or 768 Penning.

**1564** - Minting of silver Daler and copper Daler.

**1661** - Stockholm Banco (Bank of Stockholm) began issuing banknotes in Dalers.

**1715-1719** - Under Charles XII, minting of copper coins (Mynteken) with real value of ⅓ Oere. Issued for one silver Daler.

**18th Century** - Two systems of accounting, according to provincial area:
  - Silver Mynt (silver money): Daler, or ⅙ Riksdaler, counted for 4 Marks, 8 Skilling, 32 Oere, or 128 Oerlein.
  - Kopper Mynt (copper money): Daler, or 1/18 Riksdaler, counted for 2.7 Skilling, 4 Marks K.M., 32 Oere K.M., or 128 Oerlein K.M. Daler S.M. equivalent to 3 Daler K.M.
  Specie money: silver Daler, copper Daler, and their multiples.

**1775** (November 27th) - Under Gustave III, unification of accounting systems into one based on silver money.

**III. -** Coin of **Danish West Indies** in 1904 equal to 5 Francs or 500 Bits. Issued in 4 and 10 Daler denominations.

## DANIM

Unit of account and copper money in **Arabia** (Basra, Persian Gulf) in 18th Century. Worth $\frac{1}{1,000}$ Toman, $\frac{1}{10}$ Mahmudi, or 10 Falus.

## *DANISH ANTILLES*

See *Danish West Indies.*

## *DANISH WEST INDIES*

**18th Century** - Unit of account: Piaster (or Riksdaler) of 8 Reales (or Bits). Specie monies:

> Gold coins of Portugal and England
> Mexican silver Piasters
> Bit coin of silver/copper
> Banknotes of Riksdaler from Bank of Copenhagen, having exchange value 25% higher than their face value (banknotes of 5 Riksdaler accepted as 6.25 Riksdaler)

**1740** - Minting of Skilling and multiples in copper and silver.

**1808-1848** - Circulation of Skilling and Real equal to 10 Skilling.

**1859** - Concurrent use of Danish and American monies. American coins circulated.

**1863-1905** - Under Christian IX, use of Daler worth 5 Francs, 100 Cents, or 500 Bits.

**1905** - Use of Franc (as in French West Indies) divided into 100 Bits.

**1916** - Ceded to United States. American monetary system. - See *Dollar.*

## *DANZIG*

Predecessors - See *Prussia* and *Poland.*

**16th Century** - Minting of coins that copied Polish monies: silver $\frac{1}{2}$ Gros (1524-26), Deniers, Szelong and silver Gros, gold Ducats (1528), Thalers (1567).

**18th Century** - Circulation of Croutacs, or Danzigsoere, silver money worth 9 Groschen or 162 Pfennig.
Unit of account: Guilder (Gulden) of 30 Gros (Groschen).

**1801** - Minting of local Szelag (Schilling).

**1808-1812** - Danzig minted silver/copper Groschen, copper Szelag.

**1920** (November 9th) - With creation of Free City, circulation of German Mark until its collapse.

**1923** (December 18th) - Creation of Danzig Guilder (Gulden), of 100 Pfennig. - See

*Gulden Danzig.*

**1939** (September) - Introduction of Reichsmark.

**1945** - See *Poland* and *Zloty.*

# DARIC

Money of pure gold or of silver of the **Persian** Empire. Minted by Darius.

1 Daric = 8.40 grams of gold = 20 silver Siglos

Widespread use in **Greece** and **India** during 5th Century.

# DARIJ

Submultiple of Riyal (1/22), monetary unit of **Saudi Arabia,** and of Qurush (1/2). Minted in nickel. Made up of 4 Halalas.

Variations of name - Local Piastre, Qurush Darij, Dari.

  - See *Riyal Saudi Arabia.*

# DEBEN

Name given to metal bars (gold, silver, electrum, copper, malachite, iron and lead) which served quasi-monetary functions in **Egypt** prior to Persian conquest.

Origin of name - Deben was ancient Egyptian unit of weight equal to 91 grams and divided into 10 Kite. These metal bars, bent in form of open rings or Z's, weighed in the neighborhood of a Deben. Worth varied according to metal.

Variations of name - Uten, Utnu, Tabnau, Outen.

Predecessor - See *Egypt.*

**28th Century B.C.** - Ancient accounts showed following values of copper Deben:

  120 Deben = 1 ox

  3 Deben = 1 knife

  Workers in religious temples exacted 60 Deben per year from Treasury.

**12th Century B.C.** - Records indicated government subsidies to Asiatic rulers and Egyptian priests made in gold Deben.

**10th Century B.C.** - Deben weights of gold, silver, electrum and malachite used widely for trading and hoarding.

**525 B.C.** - Persian conquerors introduced true coinage to replace metal rings and bars.

  - See *Daric* and *Siglos.*

**3rd Century B.C.** - Ptolemies minted bronze coins called Ptolomaicii, with weights approximating Deben (90 grams) and Half Deben (45 grams).

# DECIME

Early submultiple of Franc (¹⁄10), monetary unit of **France.**

**1793** (December 7th) - Livre divided into 10 Décimes by law.

**1795** (April 7th) - Law defined Décime as ¹⁄10 Franc.

**1795** (August 15th) - Law confirming division of Franc into 10 Décimes of 10 Centimes. Minting of Décimes in copper.

**1807** (September 15th) - Minting of coins of 10 Centimes in silver / copper.

**1852** (May 6th) - Demonetization of Décimes, and minting of coins of 10 Centimes in bronze. - See *Centime.*

# DECIMO

**I.** - Submultiple (¹⁄10) of Venezolano, early monetary unit of **Venezuela.** Minted in silver (2.5 grams 845 fine) according to law of May 11, 1871. - See *Venezolano.*

**II.** - Submultiple (¹⁄10) of **Ecuadorean** Peso from 1871 to 1884. Equivalent to Real. In 1884 it became submultiple (¹⁄10) of the **Ecuadorean** Sucre. Minted in silver under name of Real at end of 19th Century (2.5 grams of silver 900 fine, or 2:25 grams fine silver), then in nickel. Double Decimo called Peseta. Half Decimo was called Medio.

**III.** - Submultiple (¹⁄10) of **Mexican** Piaster from March 15, 1861. Equal to 10 Centavos. Minted in silver.

**IV.** - Submultiple (¹⁄10) of **Chilean** Peso from 1851 to 1885. Equal to 10 Centavos.

**V.** - Submultiple (¹⁄10) of **Argentine** Peso, called Peso Fuerte (hard Peso), from 1875 to 1881. Minted in silver.

**1882** - Minting of copper Decimo equal to ¹⁄10 copper Real.

**VI.** - Small **Spanish** copper coin equal to ¹⁄10 Real. Minted from 1848 to 1859.

# DENARIO

Early **Spanish** money, derived from the Roman Denarius.

Origin of name - See *Denarius.*

Predecessors - See *Denarius.*

**5th - 8th Century** - Among monies of Visigoths, Denario was a silver coin (5.12 grams fine, then 4.31, then 3.6).

**8th Century** - Denario of Goths replaced by Dirhem of Arabs.

**12th Century** - In monetary systems of Christian Spain, Denario was submultiple of Sueldo (Sou) and Maravedi. - See *Sueldo* and *Maravedi.*

**13th Century** - See *Dinero.*

## DENARIUS

Silver, then bronze money. One of basic units of **Roman** monetary system. Replaced Drachma, basic unit of Greek monetary system.

Origin of name - Latin *decem* (ten). First Denarius, marked with an X, worth 10 Asses of bronze.

Submultiples - Quinairius (½ Denarius; or 5 Asses); Sestertius (¼ Denarius; or 2.5 Asses).

Predecessors - See *Rome, Quadrigatus* and *Bigatus.*

Plural - Denarii.

**End of 3rd Century B.C.** - First Denarius (heavy Denarius) weighted 4.50 grams of silver, and was identical with Quadrigatus, its predecessor.

**187 B.C.** - Victories over Carthage and the East permitted Rome to stabilize and revise its monetary system. Basic coins: bronze As, gold Aureus and classical silver Denarius, worth 10 Asses. This Denarius weighted 3.89 grams and succeeded the Bigatus of the same weight.
Minting of gold Denarius (10.91 grams), called Denarius Aureus, and more simply Aureus, worth 25 silver Denarii. - See *Aureus.*

**89 B.C.** - Relationship of silver Denarius to bronze As went from 10 to 16 (sign XVI replacing sign X). Sestertius became customary unit of account in place of As.

**1st Century A.D.** - Under Nero, weight of Denarius reduced to 3.41 grams. Progressive lowering of fineness.

**3rd Century** - Under Septimius Severus, fineness of Denarius fell below 500. Under Alexander Severus, it reached 330.

**214** - In order to distinguish it from Argenteus Antoninianus, created by Caracalla, Denarius named Argenteus Minutulus. The coins circulated simultaneously.

**About 240** - Minting of silver Denarius ended. Existing Denarii either hoarded or melted and cast into Argentei Antoniniani.
Word Denarius referred only to bronze coins.

**290** - Within framework of monetary reform of Diocletian, Denarius became bronze divisionary coin containing 3.16 percent silver.

**312** - Reform of Constantine. Denarius, often called Follis, used for small payments in Eastern Roman Empire. - See *Follis.* Creation of silver ½ Siliqua (see *Siliqua),* which Franks called Denier. - See *Denier.*

## DENARO

In **Italy,** silver money, then silver/copper money and unit of account derived from Roman Denarius and Carolingian Denier. Word *denaro* still used in 20th Century to mean money. Cf. *Dinero.*

Origin of name - See *Denarius.*

Variation of name - Danaro.

Plural form - Denari.

**I.** - Unit of account in **Venice.** Equal to ¹/₁₂ Soldo, ¹/₂₄₀ Lira. Since Venice adopted two types of Lire, heavy Lira (Lira di Grossi) and light Lira (Lira di Piccioli), Denaro had two values.

**9th Century** - Minting of Carolingian Denier (Denaro), derived from Denarius.

**12th Century** - Heavy Denaro was identical with Grosso (see *Grosso*); light Denaro, with Picciolo (see *Picciolo).*

**18th Century** - In value scale for accounts in Ducatos, the Denaro di Ducato (or Grossetto) represented $1/12$ Grosso, or $1/288$ Ducato.
In value scale for accounts in Lire, Denaro di Lira represented $1/12$ Soldo, $1/240$ Lira, $1/1,488$ Ducato or $1/14,880$ Lira Grossa.

**II.** - Unit of account in **Florence.** Equal to $1/12$ Soldo, $1/240$ Lira.
In four value scales of accounting in Tuscany, Denaro (of gold, of Ducato, of Pezza, of Lira) equal to $1/12$ Soldo (of gold, of Ducato, of Pezza, of Lira) and $1/240$ of unit of account (gold Scudo, Ducato, Pezza, Lira).
In Lira value scale, Denaro di Lira also valued at $1/4$ Quattrino, $1/20$ Crazia, $1/80$ Paolo, $1/480$ Testone.

**III.** - In **Naples,** minting of Carolingian Denier (Denaro) from 9th Century. Minting in silver/copper in 15th Century. Unit of account in 18th Century, also called Cavallo. Equal to $1/2$ Picciolo, $1/4$ Quattrino, $1/6$ Tornese, $1/12$ Grano, $1/30$ Cinquina, $1/120$ Carlino, $1/240$ Tarin, $1/1,200$ Ducato.

**IV.** - Unit of account, and often silver or silver/copper coin, Denaro represented $1/12$ Soldo or $1/240$ Lira in several **Italian states** before unification: in Bassano, Bergamo, Bologna, Genoa, Leghorn, Lucca, Mantua, Milan, Modena, Padua, Parma, Trieste, Turin (Piedmont, Savoy, Sardinia).
Local variations - Denaro represented $1/240$ Scudo of gold Stampa in Rome; $1/240$ Scudo in Ancona and in Nove; $1/288$ Ducato in Padua; $1/1,488$ Ducato in Bergamo and Bassano; $1/1,440$ Pezza in Leghorn.

# DENGA

In **Russia,** silver coin, then copper coin, used from 14th to 18th Century. Minted in irregular shapes, first in Novgorod, then in Pskov and in Moscow. Corresponded to Denier. Value: $1/2$ Kopek.

Plural - Dengi.

Variations of name - Denuschka, Denechka, Tenga.

# DENIER

Former specie money and unit of account in numerous countries. Derived from Roman Denarius and from Carolingian Denier and representing principal monetary unit until wide distribution of its multiples: Esterlin (4 Deniers), then Gros (12 Deniers).

Origin of name - See *Denarius.*

**I.** - In **France,** silver money, then bronze, and unit of account, until 18th Century. Multiples - Liard (3 Deniers), Sou (12 Deniers), Livre (240 Deniers).

Submultiples - Denier equal to 2 Mailles or Obols, 4 Pites, or 8 Semi-Pites.

**312** - Creation by Constantine of silver coin called 1/2 Siliqua of 1.30 grams. - See *Siliqua*. Franks, accustomed to calling silver coins Deniers (Denarii), adopted it as monetary unit. Weight: between 1.37 to 1.20 grams.

**6th Century** - According to Salic Law, Denier (Denarius) represented 1/40 Sou.

**7th and 8th Centuries** - Disorderly mintings of various Deniers (Denarii).

**8th Century** - According to law of Ripuarian Franks, Denier (Denarius) represented 1/12 Sou.

**801** - Introduction of Carolingian system of accounting: 1 Livre = 20 Sous = 240 Deniers. Attempts to unify monetary system and make silver Carolingian Denier (1.75 to 1.85 grams) principal monetary unit of Charlemagne's Empire.

**9th Century** - Successive weight reduction of Denier, and an increase of feudal varieties.

**11th Century** - Denier weighed about 1.20 grams. Silver content periodically reduced (1 gram, then 0.7 grams).

**12th Century** - Denier lightened to about 1 gram of 500 fine silver.

**13th Century** - Denier of Paris (Parisis) of Philippe-Auguste weighed 1.20 grams; Denier de Tours (Tournois) of Saint Louis, 1.13 grams.

**1305 (May 5th)** - Philip the Fair minted silver Denier Parisis (1.15 grams 430 fine) and silver Denier Tournois called Petit Tournois (1.11 grams 350 fine).

**1311** (January 27th) - Denier Parisis minted under name Bourgeois. - See *Bourgeois*.

**1344** - Petit Tournois dropped in weight and silver content (1.08 grams 90 fine).

**1346** - Minting of Double Parisis, silver/copper coin worth 2 Deniers Parisis or 2.5 Deniers Tournois.

**1347** - Minting of Double Tournois, silver/copper coin worth 2 Deniers Tournois.

**1350** - Double Tournois taken out of circulation.

**1359 to 1360** - Eight successive issues of Deniers à l'Etoile (with star). Exchange rate remained 25 Sous 6 Deniers. Silver fineness progressively reduced to 145.

**1360** - Minting of silver Denier Parisis, called Petit Parisis (1.27 grams 210 fine). Minting of silver Denier Tournois, called Petit Tournois (1.16 grams 170 fine).

**1361** - Weight and fineness of Petit Tournois improved (1.48 grams 190 fine, then 290 fine).

**1365** (April 20th) - Weight and fineness of Petit Tournois reduced (1.27 grams 210 fine).

**1421-1423** - British Occupation. Coins of 2 Deniers Tournois (Niquet) and of 3 Deniers Tournois (Tresin) minted.

**Under Charles VIII** - Final minting of silver Denier Parisis.

**1577** - Henry III minted copper Deniers with legal tender status limited to 20 Sous.

**Under Louis XIII** - Final minting of copper Denier. Remained unit of account.

**18th Century** - Denier still circulated in some of provinces south of the Loire.

**1794** (December 7th) - Denier ceased to be unit of account by law.

**II.** - In **France**, word Denier was synonym for coin, and in broader terms designated money in general. Gold monies - Denier à l'Ecu (see *Ecu*), à l'Agnel (see *Agnel* ), à la Reine. Silver monies - Denier à l'Etoile.

**III.** - In **Venice** and **Italy**, see *Denaro*.

**IV.** - Unit of account in **Malta** during domination by Knights of Malta (1530-1798) and in 19th Century; 1,440 Deniers counted for 1 Scudo (Ecu), 120 for 1 Tarin, 60 for 1 Carlino, 10 for 1 Picciolo, 6 for 1 Grano.

**V.** - For **Spain,** see *Denario* and *Dinero.*

**VI.** - For **Portugal,** see *Dinheiro.*

**VII.** - For **German states,** see *Pfennig.*

**VIII.** - In certain **Swiss** Cantons (Geneva, Vaud. . .), silver money minted in 14th Century and unit of account until 1850: $1/240$ Livre, $1/12$ Sol, in Basel, Berne, Geneva (bank and large transactions); $1/720$ Ecu in Basel; $1/144$ Guilder in Geneva (government and small trade).
Copper coin of 2 Deniers called Angster; coin of 4 Deniers called Rappe.

**IX.** - For **England,** see *Penny.*

**X.** - For **Scandinavian** countries, see *Penning.*

**XI.** - **Polish** money, first cast in silver, also unit of account. Minted in 10th Century, Denier was first national money of Poland (see *Poland*). Became submultiple of Grosz; 12 Deniers equalled one Grosz (see *Grosz*).

**XII.** - In **Bohemia,** silver money issued in 10th Century. Weight reduced in 11th Century. Minting of Petit Deniers in 12th Century, called Bracteates in 13th Century.

**XIII.** - In **Hungary,** silver money issued in 11th Century. Replaced by Bracteates in 13th Century. Return to (Petit Deniers) in 14th Century.

**XIV.** - For **Russia,** see *Denga.*

**XV.** - In **Near East,** silver or copper money introduced by Crusaders, and locally imitated in Syria, Palestine, Greece (Morea, Rhodes. . .).

**1249** - Saint Louis authorized Morea to mint Denier Tournois of French type, which spread throughout entire East and was very successful until 14th Century. Duchy of Athens, Epirus, Corfu, Zakynthos. . .minted Deniers Tournois.

**14th Century** - In Rhodes, Denier worth $1/320$ Zecchino (Sequin), $1/48$ Bezant, $1/32$ Gigliato, $1/16$ Asper, $1/2$ Carat.

**XVI.** - Denier became Dinar in **Arab** countries. - See *Dinar.*

**XVII.** - In the **Netherlands,** silver, then silver/copper money, also a unit of account.

**13th Century** - Holland used silver Denier.

**14th Century** - Blanc Denier common in Hainaut and in Brabant. Flanders minted a black Denier.

**17th and 18th Centuries** - Denier valued at $1/1,920$ Livre or $1/320$ Guilder. Usually called Penning. - See *Penning.*


## DENMARK

**10th and 11th Centuries** - Introduction and imitation of English Penny (Denier), which gave rise to silver Pfennig. - See *Pfennig.*
Progressive depreciation with intervening restorations of strong monies (13th and 16th Centuries).

From marc, a unit of weight, was derived unit of account Mark. - See *Mark*.

**14th Century** - Minting of silver/copper Pfennig, later in copper alone, and of Bracteates. - See *Bracteate*.

**15th Century** - Accounts in Guilders (Rynske Gylden, or gold Guilders of the Rhine) of 24 Skillings.

**About 1445** - Silver Skilling became principal specie money with its submultiple Korsvide, valued at ½ Skilling.

**1496** - Minting of gold Noble, modeled after English Sovereign. - See *Noble*.

**1513-1516** - Currency system included following monies:
> In gold - Gold Guilder of the Rhine worth 24 Skillings
> In silver - Guilder (Solvgylden) worth 24 Skillings; Skilling
> In silver/copper - Hvid or Blanc (⅓ Skilling); Blaffert (2
> Pfennig); Pfennig

**1534** - Minting of silver Mark.

**1537** - Under German influence, minting of silver Daler, copying Joachimsthaler. - See *Daler*.

**1563-1570** - Under Frederick II, minting of inferior monies.

**1611-1648** - Deterioration of Skilling. - See *Skilling*.

**1618** - System of accounting: Krone, divided into 8 Marks or 128 Skillings. Minting of gold Krone (Guldkrone).

**1644-1730** - Minting of gold Ducats.

**18th Century** - System of accounting: Rigsdaler, divided into 6 Marks or 48 Stuyver, or 96 Skillings, or 192 Fyrk, or 288 Hvid, or 1,152 Pfennig.
In areas of Norway under Danish rule, Rigsdaler divided into 4 Ort or 96 Skilling. Specie monies:
> In gold - Ducat
> In silver - Rigsdaler, Krone
> In silver/copper - Ebräer, Kopfstück, Riksort
> In copper - Skilling

**1775** - New gold coin: Christian d'Or, or Pistole.

**1813** (January 5th) - Monetary unit: silver Rigsbankdaler of 6 Marks or 96 Skillings. - See *Rigsdaler*.

**1827** (February 3rd) - Minting of gold Fredericks d'Or, then Christian d'Or.

**1872** (December 18th) - Scandinavian Monetary Union.

**1873** (May 27th) - Adoption of gold standard with Danish Krone as monetary base. - See *Krone Denmark*.

**1918** (December 1st) - Creation of Icelandic Króna, at par with Danish Krone. - See *Króna Iceland*.

# DEUTSCHE MARK

See *Mark German Federal Republic*.

# DIME

**I.** - In **United States,** silver coin of 10 Cents created April 10, 1792 at 900 fine.
Origin of name - Latin: *decima.*
**1853** - Weight reduced from 41.25 to 38.4 grains.
**1965** - Coinage Act of 1965 authorized minting in United States of three layer clad coin; two outer layers of 75% copper and 25% nickel and an inner core of pure copper.
**II.** - In **Canada,** silver coin of 10 Cents created May 4, 1910 at 925 fine.
**1920** (May 11th) - Fineness reduced to 800.
**1967** (August 17th) - Fineness reduced to 500.

# DINAR

Early money of **Arab** or **Islamic** countries.
Origin of name - See *Denarius.*
**I.** - Arab gold money copied from Byzantium. Also called Saracen Bezant, and in West, Mancuso. - See *Mancuso.*
**End of 7th Century** - Minting of gold Dinars (4.25 grams), copied from Bezant of Eastern Empire (see *Bezant*), and derived from Roman Solidus (see *Solidus*). First issued in Syria under Abd-el-Melek (685-705) and perhaps in Egypt. Circulation of Dinar throughout East, in North Africa, and in Spain under Abd-el-Rahman III (912-961). Value fixed by religious law.
**End of 11th Century** - Weight of fine gold content of Dinar reduced to about 3.90 grams.
**11th-14th Century** - Last mintings of Dinar: in Bagdad, 1262; in Egypt, 1346. Disappeared from Morocco in 11th Century and from India in 13th Century. In Sicily, 1/4 Dinar coin gave rise to Tarin. Castille minted coin under name Alfonsino. - See *Alfonsino.*
**Until 19th Century** - Remained unit of account in Morocco.
**1926** - In Hejaz, minting of gold Hashimi Dinar (7.24 grams).
**II.** - Gold coins, sometimes called Sarrazinos, minted by Crusaders in **Palestine.** They were copied from Arabian Dinar. Innocent IV excommunicated Christians who minted Saracen Bezants bearing name of Mohammed. He ordered "this abominable custom" be stopped. Mintings continued at Saint Jean d'Acre.
**III.** - Unit of account in **Persia** in 18th Century; 1/5 Kazbegi; 1/50 Shahi, 1/100 Mahmudi, 1/200 Abbasi, 1/10.000 Toman. Multiple: Dinar Bisti, or Decuple Dinar. Word Dinar in Persia of 18th Century usually referred to gold specie money. In 19th and 20th Centuries, submultiple of Rial (1/100) and Pahlevi (1/10.000), monetary units of **Iran.**
**IV.** - In **India,** gold coin minted by Sultan of Delhi.
- For other Dinar varieties, see the following:

## DINAR ALGERIA

Monetary unit of **Algeria.** Divided into 100 Centimes.

Bank of issue - Banque Centrale d'Algérie.

Predecessor - See *Franc Algeria.*

**1964** (April 1st) - Algerian Franc replaced by Dinar. Official parity and link to French Franc unchanged:
>1 Algerian Dinar = 180 milligrams of fine gold
>1 U.S. Dollar = 4.93706 Algerian Dinars

**1967** (November 1st) - Introduction of foreign exchange controls.

**1968** (November 24th) - Algerian Dinar deteriorated 33% from official rate on the black market.

**1969** (August 11th) - Algerian Dinar did not follow French Franc devaluation. New Link to French Franc:
>1 Algerian Dinar = 1.12499 French Francs

## DINAR BAHRAIN

Monetary unit of **Bahrain** and **Abu Dhabi.** Divided into 1,000 Fils. Circulates freely in the entire Persian Gulf Area.

Bank of issue - Bahrain Currency Board.

Predecessors - See *Persian Gulf Rupee, Indian Rupee.*

**1965** (October) - Bahrain Dinar introduced to replace Gulf Rupee:
>1 Bahrain Dinar = 1,866.20805 milligrams of fine gold
>1 Bahrain Dinar = 2.10 U.S. Dollars

**1966** (June 18th) - Abu Dhabi adopted Bahrain Dinar.

## DINAR IRAQ

Monetary unit of **Iraq.** Divided into 5 Riyals, 20 Dirhams, or 1,000 Fils.

Bank of issue - Iraqi Currency Board, then National Bank of Iraq, established in June 1948 and renamed Central Bank of Iraq in July 1956.

Predecessor - See *Iraq.*

**1931** (April 19th) - Creation of Iraqi Dinar:
>1 Iraqi Dinar = 1 Pound Sterling
>1 Iraqi Dinar = 7,322.38 milligrams of fine gold

**1932** (April 1st) - Abandonment of gold standard, and depreciation parallel to that of Pound Sterling.

**1941** (November 24th) - Foreign exchange controls.

**1946** (December 18th) - Parity registered with International Monetary Fund:
>1 Iraqi Dinar = 1 Pound Sterling
>1 Iraqi Dinar = 3,581.34 milligrams of fine gold

1 Iraqi Dinar = 4.03 U.S. Dollars

**1949** (September 20th) - Dinar devalued along with Sterling:
    1 Iraqi Dinar = 2,488.28 milligrams of fine gold
    1 Iraqi Dinar = 2.80 U.S. Dollars

**1959** (June 23rd) - Iraq withdrew from Sterling Area; currency regulations revised accordingly.

**1961** (January 6th) - Central Bank issued new currency notes bearing emblem of Republic. All old notes ceased to be legal tender by end of month.

**1970** (March) - Iraqi Dinar fell to record low of U.S. $2.33 in black market.

## DINAR JORDAN

Monetary unit of **Jordan.** Divided into 1,000 Fils.

Bank of issue - Jordan Currency Board, then Central Bank of Jordan from 1964.

Predecessor - See *Pound Palestine.*

**1950** (July 1st) - Jordan Dinar created. Jordan rejoined Sterling Area:
    1 Jordan Dinar = 1 Pound Sterling
    1 Jordan Dinar = 2.80 U.S. Dollars
Two additional selling rates existed, resulting from taxes (periodically changed) on payments for invisibles.

**1953** (October 2nd) - Initial par value established with International Monetary Fund:
    1 Jordan Dinar = 2,488.28 milligrams of fine gold
    1 Jordan Dinar = 2.80 U.S. Dollars

**1954** (February 1st) - Beirut fluctuating free market rate authorized for most transactions not covered by official buying and selling rates.

**1954** (June) - Taxes on payments for invisibles unified. Applied to both official rate and free market rate.

**1955** (January 26th) - Import and exchange restrictions eased. Free exchange market for transactions in Arab League currencies recognized as legal. Surrender requirements at official rate applied to all receipts in non-Arab League currencies.

**1957** - Jordan Dinar in unofficial dealings fell to temporary low of U.S. $2.20.

**1959** (January 7th) - Scope of free market reduced. Applied to most goods originating in or reshipped from Arab League countries.

**1964** (October 1st) - Central Bank of Jordan began operations. Tax on exchange for invisibles reduced and extended to cover import payments.

**1967** (May 1st) - Tax on exchange for invisibles abolished.

## DINAR KUWAIT

Monetary unit of **Kuwait.** Divided into 1,000 Fils.

Bank of issue - Kuwait Currency Board, then Central Bank of Kuwait from April 1, 1969.

Predecessors - See *Rupee India, Rupee Persian Gulf.*

**1961** (April 1st) - Creation of Kuwaiti Dinar linked to Pound Sterling:
1 Kuwaiti Dinar = 1 Pound Sterling

**1963** (April 26th) - Par value established with International Monetary Fund:
1 Kuwaiti Dinar = 2,488.28 milligrams of fine gold
1 Kuwaiti Dinar = 2.80 U.S. Dollars

**1967** (November 18th) - Kuwaiti Dinar did not devalue with Sterling. New relationship:
1 Kuwaiti Dinar = 1 Pound 3 Shillings 4 Pence

## DINAR SERBIA

Monetary unit of **Serbia.** Divided into 100 Paras.

Bank of issue - Banque Nationale Privilégiée du Royaume de Serbie, established 1883.

Predecessor - See *Serbia.*

Plural - Dinara.

**1873** (November 8th) and **1875** (June 20th) - Adoption of Dinar under bimetallic standard. Linked to French monetary system:
1 Serbian Dinar = 4.50 grams of fine silver
1 Serbian Dinar = 290.322 milligrams of fine gold
1 Serbian Dinar = 1 French Franc

Minting on this base of gold coins similar to French type. Dinar also minted in silver, as was Franc.

**1878** (December 10th) - Limitations on legal tender status of silver money.

**1913** - Forced parity.

**1918** - Incorporation into Yugoslavia. - See *Dinar Yugoslavia.*

**1941-1945** - During war, Yugoslav Dinar devalued and replaced again by Serbian Dinar (Dinar Neditch):
1 Serbian Dinar = 17.9 milligrams of fine gold

**1945** (April) - Liberation of Yugoslavia. Serbian Dinar replaced by Yugoslav Dinar:
1 Yugoslav Dinar = 20 Serbian Dinars
See *Dinar Yugoslavia.*

## DINAR SOUTH ARABIA

Monetary unit of **Federation of South Arabia,** then of **Southern Yemen.** Divided into 1,000 Fils.

Bank of issue - Southern Yemen Currency Authority.

Predecessors - See *Arabia* (before 20th Century), then *Shilling East Africa.*

**1965** (April 1st) - Introduction of South Arabian Dinar at par with Sterling, replacing East African Shilling as monetary unit of Federation of South Arabia:
1 South Arabian Dinar = 20 East African Shillings = 1
Pound Sterling

1 South Arabian Dinar = 2.80 U.S. Dollars

**1967** (November 18th) - South Arabian Dinar devalued parallel with Sterling:
　　　　1 South Arabian Dinar = 2,132.81 milligrams of fine gold
　　　　1 South Arabian Dinar = 2.40 U.S. Dollars

**1967** (November 30th) - Creation of Southern Yemen from Federation of South Arabia. Currency remained unchanged.

**1968** - Name of currency changed to Southern Yemen Dinar. Value remained the same.


## DINAR SOUTHERN YEMEN

Monetary unit of **People's Republic of Southern Yemen.** Divided into 1,000 Fils.

Predecessor - See *Dinar South Arabia.*

**1968** - South Arabian Dinar renamed Southern Yemen Dinar. Value remained the same:
　　　　1 Southern Yemen Dinar = 2,132.81 milligrams of fine gold
　　　　1 Southern Yemen Dinar = 2.40 U.S. Dollars


## DINAR TUNISIA

Monetary unit of **Tunisia.** Divided into 1,000 Millimes.

Bank of issue - Banque Centrale de Tunisie (Central Bank of Tunisia), established 1958.

Predecessor - See *Franc Tunisia.*

**1958** (November 1st) - Tunisian Dinar created to replace Tunisian Franc:
　　　　1 Tunisian Dinar = 1,000 Tunisian Francs

**1958** (December 30th) - Official rate defined by law:
　　　　1 Tunisian Dinar = 2,115.88 milligrams of fine gold
　　　　1 Tunisian Dinar = 11.7549 French Francs
　　　　1 U.S. Dollar = 0.42 Tunisian Dinars
Dinar fell on black market to record low of 1.90 per U.S. Dollar, a premium of 352% for the latter. Subsequently improved in value.

**1964** (September 28th) - Devaluation. New par value registered with International Monetary Fund:
　　　　1 Tunisian Dinar = 1,692.71 milligrams of fine gold
　　　　1 Tunisian Dinar = 1.90476 U.S. Dollars


## DINAR YUGOSLAVIA

Monetary-unit of **Yugoslavia.** Divided into 100 Paras.

Bank of issue - In 1920, Banque Nationale du Royaume des Serbes, Croates et Slovènes and in 1929 name changed to Banque Nationale du Royaume de Yugoslavie. Operations interrupted in April 1941, resumed in October 1944. In January 1946, name changed to Banque Nationale de la République Fédérative Populaire de

Yugoslavie. Nationalized in September 1946, and in April 1963 name changed to Banque Nationale de Yugoslavie (National Bank of Yugoslavia).

Predecessors - See *Dinar Serbia, Serbia* and *Turkey.*

**1918** (December 25th) - Dinar became principal monetary unit in Yugoslavia. Austrian Krone (Krone of 100 Heller, or Xelera) circulating in Yugoslavia were counter-marked.

**1919** (November 5th) - Second marking, 20% withdrawn from circulation. Exchange rate:
    1 Yugoslav Dinar = 4 Kronen

**1922** (December 30th) - Foreign exchange controls.

**1925** - De facto stabilization.

**1931** (May 12th) - De jure stabilization with a 90.8% devaluation:
    1 Yugoslav Dinar = 26.5 milligrams of fine gold
    1 U.S. Dollar = 56.40 Yugoslav Dinars

**1931** (June 28th) - Foreign exchange controls lifted.

**1931** (October 7th) - Foreign exchange controls reimposed. Creation of blocked accounts, and rising black markets.

**1932** (October) - National Bank granted 20% premium on foreign exchange.

**1933** (January 2nd) - Premium raised to 28.8%, signifying devaluation of Dinar by 22.18% in relation to parity of 1931:
    1 U.S. Dollar = 44.00 Yugoslav Dinars

**1935** (January 16th) - Devaluation confirmed on foreign exchange market in Belgrade.

**1936** (April 7th) - Controls on imports.

**1937** (April 3rd) - Creation of Tourist Dinar:
    1 Pound Sterling = 250 Yugoslav Dinars

**1939** - Exchange rate for Reichsmark raised from 14.80 to 17.82 Dinars.

**1941** (April) - German Occupation: 1 Reichsmark = 20 Yugoslav Dinars.

**1941** (July) - In territories incorporated with Croatia, creation of Kuna. - See *Kuna.* In territories annexed to Italy (Ljubljana and Dalmatia), introduction of Lira; first at 3.33 Dinars, then at 2.63 Dinars.
In Serbia, devaluation of Yugoslav Dinar, which became Serbian Dinar (or Dinar Neditch):
    1 Serbian Dinar = 17.9 milligrams of fine gold

**1945** (April) - Liberation of Yugoslavia. Introduction of new Dinar:
    1 Yugoslav Dinar = 20 Serbian Dinars

**1945** (May) - All transactions placed under control of National Bank:
    1 U.S. Dollar = 50 Yugoslav Dinars

**1945** (September) - New Yugoslav Dinar, issued by Treasury (Dinar Y.D.F. or Dinar of Democratic and Federal Yugoslavia), replaced monies used during war:
    1 Yugoslav Dinar = 20 Serbian Dinars, 40 Croatian Kuna,
                       3.33 Italian Lire, 10 Bulgarian Leva, 1 Hungarian Pengoe, 0.40 Albanian Francs, 2 Albanian Leks

**1945** (November 29th) - Monarchy abolished and Federal Republic declared:
    1 Yugoslav Dinar = 17.7734 milligrams of fine gold

1 U.S. Dollar = 50 Yugoslav Dinars

**1951** (December) - Dinar fell to low of 750 per U.S. Dollar in black market, premium for latter of 1,400%.

**1952** (January 1st) - Devaluation accepted by International Monetary Fund:
1 Yugoslav Dinar = 2.96223 milligrams of fine gold
1 U.S. Dollar = 300 Yugoslav Dinars

**1952** (July 1st) - Coefficients (multipliers) applied to official rate of exchange to stimulate exports and discourage imports. Resulted in numerous multiple rates, constantly revised. A retained (free) exchange market also existed.

**1954** (January 1st) - Import coefficients applied to retained (free) exchange market rate.

**1954** (December 1st) - Settlement rate established. Initially 632 Dinars per U.S.Dollar, periodically adjusted by National Bank. Export coefficients applied to this rate.

**1954** (December 28th) - Premium of 100% of official rate applied to emigrant remittances and other invisibles. Created special rate of 600 Dinars per U.S. Dollar. Auction sales of foreign exchange for official import organizations.

**1956** (January 1st) - Exporters required to surrender receipts to National Bank at settlement rate in almost all cases. Special diplomat and tourist rate of 400 Dinars per U.S. Dollar decreed. Sales of exchange in free market made only by National Bank and used for some specialized imports. Rates in this market subsequently deteriorated to near 10,000 Dinars per U.S. Dollar.

**1958** (January 1st) - New rates established by National Bank for government and social organizations:
1 U.S. Dollar = 600 Yugoslav Dinars (noncommercial payments)
1 U.S. Dollar = 632 Yugoslav Dinars (settlement rate for commercial payments)

**1961** (January 1st) - Currency reform. Multiple rate system greatly simplified. Practically all transactions in foreign exchange took place at unified settlement rate of:
1 U.S. Dollar = 750 Yugoslav Dinars
Basic rate of 300 Dinars per U.S. Dollar officially maintained, but inoperative.

**1961** (February 15th) - Special diplomatic and tourist rate adjusted:
1 U.S. Dollar = 600 Yugoslav Dinars

**1962** (January 1st) - Exchange rate structure unified. Special diplomatic and tourist rate abolished. Rate of 750 Dinars per U.S. Dollar applicable to all transactions.

**1965** (July 26th) - Devaluation and new par value established with International Monetary Fund:
1 Yugoslav Dinar = 0.710937 milligrams of fine gold
1 U.S. Dollar = 1,250 Yugoslav Dinars
Temporary rate of 1,000 Dinars per U.S. Dollar established (early July 1965) and made applicable to all transactions.

**1965** (December) - Dinar on black market fell to low of 1,570 per U.S. Dollar.

**1966** (January 1st) - Introduction of Hard Dinar for 100 Old Dinars:
1 Hard Dinar = 71.0937 milligrams of fine gold
1 U.S. Dollar = 12.50 Yugoslav Dinars

**1966** (November) - Dinar on black market fell to 16.00 per U.S. Dollar.
**1971** (January 23rd) - Devaluation of 16.7% in terms of gold:
     1 Dinar = 59.2447 milligrams of fine gold
     1 U.S. Dollar = 15.00 Yugoslav Dinars
**1971** (February) - Dinar on black market fell to 16.45 per U.S. Dollar.

## DINERO

**I.** - Early money of **Spain.**
Origin of name - See *Denarius.*
Variation of name - *Denario.*
Predecessor - See *Spain, Denario.*
**1230-1252** - Ferdinand III minted silver Dinero, called Pépion - See *Pépion.*
**1258** - Minting of Dinero Prieto (brown Dinero), or Negro, weighing 8.53 grams with 2.84 grams of fine silver. - See *Negro.*
**14th Century** - In Majorca and Barcelona, a copper coin called Malla, equal to ½ Dinar. - Cf. *Maille.*
**Until 19th Century** - Dinero was unit of account in various provinces of Spain: ¹/₁₂ Sueldo (Sou) and ¹/₂₄₀ Libra (Livre) in Alicante, Catalonia, Majorca and Valencia; ¹/₁₆ Sueldo and ¹/₃₂₀ Libra in Aragon; ¹/₃₄₀ Real in Malaga.
Submultiple of unit of account in Catalonia: 1 Dinero = 2 Mallas.
Term Dinero in Spain meant money in general.
**II.** - Submultiple (¹/₁₀) of **Peruvian** Sol. Minted after 1857 in the form of silver coin: 2.50 grams 900 fine, or 2.25 grams of fine silver.

## DINHEIRO

In **Portugal,** unit of account and specie money used after 12th Century.
Origin of name - See *Denarius.*
Predecessor - See *Portugal.*
**12th Century** - Derived from Carolingian Denier, Dinheiro used as a unit of account. Corresponded to ¹/₂₄₀ Livre or ¹/₁₂ Soldo. Minted in silver/copper from reign of Alfonso I (1128-1185) to reign of Alfonso II (1248-1279).
**14th Century** - Dinheiro still circulated under Peter I (1357); Denier Alfonsin (Dinheiro Alfonsino) had exchange rate of ¹/₉ Soldo. Half Denier (Meio Dinheiro) minted in silver/copper under Ferdinand I (1367-1383).

## DIRHAM

**I.** - Monetary unit of **Morocco.** Divided into 100 Moroccan Francs.
Variations of name - Dirhem, Dihrem.

Plural - Dirhams.

Bank of issue - Banque du Maroc (Bank of Morocco).

Predecessor - See *Franc Morocco.*

**1960** (April) - Franc-Zone link severed. Strict exchange controls instituted. Dirham entered circulation.

**1961** (January 1st) - Dirham defined by law as:
1 Dirham = 175.61 milligrams of fine gold
1 U.S. Dollar = 5.06 Dirhams
1 French Franc = 1.026 Dirhams

**1967** (June) - Currency depreciated 28% (7.00 per U.S. Dollar) from official rate in black market to an all-time low.

**II.** - Submultiple of **Iraqi** Dinar ($1/20$) and **Iraqi** Riyal ($1/4$). - See *Dinar Iraq.*
Minted in form of silver coin (9 grams, 500 fine).

## DIRHEM

Silver money of **Arab** or **Islamic** countries.

Origin of name - Egyptian form of Greek word *Drachma.* In Egypt, Dirhem was unit of weight.

Variations of name - Dihrem, Dirham. Cf. *Dirham.*

Plural - Draham.

**I.** - In **Arabia,** silver money used before advent of Islam (4.25 grams in 3rd Century), authorized by Koran for rules covering dowries, divorces, tithes, fines.
Legal weight of Dirhem: 2.97 grams.
Minted in Damascus. Diffused by Arab expansion into North Africa and Spain. Adopted and copied by Crusaders in **Palestine.**

**II.** - In **Morocco,** silver money imported by Arabs. Circulated until 19th Century. In Hassani monetary system established by Sultan Moulay-Hassan and maintained until 1920, Dirhem equal to $1/10$ Rial. Minted in silver until 1914 (2.30 grams). - See *Ukkia.*

**III.** - In 18th Century **Persia,** word Dirhem generally meant silver coin.

**IV.** - **Turks** minted large copper Dirhem (12 grams) during 12th and 13th Centuries.

## DIWARRA

Hand-worked sea shell used as money in **Bismarck Archipelago** (New Guinea), and particularly on Island of Neupommeron.

Small shell of 1 centimeter, *nassa callosa,* brown in color and spotted with white, carved and polished into form of disk and punctured in center.
Shells strung on cords as long as 20 meters.

Value varied according to color: the redder the shell, the higher its value.

## *DJIBOUTI*

See *French Territory of the Afars and the Issas.*

## DOBLA

See *Doubloon.*

## DOBLADO

In **Ecuador,** gold coin struck in 1835. Equal to 2 Escudos.

## DOBLON

In early **Mexico,** gold coin equal to Onza of 8 Escudos. In **Chile** and **Uruguay,** name for coin of 10 Pesos. In **Spain,** the name for Dobla or Doubloon.

## DOBRA

**I.** - Gold coin in **Portugal** from 14th to 19th Century.

Origin of name - See *Doubloon.*

Variations of name - Doubloon, Double, Dobrao, Dobraon.

**14th Century** - Peter I minted gold Dobra (4.97 grams) valued at 4 Livres 2 Soldos. Ferdinand I minted one valued at 6 Livres.

**Before 1722** - Dobra (53.79 grams 916 fine) valued at 20,000 Reis. The 1/20 Dobra coin (2.69 grams 916 fine) worth 1,000 Reis.

**1722-1835** - Dobra (28.69 grams 916 fine) worth 12,800 Reis. The 1/2 Dobra, or Moeda, worth 6,400 Reis. The former commonly known as Joannes and as Joe in British West Indies. - See *Joe.* The 1/8 Dobra, or Escudo, worth 1,600 Reis. Dobra valued at 12,800 Reis until 1854.

**II.** - Minted in **Brazil** during Brazilian Empire (1822-1889).

## DOHOZARI

Gold coin in **Persia** in late 19th and early 20th Century. Valued at 1/5 Toman, Dohozari was 0.575 grams 900 fine gold.

## DOLERA

Name given to Duro in **Spain** under Charles V. - See *Duro.*
Origin of name - See *Thaler.*
Word Dollar derived from this name.

## DOLLAR

Monetary unit of the **United States.** Divided into 100 Cents.

Origin of name - Spanish money, *Dolera,* which originated from Thaler of German states. - See *Thaler.* In Southern United States, Dollar sometimes called Piaster.

Bank of issue - First by the Treasury (Greenbacks) and many private banks (89 issuing banks in 1811, 800 in 1837, 7,355 in 1912). Since December 23, 1913 by Federal Reserve Banks, controlled in Washington by Federal Reserve Board; also by the Treasury.

Predecessors - Before independence, circulation of Pound Sterling. - See *United States.*

**1775** (June 22nd) - With increasing economic independence, creation of autonomous monetary unit called Continental Dollar based on heavy Spanish Piaster (Dolera). Congress authorized issue of paper money.

**1776** - During the Revolutionary War, forced parity and inflation.

**1779** (November) - $241.5 million in circulation, including issues of various State governments.

**1780** (March 18th) - Exchange of paper Dollars for silver Dollars at a rate of 40 to 1.

**1780** - Colonial States minted copper Cents.

**1781** - Continental Dollar depreciated to $1/100$ , then to $1/1.000$ of a silver Dollar.

**1786** - Elimination of Pound Sterling. Definition of Dollar in silver:
$$1 \text{ U.S. Dollar} = 24.3 \text{ grams of silver}$$

**1792** (April 4th) - Adoption of bimetallism with ratio of silver to gold of 15 to 1:
$$1 \text{ U.S. Dollar} = 24.06 \text{ grams fine silver} = 1,603.8 \text{ milligrams fine gold}$$
Dollar copied from Spanish Piaster, but weighed somewhat less. Minting of gold coin (Eagle) of 17.50 grams 916 fine, or 16.038 grams of fine gold, valued at $10. - See *Eagle.*

**1834** - Bank of United States dissolved. Issue of paper money by private institutions.

**1834** (June 28th) - Weight of gold coin lowered to 16.72 grams 899225 fine, or 15 grams fine gold.

**1837** (January 18th) - In face of flight of gold, modification of currency's gold definition by reducing fineness to 900 and establishing ratio of 16 (silver) to 1 (gold).
$$1 \text{ U.S. Dollar} = 24.06 \text{ grams fine silver} = 1,504.656 \text{ milligrams fine gold}$$

**1837** (May 10th) - Numerous private banks suspended convertibility of banknotes into metal until 1843.

**1845** - In California, hallmarked gold cylinders minted and accepted in business transactions.

**1849** (March 3rd) - After discovery of gold in California, gold Dollar coins and 20 Dollar Coins (Double Eagles) were minted. - See *Eagle.*

**1853** (February 24th) - Minting of divisionary silver coinage 900 fine, but of reduced weight. Legal tender status limited to 5 Dollars.

**1861** (December 30th) - Suspension of specie payments.

**1862-1876** - Issue of fractional paper currency called Shin Plasters, denominated from 3 to 50 Cents.

**1862** (February 25th) - Civil War. Only paper money had legal tender status. Inflation of Government's paper money (Greenbacks) up to 2,100 million Dollars. Currency depreciation (maximum of 65% in November 1864 for banknotes of Federal Government). - See also *Dollar Confederate States.*

**1873** - Suspension of free minting of silver. Limitations on legal tender status of silver coins.
Creation of Trade Dollar. - See *Trade Dollar.*

**1878** - Bland Act reinstated silver to full legal tender status, under pressure of silver lobby.

**1879** (January 1st) - After progressive revaluation of paper Dollar, forced parity lifted and gold convertibility reinstated.

**1890** (July 14th) - Sherman Act obligated Treasury to buy silver against issue of Treasury banknotes.

**1893** (November 1st) - In face of flight of gold (exported and hoarded), abolition of legislation favoring silver.

**1900** (March 14th) - Currency Act linked Dollar to gold monometallic standard through limitations placed on legal tender status of silver:
      1 troy ounce of gold = 20.67 U.S. Dollars
      1 U.S. Dollar = 1,504.656 milligrams of fine gold

**1917** (September 7th) - Embargo on gold. Currency depreciation (42% maximum).

**1919** (June 30th) - Lifting of embargo on gold. Return of Dollar to parity. Progressive increase of American gold reserves.

**1933** (January) - Banking and agricultural crises resulted in flight of gold.

**1933** (March 6th) - Roosevelt Proclamation resulted in embargo on gold and establishment of foreign exchange controls.

**1933** (March 9th) - Suspension of gold convertibility.

**1933** (April 5th) - Compulsory surrender of gold (more than $100) held by private individuals.

**1933** (May 12th) - Authorization given to President by Congress to devalue the Dollar to maximum of 50%.

**1933** (October 25th) - Gold purchased from American mines at increased price of $31.36 per troy ounce against former $20.67. Price subsequently raised in stages.

**1934** (January 15th) - Roosevelt asked Congress for devaluation of between 40% and 50%.

**1934** (January 30th) - Congressional approval of full powers to devalue the Dollar.

**1934** (January 31st) - Presidential Proclamation. Dollar devalued by 40.94%:
   1 troy ounce of gold = 35.00 U.S. Dollars
   1 U.S. Dollar = 888.6706 milligrams of find gold
Transfer of gold from Federal Reserve Banks to Treasury. Creation of Exchange Stabilization Fund.

**1934** (June 19th) - Silver Purchase Act obligated Treasury to buy silver until price rose to $1.29.

**1934** (November 12th) - Foreign exchange controls lifted.

**1946** (December 18th) - Parity registered with International Monetary Fund:
   1 U.S. Dollar = 888.6706 milligrams of find gold

**1960** (October) - Free market gold price in London hit record high.

**1961** (January 16th) - Restriction prohibiting Americans from purchasing or holding gold abroad.

**1961** (October-November) - Formation of Gold Pool to maintain free market price of gold in London at $35 per ounce.

**1961** (November 28th) - After exhaustion of free silver stocks, U.S. Treasury abandoned efforts to hold silver price at 91 1/8 cents per ounce, and allowed silver price to float.

**1962** (July 20th) - Import of gold coins required licensing.

**1963** (June 4th) - Silver Act called for withdrawal from circulation of Silver Certificates, replaced by Federal Reserve Notes.

**1963** (July) - Interest Equalization Tax imposed on most foreign securities.

**1963** (September) - Silver price in free market reached official value of 129.3 cents per ounce. Treasury intervened to maintain silver price at this level.

**1965** - Coinage Act. Minting of silver coins discontinued. Subsidiary coins henceforth made of nickel clad copper.

**1965** (February) - "Voluntary" restraints on foreign investments proposed.

**1965** (March) - Gold cover for Federal Reserve bank deposits removed.

**1967** (May 18th) - U.S. Treasury withdrew ceiling on silver price. Ban on melting of silver coins and export of more than $5 worth.

**1967** (July 14th) - Redemption of Silver Certificates ended by Treasury, and existing silver stocks transferred to General Services Administration.

**1967** (November) - Following Sterling devaluation, run on Gold Pool. Dollar under attack.

**1968** (March 18th) - Gold pool dissolved. Two-tier gold market established. Official price maintained at $35 per ounce for foreign Central Banks. Free market price allowed to float, as intervention ended. Formal removal of 25% gold cover on Federal Reserve Notes.

**1969** (April 26th) - Ban removed on free import of gold coins minted prior to 1934.

**1969** (May 12th) - Ban on melting and exporting of silver coins lifted.

**1970** (October 26th) - Foreign exchange controls decreed.

**1970** (December) - Dollar in terms of 1940 value worth only 36 cents.

## DOLLAR AUSTRALIA

Monetary unit of **Australia.** Divided into 100 Cents.

Bank of issue - Reserve Bank of Australia.

Predecessor - See *Pound Australia.*

**1966** (February 14th) - Australian Dollar created. Adoption of decimal system for subsidiary coinage:

1 Australian Dollar = 995.311 milligrams of fine gold

1 Australian Dollar = 1.12 U.S. Dollars

## DOLLAR BAHAMA ISLANDS

Monetary unit of **Bahama Islands.** Divided into 100 Cents.

Note-issuing authority - Bahamas Monetary Authority, established November 1968.

Predecessor - See *Pound Bahama Islands.*

**1966** (May 25th) - Bahama Dollar replaced Bahama Pound. Decimal system introduced:

1 Bahama Dollar = 870.898 milligrams of fine gold

1 Bahama Dollar = 7 Shillings = 0.98 U.S. Dollars

**1967** (November 18th) - Pound Sterling devaluation:

1 Bahama Dollar = 8 Shillings 2 Pence = 0.98 U.S. Dollars

**1970** (February 2nd) - New par value:

1 Bahama Dollar = 888.6705 milligrams of fine gold

1 U.S. Dollar = 1 Bahama Dollar

## DOLLAR BARBADOS

Proposed (1971) monetary unit of **Barbados.** To be divided into 100 Cents. Will replace East Caribbean Dollar.

## DOLLAR BERMUDA

Monetary unit of **Bermuda.** Divided into 100 Cents.

Note-issuing authority - Currency and Exchange Control Board.

Predecessor - See *Pound Bermuda.*

**1970** (February 6th) - Creation of Bermuda Dollar to replace Bermuda Pound. Decimal system introduced:

1 Bermuda Pound = 2.40 Bermuda Dollars

1 Bermuda Dollar = 888.6705 milligrams of fine gold

1 U.S. Dollar = 1 Bermuda Dollar

## DOLLAR BRITISH HONDURAS

Monetary unit of **British Honduras.** Divided into 100 Cents.

Note-issuing authority - Board of Commissioners of Currency.

Predecessor - See *British Honduras.*

**1894** (October) - Ordinance authorized issue of government banknotes by newly established Board of Commissioners of Currency. British Honduras Dollar issued at par with U.S. Dollar.

**1934** - Monetary system linked to U.S. Dollar: 1 British Honduras Dollar = 1 U.S. Dollar.

**1946** (December 16th) - Parity registered with International Monetary Fund:
1 British Honduras Dollar = 888.6705 milligrams of fine gold
1 U.S. Dollar = 1 British Honduras Dollar
1 Pound Sterling = 4.03 British Honduras Dollar

**1949** (September 18th) - Parity with U.S. Dollar retained:
1 Pound Sterling = 2.80 British Honduras Dollars

**1949** (December 31st) - Devaluation:
1 British Honduras Dollar = 622.07 milligrams of fine gold
1 U.S. Dollar = 1.42857 British Honduras Dollars
1 Pound Sterling = 4.00 British Honduras Dollars

**1967** (November 18th) - Devaluation, parity with Sterling retained:
1 British Honduras Dollar = 533.203 milligrams of fine gold
1 U.S. Dollar = 1.66667 British Honduras Dollars

## DOLLAR BRITISH WEST INDIES

Former monetary unit of **Trinidad and Tobago, Barbados, Leeward Islands, Windward Islands** and **British Guiana.** Divided into 100 Cents.

Note-issuing authority - Before 1951, individual government treasuries and some commercial banks. As of August 1, 1951, Board of Commissioners of Currency, British Caribbean Territories (Eastern Group).

Predecessor - See individual territory.

**1935** - British West Indies Dollar became monetary unit for British West Indies with fixed relationship to Pound Sterling:
1 Pound Sterling = 4.80 BWI Dollars

**1946** (December 18th) - Par value of BWI Dollar established with International Monetary Fund:
1 BWI Dollar = 746.113 milligrams of fine gold
1 U.S. Dollar = 1.19107 BWI Dollars

**1949** (September 18th) - BWI Dollar devalued parallel to Sterling:
1 BWI Dollar = 518.391 milligrams of fine gold

1 U.S. Dollar = 1.71429 BWI Dollars

**1951** (August 1st) - Board of Commissioners of Currency, British Caribbean Territories (Eastern Group), became sole note-issuing authority as per multilateral agreement among territories. Issued new currency notes at par with old BWI Dollars and bearing same name. Treasury notes of some governments continued to circulate (i.e. Trinidad, British Guiana). No new government notes issued.

**1955** (October 1st) - Subsidiary coins of silver and bronze issued.

**1962** - British Guiana, and Trinidad and Tobago withdrew from British Caribbean Currency Board.

**1965** (October 6th) - BWI Dollar replaced at par by new monetary unit. - See *Dollar East Caribbean.*

## DOLLAR BRUNEI

Monetary unit of **Brunei.** Divided into 100 Cents.

Note-issuing authority - Brunei Currency Board.

Predecessors - See *Dollar Malaya, Dollar Straits Settlements.*

**1967** (June 12th) - Brunei Dollar created. At par with, but not linked to Malayan Dollar.

>1 Brunei Dollar = 290.299 milligrams of fine gold
>1 U.S. Dollar = 3.06122 Brunei Dollars

Multilateral agreement made Brunei Dollar interchangeable at par with newly created Malaysian Dollar and Singapore Dollar.

## DOLLAR CANADA

Monetary unit of **Canada.** Divided into 100 Cents. In French Canada, sometimes called Piastre, or Pièce, divided into 100 Sous.

Bank of issue - By Treasury (Dominion notes) and Chartered Banks, then by Bank of Canada (created July 3, 1934).

Predecessor - British monetary system. - See *Canada* and *Pound Sterling.*

**1853** - Provinces of Canada Currency Act legalized transactions in decimal currency. Gold coins made legal tender. Adoption of gold standard.

**1870** - Appearance of Canadian Dollar notes.

**1910** (May 4th) - Definition of monetary unit:

>1 Canadian Dollar = 1,504.656 milligrams of fine gold
>1 U.S. Dollar = 1 Canadian Dollar

**1914** - Suspension of gold standard.

**1926** (July 1st) - Restoration of gold standard at former parity. British and American gold coins were legal tender.

**1931** (October 19th) - Following Pound Sterling, currency depreciation of 12%. Embargo on gold exports.

**1933** (April 10th) - Canada, along with United States, suspended gold standard. Further depreciation of 23%.

**1935** (March 11th) - Bank of Canada became sole monetary authority.

**1935** (June 19th) - Revaluation of gold reserves of Dominion at $35 per ounce from $20.67, devaluation of 40.94%:

    1 Canadian Dollar = 888.6706 milligrams of fine gold
    1 U.S. Dollar = 1 Canadian Dollar

**1935** (July 3rd) - Creation of Exchange Equalization Fund.

**1939** (September 16th) - Foreign exchange controls:

    1 U.S. Dollar = 1.11 Canadian Dollars

Appearance on New York foreign exchange market of official free rate, used for tourists and investments in Canada.

**1946** (July 5th) - Upvaluation of 10%; Canadian Dollar raised to parity with U.S. Dollar:

    1 Canadian Dollar = 888.6706 milligrams of fine gold
    1 U.S. Dollar = 1 Canadian Dollar

**1946** (December 18th) - Parity registered with International Monetary Fund.

**1949** (September 20th) - Devalued with Pound Sterling:

    1 Canadian Dollar = 807.883 milligrams of fine gold
    1 U.S. Dollar = 1.10 Canadian Dollars

**1950** (October 1st) - Influx of capital from United States. Free foreign exchange market opened. Canadian Dollar drew nearer to U.S. Dollar in free market.

**1951** (December 14th) - Foreign exchange controls abolished.

**1952** (January 22nd) - Canadian Dollar reached, then rose above, parity of U.S. Dollar in the free market.

**1956** (March 19th) - Reestablishment of free gold market with unrestricted exports and imports of the metal.

**1959** (October) - Canadian Dollar rose to 6% premium over U.S. Dollar.

**1961** (June) - Premium for Canadian Dollar disappeared.

**1962** (May 2nd) - Fluctuating rate system abolished. De facto devaluation:

    1 Canadian Dollar = 822.021 milligrams of fine gold
    1 U.S. Dollar = 1.081 Canadian Dollars

**1970** (May 31st) - Floating exchange rate reestablished. De facto upvaluation in relation to the U.S. Dollar. By end of August, Canadian Dollar almost at par with U.S. Dollar.

## DOLLAR CANTON

Early monetary unit of **Southern China** (Kwantung and Kwangsi. Created after monetary reform of 1935.

Bank of issue - Central Bank of Canton.

Predecessor - See *Dollar China.*

**1935** - After reform of November 3rd, involving abandonment of silver standard and confiscation of silver holdings, monetary secession of Southern provinces. Creation of independent monetary unit, the Canton Dollar.

**1936** (October) - Issue of bonds for 120 million U.S. Dollars to stabilize Canton Dollar.

**1937** (June) - Stabilization on basis of:

1 Canton Dollar = 1.44 Chinese Dollars

**1938** (October 31st) - Japanese Occupation. - See *Yuan Nanking.*


## DOLLAR CAYMAN ISLANDS

Proposed (February 1972) monetary unit of **Cayman Islands.** To be divided into 100 Cents. Will replace Jamaican Dollar.


## DOLLAR CHINA

In **China,** silver money in 19th Century, then monetary unit from 1910 to 1948. At first, divided into 100 Fen or 1,000 Li, and from 1895 into 100 Cents.

Chinese names - Yuan, then Fa Pi or Fapi after 1933.

Bank of issue - Completely free and disorganized until 1931. Then, until the Communist conquest, undertaken by several government banks (Central Bank, Bank of China, Bank of Communications, Chinese Farmers' Bank) and by provincial banks.

Predecessor - See *China.*

**1838** - Minting of Dollar similar to Mexican Piaster by Provincial Treasury of Fukien.

**1887** - Opening of first mint in Kwantung.

**1890** - After Imperial approval, issue of first Chinese Dollar by Mint of Canton. "Dragon Piaster", as it was called, weighed 29.95 grams of silver 900 fine in Canton, 28.20 grams 820 fine in Pehtang. Numerous provincial imitations circulated in limited areas beyond Imperial control.

**1910** (May 25th) - Decree establishing Chinese Dollar (Yuan): 1 Chinese Dollar = 72/100 Tael = 27.216 grams of silver 900 fine = 24.494 grams of fine silver.

**1914** (February) - After Revolution, minting of Chinese Dollar called Yuan Shih Kai with imprint of President of the Republic. Minted to replace foreign and provincial varieties of coins. This Yuan distributed throughout national business community. Value fluctuated according to price of silver.

**1931** (May 1st) - Paper currency in circulation revamped through elimination of nonofficial issues; replaced with banknotes issued by provincial, national, and foreign banks in China.

Issue of banknotes backed by gold by Central Bank of China, in order to facilitate collection of customs duties.

**1933** (March 8th) - Replacement of Sycees and Taels, and adoption of Chinese Dollar as sole monetary unit: 1 Chinese Dollar = 0.715 Shanghai Tael = 26.6971 grams of silver 880 fine = 23.4934 grams of fine silver.

**1935** (November 3rd) - Monetary reform, with confiscation of silver metal and silver Dollar coins and abandonment of gold standard. Forced parity established for banknotes of three State Banks. Parity of Chinese paper Dollar (Fa Pi) in relation to Pound Sterling maintained:

1 Chinese Dollar = 14½ Pence

**After 1935** - Monetary breakup: in Northern China (see *Dollar Northern China*), in Southern China (see *Dollar Canton* ).

**1936** (May 17th) - Decree ordering minting of Chinese silver Dollars (coins of ½ and 1 Dollar) with very reduced fineness for divisionary coins.

**1938** (March 14th) - Foreign exchange controls.

**1938** (March 28th) - Termination by foreign banks of stabilization agreement by which they would not deal in Chinese Dollar below 14½ Pence. Decline of Chinese Dollar to 8⅜ Pence in June 1938, to 3½ Pence in August 1939.

**1939** - Appearance of free market where Chinese Dollar, then called Shanghai Dollar, depreciated sharply.

**1941** (August 18th) - Creation of Stabilization Board pegging Chinese Dollar at 3³/₁₆ Pence.

**1942** (July 10th) - Official exchange rate:

1 U.S. Dollar = 20 Chinese Dollars

**1945** (June) - Gold price raised; new parity:

1 U.S. Dollar = 1,430 Chinese Dollars

**1946** (March 8th) - Official exchange rate:

1 U.S. Dollar = 2,020 Chinese Dollars

**1946** (August 19th) - Official exchange rate:

1 U.S. Dollar = 3,350 Chinese Dollars

Hyper-inflation (4,084 billion Chinese Dollars in circulation at end of 1946).

**1947** (February 17th) - Official exchange rate:

1 U.S. Dollar = 12,000 Chinese Dollars

**1947** (August 17th) - Creation of open market valid for most transactions, official rate being retained for some imports (cotton, wheat, flour, rice, coke. . .).

Open market rate:

1 U.S. Dollar = 90,000 Chinese Dollars

Free market rate:

1 U.S. Dollar = 145,000 Chinese Dollars

**1948** (January) - Official rate limited essentially to government transactions.

**1948** (May 31st) - Introduction of system of certificates, whereby exporters received certificates against deposits of foreign exchange.

**1948** (August 18th) - Official exchange rate:

1 U.S. Dollar = 20,000 Chinese Dollars

Open market rate, with certificates:

1 U.S. Dollar = 8,287,000 Chinese Dollars

Free market rate:

1 U.S. Dollar = 12,000,000 Chinese Dollars

**1948** (August 19th) - Creation of new monetary unit. - See *Gold Yuan.*

**1949** (September 21st) - Communist victory. Issue of new monetary unit. - See *Jen Min Piao.* On Taiwan (Formosa), adoption of independent monetary unit. - See *Dollar Taiwan.*

## DOLLAR CHUNGKING

Name frequently given to **Chinese** Dollar from 1939 to 1945. - See *Dollar China.*
Variation of name - Yuan Chungking.

## DOLLAR CONFEDERATE STATES

Monetary unit of **Confederate States of America.** Divided into 100 Cents.
Bank of issue - State Banks and Treasuries, and private banks.
**1861** (February) - Confederate Dollar banknotes issued to replace U.S. Dollar at par.
Subject to widespread counterfeiting.
**1865** (April) - End of Civil War. Confederate Dollar rendered useless and valueless.
**1868** (July 28th) - Constitutional amendment (Article XIV, Section 4) officially demonetized Confederate Dollar.

## DOLLAR EAST CARIBBEAN

Monetary unit of **Barbados, Leeward Islands** (Antigua, St. Kitts-Nevis-Anguilla, Montserrat), and **Windward Islands** (Granada, St. Vincent, St. Lucia, and Dominica). - Circulates freely in Trinidad and Tobago. Divided into 100 Cents.
Note-issuing authority - East Caribbean Currency Authority.
Predecessor - See *Dollar British West Indies.*
**1965** (October 6th) - East Caribbean Dollar issued pursuant to East Caribbean Currency Agreement of 1965. Replaced BWI Dollar at par. Fixed relationship to Pound Sterling:
   1 East Caribbean Dollar = 518.391 milligrams of fine gold
   1 Pound Sterling = 4.80 East Caribbean Dollars
   1 U.S. Dollar = 1.71429 East Caribbean Dollars
**1967** (November 23rd) - East Caribbean Dollar devalued with Sterling:
   1 East Caribbean Dollar = 444.335 milligrams of fine gold
   1 U.S. Dollar = 2.00 East Caribbean Dollars

## DOLLAR EAST INDIA COMPANY

**I.** - Silver coin first minted in 1788. Used in **Far Eastern** trade (especially Straits Settlements). Submultiples - Cent coinage minted in silver (half, quarter and tenth of Dollar) and in copper (one, quarter and tenth of Cent).
Predecessor of Straits Settlements Dollar - See *Dollar Straits Settlements.*
**II.** - Copied for special colonial silver and copper coinage in **Sierra Leone** (1791). - See *Sierra Leone.*

## DOLLAR ETHIOPIA

Monetary unit of **Ethiopia** since 1945. Divided into 100 Cents.

Origin of name - Ethiopian, *Talari* (from Thaler). - See *Talari.*

Bank of issue - State Bank of Ethiopia created July 1945, then National Bank of Ethiopia created January 1964.

Predecessor - See *Ethiopia.*

**1945** (July 23rd) - Creation of Ethiopian Dollar:
  1 Talari = 1.50 Ethiopian Dollars
  2 East African Shillings = 1.00 Ethiopian Dollar
  1 U.S. Dollar = 2.48417 Ethiopian Dollars
 Parity corresponded to:
  1 Ethiopian Dollar = 357.690 milligrams of fine gold
 Debt obligations in Maria Theresia Thalers convertible into Ethiopian Dollars at ratio of 1:1.

**1946** (December 18th) - Gold parity confirmed by International Monetary Fund.

**1949** (September 11th) - Foreign exchange controls instituted. Black market resulted, with Ethiopian Dollars traded at more than 4.00 per U.S. Dollar, premium on latter of 61%.

**1950** - Control restrictions eased; black market still existed for various transactions. Dollar premium in this market ranged from 10%-20%.

**1964** (January 1st) - Small adjustment in official parity:
  1 Ethiopian Dollar = 355.468 milligrams of fine gold
  1 U.S. Dollar = 2.50 Ethiopian Dollars

## DOLLAR FIJI ISLANDS

Monetary unit of **Fiji Islands.** Divided into 10 Shillings, or 100 Cents.

Note-issuing authority - Commissioners of Currency.

Predecessor - See *Pound Fiji Islands.*

**1969** (January 13th) - Currency decimalized. Fiji Dollar issued to replace Fiji Pound:
  1 Fiji Dollar = 10 Shillings
  1 Fiji Dollar = 1,020.48 milligrams of fine gold
  1 Fiji Dollar = 1.148 U.S. Dollars

**1969** (May 14th) - Parity registered with International Monetary Fund.

## DOLLAR GUYANA

Monetary unit of **Guyana.** Divided into 100 Cents.

Bank of issue - Bank of Guyana.

Predecessor - See *Dollar British West Indies.*

**1965** (November 15th) - Guyana Dollar issued to replace British West Indies Dollar at par. Fixed relationship to Sterling:
1 Pound Sterling = 4.80 Guyana Dollars

**1966** (September 30th) - BWI Dollar ceased to be legal tender in Guyana.

**1967** (February 13th) - Initial par value established with International Monetary Fund:
1 Guyana Dollar = 518.391 milligrams of fine gold
1 U.S. Dollar = 1.71429 Guyana Dollars

**1967** (November 20th) - Guyana Dollar devalued with Sterling:
1 Guyana Dollar = 444.335 milligrams of fine gold
1 U.S. Dollar = 2.00 Guyana Dollars

## DOLLAR HONG KONG

Monetary unit of **Hong Kong.** Divided into 100 Cents.

Bank of issue - By Hong Kong and Shanghai Banking Corporation, Chartered Bank, and Mercantile Bank, as well as Treasury (from 1935).

Predecessors - See *Hong Kong, Piaster Mexico.*

**1895** (February 2nd) - Creation of autonomous money, Hong Kong Dollar, silver coin similar to Mexican Piaster: 1 Hong Kong Dollar = 26.9568 grams of 900 fine silver = 24.2611 grams of fine silver
Fluctuated in value with price of silver.

**1917** - Hong Kong Dollar weighed about 20 grams 900 fine.

**1931** - Hong Kong Dollar = 12 Pence.

**1935** (May) - Hong Kong Dollar = 27 Pence.

**1935** (November 9th) - After Chinese monetary reform, embargo on silver exports. Issue of Treasury banknotes.

**1935** (December 5th) - Confiscation of silver bars and coins. Creation of Exchange Equalization Fund. Silver standard abandoned. Monetary unit linked to Sterling at approximate rate of:
1 Hong Kong Dollar = 15 Pence

**1939** (September 8th) - Foreign exchange controls; beginning of free market operations.

**1941** (August 1st) - Incorporated into Sterling Area until Japanese Occupation.

**1942** (January 5th) - Issue of military Yen, or Gumpyo, by Japanese. Rate of exchange:
1 Yen = 2, then 4 Hong Kong Dollars. - See *Gumpyo.*

**1943** (May 31st) - Demonetization of Hong Kong Dollar (forbidden in China in July 1942).

**1945** (September 14th) - Japan defeated, Hong Kong Dollar returned to circulation with former relationship to Sterling:
1 Hong Kong Dollar = 15 Pence

**1946** (December 18th) - Parity registered with International Monetary Fund:
1 Hong Kong Dollar = 223.834 milligrams of fine gold
1 U.S. Dollar = 3.97022 Hong Kong Dollars

**1949** (August) - Hong Kong Dollar fell to record low of 7.10 per U.S. Dollar in free market dealings.

**1949** (September 18th) - Devaluation parallel to Pound Sterling and institution of multiple rate system:

    1 Hong Kong Dollar = 15 Pence = 155.517 milligrams of fine gold

    1 U.S. Dollar = 5.71429 Hong Kong Dollars (par value)

    1 U.S. Dollar = 5.694/5.755 Hong Kong Dollars (official buying and selling rates for all transactions against Sterling, U.S. Dollar proceeds of exports not of local origin and for most authorized non-Dollar transactions).

    1 U.S. Dollar = 5.997-6.2091 Hong Kong Dollars (mixed rates resulting from surrender of export proceeds at percentage of official and free market rate for certain exports originating in Mainland China, Hong Kong, Korea and Macao and received in U.S. Dollars).

    1 U.S. Dollar = 6.30 Hong Kong Dollars (free market rate for all other transactions)

**1962** (August 22nd) - Mixed rates abolished, and export proceeds previously covered by these rates surrendered at free market rate.

**1967** (November 18th) - Devaluation parallel to Pound Sterling:

    1 Hong Kong Dollar = 15 Pence = 133.301 milligrams of fine gold

    1 U.S. Dollar = 6.66667 Hong Kong Dollars

**1967** (November 22nd) - Upvaluation. New relationship to Sterling established:

    1 Hong Kong Dollar = 16.5 Pence = 146.631 milligrams of fine gold

    1 U.S. Dollar = 6.06061 Hong Kong Dollars


## DOLLAR HUA HSING

Money issued by Japanese in region of **Shanghai** from 1939 to 1941.

Variation of name - Yuan Hua Hsing.

**1939** (May) - Creation of Hua Hsing Commercial Bank in Shanghai with participation of Japanese capital. Linking of Dollar Hua Hsing to Chinese Dollar.

**1939** (July) - Stabilization in relation to Pound Sterling:

    1 Dollar Hua Hsing = 6 Pence

Exchange rate raised in relation to Chinese Dollar (up to 1.79 Chinese Dollars).

**1941** (January) - Hua Hsing Commercial Bank stopped issuing banknotes. Exchange of banknotes against Yuan Nanking. - See *Yuan Nanking.*

## DOLLAR JAMAICA

Monetary unit of **Jamaica, Turks and Caicos Islands,** and **Cayman Islands.** Divided into 100 Cents.

Bank of issue - Bank of Jamaica.

Predecessor - See *Pound Jamaica.*

**1969** (September 8th) - Jamaica Dollar issued to replace Jamaica Pound. Decimal system introduced:

1 Jamaican Pound = 2 Jamaican Dollars
1 Jamaican Dollar = 1,066.41 milligrams of fine gold
1 Jamaican Dollar = 1.20 U.S. Dollars

## DOLLAR LIBERIA

Monetary unit of **Liberia.** Divided into 100 Cents.

Note-issuing authority - None, as there are no Liberian banknotes.

Predecessor - See *Liberia.*

**1942** (November 3rd) - Adoption of American monetary system.

**1944** (January 1st) - Creation of Liberian Dollar, linked to, and at par with U.S. Dollar.

1 Liberian Dollar = 888.671 milligrams fine gold
1 U.S. Dollar = 1 Liberian Dollar

Circulation of U.S. Dollar banknotes and subsidiary coinage. Subsequent local mintings of silver Liberian Dollar coins and subsidiary coinage of silver and copper.

British banknotes and coins ceased to be legal tender.

## DOLLAR MALAYA

Former monetary unit of **Malaya,** then **Federation of Malaysia,** Singapore, and Brunei. Divided into 100 Cents.

Note-issuing authority - Board of Commissioners of Currency, Malaya, then Board of Commissioners of Currency, Malaya and British Borneo. After September 1963, Bank Negara Malaysia.

Variations of name - Malaya and British Borneo Dollar.

Predecessor - See *Dollar Straits Settlements.*

**1946** (April 1st) - Straits Dollar became known as Malayan Dollar with dissolution of Straits Settlements.

**1946** (December 18th) - Par value of Malayan Dollar registered with International Monetary Fund:

1 Malayan Dollar = 28   Pence = 417.823   milligrams   of
                                fine gold
1 U.S. Dollar = 2.12691 Malayan Dollars

**1949** (May) - U.S. Dollar premium rose to 100% over official rate on black market.

**1949** (September 18th) - Devaluation parallel to Pound Sterling:
  1 Malayan Dollar = 28   Pence = 290.299   milligrams   of
      fine gold
  1 U.S. Dollar = 3.06122 Malayan Dollars

**1952** (January 1st) - Board of Commissioners of Currency, Malaya and British Borneo established as note-issuing authority.

**1952** (December 31st) - All silver coins ceased to be legal tender.

**1963** (September 16th) - Formation of Federation of Malaysia. Issuance of currency taken over by Bank Negara Malaysia (Central Bank).

**1967** (June 12th) - Malysian Dollar issued to replace Malayan Dollar. - See *Dollar Malaysia.*

**1967** (November 18th) - Malayan Dollar devalued 14.3% in line with Sterling devaluation:
  1 Malayan Dollar = 28   Pence = 0.8571   new   Malaysian
      Dollars

**1969** (January 1st) - Malayan Dollar demonetized.


## DOLLAR MALAYSIA

Monetary unit of **Federation of Malaysia.** Divided into 100 Cents.

Bank of issue - Bank Negara Malaysia (Central Bank).

Predecessor - See *Dollar Malaya, Dollar Straits Settlements.*

**1967** (June 12th) - Bank Negara Malaysia began issuing Malaysian Dollar at par with, but not linked to Malayan Dollar.
  1 Malaysian Dollar = 290.299 milligrams of fine gold
  1 U.S. Dollar = 3.06122 Malaysian Dollars
Multilateral agreement made Malaysian Dollar interchangeable at par with newly created Singapore Dollar and Brunei Dollar.


## DOLLAR NEW ZEALAND

Monetary unit of **New Zealand.** Divided into 100 Cents.

Bank of issue - Reserve Bank of New Zealand.

Predecessor - See *Pound New Zealand.*

**1967** (July 10th) - New Zealand Dollar replaced New Zealand Pound, and currency decimalized:
  1 New Zealand Dollar = 1,235.65 milligrams of fine gold
  1 New Zealand Dollar = 1.39 U.S. Dollar

**1967** (November 21st) - Following Sterling devaluation, New Zealand Dollar devalued 19.45% in terms of gold and 24.2% in terms of foreign currencies:
  1 New Zealand Dollar = 995.31 milligrams of fine gold
  1 New Zealand Dollar = 1.12 U.S. Dollars

**1968** (July) - Currency hit all-time low of U.S. $0.87¾ in black market, a discount of 22% from official rate.


## DOLLAR NORTHERN CHINA

Monetary unit imposed on **Northern China** during Japanese Occupation from 1935 to 1944.

Variations of name - Yuan of Peiping, Yuan of Tientsin.

Bank of issue - Federal Reserve Bank of Northern China (located in Peiping).

Predecessor - See *Dollar China.*

**1935** (November 21st) - Hostility of Northern Chinese provinces against Chinese monetary reform (abandonment of silver standard, compulsory surrender of private silver holdings). Refusal to transfer silver of Northern China to Nanking resulted in creation at Tientsin of branch of Central Bureau of Mint.

**1936** (April) - Mint at Tientsin struck autonomous copper coinage; first monetary secession.

**1936** (May) - Issue of autonomous banknotes in Hopei and Chahar by Provincial Bank of Hopei.

**1938** (March 1st) - Creation of Federal Reserve Bank of Northern China (or Reserve Bank of Peiping), entrusted with issuing Dollar of Northern China:

1 Dollar of Northern China = 1 Japanese Yen = 14 Pence

Banknotes of provincial banks withdrawn from circulation within three months. Those of Central Bank of China and of Bank of Communications withdrawn within one year.

Foreign exchange controls. Currency depreciation in relation to Yen.

**1943** (April 1st) - Adoption of new official monetary relationship:

1 Dollar Northern China = 3.80 Yuan Nanking

**1944** (April 30th) - In region of Hwei-Hai, Nanking Yuan replaced Dollar Northern China. - See *Yuan Nanking.*


## DOLLAR RHODESIA

Monetary unit of **Rhodesia.** Divided into 100 Cents.

Bank of issue - Reserve Bank of Rhodesia.

Predecessor - See *Pound Rhodesia.*

**1970** (February 17th) - Rhodesian Dollar replaced Rhodesian Pound. Decimal system introduced:

1 Rhodesian Pound = 2.00 Rhodesian Dollars
1 Rhodesian Dollar = 1,244.14 milligrams of fine gold
1 Rhodesian Dollar = 1.40 U.S. Dollars

**1970** (December) - Rhodesian Dollar fell to low of U.S. $0.87 on black market, a discount of 37 ¾% from official rate.

## DOLLAR SHANGHAI

Name frequently given to **Chinese** Dollar after monetary secessions which followed monetary reform of 1935. - See *Dollar China.*

## DOLLAR SINGAPORE

**I.** - Monetary unit of **Singapore.** Divided into 100 Cents.

Note-issuing authority - Board of Commissioners of Currency, later Monetary Authority of Singapore.

Predecessor - See *Dollar Malaya, Dollar Straits Settlements.*

**1967** (May 19th) - Singapore Dollar created at par with, but not linked to Malayan Dollar:

> 1 Singapore Dollar = 290.299 milligrams of fine gold
> 1 U.S. Dollar = 3.06122 Singapore Dollars

**1967** (June 12th) - Singapore Dollar interchangeable at par with newly created Brunei Dollar and Malaysian Dollar by multilateral agreement.

**II.** - Name sometimes used in reference to Straits Settlements Dollar, former monetary unit in **Singapore.**

## DOLLAR STRAITS SETTLEMENTS

Former monetary unit of **Singapore, Malayan States, Sarawak** and **British North Borneo.** Divided into 100 Cents.

Variations of name - Malayan Dollar, Sarawak Dollar, Singapore Dollar, Straits Dollar, S.S. Dollar.

Predecessors - See *Straits Settlements* and *Dollar East India Company.*

**1903** (June 25th) - Straits Dollar minted with weight and fineness comparable to Mexican Piaster, traditionally circulating in Far East:

> 1 Straits Dollar = 27.0695 grams silver 9027 fine = 24.-
> 4356 grams fine silver

Value fluctuated according to price of silver.

**1906** (February) - Straits Dollar linked to Pound Sterling:

> 1 Straits Dollar = 28 Pence = 854.277 milligrams of fine
> gold

**1931** (September 21st) - Adherence to Sterling Area and depreciation parallel to Pound. - See *Pound.*

**1939** (September 18th) - Foreign exchange controls.

**1942** (February 15th) - Circulation of Japanese military banknotes (Gumpyo), denominated in Straits Dollars. Declared legal tender at par with Straits Dollar. - See *Gumpyo.*

**1945** (September 2nd) - Demonetization of Gumpyo.

**1946** (January 1st) - Restoration of Straits Dollar linked to Sterling:

1 Straits Dollar = 28 Pence

**1946** (April 1st) - Straits Dollar became known as Malayan Dollar with dissolution of Straits Settlements. - See *Dollar Malaya.*


# DOLLAR TAIWAN

Former monetary unit of **National Republic of China on Taiwan** (formerly Formosa) from 1945 to 1949. Divided into 100 Cents.

Bank of issue - Bank of Taiwan.

Predecessor - From 1895 to 1945, monetary system of Japan.

**1945** - Taiwan Dollar linked to Chinese Dollar at fixed rate of exchange. Taiwan Dollar less affected by inflation. Retained premium over Chinese Dollar.

**1946** - Official rate: 1 U.S. Dollar = 95.70 Taiwan Dollars.

**1947** - Official rate: 1 U.S. Dollar = 1,000.00 Taiwan Dollars.

**1948** - Official rate: 1 U.S. Dollar = 25,850.00 Taiwan Dollars.

**1949** (June) - Official rate: 1 U.S. Dollar = 40,000.00 Taiwan Dollars.

**1949** (June 15th) - Deflationary monetary reform:
>40,000.00 Taiwan Dollars = 1.00 New Taiwan Dollar
>1 U.S. Dollar = 5.00 New Taiwan Dollars

Foreign exchange controls instituted.

See *Dollar (New) Taiwan.*


# DOLLAR (NEW) TAIWAN

Monetary unit of Nationalist Chinese **Taiwan,** formerly Formosa. Divided into 100 Cents.

Bank of issue - Bank of Taiwan. July 1961, Central Bank of China became monetary authority. Granted continuation of banknote issue to Bank of Taiwan.

Predecessor - From 1895 to 1945, monetary system of Japan. - See *Yen.* From 1945 to 1949, monetary system of National Republic of China. - See *Dollar Taiwan.* After Communist victory in China and withdrawal of Generalissimo Chiang Kai-shek to Taiwan:

**1949** (June 15th) - Official rate: 1 U.S. Dollar = 5.00 New Taiwan Dollars. Fluctuating exchange certificate rate, periodically adjusted by Bank of Taiwan, also existed as did rate for trade with Japan.

**1950** (May) - Official rate: 1 U.S. Dollar = 8.00 New Taiwan Dollars.

**1950** (June) - Official rate: 1 U.S. Dollar = 9.50 New Taiwan Dollars.

**1950** (September 15th) - Exchange certificate rate at 10.25/10.30 per U.S. Dollar. Japanese trade rate 9.75/9.80 per U.S. Dollar.

**1950** (September 20th) - Exchange controls and restrictions became effective.

**1951** (April 11th) - Exchange certificate rate changed to 15.85/15.95 per U.S. Dollar. Japanese trade rate 15.08/15.18 per U.S. Dollar.

**1951** (May 8th) - Special rate for trade with Japan abolished.

**1951** (May 21st) - Multiple rate structure:

> 1 U.S. Dollar = 5.00 New Taiwan Dollars (inoperative official rate)
>
> 1 U.S. Dollar = 10.25/10.30 New Taiwan Dollars (Bank of Taiwan rate for government transactions and essential imports)
>
> 1 U.S. Dollar = 14.49 New Taiwan Dollars (mixed rate for private exports)
>
> 1 U.S. Dollar = 15.55/15.65 New Taiwan Dollars (foreign exchange deposit certificate rate for invisibles, capital and authorized imports)

Minor rate of 12.37 New Taiwan Dollars per U.S. Dollar existed for government exports of camphor and salt.

**1953** (January 5th) - Simplification of currency structure: Official rate of 5.00 per U.S. Dollar dropped, as was 10.25/10.30 rate and the 12.37 rate. The 14.49 rate limited to sugar and rice exports.

**1953** (September 12th) - Defense tax of 20% introduced on most private imports.

**1954** (January 1st) - Rate of 14.49 per U.S. Dollar abolished. All receipts and payments settled at certificate rates of 15.55/15.65 per U.S. Dollar.

**1954** (June 29th) - Defense tax of 20% extended to most sales of foreign exchange.

**1955** (March 1st) - Negotiable exchange certificates, with either fixed or fluctuating rates, governed currency system. Fixed rate set at 6.00 per U.S. Dollar, fluctuating rate 7.00-16.00 per U.S. Dollar. Bank of Taiwan rate 15.56/15.65 per U.S. Dollar) continued to apply to government exports and imports and to specified exports. All other exports, imports and inward and outward remittances took place at exchange certificate rate of 21.55 per U.S. Dollar (fixed value of 6.00 plus Bank of Taiwan rate of 15.55).

**1955** (September 10th) - Transactions at Bank of Taiwan rate eliminated. Dealings of government agencies and specified public enterprises took place at rates based on fixed exchange certificate price, while all other transactions effected at rate based on fluctuating exchange certificate price. All exports of government agencies and specified public enterprises, and exports of various products granted exchange certificates equal to 80% of export proceeds, some at 50%. The 20% defense tax applied to all selling rates. Multiple rate structure contained 9 different rates ranging from 18.55 to 34.00 per U.S. Dollar, last being rate for foreign diplomatic and military personnel which was periodically adjusted.

**1956** - Number of mixed rates for various products removed, while others shifted. Resulting in 6 rates ranging from 20.35 to 34.00 per U.S. Dollar. The last, formerly called diplomatic rate, now referred to as preferential rate, and its use expanded throughout 1957.

**1958** (April 12th) - Multiple rate structure virtually eliminated and defense tax abolished. Two effective rates:

> 1 U.S. Dollar = 24.58/24.78 New Taiwan Dollars (official rate for various exports and imports and for invisibles for government account)
>
> 1 U.S. Dollar = 36.08/36.38 New Taiwan Dollars (official

rate plus exchange certificate rate of 11.50/11.60
for all other exports, imports and invisibles)

**1958** (November 21st) - Exchange transactions previously effected at official rate took place at rate of 36.08/36.38 New Taiwan Dollars per U.S. Dollar. Rate fluctuated.

**1960** (July) - Practically all transactions effected at fluctuating exchange certificate rate, virtually stabilized at 40.00 per U.S. Dollar.

**1961** (June 1st) - Official buying rate raised to 40.00 New Taiwan Dollars per U.S. Dollar. Previous official selling rate abandoned.

**1961** (June 30th) - New Taiwan Dollar fell to low of 53.20 per U.S. Dollar on black market, from where it improved gradually.

**1963** (October 1st) - Foreign exchange certificate system abolished. Official rates established at 40.00/40.10 per U.S. Dollar.


## DOLLAR TRINIDAD AND TOBAGO

Monetary unit of **Trinidad and Tobago.** Divided into 100 Cents. Circulates freely in Barbados, Windward Islands and Leeward Islands.

Bank of issue - Central Bank of Trinidad and Tobago.

Predecessor - See *Dollar British West Indies.*

**1964** (December 14th) - Issued at par with BWI Dollar, having fixed relationship to Sterling:
1 Trinidad and Tobago Dollar = 50 Pence

**1965** (February 10th) - Initial par value established with International Monetary Fund:
1 Trinidad and Tobago Dollar = 518.391 milligrams of
fine gold
1 U.S. Dollar = 1.71429 Trinidad and Tobago Dollars

**1967** (November 23rd) - Currency devalued with Sterling:
1 Trinidad and Tobago Dollar = 444.335 milligrams of
fine gold
1 U.S. Dollar = 2.00 Trinidad and Tobago Dollars


## *DOMINICAN REPUBLIC*

**15th-16th Century -** Called Hispaniola. Spanish monies. - See *Spain.*

**16th Century -** Minted small copper coins called Quartos, oldest metallic money of New World.

**17th Century -** Called Santo Domingo. Use of Portuguese, Spanish and English monies.

**18th Century -** See *Piaster Gourde.*

**Before 1844 -** See *Haiti.*

**After 1844 -** See *Peso Dominican Republic.*

## DOMINICANO

Early monetary unit of **Dominican Republic.** Created April 17, 1889. Divided into 100 Centesimos. Defined as equal to 0.75 Francs, or 3.375 grams fine silver. Minted in 1897 in Philadelphia.

## DONG

**I.** - Monetary unit of **North Viet Nam** (Viet Minh). Divided into 100 Xu.

Bank of issue - State Bank of Democratic Republic of Viet Nam.

Predecessor - See *Piastre Dong Viet, Piastre Indochina* and *Viet Nam (North).*

**1954** (July 20th) - Official exchange rate:
1 Indochinese Piastre = 32.00 Dongs
On cross-rate basis:
1 U.S. Dollar = 1,120 Dongs
Computed on cross-rate with Hong Kong Dollar, Dong depreciated from former 1,120 to 3,591 per U.S. Dollar by April 1958.

**1956** (March) - 1 Viet Nam Piastre = 28.00 Dongs.

**1956** (December 15th) - Exchange rate fixed with Mainland China:
1 Jen Min Piao = 1.47 Dongs

**1959** (February 28th) - Currency reform:
1,000 old Dongs = 1 new Dong
Based on cross-rate with Hong Kong Dollar:
1 U.S. Dollar = 3.59 Dongs

**1961** (January 1st) - Alignment to Soviet monetary reform:
1 new Ruble = 3.27 Dongs
1 U.S. Dollar = 2.94 Dongs (official rate)
1 U.S. Dollar = 4.20 Dongs (noncommercial rate)

**II.** - For **South Viet Nam,** see *Piastre Viet Nam.*

## DOPPIA

**I.** - Gold money of **Venice,** valued at 29 Lire (in 1686), then 37 Lire 10 Soldi (in 1739). Weight in 18th Century: 6.72 grams of gold.

Origin of name - Italian, *doppio* (double).

Variations of name - Doppie, Double.

**II.** - Gold money of Grand Duchy of **Tuscany,** valued in 18th Century at 11.50 Lire. Double Doppia valued at 23 Lire. Doppia Lira was unit of account equal to Testone (worth 2 Lire).

**III.** - Gold money used in various **Italian** states until 19th Century. Also called Pistole.
- In Genoa, exchange rate in 18th Century: 23 Lire 12 Soldi.
- In Rome, Doppia of 33 Paoli equal to Double Escudo (Doppio Scudo), or 6.9

grams 900 fine (old Pistole). In 1778, weight reduced to 5.4 grams 900 fine (new Pistole). Doppia minted by Pope Leo XII called Leonina.
- In Turin (Piedmont, Savoy), minted in 1741-1742: weighed 7.2 grams 903 fine and had value of 16 Lire 7 Soldi 6 Denari.
  Minted in 1755 and in 1814: weighed 9.6 grams 906 fine and worth 24 Lire.
- In Bologna, exchange rate during 18th Century was 15 Lire.
- In Leghorn, equal to 24 Lire in "long money ", 23 Lire in "good money".
- In Milan (Lombardy), Doppia minted by Austria circulated with exchange rate of 24 Lire. Locally minted coin (1778) also valued at 24 Lire.
- In Naples, value during 18th Century was 16 Carlini.
- In Parma, 72 Lire 12 Soldi.

IV. - In **Sardinia,** gold coin issued in 1755 equal to 24 Lire.


## DOS

Gold coin (6.2 grams 900 fine) of **Siam.** Worth 10 Ticals (Baht) according to reform of November 11, 1908. However, coin never minted.


## DOUBLE

In Latin countries, money representing twice the value of gold or silver monetary unit.

I. - For **Venice** and **Tuscany,** see *Doppia.*

II. - For **Spain** and **Mexico** (Dobla, Doblon), see *Doubloon.*

III. - For **Portugal,** see *Dobra.*

IV. - In **France,** name given to various monies:
  Silver/copper coins - Corresponded to 2 Deniers: Double Parisis, Double Tournois. Minted in 1293 by Philip the Fair and in 1346-47 by Philip VI. Became copper coin in 1577 (Henry III). Still made of copper in 18th Century.
  Gold coin - Minted by Philip VI in 1339. Exchange rate: 60 Sous, and by Dauphin Charles in 1420 (6.12 grams of fine gold). Exchange rate: 8 Livres.

V. - Copper coin of **Island of Guernsey** in 1830. Equal to ⅛ Penny. Multiple of 4 and 8 Doubles.

**1861** - Replaced by bronze Doubles.


## DOUBLOON

Gold money of **Spanish** states or territories under **Spanish** influence.

Origin of name - Spanish: *doble;* Latin: *duplus,* meaning double.

Variations of name - Doble, Dubla, Doblon.

Predecessor - See *Spain.*

I. - In **Spain,** gold money first called Dobla, then Doblo Escudo and Doblon (Doubloon).

**1284-1303** - Sancho IV or Alphonso XI minted gold coin (4.6 grams) called Dobla or Dobla Castellana.

**1391** - Enrique III minted gold Dobla with weight similar to its predecessor.

**15th Century** - Weight of coin reduced periodically.

**1497** (June 13th) - Demonetized Dobla. New coin, Excelente de Granada (3.49 grams fine gold).

**1537** - Charles V created gold Escudo (3.38 grams 917 fine) and Doblo Escudo (6.76 grams 917 fine). Coin became famous under name Pistole. - See *Pistole* and *Escudo.*

**1772** (May 29th) - Decree of Aranjuez. Doubloon (Doblon de Oro) minted with reduced fineness (893).
Multiples of Doubloon - Doblon de à Cuatro and Doblon de à Ocho, latter being the Onza.
Submultiples of Doubloon - 1/2 Doubloon or 1/2 Pistole.

**1785** - Fineness reduced (872).

**1808-1814** - Catalonia minted gold Doubloon with value of 5 Pesetas.

**1847** - Under Isabella II, Pistole disappeared. Doblon or Isabella (3.336 grams 900 fine gold) minted with value of 5 Duros or 100 Reales. Weight increased to 8.387 grams 900 fine from 1864 to 1868.

**II.** - Gold coin of **Spanish America** in 17th and 18th Centuries. Also called Onza or Doblon de Ocho.

**III.** - Gold coin (8 Escudos) of **Mexico** minted after 1675. Worth 16 Piasters.

**IV.** - Gold coin of **Chile:** 5.99 grams 916 fine before 1910; then fineness reduced to 900. Value: 5 Pesos before 1885, 10 Pesos thereafter. Equal to 1/2 Condor.

**V.** - Early coin of **Colombia:** 8.06 grams 900 fine, or 7.25 grams fine gold. Value: 5 Pesos. Equal to 1/2 Condor. Same name was sometimes given to heavier coin: 27 grams 870 fine, then 25.8 grams 900 fine.

**VI.** - In **Venezuela,** gold coin (16.129 grams 900 fine) minted under law of May 11, 1871, worth 10 Venezolanos.

**VII.** - In **Ecuador,** gold coin (6.45 grams 900 fine) minted according to monetary system of 1884.

**VIII.** - In **Bolivia,** gold coin minted in small quantities after 1863. Equal to 1/4 Onza. Value in silver Bolivianos varied according to price of gold. The 1/2 Doubloon called Escudo.

**IX.** - In **Peru,** Mint of Lima authorized to mint gold Doubloon of 8 Escudos in 1675.

**X.** - In **Uruguay,** Law of June 23, 1862, authorized minting of gold Doubloon 16.97 grams 916 fine. Exchange rate: 10 Pesos. Actually minted from 1870 to 1877.

**XI.** - In **Papal States,** gold coin minted in Bologna by Pope Benedict XIV (1740-1758). Doblone d'Oro, or Doubloon of Bologna: 37.2 grams.

# DOUZAIN

Early **French** silver money worth 12 Deniers. Beginning in the reign of Francis I, minted to replace Grand Blanc. At first 333 fine, then 285 fine. Legal tender status limited to 10 Livres in 1692.

Origin of name - Meaning 12th part.

Variation of name - Dozen.


# DRACHMA

Monies of **Greek** states or territories under **Greek** influence.

Origin of name - Greek *drachme* from *drax* (pinched, fistful of grain), *drassein* (to seize); Drachma represented fistful of Obols.

Plural - Greek: Drachmae, English: Drachmas.

I. - Silver money and basic monetary unit of **Ancient Greece.**

Multiples - Decadrachm (10), Octodrachm (8), Tetradrachm (4), Tridrachm (3), Didrachm (2).

Submultiples - Hemidrachm or Tribolon ($1/2$), Diobolon ($1/3$), Obol ($1/6$), Hemiobolion ($1/12$), Tetartemorion ($1/24$).

**6th Century B.C.** - In monetary system of Aegina, Drachma (about 6 grams of silver) was $1/60$ Mina (364 grams). Basic coin was Didrachm (2 Drachmae) of 12 grams silver imprinted with image of tortoise.

In monetary system of Thrace, Drachma was $1/90$ Mina. Basic coin was Octodrachm (8 Drachmae) of 30 to 40 grams silver imprinted with image of knight.

In system of account in Euboea, Drachma (4.25 grams of silver) worth $1/100$ Mina (425 grams), and $1/6,000$ Talent. It was worth 6 Obols, 24 Dichalkons, 48 Chalcoi or 336 Lepta.

**595 B.C.** - In Athens, Solon substituted Euboea monetary system for Aegina monetary system. This involved reduction in weight of Drachma from 6 to 4.25 grams of silver.

Basic coin in Attica: Tetradrachm (4 Drachmae) of 17 grams silver imprinted with the image of owl.

Spread of accounting system of Euboea to Corinth (Tridracham with imprint of colt), to Corfu (Tetradrachm with imprint of cow), to Magna Graecia (Tridrachm), to Sicily (Tetradrachm of 17 grams).

Didrachm of Phocis with imprint of seal (7.5 grams of silver) circulated in Western Mediterranean (Naples and Marseilles).

**478 B.C.** - Athenian League formed against Persians, adopted Tetradrachm with owl as common monetary unit.

**3rd Century B.C.** - In Egypt, Ptolemies divided Mina of 364 grams into 100 Drachmae (3.64 grams of silver). Tetradrachm weighed 14.56 grams. System adopted by Rhodes. Athens stopped minting of silver coins.

In Sicily, Syracuse minted Drachmae of 5.5 grams of silver, then 3.5 grams, also Tetradrachms of 13.5 grams.

Marseilles minted Drachmae of 3.76 grams.

**2nd Century B.C.** - In Marseilles, Drachma reduced in weight to less than 3 grams. In territories conquered by Rome, Roman silver coins replaced Drachma; Victoriatus on shores of Adriatic; Denarius on Delos at par with Drachma.

**168 B.C.** - Rhodes stopped minting Tetradrachm.

**II.** - **Persia,** under Sassanids, minted silver coin imitating Greek Drachma. Circulated in Arabia and gave rise to Dirhem. - See *Dirhem.*

**III.** - Monetary unit of **Modern Greece.** Divided into 100 Lepta (singular: Lepton). Predecessor - See *Greece.*

Bank of issue - National Bank of Greece until 1928, then Banque de Grèce (Bank of Greece).

**1833** (February 8th) - Drachma replaced Phoenix as national currency.
1 Drachma = 1 Phoenix
1 Drachma = ⅙ Spanish Piaster = 4.06 grams of fine silver
New system provided for minting of gold coins (20 and 40 Drachmae), on basis of 254.4 milligrams of fine gold per Drachma, and silver coins (1 and 5 Drachmae).

**1836** (September 26th) - Adoption of decimal system. Drachma linked with Franc Germinal:
1 Drachma = 1 Franc Germinal = 4.50 grams of fine silver
= 290.322 milligrams of fine gold

**1841** - National Bank of Greece became bank of issue.

**1848** - Increased indebtedness of government resulted in inflationary monetary policy and necessitated forced parity.

**1868** (September 26th) - Adherence to Latin Monetary Union (see *Union Latine*). Then new return to forced parity.

**1877** - Suspension of convertibility.

**1885** (January 1st) - Restoration of gold standard at former gold parity.

**1885** (September 30th) - Suspension of gold standard. Currency depreciation.

**1910** - De facto stabilization resulted from purchase of foreign exchange by National Bank.

**1920** - Inflation and progressive depreciation.

**1922** (March 25th) - Monetary reform. All banknotes in circulation cut in half. Left portion continued to circulate at half face value. Right half regarded as forced loan to government.

**1925** (October 25th) - Foreign exchange controls.

**1926** - New monetary reform. Printing of banknotes in denominations of 25 Drachmae and over, which were again cut in half. Left portion continued to circulate at 75% of face value and 25% considered loan value. Right portion again regarded as forced loan to government. All old halves from first monetary reform exchanged.

**1928** (May 14th) - Stabilization with devaluation of 93.6%:
1 Drachma = 19.526 milligrams of fine gold
1 Pound Sterling = 375 Drachmae

**1931** (September 21st) - After break between Pound and gold, Drachma convertible into Dollars, and no longer into Sterling.

**1931** (September 28th) - Monopoly on foreign exchange operations given to National Bank. Foreign exchange controls. Currency depreciation (49%).

**1932** (April 26th) - Law officially suspending Dollar standard.

**1933** - De facto stabilization after depreciation of 56% on basis of:

1 Drachma = $1/7$ Franc (Poincaré)

**1936** (September 28th) - After devaluation of Franc, link to Pound Sterling:
1 Pound Sterling = 548 Drachmae

**1940** - Rate of exchange with Reichsmark raised from 46.50 Drachmae to 48.50 Drachmae by agreement.

**1941** (April) - German Occupation:
1 Reichsmark = 60 Drachmae
Rapid inflation and sharp depreciation.

**1943** (March) - Issue by Germans of auxiliary military money denominated in Reichspfennig.

**1944** (November 11th) - Creation of new Drachma. Replaced Drachma that was victim of inflation (circulation estimated at 2,500 quadrillion Drachmae). Gold Sovereign quoted at 30 billion old Drachmae:
1 new Drachma = 50 billion old Drachmae
1 U.S. Dollar = 150 Drachmae

**1945** (June 5th) - Stabilization attempt failed. New devaluation:
1 U.S. Dollar = 500 Drachmae

**1946** (January 26th) - 1 U.S. Dollar = 5,000 Drachmae.

**1947** (February) - Sale price of gold Sovereign on free market and by National Bank rose to 140,000 Drachmae.

**1947** (October) - Obligation to sell all foreign exchange proceeds at official rate of exchange. Increased through certificate of exchange (in Dollars or Pounds) negotiable on free market. De facto exchange rate:
1 U.S. Dollar = 8,000 to 10,000 Drachmae

**1949** (September 22nd) - Stabilization of exchange certificate by Banque de Grèce, raising exchange rate to:
1 U.S. Dollar = 15,000 Drachmae

**1951** (June 1st) - Official exchange rate without exchange certificate increased to:
1 U.S. Dollar = 15,000 Drachmae

**1953** (April 9th) - Devaluation:
1 U.S. Dollar = 30,000 Drachmae
Existing de facto multiple rate practices (export subsidies) abolished.

**1954** (May 1st) - Monetary reform:
1 new Drachma = 1,000 old Drachmae
1 U.S. Dollar = 30.00 Drachmae
All prices, debts and contracts divided by 1,000.

**1956** (January 11th) - Freedom of gold imports in any form.

**1961** (March 29th) - Par value registered with International Monetary Fund:
1 Drachma = 22.622 milligrams of fine gold
1 U.S. Dollar = 30.00 Drachmae

**1964** (January) - Controls imposed on dealings in gold Sovereigns. Official market created. Sales of Sovereigns, requiring identification, could only be made to licensed stockbrokers acting as agents for Banque de Grèce. Restrictions lifted later in year.

**1965** (December 22nd) - Free market for gold coins abolished. Restrictions of January

1964 reinstituted. Price of gold Sovereign initially set at 328 Drachmae by Banque de Grèce.

**1967** (December 31st) - Drachma, at 32.50 per U.S. Dollar, reached its all-time low in unofficial dealings.

## DREIER

Early **German** money (sometimes called Dreyes in France).

Origin of name - From German *drei* (three).

**1680** - In Holy Roman Empire, money defined by Diet of Regensburg as being worth 3 Pfennige.

**During 18th Century** - In Brandenburg, silver/copper money worth 1/3 Groschen. In Trier, silver/copper money worth 3 Petermännchen.

## DREILANDER

Silver money of the **Netherlands** in 15th Century. Name reflected fact that it was common to three states (Brabant, Hainaut, Holland). Exchange rate: 2 Grooten. Cf. *Vierlander.*

Variation of name - Drielander.

## *DUBAI*

See *Trucial States.*

## DUBBELTJE

**I.** - In **Netherlands** and in Dutch possessions, name for 2 Stuyver coin. Minted in silver/copper, and later designated silver 10 Cent coin.

**II.** - In **Malay Peninsula,** equal to 2.5 Duits.

## DUCADO

In **Spain,** gold money, then unit of account, from 15th to 19th Centuries.

Origin of name - See *Ducato.*

**15th Century** - Gold coin minted in Aragon.

**1537** - Charles V adopted Ducado as unit of account:
   1 Ducado = 375 Maravedis
   12 Ducados = 10 Pesos

**1808** - Disappearance of system of accounting in Ducados. Adoption of French monetary system.

**1847** - Adoption of system of accounting in Reales. Ducado continued to exist for a time in Malaga and Navarra. It was divided into 49 Tarjas, 65 1/3 Grosos, 196 Ochavos, 392 Maravedis, or 784 Cornados.

## DUCAT

Gold, then silver money, and unit of account. Derived from Ducato of Venice. Origin of name - See *Ducato*.

**I.** - For **Venice** and **Italy,** see *Ducato*.

**II.** - For **Spain,** see *Ducado*.

**III.** - For **German States, Austria, Hungary, Switzerland,** see *Dukat*.

**IV.** - In **Netherlands,** gold money issued in 1606 (3.49 grams 978 fine) with exchange rate of 3.16 Guilders. Rate increased to 5.25 Guilders in 18th Century, to 5.60 Guilders in 19th Century. Sometimes called Noble in Orient. Minted in 19th Century: 3.496 grams 983 fine, or 3.437 fine gold. Minted in Utrecht until 1928, especially for Indonesia.
Silver Ducat, created in 1659 (28 grams 865 fine). Usually called Rix Daler.

**V.** - In **Dutch East Indies** (Indonesia), introduction of counter-marked gold Ducat in 1686. Minting of Ducats of 3.45 grams 978 fine. Use until 1936 of a Ducat of 3.49 grams 983 fine.

**VI.** - In **Liege, Maastricht** and **Westphalia,** gold coin with an exchange rate of 8.50 Guilders.

**VII.** - In **Denmark,** gold money minted in 1644 and 1660. New issue from 1714 to 1717: 2.9 grams 862 fine. Exchange rate raised to 11 Marks in 1757. Common Ducat (1757) of 3.14 grams 924 fine had a value of 12 Marks.

**VIII.** - In **Sweden,** gold money from 16th to 19th Century. First appeared in 1569. Weight: 3.48 grams 976 fine. Exchange rate: 94 Skilling.
Derivative coins: Quadruple, Double, and 1/4 Ducat.

**IX.** - In **Poland,** gold money imitating Ducat of Hungary. Issued from 1526 by Sigismund I: 3.45 grams of fine gold. Successive reduction in weight and raising of rate as unit of account from 58 Grosze in 1598 to 165 Grosze in 1631. Before Partition of 1792, gold Ducat (3.50 grams 969 fine) had exchange rate of 9 Florin Zlote, or 270 Grosze. Exchange rate doubled in Greater Poland. Minted in 1800-1813 by Grand Duchy of Warsaw, and in 1830-1831 by Polish Republic. Based on Dutch Ducat.

**X.** - In **Russia,** at first coin copied Ducat of Hungary. Struck under Ivan III by minters who came from Hungary. Then imitated Dutch Ducat under Peter I (Ukases of 1701, 1711, 1718) and Paul I (1796). Under Peter I exchange rate was 2 Rubles (3.42 grams of fine gold).
From 1834 to 1885, Imperial Ducat contained 3.92 grams 916 fine, or 3.92 grams fine gold. Exchange rate: 3 Rubles.

Other Russian Ducats: platinum Ducat and white Ducat.

**XI.** - In **Scotland,** gold money issued in 16th Century.

**XII.** - In **Morocco,** gold money of 18th Century.Worth 48 Blanquillos, or 960 Falus. Name sometimes given to Real Hassani of 10 Ukkias. - See *Hassani.*

# DUCATO

In **Italy,** gold, then silver money, and unit of account, from 13th to 19th Century.

Origin of name - General hypotheses: 1) Coin imprinted with figure of Duke (Italian: *duca*). In 6th Century, Governor of Italy, Longinus, declared himself Duke of Ravenna and minted coins bearing his image which were called Ducats. 2) In 12th Century, Bezants minted in Byzantium by Emperor Constantine X and Emperor Michael VII of Ducas family were called Ducas in Italy. Probable etymology: Zecchino of Venice, minted in 1284, bore Latin motto: *Sit tibi, Christe, datus quem tu regis iste ducatus.* Last word of motto retained to designate coin and all its derivatives. Name interchangeable with Ducat.

Plural - Ducati.

**I.** - In **Venice:**

**1284** - Minting of the first gold Ducato, equal to Fiorino (Guilder) of Florence. Generally called Zecchino. - See *Zecchino.*

**1561** - Minting of heavy silver Ducato (33 grams 945 fine). Exchange rate: 124 Soldi.

**1578** - This Ducato became the Scudo. - See *Scudo.*

**1660** - New Ducato, or Ducatello, minted (19.3 grams fine silver) with an exchange rate of 124 Soldi.

**18th Century** - Ducato both specie money and a unit of account. As unit of account, value was 6.2 Lire, 24 Grossi, 124 Soldi, 288 Denari of Ducato (Grossetti), or 1,488 Denari de Lira.

Variations in Bergamo, Bassano, Padua: Ducato equal to 24 Grossi and divided into 288 Piccioli, or 1,488 Denari.

In records of Bank of Venice, worth ¹/10 Lira Grossa. As specie money, Ducato Effettivo (effective Ducato) contained 17 grams fine silver. Worth 8 Lire de Piccioli. A ¹/2 and ¹/4 Ducato also circulated.

**II.** - In **Florence,** gold, then silver money, and unit of account.

**1531** - When Medicis created Duchy of Tuscany, gold Fiorino (1.8 grams) valued at 7 Soldi became Ducato.

**18th Century** - Ducato (or Piastra) was silver coin worth 7 Lire. As unit of account, the Ducato (also called Piastra, Ducatone, Scudo Corriente) valued at 7 Lire, 20 Soldi di Ducato, 84 Crazie, or Ducati. Denari di Ducato. Ducati

**III.** - In **Milan,** gold coin (3.50 grams) issued in 1468. Also called Zecchino (Sequin). Circulated until 19th Century (worth 14 Lire 10 Soldi in 1778). Louis XII minted coin of 10 gold Ducati. Before Italian unification, silver Ducati circulated in Lombardy (22.63 grams 820 fine, and 28.56 grams 826 fine).

**IV.** - In **Genoa,** gold coin minted between 1458 and 1461.

**V.** - In **Savoy,** gold coin issued in 1430.

**VI.** - In **Leghorn** and **Lucca,** unit of account (also called Ducatone Piastra or Scudo Corriente) worth 7 Lire.

**VII.** - In **Parma,** until Italian unification, silver money (25.7 grams 906 fine) valued at 24 Lire.

**VIII.** - In **Modena,** unit of account (also called Ducado) worth 8 Lire.

**IX.** - In **Rome** (Papal States), the Ducato di Camera, divided into 16 Paoli, was unit of account in the chancellery of Pope. Minted from 15th to 18th Century (between 3.2 and 3.5 grams of very fine gold).

**X.** - In **Sicily,** silver money created around 1140 for Duchy of Apulia; gold coin minted about 1285.

**XI.** - In **Naples,** gold coin minted as of 1465. Silver money created in 1551 (25.3 grams fine silver). Reduced to 19.7 grams fine at end of 18th Century; raised to 22.83 grams fine in 1804 and circulated until 1865. Also called Piastre, or Ducato del Regno. Exchange rate: 10 Carlini, then 12 Carlini.

**18th Century** - Unit of account worth 5 Tarin, 10 Carlini, 40 Cinquine, 100 Grani, 200 Tornesi, 300 Quattrini, 600 Piccioli, 1,200 Cavalli or Denari.

**XII.** - In Kingdom of **Two Sicilies,** Ducato worth 100 Grani or 300 Tornesi until 1869.

**XIII.** - In Republic of **Ragusa** in 18th Century, Ducato was unit of account and silver coin worth 40 Grossetti.


## DUCATON

Silver coin used in various European countries until 19th Century.

Origin of name - Diminutive of Ducat.

Variation of name - Ducatone.

**I.** - In **Netherlands,** silver coin (28.97 grams fine) imprinted with Austrian coat of arms. Exchange rate in 18th Century: 63 Stuyver. Circulated in **Belgium** until adoption of Franc. Introduced in **Indonesia** in 1726.

**II.** - In **Venice,** silver coin (27.5 grams 915 fine) called Ducatono, or Giustina. Issued in 15th Century. Exchange rate in 18th Century: 11 Lire.

**III.** - In **Florence, Leghorn** and **Lucca,** unit of account. - See *Ducato.*

**IV.** - In **Turin** (Piedmont, Savoy and Sardinia), silver coin (31.8 grams 950 fine) worth 5 Lire.

**V.** - In **Milan,** silver coin minted in 16th Century, first by Louis XII, then in 1551 by Charles V. Exchange rate in 18th Century: 8 Lire 12 Soldi.


## DUDDU

Copper coin and early division of French Rupee in **India.** - See *Rupee France.*

Variations of name - Doudou, Dudu, Tuttu.

**18th Century** - Copper money: 14 Duddus equal to gold Fanam.

**19th Century** - 24 Duddus equal to French Rupee; 3 Duddus equal to Fanam (4 Cash).

**1871** (June 7th) - Decree demonetized Duddu.

# DUIT

**I.** - Early copper money of **Netherlands** from late 16th to early 19th Century. Exchange rate in 18th Century: 2 Penninge.
Variations of name - Duyter, Dute, Doit, Duyt.
**II.** - In **Netherlands East Indies,** copper coin introduced in 1726 and 1786. Submultiple from 1817 to 1854 of Guilder (¹⁄₁₂₀) and Stuyver (¹⁄₄).
**III.** - In **Surinam,** issue in 1676 of 1, 2 and 4 Duiten copper coins.

# DUKAT

Gold money of **German States** from 14th to 19th Century.
Origin of name - See *Ducato.*
Plural - Dukaten.
**I.** - In **Hungary,** gold coin (3.49 grams 986 fine) called Dukat of Hungary, or Dukat of Kremnitz. - See *Kremnitz.*
**1382** - First minting copied Ducat of Venice (Sequin or Zecchino).
**16th Century** - Multiplication and diffusion of famous Hungarian Dukats. Copied throughout Europe (Germany, Bohemia, Poland . . .).
**II.** - In **Holy Roman Empire** and **German States,** gold money at first imitating Hungarian Dukat (Teutonic Order, 1410). Minted for Holy Roman Empire in 1559 (3.44 grams fine gold). Exchange rate: 104 Kreuzer in 1582; 114 in 1585; 178 in 1619; 960 in 1622 (30 Years War); dropped to 140 Kreuzer in December 1623; raised to 180 Kreuzer in 1667 (Bavaria, Swabia and Franconia); 210 in 1681; 240 in 1690; maintained at 240 in 1736; raised to 250 in 1753.
**1753** - According to Convention of Vienna, defined at 3.49 grams 980 fine, or 3.42 grams fine gold. Circulated in states of Holy Roman Empire under name of Reichsdukaten.
**III.** - Lighter **Austrian** Dukat (2.9 grams 966 fine gold) circulated in Vienna and in Brussels.
**19th Century** - Austrian Dukat linked to Dukat of Convention of Vienna at weight of 3.4909 grams 986 fine, or 3.442 grams fine gold. Multiple: 4 Dukaten (13.963 grams 986 fine, or 13.769 grams fine gold). Continued to be struck (restrikes) into 20th Century.
**IV.** - In **Swiss States** until 1850, gold coin of 3.49 grams 980 fine. Basel had special Dukat of 3.40 grams 917 fine. Zurich minted gold coins of 5 Dukaten (1742), 2 Dukaten (1743), 1 Dukat (1748), ¹⁄₂ Dukat (1745), and ¹⁄₄ Dukat (1743).

## DUMA MONEY

Money of **Provisional Revolutionary Government of Russia** from March to November 1917 under Kerensky regime. - See *Ruble.*

## DUPONDIUS

**Roman** bronze money equivalent to 2 Asses. - See *As.*
Origin of name - Latin *duo* (two), *ponduis* (weight).

## DURILLO

Gold money of **Spanish America** minted under Ferdinand VII (1808-1825). Equivalent to ½ Escudo.

## DURO

I. - In **Spain,** silver coin created by Catholic kings following discovery of America. Became prototype of silver coins in wake of conquest of world (Mexican Piaster, Maria Theresia Thaler . . .).
Origin of name - Spanish: *duro* (hard), Latin: *durus.* Originally, Peso Duro (hard Piaster).
Variations of name - In Spanish, Peso Duro, commonly called Duro; Peso Fuerte, Real de Ocho, worth 8 Reales.
Predecessor - See *Spain.*
**1497** (June 13th) - Decree of Medina del Campo brought about monetary reform and creation of new specie money. Silver monies were Duro (first important silver money) and Real (see *Real* ):
    1 Duro = 8 Reales = 25.92 grams of fine silver
Numerous subsequent manipulations, either of content or weight of Duro, or of its exchange rate as unit of account.
**About 1530** - Under Charles V, type of Duro took more fashionable name of Thaler (See *Thaler*), which became Dolera.
**1535** - Mint, inaugurated in Mexico, undertook to strike silver coins imitating Duro-Dolera. Mexican Piasters, which gave rise to Dollar, eventually became predominant in Pacific and Indian Oceans.
**1686** (October 14th) - Value raised from 8 to 10 Reales. Piaster had exchange rate of 8 Reales. Early Piece of Eight had an exchange rate of 10 ⅝ Reales.
**1730** - Minting of Piaster "with a column": 27.06 grams 916 fine silver.
**1772** (May 29th) - Decree of Aranjuez reduced fineness of coinage. Heaviest silver coin was Duro, or heavy Piaster, of 20 Reales (27.06 grams 892-896 fine).
**1808-1814** - Joseph Bonaparte retained Duro valued at 20 Reales.

**1847** (May 31st) - Monetary reform of Isabella II linked Duro to French coin of 5 Francs:

$$1 \text{ Duro} = 5 \text{ Pesetas} = 20 \text{ Reales} = 25 \text{ grams of silver } 900$$
$$\text{fine} = 22.50 \text{ grams of fine silver}$$

**1864-1868** - Unstable monetary system. Escudo was basic unit. Duro was silver coin of 25.96 grams 900 fine worth 2 Escudos, or 20 Reales.

**After 1868** - Word Duro continued to designate 5 Peseta coin. As unit of account, Duro corresponded to 5 Pesetas.

**II.** - Duro Azizi: **Moroccan** coin, also called Piastre, minted in 1903 of 25 grams silver 900 fine, or 22.50 grams of fine silver. Gold 20 Rial coin also called Duro.
 - Cf. *Hassani Rial.*

## *DUTCH GUIANA*

See *Surinam.*

## DVOUGRIVENIK

Coin in **Russia.** Valued at 20 Kopeks in late 19th and early 20th Century.

# EAGLE

Name given to the 10 Dollar gold coins of the **United States,** bearing image of American eagle.

**1792** (April 4th) - 17.50 grams 916 fine, or 16.038 grams of fine gold.

**1834** (June 28th) - 16.72 grams 899225 fine, or 15 grams of fine gold.

**1837** (January 18th) - 16.72 grams 900 fine, or 15.04656 grams of fine gold.

**1849** (March 3rd) - Minting of Double Eagle, 20 Dollar gold piece weighing 33.437 grams 900 fine, or 30.09 grams of fine gold. Half Eagle, or 5 Dollar gold piece, weighed 8.36 grams 900 fine, or 7.52328 grams of fine gold.

# ECU

Money of several countries. Inspired by a French coin imprinted with a shield (écu) bearing coat of arms of France.

Origin of name - Latin *scutum* (shield); old French *escut.*

**I. -** In **France,** gold money (from 13th to 17th Century), then silver money (17th and 18th Centuries); also unit of account (1577 to 1602) and a paper money (1718).

**1266** (August 15th) - Saint Louis minted Denier à l'Ecu, coin of 4.19 grams fine gold. Rate of exchange: 10 Sous Tournois. Later revived as Denier à l'Agnel. - See *Agnel.*

**1337** - Philip VI minted gold Denier à l'Ecu or Ecu (4.53 grams of fine gold). Fineness reduced to 958 in 1348 and to 875 in 1349. Rate of exchange: 16 Sous 8 Deniers in 1343, 22 Sous in 1346, 18 Sous 9 Deniers in 1348, 25 Sous in 1349, 18 Sous 9 Deniers in 1350.

**1351** - Jean II debased Ecu to 750 fine. Rate of exchange: 25 Sous.

**1385** (March 11th) - Charles V replaced gold Franc with a Crowned Ecu (Ecu à la Couronne, or Couronne) containing 4.08 grams of fine gold. Rate of exchange: 22 Sous 6 Deniers.

**1389** (September 11th) - Gold content lowered to 4 grams.

**1411** (October 20th) - Gold content further reduced to 3.82 grams.

**1417** (May 10th) - Crowned Ecu disappeared; replaced by Agnel.

**1419** (March 7th) - Charles VI minted gold Ecu (5.56 grams 915 fine) imprinted with a helmet and coat of arms of France. Rate of exchange: 30 Sous.

**1420** - King Henry V of England minted gold Ecu, which copied French coin and was worth 22 Sous 6 Deniers.

**1422** (December 31st) - Charles VII minted Ecu à la Couronne (3.82 grams fine gold) worth 25 Sous.

**1424** (August 23rd) - Minting of gold Ecu (3.49 grams 960 fine) valued at 25 Sous.

**1429** (January) - Gold fineness reduced to 745.

**1435** (September 15th) - Minting of Ecu of 3.49 grams of fine gold. Rate of exchange: 30 Sous.

**1456** - Rate of exchange of Ecu: 27 Sous 6 Deniers.

**1473** (June 18th) - Louis XI minted gold Ecu (3.68 grams 967 fine) worth 28 Sous 4 Deniers.

**1475** (January 8th) - Rate of exchange raised to 30 Sous 3 Deniers.

**1475** (November 2nd) - Louis XI minted Ecu au Soleil (Ecu-sol) with imprint of the sun (soleil) above French coat of arms. Weighed 3.68 grams 967 fine gold. Rate of exchange: 33 Sous.

**1487** (July 30th) - Charles VIII raised rate for Ecu au Soleil to 36 Sous 3 Deniers.

**1488** - Ecu minted in Naples, copying Ecu au Soleil.

**1491** - Ecu minted in Britain, copying Ecu au Soleil. Coin imprinted with image of an ermine.

**1510** (November 19th) - Louis XII added Ecu called au Porcs-epic (with porcupines), and having a similar weight and fineness as Ecu au Soleil.

**1519** (June 10th) - Francis I resumed minting of Ecu à la Couronne and au Soleil. Weight lowered to 3.41 grams 968 fine gold. Rate of exchange: 40 Sous.

**1532** (March 5th) - Rate of exchange: 45 Sous.

**1538** - Fineness reduced for a few months. Variations of Ecus minted under Francis I: à la Croisette, à la Salamandre.

**1549** - Under Henry II, Ecu took name Henri (minted until 1561). Rate of exchange: 46 Sous.

**1561** (August 30th) - Charles IX raised exchange rate of Ecu to 52 Sous.

**1573** (June 9th) - Rate raised to 54 Sous.

**1574** (September 22nd) - Henry III increased exchange rate of Ecu to 58 Sous.

**1575** (May 31st) - Henry III raised Ecu to 60 Sous. Estates-General temporarily increased it to 65 Sous.

**1577** (November 1st) - Decree making Ecu (3.36 grams 952 fine gold) the "unalterable" monetary unit and unit of account: 1 Ecu = 60 Sous.

**1594** - Ecu quoted at 64 Sous. Henry IV forbade its acceptance for more than 60 Sous, but this prohibition failed.

**1602** (September 16th) - Henry IV abolished system of accounting in Ecus, and reestablished system of Livres, Sous and Deniers Tournois. Raised exchange rate for Ecu to 65 Sous.

**1615** (February 5th) - Louis XIII raised Ecu to 75 Sous.

**1630** (February) - Rate of exchange raised to 80 Sous.

**1631** (August) - Rate raised to 83 Sous.

**1633** (July) - Rate raised to 86 Sous.

**1636** (March 5th) - Rate raised to 94 Sous.

**1636** (June 28th) - Rate raised to 104 Sous.

**1641** (December 23rd) - Monetary reform: gold Ecu replaced by Louis d'Or, but continued to circulate (for 104 Sous in 1652, 124 Sous in 1653). Minting of silver Ecu (27.3 grams 916 fine) worth 60 Sous, sometimes called Louis d'Argent or Ecu Blanc.

**1653** (March 7th) - Exchange rate of silver Ecu: 70 Sous.

**1654** (May 31st) - Rate lowered in stages to 60 Sous.

**1692 to 1700** - Rate of exchange varied between 65 and 72 Sous.

**1701** - Minting of Ecu aux Armes (27.1 grams 911 fine silver). Rate of exchange: 76 Sous, lowered in stages to 68 Sous.

**1704** - Minting of Ecu aux Livres (27.1 grams 911 fine silver). Rate of exchange: 80 Sous, lowered in stages to 67 Sous.

**1709** - Rate of exchange raised to 100 Sous.

**1715** - Rate of exchange lowered in stages to 70 Sous. Minting of Ecu aux 3 Couronnes (30.45 grams 913 fine).

**1716** (May 2nd) - Banque de John Law issued banknotes denominated in Ecus de Banque.

**1718** (March 20th) - Minting of Ecu called Ecu de Navarre (24.35 grams 912 fine silver) valued at 120 Sous.

**1718** (December 4th) - Banque de John Law became Banque d'Etat. Ceased issuing banknotes in Ecus de Banque. Henceforth, its banknotes were denominated in Livres.

**1719** - Rate of exchange of Ecu lowered to 116, then 112 Sous.

**1720** - Rate raised in stages to 160, then 240 Sous. Highest rate of exchange quoted just before collapse of Law's enterprise: 327 Sous.

**1724** - Minting of Ecu aux Lis (23.45 grams 913 fine silver).

**1726** (January) - Minting of silver Ecu aux Armes (29.35 grams 907 fine). Rate of exchange: 100 Sous, raised to 120 Sous on May 26th and maintained at this level (6 Livres) until the Revolution. Small Ecu worth 3 Livres.

**1791** - Minting of Constitutional Ecu with same weight and fineness as its predecessor.

**1793** - Minting of Republican Ecu with same weight and fineness.

**1793** (April 11th) - Payments in Ecus prohibited.

**1796** (July 23rd) - Legal tender status of Ecu restored.

**1810** - Legal tender value of Ecus of 6 Livres fixed at 5.80 Francs.

**1829** (June 14th) - Decree demonetizing Ecus.

**1834** (December 31st) - Effective demonetization of Ecus. Word Ecu persisted through 19th Century to designate sum of 3 Francs.

**II.** - Gold coin minted in several European States: **Savoy** (14th Century), **Lausanne** (14th Century), **Flanders** (Double gold Ecu, 1407), **Brabant** (14th and 15th Centuries), **Holland** (14th Century).

**III.** - For **Spain** and **Portugal**, see *Escudo*.

**IV.** - For **Italian** States and **Malta**, see *Scudo*.

**V.** - In **Liege**, **Maastricht** and **Westphalia**, specie money (22.1 grams fine silver) and unit of account, also called Patagon. - See *Patagon*.

**VI.** - In **German** States, name sometimes given to Thaler, unit of account, and to Reichsthaler, silver specie money. - See *Thaler* and *Reichsthaler*.

**VII.** - In **Swiss** cantons, until 1850, silver coin, also called Thaler, sometimes Patagon (in Geneva). In Basel, unit of account, divided into 60 Sols or 720 Deniers.

# *ECUADOR*

**16th to 19th Century** - Circulation of silver Spanish and Mexican Piasters.

**1819** - Ecuador became part of Republic of Colombia, which observed Spanish monetary system. - See *Colombia.*

**1835** - Gold coin, Doblado, equal to 2 Escudos.

**1836** - Independent Ecuador retained silver Piaster (or Peso) of 8 Reales as monetary unit.

**1856** (December 5th) - Adoption of French monetary system. Franco was basic unit. - See *Franco.* Peso remained unit of account.

**1871** (November 21st) - New monetary unit. - See *Peso Ecuador.*

**1874** (May 1st) - Peso replaced. - See *Sucre.*


# *EGYPT*

**41st Century B.C.** - King Menes (First Dynasty) gave minor monetary role to small gold cubes (14 grams) bearing his mark. Virtually all payments made in kind, and ancient Egyptian civilization rested upon state communism.

**32nd to 30th Century B.C.** - Fourth and Fifth Dynasties produced gold rings (14 grams) having no monetary function other than being store of wealth. Referred to in historical documents as "scale money", probably because transfer took place by weighing rings.

**28th Century B.C.** - Copper brought into monetary use as means of payment in bar and ring form. - See *Deben.*

**13th Century B.C.** - Ramses favored use of metal as medium of exchange.

**10th Century B.C.** - Gold, silver, electrum, copper and malechite began to replace barter in trade transactions.

**6th Century B.C.** - Persian conquest. Use of Persian monetary system. - See *Daric* and *Siglos.*

**4th Century B.C.** - Alexander the Great conquered Egypt. Introduced Macedonian gold money. - See *Stater.*

**3rd Century B.C.** - Ptolemies adopted Mina (364 grams), divided into 100 Drachmae, as unit of account. Minting of silver Drachmae (3.64 grams), Tetradrachm (14.56 grams), and bronze coins weighing 90 grams and 45 grams (based on Deben weight). Most payments made in bronze.

**1st Century B.C.** - Few mintings in silver.(sometimes copper coins coated with a layer of silver). Under Cleopatra, bronze coins (17.5 and 8.1 grams); under Augustus, bronze coins (12.5 grams). Unit of account, Talent, after Greek Talent. Talent of copper was worth 12 Denarii.

**30 B.C. to 340 A.D.** - Roman influence. - See *Rome.*

**340 to 638** - Egypt part of Eastern Roman Empire. - See *Byzantium.*

**7th to 16th Century** - Arabic monies. - See *Arabia.*

**16th to 18th Century** - Turkish domination. - See *Turkey.*

**18th Century** - Monetary system related to Turkish system.
Unit of account: Piastre equal to 33 Medini, 99 Aspers, 198 Forli, or 264 Burbes.
Multiple: Beutel (24,000 Médini or 75,000 Aspers).
Specie money: Ducatello (10 Medini); Griscio or Abuquelp (30 Medini); Turkish monies (Fonduk, Zer-mahbub, Para).

**1798 to 1801** - Mintings under French occupation similar to Turkish monetary system.

**1834** - Reform of Mohammed Ali:
1 Piastre = 40 Para = 23.4 grams of fine silver
- See *Piastre Egypt.*

**1885** - Adoption of gold standard. Egyptian Pound replaced Piastre as monetary unit.
- See *Pound Egypt.*


## EL SALVADOR

**16th to 19th Century** - Circulation of Spanish and Mexican Piasters. - See *Piaster Mexico.*

**1821** - Independence from Spain.

**1823** - Independence from Mexico.

**1823-1838** - Loosely grouped into United Provinces of Central America. - See *Peso Central America.*

**1839** - Independence. Peso of Central America gave rise to El Salvador Peso. - See *Peso El Salvador.*

**1919** - Adoption of gold standard with creation of new monetary unit. - See *Colón El Salvador.*


## ENGLAND

**Before Roman invasion** - Crude imitations of the Macedonian Stater.

**After Roman invasion** - Roman monies.

**In Saxon period** - There were some copies of Arabian Dinar. Use of silver Sceattae; additionally, gold Sous and Triens, and copper Stycas. Introduction of Carolingian units of accounting: Livres, Sols, Deniers.

**During Danish invasions** - Minting of silver Deniers and Obols by Danes.

**10th to 13th Century** - Circulation primarily composed of silver Deniers (Pennies) and foreign gold coins (Bezants, then Fiorini or Guilders of Florence). - See *Penny.*

**1257** - Introduction of a gold coin of 2.95 grams valued at 20 Pence, then at free exchange rate; raised to 40 Pence in 1265, disappeared after 1270.

**13th Century** - Circulation of Sterling-type Penny, called Esterlin on Continent. - See *Esterlin.*

**1343** - Attempt at monetary union with Flanders.

**1344** - Minting of gold coins: Florin, then Noble. - See *Noble.*

**1489** - Creation of gold Sovereign. - See *Sovereign.*

**16th Century** - Mary Tudor attempted to adopt gold standard by classifying silver coins as subsidiary coinage.

**17th Century** - In 1601, Elizabeth I reinstated silver Shilling as basic unit of monetary system. - See *Shilling.*

**1694** - Creation of Bank of England, and appearance of paper money. - See *Pound.*

**1696** - General removal of silver coins from circulation. Replaced by new coins in order to lower gold Guinea to value officially designated as unit of account. - See *Guinea.*

**1774** - Limitations on use of silver as legal tender. - See *Shilling.*

**1816** (June 22nd) - Adoption of gold standard. - See *Pound.*

**1971** (February 15th) - Decimalization of Pound Sterling, divided into 100 Pennies.


## ENRIQUE

Name used for **Spanish** gold Dobla issued by King Henry IV (1454-74). Coin of 50 Enriques weighed exeptional amount of 229 grams.


## EPU UNIT OF ACCOUNT

Unit of account adopted for **European Payments Union,** according to agreement of September 19, 1950.

Members of EPU - Austria, Belgium-Luxembourg, Denmark, France, Germany, Greece, Iceland, Italy, Netherlands, Norway, Portugal, Sweden, Switzerland, Turkey, United Kingdom.

1 EPU Unit = 888.6706 milligrams of fine gold

1 U.S. Dollar = 1 EPU Unit

**1958** (December 28th) - European Payments Union dissolved. EPU Unit no longer used in accounting.


## EQUATORIAL GUINEA

**1968** (October 12th) - Independent republic established from Spanish provinces of Fernando Po and Rio Muni. For money in circulation, see *Peseta.*

**1969** (October 12th) - New monetary unit issued to replace Spanish Peseta at par. - See *Peseta Guineana.*


## ERANAMBATRY

Early silver coin of **Madagascar.** Submultiple (1/72) of Ariary. - See *Ariary.*

## *ERITREA*

**Early monies** - See *Ethiopia.*

**1890** (August 10th) - Italian silver coins called Tallero d'Italia first minted. - See *Tallero.*

**Early 20th Century** - Circulation of Italian monies. - See *Lira.* Unsuccessful attempts made at prohibiting circulation of Maria Theresia Thaler.

**1941** - British occupation: 1 Pound Sterling = 480 Lire.

**1946** - Monetary system of Ethiopia. - See *Dollar Ethiopia.*

**1952** (October 1st) - Ethiopian Dollar became sole legal tender.

## ERNST

**I.** - Early gold coins sometimes called Carolin, in **Hesse-Darmstadt.** Issued in 1733 by Grand Duke Ernst Louis.

**II.** - Gold coin called Ernst d'Or struck by Ernst August, Duke of **Hanover** (1837-1851). Name for Pistole or 5 Thaler coin.

## ESCALIN

**I.** - Early **French** form for Schelling, Schilling, Shilling. . .

Variations of name - Schelin, Chelin.

**II.** - Name sometimes given in **France** and in **French Colonies** to Spanish coins of one Real (Double Escalin) and of ½ Real (Escalin).

**III.** - In **Santo Domingo** and **Haiti,** early submultiple of Gourde: Double Escalin, originally ⅛ Gourde, but de facto ¹⁄₁₁. Equal to Dutch Schelling of Curaçao. Single Escalin originally ¹⁄₁₆ Gourde. - See under *Schilling.*

**IV.** - Silver coin of **Netherlands** since 16th Century. Same as Schelling, but generally used to designate such coins employed in trade outside Netherlands.

## ESCUDILLO D'ORO

Early gold coin of **Spain** and territories under **Spanish** influence. Minted after 1814 in Spain by Ferdinand VII. Weighed 1.691 grams 875 fine and valued at ½ Escudo, or 20 Reales. Equal in value to Peso Fuerte (Duro).

## ESCUDO

Early money of **Spain** and **Spanish America.**

Origin of name - See *Ecu.*

**I.** - In **Spain,** gold, then silver money.

**1537** - With influx of precious metals from America, Charles V issued gold coins: Escudo or Corona (3.38 grams 917 fine), Doblado (Double Escudo 6.76 grams 917 fine) famous under name Pistole. - See *Pistole.*

As unit of account, gold Escudo was worth 350 Maravedis in 1537, 400 in 1587, 440 in 1609, 550 in 1642, 612, then 510 in 1643, 646 in 1686.

Original fineness reduced to 909, then to 893 in 1772 and to 872 in 1785.

**1566** (November 23rd) - Minting of Escudo de Quatro (Quadruple Escudo).

**1621** - Philip IV minted 100 Escudo gold coin weighing 35.92 grams.

**1686** (October 14th) - Silver Real (2.58 grams) called Escudo de Plata (silver Escudo). - See *Real.*

As unit of account, silver Escudo worth 10 Reales in 1686, 20 in 1737.

**1814** - Escudo minted in gold by Ferdinand VII. Rate of exchange: 40 Reales.

**1847** (May 31st) - Monetary reform of Isabella II: silver Escudo (12.92 grams 900 fine) equal to ½ Duro, or 10 Reales.

**1864** (June 26th) - Temporary designation (until 1868) of silver Escudo as monetary unit, divided into 100 Centesimos and 1,000 Milesimos.

**II.** - In **Castile,** until 19th Century, unit of account equal to 10 Reales, or 340 Maravedis.

**III.** - Gold money of **Spanish America.** Minted in Mexico and Peru after 1675. Half Escudo called Durillo.

**IV.** - Early gold money of **Chile:** 2.995 grams 916 fine before 1910, then reduced to 900 fine. Value: 2 Pesos before 1885, 5 Pesos after 1885.

**V.** - In **Colombia,** early gold coin (3.225 grams 900 fine). Equal to French coin of 10 Francs (Half Napoléon) worth 2 Pesos. Half Escudo, or gold Peso, weighed 1.6129 grams 900 fine.

**VI.** - In **Paraguay,** early gold coin (6.78 grams 875 fine) worth 4 Patacons.

**VII.** - In **Bolivia,** early gold coin, minted in small quantities after 1863. Equal to ⅛ Onza or ½ Doblon. Value in silver Bolivianos varied with price of gold. The Medio Escudo (½ Escudo) also minted in gold.

**VIII.** - Gold coin of **Mexico** before 1861, worth 2 Piasters.

**IX.** - In **Costa Rica,** before monetary reform of 1896, Escudo equal to 2 Pesos. Relatively few Escudo coins minted.

**X.** - In **Venezuela,** early gold coin (8.065 grams 900 fine) worth 5 Venezolanos. Minted under coinage law dated May 11, 1871.

**XI.** - In **Uruguay,** gold coin minted in 1854 (1.67 grams 875 fine). Also called Patagon.

**XII.** - For other Escudo varieties see following:

## ESCUDO ANGOLA

Monetary unit of **Angola.** Divided into 100 Centavos.

Bank of issue - Banco de Angola.

Predecessors - See *Angola* and *Angolar.*

**1958** (December 31st) - Escudo introduced to replace Angolar at par and bearing a fixed relationship with Metropolitan Escudo:
    1 Angolan Escudo = 1 Portugese Escudo
    1 Angolan Escudo = 30.9103 milligrams of fine gold
    1 U.S. Dollar = 28.75 Angolan Escudos

**1964** (February) - Escudo on black market fell to low of 43.00 per U.S. Dollar.


## ESCUDO CHILE

Monetary unit of **Chile.** Divided into 100 Centesimos.

Origin of name - See *Ecu.*

Bank of issue - Banco Central de Chile (Central Bank of Chile)

Predecessor - See *Peso Chile.*

**1960** (January 1st) - Escudo replaced Peso at rate of:
    1 Escudo = 1,000 Pesos
    1 U.S. Dollar = 1.05 Escudos

**1962** (January 15th) - Reversion to dual rate system:
    1 U.S. Dollar = 1.051/1.053 Escudos (official banking free
        market for most authorized transactions)
    1 U.S. Dollar = 1.40 Escudos (fluctuating brokers' rate for
        most invisible dealings and for luxury imports)

**1962** (October 15th) - Banking rate no longer supported, but allowed to fluctuate.

**1962** (December 29th) - Banking rate: 1.625/1.645 per U.S. Dollar; Brokers' rate: 2.384/2.416 per U.S. Dollar.

**1963** (May 8th) - Gold trading on brokers' market terminated. Central Bank retained sole right to deal in gold coins and bars.

**1963** (December 31st) - Banking rate: 2.146/2.148 per U.S. Dollar; Brokers' rate: 3.018/3.036 per U.S. Dollar.

**1964** - Steady inflation and deterioration of Escudo on black market prompted Central Bank intervention in both banking and brokers' markets.

**1964** (December 31st) - Banking rate: 2.70/2.71 per U.S. Dollar; Brokers' rate: 3.-25/3.26 per U.S. Dollar.

**1965** (December 31st) - Banking rate: 3.46/3.47 per U.S. Dollar; Brokers' rate: 4.-20/4.219 per U.S. Dollar.

**1966** - Banking and Brokers' rates fixed monthly, further depreciating Escudo.

**1966** (December 31st) - Banking rate: 4.36/4.37 per U.S. Dollar; Brokers' rate: 4.-99/5.00 per U.S. Dollar.

**1967** (December 29th) - Banking rate: 5.79/5.80 per U.S. Dollar; Brokers' rate: 6.-71/6.72 per U.S. Dollar.

**1968** - Rates fixed twice a month.

**1968** (December 30th) - Banking rate: 7.65/7.67 per U.S. Dollar; Brokers' rate: 8.-69/8.71 per U.S. Dollar.

**1969** (December 31st) - Banking rate: 9.96/9.98 per U.S. Dollar; Brokers' rate: 11.-50/11.52 per U.S. Dollar.

**1970** (July 28th) - Banking rate: 12.21/12.23 per U.S. Dollar; Brokers' rate: 14.33/14.35 per U.S. Dollar. System of monthly and/or semi-monthly devaluations suspended.

**1970** (October) - Escudo on black market fell to 50.00-60.00 per U.S. Dollar. Subsequently improved.


## ESCUDO MOZAMBIQUE

Monetary unit of **Mozambique.** Divided into 100 Centavos.

Bank of issue - Banco Nacional Ultramarino in Lisbon. Established in 1864.

Predecessor - See *Mozambique.*

**1922** (September 1st) - Mozambique Escudo created with link to Metropolitan unit:
      1 Mozambique Escudo = 1 Portuguese Escudo
   - See *Escudo Portugal.*


## ESCUDO PORTUGAL

Monetary unit of **Portugal.** Divided into 100 Centavos. Early submultiples: 10 Tostao, 50 Vintem, or 1,000 Reis.

Origin of name - See *Ecu.*

Bank of issue - By Banco de Portugal (Bank of Portugal), which has had a monopoly on banknote issue since 1887. For Cape Verde, Portuguese Guinea, Sâo Tomé and Principe, by Banco Nacional Ultramarino, established in 1864.

Predecessor - See *Portugal.*

**15th Century** - Under Alfonso V, appearance of first Portuguese gold Escudo: 4.97 grams.

**1722** (April 4th) - Following Spanish example, minting of gold coin called Escudo (3.88 grams 916 fine) worth 16 silver Tostao or 1,600 Reis. Rate of exchange subsequently raised under Joseph I.

**1835** (April 24th) - Decree reorganizing monetary system. Escudo (Escudo de ouro) became coin of 3.547 grams 916 fine, or 3.248 grams fine gold; worth 2,000 Reis.
   - See *Real* and *Milreis.*

**1854** - Escudo was minted as silver coin.

**1911** (May 22nd) - Newly proclaimed Republic repudiated name Milreis, a vestige of royalty.
   Adoption of Escudo as monetary unit of Portugal at par with Milreis. Theoretical definition:
      1 Escudo = 1 Milreis = 1,625.85 milligrams of fine gold
      1 Pound Sterling = 4.50 Escudos
   Minting of gold coins on basis of 1.8 grams 900 fine per Escudo.

**1914** (September 24th) - Foreign exchange controls.

**1918** (April 21st) - Issue of State banknotes simultaneously with banknotes of Banco de Portugal. Two ceilings on banknote issues raised. Increasing depreciation of Escudo.

**1924** (July) - Maximum depreciation of Escudo (97%).

**1924** (September 6th) - Foreign exchange controls extended to capital outflow.

**1928** (April 28th) - De facto stabilization of Escudo on basis of:
1 Pound Sterling = 108.25 Escudos

**1931** (June 9th) - De jure stabilization acknowledged devaluation of 95.91%:
1 Escudo = 66.57 milligrams of fine gold
1 Pound Sterling = 110.00 Escudos
Creation of unit of account: 1 Conto = 1,000 Escudos.

**1931** (December 29th) - Following depreciation of Pound Sterling, suspension of gold standard. Convertibility of banknotes into Sterling on unchanged basis of:
1 Pound Sterling = 110.00 Escudos.

**1937** (October 18th) - Foreign exchange controls abolished.

**1939** (November 14th) - Rate of exchange to U.S. Dollar fixed at:
1 U.S. Dollar = 27.50 Escudos

**1940** (June) - De facto stabilization in relation to U.S. Dollar:
1 U.S. Dollar = 25.00 Escudos

**1949** (September 19th) - Following Sterling, Escudo devalued, but to lesser proportion (13.04%):
1 U.S. Dollar = 28.75 Escudos
1 Pound Sterling = 80.50 Escudos

**1962** (June 1st) - Initial par value for Escudo established with International Monetary Fund:
1 Escudo = 30.910 milligrams of fine gold
1 U.S. Dollar = 28.75 Escudos

## ESPADIM

**Portuguese** coin bearing the imprint of a sword. Minted in silver on August 22, 1460, by Alfonso V, originator of the Order of the Sword (*espadim*). Struck in gold by Joannes II (1481-1495), and equal to ½ Justo.

## ESTERLIN

Silver Penny, issued in 13th Century in **England.** - See *Pound.* Weight: 1.17 grams. Reduced to 0.97 grams in 1412, to 0.78 grams in 1464.

Variation of name - Easterling, Estrelin.

First type copied in Ireland and Scotland.
Copied on Continent in 13th and 14th Centuries: in Brabant, Netherlands, German states, Luxembourg (rate of exchange: 4 Deniers) and Portugal.
Luxembourg type, widely circulated, returned to England.

Esterlin was money most generally used in Western Europe during 13th Century, before circulation of Gros.

Esterlins circulating in France had legal tender status of 4 Deniers Tournois, or 1/3 Sou. Demonetized in 1265.

## ESTONIA

**12th to 15th Century** - Prussian monies (Teutonic Order).

**15th Century** - Order of Livonia minted silver Schilling and its submultiples (Denier, or Pfennig; Obol, or Artig).

**17th Century** - Swedish monies. - See *Sweden.*

**18th Century** - Unit of account in Tallin and Narva: Ruble, divided into 10 Grivenki or 100 Kopeks, and Reichsthaler of 80 Kopeks.
Specie money in general use: Russian monies, Thalers, Swedish Carolins.
Local monies: Livonese. - See *Livonese.*

**19th Century** - Russian monetary system. - See *Russia.*

**1918** - Circulation of Ruble and Finnish Markka. Both replaced by issue of Estonian Marks. - See *Mark Estonia.*

**1924** (June) - Adoption of Estonian Kroon as unit of account.

**1928** (January 1st) - De jure creation of Estonian Kroon as monetary unit. - See *Kroon.*

**1940** (June 17th) - Russian occupation.

**1940** (August 6th) - Estonia became Estonian Soviet Socialist Republic.

**1940** (November 25th) - Introduction of Ruble. Circulated with Kroon.

**1941** (April) - Abolition of Kroon. Ruble became sole legal tender.

**1941** (July) - German occupation. Reichskreditkassen issued banknotes denominated in Reichsmark to replace Ruble.

**1942** (July 30th) - Central Bank of Ostland created and authorized to issue banknotes denominated in Ostland Mark. - See *Mark Ostland.*

**1944** - Reintroduction of Ruble. - See *Ruble.*

## ETHIOPIA

**Early monies** - Tablets of rock salt, pepper and glass pearls. - See *Amolés Borjooke.*
Salt remained a medium of exchange well into the 20th Century.

**4th to 9th Century** - Roman gold Aureus and Solidus coins circulated during Roman influence. - See *Aureus, Solidus.*

**18th Century** - Gold in sheet form used in payment for government expenditures. Introduction of Indian Rupees and Maria Theresia Thalers which remained traditional money of Ethiopia. - See *Maria Theresia Thaler.*

**1893** - Adoption of silver Talari, copied from the Maria Theresia Thaler. - See *Talari.* Copper Bokcha served as divisionary coin.

**1935** - Italian Occupation; introduction of Lira. - See *Lira.*

**1941** (April) - British Occupation; introduction of East African Shilling. - See *Shilling East Africa.*

**1945** (July 23rd) - Creation of Ethiopian Dollar. - See *Dollar Ethiopia.*


## EXCELENTE

Gold coin issued in **Spain** on June 13, 1497, under name of Excelente de la Grenada: 8.58 grams 989 fine, or 8.49 grams of fine gold with a value of 375 Maravedis. Became known as Double Ducat.


## EYRIR

Submultiple (¹/₁₀₀) of **Icelandic** Krona. - See *Krona Iceland.* Cf. *Oere.*

Plural - Aurar.

# FA PI

Popular name for Chinese Dollar in **China** after 1935. - See *Dollar China.*
Variation of name - Fapi.

# *FALKLAND ISLANDS*

**18th Century** - Temporary colonization by France, Spain and Britain with use of
Spanish specie money.
**1820** - East Falkland recolonized. Use of Spanish specie money.
**1832-1833** - British military occupation followed by introduction of British monetary
system. - See *Pound.*
Subsequent issue by Colonial government of currency notes denominated in Falkland Pounds. - See *Pound Falkland Islands.*
British money retained legal tender status.

# FALLE

Copper money used in 17th and 18th Centuries in **Egypt** and along Mediterranean
Coast of Africa. Equivalent to ¼ Asper or ¹/₁₂ Para. Called Mangir or Mangur
by Turks.
Variation of name - Folle.

# FALUCE

In **India** (Southern States, Hindu system), submultiple of Hun or Pagoda (¹/₁₆₈) and
Fanam (¼). Equal to 20 Cache or Kas.

# FANAM

Early monetary unit in India.
Variations of name - Fanos, Fanon, Faname, Fanoe, Fanoin.
**I.** - In **India** (Southern States, Hindu system), submultiple (¹/₄₂) of Hun (or Pagoda).
Equal to 4 Faluce, or 80 Cache. Minted by British East India Company from 1671.
Unit of Account:
- In Calicut and on southern coast of Malabar, equal to 15 Biche.
- In Cannanore and on northern coast of Malabar, equal to 16 Biche.
- In Madras, equal to ¹/₁₀ Rupee, or ¹/₃₆ Pagoda.
- In Ceylon, Dutch until 1802, equal to ¹/₁₂ Rijksdaalder.
- In Travancore, equal to ⅛ Rupee, or 64 Cache.
Gold specie money:

- In Calicut in 18th Century, equal to 16 silver Taré.
- In Pegu, in Assam and in Ceylon.
  Silver specie money:
- In Madras, equal to $1/10$ Rupee.

II. - In **French India,** small gold coin and silver coin in Pondicherry. During 18th Century, Fanam worth 60 Cache, 14 Duddus, $1/7$ Rupee, or $1/24$ Pagoda. In 19th Century, submultiple ($1/8$) of French Rupee. Equal to 3 Duddus or 12 Cache. Coins of $1/2$, 1 and 2 Fanams circulated until demonitized by Decree of June 7, 1871. Remained unit of account in Pondicherry, equal to 2 Anna, 128 Pice, 384 Pie.

## FARDOS

Silver money and unit of account used in Bantam **(Java)** during 18th Century.

## *FAROE ISLANDS*

Danish monetary system. - See *Denmark* and *Krone Denmark.*

## FARTHING

I. - In **England,** submultiple ($1/4$) of Penny. Also, unit of account and silver coin (minted for first time under Edward I, 1272-1307), then copper coin (2.83 grams) in 18th and 19th Centuries.

Origin of name - From English far-thing, Farthing being coin farthest from Pound. Or possibly from English term for shearing Pennies into four pieces to give change, "fourthing", which was practiced prior to first minting of Farthing coin.

**Early 19th Century** - Circulated on French Coast of English Channel prior to issue of Centimes. Value was 2 Liards (6 Deniers).

II. - In **Ireland,** $1/2$ Farthing minted in copper in 1460 under name Patrick.

## *FEDERATION OF ARAB EMIRATES*

**1969** (October 22nd) - Federation of Arab Emirates formed from Trucial States, Qatar and Bahrain, with Abu Dhabi as provisional capital. Monies in circulation, see *Trucial States, Qatar* and *Bahrain.*

## *FEDERATION OF MALAYA*

Predecessor - See *Straits Settlements.*

**1946** (April 1st) - Malayan Union formed from separate Malayan States when Straits Settlements dissolved. Money in circulation, see *Dollar Malaya.*

**1948** (February 1st) - Malayan Union became Federation of Malaya.

**1957** (August 31st) - Federation became sovereign member-state of Commonwealth.

**1963** (September 16th) - Federation of Malaya became part of Federation of Malaysia. - See *Malaysia.*

## *FEDERATION OF RHODESIA AND NYASALAND*

**1891** (May 14th) - British protectorate of Nyasaland created. Use of British monetary system. - See *Pound.*

**1911** (May 11th) - Two provinces of Northeastern and Northwestern Rhodesia amalgamated under title of Northern Rhodesia by Order-in-Council. Use of British monetary system.

**1923** (October) - Southern Rhodesia, formerly under administration of British South Africa Company, annexed to His Majesty's Dominions.

**1924** (April 1st) - British South Africa Company relieved of administration of Northern Rhodesia.

**1940** - Southern Rhodesia Currency Board issued Southern Rhodesia Pound. Issue replaced British currency and notes of two resident British Banks. - See *Pound Southern Rhodesia.*

**1953** (August 1st) - Federation of Rhodesia and Nyasaland created by Order-in-Council proclaiming Federal State.

**1956** (April 1st) - Bank of Rhodesia and Nyasaland created as Central Bank replacing Rhodesia Currency Board as note-issuing authority. Issued new currency. - See *Pound Rhodesia and Nyasaland.*

**1963** (December 31st) - Federation dissolved. Newly independent Nyasaland and Northern Rhodesia became Malawi and Zambia, respectively. - See *Malawi, Zambia.* Southern Rhodesia reverted to status of self-governing Colony. - See *Southern Rhodesia.*

## *FEDERATION OF SOUTH ARABIA*

First formed on February 11, 1959. Total membership established by March 1963. Consisted of 17 emirates, protectorates, sultanates and sheikdoms, including Aden. Money in circulation, see *Shilling East Africa.*

**1965** (April 1st) - New monetary unit introduced. - See *Dinar South Arabia.*

**1967** (November 30th) - Creation of Southern Yemen from Federation of South Arabia. Monetary unit unchanged. - See *Southern Yemen.*

## FELS

**I.** - Copper money of **Arabs** from time of Muhammad. Spread through Arab expansion into Syria, Africa and Spain. Remained unit of account in Arabia during 18th Century (Basra, Persian Gulf), equivalent to $1/10.000$ Toman, $1/100$ Mahmudi, or $1/10$ Danim.

Origin of name - Arabic *fels,* meaning money or copper money.

Variations of name - Felou, Flus, Foulous, Fluce, Flous, Flouche, Fals.

Plural - Falus.

**II.** - In **Spain,** copper Fels minted in Castile and León during 12th Century.

**III.** - In **Morocco** during 18th Century, copper Fels valued at $1/20$ silver Blanquillo, $1/960$ gold Ducat.

**19th Century** - Minted from silver/copper, Fels worth $1/240$ Miscal, $1/24$ Ukkia, or $1/6$ Muzuna. Coins of 2 and 4 Falus minted in bronze.

## FEN

**I.** - In **China,** submultiple ($1/100$) of Chinese Dollar until 1895. Equal to 10 Li. - See *Dollar China.*

**II.** - In **China,** submultiple ($1/100$) of Manchukuo Yuan until 1945. - See *Yuan Manchukuo.*

**III.** - **Chinese** name for Candareen. - See *Candareen.*

## FENNIGY

Submultiple ($1/100$) of Marka, early monetary unit of **Poland.** - See *Marka.*

## FERLING

**I.** - Small copper coin in **France.** Valued at $1/4$ Denier.

Origin of name - See *Farthing.*

Variations of name - Ferlin, Ferlinc.

Plural - Ferlinges.

**II.** - In **England,** name given to $1/4$ Noble issued by Edward III.

## *FERNANDO PO*

See *Spanish Guinea.*

## FETTMANNCHEN

Early silver/copper coin in various **German States** from 16th to 18th Century.
Origin of name - From short, stout figure depicted on coin.
**17th Century -** Under Abbesses of Essen (1646-1688), value set at ¹/₁₂₀ Thaler.
**18th Century -** In Lower Westphalia, Fettmännchen was divisionary coin valued at 4 Pfennige, or 8 Heller; in Cologne, worth 8 Heller.

## *FIJI ISLANDS*

**1872 -** Postal use of the Dollar, divided into 100 Cents.
**1874 -** Introduction of British monetary system. - See *Pound.*
Subsequent issue by Colonial government and private banks of currency notes denominated in Fiji Pounds. - See *Pound Fiji.*
**1969** (January 13th) - Introduction of decimal currency system. - See *Dollar Fiji.*

## FIL

Submultiple (¹/₁.₀₀₀) of Dinar in **Bahrain, Jordan, Kuwait** and **Southern Yemen.**

## FILIBERTO

Money of Duchy of **Savoy** during 16th Century. Issued in 1562 both in gold (9 Lire) and in silver (5 Soldi).

## FILIPPO

**I. -** Silver coin (27.8 grams 950 fine) issued by Philip II (1527-1598) for **Milan.** Valued at 106 Soldi Imperiali prior to 1750 and at 150 Soldi Corrente thereafter.
**II. -** In **Modena,** silver Filippo worth 15.5 Lire.

## FILLER

In **Hungary,** submultiple (¹/₁₀₀) of Korona, then Pengoe and finally Forint. - See *Korona, Pengoe,* and *Forint.*

## FINLAND

**Prior to 1860** - Russian monetary system. - See *Ruble.*
**After 1860** - Independent system. - See *Markka.*

## FLEUR DE LIS

Coins issued in **France** during 14th Century.

Origin of name - From imprint, which showed king in tunic decorated with lily of the valley (fleur de lis).

**1356** (July 26th) - Jean II minted silver Denier Blanc à la Fleur de Lis weighing 4.08 grams 270 fine. Exchange rate: 8 Deniers.

**1356** (November) - Exchange rate reduced to 3 Deniers.

**1358** (July 1st) - Weight reduced to 3.82 grams 248 fine. Exchange rate: 15 Deniers.

**1358** (August 5th) - Weight reduced to 3.06 grams 248 fine.

**1359** - Minting of silver Denier Blanc à la Fleur de Lis with fineness progressively reduced to 166. Exchange rate: 15 Deniers.

**1360** - Weight: 4.53 grams 267 fine. Exchange rate: 10 Deniers.

**1361** - Exchange rate reduced to 8 Deniers prior to demonetization.

**1365** (April 20th) - Creation of gold Denier à la Fleur de Lis weighing 3.82 grams. Exchange rate: 20 Sous. Replaced gold Franc.

For monies minted under Louis XIV, see *Lis.*

## FLORENCE

Roman money (see *Rome),* then introduction of Carolingian monetary system (Livre of 20 Sols or 240 Deniers), giving rise to first unit of account, Lira of 20 Soldi or 240 Denari.

**1252** - With appearance of gold in West, new minting of coins. Lira became gold Fiorino (3.5 grams), Soldo became silver Fiorino (2.1 grams). - See *Guilder.*

**1296** - Silver Fiorino (Guilder) became known as Grosso, as in Venice.

**1531** - Gold Guilder called Ducato.

**1534** - Cosimo I of Medicis minted silver Lira.

**1737** - Grand Duchy of Tuscany passed from rule of Medicis to House of Lorraine-Austria. - See *Tuscany.*

**1801** - French occupation.

**1815** - Restoration of Grand Duchy of Tuscany.

**1819** - Annexation to Italy. - See *Italy* and *Lira.*

## FLORETTE

Silver coin minted in **France** during 15th Century.

Origin of name - From imprint, which showed three fleurs de lis.

**1417** (May 10th) - Minting of Florette weighing 3.06 grams 667 fine. Exchange rate: 20 Deniers Tournois.

**1417** (October 21st) - Reduction of fineness to 457.

**1419** (March 7th) - Fineness further reduced to 349. Rivalry between Florette of Charles VI, and Florette of Dauphin.

**1420** (May 6th) - Weight and fineness reduced to 2.45 grams 228 fine. Florettes of the Dauphin and of Charles VI linked.

**1420** (June 11th) - Weight and fineness decreased by Dauphin to 2.42 grams 198 fine.

**1421** (January) - Weight and fineness lowered by Dauphin to 2.22 grams 167 fine.

**1421** (October) - Weight and fineness decreased by Dauphin to 2.05 grams 102 fine.

**1422** (July) - Weight and fineness reduced by Dauphin to 1.88 grams 042 fine.

**1426** (December 24th) - Charles VII minted silver Florette weighing 3.40 grams 394 fine. Exchange rate: 10 Deniers.

**1429** (June 10th) - After seven successive reductions, weight of Florette finally lowered to 2.91 grams 399 fine.

## FLORIN

Origin of name - French word meaning flower. Coin first referred to as Florin was Italian Fiorino, which bore a fleur de lis.

**I. - French** name for various Guilder varieties; used interchangeably with name Guilder. - See *Guilder.*

**II. - In France** during 13th and 14th Centuries, name used for various gold coins.

**13th Century -** Name sometimes given to gold coins copying Fiorino and minted by Saint Louis and later kings: Florin à l'Agnel, Florin à l'Ecu, etc.

**1346** (April 27th) - Philip VI minted Florin Georges (4.70 grams of fine gold; later 4.55 grams). Worth 1 Livre. Bore image of St. George slaying dragon.

**III. - In England,** gold, then silver coin.

**1343 -** A gold Florin minted (7.5 grams 965 fine), common to both England and Flanders. Exchange rate: 6 Shillings.

**1344** (April 20th) - Gold Florin withdrawn from circulation and later replaced by silver Florin worth 2 Shillings.

**19th Century -** Silver Florin weighed 11.31 grams 916 fine.

**20th Century -** Florin reduced to level of divisionary coin, and fineness reduced to 500.

**1971** (February 15th) - With decimalization, Florin as divisionary coin disappeared.

## FLORIN ZLOTY

Early unit of account (17th and 18th Centuries) in **Poland,** then specie money. Divided into 30 Grosze or 360 Deniers.

Predecessor - See *Poland.*

**1815** - Russian Kingdom of Poland minted gold coin called Royal Florin, or Zloty Krolewskic, and silver coin (Florin Zloty).

**1830-1831** - Polish Republic minted silver coin of 5 Zlote.

**1833** and **1834** - Poland, which became a Russian province, minted transition coins denominated in Rubles and Florin Zlote: gold coins of 1.5 Rubles (10 Florin Zlote) and 3 Rubles (20 Florin Zlote), silver coins of 30 Kopeks (2 Florin Zlote).

**1847** (April) - Florin Zloty demonetized. Russian monies only legal tender. - See *Ruble.*

**1916-1924** - German Occupation. - See *Marka.*

**1924** - Reintroduction of Zloty. - See *Zloty.*


## FOLLARO

Copper or bronze money, minted in **Southern Italy** (Naples, Capau, Salerno) from 9th Century, and in Ragusa until 14th Century. Imitated Byzantine Follis. - See *Follis.*


## FOLLIS

Name given to ordinary bronze Denarius in **Eastern Roman Empire** from time of Constantine (312). - See *Denarius.*

Origin of name - Latin *follis,* meaning leather sack filled with air.

**4th Century** - Follis, valued at 20 Nummi, was $1/288$ gold Solidus and $1/24$ silver Miliarensis.

**End of 5th Century** - Fluctuated in value according to monetary ratio of copper to gold and to silver. Exchange rate varied between $1/180$ and $1/210$ gold Bezant and $1/15$ and $1/18$ silver Miliarensis. Follis equal to 32 Nummi.

**10th Century** - After Basil I, bronze Follis, equal to 2 Obols, stabilized at $1/144$ gold Bezant, $1/12$ Miliarensis, and $1/6$ Keration (Siliqua).
Imitated in Salerno, Capua and Naples, it gave rise to Follaro.

**12th Century** - Imitated in Edessa and Antiochia by Crusaders.

**15th Century** - Disappeared along with dissolution of Eastern Roman Empire.


## FORINT

Monetary unit of **Hungary.** Divided into 100 Filler.

Bank of issue - National Bank of Hungary.

Predecessors - See *Pengoe* and *Hungary.*

**1946** (July 26th) - Decree established Forint to replace collapsing Pengoe.

**1946** (August 1st) - Forint entered circulation, replacing Pengoe:

    1 Forint = 400,000 quadrillion paper Pengoe

    1 Forint = 75.696 milligrams of fine gold

    1 U.S. Dollar = 11.74 Forints

Hungary entered Ruble Bloc.

**1956** (December) - Forint fell to all-time low of 155.00 per U.S. Dollar in black market transactions.

**1957** (April 1st) - Partial devaluation. Special premiums of 80% to 100% above official rate applied to all Capitalistic noncommercial transactions:

    1 U.S. Dollar = 21.13 Forints (tourist rate)

    1 U.S. Dollar = 23.48 Forints (support and other official payments)

**1961** (January 1st) - Soviet monetary reform. Forint upvalued 56% relative to Ruble:

    1 New Ruble = 13.04 Forints (official)

    1 New Ruble = 14.00 Forints (Ruble Area noncommercial, tourist and/or support payments)

**1963** (April) - General alignment of Ruble Bloc currencies for noncommercial transactions only. Forint upvalued in relation to Ruble:

    1 Ruble = 13.10 Forints

**1966** - Creation of Ikka-Dollar voucher resulting from hard currency remittance by nonresident to a Hungarian. Used for purchases of quality goods at special State Stores. Official rate of vouchers set at 30.00 Forints. Premium existed on black market.

**1968** (January 1st) - Economic reform with partial devaluation:

    1 U.S. Dollar = 30.00 Forints (all Capitalistic noncommercial payments)

**1968** (January 24th) - Foreign Trade Price Multiplicators created:

    1 U.S. Dollar = 60.00 Forints (for hard currencies)

    1 Ruble = 40.00 Forints (Socialist currencies)

**1968** (September) - Forint fell to 10 year low of 62.50 per U.S. Dollar in black market transactions.

# FORLI

Unit of account in **Egypt** during 18th Century. Valued at 1.33 Burbe, $1/198$ Piastre, $1/6$ Para (or Medino), and $1/2$ Asper.

# *FORMOSA*

See *Taiwan.*

## FORTE

Silver coin minted during 14th Century in **Portugal** by King Diniz (1279-1325). Worth 1 Soldo or 1 Tornez.

## FRANC

In **France,** gold, then silver money, then basic unit of French monetary system. Was also prototype for several monies in Europe. Used in **French Colonies** (except Asia) until 1945. Monetary unit of the **French Antilles, French Guiana** and **Monaco,** and of **Saarland** (1948 to 1959). Divided into 100 Centimes.

Origin of name - Imprint on coin minted in 1360 represented king brandishing sword astride a horse decorated with fleur de lis. Inscription: "Francorum rex". Coin called Franc à Cheval. Under Charles V in 1365, coin representing king on foot was, by analogy, called Franc à Pied (foot). Franc of 1360 had 20 Sous as its exchange rate (1 Livre Tournois). Association remained in public mind. Terms "Livre" or "Franc" eventually used with no difference in meaning.

Bank of issue - Banque de France (Bank of France) created January 18, 1800; nationalized December 2, 1945.

Predecessors - See *France, Livre Tournois, Assignat, Mandat.*

**1360** (December 5th) - Minting of Franc under Ordinance of Paris by Jean the Good:
   1 French Franc = 3.8773888 grams of fine gold
   1 French Franc = 20 Sous

**1365** (April 22nd) - Under Charles V, suspension of minting of earlier French Franc:
   1 New French Franc = 3.82 grams of fine gold
   1 New French Franc = 20 Sous

**1423** (November) - Under Charles VII:
   1 French Franc = 3.059411 grams of fine gold
   1 French Franc = 20 Sous

**1577** (November 1st) - Under Henry III, French Franc became silver unit:
   1 French Franc = 14.07 grams of silver 833 fine = 11.72
                    grams fine silver
Simultaneous minting of 1/2 French Franc and 1/4 French Franc.

**Beginning of 17th Century** - Under Henry IV, silver French Franc made heavier:
   1 French Franc = 23 grams of fine silver

**1641** (December 23rd) - Under Louis XIII, general debasement of French Franc. Henceforth, was only a unit of account, as was Livre.

**1795** (April 7th) (18 Germinal Year III) - Adoption of word Franc to designate future monetary unit in place of Livre.

**1795** (August 15th) (28 Thermidor Year III) - Definition of French Franc in silver:
   1 French Franc = 5 grams of silver 900 fine = 4.50 grams
                    fine silver

**1796** (April 14th) (25 Germinal Year IV) - Exchange of Livres for French Francs on basis of:
   1 French Franc = 1 Livre 3 Deniers

1 Livre = 99 Centimes

**1803** (April 7th) (17 Germinal Year XI) - Bimetallic monetary system:
1 French Franc = 5 grams of silver 900 fine = 4.5 grams fine
silver = 322.58 milligrams of gold 900 fine =
290.3225 milligrams fine gold
Corresponding parities:
1 U.S. Dollar = 5.182 French Francs
1 Pound Sterling = 25.221 French Francs

**1803** (April 14th) (24 Germinal Year XI) - Banque de France received exclusive privilege of issuing banknotes in Paris.

**1805** (September 24th) - Limitations placed on convertibility. Maximum currency depreciation of 8%.

**1806** (January 28th) - Resumption of specie payments.

**1814** (January 18th) - Forced parity.

**1814** (April 15th) - Restoration of convertibility.

**1848** (March 15th) - Creation of legal tender status, and forced parity for banknotes.

**1848** (April 27th and May 2nd) - Assimilation of local banks of issue by Banque de France.

**1850** (August 6th) - Suspension of legal tender status, and forced parity for banknotes.

**1865** (December 23rd) - Agreement of Latin Monetary Union on minting of coins (see *Union Latine*).
1 French Franc coin of 5 grams lowered to a fineness of 835.

**1870** (August 12th) - Reinstitution of legal tender status, and forced parity for banknotes. Maximum depreciation 2%.

**1878** (January 1st) - Abolition of forced parity.

**1914** (August 5th) - Forced parity. Inflation and currency depreciation. Maximum loss of 90% by July 1926.

**1916** (February 12th) - Foreign exchange controls established.

**1921** (September 15th) - French Franc coined in form of bronze aluminum tokens (91% copper, 9% aluminum). Issued by Chambers of Commerce to replace emergency banknotes issued during war.

**1928** (June 25th) - Devaluation by 79.69%, and return to convertibility into metal. Adoption of gold standard and abolishment of foreign exchange controls. Convertibility limited to gold bar of 400 ounces (215,000 Francs).
1 Franc Poincaré = 58.95 milligrams of fine gold
1 U.S. Dollar = 25.524 French Francs
1 Pound Sterling = 124.213 French Francs
With adoption of new gold definition, Stabilization Law foresaw minting of bronze/aluminum coins to be issued by Government replacing tokens of Chambers of Commerce.

**1936** (October 1st) - Forced parity. Creation of Exchange Stabilization Fund. New valuation of monetary gold stock of Banque de France:
1 French Franc = 44.1 milligrams of fine gold

**1937** (July 21st) - New valuation of monetary gold stock:
1 French Franc = 38.7 milligrams of fine gold

**1938** (November 12th) - New valuation of monetary gold stock:
  1 French Franc = 24.75 milligrams of fine gold

**1939** (September 9th) - Foreign exchange controls, freezing exchange rates at:
  1 U.S. Dollar = 43.80 French Francs
  1 Pound Sterling = 176.625 French Francs

**1940** (February 29th) - New valuation of monetary gold stock:
  1 French Franc = 21 milligrams of fine gold

**1940** (May 17th) - German Ordinance fixing Mark-Franc relationship in Occupied France at:
  1 Reichsmark = 20.00 French Francs
Subsequent inflation and currency depreciation on black markets.

**1941** (December 20th) - Decree ordering minting of 1 French Franc coins in aluminum (1.3 grams).

**1945** (June 4th-15th) - Exchange of banknotes without blockage of accounts.

**1945** (December 26th) - Devaluation and adoption of new parities:
  1 French Franc = 7.46 milligrams of fine gold
  1 U.S. Dollar = 119.10 French Francs
Inflation and depreciation continued.

**1946** (December 18th) - Parity registered with International Monetary Fund.

**1948** (January 26th) - Adoption of a system of multiple exchange rates ranging from 214.39 French Francs per U.S. Dollar (official exchange rate) for 50% of exports proceeds to 305.00 French Francs (free market rate for remainder). System not recognized by International Monetary Fund.

**1948** (January 30th) - Withdrawal from circulation of banknotes of 5,000 French Francs with partial temporary blocking of accounts.

**1948** (February 2nd) - Opening of free gold market.

**1949** (April) - Rate of exchange for U.S. Dollar raised to 330.00 French Francs (free market).

**1949** (September 20th) - Following devaluation of Pound Sterling, devaluation of French Franc:
  1 U.S. Dollar = 350.00 French Francs
Gradual evolution of multiple rate structure with premiums on U.S. Dollar ranging up to 20% or more:
  Franc Libre (Official Rate)
  Franc Capital (Registered Investments)
  Franc EFAC (Exportations-Frais Accessoires; Up to 20%
          Retention of Export Proceeds)
  Franc Intérieur Estranger (Nonregistered Investments)
  Franc Pétrole (40% of Crude Oil Imports)
  Franc Cinématographique (40% of Film Royalties)
  Devises-Titres (Foreign Securities Purchases)

**1950** (August 16th) - New valuation of monetary gold stock:
  1 French Franc = 2.52 milligrams of fine gold

**1953** (April 3rd) - Creation of Franc Touriste (for foreign tourists).

**1956** (July 12th) - Creation of Compte Etranger (balances of Sterling Area and EPU countries).

**1957** (February 13th) - Tax (F 500 - F 1,000) on foreign exchange for travel abroad.

**1957** (August 11th) - "Operation 20%"; decree levying 20% tax on sales and purchases of foreign exchange (except for imports of primary commodities and textile exports).

**1957** (October 28th) - Decree making all imports subject to 20% surcharge and all exports to 20% premium. De facto exchange rate:
> 1 U.S. Dollar = 420.00 French Francs

**1958** (July 24th) - De jure acknowledgement of this parity through new valuation of monetary gold stock:
> 1 French Franc = 2.115 milligrams of fine gold

**1958** (December 27th) - Devaluation of 14.93% approved by International Monetary Fund:
> 1 Franc Pinay = 1.80 milligrams of fine gold
> 1 U.S. Dollar = 493.706 French Francs

Restoration of convertibility of French Franc into foreign exchange for nonresidents.

Travel tax abolished; simplification of exchange rate structure:
> Franc Convertible
> Franc EFAC
> Devises-Titres

**1960** (January 1st) - Creation of "heavy" or Nouveau Franc:
> 1 Nouveau French Franc = 100 French Francs
> 1 Nouveau French Franc = 180 milligrams of fine gold
> 1 U.S. Dollar = 4.93706 Nouveau French Francs

Progressive elimination of foreign exchange controls.

**1962** (April 2nd) - Devises-Titres abolished.

**1963** (January 1st) - Designation "Nouveau" dropped.

**1966** (January 8th) - Franc EFAC abolished.

**1967** (January 31st) - Elimination of foreign exchange controls completed.

**1968** (May 29th) - Reestablishment of foreign exchange controls. Appearance of Devises-Titres.

**1968** (September 4th) - Lifting of foreign exchange controls.

**1968** (November 25th) - Reimposition of foreign exchange controls.

**1968** (December 13th) - Devises-Titres abolished.

**1969** (August 8th) - Devaluation of 11.1% and reestablishment of Devises-Titres market:
> 1 French Franc = 160 milligrams of fine gold
> 1 U.S. Dollar = 5.554 French Francs

**1969** (November) - French Franc hit historic low of 6.00 per U.S. Dollar on black market. Subsequent improvement to near official rate.

## FRANC ALGERIA

Former monetary unit of **Algeria.** Divided into 100 Centimes.

Bank of issue - Banque de l'Algérie holding privilege of banknote issue granted by law of August 4, 1851. Nationalized on May 17, 1946. Became Banque de l'Algérie et de la Tunisie January 23, 1948. Reverted to Banque de l'Algérie (1958). Replaced by Banque Centrale d'Algérie (Central Bank of Algeria) December 13, 1962.

Predecessor - See *Algeria.*

**1830** - Beginning of French conquest. Difficult introduction of French coins of 5 Francs. Legal tender status accepted for Franc only gradually, as occupation progressed.

**1878** - French Treasury account with Banque de l'Algérie established. Permitted link of Algerian Franc to Metropolitan Franc. - See *Franc.*

**1940** (May 20th) - Decree establishing foreign exchange controls between Metropolitan France and Overseas Territories.

**1942** (November) - Following landing of Allied Forces, new exchange parities:
1 Pound Sterling = 300.00 Algerian Francs
1 U.S. Dollar = 75.00 Algerian Francs
Incorporated into Sterling Area.

**1943** (February 2nd) - Exchange rates lowered:
1 Pound Sterling = 200.00 Algerian Francs
1 U.S. Dollar = 50.00 Algerian Francs

**1944** (December 6th) - Return to Franc-Zone. Subsequent developments parallel to those of French Franc. - See *Franc.*

**1945** (October 1st) - Issue of brass coins worth 2 Francs. Minted in 1944 by Philadelphia Mint.

**1964** (April 1st) - Algerian Franc replaced by new unit at par. - See *Dinar Algeria.*

## FRANC BELGIUM

Monetary unit of **Belgium.** Divided into 100 Centimes.

Bank of issue - Originally by private banks (including Société Générale de Belgique) then entrusted to Banque Nationale de Belgique (National Bank of Belgium), created May 5, 1850. Issue privilege temporarily returned to Société Général de Belgique under German Occupation from 1914 to 1918, and entrusted to Banque d'Emission in Brussels by Germans from 1940 to 1944.

Predecessors - See *Netherlands* and *Belgium.*

**14th Century** - Louis II, Count of Flanders, issued Franc à Cheval, then Franc à Pied, gold monies imitating Francs of France. William V in Holland also minted Franc à Cheval.

**15th Century** - Philip the Good minted gold Franc à Cheval in Netherlands.

**1832** (June 5th) - Independent Belgium adopted monetary system based on French system:

1 Belgian Franc = 4.50 grams of fine silver
1 Belgian Franc = 290.322 milligrams of fine gold
1 Belgian Franc = 1 French Franc

**1848** (March 4th) - Granting of legal tender status to English Sovereign.

**1848** (March 20th) - Forced parity.

**1850** (May 5th) - Restoration of convertibility.

**1850** (December 28th) - Adoption of silver standard.

**1861** (June 14th) - French gold coins made legal tender. Return to bimetallism.

**1865** - Adherence to Latin Monetary Union. - See *Union Latine.*

**1878** - Suspension of free minting of silver.

**1914** (August 4th) - Suspension of convertibility.

**1914** (August) - German Occupation. Issue of Marks:
1 Mark = 1.25 Belgian Francs

**1918** - Replacement of Mark by Belgian Franc at same ratio.

**1919** - Inflation and currency depreciation (74% at end of 1923).

**1923** (August 10th) - Foreign exchange controls.

**1926** (February 27th) - Law providing for reestablishment of gold standard.

**1926** (July 13th) - Maximum currency depreciation (88%).

**1926** (October 25th) - Reestablishment of convertibility into gold, acknowledging devaluation of 85.58%. Creation of Belga as unit of account for foreign exchange transactions:
1 Belgian Franc = 41.842 milligrams of fine gold
1 Belga = 5.00 Belgian Francs

**1933** - Gold Bloc formed.

**1935** (March 18th) - Foreign exchange controls reintroduced.

**1935** (March 30th) - Law providing for devaluation of 25% to 30%. Creation of Exchange Equalization Fund.

**1935** (March 31st) - Decree of Van Zeeland confirming devaluation of 28%:
1 Belgian Franc = 30.1264 milligrams of fine gold

**1935** (April 26th) - Lifting of foreign exchange controls.

**1936** (March 31st) - Full restoration of gold standard.

**1940** (May 10th) - Suspension of convertibility.

**1940** (May 14th) - German Occupation. Foreign exchange controls.

**1940** (May) - 1 Reichsmark = 10.00 Belgian Francs.

**1940** (July) - 1 Reichsmark = 12.50 Belgian Francs.

**1944** (October 5th) - Liberation of Belgium. Anglo-Belgian Monetary Agreement established new currency relationships:
1 Pound Sterling = 176.62 Belgian Francs
1 U.S. Dollar = 43.77 Belgian Francs

**1944** (October 6th to 13th) - Exchange of banknotes with 60% blocking of accounts.

**1945** (January) - New valuation of gold:
1 Belga = 101.40 milligrams of fine gold

**1946** (December 18th) - Parity registered with International Monetary Fund:

1 Belgian Franc = 20.2765 milligrams of fine gold
1 U.S. Dollar = 43.8275 Belgian Francs

**1949** (September 21st) - Devaluation by 12.3%, following Pound Sterling:
1 Belgian Franc = 17.7734 milligrams of fine gold
1 U.S. Dollar = 50.00 Belgian Francs

**1949** (November) - Reopening of official foreign exchange market.

**1955** (July 18th) - Reform of exchange controls making Franc financially convertible. Two exchange markets created; official regulated market for authorized banks only at rates maintained within official limits for commercial transactions, and freely fluctuating free market for noncommercial dealings.

**1956** (January 1st) - Major easing of regulations, and free gold dealings resumed.

**1957** (April 1st) - Reorganization of Transferable Franc Area to include all countries except Dollar Area and bilateral agreement countries.

**1958** (December 28th) - External convertibility established with full transferability of current balances, except for a few bilaterals, into any currency.

**1969** (August) - Belgian Franc dropped to 55.00 per U.S. Dollar on free market. Subsequent improvement to near parity.


## FRANC BURUNDI

Monetary unit of **Burundi**. Divided into 100 Centimes.

Bank of issue - Banque de la République du Burundi (Bank of Republic of Burundi), established May 19, 1964, as Banque du Royaume du Burundi. Name changed on November 28, 1966.

Predecessors - See *Franc Congo, Franc Ruanda-Burundi.*

**1964** (May 19th) - Burundi Franc replaced Ruanda-Burundi Franc at par:
1 Burundi Franc = 17.7734 milligrams of fine gold
1 U.S. Dollar = 50.00 Burundi Francs
Free market rate at near 100.00 per U.S. Dollar existed for some transactions.

**1965** (January 26th) - Free market rate abolished. New official rate established:
1 Burundi Franc = 10.1562 milligrams of fine gold
1 U.S. Dollar = 87.50 Burundi Francs

**1966** (March 31st) - Burundi Franc fell to 125.00 per U.S. Dollar on black market.


## FRANC CFA

Monetary unit of **Communauté Financière Africaine** (CFA): French West Africa, French Equatorial Africa, Cameroon, Togo, Madagascar, Comoro Islands, Réunion, as well as St. Pierre et Miquelon. Divided into 100 Centimes. Former monetary unit (from December 1945 to March 1949) of French Somaliland.

Banks of issue - 1) At first, by Caisse Centrale de la France d'Outre-Mer, created on February 2, 1944. Originally established on December 2, 1941, as Caisse Centrale de la France Libre. Name changed on December 30, 1958, to Caisse Centrale de

Coopération Economique. On October 1, 1959, lost note-issuing authority everywhere except for St. Pierre et Miquelon.

2) By Institut d'Emission des Départements d'Outre-Mer, established on January 7, 1959, as note-issuing authority for French Guiana, Guadeloupe, Martinique, all using Metropolitan Franc, and Réunion, using only CFA Franc.

3) By Banque de Madagascar established in December 1925. Renamed Banque de Madagascar et des Comores in 1950, as note-issuing authority for Comoro Archipelago and Madagascar (until April 1, 1962).

4) By Institut d'Emission Malgache, established on March 8, 1962. On April 1, 1962, assumed note-issuing authority for Malagasy Republic (Madagascar).

5) By Banque Centrale des Etats de l'Afrique Equatoriale et du Cameroun (BCEAEC) for Equatorial African and Cameroon Currency Union composed of Cameroon, Central African Republic (Ubangi-Shari until December 1, 1958), Chad, Congo-Brazzaville (Middle Congo until November 28, 1958) and Gabon. In 1959, BCEAEC replaced as note-issuing authority the Institut d'Emission de l'Afrique Equatoriale Française et du Cameroun, established on September 30, 1955 as successor institute to Caisse Centrale de la France d'Outre-Mer, serving this area in Africa.

6) By Banque Centrale des Etats de l'Afrique de l'Ouest (BCEAO) for West African Currency Union composed of Dahomey, Ivory Coast, Mauritania, Niger, Senegal, Togo and Upper Volta. On May 12, 1962, BCEAO organized to replace as note-issuing authority the Institut d'Emission de l'Afrique Occidentale Française et du Togo, established in October 1955, as successor organization to Banque de l'Afrique Occidentale, created in 1901 and serving French West Africa and Togo. Until March 8, 1960, Guinea was within framework of CFA area. Mali was also member of CFA area until July 2, 1962, and later reentered Franc-Zone in February 1967.

Predecessors - See *Franc,* and individual countries.

**1945** (December 26th) - Devaluation and dismemberment of Franc within Franc-Zone. Creation by decree of CFA Franc (linked to French Franc). Devalued in relation to foreign currencies and reduced in relation to French Franc:

    1 CFA Franc = 1.70 French Francs
    1 Pound Sterling = 282.352 CFA Francs
    1 U.S. Dollar = 70.058 CFA Francs

**1948** (January 26th) - Devaluation equal to that of French Franc. Official parity valid for commercial transactions:

    1 CFA Franc = 1.70 French Francs
    1 Pound Sterling = 508.235 CFA Francs
    1 U.S. Dollar = 126.11 CFA Francs

Capital transactions carried out at free market rate.

**1948** (October 18th) - Parity of the CFA Franc maintained in relation to foreign currencies when Metropolitan Franc devalued:

    1 CFA Franc = 2.00 French Francs
    1 Pound Sterling = 508.235 CFA Francs
    1 U.S. Dollar = 126.11 CFA Francs

**1949** (March 17th) - Withdrawal of French Somaliland from CFA Group, and creation of Djibouti Franc. - See *Franc Djibouti.*

**1949** (August 8th) - Commercial transactions regulated on basis of average rate between free market and official exchange rate:

1 U.S. Dollar = 107.195 CFA Francs

**1949** (September 20th) - With devaluation of French Franc, all transactions carried out at free market rate, or corresponding purchase price:

1 CFA Franc = 2.00 French Francs
1 Pound Sterling = 490.00 CFA Francs
1 U.S. Dollar = 175.00 CFA Francs

**1958** (December 27th) - Devaluation of French Franc:

1 CFA Franc = 2.00 French Francs
1 U.S. Dollar = 246.853 CFA Francs

**1960** (January 1st) - Creation of "heavy" or Nouveau French Franc:

1 CFA Franc = 0.02 French (Nouveau) Franc
1 U.S. Dollar = 246.853 CFA Francs

**1960** (August) - Members of this Equatorial African Currency Union each gained independence. Accord of cooperation regarding economic, monetary and financial matters signed by France and new republics.

**1962** (January 17th) - CFA Franc became only legal tender. West African Currency Union continued in reorganized form. Cameroon, although member of CFA group, had special banknote issue with an overprint "Cameroun".

**1962** (May 12th) - West African Currency Union set up by treaty, and accord with France formulated. All CFA countries had exchange value of their currencies guaranteed by France, their reserves held exclusively in French Francs. Paris handled bulk of foreign exchange transactions.

**1964** (November) - Banque Centrale des Etats de l'Afrique Equatoriale et du Cameroun legally reorganized into multinational institution with head office in each of five participating countries. Central Administrative Office in Paris.

**1967** (July 1st) - CFA Franc raised to status of almost complete convertibility.

**1968** (May) - Following France's lead, foreign exchange controls reimposed. Removed in September, and reinstated after November.

**1969** (August 8th) - Devaluation of French Franc by 11.1%:

1 CFA Franc = 0.02 French Franc
1 U.S. Dollar = 277.7095 CFA Francs

CFA Franc in black market quoted at historic low of 305.00 per U.S. Dollar. Subsequent improvement to near parity.

## FRANC CFP

Monetary unit of **French Colonies of the Pacific:** New Caledonia, French Polynesia and Wallis and Futuna Islands. Divided into 100 Centimes.

Origin of name - Colonies Françaises du Pacifique, later Comptoirs Français du Pacifique.

Bank of issue - Banque de l'Indochine. Since March 1, 1967, L'Institute d'Emission d'Outre-Mer.

Predecessors - See *New Caledonia, French Polynesia.*

**1945** (December 26th) - Devaluation and dismemberment of Franc within Franc-Zone.

Creation of CFP Franc linked to Metropolitan Franc. Consolidation of earlier parities of Pound Sterling (200.00 Francs) and of U.S. Dollar (49.625 Francs). CFP Franc aligned to devalued Metropolitan Franc:

1 CFP Franc = 2.40 Francs
1 Pound Sterling = 200.00 CFP Francs
1 U.S. Dollar = 49.625 CFP Francs

**1946** (December 18th) - Parity registered with International Monetary Fund:

1 CFP Franc = 17.9067 milligrams of fine gold
1 U.S. Dollar = 49.6278 CFP Francs

**1948** (January 26th) - Notwithstanding devaluation of Franc of Metropolitan France, maintenance of parities to Pound Sterling and U.S. Dollar:

1 CFP Franc = 4.32 Francs

**1948** (October 18th) - Same operation. New relationship:

1 CFP Franc = 5.31 Francs

**1949** (April 27th) - Raising of exchange rate of U.S. Dollar on Paris free market resulted in new modification of relationship between CFP Franc and Metropolitan Franc:

1 CFP Franc = 5.48 Francs

**1949** (September 20th) - General modification of parities. Not approved by International Monetary Fund:

1 CFP Franc = 5.50 Francs
1 U.S. Dollar = 63.63 CFP Francs
1 Pound Sterling = 178.18 CFP Francs

**1959** (January 7th) - Following devaluation of Metropolitan Franc, new parity established with International Monetary Fund:

1 CFP Franc = 9.90 milligrams of fine gold
1 U.S. Dollar = 89.7647 CFP Francs

**1960** (June 1st) - Creation of "heavy" Franc:

1 CFP Franc = 0.055 Franc

**1969** (August 10th) - Devaluation parallel to Metropolitan unit:

1 CFP Franc = 8.8 milligrams of fine gold
1 U.S. Dollar = 100.985 CFP Francs

## FRANC CONGO

Former monetary unit of **Belgian Congo** and **Ruanda-Urundi.** Divided into 100 Centimes.

Bank of issue - Banque du Congo Belge; replaced in 1951 by Banque Centrale du Congo Belge et du Ruanda-Urundi; then Conseil Monétaire de la République du Congo formed October 3, 1960; finally Banque Nationale du Congo (National Bank of Congo) established June 22, 1964.

**1887** (July 27th) - Adoption of monetary system based on gold standard, but without free minting of gold and without effective domestic circulation. Unit of account: Franc. Means of payment: gold coins of 20 Francs and divisionary silver coins.

**1911** (July 18th) - Agreement giving Banque du Congo Belge privilege of issuing banknotes redeemable in gold or silver coins of Latin Monetary Union:

1 Congolese Franc = 1 Belgian Franc

**1914** - Forced parity.

**1919** (June) - Reestablishment of Congolese Franc at par with Belgian Franc. Circulation of banknotes and Belgian monies and some local divisionary coinage (5 to 20 Centimes in nickel, 1 and 2 Centimes in copper).

**1920** (December 28th) - Local issue of copper/nickel coins in denominations of 1 Franc and 50 Centimes.

**1925** and **1935** - Parallel devaluations with Belgian Franc. - See *Franc Belgium.*

**1940** (June 7th) - Linked to French Franc:
    1 Congolese Franc = 1 French Franc
    1 Pound Sterling = 176.625 Congolese Francs
    1 U.S. Dollar = 43.80 Congolese Francs

**1941** (January 21st) - Anglo-Belgian Agreement provided for entrance of Congolese Franc into Sterling Area.

**1944** (October 5th) - Congolese Franc linked to Belgian Franc. Common evolution of the two currencies. Congolese Franc left Sterling Area.

**1949** (September 21st) - Devaluation along with Pound Sterling and Belgian Franc:
    1 Congolese Franc = 17.7734 milligrams of fine gold
    1 U.S. Dollar = 50.00 Congolese Francs

**1951** (July 30th) - Banque Centrale du Congo Belge et du Ruanda-Urundi became note-issuing authority.

**1952** (December) - Colonial Council specified Congolese Franc distinct from Belgian Franc and that relationship could be modified. Valuation of monetary gold stock by Central Bank at rate of 56.26 Congolese Francs per gram of fine gold.

**1960** (July 11th) - Secession of Katanga Province - See *Franc Katanga.*

**1960** (September 22nd) - Congolese Franc replaced by Ruanda-Burundi Franc in Ruanda Urundi. - See *Franc Ruanda-Burundi.*

**1960** (October 3rd) - Conseil Monétaire formed to plan monetary policy prior to creation of new Central Bank.

**1962** (November 6th) - Partial devaluation. Commercial rate of 65.00 Congolese Francs per U.S. Dollar established for most trade transactions. Based on 80% of official rate and 20% of free rate of 125 Congolese Francs per U.S. Dollar.

**1963** (October) - Franc on black market fell to 435 per U.S. Dollar, premium of 770% over official rate.

**1963** (November 9th) - Devaluation, and mixed rates abolished:
    1 Congolese Franc = 5.924 milligrams of fine gold
    1 U.S. Dollar = 150.00/180.00 Congolese Francs (buying-
                /selling)

**1967** (June 24th) - Devaluation:
    1 Congolese Franc = 1.77734 milligrams of fine gold
    1 U.S. Dollar = 500.00 Congolese Francs

**1967** (July 23rd) - Creation of new unit, Zaire, equal to 1,000 Congolese Francs. - See *Zaire.*

**1967** (September) - Congolese Franc hit record low of 715 per U.S. Dollar in the black market, prior to removal.

# FRANC DJIBOUTI

Monetary unit of **French Territory of the Afars and the Issas** (formerly called French Somaliland). Divided into 100 Centimes.

Note-issuing authority - Public Treasury, which took over earlier banknotes of branch of Banque de l'Indochine.

Predecessors - See *French Somaliland, Franc CFA.*

**1949** (March 17th) - Decree substituting Djibouti Franc for CFA Franc. Currency unit withdrawn from Franc-Zone. Technically in Dollar Area. Defined in gold and freely convertible into U.S. Dollars:
>    1 Djibouti Franc = 4.14507 milligrams of fine gold
>    1 U.S. Dollar = 214.392 Djibouti Francs

Parity registered with International Monetary Fund.

**1949** (March 23rd) - Introduction of unit on free exchange market in Paris (exchange rate applicable to financial transactions).

**1949** (September 20th) - Extension of free market exchange rate to commercial transactions:
>    1 Djibouti Franc = 1.635 French Francs

Rate varied with quotation for U.S. Dollar in Paris.

**1958** (December 29th) - After devaluation of French Franc:
>    1 Djibouti Franc = 2.30 French Francs

**1960** (January 1st) - After creation of hard French Franc:
>    1 Djibouti Franc = 0.0230 French Francs

**1969** (August 8th) - After devaluation of French Franc:
>    1 Djibouti Franc = 0.0259 French Francs

# FRANC GUIANA

Monetary unit of **French Guiana,** directly linked to Metropolitan Franc. Divided into 100 Centimes. Circulates freely in French West Indies.

Note-issuing authority - Banque de la Cuyane, established July 11, 1851; Caisse Centrale de la France d'Outre-Mer from June 1944 (renamed Caisse Centrale de Coopération Economique on December 30, 1958); replaced by Institut d'Emission des Départments d'Outre-Mer on January 7, 1959).

Predecessor - See *French Guiana.*

**1820** (February 2nd) - Monetary system linked to that of Metropolitan France. Legal tender status given only to French monies.

**1851** (July 11th) - Banque de la Cuyane established to issue Franc banknotes in French Guiana.

**1855** (April 23rd) - Decree revoked legal tender status of foreign monies.

**1916** (December 16th) - Issue of treasury vouchers (1 and 2 Francs), which circulated until 1921.

**1920** (August 8th) - Legal tender status given all monies of Metropolitan France, including divisionary coinage.

**1939** (September 9th) - Foreign exchange controls within framework of Franc-Zone.

**1940** (May 20th) - Decree establishing foreign exchange controls between Metropolitan France and Overseas Territories.

**1943** (February 2nd) - Allied agreement fixing 1 Pound Sterling at 200 Guiana Francs and 1 U.S. Dollar at 50 Guiana Francs.

**1944** (August 28th) - Decree transferring privilege of banknote issue to Caisse Centrale de la France d'Outre-Mer. Subsequent history parallel to Metropolitan Franc. - See *Franc*.


## FRANC GUINEA

Monetary unit of **Guinea**. Divided into 100 Centimes.

Bank of issue - Banque Centrale de la République de Guinée (Central Bank of Republic of Guinea).

Predecessors - See *French Guinea* and *Franc CFA*.

**1960** (March 1st) - Guinea withdrew from Franc-Zone. Creation of Guinea Franc to replace CFA Franc at par:

    1 Guinea Franc = 0.02 French Francs
    1 U.S. Dollar = 246.853 Guinea Francs

**1969** (March) - Guinea Franc fell to record low of 2,000 to 3,000 per U.S. Dollar on the black market.


## FRANC KATANGA

Monetary unit of former **Republic of Katanga**. Divided into 100 Centimes.

Bank of issue - Banque Nationale du Katanga (National Bank of Katanga) established August 2, 1960.

Predecessor - See *Franc Congo Democratic Republic* (Belgian Congo).

**1960** (July 11th) - Secession from Congo Democratic Republic (Belgian Congo).

**1960** (August 10th) - Creation of Katanga Franc and institution of foreign exchange controls:

    1 Katanga Franc = 17.7734 milligrams of fine gold
    1 U.S. Dollar = 50.00 Katanga Francs

**1960** (December) - Katanga Franc declared legal tender.

**1961** (January 26th) - Circulation and acceptance of Congolese Francs in territory of Katanga Republic prohibited.

**1961** (August) - Partial devaluation. Commercial Franc created for most licensed trade transactions at 50% of official rate and 50% of free market rate.

**1962** (August) - Katanga Franc declined to low of 195.00 per U.S. Dollar on free market, premium of 290% for the Dollar over official rate.

**1963** (January 10th) - Breakdown of Katanga's currency system. Katanga Franc ceased to exist, and Katanga annexed to Congo Democratic Republic again as province with Congolese Franc as legal tender. - See *Franc Congo*.

## FRANC LUXEMBOURG

Monetary unit of Grand Duchy of **Luxembourg**. Divided into 100 Centimes.

Bank of issue - Banque Internationale à Luxembourg (International Bank of Luxembourg), authorized in 1856, and since 1922 guaranteed by Banque Nationale de Belgique. Luxembourg government also issues banknotes from 5 to 100 Francs and coins.

Predecessor - See *Luxembourg*.

**1848** (December 20th) - Adoption of Franc as unit of account in place of Dutch Guilder:
　　1 Franc = 290.322 milligrams of fine gold
Circulation of German money. Banque Internationale à Luxembourg issued banknotes in Francs, Dutch Guilders, German Gulden and Thalers.

**1914** (August 3rd) - Forced parity.

**1914** (November) - Issue by Treasury of Francs backed by German Mark.

**1918** (November 11th) - Elimination of Mark as currency cover.

**1922** (May 1st) - Belgo-Luxembourg Economic Union came into force, and placed in circulation banknotes of Banque Nationale de Belgique:
　　1 Luxembourg Franc = 1 Belgian Franc

**1929** (December 19th) - Stabilization, with devaluation of 85.57%:
　　1 Luxembourg Franc = 1 Belgian Franc
　　1 Luxembourg Franc = 41.8422 milligrams of find gold

**1935** (March 18th) - Foreign exchange controls.

**1935** (April 1st) - Devaluation of 10%:
　　1 Luxembourg Franc = 1.25 Belgian Francs
　　1 Luxembourg Franc = 37.658 milligrams of find gold

**1940** (May) - Foreign exchange controls distinct from Belgian controls:
　　1 Reichsmark = 8.00 Luxembourg Francs
During entire German Occupation, Luxembourg Franc maintained at 1.25 Belgian Francs.

**1940** (July) - 1 Reichsmark = 10.00 Luxembourg Francs

**1940** (August 26th) - Reichsmark declared legal money along with Luxembourg Franc and Belgian Franc.

**1941** (January 20th) - Reichsmark declared only legal money.

**1944** (September 4th) - With liberation, Luxembourg Franc linked at par to Belgian Franc. Parallel monetary developments. - See *Franc Belgium*.

## FRANC MALAGASY

Monetary unit of **Malagasy Republic.** Divided into 100 Centimes.

Variation of name - Malgache Franc.

Note issuing authority - Institut d'Emission Malgache, established March 8, 1962.

Predecessors - See *Madagascar* and *Franc CFA.*

**1963** (July 1st) - Malagasy Franc established as legal tender to replace CFA Franc:
1 Malagasy Franc = 1 CFA Franc = 0.02 French Franc
1 U.S. Dollar = 246.853 Malagasy Francs

**1969** (August 11th) - Devaluation (11.1%) following French Franc. Exchange rate for French Franc and CFA Franc unchanged:
1 U.S. Dollar = 277.71 Malagasy Francs

## FRANC MALI

Monetary unit of **Mali.** Divided into 100 Centimes.

Bank of issue - Banque de la République du Mali. Established July 1, 1962; dissolved March 29, 1968. Replaced by Banque Centrale du Mali (Central Bank of Mali).

Predecessors - See *French Sudan* and *Franc CFA.*

**1962** (July 2nd) - Mali withdrew from Franc-Zone. Creation of independent monetary unit to replace CFA Franc at par.
1 Mali Franc = 1 CFA Franc
1 U.S. Dollar = 246.853 Mali Francs

**1967** (May 5th) - Devaluation of 50%:
1 Mali Franc = 0.50 CFA Francs
1 U.S. Dollar = 493.706 Mali Francs

**1967** (February) - Mali reentered Franc-Zone.

**1968** (March 29th) - Mali Franc became convertible at rate of:
1 Mali Franc = 0.01 French Francs

**1969** (August 10th) - Devaluation of 11.1% parallel to that of French Franc:
1 U.S. Dollar = 555.419 Mali Francs

## FRANC MOROCCO

**I.** - Former monetary unit of **Morocco.** Divided into 100 Centimes.

Variation of name - Franc Cherifien.

Bank of issue - Banque d'Etat du Maroc chartered April 7, 1906. Replaced by Banque du Maroc (Bank of Morocco) July 1, 1959.

Predecessors - See *Morocco* and *Hassani.*

**1920** (June 21st) - Decree made Moroccan Franc legal money of French Morocco.

**1920** (November) - Banque d'Etat du Maroc issued banknotes denominated in Francs.

**1922** (March 4th) - Decree of Vizier forbidding circulation of banknotes of Banque de

.France,Banque de l'Algérie, and Banque Algéro-Tunisienne (subsidiary of Banque de l'Algérie).

**1924** (December 29th) - Accord opening an account in French Treasury with Banque d'Etat du Maroc to maintain parity of Moroccan currency with French Franc of Metropolitan France.

**1924** (December 30th) - Sole right of banknote issue entrusted to Banque d'Etat du Maroc:

> 1 Moroccan Franc = 1 French Franc

See *Franc.*

**1925** (January 14th) - Closing of Banque Algéro-Tunisienne.

**1928** (September 5th) and **1936** (December 31st) - Stabilization, and devaluation parallel to French Franc.

**1939** - Foreign exchange controls within framework of Franc-Zone.

**1940** (May 20th) - Decree establishing foreign exchange controls between Metropolitan France and Overseas Territories.

**1942** (November) - Following landing of Allied troops, new exchange parities established. Differed from exchange rates of French Franc:

> 1 Pound Sterling = 300.00 Moroccan Francs
> 1 U.S. Dollar = 75.00 Moroccan Francs

Incorporated into Sterling Area.

**1943** (February 2nd) - Exchange rates lowered:

> 1 Pound Sterling = 200.00 Moroccan Francs
> 1 U.S. Dollar = 50.00 Moroccan Francs

**1944** (February 8th) - Exchange rate ratified.

**1944** (December 6th) - Return to Franc-Zone.

**1945** (December 26th) - Devaluation parallel to French Franc. Henceforth, similar evolution of both monetary units. - See *Franc.*

**1952** - International Court of Justice Decree in the Hague condemned discriminatory practice of "imports without currency," but allowed Morocco to remain within Franc-Zone.

**1956** (October 29th) - Independence. Spanish banknotes exchanged for Moroccan Francs:

> 1 Spanish Peseta = 10.00 Moroccan Francs

**1958** (December 29th) - French Franc devalued. New link established:

> 1 Moroccan Franc = 1.175 French Francs

**1959** (July 1st) - Banque d'Etat du Maroc stripped of power. New Banque du Maroc assumed note-issuing authority.

**1959** (October 17th) - Moroccan Franc devalued 20.4% in terms of U.S. Dollar, 17% in terms of gold content:

> 1 Moroccan Franc = 1.7561 milligrams of fine gold
> 1 U.S. Dollar = 506.00 Moroccan Francs.

Creation of new monetary unit equal to 100.00 Moroccan Francs. - See *Dirham.*

**II.** - Submultiple (¹/₁₀₀) of Dirham, monetary unit of **Morocco.**

## FRANC NEW HEBRIDES

Monetary unit (simultaneously with Australian Pound) of **New Hebrides.** Divided into 100 Centimes.

Bank of issue - Banque de l'Indochine and Institut d'Emission d'Outre-Mer (notes stamped "Nouvelles-Hebrides").

Predecessor - See *New Hebrides.*

**1941** (August 31st) - Creation by decree of New Hebrides Franc, distinct from Metropolitan Franc. Banque de l'Indochine banknotes overprinted with Cross of Lorraine and statement "Nouvelles-Hébrides-France Libre." Exchange of earlier banknotes against overprinted banknotes from September 1st to December 1st. Convertible into Australian Pounds at Service du Contrôle du Franc Néo-Hébridais:

1 Australian Pound = 141.30 New Hebrides Francs

**1941** (September 1st) - Inclusion of New Hebrides in Sterling Area.

**1941** (October 1st) - Sole legal tender status to overprinted Franc banknotes and Australian currency.

**1943** (September 30th) - Decree temporarily authorizing Service du Contrôle du Franc Néo-Hébridais to issue banknotes, convertible into Australian Pounds, in order to augment circulation of banknotes from Banque de l'Indochine.

**1944** (February 22nd) - New parities established:

1 Australian Pound = 160.00 New Hebrides Francs
1 Pound Sterling = 200.00 New Hebrides Francs

**1945** (March 27th) - Franco-British Agreement based on an accord of February 8, 1944 placed New Hebrides in Franc-Zone. Although for "certain purposes of foreign exchange control" was considered as being within jurisdiction of Sterling Area.

**1945** (December 26th) - Creation of Franc des Colonies Françaises (CFP Franc). New Hebrides Franc placed on same footing as CFP Franc. - See *Franc CFP.*

**1949** (October 4th) - Following Pound Sterling and Metropolitan Franc devaluations, new exchange rate:

1 Australian Pound = 140.00 New Hebrides Francs

**1959** (January 7th) - Following devaluation of Metropolitan Franc, new parity established with International Monetary Fund:

1 New Hebrides Franc = 9.90 milligrams of fine gold
1 U.S. Dollar = 89.7647 New Hebrides Francs

**1960** (January 1st) - Creation of "heavy", or Nouveau Franc:

1 New Hebrides Franc = 0.055 French Francs

**1969** (August 10th) - Break with CFP Franc after Metropolitan Franc devaluation. New relationship with devalued Metropolitan unit:

1 New Hebrides Franc = 0.061875 Francs

**1971** (January 6th) - Dealings involving United Kingdom and residents of New Hebrides to be henceforth treated as other transactions involving nonresidents of Sterling Area.

## FRANC RUANDA-BURUNDI

Former monetary unit of **Ruanda-Urundi, Rwanda,** and **Burundi.** Divided into 100 Centimes.

Bank of issue - Banque d'Emission de Ruanda-Urundi (Bank of Issue of Ruanda-Urundi), established September 1960.

Predecessor - See *Franc Congo.*

**1960** (September 22nd) - Ruanda-Burundi Franc issued to replace Congolese Franc at par:
1 Ruanda-Burundi Franc = 17.7734 milligrams of fine gold
1 U.S. Dollar = 50.00 Ruanda-Burundi Francs
Official rate applied to essential imports and some exports. Free market rate, in the range of 100 Francs per U.S. Dollar, applied to all other transactions.

**1964** - Monetary unit replaced by two new issues. - See *Franc Rwanda* and *Franc Burundi.*

## FRANC RWANDA

Monetary unit of **Rwanda.** Divided into 100 Centimes.

Bank of issue - Banque Nationale du Rwanda (National Bank of Rwanda), established 1964.

Predecessors - See *Franc Congo, Franc Ruanda-Burundi.*

**1964** (May 19th) - Rwanda Franc issued to replace Ruanda-Burundi Franc at par:
1 Rwanda Franc = 17.7734 milligrams of fine gold
1 U.S. Dollar = 50.00 Rwanda Francs
Free market rate in range of 118 Francs per U.S. Dollar existed for some transactions.

**1966** (March 31st) - Rate of Rwanda Franc fell to 165 per U.S. Dollar on black market.

**1966** (April 7th) - Currency devalued, and free rate abolished:
1 Rwanda Franc = 8.88671 milligrams of fine gold
1 U.S. Dollar = 100.00 Rwanda Francs

## FRANC SWITZERLAND

Monetary unit of **Switzerland.** Divided into 100 Centimes or Rappen.

Bank of issue - By 35, then 18 local banks, established between 1833 and 1862: Banks of Aargau, Basel, Berne, Fribourg, Geneva; Commercial Banks of Geneva, Graubünden, Glarus, Lucerne, Neuchatel, Solothurn, Vaud, Valais. . .then by Banque National Suisse (Swiss National Bank), created October 6, 1905 and operative from June 20, 1907. Withdrawal of banknotes of cantonal banks completed June 20, 1910.

Predecessor - See *Switzerland.*

**1799** (March 17th) - Helvetian Republic adopted Swiss Franc as monetary unit. Equal to 1.5 Livre Tournois (6.66 grams of fine silver). Divided into 10 Batzen or 100 Rappen. Minting of gold coins (16 and 32 Francs) and silver coins (4 Francs).

**1803** (August 11th) - Law defining Swiss Franc equal to 1/5 French Franc (6.75 grams of fine silver). This system superimposed on cantonal monetary system.

**1806** - Canton of Neuchatel adopted French monetary system.

**1815** - Privilege of coining money returned to cantons.

**1819** (July 14th) - Agreement of 19 cantons adopting Swiss Franc as monetary unit equal to 1.5 Livre Tournois (6.66 grams of fine silver).Only small coins minted.

**1838** (February 7th) - Geneva linked to French monetary system: Franc of 4.50 grams of silver, divided into 100 Centimes.

**1848** (September 12th) - Federal Constitution reserved monetary privilege to Confederation, and put an end to minting in cantons.

**1850** (May 7th) - Monetary unification of Switzerland on basis of silver monometallic standard, with adoption of Swiss Franc equal to French Franc:
 1 Swiss Franc = 4.5 grams of fine silver
Minting of coins of 5 and 20 Centimes in argenton (alloy of silver, copper, nickel and zinc), replaced in 1879 by nickel coins.

**1860** (January 15th) - Because of influx into Switzerland of French gold coins, recognition of legal tender status for French coins. Silver coins (except those of 5 Francs) became divisionary coinage. Establishment of bimetallic standard:
 1 Swiss Franc = 290.3225 milligrams of fine gold
 1 Swiss Franc = 4.50 grams of fine silver

**1865** (December 23rd) - Convention of Latin Monetary Union. - See *Union Latine.*

**1914** (August 3rd) - Suspension of convertibility of banknotes.

**1920** - Temporary depreciation (22% in November).

**1925** - Return of gold into circulation. Lifting of embargo on gold shipments.

**1929** (December 20th) - Adoption of gold standard and return to former parity:
 1 Swiss Franc = 290.3225 milligrams of find gold

**1931** (June 3rd) - Law outlining monetary legislation of Switzerland (gold standard).

**1934** (November) - Creation of Tourist Franc:
 1 Pound Sterling = 15 Swiss Francs

**1935** - Abolition of Tourist Franc.

**1935** (June 20th) - Agreement between Swiss National Bank and private banks to prevent speculation in gold and foreign exchange.

**1936** (September 27th) - Forced parity. Devaluation provided for, between limits of 190 and 215 milligrams of fine gold per Franc. De facto stabilization on basis of 4.15 Francs per U.S. Dollar.

**1936** (September 30th) - Creation of Exchange Stabilization Fund.

**1940** (May 31st) - New valuation of gold stock on basis of:
 1 Swiss Franc = 205.35 milligrams of fine gold
 1 U.S. Dollar = 4.32 Swiss Francs

**1942** (January 19th) - Exchange controls, with dual rate system (commercial rate at par and fluctuating financial free rate).

**1943** (December) - Free rate rose to as high as 2.27 per U.S. Dollar, discount of 47%

for the Greenback.

**1949** (September 25th) - Abolition of all controls on exchange of U.S. Dollars.

**1952** (December 17th) - New monetary statute, which came into force on April 20, 1953. Gold standard at fixed parity:
 1 Swiss Franc = 203.226 milligrams of fine gold
 1 U.S. Dollar = 4.37282 Swiss Francs

**1954** (July 1st) - Decree relieving Swiss National Bank of obligation to redeem banknotes for gold.


## FRANC TUNISIA

Former monetary unit of **Tunisia**. Divided into 100 Centimes.

Bank of issue - Banque de l'Algérie, and from 1948, Banque de l'Algérie et de la Tunisie (Bank of Algeria and Tunisia). Notes distinct from those of Algeria.

Predecessor - See *Tunisia*.

**1881** - French Occupation and introduction of French Franc:
 1 Tunisian Piastre = 0.60 French Franc

**1891** (July 1st) - Decree of the Bey made Franc monetary unit of Tunisia. Withdrawal of all other specie monies. Circulation of banknotes of Banque de l'Algérie. Special minting of Tunisian gold coins, copying French coins.

**1904** (January 8th) - Note-issuing authority granted to Bank de l'Algérie.

**1918** (February 16th) - Issue of Treaury notes (1 to 5 Francs) by Tunisian Government.

**1929** (May 2nd) - Decree of the Bey conforming to new monetary law of June 25, 1928:
 1 Tunisian Franc = 58.95 milligrams of fine gold

**1936** - Devaluation parallel to French Franc.

**1939** (September 9th) - Foreign exchange controls within Franc-Zone.

**1940** (May 20th) - Decree instituted foreign exchange controls between Overseas Territories and Metropolitan France.

**1943** (June) - Allied occupation . Adoption of parities fixed in Algeria during February:
 1 Pound Sterling = 200.00 Tunisian Francs
 1 U.S. Dollar = 50.00 Tunisian Francs

**1944** (December 6th) - Return to Franc-Zone. Subsequent developments parallel to those of French Franc. - See *Franc*.

**1958** (November 1st) - Adoption of new monetary unit to replace Tunisian Franc. - See *Dinar Tunisia*.


## FRANC WEST INDIES

Monetary unit of **French West Indies** (Martinique, Guadeloupe), directly linked to Metropolitan Franc. Divided into 100 Centimes. Circulates in French Guiana.

Note-issuing authority - Banque de la Martinique and Banque de la Guadeloupe, established 1851; Caisse Centrale de la France d'Outre-Mer from June 1944 (renamed Caisse Centrale de Coopération Economique on December 30, 1958); replaced by Institut d'Emission des Départments d'Outre-Mer on January 7, 1959.

**Predecessor** - See *French West Indies.*

**1820** (February 2nd) - Monetary system linked to that of Metropolitan France. Legal tender status given only to French monies.

**1848** - Abolition of slavery gave rise to wage earning class and required new means of payment. Issue of "bons de caisse" on Martinique and "bons de prêts" on Guadeloupe, both having forced parity.

**1851** (July 11th) - Legal creation of Banque de la Martinique and Banque de la Guadeloupe, having privilege of banknote issue. Began functioning in 1853. Progressive withdrawal of "bons de caisse" and "bons de prêts."

**1855** (April 23rd) - Decree cancelling legal tender status for foreign monies, and authorizing supplementary issue of "bons de caisse" with forced parity (continued until end of century).

**1897** - As result of poor harvest, depreciation of West Indies Franc (up to 35% discount).

**1896 to 1899** - Replacement of "bons de caisse" by nickel/silver coins.

**1916** (March 9th) - Issue of "bons de caisse" for use as divisionary money.

**1920** (August 6th) - Legal tender status given all monies of Metropolitan France, including divisionary coinage. - See *Franc.*

**1939** (September 9th) - Foreign exchange controls within framework of Franc-Zone.

**1940** (May 20th) - Decree establishing foreign exchange controls between Metropolitan France and Overseas Territories.

**1943** (February 2nd) - Allied agreement fixing 1 Pound Sterling at 200 West Indies Francs and 1 U.S. Dollar at 50 West Indies Francs.

**1944** (June 27th) - Decree transferring privilege of banknote issue to Caisse Centrale de la France d'Outre-Mer. Subsequent history parallel to Metropolitan Franc. - See *Franc.*

## *FRANCE*

**Until 1st Century B.C.** - See *Gaul.*

**1st to 5th Century** - See *Rome, Solidus,* and *Denarius.*

**5th to 8th Century** - Under Merovingians, continued use of Roman coins. Solidus gave rise to gold Sou (and its third, Triens), which became Sou of account (see *Sou*); Denarius gave rise to silver Denier (see *Denier*).

**8th Century** - Carolingian system of accounting (see *Livre*).

**12th Century** - Carolingian Livre gave rise to French Livre and its local variations (Parisis, Tournois. . .).

**13th Century** - Adoption of Tournois system of accounting (see *Tournois*) in preference to Parisis system of accounting (see *Parisis*). Definitely supplanted in 17th Century:

      1 Livre Tournois = 20 Sous Tournois = 240 Deniers Tournois

See *Livre Tournois.*

**1789-1796** - Inflation during the Revolution. - See *Assignat* and *Mandat.*

**1795-1803** - Substitution of Franc for Livre Tournois. - See *Franc.*

## FRANCESCINO

Silver coin of Grand Duchy of **Tuscany.** Worth ½ Francescone or 5 Paoli.

Origin of name - See *Francescone.*

Plural - Francescini.

## FRANCESCONE

Silver coin of Grand Duchy of **Tuscany** and **Leghorn.**

Origin of name - From Francis II, Duke of Lorraine, who became Grand Duke of Tuscany.

Plural - Francesconi.

**1737** - First minting of Francescone (27.30 grams 916 fine), valued at 10 Paoli or 2 Francescini.

**1766** - Francescone renamed Leopoldino upon accession of Leopold to Grand Duchy of Tuscany. Weight and exchange rate unchanged.

**1801** - Disappeared with establishment of Kingdom of Etruria.

**1826** - Name Francescone often given to Leopoldino - See *Leopoldino.*

## FRANCHO

**I.** - Silver coin minted in **Lucca** and **Piombino** (1805-1808). Copied the Franc.

Plural - Franchi.

**II.** - Monetary unit of Kingdom of **Naples,** under Murat (1810-1813). Divided into 100 Centesimi.

Gold coins worth 40 Franchi minted in this period.

## FRANCISCUS

**French** silver coin, created by Francis I (July 19, 1519) and minted until 1539. Also called Dixain. Rate of exchange: 10 Deniers.

## FRANCO

**I.** - Monetary unit of **Ecuador** from 1856 to 1871. Defined like the Franc Germinal: 290.3225 milligrams of fine gold, or 4.5 grams of fine silver.

**1871** (November 21st) - Adoption of silver Peso as monetary unit. Franco became ⅕ Peso. - See *Peso Ecuador.*

**II.** - In **Dominican Republic,** silver coin introduced in 1891. Equal to 100 Centimos.


## FRANKA

Early monetary unit of **Albania** from 1925 to 1947. Divided into 5 Leks or 100 Centimes (Qindars).

Bank of issue - National Bank of Albania.

Variation of name - Franc, Frank, Franca Ari (gold Franc).

Predecessor - See *Albania.*

**1925** (July 5th) - Adoption by Albania of independent monetary system:
    1 Franka = 1 Franc Germinal = 290.3225 milligrams of fine
                        gold
Minting of gold coins (100, 20, 10) in Rome and Vienna.

**1938** - Italian Occupation:
    1 Lira = 6.25 Frankas

**1940** - Inflation, and currency depreciation.

**1945** (September) - In territories recovered by Yugoslavia, exchange of banknotes:
    1 Dinar = 0.40 Franka = 2 Leks

**1946** (November) - Currency union with Yugoslavia. The Lek, formerly a submultiple of Franka, became monetary unit. - See *Lek.*


## FREDERICKS D'OR

Gold money of Denmark. Minted in 1827 (reign of Frederick VI), and after 1848 (accession of Frederick VII). Patterned after Christian d'Or: 6.65 grams, of which 6 grams were fine gold. Exchange rate varied according to fluctuations of gold price. In principle: 4 Rigsdaler.


## *FRENCH ANTILLES*

See *French West Indies.*

## FRENCH CONGO

Designation for French Equatorial African territories, prior to formation of French Equatorial Africa (January 15, 1910). Monetary history, see *French Equatorial Africa.*

## FRENCH EQUATORIAL AFRICA

**Native monies** - Knives called quindias in Upper Ubangi; spearheads and knife blades in Gabon and Ubangi-Shari; raw iron(aités) among the Gollos.

**19th Century** - Prior to French influence, Maria Theresia Thalers entered into circulation for trade purposes. - See *Maria Theresia Thaler.*

**Early missionaries** - Payments made to native bearers and boatmen in form of vouchers exchangeable for merchandise.

**1839-1862** - French settlers on Gabun River (Libreville) and in Cape Lopez introduced and applied French monetary system.

**1883** - Merchandise voucher system replaced. Use of zinc plaque money (from 10 Centimes to 1 Franc) and copper tokens (from 5 to 50 Francs). Coastal areas of Gabon used Banque de France banknotes.

**1890** - Copper tokens withdrawn from circulation.

**1893** - New issue of zinc tokens in denominations of 1 Franc and submultiples.

**1895** (March 22nd) - Maria Theresia Thaler recognized as legal tender in area of Upper Sanga:
1 Maria Theresia Thaler = 3.00 French Francs
British monies accepted by public financial institutions.

**1901** (January 29th) - Note-issuing privilege granted to Banque de l'Afrique Occidentale.

**1910** (January 15th) - French Congo became French Equatorial Africa, divided into Gabon, Middle Congo and Ubangi-Shari.

**1917** (October 17th) - Issue of divisionary banknotes by Government-General of French Equatorial Africa. Remained in circulation until 1924.

**1920** (March 17th) - Chad made into separate Colony, carved out of Ubangi-Shari.

**1920** (August 8th) - Legal tender status conferred on all monies of Metropolitan France, including divisionary coins.

**1925** (June 6th) - Brazzaville branch of Banque de l'Afrique Occidentale issued banknotes which became sole legal tender.

**1939** (September 9th) - Foreign Exchange controls introduced within Franc-Zone.

**1940** (May 20th) - Decree established foreign exchange controls between Metropolitan France and Overseas Territories.

**1940** (September 16th) - Decree authorized Governor-General to issue "monetary exchange certificates" backed by gold. Certificates never issued.

**1940** (October 9th) - Decree abrogated law of September 16th. Authorized issue of banknotes of 1,000 and 5,000 Francs, bearing no special guarantee and called "Larminat bonds."

**1941** (March 19th) - Anglo-French accord incorporated French Equatorial Africa into Sterling Area. In Free Africa, parity established:

1 Pound Sterling = 176.625 French Francs

**1941** (December 2nd) - Creation of Caisse Centrale de France Libre. Decree acknowledged that "monetary unit of Free France is the Franc."

**1942** (January 30th) - Legal tender status in French Equatorial Africa and French Cameroon given to banknotes issued by Caisse Centrale de France Libre.

**1942** (July 24th) - Temporary suspension in French Equatorial Africa and French Cameroon of note-issuing privilege of Banque de l'Afrique Occidentale. Exchange of latter's banknotes for those of Caisse Centrale de France Libre ordered. New notes printed in England.

**1942** (October 1st) - Legal tender status for banknotes of Banque de l'Afrique Occidentale and for "Larminat bonds" revoked.

**1943** (February 2nd) - Caisse Centrale de France Libre renamed Caisse Centrale de la France d'Outre-Mer and given note-issuing privilege for French Equatorial Africa and Cameroon.

**1944** (February 8th) - Anglo-French accord confirmed exchange rate of:

1 Pound Sterling = 200.00 French Francs

**1944** (June) - Franco-American agreement sanctioned exchange rate:

1 U.S. Dollar = 50.00 French Francs

**1944** (December 6th) - Parities declared and redefined:

1 Pound Sterling = 200.00 French Francs

1 U.S. Dollar = 49.625 French Francs

**1945** (December 26th) - Creation of Franc des Colonies Françaises d'Afrique (Franc CFA), and integration of French Equatorial Africa into CFA group. - See *Franc CFA.*

**1958** (November 28th; December 1st) - French Equatorial Africa dissolved. Territories became member states of French Community. - See *Gabon, Congo People's Republic (Brazzaville), Chad* and *Central African Republic.*

## *FRENCH GUIANA*

**18th Century** - Monetary system analagous to that of French West Indies, involving a Livre depreciated in relation to Livre Tournois. - See *French West Indies* and *Livre Coloniale.*

**1779** (December 10th) - To mitigate scarcity of specie money, issue of 442,500 Livres in playing card money authorized (see *Canada* ). Circulation of coins of 2 Sous, called Tampé, in rolls of 60 coins. - See *Tampé.*

**1781** (November 10th) - Declaration of Versailles calling for withdrawal of card money.

**1782** - Issue of silver/copper coins of 2 Sous with exchange rate of 3 Sols, in rolls of 60 coins. Exported to, and counter-marked in, foreign colonies.

**1793** (September 15th) - Decree authorized issue of Treasury vouchers to replace paper money.

**1818** (October 4th) - Minting of silver/copper 10 Centime coin called Marqué Blanc worth 13.5 Centimes in colonial silver (6 coins for 1 Livre Coloniale). Circulated in rolls of 30, then 60 coins.

**1820** (February 2nd) - Abolition of Livre Coloniale and adoption of decimal currency system. Marqué Blanc thereafter worth 10 Centimes. Legal tender status applicable only to French money.

**1834, 1838** and **1844** - Issue of Treasury vouchers to replace copper coins too heavy to circulate.

**1844** (June 8th) - Demonetization of Marqué Blanc.

**1845** (March 23rd) - Demonetization of Marqué Noir.

**1846** - Recoining of withdrawn money into 10 Centime coins.

**1851** (July 11th) - Following abolition of slavery, creation of class of salaried employees requiring new means of payment. Banque de la Cuyane established as note-issuing authority for Franc banknotes. - See *Franc Guiana*.


## FRENCH GUINEA

**Early native monies** - Bars of iron flattened at ends (20 centimeters long); Cowrie shells (16th to 19th Century) imported from Maldive Islands. Primitive unit of account: the slave. Gold powder during 14th Century (see *Miscal* ).

**18th Century** - Monetary use of white and blue striped cloth (4.16 x 0.79 meters). Manufactured in India, particularly on Coromandel Coast, and introduced by European traders into Guinea.

**19th Century** - Increasing French influence and gradual acceptance of French monetary, system. Franc banknotes issued by Banque du Senegal. - See *Franc*.

**1891** - Given French Protectorate status, separate from Senegal.

**1895** - Became part of French West Africa. - See *French West Africa*.

**1945** (December 26th) - Creation and use of CFA Franc. - See *Franc CFA*.

**1958** (October 2nd) - French Guinea became independent Republic of Guinea. - See *Guinea*.


## FRENCH INDIA

**Before 18th Century** - See *India*.

**18th Century** - Circulation of Mexican Piasters, silver coins of 24.4356 grams fine silver. - See *Piaster Mexico*. Local coins, minted by neighboring Indian princes, also circulated. - See *Rupee India*.

**1700** - Opening of mint in Pondicherry. Minting of silver Fanams, copper Duddus (Doudous) and Cache (Kas); and in city of Mahé copper Biches.

**1705** - Minting in Pondicherry of gold Pagode (Pagoda) of local type. Continued until 1789.

**1736** - Dumas obtained from the Mogul Mohammed Shah perpetual right for Pondicherry to mint silver Rupees of Arcate type. - See *Rupee France*.

**1817** - Minting operations, which had been interrupted since 1793, resumed in Pondicherry.

**1837** - Minting in Madras of Double Fanams, Fanams and 1/2 Fanams, having legal tender status in French India.

**1841** - Closing of mint in Pondicherry.

**1871** - Withdrawal of legal tender status from Fanams and Rupees minted in Pondicherry. Only specie money of India regarded as legal tender.

**1875** (January 21st) - Pondicherry branch of Banque de l'Indochine granted privilege of issuing banknotes secured by specie monies and banknotes of India.

**1940** (May 20th) - Decree establishing foreign exchange controls between Metropolitan France and Overseas Territories.

**1941** (January 28th) - Agreement for customs union with British India.

**1950** (May 2nd) - Transfer of Chandernagor to Indian Administration.

**1954** (November 1st) - Transfer of four remaining French settlements to India. French Rupee replaced by Indian Rupee. - See *Rupee India.*

## *FRENCH OCEANIA*

Former title for French Settlements in South Pacific Ocean. - See *French Polynesia.*

## *FRENCH POLYNESIA*

**18th Century** - Circulation of Mexican Piasters (24.43 grams fine silver), then Chilean, Peruvian and Greek silver coins.

**1848** (September 4th) - Use of coins of Metropolitan France authorized by decree.

**1867** (March 31st) - Adoption of French 5 Franc silver coin, weighing 22.50 grams, as basic unit. Simultaneous use of Piaster for payments made by French Treasury.

**1879** (October 24th) - Attempt to demonetize foreign monies.

**1880** (March 9th) - Treasury authorized to issue banknotes (Treasury bonds) with 100% metallic backing.

**1882** (June 3rd) - Decree designated Franc as official monetary unit and gave legal tender status to multiples and submultiples. - See *Franc.*

**1888** (February 20th) - Right of banknote issue granted to Banque de l'Indochine.

**1905** (December 5th) - Opening of bank branch at Papeete, Tahiti.

**1906** (October 20th) - Importation and circulation of Chilean coins prohibited.

**1911** (November 7th) - Prohibition on importation of Peruvian coins.

**1920** - Legal tender status for all monies of Metropolitan France, including divisionary metal coinage.

**1939** (September 8th) - Foreign exchange controls within Franc-Zone.

**1940** (May 20th) - Decree instituting foreign exchange controls between Metropolitan France and Overseas Territories.

**1941** - Incorporation into Sterling Area.

**1944** (February 8th) - Franco-British agreement fixed rate of exchange of Free Territories:

      1 Pound Sterling = 200.00 Francs

**1944** (June) - Franco-American agreement confirmed February 8th exchange rate and fixed exchange rate for U.S. Dollar:

      1 U.S. Dollar = 50.00 Francs

**1944** (December) - Parities confirmed and specified:

      1 Pound Sterling = 200.00 Francs

      1 U.S. Dollar = 49.625 Francs

Return to Franc-Zone.

**1945** (December 26th) - Creation of CFP Franc. Consolidation of earlier parities with Pound Sterling and U.S. Dollar. Lowering of parity with Metropolitan Franc. - See *Franc CFP.*


## FRENCH SOMALILAND

Primitive tribes made monetary use of salt. - See *Ethiopia.*

**Mid-19th Century** - Circulation of Maria Theresia Thaler. - See *Maria Theresia Thaler.*

**1885** (November 21st) - Decree giving legal tender status to Franc, Maria Theresia Thaler and Indian Rupee:

      1 Maria Theresia Thaler = 4.20 Francs

      1 Indian Rupee = 2.00 Francs

Actual exchange rates varied. Range: 3.90 - 4.10 Francs per Maria Theresia Thaler; 1.80 - 4.90 Francs per Indian Rupee.

**1907** (May 21st) - Issue of Franc banknotes entrusted to Banque de l'Indochine (Djibouti Branch). - See *Franc.*

**1919** (November 30th) - Chamber of Commerce of Djibouti issued Treasury vouchers for use as subsidiary coinage.

**1920** (August 8th) - Legal tender status given to all monies of Metropolitan France, including metallic divisionary coinage.

**1939** (September 8th) - Exchange controls within framework of Franc-Zone.

**1940** (May 20th) - Decree establishing exchange controls between Metropolitan France and Overseas Territories.

**1942** (March 12th) - Local Treasury issued aluminum coins (5 and 25 Centimes) at fixed exchange rate of 50 Centimes and 1 Franc.

**1943** (January 25th and 26th) - Census of banknotes in circulation (banknotes of Banque de l'Indochine and banknotes issued provisionally by Caisse Centrale of French military forces overstamped with B.I.C. Djibouti). Legal tender status of Maria Theresia Thaler and Indian Rupee withdrawn.

**1943** (February 18th) - Decree calling for exchange of banknotes:

At par - up to 5,000 Francs;

20% discount - from 5,000 to 100,000;

50% discount - above 100,000;

90% discount - all banknotes deposited between January 26th and March 31, 1943. Discounted amounts blocked.

By same decree, parity in force within Free France for Pound Sterling made applicable to French Somaliland:

    1 Pound Sterling = 176.625 French Francs

**1943** (May 24th) - Introduction of banknotes by Caisse Centrale de France Libre through Djibouti branch of Banque de l'Indochine.

**1944** (February 8th) - Parity with Pound Sterling raised to 200.00 Francs.

**1944** (June) - Franco-American agreement fixed parity of U.S. Dollar at 50.00 Francs.

**1944** (December 6th) - Parities confirmed and specified:

    1 Pound Sterling = 200.00 Francs

    1 U.S. Dollar = 49.625 Francs

**1945** (December 26th) - Creation of CFA Franc. Devalued relative to foreign exchange and lowered relative to Metropolitan Franc. French Somaliland incorporated into CFA Franc-Zone. - See *Franc CFA.*

**1948** (September 23rd) - Withdrawal of privilege of banknote issue from Banque de l'Indochine.

**1948** (December 27th) - Deliberation of Council of French Somaliland for reshaping territory into a free zone and instituting customs and monetary reforms.

**1949** (March 17th) - Creation by decree of Djibouti Franc, divorced from Franc-Zone and defined in gold. Freely convertible into U.S. Dollars. - See *Franc Djibouti.*

**1949** (March 20th) - Treasury assumed responsibility for banknotes formerly issued in French Somaliland by Banque de l'Indochine.

**1950** (December 31st) - Withdrawal of coins issued in 1942.


## FRENCH SUDAN

For types of monies prior to 19th Century, see *French Guinea.*

**19th Century** - Increasing French influence. Gradual acceptance of French monetary system and Franc banknotes issued by Banque du Senegal. - See *Franc.*

**1899** (April 1st) - Official exchange rate for Cowries established:

    1 bag of 20,000 Cowries = 7 Francs

**1904** - Colony became a part of French West Africa under name Upper Senegal and Niger. - See *French West Africa.*

**1907** (January 28th) - Cowries officially demonetized.

**1945** (December 26th) - Creation and use of CFA Franc. - See *Franc CFA.*

**1959** (January 17th) - French Sudan together with Senegal formed Federation of Mali. Monetary unit unchanged.

**1960** (September 22nd) - French Sudan became Republic of Mali. - See *Mali.*

## *FRENCH TERRITORY OF THE AFARS AND THE ISSAS*

Predecessor - See *French Somaliland.*

**1967** (July 5th) - Territory renamed under new statute. Monetary unit unchanged. - See *Franc Djibouti.*


## *FRENCH WEST AFRICA*

For early monies, see *Dahomey, French Guinea, French Sudan, Ivory Coast, Niger, Senegal.*

**1901** (June 29th) - Transfer of privilege of banknote issue to Banque de l'Afrique Occidentale. - See *Franc.*

**1904** (June 15th) - Ban on import of Piasters and silver bullion.

**1920** (August 8th) - Legal tender status conferred on all monies of Metropolitan France, including divisionary coinage.

**1924** (July 27th) - Decree authorizing public offices to accept English monies, but not to distribute them.

**1934** (July 21st) - Exchange tax on transfers between French West Africa and Metropolitan France (highest: 0.35 per 100 units; lowest: 0.10 per 100 units).

**1939** (September 9th) - Foreign exchange controls introduced within Franc-Zone.

**1942** (April 17th) - Elimination of exchange tax.

**1942** (August 3rd) - Decree tolerating continued circulation of banknotes of Banque de France.

**1942** (December) - Incorporated into Sterling Area.

**1943** (February 2nd) - Allied agreement:
    1 Pound Sterling = 200.00 French Francs
    1 U.S. Dollar = 50.00 French Francs

**1944** (February 8th) - Anglo-French agreement sanctioning exchange rate in Free Territories at 200.00 French Francs per Pound Sterling.

**1944** (March 13th) - Issue by Treasury of divisionary banknotes of ½, 1 and 2 Francs.

**1944** (June) - Franco-American agreement sanctioning parity of U.S. Dollar at 50.00 French Francs.

**1944** (December 6th) - Parities redefined and confirmed:
    1 Pound Sterling = 200.00 French Francs
    1 U.S. Dollar = 49.625 French Francs
Return to Franc-Zone.

**1945** (December 26th) - Creation of Franc des Colonies Françaises d'Afrique (Franc CFA) and incorporation of French West Africa into CFA Group. - See *Franc CFA.*

**1945** (December 28th) - Decree repealing the toleration of continued circulation of Banque de France banknotes.

**1958** (November 28th; December 4th) - French West Africa ceased to exist. - See *Dahomey, Guinea, French Sudan, Senegal, Ivory Coast, Niger, Upper Volta.*

## FRENCH WEST INDIES

**Until 1670** - Barter and payments by means of commodities (first tobacco, then sugar).

**1670** (February 19th) - Declaration of Saint-Germain decreed minting and introduction in French America of coins of 5 and 15 Sols. Continued use of sugar as usual means of payment (especially for taxes) with coins serving only to even out balances. General rule: specie money in terms of Livres, Sols and Deniers were worth 50% more in Islands than in France. - See *Livre Coloniale.*

    100 Livres Tournois = 150 Livres in French West Indies

**1720** (March 17th) - Issue of coins of 12 Deniers.

**1721** (June) - Issue of copper coins of 9 Deniers.

**1730** (December) - Edict called for minting of silver coins of 6 and 12 Sols for Windward Islands (subsequently exported to and counter-marked in British Antilles).

**1738** (October) - Minting of coin of 2 Sols of low silver fineness with rate of exchange of 2 Sols 6 Deniers. Coin was called Marqué (in contrast to worn-out coins), or Noir (because of its low silver content). - See *Marqué.*

**1763** (January) - Stamping of these coins in Paris Mint. Marqué thus became known as Tampé (for Etampé). - See *Tampé.*

**1766** (October) - Minting of 1 Sol copper coins, weighing 12.5 grams, for Windward Islands. Failed to circulate, as coins were too heavy.

**1793** (September 28th) - Circulation of 1 Sol coins generally called Collot, with legal tender status in amounts up to 8 Livres 5 Sols.

**1803-1805** - Assay and marking of "nailed Moeda", Portuguese gold coin with hole that was plugged with gold. - See *Moeda.*

**1797 to 1813** - Scarcity of means of payment. Spanish Gourde Piasters cut into pieces called Mocos and given legal tender status. - See *Moco.*

**1811** - Counter-marking of all silver and silver/copper coins.

**1817** - General demonetization of Mocos. Replaced by coins denominated in Francs.

**1818** - Introduction of 10 Centime silver/copper coins called Marqués Blancs. Circulated in rolls of 30, then 60 coins. Each coin was worth 13.5 Centimes in colonial silver.

**1820** (February 2nd) - Monetary system linked to that of Metropolitan France. Abolition of Antilles Livre. Decimalization of currency. French monetary units declared sole legal tender. Marqué Blanc worth 10 Centimes; Marqué Noir 7½.

**1828** (February 24th) - Tampés and Marqués Noirs withdrawn from circulation.

**1844** (June 8th) - Marqués Blancs withdrawn from circulation. - See *Franc West Indies.*

## FRIEDRICHSDOR

Gold money of **Prussia** (sometimes called Pistole, by virtue of its weight).

Origin of name - Coin minted with effigy of King Frederick.

    Weight: 6.6 grams, of which 5.9 were fine. Rate of exchange provided for by Convention of Vienna (1753): 9 Guilders. Exchange rate in Prussia, Brandenburg, Silesia, Hesse-Kassel: 5 Thaler.

Multiple and submultiple - Double Friedrichsdor, ½ Friedrichsdor.

**1821** - Minting of Friedrichsdor (6.68 grams of gold), having 5 Thaler as exchange rate.

## FUANG

**I.** - Early unit of account and silver coin in **Siam.** Originally equal to 800 Bias (Cowries). - See *Bia.*

Variation of name - Fouang.

**18th Century** - Minted in silver, Fuang was equal to 800 Bias, 8 Clam, 4 Pais, 2 Song Pais, ½ Salung, ⅛ Tical, 1/32 Tael, 1/640 Catty.

**Early 20th Century** - Continued to circulate as silver coin with three different weights and finenesses: 1.944 grams 907 fine; 1.93 grams 903 fine; and 1.875 grams 900 fine.

**II.** - Extensively copied in **Cambodia.**

## FUNDUK

**Turkish** and **Egyptian** gold coin, also called Sequin or Sultanine. Weight: 3.5 grams 800 fine. Fineness varied considerably.

Origin of name - Turkish word *Funduk,* meaning grain.

Variations of name - Foundouc, Fondoukali, Fondukly.

**17th Century** - Altyn came to be known as Funduk. Minted in Cairo of Abyssinian gold and in Constantinople.

**1764** - Mustapha raised Funduk in value from 3 Piastres 80 Aspers to 3 Piastres 105 Aspers, at par with Venetian Zecchino.

**1769** - Withdrawal from circulation (theoretical) of Funduk. Subsequent minting of Roob, or quarters of Funduk (roob = quarter).

**19th Century** - Circulation of Funduk and Double Funduk (Sequin and Double Sequin), worth 50 and 100 Piastres.

## FYNG

Submultiple of Tsjao (1/10) and of Jen Min Piao (1/100), monetary unit of **China.**

Variation of name - Fen.

## FYRK

**I.** - Unit of account in **Denmark** during 18th Century. Equal to 1/192 Rigsdaler, 1/48 Oere, 1/32 Mark, ¼ Stuyver and ½ Skilling, or 1.50 Hvid, 6 Pfennig.

Origin of name - From *fyr* (four). Stuyver equalled 4 Fyrk.

**II.** - A copper coin of **Sweden** from 1522 to early 17th Century. Variation of name - Fyrkar.

## *GABON*

Predecessor - See *French Equatorial Africa.*

**1960** (August 17th) - Became independent nation within French Community. Money in circulation, see *Franc CFA.*

## GALEAZZO

Silver coin issued in early 18th Century for **Dalmatia** and **Albania.** Valued at 3 Lire. Submultiples of halves and quarters.

Origin of name - From imprint of a galley (Italian *galea* ).

Plural - Galeazzi.

## *GAMBIA*

Native monies - See *Gold Coast.*

**Early 19th Century -** British trading posts introduced specie monies of United Kingdom.

**1843** - Became British Colony. Monetary system of United Kingdom. - See *Pound.*

**1913** - Newly formed West African Currency Board minted special coinage for British West Africa. - See *Pound West Africa.*

**1964** (May 13th) - Creation of new monetary unit to replace West African Pound· at par. - See *Pound Gambia.*

## GANZA

Money made of a coarse alloy of copper and tin. Freely minted in 18th Century in Kingdom of Pegu **(Burma).**

Variations of name - Ganzas, Gauza.

## GARI

In **India** (States of the Mogul), unit of account equal to 4,000 Rupees.

## GASS

Early unit of account used on south bank of **Persian Gulf** in Goumron (Persian possession until 1800). Equal to $1/2,000$ Toman or $1/20$ Mahmudi.

## GAUL

**Primitive monies** - Stone hatchets, called celts; metal wheels (gold, bronze. . .) called *rouelles;* gold rings.

**600 B.C.** - In Marseilles, Phocaeans imported their coins made of electrum: Stater (17. grams), Hecté (⅙ Stater).
Subsequent introduction of Greek silver coins, and local minting of coins copying Didrachm (7.5 grams), Drachma (3.80 grams, then 2.75 grams), Obol (0.53 grams to 0.71 grams) and multiples and submultiples. Circulated in Gaul.

**250 B.C.** - Mintings of monies imitating Stater.

**150 B.C.** - Indiscriminate minting of coins no longer patterned after Greek prototypes. Minted from gold, electrum, bronze, copper, lead, with weights progressively reduced.

**1st Century B.C.** - Imitation of Roman silver Denarius, then introduction of monetary system of Rome. - See *Rome.*
For later history of money in Gaul, see *France.*

## GAZZETTA

**I.** - **Venetian** money in 17th Century. Minted in copper and valued at 2 Soldi. It gave its name to the first "gazette" (newspaper) payed for with one Gazzetta.

**II.** - Minted in Venice for **Morea, Crete** (1658) and **Ionian Islands** (1700, 1730, 1735, 1801).

## GENOA

Roman monies (see *Rome* ), then Carolingian monetary system (see *Lira* ).

**13th Century** - Republic of Genoa kept accounts in Lira, of 20 Soldi or 240 Denari.
Specie monies:
      In gold - Genovino (8 Soldi), Quartarola (2 Soldi)
      In silver - Grosso (4 Denari), Denaro, Medaglia,or Pitta (½ Denaro)
      In copper - Quartaro

**1458 to 1461** - During French Occupation, issue of gold Ducat.

**15th Century** - Minting of a silver Testone.

**18th Century** - Units of account: Lira of 20 Soldi or 240 Denari; gold Scudo; gold Scudo of Le Marche; silver Scudo; silver Scudo di Cambio; Piastre, or Pezza.
Specie monies:
      In gold - Doppia, Scudo, Zecchino
      In silver - Scudo, Scudo di Cambio, Giorgino
      In silver/copper - Madonnina, Cavallotto
      In copper - Soldo, multiples of Denaro

**1798 to 1805** - Liguria minted gold coins of 12, 24, 48 and 96 Lire; silver coins of 1, 2, 4 and 8 Lire; silver/copper coins of 10 Soldi.

**1814** - Monies of Piedmont. - See *Piedmont.*

**1865** - After unification of Italy, linking of currency to system of Latin Monetary Union. - See *Italy* and *Lira.*


## GENOVINO

Early monetary unit of **Genoa.**

Variations of name - Genoite, Genoise, Genovina, Genovine, Croizat, Croisat.

**12th Century** - Gold coin worth 8 Soldi. The 1/3 Genovino called Terzarola, the 1/4 Genovino called Quartarola.

**16th Century** - Minting of silver Genovino equal to Scudo. - See *Scudo.*


## GENTIL

Gold coin of **Portugal** issued in 14th Century by Fernando I (1367-1383). Also called Dobra Gentil.


## GEORGE

**I.** - Gold coin (6.05 grams fine) of **Hanover** in 18th Century with name of Elector George, King of England. Exchange rate 4.66 Thaler.

**II.** - Name given to 5 Dollar gold coin in **Canada** in 1912.


## *GEORGIA*

Greek, Persian, Arab, Byzantine monies.

**10th Century** - Local minting of coins imitating Byzantine and Arab monies.

**15th Century** - See *Turkey.*

**18th Century** - Circulation of Chaouri (silver coins), and of Carbequi (copper coins):
    1 Piastre = 10.50 Chaouri
    1 Chaouri = 1/4 Abbasis, 1/2 Usalton, or 10 Carbequi (As-
            pers)

**1802** (October 21st) - In Georgia annexed by Russia, minting of monies conforming to early types: Abbasis of 20 Kopeks (issued until 1833), Grocheviki, Deniejki and Kopek (minted until 1810).

Subsequent use of Russian monetary system. - See *Ruble.*

## GERMAN EAST AFRICA

See *Tanganyika.*

## GERMANY

For monetary history of German states before 19th Century, see *Holy Roman Empire, Hamburg, Bavaria, Prussia, Saxony...*

**1807** (December 7th) - Introduction of French monetary system in Westphalia. Minting of gold coins of 40, 20, 10 and 5 Francs and silver pieces of 5, 2 and 1 Franc.

**1838** (July 30th) - Dresden Convention attempted to link together various German monetary systems on silver standard basis.

**1857** (January 24th) - Germanic Monetary Agreement made silver Thaler monetary unit of North German Confederation. - See *Thaler.* Fixed relationship established between Thaler (money of Northern States), Gulden (Guilder) (money of Southern States) and Austrian Gulden. - See *Guilder, Gulden* and *Gulden Austria.*

**1871** (December 4th) - Law creating 10 and 20 Mark gold coins. Suspension of minting of silver coinage. Its replacement and redemption at rate of 10 new Marks for 3.33 Thaler, 5.50 Gulden, 8 Marks, or 5.33 Schillings of Hamburg and Lubeck. - See *Mark.*

**1873** (July 12th) - Law establishing gold standard as monetary base of Mark.

**1923** (October 15th) - After collapse of Mark, creation of a money guaranteed by a gold-linked mortgage on landed properties. - See *Rentenmark.*

**1924** (August 30th) - Law establishing Reichsmark equal to 1 Rentenmark or 1 trillion paper Mark. - See *Reichsmark.*

**1948** (June 20th) - With collapse of inflated Reichsmark, currency reform declared. Western Occupation zones exchanged banknotes and substituted Deutsche Mark at rate of 1 for 10. - See *Mark German Federal Republic.* Russian zone created Ostmark. - See *Mark Coupon* and *Mark German Democratic Republic.* For money in Berlin, see *Berlin.*

## GERMANY EAST

See *Mark Coupon, Mark German Democratic Republic* and *Berlin.*

## GERMANY WEST

See *Mark German Federal Republic.*

## GHANA

Predecessor - See *Gold Coast.*

**1957** (March 6th) - Gold Coast became independent Republic of Ghana. Monetary unit remained West African Pound. - See *Pound West Africa.*

**1958** (July 14th) - Ghana Pound issued by Bank of Ghana to replace West African Pound at par. - See *Pound Ghana.*

**1965** (July 19th) - Creation of new monetary unit. - See *Cedi.*


## GHRUSH

**I.** - A silver money of **Turkey** in 18th and 19th Centuries. - See *Piastre Turkey.*
Variation of name - Grouch, Grush, Gurush.

**II.** - In **Turkey**, a silver/copper coin called Gersch. Valued at 40 Paras.
**20th Century** - See *Kurus.*

**III.** - In **Egypt**, a silver/copper coin valued at 40 Medinos.


## GIBRALTAR

**Until 1704** - Spanish monies. - See *Spain.*

**1704** - Simultaneous use of Spanish and English monies.

**1842** - Issue of copper coins of 2, 1 and ½ Quarto conforming to Spanish type.

**1889 to 1895** - Postal use of Peseta of 100 Centimos. - See *Peseta.*

**1914** - Issue of local banknotes on basis of Pound Sterling. - See *Pound Gibraltar.*

**1936** - Demonetization of Spanish monies. Official exchange rate applicable only to banknotes issued by local government (banknotes of Bank of England withdrawn from circulation), and to British silver coins.


## GIGLIATO

In **Italy** and countries under Italian influence, monies bearing fleur de lis.
Origin of name - Italian *giglio* (lily).
Variation of name - Gillat (in French).

**I.** - Money issued in **Naples** and **Sicily** in 1304 by Charles II of Anjou (called Carlino of Majesty). Issued again in 15th Century (called Alfonsino).

**II.** - Name for **Florentine** Zecchino. - See *Zecchino.*

**III.** - In **Rhodes,** money circulating in 14th Century as ¹/₁₀ Zecchino (Sequin), or ²/₃ Bezant. Worth 2 Aspers, 16 Carats, or 32 Deniers.

**IV.** - Also circulated in **Chios.**

## *GILBERT AND ELLICE ISLANDS*

**1892** - Proclaimed British Protectorate. Use of British monetary system. - See *Pound.*

**20th Century** - Use of Australian monetary system. - See *Pound Australia.*

**1941** (December) - Japanese Occupation. Temporary use of Japanese Military Yen. - See *Gumpyo.*

**1943** (November) - Allied liberation and return to Australian monetary system.

## GIORGINO

**I.** - In Republic of **Genoa** in 1668, silver money with imprint of Saint George. Worth 1 Lira 6 Soldi. Weight: 5.9 grams 864 fine, or 5.1 grams fine silver.

Variation of name - Georgine (in French).

**II.** - In **Modena,** silver/copper coin in 1598 with imprint of Saint Geminian. Worth 5 Soldi.

## GIULIO

**Italian** money bearing name of Pope Julius.

Variation of name - Jules (French).

**I.** - In **Papal States,** silver coin minted in 16th Century, then unit of account as well as silver/copper coin. Also called Paolo. - See *Paolo.*

**II.** - In Grand Duchy of **Tuscany,** unit of account and silver/copper coin equivalent to Paolo.

**III.** - In **Bologna,** unit of account and silver/copper coin equivalent to Paolo.

## GIUSTINA

In **Venice** and in **Italian States** under Venetian influence, silver money with imprint of Saint Giustina, patron of Venice.

**I.** - Name often given to Ducatono, silver money of **Venice.** Giustina Maggiore, issued about 1580, had 8 Lire as exchange rate. Giustina Minore had exchange rate of 6 Lire 4 Soldi. - See *Ducaton.*

**II.** - In **Bologna,** Giustina (or Giustino) was silver money worth 26 Soldi in 18th Century.

## GIZZI PENNY

Slender, hand forged, twisted iron rod, 15 to 18 inches long, used as early money of Gizzi (Kissi) tribe in **West Africa.** Still used to limited extent. If broken, "soul" escaped and money became worthless, only exception being when high priest broke it for small transactions.


## *GOA*

See *Portuguese India.*


## *GOLD COAST*

Includes Ashanti (from 1896), Northern Territories (from 1901), British Cameroons (from 1916), and British Togoland (from 1920).

**Early native monies** - Bars of iron flattened at ends (20 centimeters long); Cowrie shells imported from Maldive Islands by gold and slave traders.

**17th Century** - Introduction of specie monies of Netherlands in Dutch coastal settlements. - See *Netherlands.*

**1796** and **1818** - Mintings of silver Ackey of 8 Takoe.

**1821** - Introduction of British specie monies and Maria Theresia Thalers. - See *Maria Theresia Thaler.*

**1886** - Became British Protectorate. Monetary system of United Kingdom. - See *Pound.*

**1913** - Newly formed West African Currency Board minted special silver coinage for British West Africa. - See *Pound West Africa.*

**1957** (March) - Bank of Ghana established as Central Bank.

**1957** (March 6th) - Gold Coast became independent Republic of Ghana. Monetary unit remained West African Pound. - See *Ghana.*


## **GOLD UNIT**

Unit created in **China** for calculation and collection of customs duties.

Variation of name - Custom Gold Unit.

Predecessors - Until February 1, 1930, customs duties collected and Chinese foreign trade statistics maintained in Tael Haikuan. - See *Tael.*

**1930** (February 1st) - Introduction of customs unit of account on gold basis:
  1 Gold Unit = 601.886 milligrams of fine gold
  1 Gold Unit = 0.40 U.S. Dollars

**1931** - Issue of banknotes denominated in Gold Units, covered 100% by United States Dollars.
  Variable relationship between Gold Unit and Chinese Dollar according to price of silver and exchange rate for United States Dollar.

**1933** (March 8th) - Adoption of Chinese Dollar as common monetary unit. - See *Dollar China.*

**1935** (November 3rd) - Monetary reform. Gold standard abandoned.

## GOLD YUAN

Former monetary unit of **China**. Divided into 100 Cents.

Predecessor - See *Dollar China*.

**1948** (August 19th) - After galloping inflation and collapse of Chinese Dollar (12 million Chinese Dollars = 1 United States Dollar on the free market) creation of new monetary unit called Gold Yuan (Gold Dollar).

  1 Gold Yuan = 3 million Chinese Dollars
  1 Gold Yuan = 222 milligrams of fine gold
  1 U.S. Dollar = 4.05 Gold Yuan

**1948** (November 11th) - Devaluation of Gold Yuan:

  1 U.S. Dollar = 20.00 Gold Yuan

Establishment of exchange clearance certificate system (all foreign currency receipts surrendered to Central Bank in exchange for negotiable clearance certificates denominated in U.S. Dollars).

**1949** (February) - Creation of Customs Yuan, worth 0.40 U.S. Dollars, for collection of customs receipts.

**1949** (May 18th) - Exchange clearance certificate system replaced by exchange deposit certificates issued in amount of 80% of all foreign exchange deposited. Exchange deposit certificates freely negotiable.

**1949** (September) - After galloping inflation, final collapse of Gold Yuan. On the free market:

  1 U.S. Dollar = 425 million Gold Yuan

**1949** (September 21st) - Communist victory. Issue of new monetary unit. - See *Jen Min Piao*. On Taiwan (Formosa), adoption of independent monetary unit. - See *Dollar Taiwan*.

## GOURDE

**I.** - Name given to silver Spanish Piaster and Mexican Piaster circulating in **Antilles** and **Mexico**. - See *Piaster Spain, Piaster Mexico*.

Origin of name - Spanish *gordo*, (fat, thick).

**1732** - Newly minted Piasters, accepted at nominal value, called heavy Piaster or Peso Gordo (Gourde). Earlier minted Piasters accepted only by weight. - See *Piaster Mexico*.

**Beginning of 19th Century** - Cutting of Gourdes into pieces called Mocos. - See *Mocos*.

**1817** - Demonetization of Mocos.

**II.** - Monetary unit of **Haiti**. - See *Gourde Haiti*.

## GOURDE HAITI

Monetary unit of **Haiti**. Divided into 100 Centimes, or Centièmes.

Origin of name - See *Gourde*.

Bank of issue - Banque Nationale d'Haiti in 1880, followed by Banque Nationale de la République d'Haiti (National Bank of Republic of Haiti) in 1910, which was first controlled by Banque d'Union Parisienne, then by National City Bank of New York. Returned to Haiti in 1935.

Predecessors - See *Haiti, Piaster Gourde.*

**1814** (June 30th) - Minting of silver Gourde.

**1817** (July 1st) - Demonetization of all existing paper money issued by government.

**1817** (August 4th) - Minting of silver Gourde having reduced fineness (666).

**1822-1843** - Minting of silver coins of 6, 12 and 25 Centimes.

**1826** (September 25th) - Decree ordering new issue of paper money in denominations of 1, 2 and 5 Gourdes (beginning in 1827, of 10 Gourdes).

**1841** - Depreciation of banknotes by two-thirds. Numerous counterfeits.

**1842** (August 6th) - Order calling for exchange of 10 Gourde banknotes for half-value against banknotes of 1 and 2 Gourde denominations, and for half-value against customs vouchers. Further depreciation of banknotes that remained in circulation.

**1843-1880** - Minting of Centimes in copper, then bronze.

**1869** - Runaway inflation, and severe depreciation:
1 U.S. Dollar = 4,000 Gourdes

**1870** - Demonetization and exchange of banknotes of 5, 10 and 20 Gourdes:
1 new Gourde = 10 old Gourdes

**1872** (August 26th) - Withdrawal from circulation of all paper money on basis of:
1 heavy silver Gourde = 300 paper Gourdes
1 U.S. Dollar = 1 heavy silver Gourde

**1873** (May 15th) - Withdrawal of banknotes from circulation completed.

**1880** (September 28th) - Gourde defined in gold replaced silver Gourde:
1 Gourde = 5 Francs
1 Gourde = 1,451.6 milligrams of fine gold
De facto inconvertibility of paper money.
Silver coin of 5 Gourdes linked to French 5 Franc coin: 25 grams 900 fine, or 22.5 grams fine silver.

**1880** - Banque Nationale d'Haiti established as banknote-issuing authority.

**1892** - Beginning of massive issues of paper money.

**1905** - Depreciation of currency. Premium for gold rose to over 500%.

**1910** (October 21st) - Banknote issue entrusted to Banque Nationale de la République d'Haiti.

**1915** (September 16th) - Agreement between Haiti and United States linked Gourde to U.S. Dollar:
1 Gourde = 300.92 milligrams of fine gold
1 U.S. Dollar = 5.00 Gourdes

**1916** - Banque Nationale de la République d'Haiti controlled by National City Bank of New York.

**1916-1919** - Fiduciary paper money replaced by new banknote issue.

**1922** - Banque Nationale de la République d'Haiti became an affiliate of National City Bank of New York.

**1934** (February) - Devaluation parallel to that of U.S. Dollar:
   1 Gourde = 177.734 milligrams of fine gold
   1 U.S. Dollar = 5.00 Gourdes

**1935** - Banque Nationale de la République d'Haiti sold to government of Haiti by National City Bank of New York.

**1951** (August 20th) - Agreement between Haiti and United States confirming parity of 1934.

**1954** (April 9th) - Parity of 1934 registered with International Monetary Fund.

**1958-1970** - Although there was no black market for the Gourde, premiums of up to 10%-15% had been offered for "Payments New York." Gourde in New York quoted at 5.71-5.88 per U.S. Dollar.


# GRACE

Silver/copper money of Grand Duchy of **Tuscany** in 18th and 19th Centuries. Equal to 5 Quattrini.


# GRANO

**I.** - Unit of account and specie money of **Malta** during domination of Island by Knights of Malta (1530 to 1798) and in 19th Century.

Origin of name - Italian *Grano,* meaning grain. It was a unit of weight and a subdivision of gros, mark and livre.

Variation of name - Grain.

Plural - Grani.

**Until 1730** - Worth 1/20 Tarin, 1/10 Carlino, 1/5 Cinquina, or 6 Piccioli.

**After 1730** - 240 Grani equalled 1 Scudo (Ecu), 20 equalled 1 Tarin, 10 equalled 1 Carlino, and 12/3 equalled 1 Picciolo.

**18th Century** - Grano worth 6 Deniers.
   Specie coins ranging from 1/2 Grano to 15 Grani. Minted in copper beginning in 16th Century.

**II.** - Unit of account and silver coin in **Naples** until 1865. Grano was worth 1/100 Ducato, 1/20 Tarin, 1/10 Carlino, or 2 Tornesi, 3 Quattrini, 12 Cavalli 12 Denari.

**III.** - In **Sicily,** unit of account worth 1/600 Oncia, 1/240 Scudo, 1/120 Fiorino, 1/20 Tarin, 1/10 Carlino, or 6 Piccioli. Grano of Sicily, minted in copper, worth 1/2 Grano of Naples. Unified monetary system between Naples and Sicily in 1828.

**IV.** - Money of Kingdom of **Two Sicilies** until 1860, worth 1/100 Ducato or 3 Tornesi.

**V.** - Submultiple of **Mexican** Piaster (1/32) and of Real (1/4) until 1861. Also a copper coin.

Variation of name - Cuartilla.

# GRAVE

Silver money of **Portugal** issued by Fernando I (1367-1383). Worth 3 Dinheiros.

## *GREAT BRITAIN*

See *England.*

## *GREECE*

**Primitive monies** - Cattle. In Sparta until 3rd Century, bars and iron money.

**7th Century B.C.** - Minting of first coins, called Staters, in electrum (alloy of gold and silver) generally being 700 fine gold: in Lydia by King Gyges; in Ionia (Ephesus, Miletus). - See *Stater.*

**6th Century B.C.** - Simultaneous use of two Greek systems of accounting (that of Aegina and that of Euboea), dividing Talent into Minas, Drachmae and Obols. - See *Mina.*
Minting of silver Drachma, hereafter basic coin of Greek monetary system. Multiples - Didrachm, Tetradrachm, Tridrachm, . . .etc. - See *Drachma.*

**5th Century B.C.** - Gold Darics, minted by Persians and introduced by mercenaries, circulated in Greece.

**356 B.C.** - In Macedonia, owing to mines of Mount Pangaeus, Philip minted gold Stater that overran Greece along with Macedonians.

**4th Century B.C.** - Rhodes, after Ptolemies in Egypt, divided Mina of Aegina into 100 Drachmae, thus reducing weight of Drachma.

**2nd Century B.C.** - Roman Denarius replaced Drachma. - See *Denarius* and *Rome.*

**5th Century** - See *Byzantium.*

**13th Century** - Latins of Morea, of Duchy of Athens, etc., introduced their monies: the Denier Tournois of French type, Obol, etc.

**14th Century** - In Rhodes and Chios, monies copied from those of Venice (Zecchino, Grosso), Byzantium (Bezant) and Turkey (Asper). - See *Sequin* and *Zecchino.*

**15th Century** - See *Turkey.*

**18th Century** - Turkish monies. On islands belonging to Republic of Venice, accounting system based on Reale of 10 Lira, 100 Soldi or 100 Aspers.
Specie monies⁻ on same islands were coins of Venice. - See *Venice.*

**1828** - Independent Greece established national silver money, Phoenix of 100 Lepta. - See *Phoenix.*

**1838** - Drachma reintroduced, replacing Phoenix. - See *Drachma.*

## GREENLAND

Danish monetary system. - See *Denmark* and *Krone Denmark.*
Concurrent circulation of local banknotes (from 5 to 10 Kroner) and divisionary coinage (from 25 Oere to 5 Kroner).
**1967** (July 1st) - Greenland notes and coins withdrawn from circulation and replaced by Danish money.

## GREGORINA

Gold coin of **Papal States** minted by Gregory XVI beginning in 1835. Weight 8.66 grams 900 fine. Value: 5 Scudi.

## GRENADINO

Monetary unit of early **Colombia** from 1847 to 1871, simultaneous with Peso. Silver coin with same weight as Spanish Piaster. Divided into 8 Reales.

## GRIFFON

Silver money of the **Netherlands** issued in 1487 by Maximilian of Austria, and worth ¼ Real.
Origin of name - From imprint of a griffon holding a sword.

## GRIMELLIN

Unit of account in **Tripoli** in 18th and 19th Centuries. Equivalent of ¹⁄₁₃ Piastre, or 4 Aspers.
Variations of name - Grimelin, Grimellino.
Plural- Grimellini.

## GRIVNA

I. - In **Russia,** before 15th Century (?), gold, silver and silver/copper monies. Gold Grivna worth 6 silver Grivenki or 24 silver/copper Grivenki. First types were oblong and in silver. In 1701, Grivna appeared in form of round silver coin. In 1726, minting of copper Grivna. Circulated in 18th, 19th and beginning of 20th Century.
Variations of name - Grivennik, Griwne, Grive, Grif.
Plural - Grivenki.

**II.** - In **Ukraine,** from 1919 to 1923, equal to ½ Ruble.

## GROAT

**I.** - Early **English** silver money.

Origin of name - From French Gros. - See *Gros.*

**1299** - Minting of Groat in silver by Edward I. Worth 4 Pence or 4 Deniers. Debasements. - See *Penny.*

**1543** - Henry VIII reduced weight and fineness of Groat from 2.72 grams 425 fine, or 2.52 grams fine silver to 2.59 grams 833 fine, or 2.16 grams fine silver.

**1551** - Exchange rate reduced to 3 Pence (April 3rd), then to 2 Pence (July).

**1561** - Exchange rate raised back to 4 Pence.

**End of 18th Century** - Groat was still small silver coin worth 4 Pence.

**19th Century** - Groat, worth 4 Pence, was silver coin weighing 1.88 grams 925 fine, or 1.74 grams fine silver.

**II.** - **Irish** silver money, progressively reduced in weight in 15th Century from 2.92 grams (1465) to 2 grams (1483).

**III.** - Silver money of **Scotland** issued in 1358.

**IV.** - Silver coin in **British Guiana** (1888) and in **British West Indies.**

## GROCHEVIK

**Russian** coin of 2 Kopeks. Issued in copper in 1655 at forced parity against silver coins. Rapidly depreciated to ¼ of its former value in 1662 and to ¹/₁₅ in 1663, when it was withdrawn from circulation.

## GROOT

**I.** - Early money of the **Netherlands.** In method of accounting derived from Carolingian system, Livre consisted of 20 Schelling (Sols) or 240 Grooten. Groot equivalent to Denier.

Origin of name - See *Gros.*

Plural - Grooten.

**14th Century** - Groot was silver money in Flanders, Brabant, Hainaut, Holland.

**1300** - Minting of Groot used by Flanders and Brabant.

**1355** - In accounting system using Guilder (Florin), Groot equal to ¹/₄₀ Guilder (Florin). Simultaneous existence of two systems, Livre and Guilder (Florin).

**1364** - Double Grooten (2 Grooten coin) called silver Livre or Botdrager.

**1384** - For five years use of monies common to both Flanders and Brabant: Groot and

Double Groot, minted in gold and called Roosebeker (crown of roses).

**15th Century** - Minting of silver Groot in various states of Netherlands.

**1420** - The Double Groot, or Dreilander, common to three countries.

**1474** - Charles the Bold minted Groot or 1/2 Briquet. Double Groot was called Briquet.

**1520** - Charles V minted silver Groot.

**18th Century** - Groot worth 1/240 Livre (Pondt Vlaams), 1/40 Guilder (Florin), 1/12 Schelling, 1/2 Stuyver, 8 Penning (Deniers), and in Brabant, 24 Myten.

**II.** - Unit of account in **Bremen** and **Oldenburg.** Minted in silver in 1429.

**18th Century** - Groot worth 1/72 Thaler, 4 Pfennig, or 5 Schwaren.

**19th Century** - Groot worth 1/72 gold Thaler (Louis d'Or), or Pistole.


# GROS

Early unit of account and silver specie money in numerous countries. Patterned after Gros of Saint Louis, first heavy silver money of the West.

Origin of name - Vulgar Latin *grossus* (gros): Gros was exceptionally heavy money at its inception.

Variations of name - In Germany, *Groschen;* in Netherlands, *Groot;* in Poland and Russia, *Grosz;* in Italy and Portugal, *Grosso.*

**I.** - In **France,** silver money from 13th to 18th Century.

**1266** (August 15th) - Saint Louis minted Gros Tournois, heavy silver coin (4.22 grams 957 fine, or 4.04 grams fine). Exchange rate: 1 Sou Tournois, or 12 Deniers. Subsequent minting of other Gros varieties in countries of Holy Roman Empire (Lorraine, Flanders, Burgundy).

**1290** - Exchange rate of Gross increased to 13 Deniers.

**1295** - Exchange rate of Gros raised to 15 Deniers.

**1303** (August 15th) - Weight of Gros lowered to 3.03 grams fine silver, and exchange rate raised to 26 Deniers.

**1305** (June 21st) - Exchange rate of Gros of Saint Louis (4.04 grams of fine silver) raised to 39.375 Deniers.

**1306** (June 8th) - Exchange rate of Gros lowered to 1 Sou. Repudiation of Gros of 1303.

**1308** - Exchange rate of Gros: 13.125 Deniers.

**1311** - Exchange rate of Gros: 15 Deniers.

**1313** - Exchange rate of Gros: 1 Sou.

**1316** - Exchange rate of Gros: 15 Deniers.

**1326** - Exchange rate of Gros: 15 Deniers, raised by general public to as high as 25 Deniers (1328).

**1330** - Gros of 3.90 grams of silver worth 12 Deniers.

**1329-1349** - Under Philip VI, numerous changes in Gros: fineness reduced to 500 (Gros au Lis in 1341; Gros à la Queue in 1349); exchange rate raised to 60 Deniers (in 1343).

**1337** - Creation of Gros à la Couronne. - See *Crown.*

**1355** - Minting of Gros à la Queue by Jean the Good. Exchange rate: 15 Deniers.

**1360** - Maximum debasement of Gros to fineness of 125 (Gros à la Couronne). Exchange rate of Gros Blanc: 15 Deniers.

**1361** (April 10th) - Gros, containing 2.79 grams of pure silver, worth 15 Deniers or 1 Sou Parisis. Fineness of coin often modified.

**1369** (August 2nd) - Minting of a pure silver Gros (2.44 grams) equal to 15 Deniers.

**1385** (March 11th) - Minting of Gros discontinued.

**1411** (June 7th) - Minting of a Gros au Lis (2.79 grams 971 fine, or 2.71 grams fine silver). Exchange rate: 1 Livre.

**1411** (September 5th) - Weight of Gros, maintained at value of 1 Livre, raised to 3.76 grams 750 fine, or 2.82 grams find silver.

**1420** - Minting of Gros Heaumé by English in France: 2.84 grams 958 fine, or 2.72 grams fine silver. Exchange rate: 20 Deniers.

**1422** - Creation of Gros Blanc, worth 19 Deniers Tournois, by Charles VII; weight and fineness subjected to frequent variations.

**17th Century** - Some silver/copper Gros, minted at Dôle and Besancon, circulated in Franche-Comté until reunited with France (1678). Exchange rate: 10 Deniers.

**18th Century** - Gros still circulated in Lorraine. Exchange rate: 10 Deniers.

**II.** - Gros of Saint Louis became international money of **Europe.** Copied in numerous countries (end of 13th, 14th and 15th Centuries):
  - In **Switzerland:** Vaud, Lausanne. . .
  - In **Luxemburg:** corresponded to $1/22$ Guilder (Florin) in 1424.
  - In **Netherlands:** see *Groot.*
  - In **Scotland** (appeared in 1358). - See *Groat.*
  - In **Holy Roman Empire** and the German states (see *Groschen* ). First Imperial Gros under Henry VII (1308-13), Saxony (14th Century), Brandenburg (1463).
  - In **Austria** (under Frederick III).
  - In **Bohemia** minted in 1300 by Wenceslaus II from Gros of Prague, similar to Gros Tournois. Became prototype money. Minted in 16th Century in Joachimsthal. - See *Joachimsthaler.*
  - In **Hungary** (14th Century).
  - In **Poland:** Casimir the Great (1333-1370) imitated Gros of Prague in Cracow (see *Grosz* ).
  - In **Prussia** (Teutonic Order), free circulation of Gros of Prague and Cracow. Minting of Gros worth 3 Schillings or 36 Pfennig at end of 15th Century.
  - In **Spain,** under name of Real.
  - In **Portugal:** Alfonso V (1438-1481) issued silver Gros, or Alfonsin.
  - In **Italy:** Genoa (1458 to 1461); Savoy and Piedmont adopted French type Gros (14th Century); Asti.
  - In **Levant** as result of Crusades: in Cyprus, Rhodes, Syria.

**III.** - For **Venice** and other **Italian** states, see *Grosso.*

**IV.** - For **Russia,** see *Grosz.*

## GROSCHEL

Copper money of various **German** states in 18th Century.

Oirgin of name - Derived from French *Gros,* German *Groschen.* - See *Gros.*

I. - In **Austria,** Groschel worth $1/80$ Gulden (Florin), or $1/4$ Groschen. Corresponded to 3 Pfennig or 6 Heller.

II. - In **Silesia,** Groschel worth $1/96$ Thaler, and corresponded to 3 Deniers.

## GROSCHEN

I. - **German** silver money, then of silver/copper. Also unit of account.

Origin of name - German diminutive *(chen)* of French *Gros.* - See *Gros.*

**1296** - Imitating Gros Tournois, silver Groschen minted in Bohemia as heavy money in relation to debased Pfennig (Denier). Weight: 4.25 grams 940 fine, or 4 grams fine silver.

**1378** - Debasement and depreciation of Groschen. Weight: 3.34 grams 868 fine, or 2.9 grams fine silver.

**1490** - Weight of Groschen reduced to 2.27 grams 308 fine, or 0.70 grams fine silver. Minting of new, heavier silver coins in Saxony worth one gold Florin (Gulden), and called Guldengroschen. - See *Guldengroschen.*

**1524** - In monetary system of Charles V, Groschen weighed 1.7 grams 765 fine, or 1.3 fine silver. Equivalent to $1/21$ Reichsgulden, a new, heavy silver coin (29.2 grams 935 fine, or 27.3 grams fine silver), or 4 Kreuzer.
Saxon variation - Mariengroschen, or Gros of Virgin Mary, equal to $2/3$ Groschen. - See *Mariengroschen.*

**1623** - Minting of new Groschen in Saxony: Gute Groschen equal to $1/24$ Thaler or 12 Pfennig. - See *Gute Groschen.*
As a unit of account, Groschen was worth $1/30$ Thaler or 12 Pfennig in Southern and Western States (Austria, Bavaria, Swabia, Franconia, Rhineland) which kept accounts in Thaler, Groschen and Pfennig.
Valued at $1/20$ Guilder (Guilden), or 3 Kreuzer in Eastern States (Saxony. . .) which kept accounts in Guilder (Guilden), Kreuzer and Pfennig.

**1667** - Decisions of Conference of Zinna (electoral Saxony, Brandenburg, Brunswick-Lüneburg): silver coin equal to $2/3$ Thaler corresponded to 16 Gute Groschen or 24 Mariengroschen.

**1690** - Decisions of Conference of Leipzig (electoral Saxony, Brandenburg, Brunswick-Lüneburg): Gute Groschen corresponded to $1/24$ Thaler or 12 Pfennig.

**1693** - Application of Decisions of Leipzig to entire Holy Roman Empire (except in Hamburg and Lübeck).

**1753** - Convention of Vienna defined silver Groschen as worth 3 Kreuzer.

**18th Century** - As a unit of account, Groschen worth $1/30$ Livre or 12 Pfennig in Brandenburg (bank money), $1/24$ Reichsthaler or 16 Heller in Hesse-Kassel, $1/20$ Guilden in Upper Palatinate (Heidelberg), $1/30$ Guilden or 18 Pfennig in Prussia

(Königsberg), 1/164 Livre, 1/4 Schilling, 3 Regensburger or 15 Heller in Regensburg (for payment of taxes and fines).

Silesian variation - See *Silbergroschen.*

Bremen variation - See *Groot.*

In Austria and Bavaria, Groschen worth 3 Kreuzer. Austrian 1/2 Groschen called Pultura.

**19th Century -** Groschen worth 1/30 Thaler or 12 (then 10) Pfennig in Brunswick and Hanover in North German Confederation until 1871.

Variations - Silbergroschen, worth 1/30 Thaler or 12 Pfennig in Anhalt. Mariengroschen, worth 1/36 Thaler or 8 Pfennig in Brunswick (Hanover before 1817). Neugroschen worth 1/30 Thaler or 10 Pfennig in Saxony.

**II. -** Submultiple of Schilling (1/100), monetary unit of **Austria.** - See *Schilling Austria.*


## GROSCHLEIN

Under monetary system of Charles V (Ordinance of Essling of 1524), silver money circulating in the **Holy Roman Empire.** Worth 1/4 Groschen or 1/84 Guilder (Florin).


## GROSSETO

**I. -** Silver coin and unit of account in **Venice,** corresponding to Denaro de Ducato.

Origin of name - Diminutive of Grosso. - See *Gros.*

Plural - Grosseti.

**14th Century -** As silver coin, Grosseto replaced Matapan. Value: 4 Soldi.

**18th Century-** 2.32 Grosseti required for 1 Soldo or Marchetto, 12 Grosseti for 1 Grosso, 46.4 Grosseti for 1 Lira, 288 Grosseti for 1 Ducato (Ducat). In records of Bank of Venice, 2.88 Grosseti equivalent to 1 Lira grossa. Grosseto equalled 5.6 Denari de Lira.

**II. -** In Republic of **Ragusa,** silver money and unit of account from 16th to 18th Century.


## GROSSO

Silver money, then unit of account. Originated in **Venice,** and imitated in **Italian States** and **Near East.**

Origin of name - See *Gros.*

Plural - In Italian, *Grossi.*

**I. -** In **Venice,** silver money, then unit of account. Sometimes called Matapan, Matagan, or Matopan.

**1192 -** Doge Enrico Dandolo created Grosso of 2.1 grams of silver. Exchange rate: 26 Piccioli.

**1278** - Grosso raised to 28 Piccioli.

**1282** - Grosso raised to 32 Piccioli.

**1350** - Grosso raised to 48 Piccioli.

**1379** - Weight of Grosso lowered to 2 grams of silver.

**1399** - Weight of Grosso lowered to 1.8 grams of silver.

**1472** - Silver Grosso took the place of Lira de Piccioli which became specie money.

**18th Century** - Unit of account in Venice, Bergamo, Padua and Bassano: 3.87 Grossi needed for 1 Lira, 24 Grossi for 1 Ducato (Ducat), 240 Grossi for 1 Lira Grossa. Grosso equal to 5.166 Soldi (Marchetti), 12 Grosseti, or 62 Denari de Lira (Deniers).

**II.** - Name used after 1296 for silver Guilder (Florin) of **Florence.** - See *Guilder.*

**III.** - In **Rome,** silver money at first minted by Senate about 1255, then by Popes (Papal States); worth 5 Baiocci. Grosso Papalo (1/10 Ducato) was identical with Carliño.

**IV.** - In **Milan,** silver coin worth 1/2 Teston or 10 Soldi, issued in 1468.

**V.** - In **Genoa,** silver coin from 13th to 15th Century. Worth 4 Denari or 1/3 Soldo.

**VI.** - In **Sardinia,** silver money issued at end of 13th Century.

**VII.** - Imitation of Grosso of Venice in countries of **Near East:** In Bulgaria (13th Century), in Serbia (13th and 14th Centuries), in Albania (14th Century), in Ragusa (13th to 16th Century), in Walachia (14th Century), in Armenia (12th to 14th Century under name of Tahégan), in Rhodes and Chios (14th Century).

**VIII.** - In **Portugal,** silver coin minted in 15th Century by Alfonso V (also called Alfonsin). The 1/2 Grosso was called Chimfram. - See *Chimfram.*


## GROSSONE

Silver coin of various **Italian States** in 13th and 14th Centuries.

Origin of name - Derived from Grosso. - See *Gros.*

Variation of name - Grossono.

**I.** - Name used for silver Guilder (Florin) of **Florence** after 1296. - See *Guilder.*

**II.** - Name given to silver Lira issued in **Milan** in 1474. - See *Testone.*

**III.** - Money in **Venice,** issued in 1423 by Francesco Foscari, equal to 8 Soldi.


## GROSZ

**I.** - Unit of account in early **Russia.** Equal to 1/50 Ruble and worth 2 Kopeks, 4 Dengi, or 8 Poluschkas.

**II.** - Early money of **Poland** in silver, then copper.

Origin of name - Variation of Gros. - See *Gros.*

Variation of name - Groszy.

Predecessor - See *Poland.*

Plural - Grosze.

**13th Century** - King Wenceslaus II issued silver Grosz.

**14th Century** - Casimir the Great issued silver Grosz, imitating Gros of Prague, divided into Deniers.

**1526** - Sigismund I strengthened Grosz and Denier.

**1623** - Alteration of fineness of Grosz.

**1650** - Minting of lighter Grosz.

**1764** - Grosz minted in copper.

**1785** - Before partition of Poland, Grosz simultaneously unit of account ($1/30$ Florin Zloty) and divisionary specie money (1.95 grams of copper). As unit of account, worth 12 Deniers. As specie money, divided into 4 Szelong.

**1810-1813** - Minting of copper Grosz by Grand Duchy of Warsaw.

**1815** - Minting of 3 Grosze copper coins for Russian Kingdom of Poland, of 5 and 10 Grosze copper coins for Republic of Cracow.

**1922 and 1924** - Creation of new Zloty. - See *Zloty*.

**III.** - Submultiple ($1/100$) of Zloty, monetary unit of **Poland.**


## *GUADALOUPE*

See *French West Indies.*


## *GUAM*

**18th and 19th Centuries** - Spanish domination. Use of Spanish monies for trade transactions.

**1898** - Ceded to United States. Introduction of United States monetary system. - See *Dollar.*


## GUARANI

Monetary unit of **Paraguay** since 1943. Divided into 100 Centimos.

Origin of name - From the Guaraníes, native people of the banks of Paraguay River.

Bank of Issue - National Bank of Paraguay, organized in March 1943 and reorganized as Banco del Paraguay in September 1944. Banco Central del Paraguay (Central Bank of Paraguay) established on March 25, 1952.

Predecessors - See *Paraguay* and *Peso Paraguay.*

Plural - Guaraníes.

**1943** (October 5th) - Paraguayan Peso replaced by Guaraní.

    1 Guaraní = 100.00 Paraguayan Pesos
    1 U.S. Dollar = 3.09 Guaraníes

**1946** (December 18th) - Parity registered with International Monetary Fund:

    1 Guaraní = 287.595 milligrams of fine gold

        1 U.S. Dollar = 3.09 Guaraníes (3.059/3.121 buying and
           selling)

**1949** (November 5th) - Multiple rate structure established:
        1 U.S. Dollar = 3.059/3.121 Guaraníes (government re-
           ceipts and payments, essential imports)
        1 U.S. Dollar = 4.92/4.9821 Guaraníes (basic exports,
           capital goods imports)
        1 U.S. Dollar = 6.02/6.0821 Guaraníes (favored exports,
           various consumer imports)
        1 U.S. Dollar = 7.99/8.0521 Guaraníes (invisibles and
           capital, nonessential and luxury imports)
In addition, export rates burdened with taxes ranging up to 15%.

**1950** (April 11th) - Favored exports shifted to 7.99 Guaraníes per U.S. Dollar rate; 6.02 Guaraní rate now applied to miscellaneous exports. Imports classified into four categories, three of which subject to exchange taxes of from 2% to 10%, widening exchange rate structure to as high as 8.85732 Guaraníes per U.S. Dollar.

**1951** (March 5th) - Devaluation of Guaraní and regrouping of exchange rates:
        1 Guaraní = 148.112 milligrams of fine gold
        1 U.S. Dollar = 6.00 Guaraníes (government receipts and
           nontrade payments, basic exports and Category
           I imports)
        1 U.S. Dollar = 9.00 Guaraníes (other exports and Cate-
           gory II imports, registered capital and specified
           invisibles).
        1 U.S. Dollar = 19.00 Guaraníes (free market rate for other
           invisibles and nonregistered capital)
Taxes on sales of exchange removed, and export taxes raised to range of 11% to 33%.

**1951** (September) - Free market rate dropped to 36.00 Guaraníes per U.S. Dollar.

**1952** (March 25th) - Banco Central del Paraguay established as bank of issue and Central Bank.

**1952** (April) - Restrictions in free market. Controlled free rate established and pegged at 30.00 Guaraníes per U.S. Dollar.

**1952** (June 21st) - Emergency change in exchange system. Basic import rate devalued from 6.00 to 15.00 Guaraníes. Exchange surcharge of 6.00 Guaraníes, added to import rate, yielded effective rate of 21.00 Guaraníes for imports formerly affected at 9.00 Guaraní rate.

**1952** (August 1st) - Exchange reform completed:
        1 U.S. Dollar = 6.00 Guaraníes (government nontrade pay-
           ments)
        1 U.S. Dollar = 15.00 Guaraníes (Group I for all exports,
           essential imports)
        1 U.S. Dollar = 21.00 Guaraníes (Group II for semi-essen-
           tial imports)
        1 U.S. Dollar = 30.00 Guaraníes (Group III for nonessen-
           tial imports)

> 1 U.S. Dollar = 30.00 Guaranies (Controlled "Free" Market for invisibles and nonregistered capital)

**1952** (November 4th) - Controlled free market rate pegged at 49.00 Guaranies per U.S. Dollar.

**1953** (January 1st) - Imports regrouped. Multiple rates unchanged.

**1953** (September 23rd) - Fluctuating free market established. Controlled free market continued to function.

**1954** (January 1st) - New parity:
> 1 Guarani = 59.2447 milligrams of fine gold
> 1 U.S. Dollar = 15.00 Guaranies

Multiple rates varied from 15.00 to 54.00 Guaranies per U.S. Dollar. Controlled free rate reached 56.00 Guaranies, and fluctuating rate hit 61.00 Guaranies.

**1954** (August 10th) - Guarani devalued:
> 1 Guarani = 42.3176 milligrams of fine gold
> 1 U.S. Dollar = 21.00 Guaranies

Multiple exchange rates ranged from 27.00 to 73.70 Guaranies per U.S. Dollar.

**1954** - Controlled free market peg lowered 7 times from 56.00 to 63.30 Guaranies.

**1955** (June 15th) - Private gold holdings outlawed.

**1955** - During the year numerous changes made in multiple rate structure, both in terms of rates and groupings.

**1956** (February) - Obligation to declare gold and foreign exchange cancelled.

**1956** (March 1st) - New par value established:
> 1 Guarani = 14.8112 milligrams of fine gold
> 1 U.S. Dollar = 60.00 Guaranies

Exchange rate structure greatly simplified:
> 1 U.S. Dollar = 60.00 Guaranies (Group I for exports, essential imports, government receipts)
> 1 U.S. Dollar = 85.00 Guaranies (Group II for nonessential imports)
> 1 U.S. Dollar = 109.85/126.00 Guaranies (Fluctuating "Free" Market for other invisibles and capital)

**1957** (August 12th) - Exchange reform introduced. Official rate ceased to function for all practical purposes. Rate system based on fluctuating free market, initially 98.00 Guaranies per U.S. Dollar.

**1959** (February 10th) - Reintroduction of taxes and surcharges on exports and imports.

**1960** (October) - Fluctuating free rate stabilized at 123.60/126.00 Guaranies per U.S. Dollar.

**1964** (September) - Black market rate fell to all-time low of 164.00 Guaranies per U.S. Dollar, against 126.00 Guaranies per U.S. Dollar in official free market.

**1969-1970** - Guarani on black market hovered near 145.00 per U.S. Dollar.


## *GUATEMALA*

**16th to 19th Century** - Circulation of Spanish and Mexican Piasters.

**1701** - Establishment of a mint in Guatemala. Minting of Piasters.

**1821** - Revolted from Spain.

**1822** - Joined Mexican Empire.

**1823** - Loosely grouped into United Provinces of Central America. - See *Peso Central America.*

**1839** - Became independent Republic. Continued to use Central American Peso.

**1847** - Central American Peso replaced by Guatemalan Peso. - See *Peso Guatemala.*

**1925** (May 7th) - Substitution of Quetzal linked to U.S. Dollar for Peso. - See *Quetzal.*


## GUELFO

A variety of silver Guilder (Florin) of **Florence** after 1296. Value: 4 Soldi or ½ Popolino. - See *Guilder.*


## GUENAR

Silver coin issued in **France** in 14th Century.

**1385** (March 11th) - Creation of Guénar under Charles VI, destined to succeed Gros. Weight 3.26 grams, of which 1.63 grams was silver. Exchange rate 10 Deniers.

**1389** (September 11th) - Weight raised to 3.30 grams, of which 1.51 grams were silver.

**1411** (October 20th) - Weight lowered to 3.06 grams, of which 1.28 grams were silver.

**1417** (May 10th) - Weight maintained at 3.06 grams, but with 1.02 grams of silver. Exchange rate remained 10 Deniers.

**1417** (October 21st) - New reduction of fineness to 0.68 grams of silver.

**1415-1422** - Under Henry V, rival Guénar issued by the English.


## GUILDER

Originated in Florence, subsequently influenced Italian states (Savoy, Savona, Sicily, Montferrat. . .), German states (Holy Roman Empire, Austria, Switzerland, Luxembourg. . .), Netherlands and the rest of Europe (France, Aragon, England, Bohemia, Hungary, Poland, Denmark. . .).

Origin of name - English modification of Dutch word *Gulden* (gold).

Variations of name - Italian: *Fiorino,* French: *Florin,* German and Dutch: *Gulden,* Danish: *Gylden,* Hungarian: *Forint.*

**I.** - Money of **Florence** from 13th to 19th Century.

**1252** - With reappearance of gold in Western Europe, Florence minted gold Guilder (3.56 grams) worth 1 Lira, and silver Guilder (2.1 grams) worth 1 Soldo: 1 gold Guilder = 20 silver Guilders.
Evolution of these two coins:

| | GOLD GUILDERS | | SILVER GUILDERS | | |
| | Weight in Grams | Rate in Soldi | Weight in Grams | Rate in Soldi | Denari |
|---|---|---|---|---|---|
| 1252 | 3.5 | 20 | 2.1 | 1 | – |
| 1275 | 3.5 | 30 | 2.1 | 1 | – |
| 1296 | 3.5 | 40 | 1.9 | 2 | – |
| 1321 | 3.5 | 51 | 1.9 | 2 | – |
| 1324 | 3.5 | 60 | 1.9 | 2 | – |
| 1345 | 3.5 | 60 | 2.4 | 4 | – |
| 1356 | 3.5 | 70 | 2.4 | 4 | – |
| 1390 | 3.5 | 70 | 2.7 | 5 | 6 |
| 1422 | 3.5 | 80 | 2.7 | 5 | – |
| 1460 | 3.5 | 80 | 2.5 | 6 | 8 |
| 1462 | 3.5 | 87 | 2.5 | 6 | – |
| 1464 | 3.5 | 106 | 2.5 | 6 | – |
| 1489 | 3.5 | 106 | 2.2 | 6 | – |
| 1501 | 3.5 | 140 | 2.2 | 6 | – |
| 1503 | 3.5 | 140 | 3.4 | 7 | – |
| 1506 | 3.5 | 140 | 1.9 | 7 | – |
| 1531 | 3.5 | 150 | 1.8 | 7 | – |

**1296** - Silver Guilder called Grosso, Grossono, or Guelfo.

**1321** - Gold Guilder called Guilder of Public Seal (Fiorino di Sugello).

**1464** - Guilder became known as Large Guilder (Fiorino Largo).

**1531** - Name Ducato was applied to gold Guilder.

**18th Century** - Name Zecchino applied to gold Guilder.

**1826** - In Grand Duchy of Tuscany, silver Guilder worth 1.66 Lire, 2.5 Paoli, 100 Quattrini, or 400 Denari.

**II.** - In **Italian states,** gold money imitating or inspired by Fiorino (Guilder) of Florence or Zecchino of Venice.

- In Milan (13th Century), in Rome (1350).
- In Savoy, gold coin minted under Amadeus VI (1285-1323). Worth ½ Livre Tournois, it circulated until 1717.
- In Sicily, until Italian unification, unit of account equivalent to ⅕ Oncia, ½ Scudo, or 6 Tarin, 12 Carlini, 90 Ponti, 120 Grani, 720 Piccioli.
- In Trieste, under Austrian rule in the 18th and 19th Centuries, unit of account worth 5 Lire, 60 Crazia (Kreuzer), or 100 Soldi. Also minted in silver.

**III.** - In **Aragon,** minting of gold Guilder imitating the one of 14th Century Florence.

**IV.** - In **England,** gold, then silver money. - See *Florin.*

**V.** - For **Austria,** see *Gulden* and *Gulden Austria.*

**VI.** - In **Switzerland,** gold, then silver money and unit of account.

- In Basel, gold coin minted after 1429. As unit of account, Guilder (Gulden)

equivalent to 15 Batzen, 25 Blafferts, 60 Kreuzer, 150 Rappen, 300 Pfennig. Also silver coin (sometimes called Ecu).
- In Geneva, government and small businesses kept accounts in Guilders of 12 Sols, 48 Quarts and 144 Deniers.
- In Zurich and Saint Gall, Guilder worth 60 Kreuzer or 480 Heller (and, in Zurich: 40 Schillings; in Saint Gall: 10 Schillings or 15 Batzen).
- In Lucerne, Guilder equalled 40 Schillings.
- In Neuchatel, Guilder divided into 15 Batzen or 60 Kreuzer.
- Berne minted its first gold Guilder in 1479.

**VII.** - For **Hungary,** see *Gulden Hungary* and *Forint.*

**VIII.** - In **Bohemia,** Jean de Luxembourg (1309-1346) minted first gold Guilder.

**IX.** - For **Poland,** see *Florin Zloty,* and for **Danzig,** see *Gulden Danzig.*

**X.** - In **Denmark** and **Norway,** unit of account in 15th and 16th Centuries. Divided into 24 Skillings. Gold money minted at end of 15th Century and in 1513 (gold Guilder of Rhineland, or Rynske Gylden); silver money minted in 1516 (Sölvgylden).

**XI.** - In **Brazil** (1645-46), Dutch West Indies Company minted square gold coins worth 3, 6 and 12 Guilders (Gulden).

**XII.** - In **Liege, Maastricht,** and **Westphalia,** in 18th Century, gold money (5 Guilder coin) and unit of account equal to ¼ Patacon, 2 Schellings, 3 Stuyvers, 80 Oord, or 320 Penning.
- For other Guilder varieties, see the following:

## GUILDER INDONESIA

See *Guilder Netherlands East Indies.*

## GUILDER NETHERLANDS

Monetary unit of the **Netherlands.** First divided into 20 Stuyver, 40 Grooten, or 320 Pennengen or Penning, then from 18th Century divided into 100 Cents. The ¼ Guilder was called Kwartje; ¹⁄₁₀ Guilder, Dubbeltje; ¹⁄₂₀ Guilder, Stuyver).

Variation of name - *Gulden* (Dutch).

Bank of issue - By Bank of Amsterdam from 1609 to 1794 (constant premium of from 3% to 9% on banknotes over specie money), except during time of French invasions of 1672 and 1794; then by Nederlandsche Bank (Netherlands Bank) since 1814. Issue by Treasury of "Muntbiljetten" (banknotes of 1 and 2.5 Guilders, theoretically convertible into silver) beginning in 1914.

Predecessor - See *Netherlands.*

**14th Century** - Gold Guilder imitated that of Florence. Minted in Luxembourg (by Jean the Blind, 1309-1346), Hainaut (before 1345), Flanders, Brabant (before 1355), and Holland.

**1355** - Guilder became unit of account equal to ⅙ Livre, 20 Stuyver, or 40 Grooten.

**1466** - Philip the Good minted Guilder of Bourgogne, gold coin worth 41 Grooten.

**1467** - Charles the Bold raised exchange rate for Guilder of Bourgogne to 42 Grooten.

**1487** - Maximilian of Austria fixed rate of exchange of Guilder of Bourgogne at 4 Reales.

**1496** - Philip the Fair minted Guilder Philippus with image of Saint Philip.

**1520** - Charles V lowered exchange rate for Guilder to 40 Grooten.

**15th to 18th Century** - As unit of account, Guilder divided into 20 Patards or 320 Penning. As specie money, minted in gold and in silver. Ratio of Guilder of account to specie monies:

|  | In grams of fine gold | In grams of fine silver |
|---|---|---|
| 1489 (December 14th) .......... | 2.70 | – |
| 1520 (February 4th) .............. | 1.80 | – |
| 1542 (July 11th) .................... | – | 19.4 |
| 1573 (February 7th) .............. | 1.20 | – |
| 1577 (February 10th) ............ | – | 14.5 |
| 1603 (April 2nd) .................... | 0.90 | – |
| 1606 (March 21st) .................. | – | 11.0 |
| 1645 (March 6th) ................... | – | 9.8 |
| 1686 (December 22nd) .......... | – | 9.6 |
| 1749 (March 31st) .................. | 0.66 | – |

**1609** - Bank of Amsterdam maintained accounts in Banco Guilders, money representing fixed weight of metal. - See *Banco*.

**1694** (March 17th) and **1699** (December 31st) - Adoption of Guilder of 20 Stuyver as monetary unit by Estates-General.

**1816** (December 15th) - After elimination of French monetary system, adoption of bimetalic standard: 1 Guilder = 6.0565 milligrams of fine gold = 9.615 grams of fine silver (15.88 to 1 ratio). Guilder divided into 100 Cents. Franc retained its legal exchange rate of 47 Cents until December 22, 1825.

**1839** (March 22nd) - After disappearance of silver coins, minting of Guilders of 10 grams 945 fine.

**1850** - With decline of price of gold, demonetization of gold coins, and adoption of silver standard:

1 Guilder = 9.451 grams of fine silver

**1874** (December 3rd) - Suspension of free minting of silver coins.

**1875** (June 6th) - With depreciation of price of silver, adoption of gold standard:

1 Guilder = 604.8 milligrams of fine gold

**1877** (March 28th) - Bronze Cent replaced copper Cent.

**1914** (July 31st) - Embargo on gold shipments; forced parity.

**1920** - Depreciation (26% in November). Fineness of silver Guilder coin (10 grams) reduced from 945 to 720.

**1925** (April 28th) - Lifting of embargo on gold shipments. Convertibility reestablished only with countries whose Central Banks permitted gold shipments.

**1925** (November 17th) - Issue of gold coins.

**1933** (July 3rd) - Formation of Gold Bloc with France, Switzerland and Belgium.

**1936** (September 27th) - Embargo on gold shipments.

**1936** (September 30th) - Forced parity of banknotes. Creation of Exchange Equalization Fund. Currency depreciation.

**1938** (August 7th) -Lifting of embargo on gold shipments.

**1940** (March 16th) - Guilder redefined in terms of gold:
    1 Guilder = 497.76 milligrams of fine gold

**1940** (May 10th) - German Occupation. Foreign exchange controls. Free gold market closed:
    1 Guilder = 1.50 Reichsmark

**1940** (July 17th) - 1 Guilder = 1.327 Reichsmark.

**1943** (March 14th) - Banknotes of 500 and 1,000 Guilders cancelled. Deposit of these banknotes for exchange before the 31st (after deduction of taxes and debts owed to State).

**1943** (June 26th) - Definition of monetary gold decreed by German authorities:
    1 Guilder = 476.69 milligrams of fine gold

**1944** (September 14th) - Liberation of Netherlands. Anglo-Netherlands payments agreement:
    1 Pound Sterling = 10.691 Guilders
    1 U.S. Dollar = 2.652 Guilders

**1945** (June 9th) - Withdrawal from circulation and blocking of banknotes of 100 Guilders.

**1945** (September 13th) - Withdrawal from circulation of all other banknotes.

**1945** (September 26th) - Blocking of bank accounts.

**1946** (December 18th) - Parity registered with International Monetary Fund:
    1 Guilder = 334.987 milligrams of fine gold
    1 U.S. Dollar = 2.65285 Guilders

**1949** (September 20th) - Devaluation following Pound Sterling:
    1 Guilder = 233.861 milligrams of fine gold
    1 U.S. Dollar = 3.80 Guilders

**1952** (September 26th) - Obligation to surrender precious metals except for gold ended.

**1955** (July 11th) - Obligation to surrender gold ended.

**1956** (January) - Issue of silver Guilders (6.5 grams 720 fine).

**1961** (March 7th) - Upvaluation parallel to that of West German Mark:
    1 Netherlands Guilder = 245.489 milligrams of fine gold
    1 U.S. Dollar = 3.62 Netherlands Guilders

**1968** (March 20th) - Organized gold market established in Amsterdam. Netherlands Bank abolished restrictions on ownership, negotiation, import and export of gold.

**1968** (July 16th) - Rise in price of silver resulted in replacement of 2 and 2½ Guilder silver pieces with nickel coins. Melting silver coins banned as was exports of more than 25 Guilders worth.

## GUILDER NETHERLANDS ANTILLES

Monetary unit of the **Netherlands Antilles.** Divided into 100 Cents.

Bank of issue - De Curacaosche Bank, established December 31, 1928. Renamed Bank Van De Nederlandse Antillen (Bank of the Netherlands Antilles).

Predecessor - See *Netherlands Antilles.*

**Early 20th Century -** Antillean Guilder equal to Netherlands Guilder and represented colonial issue of Metropolitan unit. - See *Guilder Netherlands.*

**1940** (May 10th) - Following German occupation of Netherlands, break between Netherlands Guilder and Antillean Guilder:

> 1 Netherland Guilder = .710878 Antillean Guilders

Unit linked to U.S. Dollar:

> 1 U.S. Dollar = 1.88585 Antillean Guilders
> 1 U.S. Dollar = 1.885/1.905 Antillean Guilders (buying-
> /selling)

**1946** (December 18th) - Parity registered with International Monetary Fund:

> 1 Antillean Guilder = 471.230 milligrams of fine gold
> 1 U.S. Dollar = 1.88585 Antillean Guilders

**1949** (September 20th) - Following Netherlands Guilder devaluation:

> 1 Netherland Guilder = .496278 Antillean Guilders

**1952** - Exchange tax of Netherlands Antillean Guilder 0.015 per U.S. Dollar made applicable to sales of foreign exchange. Effective selling rate of 1.92 Antillean Guilders per U.S. Dollar.

**1961** (March 8th) - Following upvaluation of Netherlands Guilder, alteration of buying and selling rates, but official rate remained unchanged:

> 1 U.S. Dollar = 1.87/1.89 Antillean Guilders (buying/sell-
> ing)

Exchange tax of Netherlands Antillean Guilder 0.015 per U.S. Dollar made effective selling rate of 1.905 Antillean Guilders per U.S. Dollar.

New relationship to Metropolitan unit:

> 1 Netherlands Guilder = .520954 Antillean Guilders

## GUILDER NETHERLANDS EAST INDIES

Monetary unit of **Netherlands East Indies.** Divided into 30 Stuyvers (equivalent to 20 Dutch Stuyvers) or 120 Duiten, and from 1854 into 100 Cents.

Variation of name - Indonesian Guilder, especially after 1945.

Bank of issue - Bank of Java established 1828.

Predecessor - See *Netherlands East Indies.*

**1817** (January 14th) - Netherlands Guilder adopted as monetary unit:

> 1 Guilder = 605.65 milligrams of fine gold

**1828** - Circulation of East Indies Guilder banknotes linked to, and at par with, Netherlands Guilder.

**1832** - Adoption of copper standard.

**1877** - Introduction of gold standard:
  1 East Indies Guilder = 604.8 milligrams of fine gold
**1940** (March 16th) - New parity conforming to that of Netherlands Guilder:
  1 East Indies Guilder = 497.76 milligrams of fine gold
  1 U.S. Dollar = 1.80 East Indies Guilders
**1940** (September) - After German occupation of Netherlands, linking of East Indies Guilder to Pound Sterling:
  1 Pound Sterling = 7.60 East Indies Guilders
**1942** - Japanese Occupation. Introduction of military Yen, or Gumpyo, denominated in Guilders.
**1942** (March) - Hyper-inflation through increase of local money (between 1942 and 1945 expanded from 367 to 670 million Guilders) and by issue of 3.5 billion of occupation banknotes (1.6 billion in Sumatra and 1.57 billion in Java).
**1943** (April 1st) - Issue of banknotes denominated in Guilders by Bank for·Development of South Seas, established by Japanese. Linking of Guilder to Yen involving devaluation of 56%:
  1 East Indies Guilder = 1 Japanese Yen
**1945** (September) - Anglo-Dutch Agreement:
  1 Pound Sterling = 7.60 East Indies Guilders
Indonesian Guilder became more commonly used name for currency of Netherlands East Indies.
**1946** (March 7th) - General withdrawal of occupation banknotes from circulation and substitution of new notes printed in Australia, denominated in Indonesian Guilders:
  1 Japanese Guilder = 0.03 Indonesian Guilder
New parity fixed and Dollar quotations, suspended since 1941, resumed:
  1 Indonesian Guilder = 1 Netherlands Guilder
  1 Indonesian Guilder = 334.987 milligrams of fine gold
  1 U.S. Dollar = 2.65285 Indonesian Guilders
**1949** (September 20th) - Following Pound Sterling and Netherlands Guilder, devaluation of Indonesian Guilder:
  1 Indonesian Guilder = 1 Netherlands Guilder
  1 Indonesian Guilder = 233.861 milligrams of fine gold
  1 U.S. Dollar = 3.80 Indonesian Guilders
**1949** (November 2nd) - Independence of Indonesia. Indonesian Guilder became Indonesian Rupiah. - See *Rupiah Indonesia.*
**1950** (March 13th) - Banknotes of Java Bank and Treasury of more than 5 Indonesian Guilders were reduced in value by one-half.


## GUILDER NEW GUINEA

Monetary unit of **Netherlands New Guinea.** Divided into 100 Cents.
Bank of Issue - Nederlandsche Bank (Netherlands Bank).
Predecessor - See *Guilder Netherlands East Indies.*

**1950** (March 30th) - Creation of New Guinea Guilder equal to Netherlands Guilder. - See *Guilder Netherlands*.

**1963** (May 1st) - Netherlands New Guinea changed name to West Irian. Creation of Irian Barat Rupiah to replace New Guinea Guilder. - See *Rupiah Irian Barat*.


## GUILDER SURINAM

Monetary unit of **Surinam** (Dutch Guiana). Divided into 100 Cents.

Bank of issue - De Surinaamsche Bank, established 1865. Then from April 1, 1957, Centrale Bank Van Suriname (Central Bank of Surinam).

Prececessor - See *Surinam*.

**19th and early 20th Century** - Surinam Guilder equal to Netherlands Guilder and represented a colonial issue of Metropolitan unit. - See *Guilder Netherlands*.

**1940** (May 10th) - Following German occupation of Netherlands, break between Netherlands Guilder and Surinam Guilder:
> 1 Netherlands Guilder = .710878 Surinam Guilder

Unit linked to U.S. Dollar:
> 1 U.S. Dollar = 1.88585 Surinam Guilders
> 1 U.S. Dollar = 1.885/1.905 Surinam  Guilders  (buying-
> /selling)

**1946** (December 18th) - Parity registered with International Monetary Fund:
> 1 Surinam Guilder = 471.230 milligrams of fine gold
> 1 U.S. Dollar = 1.88585 Surinam Guilders

**1949** (September 20th) - Following Netherlands Guilder devaluation:
> 1 Netherlands Guilder = .496278 Surinam Guilder

**1961** (March 8th) - Following upvaluation of Netherlands Guilder, alteration of buying and selling rates, but official rate remained unchanged:
> 1 U.S. Dollar = 1.87/1.90 Surinam  Guilders  (buying/sell-
> ing)

New relationship to Metropolitan unit:
> 1 Netherlands Guilder = .520954 Surinam Guilder


## GUILLAUME D'OR

Early gold money of some European states. Minted by a Prince Guillaume (William).

**I.** - In the **Netherlands**, gold coin (6.05 grams fine) minted in 19th Century, from 1841 to 1847, worth 10 Guilders (Florins). Minting of Double Guillaume and ½ Guillaume.

**II.** - In electoral **Hesse**, gold money of 19th Century.

## GUINEA

**I.** - Early **English** gold coin, later unit of account.

Origin of name - Coin crudely minted from gold mined in region of Guinea by British African Company.

**1661** (August 26th) - Minting by Charles II of gold coin called Guinea, closely akin to French Louis, and equal to 20 silver Shillings.

**1694** - Because of depreciation of silver coins (see *Shilling*), accounting value of Guinea rose to 22 Shillings, then 22 Shillings 6 Pence.

**1695** - Value of Guinea increased to 23 Shillings (January), 25 Shillings (February), and 30 Shillings (June).

**1696** (February) - Because of progressive withdrawal of worn silver coins and replacement by new coins, value of Guinea declined to 28 Shillings.

**1696** (March 25th) - Official value of Guinea: 26 Shillings.

**1696** (April 10th) - Official value of Guinea: 22 Shillings.

**1699** - Official value of Guinea: 21 Shillings 6 Pence.

**1717** (December 22nd) - Guinea lowered to 21 Shillings.

**1774** (May 10th) - In order to eliminate badly worn-out Guineas, minting of new Guineas (8.39 grams 916 fine, or 7.69 grams fine gold).

**1817** - Halt in minting of Guineas, but legal tender status of 21 Shillings retained.

**20th Century** - As unit of account, term Guinea designated sum of 21 Shillings.

**II.** - In **Saudi Arabia**, Saudi Monetary Agency issued gold Guinea equal to 40 Riyals in October 1952. - See *Riyal Saudi Arabia*.

## *GUINEA*

**1958** (October 2nd) - Independent nation formed from French Guinea. Money in circulation, see *Franc CFA*.

**1960** (March 1st) - Withdrew from Franc-Zone. Banque Centrale de la République de Guinée issued Guinea Franc to replace CFA Franc at par. - See *Franc Guinea*.

## GUIOTIN

Name given in **British** and **Dutch Antilles** to chopped coins, called Mocos in French Antilles. - See *Moco*.

Origin of name - From French *guillotine*.

Variation of name - Guillotinacorta.

## GULDEN

German and Dutch name for Guilder, gold money.

Origin of name - Germanic root *gold*, which gave rise to Dutch *gulden*, English *gold*, Polish *zloty*. From Indo-European root *ghel*, meaning brilliant.

**I. -** Monetary unit of **Netherlands**. - See *Guilder Netherlands*.

**II. -** In **Holy Roman Empire** and **German** states, gold money and unit of account, then silver money.

**13th Century -** Introduction of Guilder of Florence.

**14th Century -** Gold Gulden (4.3 grams) minted by Holy Roman Empire and by Austria.

**1375 -** First debasement of Gulden.

**1386 -** Weight of Gulden reduced to 3.54 grams 938 fine by Electors of the Rhine. Attempt at monetary union among Speyer, Worms, Frankfurt and the Four Princes.

**15th and 16th Centuries -** Gulden minted of gold by German States: Brandenburg, Pomerania in 1499, Bavaria in 1506, Prussia about 1520.

**1409 -** In all states of Holy Roman Empire, Gulden debased to 3.54 grams 915 fine gold.

**1497 -** After Diet of Worms, minting of Gulden of 2.6 grams 885 fine gold.

**1524 -** Decree of Essling (suspended monetary system of Charles V): Gulden of 2.6 grams 885 fine gold.

**1524-1551 -** Development of system of accounting used especially in South and West (Austria, Bavaria, Swabia, Franconia, Rhineland):
    1 Gulden = 60 Kreuzer = 240 Pfennig
Changes in accounting relationship of gold Gulden to Kreuzer: 75 Kreuzer in 1551, 82 in 1585, 94 at beginning of 17th Century, 120 in 1617, 720 in 1622 (30 Years War), 104 in 1623, 130 in 1667, 150 in 1681, 176 in 1690 and 180 in 1736.

**1549** (May 5th) - Minting of Gulden forbidden in states of Empire.

**1559 -** Minting of silver Gulden (24.6 grams) worth 60 Kreuzer.

**18th Century -** Gold Gulden circulated in Hanover, Swabia, Saxony (3.2 grams 813 fine), and the Rhineland (3.2 grams 781 fine).
Silver Gulden (13 grams fine in 1690, then 14.3 grams fine) was money of Holy Roman Empire. Bavaria, Brunswick, Hanover, Westphalia, Cologne, Frankfurt, Friesland, minted silver Gulden of lighter weight. Swabia minted silver/copper Gulden.
Gulden of account (equal to 60 Kreuzer or 240 Pfennig), remained in use in Austria, Bavaria, Swabia, Franconia, Upper Palatinate, Frankfurt. Sometimes divided into 15 Batzen (Swabia, Upper Palatinate), into 20 Kaisergroschen (Swabia, Franconia) into 30 Albus (Upper Palatinate), into 30 Groschen or 540 Pfennig (Prussia), into 10 Schaap, 20 Stuyver or 200 Witten (Friesland), into 28 Schillings or 336 Pfennig (Münster), into 28 Schillings or 168 Pfennig (Württemberg).

**1837** (August 25th) - Treaty of Munich unified Gulden among Bavaria, Württemberg, Hesse-Darmstadt, Frankfurt. New definition:
    1 Gulden = 9.55 grams of fine silver

**1838** (July 30th) - Accord of Dresden attempted to establish unified monetary system (Prussia, Bavaria, Saxony, Württemberg, Baden, Hesse. . .) based on silver standard. Creation of common silver coin (Vereinsmünzen) worth 2 Thalers or 3.50 Gulden.

Thaler, unit of account in Prussia, Saxony. . ., equal to 1.75 Guilders.

Gulden as unit of account in Bavaria, Baden, Württemberg. . ., equal to 4/7 Thaler.

**1857** (January 24th) - Austro-German Monetary Agreement: Thaler, equivalent to 1.50 Austrian Gulden, or 1.75 Gulden of South German States, became unit of account of North German Confederation.

Gulden of South equal to 4/7 Thaler or 6/7 Austrian Gulden.

**1871** (December 4th) - Law of German Empire created gold coins of 10 and 20 Mark, suspended minting of silver monies and authorized their withdrawal from circulation: 10 Mark replaced 5.50 Gulden. - See *Mark.*

**III. -** Money of **Swiss Cantons. -** See *Guilder.*

For other Gulden varieties see following:

## GULDEN AUSTRIA

Silver money and unit of account. Became monetary unit of **Austria** from 1748 to 1892. Divided into 60 Kreuzer until 1857, then into 100 Kreuzer (in Bosnia, divided into 100 Novtchitcha).

Origin of name - See *Guilder.*

Bank of issue - By Austrian Government, Wiener Stadtbank, Oesterreichische National-al-Zettel-Bank, Oesterreichisch-Ungarische Bank (Austro-Hungarian Bank) and by the State.

Predecessors - See *Austria* and *Gulden.*

**1748** - After War of Austrian Succession, Gulden became general monetary unit. Sanctioned by Convention of 1753 between Austria and Bavaria:

Specie money: 1 Gulden = 11.5 grams of fine silver

Unit of account: 1 Gulden = 60 Kreuzer

**1762** - Issue of Gulden in Banco-Zettel (banknotes) by Wiener Stadtbank. Inflation and depreciation.

**1810** - Circulation exceeded 1 billion Gulden. Depreciation, which at its highest point made silver Gulden equal to 12 paper Gulden (1 paper Gulden worth less than 1 gram of silver).

**1811** (February 20th) - Imperial decree ordering exchange of Banco-Zettel for Einlösungsscheine (redemption certificates):

1 Gulden-Einlösungsschein = 5 Gulden-Banco-Zettel (Wiener Währung).

Circulation thus reduced from 1,060 million to 212 million Gulden.

**1813** - New inflation with issue of Anticipationsscheine (anticipation notes).

**1816** - Devaluation of 60%:

2.5 paper Gulden = 1 silver Gulden

1 paper Gulden = 4.6 grams of fine silver

Creation of Oesterreichische National-Zettel-Bank as Central Bank.

**1820** (March 20th) - Exchange of government paper money for shares, debentures or banknotes of Oesterreichische National-Zettel-Bank, established for this "deflation" and given right of banknote issue. Convertibility of new banknotes into silver. Maintenance of forced parity for government paper money with circulation reduced.

**1848** (May 22nd) - Loans to government by Central Bank; issue of Treasury notes; forced parity of banknotes and Treasury notes; and progressive inflation.

**1857** (January 24th) - Convention of Germanic Monetary Union making Austrian Gulden one of the three units of account along with Thaler and Gulden of South German States:

> 1 Austrian Gulden = 0.66 Thaler = 1⅙ South German
> Gulden = 11.11 grams of fine silver

**1857** (September 19th) - Definition of silver coin, divided into 100 Kreuzer:

> 1 Gulden = 12.345 grams 900 fine

**1859** (January 1st) - Unsuccessful attempt at return to convertibility. Continued inflation.

**1867** - Austria left Germanic Monetary Union, but retained same system.

**1870** (March 9th) - Imperial decree authorizing minting of gold coins patterned on type of Latin Monetary Union: coins of 8 Gulden equal to Napoléon (6.45 grams 900 fine) and of 4 Gulden equal to coin of 10 Francs (3.225 grams 900 fine). Issued until 1892.

**1873** - Persistent inflation: 300 million banknotes and 370 million Treasury notes in circulation.

**1878** - Recovery of banknotes to par with silver which had itself depreciated 16% in relation to gold.

**1879** - Suspension of silver standard. Paper standard instituted because of short supply of gold.

**1892** (August 2nd) - Adoption of gold standard with introduction of a common monetary system for Austria-Hungary. Gulden devalued 15% and replaced by Krone as monetary unit. - See *Krone Austria.*
Gulden remained a silver coin (12.345 grams 900 fine) worth 2 Kronen.


## GULDEN DANZIG

Early monetary unit of Free City of **Danzig.** Divided into 100 Pfennig.

Bank of issue - By Bank of Danzig, as of February 5, 1924.

Predecessor - At creation of Free City (November 15, 1920), circulation of German Mark.

**18th Century** - Unit of account: Gulden (Guilder) of 30 Groschen (Gros).

**1923** (December 18th) - After collapse of German Mark, creation and circulation of Danzig Gulden:

> 1 Gulden = 292.895 milligrams of fine gold
> 1 Pound Sterling = 25.00 Gulden

**1935** (May 2nd) - Devaluation of 42.37%:

> 1 Gulden = 168.7923 milligrams of fine gold = 1 Zloty

**1935** (June 5th-11th) - Foreign exchange controls instituted.

**1939** (September) - German Occupation and substitution of Reichsmark for Gulden:
1 Gulden = 0.70 Reichsmark

**1945** - Danzig became part of Poland. - See *Poland* and *Zloty.*

## GULDEN HUNGARY

In **Hungary,** gold money and unit of account from 14th to 19th Century. Divided into
100 Krajczár.

Bank of issue - National Bank of Hungary.

Predecessor - See *Hungary.*

**Beginning of 14th Century** - First minting of gold Gulden.

**18th Century** - Hungarian Gulden, unit of account, derived from Gulden of Holy
Roman Empire. Under name of Egyforint, equal to 10 Chustaken, 20 Caszarsgara
(Grochen), 40 Poltura, 60 Krajczár, 100 Penz-Kraslowski, 240 Rhine Deniers, or
720 Babka. Specie money, Hungarian Gulden called Uherszky-Zlaty and worth
17.5 Groschen of Holy Roman Empire.

**During 19th Century** - Hungarian Gulden equivalent to Austrian Gulden, and disappeared with it in 1892. - See *Gulden Austria.*

## GULDENGROSCHEN

**German** gold, then silver money.

Origin of name - From Groschen and Gulden (Guilder).

Predecessor - See *Groschen.*

**End of 15th Century** - In Saxony, minting of heavy silver Groschen worth 1 gold
Gulden, called Guldengroschen.

**1524** - Monetary system of Charles V: minting of Guldener, or Reichsguldener, silver
coin (29.2 grams 935 fine, or 27.3 grams fine silver), worth 1 gold Gulden. - See
*Reichsguldener.*

## GULDENTHALER

See *Thaler.*

## GUMPYO

Japanese name for Military Yen, issued by **Japanese** in territories occupied from 1941
to 1945.

**1941** - In China, issue of small banknotes denominated in Yen. For exchange ratio to local monies, see *Yuan Nanking.*

**1942** - In the Pacific, issue of Gumpyo at par with and denominated in local currency: Military Peso in Philippines, Military Guilder (Florin) in Indonesia, Military Dollar of Straits Settlements, Military Rupee in Burma. In Hong Kong, issue of Military Yen equal to 2 then 4 Hong Kong Dollars.

**1942** (April) - Issue of new banknotes to replace earlier as well as military monies in circulation: in the Philippines (Peso, Dollar, Gumpyo), in Indonesia (Guilder, Gumpyo).

**1943** (May 31st) - In Hong Kong, Hong Kong Dollar no longer exchanged for Gumpyo (only legal money and linked to the Yen).

**1945** - General withdrawal from circulation of Gumpyo.


## GUNDA

In ancient **Mogul Empire** and in **Bengal,** unit of account worth $1/5$ Burrie, $1/20$ Poni, $1/40$ Anna, $1/320$ Cawne and $1/640$ Rupee. - See *Rupee India.*

Submultiple - Gunda divided into 4 Cowries.


## GUTE GROSCHEN

Early **German** silver money, and unit of account.

Origin of name - German *gut* (good) and *Groschen* (gros). - See *Gros.*

Variation of name - *Bon Gros* (French).

Predecessor - See *Groschen.*

**1623** - Minting in Saxony of new Groschen, Gute Groschen of $1/24$ Thaler or 12 Pfennig, which replaced Mariengroschen.

**1667** - Conference of Zinna (electoral Saxony, Brandenburg, Brunswick, Lüneburg): silver coin of $2/3$ Thaler made equal to 16 Gute Groschen.

**1690** - Conference of Leipzig (electoral Saxony, Brandenburg, Brunswick, Lüneburg): value of Gute Groschen confirmed at $1/24$ Thaler or 12 Pfennig.

**1693** - Extension of agreement reached at Leipzig throughout Holy Roman Empire (except Hamburg and Lübeck).

**18th Century** - As unit of account, Gute Groschen worth $1/24$ Thaler or 12 Pfennig in Brandenburg, Saxony, Thuringia, and Lüneburg.
Silver specie money in Saxony, silver/copper money in Brandenburg, Brunswick and Silesia.

**19th Century** - Specie money in Hanover until 1871.

## *GUYANA*

Name of British Guiana upon independence on May 26, 1966. Money in circulation, Guyana Dollar. - See *Dollar Guyana.*

## GYLDEN

**Danish** name for the Guilder (Florin), unit of account in 15th Century Denmark. Minted in gold (Rynske Gylden) and in silver (Sölvgylden). Exchange rate: 24 Skilling.

Variation of name - *Gyllen* (Swedish).

## HAIES D'OR

See *Ange d'Or.*

## *HAITI*

**15th-16th Century** - Called Hispaniola. Spanish monies. - See *Spain.*

**16th Century** - Pirates imported French copper coins (Liards, Sols or Sous) and some silver coins (Testons).

**17th Century** - Called Saint Domingue. Use of Portuguese monies, English gold coins (Jacobus) and Spanish silver Piasters of 8 Reales, called Pieces of Eight, supplementing gold Escudos (worth 2 Pieces of Eight) and gold Pistoles (worth 2 Escudos). These coins used for foreign trade, i.e., purchase of slaves from Dutch and English, and imports of European goods. Most domestic payments made with tobacco and sugar.

**1697** - Treaty of Rijswijk. Division of Island: Eastern or Spanish part continued to use monies then circulating, principally heavy Piaster, or Gourde. - See *Piaster Gourde.* Western part, ceded to France, adopted monetary system of French Antilles with Livre Coloniale. - See *Livre Coloniale.*

**1781** (July 13th) - Ordinance prescribing recoinage of Spanish 1 and 1/2 Real pieces (generally called Double Escalin and ordinary Escalin), weighing 2.39 and 1.19 grams, with the countermark of Colony. This was the method for Mocos. - See *Moco.*

**1793-1798** - British Occupation.

**1801** (November 11th) - Ordinance of Toussaint-L'Ouverture deciding on local minting of silver coins of 2, 1 and 1/2 Escalin (names given to 1, 1/2 and 1/4 Real).
1 Escalin = 10 Sols or Sous
11 Escalin = 1 Spanish Piaster or Piaster Gourde
- See *Piaster Gourde.*

**1802** - Revolt from France. Proclaimed Republic of Haiti.

**1814-1822** - Minting by Spaniards of copper Cuartillo.

**1822-1843** - In unified Island, minting of silver coins of 6, 12 and 25 Centimes.

**1844** - Secession of Eastern part of island. - See *Peso Dominican Republic.* For Western part, see *Gourde Haiti.*

## HALALA

**I.** - Submultiple of Riyal (1/88), monetary unit of **Saudi Arabia.** Also of Darij (1/44) and Qurush (1/8). - See *Riyal.*
Variation of name - Hilala.

**1960** (January 8th) - Riyal subdivided into 20 Qurush or 100 Halalas.

**II.** - In **Yemen,** submultiple of Imaldi, or Maria Theresia Thaler (1/80). Also equal to 1/2 Bogache.

## HALBLING

Name given in feudal **Germany** to ½ Pfennig (Obol).
Origin of name - From German *halb*, (half).
**15th Century** - The ½ Pfennig identical with Heller.

## HALBSKOTER

Silver **Prussian** money of the Teutonic Order in the 14th Century. Equal to 16 Pfennig.
The ½ Halbskoter called Vierchen.

## HALER

Submultiple (¹⁄₁₀₀) of Koruna, monetary unit of **Czechoslovakia**. Also submultiple
( ¹⁄₁₀₀) of earlier Czech Koruna and Slovak Koruna, monetary units of **Bohemia-Moravia** and **Slovakia** (1939-1945).
Origin of name - See *Heller*.
Plural - Czech (*Haleru*); Slovak (*Haliérov*).

## HALF OERE

Small copper coin in **Sweden** in 18th Century worth ½ Oere.
Origin of name - *Alleveure* (French).

## HALFPENNY

**English** and **Irish** money equivalent to ½ Penny. - See *Penny*. First minted in silver
in England under Edward I (1272-1307).
Origin of name - Penny of Edward the Confessor (1042-1066) was cut in half to make
change. Penny marked with cross which probably encouraged cutting.

## *HAMBURG*

**10th Century** - Carolingian monetary system. - See *Livre*.
**13th Century** - System of accounting in Mark of 16 Schilling or 192 Pfennig. - See *Mark*.
Money of Hamburg became autonomous.
Decline of Mark of Hamburg in grams of fine silver: 109 in 1226; 77 in 1325; 64
in 1375; 40 in 1430; 24 in 1450; 19 in 1461; 17 in 1506.
**1432** - First minting of Schilling.

**1475** - Minting of gold Ducat.

**18th Century** - System of accounting in Lübsk (Mark Lübsk, Schilling Lübsk, Pfennig Lübsk). - See *Lübsk*.

This system became Banco monetary system (bank money), designating an unvarying weight of metal on deposit in coffers of Bank of Hamburg. Mark-Banco (bank paper money) commanded premiun of 23% - 25% over Mark coinage.

Specie monies:

In gold - Portugalöser, Dukaten
In silver - Reichsthaler, Thaler, Mark
In silver/copper - multiples of Schilling

**1871** - Monetary system of unified Germany: 10 new Mark replaced 8 Mark 5⅓ Schillings of Hamburg and Lübeck.


# HANSATSU

Paper money issued in **Japan** from 17th to 19th Century for private usage.

Three types - Kinsatsu (banknotes redeemable for gold), Ginsatsu (banknotes redeemable for silver), Zenisatsu (banknotes redeemable for copper).

Predecessor - See *Japan.*

**1617** - Issue of Ginsatsu by merchant in Osaka.

**1686** - First feudal issue. Increase in number of issues more or less authorized by military regime.

**1868** (May) - Issue of State banknotes called Dajokwansatsu or Kinsatsu, denominated in gold, at forced parity.

**1871** (August) - Abolition of private paper money (1,694 types issued by 244 groups). Replaced by State banknotes in Yen.

**1879** - End of exchange of paper monies. - See *Yen.*


# HARDI

Gold money of **Flanders** in the 14th Century. Also called Chaise.


# HASSANI

Silver coinage of **Morocco** minted during Sultanate of Moulay-Hassan (1881-1920).

Origin of name - From Sultan Moulay-Hassan.

Types - See *Peseta Hassani, Rial Hassani.*

Predecessor - See *Morocco.*

## *HAWAII*

**1847** - Issue of copper Cents.

**1883** - Issue of silver Dollars.

**1898** - Annexation by United States. American monetary system. - See *Dollar.*

## HEAUME

**I.** - Name given to helmeted silver Ecu of France. Created in 1419 by Charles VI. - See *Ecu.*

Variation of name - *Helm* (German).

**II.** - Gold money of **Netherlands.** In Flanders (14th Century and 1419). Double Heaume of 1386 worth 40 Grooten.

**III.** - Silver money of **Netherlands.** Generally called Helmeted Lion (see *Botdrager*) in Flanders 1364. In Holland under William V (1346-89).

## HECTE

**I.** - Money of **Phocaea** and **Mytilene** made of electrum (gold and silver alloy) and minted in 5th Century B.C. Equal to ⅙ Phocaean Stater (17 grams). Hecté weighed 2.8 grams.

Origin of name - From Greek *hex* (six).

**II.** - Gold coin of ancient **Greece** equal to ⅙ Stater.

## *HELGOLAND*

Predecessor - See *Hamburg.*

**Until 1875** - Use of Mark of Hamburg worth 16 Schillings.

**1875** - Combination of German and English monetary systems. Mark of Helgoland worth either 12 Pence or 100 Pfennig.

**1890** - Cession of Helgoland to Germany by Britain. German monetary system. - See *Germany* and *Mark.*

## HELLER

Germanic money, at first in silver, later in copper, and unit of account.

Origin of name - From Hall in Swabia, first city to mint Heller.

Variations of name - Haller, Haler, Haliérov (Slovak).

**I.** - **German** money derived from Pfennig.

**1224 or 1228** - In Hall in Swabia, minting of silver Pfennig, called Denarius Hallensis, or Heller. - See *Pfennig.*

**14th Century** - Imitation of Heller in Swabia, Franconia, Bavaria, Saxony, Bohemia.

**1420** - Disassociated from and more depreciated than Pfennig, the Heller worth only 1/2 Pfennig. Minted by Holy Roman Empire and German states.

**1524** - In monetary system of Charles V, minting of Heller left to states. Authority confirmed in 1559.

**18th Century** - Heller was unit of account in Bavaria valued at: 1/2 Pfennig, 1/8 Kreuzer, 1/480 Gulden. In Hesse-Kassel (1/12 Albus, 1/16 Groschen, 1/384 Reichsthaler); in Lower Westphalia (1/16 Stuyver, 1/960 Reichsthaler); in Cologne (1/12 Albus, 1/78 Thaler, 1/80 Speciesthaler); in Regensburg for payment of taxes and fines (1/2 Pfennig, 1/15 Groshen, 1/60 Schilling, 1/2,460 Livre). Was copper specie money in Bavaria, Hesse-Kassel, Saxony. In Regensburg, 5 Heller equalled 1 Regensburger. 4 Heller coin called Busch in Aachen, Frichs in Cleves.

**II.** - In **Austria,** Heller was 1/100 of monetary unit based on gold, the Krone, created August 2, 1892.

In Montenegro, Heller, being 1/100 Krone, regarded as identical with Para from 1902 to 1910.

**III.** - Unit of account in certain **Swiss** cantons in 18th Century until 1850: 1/8 Kreuzer, 1/480 Guilder (Florin) in Zurich and Saint Gall.

In Zurich, 2 Heller coin called Angster.


## HENRI D'OR

Name given in **France,** under Henry II, to gold Ecu minted with imprint of the king. First minted in 1549; last minted in 1553; circulated until 1561. Minting of 1/2 Henri d'Or. Weight: 3.61 grams 970 fine, or 3.5 grams fine gold. Exchange rate: 50 Sous, then 46 Sous. - See *Ecu.*


## HIDALGO

**Mexican** gold coin of 10 Pesos weighing 8.333 grams 900 fine, or 7.5 grams fine gold. Also minted in form of Medio Hidalgo (5 Pesos), Quarto de Hidalgo (2.5 Pesos), and Quinto de Hidalgo (2 Pesos).


## HOLER

Early copper money of several **German** states.

Origin of name - From the German *hohl,* hollow. According to Diderot's Encyclopedia, Holer was so light and thin, that in order to make it more acceptable as means of payment, was given form of a head of a beaten down nail.

## *HOLLAND*

See *Netherlands.*

## *HOLY ROMAN EMPIRE*

Roman monies from left bank of Rhine to as far as countries on Danube. - See *Rome.*

**9th Century** - Use of Carolingian Denier (see *Denier).* Adoption of Carolingian system of accounting, from which Livre of 20 Schillings or 240 Pfennig derived. - See *Schilling* and *Pfennig.*

**11th Century** - From ½ Livre came Marc of Cologne (unit of weight of 233.856 grams) which gave rise to Mark, unit of account. - See *Mark.* Minting of Denier (Pfennig) and of its submultiple (Obol or Halbling).

**12th to 14th Century** - Variations of Pfennig. - See *Heller, Kreuzer.* Minting of ¼ Pfennig (Vierling) in certain countries.

To the East (Saxony, Swabia, East Franconia), issue of Bracteates. - See *Bracteate.*

**1296** - Minting of silver Groschen imitating Gros Tournois. - See *Groschen.*

**14th Century** - Minting of gold Florin (Gulden) copying Guilder of Florence (see *Florence* ) and Chaise d'Or. Counter-marking of Gros of Prague.

Other silver monies: Esterlin, Pfennig.

**1437-1447** - Diets regulated coinage of gold.

**1486** - In Tyrol, minting of first coins from thick discs, followed by Guldengroschen. Worth 1 Gulden.

**1500-1512** - Diets attempted to place coinage of silver under central control.

**1519** - On south side of Harz Mountains, Schlick family, owners of silver mines of Joachimsthal, minted silver coins of same weight as Guldengroschen, with alloy that was a bit weaker. These coins became famous under name of Joachimsthaler, abbreviated Thaler. - See *Thaler.* Thaler worth 15 Batzen or 60 Kreuzer.

**1524** - Charles V tried vainly to regulate coinage. Decree of Essling allowed states to mint Pfennig and Heller and designated the following as monies of Holy Roman Empire:

     In gold - Gulden

     In silver - Reichsguldener (worth 1 Gulden), Oerterer (¼),
          Zehner (1/10), Groschen (1/21), Gröschlein (1/84)

**1549** (May 5th) - Charles V unsuccessfully prohibited states from minting gold Gulden and silver Thalers.

**1551** (July 28th) - New attempt of alleviating money confusuon by giving Empire common monetary system. Only states which owned mines authorized to mint larger specie monies.

Unit of account: Gulden of 60 Kreuzer.

Specie monies:

     In gold - Gulden

     In silver - Reichsguldener (72 Kreuzer), Zwanziger (20
          Kreuzer), Zwölfer (12), Zehner (10), Sechser (6),
          Kreuzer

Coinage of Thaler theoretically banned. Resistance of states.

**1555** - States of North adopted Thaler of 24 Silvergroschen or 32 Mariengroschen as unit of account. States of South remained faithful to accounting in Gulden of 60 Kreuzer or 240 Pfennig. Hamburg maintained accounts in Mark of 16 Schilling or 192 Pfennig.

**1559** - Monetary decree of Ferdinand I, renewing attempts at uniformity of monies. States allowed to mint Pfennig and Heller.
Specie monies:
>      In gold - Dukaten of 3.44 grams
>      In silver - Reichsguldener (60 Kreuzer) and its submultiples
>      up to Kreuzer

**1566** - Thaler became money of Holy Roman Empire under name of Reichsthaler. Reichsguldener, no longer coined, became Guldenthaler. - See *Reichsthaler.*

**1585** - Assembled at Frankfurt, merchants and traders raised exchange rates 8%-10% for gold monies (Dukaten, Gulden), and for silver (Reichsthaler, Guldenthaler).

**1618** - Large rise in exchange rates for specie monies during 30 Years War.

**1623** - Edict of Ferdinand II stabilizing exchange rate for specie monies. Coexistence of three systems of accounting: in Gulden of 60 Kreuzer or 240 Pfennig (Austria, Bavaria, Rhineland. . .), in Thaler of 30 Groschen (states of Northeast), in Mark of 16 Schilling or 192 Pfennig (Hamburg. . .).

**1667** - Diet of Regensburg raised exchange rate for specie monies. Electoral Saxony, Brandenburg and Brunswick-Lüneburg opposed this decision, and at Zinna, adopted Thaler of 90 Kreuzer or 24 Gute Groschen as monetary unit.

**1690** - Decisions of Conference of Leipzig (electoral Saxony, Brandenburg, Brunswick-Lüneburg): Thaler of 24 Gute Groschen or 288 Pfennig, became unit of account. Exchange rates for specie money raised (Dukaten, Gulden, and Reichsthaler which became Speciesthaler). - See *Speciesthaler.*

**1693** - New rates of exchange were adopted by Rhineland, Bavaria, Swabia, Franconia, Austria. . .

**1753** (September 21st) - Convention of Vienna (Austria-Bavaria) fixing Thaler of account at 1.50 Gulden, and defining specie monies:
>      In gold - Dukaten
>      In silver - Speciesthaler, Kopfstück, Groschen

**1761** - This system adopted by Swabia.

**1763** - Adherence of other states (except Prussia and Hanover).

**19th Century** - Political and monetary unification in stages (1838, 1857, 1871, 1873).
- See *Germany.*


# *HONDURAS*

**16th to 19th Century** - Circulation of Spanish and Mexican Piasters.

**1821** - Revolted from Spain.

**1822** - Joined Mexican Empire.

**1823** - Loosely grouped into United Provinces of Central America. - See *Peso Central America.*

**1838** - Became independent Republic. Central American Peso replaced by Honduran Peso. - See *Peso Honduras.*

**1926** (April 3rd) - Creation of new monetary unit linked to U.S. Dollar. - See *Lempira.*

## *HONG KONG*

**Before 1895** - Monetary anarchy as in China (see *China*) with currency in circulation predominantly Mexican Piasters, coins of 24.4356 grams of fine silver. - See *Piaster Mexico.*
Punctured Mexican Piasters called Chopped Dollars. Others, called Clean Dollars, were weighed at each payment.

**1895** (February 2nd) - Creation of Hong Kong Dollar. - See *Dollar Hong Kong.*

**1942** - Issue of military Yen during Japanese Occupation. - See *Gumpyo.*

**1945** (September 14th) - Restoration of Hong Kong Dollar. - See *Dollar Hong Kong.*

## HOR

See *Kran.*

## HUN

In **India,** in Hindu system (Southern States), gold coin equal to 42 Fanams, 168 Faluce, or 3,360 Cache. Also called Pagoda. - See *Pagoda.*

## *HUNGARY*

**11th Century** - Simultaneous introduction of coins coming from West (Deniers, then silver Obols) and from East (Mongolian copper coins).

**12th Century** - Appearance of 1/2 Obols.

**13th Century** - Issue of Bracteates, then return to small Deniers.

**14th Century** - Imitation of gold Gulden (Florin) and silver Gros. Minting of Deniers and Obols.

**1382** - Minting of gold Dukaten which spread over all of Europe in 16th Century (Hungarian Ducat). Minting of silver Thaler.

**1521** - General reduction of fineness of silver monies from 500 to 250.

**1540** - Austrian coinage: Dukat, Thaler, Groshen, Pfennig. - See *Austria* and *Holy Roman Empire.*
In area of Hungary occupied by Turks, Ottoman coinage. - See *Turkey.*

**18th Century** - Unit of account: Egyforint (Gulden of Holy Roman Empire) equal to 10 Chustaken, 20 Caszarsgara (Groschen), 40 Poltura, 60 Kreytzar (Krajczár), 100 Penz-Kraslowski, 240 Deniers of the Rhine, or 720 Babka.
Specie monies of Austria and Holy Roman Empire under local names and local mintings: Kremnitz (Dukat), Egysthaller (Speciesthaler), Egymagiartaller (Thaler), Uherszky-Zlatý (Hungarian Gulden), Seztak or Mariasz (17 Kreuzer), Hetes or Szedmak (7 Kreuzer), Pataz (Groschen), Babka. . .
**19th Century** - Hungarian Gulden (Florin) of 100 Krajczár equivalent to Austrian Gulden. - See *Gulden Austria.*
**1892** - Substitution of gold Krone for silver Gulden (Florin). - See *Krone Austria.*
**1920** - Independence of Hungary. Creation of Hungarian Korona. - See *Korona.*
**1921-1924** - Inflation, and depreciation of Korona. In order to provide a more stable monetary unit for business, introduction of so-called "Sparkrone". - See *Sparkrone.*

## HVID

**Danish and Norwegian** money, minted in 15th Century in silver and in 16th Century in silver/copper. Worth 1/2, later 1/3 Skilling. Minted in Gotland in 14th Century.
**18th Century** - Unit of account valued at 1/288 Rigsdaler, 1/192 Daler, 1/72 Oere, 1/48 Mark, 1/6 Stuyver, 1/3 Skilling, 2/3 Fyrk, or 4 Pfennig.
Variations of name - Witten, Hvide, Korsvide.
Cf. *Albus, Witten, Blanc.*

## HWAN

Money of **South Korea** from 1953 to 1962.
Bank of issue - Bank of Korea.
Predecessors - See *Korea* and *Won.*
Variations of name - Hwon, Houan.
**1953** (February 15th) - Hwan replaced depreciated Won through exchange of banknotes:
      1 Hwan = 100.00 Won
      1 U.S. Dollar = 60.00 Hwan
**1953** (December 15th) - New official rate:
      1 U.S. Dollar = 180.00 Hwan
Hwan on black market depreciated rapidly, listing at 275.00 per U.S. Dollar at end of 1953.
**1954** (October) - Multiple rate system:
      1 U.S. Military Dollar = 310.00 Hwan (military expenditures of U.S. Army)
      1 U.S. Dollar = 379.00 Hwan (sales of foreign exchange at auction)

Continued depreciation of Hwan on black market.

**1955** (August 15th) - Official exchange rate for all transactions except certain U.S. aid imports:

> 1 U.S. Dollar = 500.00 Hwan

Multiple rates for imports.

**1955** (August 26th) - Korea became member of International Monetary Fund.

**1956** - Import Account Hwan resulting from export proceeds, receipts from invisibles and U.N. military expenditures. For import payments at official rate of 500 per U.S. Dollar. Unofficial market offered up to 60% premium, or 800 per U.S. Dollar.

**1957** - Foreign exchange sold to bidders offering to buy largest amount of National Bonds for each U.S. Dollar they wished to purchase.

**1958** (August 28th) - Foreign exchange taxes replaced system of tying sales of National Bonds to sales of exchange. Auctioning continued, but difference between successful bid price and official rate had to be paid government as exchange tax. Additional tax of 150 Hwan per U.S. Dollar applied, resulting in U.S. Dollar rate of at least 650 Hwan and as much as 768 Hwan at end of 1958.

**1960** (February 23rd) - New multiple rate structure:

> 1 U.S. Dollar = 650 Hwan (official rate for sales of exchange to Bank of Korea, U.S. offshore procurement, sales of Hwan to U.N. forces, other invisibles, government imports, aid-financed imports)
>
> 1 U.S. Dollar = 800 Hwan (official rate plus 150 Hwan Flat Tax for specified aid-financed imports)
>
> 1 U.S. Dollar = 1,233 Hwan (official rate plus 150 Hwan Flat Tax and 933 Variable Tax for other aid-financed imports)
>
> 1 U.S. Dollar = 1,105 Hwan (official rate plus 150 Hwan Flat Tax, 303 Hwan Variable Tax and 2 Hwan Fee for imports financed with government supplied exchange)
>
> 1 U.S. Dollar = 1,330/1,340 Hwan (transfer rate for imports paid with exchange purchased from holders of Import Accounts)

**1961** (January 1st) - Official rate of Hwan set at 1,000 per U.S. Dollar. Foreign exchange taxes abolished.

**1961** (February 2nd) - New exchange system. Previous multiple rate practices abolished, and flexible rate established to govern all transactions:

> 1 U.S. Dollar = 1,250 Hwan (fixed basic rate)
>
> 1 U.S. Dollar = 50 Hwan (certificate rate)
>
> 1 U.S. Dollar = 1,300 Hwan (banking rate)

Certificate rate to be varied from time to time by Monetary Board of Bank of Korea.

**1961** (August 30th) - Hwan on black market deteriorated to all-time low of 1,800 per U.S. Dollar.

**1962** (June 10th) - Currency unit changed back to Won. - See *Won.*

## ICELAND

Primative money - Dried fish. Decree issued about 1420, which stayed in force for several centuries, placed tax of dried fish on various merchandise (large barrel of butter, 120; cask of wine, 100; pair of leather shoes, 4. . .).

**Before 1873** - Danish monetary system and circulation of Danish monies:
1 Rigsdaler = 96 Skilling

**1873** - Circulation of new Danish money: 1 Krone = 100 Aurar (singular Eyrir).

**1918** - Independent Kingdom in union with Denmark. Autonomous monetary system established. Creation of Icelandic Króna of 100 Aurar. - See *Króna Iceland.*

## ICHI BU BAN

**I.** - Gold piece of rectangular form, used as money in **Japan** from 16th to 19th Century. Name meaning 1 Bu.
Equivalent to 1/40 Oban, 1/4 Coban (or Ryo), or 4 Shu kin.

Variations of name - Itzi Bu, Jehebo, Buban, Bukin (this term was used to designate the unit of account).

**1589** - Melting of gold into small pieces called Ichi Bu ban. Weight: 4.45 grams 843 fine.

**1601** - Weight of Ichi Bu ban: 4.45 grams 843 fine

**1695** - Weight of Ichi Bu ban: 4.43 grams 574 fine

**1710** - Weight of Ichi Bu ban: 2.23 grams 843 fine

**1714** - Weight of Ichi Bu ban: 4.43 grams 843 fine

**1716** - Weight of Ichi Bu ban: 4.43 grams 867 fine

**1736** - Weight of Ichi Bu ban: 3.26 grams 657 fine

**1819** - Weight of Ichi Bu ban: 3.27 grams 564 fine

**1837** - Weight of Ichi Bu ban: 2.80 grams 568 fine

**1859** - Weight of Ichi Bu ban: 2.25 grams 568 fine

**1860** - Weight of Ichi Bu ban: 0.83 grams 568 fine

**1871** - Monetary reform abolishing earlier monies. - See *Yen.*

**II.** - Silver Ichi Bu introduced in **Japan** in 1830 and used until 1870.

**III.** - Ichi Bu, marked with imprint of a lion, introduced to **Netherlands East Indies** in 1690. Equal to 20 Schelling.

## ICHI BU GIN

Silver piece of rectangular form, used as money in **Japan** in 19th Century.

## IFNI

**Prior to 1860** - Part of Morocco. - See *Morocco.*
**1860** - Introduction of Spanish monetary system. - See *Spain* and *Peseta Spain.*
**1969** (June 30th) - Incorporated into Morocco. - See *Morocco* and *Dirham.*

## IKILIK

Silver coin of **Turkey** under Selim III (1789-1807): 25.35 grams 465 fine, equal to 2
    Piastres.
Origin of name - Derived from Turkish *iki* (two).
**19th Century** - 2.405 grams 830 fine silver, equal to 2 Piastres.

## ILAVOAMENA

Submultiple of Ariary (1/48), early monetary unit of **Madagascar.** - See *Ariary.*

## IMADI

Former monetary unit of **Yemen.** Divided into 40 Bugshas or 80 Halala.
Other names - Yemen Thaler and Riyal.
Predecessor - See *Maria Theresia Thaler.*
**1923** - Minting of silver coin copying Maria Theresia Thaler, and of copper or bronze
    submultiples.
**1964** (February) - Creation of Yemen Riyal in newly formed Yemen Arab Republic.
    Imadi withdrawn from circulation in June. - See *Riyal Yemen.*

## IMPERIAL

**I.** - Gold coin in **Russia** minted from 1755 (decree of November 23rd) by Elizabeth I.
    Initial weight 16.695 grams of fine gold, then 13.08 grams 916 fine. Lowered
    November 27, 1885, through alignment to French coin of 40 Francs, to 12.903
    grams 900 fine, or 11.613 grams fine gold.
    Rate of exchange: 10 Rubles. Gold 1/2 Imperial: 8.34 grams of fine gold from 1755
    to 1885; then 6.45 grams 900 fine, or 5.80 grams fine gold (weight of Napoléon).
    Was worth 5 Rubles until 1897, them 7.50 Rubles.
**1897** (January) - After monetary reform, exchange rate of Imperial raised to 15 Rubles.
    Minting of another gold coin of 10 Rubles, having 8.602 grams 900 fine. The
    1/3 Imperial weighed 4.301 grams 900 fine, or 3.871grams fine gold, and equal to

5 Rubles.

**II.** - Gold coins of **Flanders** in the 17th Century.

**III.** - Silver coin in **Milan** in 13th and 14th Centuries. Called Imperiale.

## INCA

In **Peru,** gold coin worth ½ Peruvian Libra (Pound) or 5 Soles. Equal to English ½ Sovereign: 3.99 grams 916 fine gold.

Origin of name - From title of Pre-Colombian rulers in Peru.

**1881** - Issue of Inca banknotes at forced parity of 5 Soles.

## *INDIA*

**Aryan era** - Ox used as unit of account.

**End of Vedic age** - Appearance of copper coins (Karsha), then of silver and of gold (Nishka or Satamana).

**5th Century B.C.** - Use of copper or bronze coins (Pada, Kamsa, Kakanika, Masaka) and gold coins (Nishka, Karsha).
Introduction of Persian gold coins (Daric) and silver coins (Siglos).

**4th Century B.C.** - After invasion of Alexander, introduction of Greek coins (Drachma) within borders of Bactria.

**1st Century A.D.** - Circulation of Persian monies in the Deccan. Minting of silver and copper coins in Northern India. Traditional hoarding of silver and gold in form of idols, jewelry, bullion, house utensils.
Native monies: Shells, shell necklaces (see *Cowrie*); bitter almond (see *Badam*).

**8th Century** - Circulation of Byzantine, Iranian and Arab monies in the Deccan.

**After 11th Century** - Moslem coinage: Tankah, silver coin divided into 4 Shashani, 24 Jettal, 48 Adhâ, or 96 Biche. For minor payments, use of Cowrie or Kaoli.

**14th Century** - Minting in Delhi of gold Dinar and silver Adli.

**1329** - Issue in Delhi of copper tokens with value of one silver Tankah. Inflation and collapse of this fiduciary money.

**16th Century** - Minting of Buhloli worth 1.6 Jettal. Introduction of Portuguese monies. - See *Portuguese India.*

**End of 16th Century** - Two indigenous monetary systems divided India. In Southern India, Hindu monetary system with gold Hun, which Portuguese called Pagoda, as monetary unit:
1 Hun = 42 Fanams = 168 Faluce = 3,360 Cache (Kas)
In Central and Northern India, Moslem monetary system with silver Rupee (see *Rupee India*) as monetary unit:
1 Rupee = 16 Annas = 64 Pice = 192 Pies
Gold Mohur worth 14-16 Rupees according to price of gold bullion.

**1600** - Appearance of English specie monies: Crown, Shilling, Penny.

**1671** - British East India Company minted Pagoda, Fanam and Rupee copied from local types. Simultaneous circulation of Mexican Piasters (equal to 2-3 Rupees), Venetian Zecchini and Turkish Sequins.

*Unit of account:* Rupee of 2 Cawne, 16 Annas, 32 Ponis, 128 Burries, 640 Gundas, or 2,560 Cowries.

Multiples - Crore of 100 Lakhs or 10 million Rupees.

- In Surat: Nil of 100 Badams, 10,000 Crores, 1 million Lakhs, or 100 billion Rupees.
- In Calicut: Fanam of 15 Biche.
- In Cannanore: Fanam of 16 Biche.
- In Madras: Pagoda of 36 Fanams.

    *Specie monies:*

        In gold - Pagoda (3.60 silver Rupees)

        In silver - Rupee of varying types and weights: Mogul Rupee, Bombay Rupee (minted by English); Arcate Rupee (minted by French); Mahmudi (2.50 silver Rupees)

        In copper (in Surat) - Pacha of 40-68 Badams. - See *Pacha* and *Badam.*

    *Local specie monies:*
- In Golconda: gold Rupee equal to 14 silver Rupees.
- In Madras: silver Fanam worth 1/10 Rupee.
- In Calicut: gold Fanam equal to 16 Tarés, silver Taré.
- In Bombay (English mintings): Budgrook of 16 Serafins (or tin Xerafins), silver Rupee worth 24 copper Rupees, gold Mohur of 12.50 silver Rupees or 300 copper Rupees.

**1700** - See *French India.*

**1835** - Fixing of silver fineness of Rupee at 10.684 grams fine.

**1862** - Issue of paper Rupees.

**1948** - Pakistan adopted independent monetary system. - See *Rupee Pakistan.*

**1950** - Ceylon adopted independent monetary system. - See *Rupee Ceylon.*

## INDIO

Silver coin issued in **Portugal** in 1499; worth 33 Reis.

## *INDOCHINA*

Traditional circulation of Chinese zinc, then copper Sapèques, often fastened in rolls. - See *Sapèque.*

**541** - Minting of Annamite Sapèques by Ly Nam-Dé.

**After 16th Century** - Introduction of silver Mexican Piasters of 27.0695 grams 903 fine, or 24.4356 grams fine.

**1801** - Nguyen-Anh, Emperor of Annam, created Nên Bac, rectangular gold or silver bar bearing inscriptions. Free minting. Making of Sapèques remained monopoly of government.

**19th Century** - Native money: Sapèque in addition to silver Nên Bac.
In seaports, use of Mexican Piaster. Indochinese refused all coins not bearing a heaviness approximating that of silver Piaster. Failure of Emperors in attempts to introduce coins of different weight.
Coins of similar silver weight accepted: United States Trade Dollar (24.4935 grams fine), Hong Kong Dollar (24.2611 grams fine), French Piastre of 1885 (24.4935 grams fine).

**1862** (April 10th) - After arrival of French, legal tender status given to Mexican Piasters in Cochin China.

**1863** (March 5th) - Issue of coins in Francs (from 0.05 to 2 Francs). Attempt at fixing stable exchange ratios between various monies:
> 1 Mexican Piaster = 5.37 Francs = 5 bundles of 600 Sapèques

**1863** (June 13th) - Decree generalizing exchange rate of bundle to 1 Franc. Actually, varying rates of exchange. Circulation of Mexican Piasters, whole, or cut into 2 or 4 pieces.

**1864** (January 25th) - Legal tender status given to French monies.

**1865** - French military campaign in Annam. Increasing use of Mexican Piasters. Exchange rate: 6.25 Francs, 5.55, then 5.35.

**1874** (June 30th) - Trade Dollar accepted by government offices.

**1875** (January 21st) - Privilege of banknote issue given to Banque de l'Indochine.

**1878** (May 5th) - Introduction without success of French coins of 5 Francs.

**1885** (December 22nd) - Issue of French Piastres, called Piastres de Commerce, similar to Trade Dollar: 27.215 grams 900 fine,.or 24.4935 grams fine silver. Submultiples: 50, 20 and 10 Centièmes.

**1895** (July 8th) - Decree reducing weight of Piastre de Commerce, which became Indochinese Piastre, to 27 grams 900 fine, or 24.30 grams fine silver, Simultaneous circulation of Indochinese Piastre and Mexican Piaster. (Latter minted with 3% duty levied for export from Indochina).

**1903** (June 3rd) - Withdrawal of Mexican Piasters, and their importation banned. Abolishment of the duty levied on their export.
Indochinese Piastre remained only monetary unit of Indochina. Free minting, free convertibility (silver standard), full power of legal tender. - See *Piastre Indochina*.

**1948** - Issue of autonomous banknotes in territories controlled by Viet Minh. - See *Piastre Dong Viet*.

**1949** (March-November) - Cambodia, Laos and Viet Nam granted independence within framework of French Union. - See *individual countries*.


## *INDONESIA*

Primitive monies - Chinese porcelain vases, Chinese bronze knives, Tibetan bricks of pressed tea.

Other native monies - See *Java, Sumatra,* and *Moluccas.*

**1601** (March 1st) - Van Verre Company of Amsterdam authorized to mint Piastres of 8 Reales and their submultiples in silver.

**1645** - East India Company issued silver Crowns (of 48 Stuyver). Withdrawn in 1647.

**1686** - Introduction of counter-marked Dutch Ducats.

**1690** - Use of specially marked Japanese specie monies: Coban, Ichi Bu ban.

**18th Century** - Institution of Dutch monetary system: silver Ducatons and copper Duiten in 1726; silver Guilders, Stuyver and Duiten in 1786.

**1817** (January 14th) - Official adoption of monetary system based on Netherlands Guilder. - See *Guilder Netherlands East Indies.*

**1946** (March 7th) - Introduction of banknotes denominated in Indonesian Guilders.

**1949** (November 2nd) - Guilder replaced by Indonesian Rupiah. - See *Rupiah Indonesia.*


# IONIAN ISLANDS

Greek (see *Greece*), Roman (see *Rome*), Byzantine (see *Byzantium*), Venetian (see *Venice*), and French monies (see *France*).

**1815** - British Protectorate. Use of English monies: Pound, Shilling and Pence. - See *Pound.*

**1864** - Ceded to Greece. Use of Greek monies. - See *Greece* and *Drachma.*

**1941** - Italian Occupation. - See *Italy* and *Lira.*

**1944** - Returned to Greece. - See *Drachma.*


# IRAN

For ancient and recent history, see *Persia.*

**1935** (March 22nd) - Official name of modern Persia changed to Iran. For monetary unit, see *Rial Iran.*


# IRAQ

**3,000 B.C.** - Sumerian civilization: payment transactions settled with grain (Qua), then with silver bars (siglos).

**600 B.C.** - Assyrian civilization: barley used as money, later lead bars. Followed by Persian, Greek, Roman, Byzantine, Arab, Turkish monies.

**Before 1931** - Circulation of Egyptian Pounds and Indian Rupees.

**1931** (April 19th) - Creation of Dinar. - See *Dinar Iraq.*

# IRELAND

**10th Century** - Danish kings copied English Penny.

**12th Century** - After English conquest, introduction of English monetary system, using Pounds, Sols and Deniers. - See *England* and *Pound.* Local minting of Halfpenny and silver Farthing.
Simultaneous appearance of an Irish Pound, constantly having lower value than Pound Sterling.

**15th Century** - Debasement of silver Groat. Issue of copper Patrick. Distrust of money revived system of payments by weights.

**17th Century** - Simultaneous circulation of English, Irish, and foreign (especially Portuguese) coins.

**1825** - Introduction of British monetary system.

**1921** (December 6th) - Political independence, but British monetary system continued.

**1927** (August 20th) - Law assimilating Irish Pound with Pound Sterling. - See *Pound Ireland.*

# IRELAND (NORTHERN)

Circulation of British banknotes and coins, as well as banknotes of local banks with note-issuing privilege: Bank of Ireland, Belfast Banking Company, Provincial Bank of Ireland, Ulster Bank.

# IRMILIK

See *Medjidie.*

# IRRISH

Name formerly given to **Irish** Penny (Irish Denier), 1/240 Irish Pound. - See *Pound Ireland.*

# ISABELLA

Name given to gold **Spanish** coin called Doubloon, or Dubla. Worth 5 Duros. Created by Isabella II, circulated until 1868. - See *Doubloon.*

# ISRAEL

Predecessor - See *Palestine.*

**1948** (May 14th) - Independent state established.

**1948** (August 16th) - Creation of Israel Pound, replacing Palestinian Pound at par. - See *Pound Israel.*

## ITALY

Primitive money - Cattle.

**7th Century B.C.** - In Sicily, introduction of system of accounting of Euboea. - See *Sicily.*

**6th Century B.C.** - In Southern Italy, minting of coins copied from Corinth (7.5 to 8 grams of silver). Native coinage: bronze bar, called As. In Campania, as in Sicily, silver coin called Litra. - See *As* and *Litra.*

**5th Century B.C.** - Etruscans minted silver (8.5 grams), gold, and copper coins. Rome substituted payment in bronze bars (pecunia) for payment in cattle (pecus).

**4th Century B.C. to 5th Century A.D.** - See *Rome.*

**7th and 8th Centuries** - Lombards used Triens, or 1/3 Sou.

**9th Century** - Minting of Carolingian Denier. Carolingian system of accounting based on Livre of 20 Sols or 240 Deniers, with Lira of 20 Soldi or 240 Denari.
In Southern Italy (see *Naples, Sicily*) mixture of Byzantine and Arab monetary influences.

**10th to 19th Century** - Subsequent development of monetary system within framework of various provinces: see *Ancona, Bergamo, Bologna, Papal States, Florence, Genoa, Leghorn, Mantua, Milan, Naples, Piedmont, Sardinia, Savoy, Sicily, Tuscany, Trieste, Venice.*

**19th Century** - Unification of Italy with the Lira as monetary unit. - See *Lira* and *Lira Italy.*

## IVORY COAST

**Native money** - Metallic bracelets. - See *Manilla.*

**17th and 18th Centuries** - Irregular circulation of British and French specie monies.

**1817** - French domination and gradual acceptance of French Franc. - See *Franc.*

**1904** - Became part of French West Africa. - See *French West Africa.*

**1945** (December 26th) - Creation and use of CFA Franc. - See *Franc CFA.*

**1960** (August 7th) - Became independent republic. Monetary unit unchanged.

## JACOBUS

Gold money of **England,** minted under reign of James I, hence the name. Weight: 2.34 grams 915 fine, or 2.14 grams fine. Converted into Guineas from 1660 to 1689.

## JAFIMSKE

In **Russia,** name given to German Thaler in 16th and 17th Centuries. Stamped with Russian imprint, these coins equalled ½ Ruble.

Origin of name - Russian distortion of Joachim, for Joachimsthaler. - See *Joachimsthaler.*

**1654** - Exchange rate of Jafimske doubled to 1 Ruble.

**1655** - Jafimske cut into two parts, each piece worth ½ Ruble, or 1 Poltina; or into four parts, each piece worth ¼ Ruble, or 1 Polpoltin.

**About 1700** - Peter the Great upheld assimilation of Jafimske into Ruble.

## *JAMAICA*

Note: **Turks and Caicos Islands** and **Cayman Islands** had parallel monetary experience.

**Prior to 1655** – Spanish specie money, then introduction of British monetary system.

**18th Century** - Jamaica Pound served as unit of account. - See *Pound Jamaica.* Circulation of English and Portuguese specie monies. Limited use of English banknotes.

**19th Century** - Accounting value of Jamaican Pound adjusted to equal Pound Sterling. - See *Pound.* Circulation of English specie monies and coinage of United States and Canada.

**1846** - Silver Farthings minted for Jamaica.

**1863** (October 23rd) - Fractional coinage of United States and Canada ceased to be legal tender.

**1869-1870** - Minting of local subsidiary coinage in nickel: Pennies, Halfpennies and Farthings.

**1876** - Silver Dollar no longer legal tender. Continued circulation of American gold coins. Subsequent issue of 10, 5, and 1 Pound banknotes by several private banks (Barclays Bank, Bank of Nova Scotia, Canadian Bank of Commerce and Royal Bank of Canada).

**1917** - British Treasury notes in denominations of 1 Pound and 10 Shillings issued under Currency and Banknotes Act of 1914 declared legal tender.

**1919** (July 3rd) - British banknotes ceased to be legal tender. Banknotes of private banks continued to circulate.

**1920** (March) - First issue of local currency notes under Currency Note Law of 1904 (No. 27). - See *Pound Jamaica.*

**1951** - BWI Dollar became legal tender. Limited circulation. - See *Dollar British West Indies.*

**1958** - Notes of commercial banks and Bank of England ceased to be legal tender. English coins, Jamaican Pound notes and coins and BWI Dollar notes remained legal tender.

**1961** (May 1st) - Bank of Jamaica established as Central Bank and note-issuing authority.

**1962** (August 6th) - Jamaica became independent. Turks and Caicos Islands, and Cayman Islands became separate British Colony and continued to use monetary unit of Jamaica.

**1969** (September 8th) - Jamaican Dollar replaced Jamaican Pound as monetary unit. - See *Dollar Jamaica.*


## *JAPAN*

Appearance in Japan of Chinese Sapèques, often in bundles of a thousand (Kuan).

**708** - Minting of copper coins imitating Sapèque: Wado Kaiho weighing 7.9 grams, one of twelve ancient Sen. Weight reduced in 907 and 958. Monetary use of gold and silver bars for large payments.

**10th to 16th Century** - Suspension of all official mintings in Japan. Use of earlier monies and Chinese imported coins (called Eiraku Sen). Some poor privately minted counterfeits in copper.

**13th to 19th Century** - Issue of Tagata, paper chits replacing Sen or rice money.

**1589** - As result of gold mining, and imitating Portuguese example, striking of gold plaques in elliptical form called Oban and Coban, and of rectangular pieces, called Ichi Bu ban. These three gold monies, with various modifications, used until 19th Century. - See *Oban, Coban, Ichi Bu ban.*

**1617** - First private issue of paper money. - See *Hansatsu.*

**1636** - Minting of copper coins called Sen. - See *Sen.*

**1695** - Casting of silver elliptical bars, called Cho Gin, and round pieces of silver called Mame Gin (see Cho Gin and Mame Gin). Circulated until 1722.

**18th Century** - Units of account: Tael of 10 Mace or 100 Candareens; Cockien.

**1772** - Striking of Ni Shu gin, silver coin. - See *Ni Shu gin.*

**1824** - Issue of Shu kin, small gold coin. - See *Shu kin.*

**1829** - Issue of Shu gin, small silver coin. - See *Shu gin.*

**1837** - Issue of Ichi Bu gin, silver bar. - See *Ichi Bu gin.*

**1868** - Issue of State banknotes, called Kinsatsu (Dajokwansatsu). Denominated in gold, at forced parity.

**1869** - Minting of silver coins called Yen weighing 27.07 grams 900 fine.

**1871** - Abolition of private paper money (Hansatsu).

**1871** (June) - Minting of gold Yen coins:
    1 Yen = 1,504.656 milligrams of fine gold
    1 Yen = 100 Sen = 1,000 Rin

Bimetallic standard resulted in silver/gold ratio of 16 to 1.

**1872** - Silver coinage ceased.

**1875** - Coinage of silver resumed in form of Trade Dollar weighing 27.216 grams 900 fine.

**1878** - Trade Dollar made legal tender, but did not succeed in driving out Mexican Piaster used in Asiatic trade.

**1879** (September) - Silver Yen weighing 26.957 grams 900 fine declared legal tender. Circulated at par with Mexican Piaster, which it eventually replaced.

**1897** (October 1st) - Adoption of gold standard: 1 Yen = 750 milligrams of fine gold. Circulation of banknotes issued by Bank of Japan and convertible into gold. - See *Yen*.

**1942** - In the occupied territories, issue of Military Yen, called Gumpyo. - See *Gumpyo*.


## JAVA

**896-1158** - Hindu period. Use of square gold pieces weighing up to 10 grams, similar to those in Southern India.

**13th Century** - Local units of account: Bahar of 10 Utas, 100 Catties, 1,000 Laxsan, 10,000 Peccoes, 250,000 Tayell, 500,000 Sata, 2,500,000 Mas, 10 million Cash, or 100 million Candareens.
Other local system of accounting: Soekoe worth 5 Sata or 1,000 Caixa.
Specie monies: Pataca of 6 Mas or 24 Cash, Cash.

**After 17th Century** - Introduction of European coins (Spanish, French, Dutch, German . . .), especially Spanish Piasters.
Unit of account used by Europeans: Piaster of 60 Stuyver, worth from 20,000 to 35,000 Cash.

**1686-1700** - East India Company had gold Ducats counterstamped "B" (Batavia).

**18th Century** - In Mohammedan State of Bantam, use of Fardos, silver money and unit of account.

**1802** - Introduction of silver Guilders and copper Duiten of Batavian Republic.

**1810** - Reign of Louis Napoléon in Holland. Use of copper Stuyver and Duiten marked "LN".

**1811-1816** - Under English domination, British East India Company minted gold Mohurs, silver Rupees, copper Stuyver and lead Duiten.

**1816** - Return to Dutch control. - See *Netherlands East Indies*.


## JEN MIN PIAO (YUAN)

Monetary unit of **Communist China.** Divided into 10 Tsjao and 100 Fyng.

Variation of name - Yen Min Piao, Dollar of People's Bank, People's Bank Dollar, Yuan.

Bank of issue - People's Bank of China, established December 1948.

Predecessors - See *China, Dollar China, Gold Yuan.*

**1948** - Mao Tse Tung created People's Yuan during Civil War. Issued by People's Bank in conquered areas, with exchange rate varying according to provinces. People's Yuan gave rise to Jen Min Piao, after elimination of Nationalist Government's inflation.

**1949** (April) - Parity fixed by People's Bank:
1 U.S. Dollar = 600 Jen Min Piao
Parities subsequently fixed each month.

**1950** (January) - 1 U.S. Dollar = 21,000 Jen Min Piao.

**1950** (April) - 1 U.S. Dollar = 45,000 Jen Min Piao.

**1950** (December) - Black market rate of Jen Min Piao hit record 47,000 per U.S. Dollar.

**1951** (January) - 1 U.S. Dollar = 22,890 Jen Min Piao.

**1952** (September) - 1 U.S. Dollar = 22,267 Jen Min Piao.

**1952** (December 8th) - 1 U.S. Dollar = 23,430 Jen Min Piao.

**1955** (March 1st-April 30th) - General exchange of banknotes:
10,000 Old Jen Min Piao = 1 New Jen Min Piao
1 U.S. Dollar = 2.46 Jen Min Piao

**1962** (June) - Black market rate of Jen Min Piao hit record 21.25 per U.S. Dollar, a premium of 764% for Greenback.

**1967** (November 18th) - Following British devaluation of Sterling, Bank of China in Hong Kong reduced official rate from 42.50 to 36.60 Jen Min Piao per 100 Hong Kong Dollars and kept U.S. Dollar parity unchanged.

**1969** (June) - Name of Chinese currency unit (Jen Min Piao, or Yuan) changed to Renminbi, which served as legal tender. Yuan remained monetary unit of account.
- See *Renminbi.*


## JETTAL

Coin used in **India** after Moslem invasions. Equivalent to 1/24 Tankah or 1/6 Shashgani. Consisted of 2 Adhâ, or 4 Biche.


## JOACHIMSTHALER

See *Thaler.*


## JOE

Portuguese gold coin circulating in **British West Indies** during late 18th Century. Same as Dobra de Oito Escudos and valued at 12,800 Reis. The 1/2 Joe or Dobra de Quatro Escudos valued at 6,400 Reis.

Origin of name - From Joannes, another name for Dobra.

## *JORDAN*

Predecessor - See *Transjordan* and *Palestine*.

**1946** (June 17th) - Kingdom established from former territory of Transjordan. Monetary unit Palestinian Pound. - See *Pound Palestine*.

**1950** (July 1st) - Creation of Jordan Dinar to replace Palestinian Pound at par. - See *Dinar Jordan*.

## JUIK

Unit of account in **Turkey.**

Variations of name - Jux, Juk.

**18th and 19th Centuries** - Juik consisted of 2 Beutels, 1,000 Piastres, 12,000 Timmins, 40,000 Paras, 100,000 Minas or 120,000 Aspers.

## JUSTO

Gold coin of **Portugal** issued in 1485 and valued at 600 Reis. The ½ Justo was called Espadim.

## KABIR

Unit of account of **Arabia** in 18th Century. Equivalent to ¹⁄₈₀ Piastre.
Variations of name - Kabukt, Caveer.

## KABULI

Name used for **Afghanistan** currency until 1927. - See *Rupee Afghanistan.*

## KANTOU

Bar of salt in the form of cone weighing 10 to 20 kilos Used as money in the **Sahara** (between Fezzan and Chad) at end of 19th Century.
Cf. *Amolés.*

## KAPANG

**I.** - In Kingdom of Achin in **Sumatra,** unit of account (called Koupan): ¹⁄₆₄ Tayell, ¹⁄₁₆ Pardaw, ¹⁄₄ Mas, or 400 Cash. Copper coin minted in 1786 by British East India Company.
Variations of name - Kepeng, Keping, Kupang, Koupan.
**II.** - Copper coin minted in 1835 for **Malacca** by British East India Company. Valued at ¹⁄₄₀₀ Spanish Dollar.
**III.** - In **Japan,** gold money, also called Coban, Coupang, Cobang or Kobang. - See *Coban.*

## *KATANGA*

Predecessors - Belgian Congo, Congo Democratic Republic.
**1960** (August 10th) - Following secession from Congo Democratic Republic (July 11, 1960), creation of independent monetary unit. - See *Franc Katanga.*
**1963** (January 10th) - Katanga annexed to Congo Democratic Republic. Katanga Franc abolished and replaced by Congolese Franc. - See *Franc Congo.*

## KAZBEGI

Unit of account and copper money of **Persia** in 18th and 19th Centuries. Equal to ¹⁄₂,₀₀₀ Toman, ¹⁄₂₀₀ Hor or Kran, ¹⁄₄₀ Abbasi, ¹⁄₂₀ Mahmudi, ¹⁄₁₀ Shahi, or 5 Dinars.

## KENYA

7th Century - Arab colonization of coastal area with use of Arab specie monies.

16th Century - Portuguese domination, and introduction of Portuguese specie monies.

1740 - Reintroduction of Arab monies on coast. Use of Cowries for ivory and slave trade in interior.

Early 19th Century - Free trade with India resulted in gradual importance of Indian Rupee.

1888 - Imperial British East Africa Company minted East African Rupee - See *Rupee East Africa.*

1922 (January 1st) - Introduction of East African Shilling equal to English Shilling. - See *Shilling East Africa.*

1966 (September 14th) - Kenya Shilling replaced East African Shilling at par. - See *Shilling Kenya.*

1967 (September 14th) - East African Shilling ceased to be legal tender.

## KERATION

I. - Smallest unit of weight in **Roman Empire**, equal to $1/1.728$ Libra.

II. - Name given during **Eastern Empire** to Roman Siliqua. - See *Siliqua.*

Variation of name - Keratium.

Plural - Keratia.

## KESER

See *Beutel.*

## KHARUB

**Tunisian** copper, silver, and silver/copper coins, equivalent to $1/16$ Tunisian Piastre. Minted in 1864 at Paris Mint. Continued as unit of account after 1891 and introduction of French monetary system.

Variations of name - Caroube, Kharrube, Karub, Kharoube.

## KHODABANDI

Silver/copper coin in **Persia** in 18th Century, equal to Mahmudi. - See *Mahmudi.*

Variation of name - Chodabende.

## KIAO CH'AO

Paper money (Ch'ao meaning banknote) issued in **China** in 12th Century.

**1154** - Issue of Kiao Ch'ao in Peking.

**1190** - Inflation of Kiao Ch'ao. Collapse of its value.

**1217 to 1233** - Five issues of paper money.

**1233** - Silver bars substituted for discredited paper money.

**1260** - New issue of Kiao Ch'ao secured by silver and gold reserve, denominated in Kuan and in Wen (1 Kuan = 1,000 Wen). Imitated by Mongols, dating from Genghis Khan to Kublai Khan.

**14th Century** - Depreciation and decline of Kiao Ch'ao.

## KIAO TZE

Paper money issued in **China** from 10th to 12th Century.

**About 990** - Issue of Kiao tze by group of merchants in order to relieve scarcity of copper Tsien and compensate for depreciation of iron Tsien.

**1011** - In order to neutralize wear and tear of banknotes, exchange of paper money decreed for every three years.

**1023** - Monopoly of issue reserved to provincial administration of Szechwan.

**1069** - Spread of Kiao tze to neighboring provinces.

**1100** : Inflation to accommodate needs of Treasury.

**1105** - Expansion of Kiao tze under name of Tsien Yin (banknotes for "withdrawing" Tsien) throughout China.

**1106** - Withdrawal of banknotes, except in Szechwan.

**1126** - Heavy depreciation.

**1136** - Introduction of Kiao tze in Southern China, where they became Kuan tze, then Hwai tze, more or less convertible into Tsien. Continued inflation until end of the century.

## KIP

Monetary unit of **Laos**. Divided into 100 At.

Bank of issue - Banque Nationale du Laos (National Bank of Laos), established December 29, 1954.

Predecessor - See *Piastre Indochina.*

**1955** (May 5th) - Kip replaced Piastre as national currency:
    1 Kip = 10 French Francs
    1 Kip = 25.391 milligrams of fine gold
    1 U.S. Dollar = 35.00 Kips
    Special EFAC (Exportations-Frais Accessories) Account existed, resulting from retention of 40% of export receipts and used for certain payments abroad.

Exchange controls also led to blocked Kip variety.

**1955** (November) - Domestic inflation and external depreciation of monetary unit. Kip on black market fell to low of 110.00 per U.S. Dollar, premium of 214% for Greenback. Subsequent improvement in black market rate of Kip.

**1958** (October 10th) - Currency reform and devaluation. Exchange controls abolished:
1 Kip = 11.084 milligrams of fine gold
1 U.S. Dollar = 80.00 Kips

**1960** (August 9th) - Convertibility of Kip temporarily suspended.

**1961** (January 1st) - Convertibility of Kip restored.

**1961** (July 5th) - Laos became member of International Monetary Fund.

**1962** (January 1st) - Convertibility of Kip suspended. Exchange controls.

**1962-1963** - Depreciation of Kip on black market, hitting record low of 575.00 per U.S. Dollar at end of 1963.

**1964** (January 1st) - Devaluation of Kip. Multiple rates established:
1 U.S. Dollar = 240.00 Kips (official rate for imports of aid
goods, government requirements, 60% of export
proceeds, and specified invisibles)
1 U.S. Dollar = 344.00 Kips (mixed export rate)
1 U.S. Dollar = 480.00 Kips (free market rate for all other
transactions)
Official free market rate settled around 500.00 per U.S. Dollar. Supported by stabilization program (Foreign Exchange Operations Fund) backed by U.S., U.K., Australia and France. Later joined by Japan.

**1965** (March) - Black market rate of Kip abroad hit record 1,100.00 per U.S. Dollar, premium of 358% for Greenback over official rate and 120% over official free market rate. After stabilization, unofficial rate fluctuated between 475.00-580.00 per U.S. Dollar.

**1965** (September 28th) - Percentage of export earnings required to be surrendered at official rate reduced to 10%, except for tin ore and concentrates, where rates of 20%, 40% and 60% applied, depending on grade and source. Percentages changed periodically for various exports.

## KIROBO

Early silver money of **Madagascar,** corresponding to 1/4 Mexican Piaster (6.52 grams). Equal to 1/4 Ariary, 1/2 Loso, or 2 Sikajy, 3 Roavoamena, 12 Ilavoamena, 18 Eranambatry, 24 Varifitoventy, 36 Varidimoventy.

## KITE

Subdivision (1/10) of Deben, metal bars used as money in ancient **Egypt.** - See *Deben.*

## KITZE

See *Beutel.*


## KLIPPE

Square or polygonal silver coins of a low fineness issued in **Denmark** and in **Sweden** between 1540 and 1557, during the war between the two nations.
Origin of name - From Swedish *klippa* (cut, or clip).
Variation of name - Klipping.


## KOMMASSI

Silver/copper coin used in **Arabia** during 18th Century. Valued at $1/16$ Spanish Dollar. Later struck in copper and value depreciated, 350-500 being equivalent of Spanish Dollar.
Variations of name - Comasse, Commassee, Comassir.


## KOPEK

**I.** - Submultiple ($1/100$) of Ruble, monetary unit of **Russia,** then of the U.S.S.R.

Variations of name - Copec, Kopeck, Kopeika (Russian).

Origin of name - Word kopeijka refers to lance held in hand of Czar. Pictured on first coins.

Plural - Kopeiki (Russian), Kopeks (English).

Early submultiples - Denga or Denuschka ($1/2$); Poluschka ($1/4$).

Multiples - Grivna (10), Pialtinik (15), Dwon-Grivna (20), Poltinik (50).

**16th Century** - Circulated in form of small oblong silver coins. Kopek equal to 2 Dengi (singular: Denga).

**1655** - Issued in copper at forced parity, as well as in multiples (Grochevik = 2 Kopeks; Altyn = 3 Kopeks). Depreciated to $1/4$ in 1662, to $1/15$ in 1663. Withdrawn from circulation in 1663.

**About 1700** - Issued in silver (irregular form).

**1714** (May 20th) - Silver Kopek given a round form.

**1725** - Minting of silver plaques.

**18th to 20th Century** - Small copper coins.

**II.** - Submultiple ($1/100$) of Tug and Aksa, monetary units of **Tuva** in 1935 and 1936, respectively, and equal to Ruble.

## KOPFSTUCK

**I.** - Early **German** money.

Origin of name - German *kopf* (head) and *stück* (piece).

**18th Century** - Kopfstück equivalent to ⅙ Reichsthaler (Ecu), according to Monetary Convention of Holy Roman Empire of 1753. Weight 6.7 grams, of which 3.8 were fine silver.

In Bremen, silver/copper money worth 12 Groten.

**1753** - Silver money of Austria worth 20 Kreuzer or 5 Batzen, and Bavarian silver coin worth 24 Kreuzer.

**II.** - Silver/copper coin of **Denmark** in 18th Century, exchangeable for 10 Stuyver or 20 Skilling.


## *KOREA*

Primitive money - Rice. - See *China.*

**19th Century** - Minting of a copper Sapèque worth about ¹⁄₅₂₅ Dollar. Attempt at introducing Mexican Piaster, but Koreans preferred Japanese Yen.

**1905** - Autonomous monetary system based on Won, identical to Yen. - See *Won.* Free circulation of Japanese monies.

**1910 to 1945** - Japanese Occupation. Issue of Yen of Bank of Korea (Chosen), linked to Yen. - See *Yen.*

**1945** (August 8th) - Soviet Occupation (North Korea). September 8th, U.S. Occupation (South Korea). - See *Won.*

**1953** - Issue of new money in South Korea. - See *Hwan.*

**1962** (June 10th) - Currency changed back to Won. - See *Won.*


## KORONA

Monetary unit of **Hungary** from 1920 to 1925. Divided into 100 Filler.

Bank of issue - In 1919, by Hungarian Section of Austro-Hungarian Bank, then by State Note Institute of Ministry of Finance. After June 24, 1924, by National Bank of Hungary.

Predecessors - See *Krone Austria, Austria* and *Hungary.*

**1920** - Stamping of Austrian Krone banknotes issued both by Austro-Hungarian Bank and by government of Bela Kun.

**1921** (May 4th) - Creation of Hungarian Korona. Inflation and depreciation.

**1922** (August 8th) - Foreign exchange controls.

**1924** (August) - Stabilization of Korona under auspices of League of Nations:
1 Pound Sterling = 346,000 Koronas

**1925** (November 4th) - Adoption of Pengoe as new monetary unit. - See *Pengoe.*

## KORTEN

Money of silver/copper, then copper, in **Netherlands** during 15th and 16th Centuries.
Value: 2 Myten of Flanders, 3 Myten of Brabant, or ¹/₁₂ Groot.
Also called Double Myte.

**1466** - Issued by Philip the Good; in 1467 by Charles the Bold, and in 1520 by Charles V in pure copper.

## KORUNA CZECH

Money created by Germans in Protectorate of **Bohemia-Moravia.**
Divided into 100 Haleru (singular: Haler).

Bank of issue - Bank of Bohemia and Moravia in Prague.

Predecessor - See *Koruna Czechoslovakia, Koruna Slovak.*

Plural - Koruny.

**1939** - Dismemberment of Czechoslovakian Koruna, which gave rise to Czech Koruna and Slovak Koruna:
1 Reichsmark = 10 Czech Koruny
Retention of old parity (11.73 Czech Koruny per Reichsmark) for calculating exchange ratio between Koruna and other currencies.

**1940** (October 1st) - With abolition of borders between Germany and Protectorate, value of Koruna raised by 17% in relation to currencies other than Reichsmark:
1 Czech Koruna = 1.162 Slovak Koruny

**1945** (May) - With liberation of Czechoslovakia, return to old parity. - See *Koruna Czechoslovakia.*

## KORUNA CZECHOSLOVAKIA

Monetary unit of **Czechoslovakia.** Divided into 100 Haleru (singular: Haler).

Bank of issue - Until April 1, 1926, by State. Since 1926, by National Bank of Czechoslovakia, nationalized March 11, 1948. In 1950 by Státni Banka Ceskoslovenská ( State Bank of Czechoslovakia).

Predecessors - See *Austria, Bohemia* and *Krone Austria.*

Plural - Koruny.

**1918** - Circulation of Austrian Krone multiplied by inflation.

**1919** (February 25th) - Closing of borders prohibiting export and import of banknotes. Foreign exchange controls.

**1919** (March 3rd through 9th) - Overprinting of banknotes, with 25% of total 'withdrawn from circulation as forced loan.

**1919** (April 10th) - Creation of Czechoslovakian Koruna:
1 Koruna = 304 milligrams of fine gold

**1925** (March 12th) - After depreciation (from 1920 to 1922), de facto stabilization at:

1 U.S. Dollar = 33.78 Koruny

**1927** (April 4th) - Removal of foreign exchange controls.

**1929** (November 27th) - De jure stabilization, with devaluation of 85.3%:
1 Koruna = 44.58 milligrams of fine gold

**1931** (September 26th) - Foreign exchange controls again decreed.

**1932** (July 15th) - Tightening of foreign exchange controls.

**1934** (February 17th) - Devaluation of 16.66%:
1 Koruna = 37.15 milligrams of fine gold
1 U.S. Dollar = 23.92 Koruny

**1936** (October 9th) - Authorization given to government to fix Koruna at between 32.21 and 30.21 milligrams of fine gold. New devaluation:
1 Koruna = 31.21 milligrams of fine gold
1 U.S. Dollar = 28.47 Koruny

**1938** (October) - In Sudetenland, introduction of Reichsmark as substitute for Czechoslovakian Koruna:
1 Reichsmark = 8.33 Koruny

**1939** (March) and **1940** (October) - Introduction of Reichsmark in Protectorate of Bohemia-Moravia, and Slovakia and simultaneous circulation of each Koruna with Reichsmark. - See *Koruna Czech, Koruna Slovak.*

**1945** (May) - With liberation of Czechoslovakia, return to old parity:
1 U.S. Dollar = 28.47 Koruny

**1945** (October 21st) - General withdrawal before November 15th of all means of payment (Czech Koruna, Slovak Koruna, Reichsmark, Pengoe), and introduction of new Czechoslovakian Koruna. Banknote amounts in excess of 500 Koruny per person had to be deposited in bank.

**1945** (November 1st) - New exchange rate established:
1 U.S. Dollar = 50.00 Koruny

**1946** (December 18th) - Parity registered with International Monetary Fund:
1 Czechoslovak Koruna = 17.7734 milligrams of fine gold
1 U.S. Dollar = 50.00 Koruny

**1949** (March) - Dollar premium on black market reached high of 1,350%.

**1953** (June 1st) - Koruna linked to U.S.S.R. Ruble:
1 Ruble = 1.80 Koruny
1 Koruna = 123.4266 milligrams of fine gold
1 U.S. Dollar = 7.20 Koruny

**1953** (June 1st to 4th) - New exchange of banknotes and conversion of debts:
General rate of exchange and rate for Government debts:
1 new Koruna = 50.00 old Koruny
Salaries, pensions and debts to Government:
1 new Koruna = 5.00 old Koruny
Bank accounts and savings deposits:
1 new Koruna = 5.00 to 30.00 old Koruny

**1954** (April) - Dollar premium on black market fell to 403% after devaluation and harsh state bankruptcy.

**1954** (September) - Czechoslovakia expelled from International Monetary Fund.

**1956** (July) - Partial devaluation. Foreign tourists could purchase Cedok (Czechoslovak Tourist Bureau) coupons abroad for hard currencies at official rate. Entitled owners to change twice their face value (four times, if traveler was of Czech origin) at preferential rate of 20.00 Koruny per U.S. Dollar.

**1957** (July 1st) - Ruble Area currency reform:
  1 Ruble = 1.15 Koruny (some local financial dealings)
  1 U.S. Dollar = 14.36 Koruny (Capitalistic tourist and/or
        support rate)
Coupon system abolished.

**1961** (January 1st) - Soviet monetary reform:
  1 New Ruble = 8.00 Koruny (official)
  1 New Ruble = 11.60 Koruny (Ruble Area noncommer-
        cial, tourist and/or support rate)

**1961** (June) - Premium for U.S. Dollar on black market fell to 248%.

**1963** (April) - U.S.S.R. revalued Ruble in relation to other Socialist lands, for noncommercial transactions only:
  1 Ruble = 9.66 Koruny

**1964** (May 20th) - Capitalistic tourist and support rate devalued to 28.80 per U.S. Dollar, based on 300% premium on exchange above U.S. $4.00 per day.

**1965** (January 1st) - Capitalistic tourist and/or support rate split into two varieties:
  1 U.S. Dollar = 14.36 Koruny (support rate)
  1 U.S. Dollar = 16.20 Koruny (125% premium on tourist
        exchange above U.S. $3.00 per day)

**1966** - Existence of black market in Tuzex bonds, form of scrip bought with gold or hard currencies and entitling owner to purchase imported luxury goods. Rate for Tuzex Koruna fluctuated between 35.00 - 40.00 per U.S. Dollar. Resident travel Dollar existed for Czech citizens with exit permit who exchange their currency at official rate plus 125% premium and 125% administrative fee, making total surcharge of 400%. Resulted in Dollar rate of 36.00 Koruny.

**1969** (October) - Koruna on black market fell to 72.50 per U.S. Dollar, premium for the Greenback of 907% over official rate. Tuzex Koruna also deteriorated to level of 50.00 to 60.00 per U.S. Dollar, then in 1970 to 60.00 to 70.00 per U.S. Dollar.

**1970** - Subsequent sharp improvement in black market rate.


## KORUNA SLOVAK

Money created by Germans in **Slovakia.** Divided into 100 Haliérov (singular: Haler).
Bank of issue - By Bank of Slovakia, and by State for small denomination banknotes.
Predecessors - See *Koruna Czechoslovakia, Koruna Czech.*

**1939** - Dismemberment of Czechoslovakian Koruna:
  1 Slovak Koruna = 1 Czech Koruna = 1/10 Reichsmark

**1940** (October 1st) - New parity:
  1 Reichsmark = 11.62 Slovak Koruny
  1 Czech Koruna = 1.162 Slovak Koruny

Tax of 16% on exports to Bohemia-Moravia.

**1943** - At unofficial price for gold, 1 Slovak Koruna equalled 10 milligrams of fine gold, compared to 31.21 milligrams at official price.

**1945** (May) - With liberation of Czechoslovakia, return to old parity. - See *Koruna Czechoslovakia.*


# KOUPAN

See *Kapang.*


# KRABBELAAR

Silver/copper money of **Brabant,** according to monetary system of Netherlands (1520). Exchange rate: 4 Stuyver or Patards.

Variations of name - Crabbelaer, Vlieger.


# KRAN

**I.** - Monetary unit of **Persia** prior to Rial. Consisted of 10 Tomans and 20 Shahis. As unit of account, called Hor and worth 1/10 Toman, 5 Abbasis, 8 Larins, 10 Mahmudis, 20 Shahis, 2,000 Kazbegi, or 1,000 Dinars.

Predecessor - See *Persia.*

Variations of name - Giran, Karen.

**1857** - Kran was silver coin of 4.987 grams 900 fine, or 4.49 grams fine silver.

**1877** - Silver standard: 1 Kran = 4.603 grams of silver 900 fine, or 4.14 grams fine silver. Exchange rate varied according to price of silver bullion.

**1930** (February 25th) - Foreign exchange controls.

**1932** (March 13th) - Rial replaced Kran as monetary unit. Adoption of principle of gold standard. - See *Rial.*

**II.** - Submultiple (1/2) of Afghanistan Rupee (until 1927) and Afghani, monetary unit of **Afghanistan.** Corresponded to 30 Passa. - See *Rupee Afghanistan* and *Afghani.*


# KREMNITZ

Name of gold Dukat (Ducat) in **Hungary,** minted with initials K.B. (from *Kermecz Banya,* name of Hungarian gold mines).

Weight: 3.49 grams 986 fine, or 3.44 grams fine gold. Exchange rate: 4.20 Gulden of Holy Roman Empire. - See *Dukat.*

## KREUZER

Money of German States, derived from Pfennig.

Origin of name - From imprint of a cross (*Kreuz*).

Variations of name - French (Kreux, Creuxer, Creitzer, Cruche); Italian (Crazia). - See *Crazia*.

**I. - German** money.

**15th Century** - Appearance of Kreuzer as variation of Pfennig (see *Pfennig*). In 1490 in Tyrol, minting of Kreuzer equal to 1/60 Thaler.

**16th Century** - Kreuzer became unit of account in monetary system of Holy Roman Empire. Using Gulden, it was worth 1/60 Gulden and equal to 4 Pfennig. System used mainly in South and West (Austria, Bavaria, Swabia, Franconia, Rhineland).

**1551** - Minting of silver Kreuzer of 1.19 grams 370 fine, or 0.44 grams fine. Classified as money of Holy Roman Empire.

**1559** - Kreuzer of 1.15 grams 386 fine, or 0.44 grams fine, continued as money of Holy Roman Empire.

**17th Century** - As unit of account, Kreuzer still represented 1/60 Gulden, or 4 Pfennig. In countries to East (Saxony. . .) where accounts were kept in Thaler and Groschen, Kreuzer worth 1/90 Thaler, or 1/3 Groschen.

**18th Century** - As unit of account, Kreuzer worth 1/60 Gulden or 4 Pfennig in Austria, Bavaria, Frankfurt, Swabia, Upper Palatinate, and Franconia.

**19th Century** - Specie money until 1874 worth 1/60 Gulden or 1/90 Thaler in Prussia, Baden, Württemberg, Bavaria, North Germany. . .

**II. - In Austria,** Kreuzer in 1857 became 1/100 Gulden. Minted in copper.

**III. - In Swiss** cantons during 18th Century and until 1850, unit of account and silver/copper money.

- In Basel, 1/60 Guilder, 1/108 Thaler, 25 Rappen or 50 Pfennig.

- In Berne, 1/100 Krone, 1/40 Pfund, 1/4 Batz.

- In Zurich and Saint Gall, 1/60 Guilder or 8 Heller.

- In Neuchatel, 1/60 Guilder, 1/4 Batz.

**1798** - Helvetic Republic minted 1 and 2 Kreuzer coins.

**1799** (March 17th) - Minting of silver/copper Kreuzer.

**1806 to 1818** - Neuchatel minted silver/copper Kreuzer.

## KROISEIOI

**I. -** Name given to different Staters (of electrum, gold, or silver) minted by Croesus, in **Lydia** during 6th Century B.C. - See *Stater*.

**II. -** Coins which circulated in **Orient** until appearance of Daric. - See *Daric*.

Plural - Kroiseios.

## KRONA ICELAND

Monetary unit of **Iceland**. Divided into 100 Aurar (singular: Eyrir).

Bank of issue - By State banks (Landsbanki and Bunadarbanki Islands) and by private bank under control of State (Utvegsbanki), then by Landsbanki Islands until 1961 when Sedlabanki Islands (Central Bank of Iceland) was established.

Predecessor - See *Iceland.*

Plural - Krónur.

**1918** (December 1st) - Creation of Icelandic Króna, at par with Danish Krone, and without convertibility:

    1 Króna = 403.227 milligrams of fine gold
    1 Pound Sterling = 18.1595 Krónur
    1 U.S. Dollar = 3.73 Krónur

**1925** (October) - De facto stabilization in relation to Pound Sterling:

    1 Pound Sterling = 22.15 Krónur
    1 U.S. Dollar = 4.55 Krónur

**1931** - Depreciation parallel to that of Pound Sterling.

**1931** (October 2nd) - Foreign exchange controls within framework of Sterling Area.

**1939** (April 15th) - New exchange relationship:

    1 Pound Sterling = 27.00 Krónur
    1 U.S. Dollar = 5.75 Krónur

**1939** (September 20th) - 1 U.S. Dollar = 6.49 Krónur

**1941** - Adherence to Sterling Area.

**1946** (December 18th) - Parity registered with International Monetary Fund:

    1 Króna = 136.954 milligrams of fine gold
    1 U.S. Dollar = 6.49 Krónur

**1949** (December 20th) - Devaluation following Pound Sterling:

    1 Króna = 95.1359 milligrams of fine gold
    1 U.S. Dollar = 9.34 Krónur

**1950** (March 20th) - New devaluation:

    1 Króna = 54.5676 milligrams of fine gold
    1 U.S. Dollar = 16.29 Krónur

**1951** (March 8th) - Multiple rate structure:

    1 U.S. Dollar = 16.26/16.32 Krónur (basic buying and selling rates for certain trade transactions, invisibles and capital movements)

    1 U.S. Dollar = 18.22 Krónur (basic rate plus 24% premium certificate on half the amount of the value of exports to clearing agreement countries of most products of small fishing boat industry)

    1 U.S. Dollar = 20.39 Krónur (basic rate plus 25% premium certificate for listed imports from clearing currency countries)

    1 U.S. Dollar = 21.07 Krónur (basic rate plus 59% premium certificate on half the amount of the value of exports to EPU and Dollar Area coun-

tries of most products of small fishing boat industry)
  1 U.S. Dollar = 26.09 Krónur    (basic   rate   plus   60%
        premium certificate for listed imports from EPU
        and Dollar Area countries)

**1952** - Allocations for travel purposes subject to tax of 25%, resulting in rate of:
  1 U.S. Dollar = 20.39 Krónur
Imports of automobiles subject to 35% tax, resulting in rate of:
  1 U.S. Dollar = 22.03 Krónur

**1954** (August 6th) - Additional tax of 100% on automobiles.

**1955** (January 1st) - Percentage of value of exports for which premium certificates were issued reduced from 50% to 45% for January 1st - May 5th season.

**1955** (November 4th) - Premiums on special import certificates for Dollar Area, EPU countries and U.S.S.R. raised from 60% to 70%, and from 25% to 35% for clearing countries except for U.S.S.R.

**1956** (December 22nd) - Certificate system abolished and replaced by complex arrange-ment of taxes on foreign exchange sales:
  1 U.S. Dollar = 16.26/16.32 Krónur (basic rate for all ex-
        change proceeds and imports and invisibles ex-
        empt from tax)
  1 U.S. Dollar = 18.93 Krónur (basic rate plus 16% tax for
        most imports and invisibles)
  1 U.S. Dollar = 25.46 Krónur (basic rate plus 16% tax and
        40% license fee for business and tourist travel)
In addition, import fees of from 8% to 160% applied, resulting in rates of from 20.44 to 42.35 Krónur per U.S. Dollar.

**1958** (May 29th) - Major changes in exchange rate system:
  1 U.S. Dollar = 16.26/16.32 Krónur (basic rate for receipts
        and payments related to military installations)
  1 U.S. Dollar = 21.22 Krónur (basic rate plus 30% for basic
        consumer goods imports)
  1 U.S. Dollar = 19.91-42.43 Krónur (basic rate plus tax of
        from 22% to 160% for less essential goods)
  1 U.S. Dollar = 25.20-29.27 Krónur (basic rate plus 55% to
        80% Exchange Premium on exports of herring
        and other fish products depending on season)
  1 U.S. Dollar = 25.30 Krónur (basic rate plus 55% tax for
        all other imports, all other invisibles except
        travel and capital)
  1 U.S. Dollar = 32.64 Krónur (basic rate plus 55% tax and
        45% license fee for business and tourist travel)

**1960** (February 20th) - Exchange system revised and simplified:
  1 Króna = 23.386 milligrams of fine gold
  1 U.S. Dollar = 38.00 Krónur
Applicable to all transactions. Imports subject to taxes of 16½% - 100%.

**1961** (August 4th) - Devaluation of Króna:
  1 Króna = 20.667 milligrams of fine gold

1 U.S. Dollar = 43.00 Krónur

**1961** (October) - Black market value of Króna, having depreciated almost constantly since mid-1954, hit record 50.50 per U.S. Dollar. Minor improvement followed.

**1963** - Import taxes removed except for charge of ½ of 1% (minimum 10.00 Krónur) as license fee for imports.

**1965** (January 1st) - Imports of automobiles subject to 125% tax.

**1965** (July 1st) - Sales of foreign exchange subject to fee of ½ of 1%.

**1967** (November 27th) - Devaluation of Króna:
  1 Króna = 15.591 milligrams of fine gold
  1 U.S. Dollar = 57.00 Krónur
Fee of ½ of 1% on sales of foreign exchange abolished. Tax on automobile imports reduced to 90%.

**1967** (December) - Black market rate of Króna, after having been rather stable, rose sharply to 66.00 per U.S. Dollar.

**1968** (September 3rd) - Import surcharge of 20% and a 20% tax on purchase of foreign exchange for travel instituted.

**1968** (November 12th) - Devaluation of Króna:
  1 Króna = 10.098 milligrams of fine gold
  1 U.S. Dollar = 88.00 Krónur
Travel Króna rate abolished.

**1969** (March 1st) - Tax on imports of automobiles reduced to 60%.

**1969** (July) - Black market rate of Króna reached record 101.00 per U.S. Dollar.

## KRONA SWEDEN

Monetary unit of **Norway** (1873-1905) and **Sweden.** Divided into 100 Oerer (singular: Oere). In earlier years called Krondaler.

Bank of issue - Until 1904, by about 30 private banks, then by Sveriges Riksbank (Royal Bank of Sweden) established in 1668.

Predecessor - See *Sweden.*

Plural - Kronor.

**1873** (May 30th) - Adoption of gold standard (Scandinavian Monetary Union):
  1 Krona = 403.226 milligrams of fine gold
  1 Pound Sterling = 18.1595 Kronor
Minting of 10 and 20 Krona gold coins at 4.48 and 8.96 grams 900 fine.
Danish and Norwegian gold and silver coins legal tender in Sweden.

**1900** - 1 U.S. Dollar = 3.73 Kronor.

**1914** (August 3rd) - Suspension of convertibility.

**1916** (January) - Restoration of convertibility, but without free minting of gold.

**1920** - Suspension of convertibility.

**1924** (April 1st) - Restoration of convertibility.

**1931** (September 28th) - Suspension of convertibility. Joined Sterling Area on basis of:

1 Pound Sterling = 19.40 Kronor (depreciation of 6.41% in
relation to Pound)

**1939** (September) - Abandonment of Sterling Area:
1 Pound Sterling = 16.90 Kronor
1 U.S. Dollar = 4.20 Kronor

**1940** (February 26th) - Foreign exchange controls instituted.

**1946** (July 13th) - Easing of exchange controls, and upvaluation of 16.6%.
1 U.S. Dollar = 3.60 Kronor

**1949** (September 20th) - Devaluation following Pound Sterling:
1 U.S. Dollar = 5.17 Kronor

**1949** (November) - Unofficial rate of Krona reached record of 6.60 per U.S. Dollar,
premium of 27½% for Greenback.

**1950** (January 30th) - "Uniscan" Agreement facilitating transfers between three Scandinavian countries and United Kingdom.

**1951** (November) - Parity registered with International Monetary Fund:
1 Krona = 171.783 milligrams of fine gold
1 U.S. Dollar = 5.17 Kronor

**1959** (July 1st) - Investment Dollar Krona established, resulting from sales and purchases of foreign securities by Swedish residents and available at premium.

## KRONE AUSTRIA

Gold money of **Austria** after 1857. Then monetary unit of Austria from 1892 to 1923.
Divided into 100 Heller (100 Heller or Para in Montenegro).

Bank of issue - Until 1920 by Austro-Hungarian Bank, from 1920 to 1923 by Austrian
Economic Administration (Oesterreichische Geschäftsführung) and after 1923 by
Oesterreichische Nationalbank (National Bank of Austria).

Predecessors - Autonomous monetary systems of member states until 1892. See especially *Austria* and *Gulden.*

Plural - Kronen.

**1857** (January 24th) - Gold coin common to Austria and Bavaria, according to their
monetary agreement. No fixed exchange rate for silver Gulden.

**1892** (August 2nd) - Adoption of gold standard:
1 Krone = 304.9 milligrams of fine gold.
Minting of gold coins: 20 Kronen (6.775 grams fine), 10 Kronen (3.387 grams 900
fine).
Minting of Krone in silver (5 grams 835 fine), similar to Franc.
Gulden remained silver coin worth 2 Kronen.

**1914** (August 4th) - Suspension of gold standard. Inflation and depreciation.

**1916** (December 19th) - Exchange controls.

**1919** - Stamping of banknotes circulating within borders of new Austria.

**1922** - Galloping inflation. Collapse of Krone.

**1922** (October 4th) - Signing of plan for Financial Reconstruction (Geneva Protocols)
under auspices of League of Nations.

**1922** (November 14th) - Creation of National Bank of Austria.

**1922** (November 18th) - Issue of Kronen suspended.

**1923** - Creation of new monetary unit. - See *Schilling.*

## KRONE DENMARK

Monetary unit of **Denmark**. Divided into 100 Oerer (singular: Oere). In earlier years called Krondaler.

Bank of issue - By National Bank of Copenhagen, founded in 1818 to continue operations of Royal Bank, founded in 1813. Nationalized May 28, 1936 under name of Danmarks Nationalbank (National Bank of Denmark).

Predecessor - See *Denmark.*

Plural - Kroner.

**1618** - Krone became unit of account for Denmark. Divided into 8 Mark or 128 Skilling. Minted in gold (Guldkrone, equal to 1¾ Ducats).

**18th Century** - Silver money of 22.3 grams 668 fine, or 14.9 grams fine. Exchange rate: 34 Stuyver.

**1872** (December 18th) - Scandinavian Monetary Union.

**1873** (May 27th) - Adoption of gold standard, patterned after German model.

1 Krone = 403.226 milligrams of fine gold
1 Pound Sterling = 18.1595 Kroner

Gold and silver coins of Sweden and Norway were legal tender in Denmark. Minting of gold coins on basis of: 10 Kroner = 4.48 grams 8995 fine. Krone minted in silver (7.50 grams 800 fine).

**1914** (August 2nd) - Suspension of convertibility.

**1918** (December 1st) - Creation of Icelandic Króna at par with Danish Krone - See *Króna Iceland.*

**1924** (March) - Sharpest depreciation of Krone.

**1924** (December 20th) - Currency Stabilization Law to gradually raise exchange value of Krone. First 5.74, then 5.64 and finally 5.32 per U.S. Dollar.

**1925** (December 15th) - Currency Stabilization Law amended to maintain minimum U.S. Dollar exchange rate between 4.20 and 4.35 Kroner.

**1926** (December 22nd) - Restoration of gold standard at old parity:

1 Krone = 403.226 milligrams of fine gold

**1931** (September 22nd) - Embargo on gold shipments.

**1931** (September 29th) - Suspension of convertibility. Joined Sterling Area initially at:

1 Pound Sterling = 18.50 Kroner

**1931** (November 18th) - Foreign exchange controls.

**1932** (January 30th) - Imports of merchandise and securities, and exports of foreign exchange subject to approval of National Bank.

**1933** (January) - Under pressure of farmers, depreciation of 19% in relation to Pound Sterling:

1 Pound Sterling = 22.40 Kroner

**1936** (November) - Tightening of exchange controls. Central currency office (Valuta Central) made subordinate to Ministry of Commerce.

**1939** (September) - Pound Sterling slid from 22.40 to 20.48 Kroner.

**1940** (April) - German Occupation:
      1 Krone = 0.50 Reichsmark

**1940** (May) - 1 Krone = 0.48 Reichsmark.

**1942** (January) - 1 Krone = 0.52 Reichsmark.

**1945** (July 21st) - Calling in of banknotes exceeding sum of 100 Kroner per person. Deposit of balance in bank account, temporarily blocked.

**1945** (August) - New exchange rate parities:
      1 Pound Sterling = 19.36 Kroner
      1 U.S. Dollar = 4.80 Kroner

**1946** (December 18th) - Parity registered with International Monetary Fund:
      1 Krone = 185.178 milligrams of fine gold
      1 Pound Sterling = 19.36 Kroner
      1 U.S. Dollar = 4.80 Kroner

**1948** (September) - Unofficial rate of Krone reached 10.15 per U.S. Dollar, premium of 111% for Greenback. Gradual improvement to near official parity.

**1949** (September 18th) - Devaluation by 30.54%:
      1 Krone = 128.660 milligrams of fine gold
      1 Pound Sterling = 19.36 Kroner
      1 U.S. Dollar = 6.91 Kroner

**1950** (January 30th) - "Uniscan" Agreement facilitating transfers between three Scandinavian countries and United Kingdom.

**1950** (September 18th) - Tax of 20% on foreign travel allocations imposed, creating second official rate of 1 U.S. Dollar = 8.30 Kroner. Discontinued after October 17, 1951.

**1967** (November 21st) - Devaluation of 7.9% following cut in value of Pound Sterling:
      1 Krone = 118.49 milligrams of fine gold
      1 U.S. Dollar = 7.50 Kroner

## KRONE NORWAY.

Monetary unit of **Norway.** Divided into 100 Oerer (singular: Oere).

Bank of issue - By Norges Bank (Bank of Norway) incorporated in 1892 with its capital stock owned by State. Small denomination banknotes issued by Treasury.

Predecessors - See *Norway* and *Krona Sweden.*

Plural - Kroner.

**1905** - Creation of Norwegian Krone, linked to Swedish and Danish units:
      1 Krone = 403.226 milligrams of fine gold
      1 Pound Sterling = 18.1595 Kroner
Minting of 10 and 20 Krone gold coins of 4.48 and 8.96 grams 900 fine.
Gold and silver coins of Denmark and Sweden were legal tender in Norway (March 8, 1875).

**1914** (August 4th) - Suspension of convertibility.

**1916** (March 8th) - Restoration of convertibility, but without free minting of gold.

**1920** (November) - Suspension of convertibility.

**1928** (April 14th) - Return to convertibility at old parity.

**1931** (September 28th) - Suspension of gold standard. Joined Sterling Area:
    1 Pound Sterling = 19.90 Kroner
Depreciation of 8.75% in relationship to Pound Sterling. Breakup of Scandinavian Monetary Union.

**1939** (August 29th) - Abandonment of Sterling Area:
    1 Pound Sterling = 17.47 Kroner
    1 U.S. Dollar = 4.40 Kroner

**1940** (April) - German Occupation:
    1 Krone = 0.60, then 0.57 Reichsmark

**1940** (May 18th) - Foreign exchange controls.

**1945** (May 16th) - With liberation of Norway, new exchange rates:
    1 Pound Sterling = 20.00 Kroner
    1 U.S. Dollar = 4.963 Kroner

**1945** (September 5th) - Calling in of banknotes, 60% retained by State and 40% deposited in bank accounts.

**1946** (December 18th) - Parity registered with International Monetary Fund:
    1 Krone = 179.067 milligrams of fine gold
    1 U.S. Dollar = 4.963 Kroner

**1949** (September 20th) - Devaluation of 30.52% following Pound Sterling:
    1 Krone = 124.414 milligrams of fine gold
    1 Pound Sterling = 20.00 Kroner
    1 U.S. Dollar = 7.142 Kroner

**1950** (January 30th) - "Uniscan" Agreement, facilitating transfers between three Scandinavian countries and United Kingdom.

**1951** (October) - Unofficial rate of Krone reached record 10.10 per U.S. Dollar, premium of 41½% for Greenback. Subsequent improvement to near official parity.

**1967** - Investment Dollar Krone established, resulting from sales and purchases of foreign securities by Norwegian residents. Available at premium.


# KRONENTHALER

Silver money used in 18th and 19th Centuries in various **German** states (Bavaria, Baden, Hesse-Darmstadt, Nassau). Disappeared in 1857 after unification of all Thaler varieties.

Origin of name - German *kroner* (crown) and Thaler.

# KROON

Monetary unit of **Estonia** from 1928 to 1944. Divided into 100 Sents.

Bank of issue - By Eesti Pank (Bank of Estonia), given monopoly of banknote issue on January 1, 1928.

Predecessors - See *Estonia* and *Mark Estonia.*

Plural - Krooni.

**1924** (June) - Adoption of Estonian Kroon as unit of account.

**1928** (January 1st) - Effective creation of Kroon:
        1 Kroon = 100 Estonian Mark = 1 Swedish Krona
        1 Kroon = 403.2258 milligrams of fine gold
        1 Pound Sterling = 18.159 Krooni

**1931** (November 18th) - Foreign exchange controls.

**1932** (December) - Levying of 15% tax on foreign exchange transactions.

**1933** (June 28th) - Suspension of gold standard, and currency depreciation.

**1933** (September) - Adherence to Sterling Area at former parity:
        1 Pound Sterling = 18.159 Krooni

**1940** (November 25th) - Introduction of Ruble to circulate with Kroon:
        1 Ruble = 0.80 Kroon

**1941** (April) - Abolition of Estonian Kroon. Ruble became sole legal money.
For subsequent developments, see *Estonia* and *Mark Ostland.*


# KUAN

Early **Chinese** monetary unit, divided into 1,000 Wen, or 1,000 Cash. Appeared in form of copper (Tsien), or in banknotes (Pao Ch'ao).
In the beginning (621), Kuan represented a bundle of 1,000 coins of copper Yuan Pao.


# KUNA

Monetary unit of **Croatia** from 1941 to 1945. Divided into 100 Baniu.

Bank of issue - By Croatian State Bank, established May 10, 1941; by City of Zagreb (September 1942), and by the State (October 1942) for small denomination banknotes.

Predecessor - Monetary system of Yugoslavia. - See *Dinar Yugoslavia.*

**1941** (July) - With independent Croatia (under Italian control), creation of Kuna. Exchange of banknotes denominated in Dinars and Reichskreditkassen vouchers denominated in Reichsmark for banknotes denominated in Kuna:
        1 Kuna = 0.38 Lira = 1 Yugoslavian Dinar
        1 Kuna = 17.9 milligrams of fine gold

**1943** (September 15th) - New parity: 1 Kuna = 0.50 Lira.

Premium of 2 Kuna per Lira by Croatian State Bank, bringing exchange rate to:
1 Kuna = 0.25 Lira
In territories along Adriatic Coast (Ljubljana and Dalmatia) reincorporated into
Croatia, introduction of Kuna with double exchange rate (official rate and
premium rate).

**1945** (September) - With liberation of Yugoslavia, abolishment of Kuna and restoration
of Yugoslavian Dinar at a rate of 1 Dinar for 40 Kuna. - See *Dinar Yugoslavia.*

## KURUS

Submultiple (¹/₁₀₀) in bronze of **Turkish** Lira since 1929. Previously called Piastre.
Equal to 40 Paras.
Variation of name - Qurush.

## *KUWAIT*

Arabic monies (see *Arabia*), followed around 1899 by introduction of money of British
India (see *Rupee India*) as official currency.

**Early 20th Century** - Popular use of British gold Sovereign, Maria Theresia Thaler (in
interior), and Saudi Riyal from 1928.

**1959** (April 28th) - Gulf (External) Rupee issued to replace Indian Rupee as official
currency. - See *Rupee Persian Gulf.*

**1961** (April 1st) - Creation of Kuwait Dinar as independent monetary unit. - See *Dinar
Kuwait.*

## KWACHA MALAWI

Monetary unit of Malawi. Divided into 100 Tambala.
Origin of name - See *Kwacha Zambia.*
Bank of issue - Reserve Bank of Malawi.
Predecessor - See *Malawi* and *Pound Malawi.*
Plural - Kwacha.

**1971** (February 15th) - Decimalization and creation of Kwacha to replace Pound
Malawi:
     1 Pound Malawi = 2 Malawi Kwachas
     1 Malawi Kwacha = 1,066.41 milligrams of fine gold
     1 Malawi Kwacha = 1.20 U.S. Dollars

## KWACHA ZAMBIA

Monetary unit of **Zambia** created in 1968 and divided into 100 Ngwee.

Origin of name - Native word for dawn.

Bank of issue - Bank of Zambia.

Predecessors - See *Pound Zambia, Pound Rhodesia and Nyasaland, Pound Southern Rhodesia, Pound.*

**1968** (January 16th) - Kwacha issued, replacing Zambian Pound. Equal to half the old unit.

> 1 Zambian Kwacha = 1,244.14 milligrams of fine gold
> 1 Zambian Kwacha = 1.40 U.S. Dollars

**1969** (February) - Zambian Kwacha offered at 40% discount on black market.


## KWARTNIK

**Polish** money of 14th Century. Progressively depreciated from ½ to ⅙ Grosz.


## KYAT

Monetary unit of **Burma** since 1952. Divided into 100 Pyas.

Bank of issue - Union Bank of Burma. Name changed to People's Bank of the Union of Burma in 1969.

Predecessors - See *Burma* and *Rupee Burma.*

**1952** (July 1st) - Union Bank of Burma succeeded Burma Currency Board in London. Creation of new monetary unit, the Kyat:

> 1 Kyat = 1 Burmese Rupee = 1 Indian Rupee
> 1 Kyat = 18 Pence
> 1 U.S. Dollar = 4.76 Kyats

Almost immediate depreciation of Kyat on black market.

**1953** (August 7th) - Parity registered with International Monetary Fund:

> 1 Kyat = 186.621 milligrams of fine gold
> 1 U.S. Dollar = 4.76 Kyats

**1959** (September) - Black market rate of Kyat reached record 13.70 per U.S. Dollar, premium of 188% for Greenback.

**1966** (October 17th) - Burma withdrew from Sterling Area.

**1966** (October) - Kyat on black market reached new record of 28.75 per U.S. Dollar, premium of 504% for Greenback.

**1967** (November 18th) - Pound Sterling devalued, State Commercial Bank quoted Sterling at:

> 1 Kyat = 21 Pence

**1968** (March) - Dollar premium on black market fell to 172%, but rose again during remainder of year.

**1969** (November 1st) - Union Bank of Burma called People's Bank of the Union of Burma.

## *LACCADIVE ISLANDS*

**19th Century** - British control. Introduction of monetary system of India. - See *Rupee India.*

## LAKH

In **Mogul Empire** and **Bengal,** unit of account used as multiple of Rupee (see *Rupee India*):
>1 Lakh = 100,000 Rupees

Multiples:
>1 Crore = 100 Lakhs
>
>1 Areb = 25 Lakhs

In Surat:
>1 Nil = 100 Badams = 10,000 Crore = 1,000,000 Lakhs

Variations of name - Lack, Lac, Leck, Lacre, Laes, Lecth, Lecque.

## LANTERNINA

Silver money of the Grand Duchy of **Tuscany.** Generally called Tollero delle Torre. - See *Tollero.*

## *LAOS*

Predecessor - See *Indochina.*

**1949** (July 11th) - Laos recognized as independent associated state within French Union. Currency remained Indochinese Piastre:
>1 Piastre = 17 French Francs
>
>1 U.S. Dollar = 20.59 Piastres

**1951** (December 21st) - Banknote issue turned over to Institut d'Emission Quadripartite, functioning as Central Bank.

**1953** (May 11th) - Devaluation of Piastre:
>1 Piastre = 25.391 miligrams of fine gold
>
>1 Piastre = 10 French Francs
>
>1 U.S. Dollar = 35.00 Piastres

**1954** (July 20th) - Geneva Accord partitioned Indochina. - See also *Cambodia* and *Viet Nam.*

**1954** (December 29th) - Laos recognized as independent nation, and Banque Nationale du Laos (National Bank of Laos) established as Central Bank and note-issuing authority.

**1955** (May 5th) - Kip became national currency, equal to Piastre. Retained old relationship to Franc. - See *Kip*.

**1955** (October) - Old Piastres removed from circulation.

## LARI

Basic copper coin of **Maldive Islands.** Currently submultiple ($1/100$ ) of Maldivian Rupee. Also called Cent.

Origin of name - From Persian *Larin*. - See *Larin*.

Plural - Laree.

**18th Century** - First minting of coin weighing about 9.46 grams.

**Early 20th Century** - Minted under British auspices along with silver/copper multiple. - See *Bodulari*.

## LARIN

Money of **Perisa** and of **Orient** (from Arabia to India). In circulation until 19th Century. Strand of round silver, 6 centimeters long, folded in two and flattened to receive imprint of Persian or Arabic letters. Weight of Arabian Larin: 4.8 grams 9.17 fine, or 4.4 grams fine silver.

Origin of name - From City of Lar, capital of Carmania, where first Larins minted.

**18th Century** - In Persia, exchange rate: $1/8$ Hor, or $1/80$ Toman. Used as unit of account throughout Persian East.

## LAT

Copper bar used as money in Northern **Siam.** Valued at $1/16$ to $1/64$ Tical.

## LAT LATVIA

Monetary unit of **Latvia** from 1922 to 1940. Divided into 100 Santimi (singular: Santim).

Origin of name - Root of word Latvia.

Bank of issue - By Latvijas Banka (Bank of Latvia).

Predecessors - See *Latvia* and *Ruble Latvia*.

Plural - Latos.

**1922** (August 3rd) - Creation of Lat based on gold: 1 Lat = 50 Latvian Rubles = 290.322 milligrams of fine gold = 1 Franc Germinal.

**1922** (November 1st) - Note issue by Bank of Latvia.

**1931** (October 8th) - Foreign exchange controls.

**1936** (September 28th) - Abandoned gold standard. Joined Sterling Area based on earlier exchange rate of:

> 1 Pound Sterling = 25.22 Latos

Valuation of gold stock on this basis.

**1936** (October) - Creation of Exchange Stabilization Fund.

**1940** (Novemebr 25th) - Annexation by U.S.S.R. Ruble circulated with Lat.

**1941** (April) - Abolition of Lat, Ruble being only legal money.

**1941** (July) - German Occupation. Issue of banknotes denominated in Reichsmark by Reichskreditkassen. Gradually substituted for Rubles.

**1942** (July 20th) - Creation of Central Bank of Ostland. Authorized to issue banknotes denominated in Ostland Mark. - See *Mark Ostland.*

## LATIN MONETARY UNION

See *Union Latine.*

## *LATVIA*

**12th to 15th Century** - Prussian monies (Order of Teutonic Knights).

**15th Century** - Archdiocese of Riga minted silver Obol called Artig, then Schilling and some copper Bracteates.
Livonian Brothers of Sword simultaneously minted Schilling and its submultiples (Denier or Pfennig, Obol or Artig).

**16th Century** - Polish monies. - See *Poland.*

**17th Century** - Swedish monies. - See *Sweden.*

**18th Century** - In Riga, accounts kept in Reichsthaler of 90 Groschen, or in Guilders (Gulden) of 30 Groschen.
Specie monies:
> In gold - Ducat (Dukat)
> In silver - Reichsthaler, Livonine, and all Russian monies

**19th Century** - Russian monetary system. - See *Russia.* In Latvia, Russian Ruble called Rublia, divided into 100 Kopeks.

**1920** - Issue of Latvian Ruble, theoretically equal to Russian Ruble.

**1922** (August 3rd) - Creation of Lat. - See *Lat Latvia.*

## LAUREL

Silver money minted in **England** during reign of James I about 1619. A variety (fourth minting) of Unite. - See *Unite.* Reminted during reign of Charles II.

Origin of name - From laurel branch crowning King, imprinted on coin.

## LAXSAN

Early unit of account used in **Java:** $1/1,000$ Bahar, $1/100$ Uta, $1/10$ Catty, or 10 Peccoes, 250 Tayell, 500 Sata, 2,500 Mas, 10,000 Cash, or 100,000 Candareens.

## *LEBANON*

For monetary history prior to 1902, see *Syria.*

**1920** (May 1st) - Introduction of Lebanese-Syrian Pound as official monetary unit in Lebanon and Syria. - See *Pound Lebanon-Syria.*

**1948** (January 1st) - Breakup of common exchange control and monetary system for Lebanon and Syria. Creation of separate and distinct monetary unit in Lebanon. - See *Pound Lebanon.*

## *LEEWARD ISLANDS*

Consists of Antigua, St. Kitts-Nevis-Anguilla, Monserrat, and British Virgin Islands.

**Before 19th Century** - For money in circulation, see *British West Indies.*

**19th Century** - Counter-marked Spanish Piasters and money of Dutch Antilles circulated.

**Early 20th Century** - British coins and U.S. gold coins began to replace other specie monies.

**1935** - British West Indies Dollar introduced in form of government notes of Trinidad, Barbados and British Guiana. - See *Dollar British West Indies.*

**1951** - Unified currency of Currency Board of British Caribbean territories (Eastern Group) began circulating as legal tender along with Pound Sterling.

**1956** - British Virgin Islands became a separate British Colony. - See *British Virgin Islands.*

**1965** - BWI Dollar replaced by East Caribbean Dollar as monetary unit. - See *Dollar East Caribbean.*

## *LEGHORN*

Monies of Rome (see *Rome*), Carolingian monetary system (see *Lira*), then Florentine monetary system (see *Florence* and *Tuscany*).

**18th Century** - Units of account: Pezza, or Livornino, of 20 Soldi or 240 Denari; gold Scudo; Scudo Corrente, Ducaton, or Piastra; Testone of 2 Lire, 3 Paoli (Reali), 24 Crazie, or 120 Quattrini.
Specie monies of Tuscany. - See *Tuscany.*

## LEK

**I.** - Submultiple (¹/₅) of **Albanian** Franc from 1925 to 1946. Equal to 20 Centimes. - See *Franc Albania.*

**II.** - Monetary unit of **Albania** since 1946. Divided into 100 Qindars.

Bank of issue - By Banque Nationale de la République Populaire d'Albanie, renamed Banque de l'Etat Albanais (State Bank of Albania).

Predecessors - See *Albania, Franc Albania.*

**1946** (November) - Lek became monetary unit of Albania. Monetary agreement with Yugoslavia:
> 1 Lek = 1 Yugoslavian Dinar
> 1 U.S. Dollar = 50.00 Leks

**1948** (June) - Yugoslavia cancelled monetary agreement with Albania. Albania joined Ruble Area with Lek linked to Ruble at:
> 1 Ruble = 12.50 Leks

Official Dollar value remained same:
> 1 Lek = 17.773 milligrams of fine gold
> 1 U.S. Dollar = 50.00 Leks

**1957** (July 29th) - Ruble Area currency reform establishing Capitalistic tourist and/or support rate:
> 1 U.S. Dollar = 150.00 Leks

**1961** (January 1st) - Soviet monetary reform:
> 1 New Ruble = 55.55 Leks (official)
> 1 New Ruble = 100.00 Leks (Ruble Area noncommercial, tourist and/or support rate)
> 1 U.S. Dollar = 125.00 Leks (Capitalistic tourist and/or support rate)

**1963** (April) - U.S.S.R. revalued Ruble in relation to other Socialist lands for noncommercial transactions only:
> 1 Ruble = 83.75 Leks

**1965** (August 16th) - Introduction of "heavy" Lek at 10 old for 1 new:
> 1 Lek = 177.73 milligrams of fine gold
> 1 Ruble = 5.555 Leks (official)
> 1 Ruble = 8.375 Leks (noncommercial tourist and/or support rate)
> 1 U.S. Dollar = 5.00 Leks (official)
> 1 U.S. Dollar = 12.50 Leks (Capitalistic tourist and/or support rate)

All wages, pensions, savings and prices adjusted at same ratio.

**1967** (March) - U.S. Dollar commanded premium of 1,540% on black market.

**1970-1971** - Gradual improvement of Lek on black market to about 52.00 per U.S. Dollar in early 1971.

## LEMPIRA

Monetary unit of **Honduras** since 1926. Divided into 100 Centavos.

Origin of name - From a local chief.

Bank of issue - By Banco de Honduras and Banco Atlantida, then after June 30, 1950, by Banco Central de Honduras (Central Bank of Honduras).

Predecessor - See *Honduras, Peso Honduras.*

**1926** (April 3rd) - National money, defined in Dollars, substituted for U.S. Dollar:
  1 Lempira = 752.3 milligrams of fine gold
  1 U.S. Dollar = 2.00 Lempiras
  U.S. banknotes and coins continued to circulate.

**1934** (February) - Devaluation conforming to that of U.S. Dollar:
  1 Lempira = 444.335 milligrams of fine gold
  1 U.S. Dollar = 2.00 Lempiras

**1934** (March 27th) - Foreign exchange controls. Selling rate:
  1 U.S. Dollar = 2.025 Lempiras (North Coast)
  1 U.S. Dollar = 2.04 Lempiras (Tegucigalpa)

**1946** (December 18th) - Parity registered with International Monetary Fund:
  1 Lempire = 444.335 milligrams of fine gold
  1 U.S. Dollar = 2.00 Lempiras

**1950** (June 30th) - Exchange controls removed. Circulation of U.S. banknotes and coins replaced by Honduran currency.

**1950** (July 1st) - New selling rate:
  1 U.S. Dollar = 2.02 Lempiras

## LEONE

Monetary unit of **Sierre Leone.** Divided into 100 Cents.

Bank of issue - Bank of Sierra Leone. Established November 1963, began activities August 4, 1964.

Predecessors - See *Pound West Africa* and *Sierra Leone.*

**1964** (August 4th) - Creation of new monetary unit to replace West African Pound:
  1 Leone = 0.50 West African Pounds
  1 Leone = 1,244.14 milligrams of fine gold
  1 Leone = 1.40 U.S. Dollars

**1965** (August 6th) - Par value registered with International Monetary Fund.

**1966** (February 4th) - West African Pound ceased to be legal tender.

**1967** (November 22nd) - Devaluation of 14.3%, parallel to Pound Sterling:
  1 Leone = 1,066.41 milligrams of fine gold
  1 Leone = 1.20 U.S. Dollars

## LEONINA

Gold coin minted by **Papal States** under Leo XII (1823-1829). Corresponded to new Pistole, or Doppia, and worth 5 Scudi or 2 gold Zecchini.


## LEOPARD

Silver coin minted in **France** by English occupiers (Henry V) during Hundred Years War.

**1421** (May 6th) - Minting of silver Leopard similar to Helmeted Gros: 2.84 grams 958 fine, or 2.72 grams fine. Exchange rate: 20 Deniers.


## LEOPOLDINO

Silver money of Grand Duchy of **Tuscany.**

Origin of name - See *Leopoldine d'Oro.*

Plural - Leopoldini.

**1766** - Francescone, silver coin of 27.30 grams 916 fine having exchange rate of 10 Paoli, became Leopoldino upon accession of Leopold to throne. Same weight and exchange rate.

**1801** - Disappearance with establishment of Kingdom of Etruria.


## LEOPOLDINO D'ORO

Gold coin of Grand Duchy of **Tuscany** from 1826 to 1859. Worth 80 Guilders (Fiorini), 200 Paoli, 8,000 Quattrini, or 32,000 Denari.

Origin of name - From Leopold II, Grand Duke of Tuscany.


## LEOPOLDO

**I.** - Gold coin minted in **Lorraine** by Duke Leopold Joseph.
After Treaty of Rijswijk (1697): Conforming to French regulations and having same weight and metal content as Louis and Ecu, Leopoldo was legal tender in France (Decree of Council of August 3, 1700). Circulated until 1766.

**II.** - Silver coin of Grand Duchy of **Tuscany** from 1826 to 1859. Valued at 4 Guilders (Fiorini), 10 Paoli, 400 Quattrini, or 1,600 Denari.

## LEPTON

I. - Small coin of ancient **Greece**.

Origin of name - Greek *leptos* (thin).

Plural - Lepta.

**6th Century B.C.** - Lepton was last submultiple of Obol: 7 Lepta equal to 1 Chalcus, 56 Lepta to 1 Obol, 336 Lepta to 1 Drachma, 33,600 Lepta to 1 Mina, 2,016,000 Lepta to 1 Talent (according to system of accounts used in Euboea and adopted by Athens under Solon). Divided into 2 Hemilepta.

II. - Submultiples ($^1/_{100}$) of Phoenix from 1828 to 1833, then Drachma, monetary units of **Greece**. - See *Phoenix* and *Drachma*.

## *LESOTHO*

Independent Kingdom (1966), formerly called Basutoland. Monetary system of South Africa. - See *South Africa*.

## LEU

I. - Silver coin of **Romania**. Divided into 28 Parali.

II. - Monetary unit of **Romania** since 1867. Divided into 100 Bani (singular: Banu).

Bank of issue - By Banque Nationale de Roumanie. Name changed in November 1948 to Banque d'Etat de la République Populaire Roumaine and in June 1965 to Banque Nationale de la République Socialiste de Roumanie (National Bank of Romanian Socialist Republic).

Predecessor - See *Romania*.

Plural - Lei.

**1867** (April 14th) - Introduction of bimetallic monetary system of Latin Monetary Union, but without formal membership: 1 Leu = 4.5 grams of fine silver = 290.322 milligrams of fine gold = 1 Franc Germinal.

**1880** - Paper money issue entrusted to National Bank of Romania.

**1890** (April 14th) - Adoption of gold standard using same gold base.

**1914** - Suspension of gold standard. Depreciation of currency.

**1929** (February 7th) - Stabilization with devaluation of 96.9%:
   1 Leu = 9.0 milligrams of fine gold
   1 U.S. Dollar = 167.20 Lei

**1932** (May 7th) - Foreign exchange controls instituted.

**1934** (May 1st) - Exporters granted varying premiums arising from additional exports of petroleum, cereal and wood products.

**1935** (June 11th) - Premiums of 10% to 40%, depending on export; 44% surtax on imports. National Bank of Romania fixed 30% premium for gold purchases, creating gold value of:

1 Leu = 6.923 milligrams of fine gold

**1935** (December) - Unification of premiums at 38%.

**1936** (June 14th) - National Bank of Romania raised buying price for gold produced from Romanian mines by 38%, establishing gold value of:
1 Leu = 6.522 milligrams of fine gold

**1936** (November 6th) - Revaluation of gold reserve of National Bank on same gold basis, implying devaluation of 27.54%:
1 U.S. Dollar = 135.95 Lei

**1940** (May 18th) - Gold content of Leu reduced to 4.35 milligrams of fine gold:
1 U.S. Dollar = 204.29 Lei

**1941** (March 31st) - Gold content of Leu raised to 4.74 milligrams of fine gold:
1 U.S. Dollar = 187.48 Lei

**1941** (April) - Exchange rate for Reichsmark increased by agreement from 49.50 to 59.50 Lei.

**1941** (July) - In Bucovina and Bessarabia, issue of special Leu banknotes. Substituted for Rubles on basis of:
1 Leu = 1 Ruble

**1943** - Farmers asked to pay their debts in wheat.

**1944** - Russian Occupation:
1 Ruble = 100 Lei.

**1946** (February 6th) - 1 U.S. Dollar = 3,500 Lei

**1946** (May) - 1 U.S. Dollar = 15,000 Lei

**1947** (March 15th) - Exchange rates:
1 U.S. Dollar = 150,195 Lei (government payments)
1 U.S. Dollar = 225,195 Lei (private payments)

**1947** (June 17th) - 1 U.S. Dollar = 650,000 Lei

**1947** (July) - Accelerated depreciation of Leu on black market:
1 U.S. Dollar = 2,000,000 Lei

**1947** (August 15th) - General exchange of banknotes on basis of:
1 new Leu = 20,000 old Lei
1 new Leu = 5.94 milligrams of fine gold
1 U.S. Dollar = 150.00 new Lei
Partial blocking of accounts. Banknote exchange limited to 5 million Lei (farmers), 3 million (salaried employees), 1.5 million (unskilled labor).
Depreciation on black market to 675 Lei per U.S. Dollar in February 1950.

**1952** (January 28th) - General exchange of banknotes on basis of:
1 new Leu = 400 old Lei
Banknotes: 1 per 100 up to 1,000 Lei, 1 per 200 from 1,000 to 3,000 Lei.
Deposits in savings bank: 1 per 50 up to 1,000 Lei, 1 per 100 from 1,000 to 3,000 Lei, 1 per 200 above 3,000 Lei.
Deposits in commercial banks: 1 per 20 Lei for amounts needed to pay two weeks salaries, 1 per 200 Lei above this amount.
Public sector: banknotes, 1 per 200 Lei; deposits in commercial banks, 1 per 20 Lei.
New definition of Leu:

1 Leu = 79.346 milligrams of fine gold
1 Ruble = 2.80 Lei
1 U.S. Dollar = 11.20 Lei

**1953** (December) - Leu offered at 78% discount on black market.

**1954** (February 1st) - Currency reform. Leu aligned to Ruble:
1 Ruble = 1.50 Lei
1 Leu = 148.112 milligrams of fine gold
1 U.S. Dollar = 6.00 Lei

**1954** (March) - Leu offered at 77% discount on black market.

**1957** (July) - Ruble Area currency reform establishing Capitalistic tourist and/or support rate:
1 U.S. Dollar = 12.00 Lei

**1960** (June) - New tourist rate of 15.00 Lei per U.S. Dollar established for Capitalistic tourism arranged by National Tourist office. Previous rate still applied for all other Capitalistic noncommercial transactions.

**1961** (January 1st) - Soviet monetary reform:
1 New Ruble = 6.67 Lei (official)
1 New Ruble = 9.70 Lei (Ruble Area noncommercial, tourist and/or support rate)

**1963** (April 1st) - U.S.S.R. revalued Ruble in relation to other Socialist lands for noncommercial transactions only:
1 Ruble = 8.30 Lei

**1964** (June 15th) - Partial devaluation. New Capitalistic tourist and/or support rates established:
1 U.S. Dollar = 18.00 Lei (U.S. Dollars and equivalent Western banknotes)
1 U.S. Dollar = 15.00 Lei (various other banknotes)
1 U.S. Dollar = 12.00 Lei (Capitalistic noncommercial and support transactions)
Collectivistic noncommercial, tourist and/or support rate revalued. Percentages averaged between 64% discount to 114% premium against official rate. Percentages changed periodically.

**1967** (December) - U.S. Dollar on black market commanded premium of 916% over basic official rate and 433% over Capitalist noncommercial or support rate.

**1968** (October) - Capitalistic noncommercial or support rate and 15.00 Lei per U.S. Dollar tourist rate abolished. Replaced by 18.00 per U.S. Dollar rate.

**1961-1970** - Except for short time near end of 1967, Leu on black market fluctuated between 23.00 and 47.00 per U.S. Dollar.

# LEV

Monetary unit of **Bulgaria** since 1880. Divided into 100 Stotinka (Singular: Stotinki). Origin of name - From Bulgarian *lew* (lion) on coat of arms of Principality of Bulgaria. Variation of name - Lew.

Bank of issue - By Banque Nationale de Bulgarie (National Bank of Bulgaria) and by Treasury for small denomination banknotes.

Predecessor - See *Bulgaria*.

Plural - Leva.

**1880** (May 27th) - Following independence, adoption of monetary unit linked to Franc Germinal:
    1 Lev = 1 Franc = 290.322 milligrams of fine gold
Minting on this basis of coins of 100 Leva and 20 Leva (Alexander).

**1899** - Suspension of gold standard.

**1906** - Restoration of gold standard on basis of former parity.

**1912** - Suspension of gold standard. Depreciation of currency.

**1918** (November) - Foreign exchange controls.

**1923** - Monopoly of foreign exchange transactions relegated to National Bank of Bulgaria.

**1924** - De facto stabilization.

**1928** (December 3rd) - De jure stabilization of Lev after devaluation by 96.2%, without elimination of foreign exchange controls:
    1 Lev = 10.86956 milligrams of fine gold

**1931** (October) - Foreign exchange controls tightened. New depreciation of currency.

**1936** (April 1st) - National Bank bought foreign exchange at maximum premium of 35%.

**1940** - Maximum premium lowered to 25%. Relationship to Reichsmark fixed at:
    1 Reichsmark = 32.75 Leva

**1942** (August) - Issue of auxiliary military money by Germans. Denominated in Reichspfennig.

**1944** (September) - Soviet Occupation:
    1 Ruble = 15.00 Leva

**1945** (September) - In territories regained by Yugoslavia, exchange of banknotes on basis of:
    1 Yugoslavian Dinar = 10.00 Leva

**1945** (October) - Theoretical exchange rate:
    1 U.S. Dollar = 120.00 Leva.

**1945** (December) - Devaluation of 58%:
    1 U.S. Dollar = 286.50 Leva

**1949** (February) - On black market, Lev reached record 1,800 per U.S. Dollar.

**1952** (May 12th-15th) - Exchange of banknotes:
    1 new Lev = 100 old Leva
Prices, salaries, debts, pensions: 1 for 25 Leva
Deposits: varying rates of exchange ranging from 1 for 25 Leva to 1 for 100 Leva. Liquid assets of enterprises exceeding amount equal to one month of salaries: 1 for 200 Leva.
New definition in terms of gold:
    1 Lev = 130.687 milligrams of fine gold
    1 Ruble = 1.70 Leva
    1 U.S. Dollar = 6.80 Leva

**1953-1957** - Lev on black market deteriorated from 29.00 to 46.50 per U.S. Dollar, premium of 584% for Greenback.

**1957** (July 29th) - Ruble Area currency reform establishing Capitalistic tourist and/or support rate:
  1 U.S. Dollar = 9.52 Leva

**1959** (September) - Dollar premium on black market fell to 352%.

**1961** (January 1st) - Soviet monetary reform:
  1 New Ruble = 7.56 Leva (official)
  1 New Ruble = 8.99 Leva (Ruble Area noncommercial, tourist and/or support rate)

**1962** (January 1st) - Introduction of heavy Lev:
  10 old Leva = 1 new Lev
  1 Lev = 759.548 milligrams of fine gold
  1 Ruble = 0.89 Leva (Ruble Area noncommercial, tourist and/or support rate)
  1 Ruble = 1.30 Leva (official)
  1 U.S. Dollar = 1.17 Leva (official, tourist and/or support rate)
All wages, pensions, savings and prices adjusted at same ratio.
Although changeover to heavy Lev a "nominal" upvaluation, in terms of gold it represented 42% devaluation.
Dollar premium on black market fell to 269%.

**1963** (April) - Ruble Area monetary realignment:
  1 Ruble = 0.78 Leva (noncommercial, tourist and/or support rate)

**1964** (February 1st) - Capitalistic tourist and/or support rate devalued 70%:
  1 U.S. Dollar = 2.00 Leva

**1967** (March) - Dollar premium on black market fell to 131%. Subsequently fluctuated between 157% and 242% to end of 1970.


# LEVANT DOLLAR

I. - Name given in **Austria** to Maria Theresia Thaler of 1780 used in trade with Levant.
  - See *Maria Theresia Thaler.*
Variation of name - Levantin.
II. - Coin of **Prussia** issued in 1766 and 1767 for trade with Orient.


# LEWEKIN

Silver money of **Luxembourg** in 15th Century. Exchange rate: 1/12 Groschen.
Variation of name - Lionceau.

# LI

**I.** - Name sometimes given to **Chinese** Tsien or Cash. - See *Tsien.*

**II.** - Submultiple of **Chinese** Dollar ($\frac{1}{1,000}$) and of Fen ($\frac{1}{10}$) until 1895. - See *Dollar China.*

**III.** - Submultiple of **Manchukuo** Yuan ($\frac{1}{1,000}$), Chiao ($\frac{1}{100}$) and Fen ($\frac{1}{10}$). - See *Yuan Manchukuo.*

# LIANG

Variation of Tael, unit of account and weight in **China.** - See *Tael.*

# LIARD

**I.** - Silver, silver/copper, then copper coin, and unit of account. First used in **Dauphiné,** then in **France.**

Origin of name - Possible etymologies: from Gigue Liard, master of monies in Dauphiné, and creator of the coin; from Le Hardi (Philippe the Bold), under whose reign the coin may have been minted; from Miliarensis, silver coin of Byzantium; from early French *liart,* (gray).

**15th Century** - Originally, multiple of Denier in Dauphiné: 3 Denier coin of Dauphiné called Patard, 6 Denier coin called Liard. Latter equal to 3 Deniers Tournois or $\frac{1}{4}$ Sou.

**1457** - Annexation of Dauphiné, whereupon Louis XI introduced Liard throughout Kingdom. Exchange rate: 3 Deniers.
Various types: Liard of silver/copper (Lyon and Dauphiné), Liard of pure copper (other provinces).
There were numerous local mintings of Liard coins.
Liard, minted by Henry IV for Navarre, called Baquette.

**1654** (July 1st) - Minting of Liards of France containing 3.82 grams pure copper.

**1658** - Exchange rate for Liard lowered to 2 Deniers. At end of 18th Century, circulated in Canada with value of 4 Deniers under name Double.

**1694** - Exchange rate for Liard raised to 3 Deniers.

**1719** (July) - Minting of Liards of 3.06 grams pure copper.

**1728** (July 27th) - Decree demonetized foreign and feudal Liards (of Lorraine, Bouillon, Montbeliard, Dombes, Savoy. . .).

**1738** - Minting of silver/copper coins of 6 Liards (or 18 Deniers), which increased until 1764.

**1791 to 1793** - Minting of coins of 3 Deniers and 6 Liards in metal obtained from melting of church bells.

**1845** (April 11th) - Law decreeing demonetization of 1, 2, and 6 Liard coins.

**1856** (July 1st) - Final withdrawal from circulation of Liard. Expression "2 Liards" existed for long time to designate $2\frac{1}{2}$ Centimes. Word Liard persisted in French language (not to have a Liard, to cut a Liard in half, not to have two Liards worth of good sense. . .).

II. - In **Liege, Maastricht** and **Westphalia,** unit of account also called Oord (Ortje) or Aidan. Liard worth $1/320$ Patagon (Ecu), $1/80$ Gulden (Guilder), $1/40$ Schelling (Escalin), $1/4$ Stuyver (Sol). Was equivalent of 4 Pfennig (Deniers).

## LIBELLA

Bronze money lighter than As. Minted by **Rome** in 3rd Century B.C. (coins of 1 to 4 Libella), and progressively reduced in weight like bronze As.

Submultiple - Sembella ($1/2$ Libella), Teruncia ($1/4$ Libella).

Origin of name - Latin *libella,* diminutive of *libra* (pound).

## *LIBERIA*

**Primitive money** - Iron bars of 20 centimeters, flattened at ends.

**Early 19th Century** - Introduction of British and American coinage.

**1822** - Following American colonialization, official accounts kept in U.S. Dollars. Commercial accounts generally kept in English Pounds.

**1833-1847** - Local mintings of copper cents.

**Early 20th Century** - Liberian coinage of silver and copper. Dominance of British silver coinage.

**1944** (January 1st) - British currency ceased to be legal tender. Creation of Liberian Dollar linked to, and at par with, U.S. Dollar. - See *Dollar Liberia.*

## LIBERTINA

Silver coin issued in **Ragusa** in 1795 bearing imprint of Liberty. Copied after Maria Theresia Thaler. Exchange rate: 80 Grossetti.

Also called Tallero.

## LIBKAMARK

See *Mark German Federal Republic.*

## LIBRA

I. - **Roman** unit of weight. - See *Livre.*

II. - **Spanish** unit of account used until 14th Century in various provinces.

In Alicante, Catalonia, Majorca, Valencia:
     1 Libra = 1 Peso = 10 Reales = 20 Sueldos = 240 Dineros
     = 480 Mallas (in Catalonia)
In Aragon:
     1 Libra = 1 Peso = 10 Reales = 20 Sueldos = 320 Dineros
Origin of name - See *Livre.*


## LIBRA PERU

**I.** - Monetary unit and gold coin of **Peru** after reform of 1901 and until 1930. Equal to Sovereign: 7.9881 grams 916 fine, or 7.322382 grams fine gold. Value: 10 Soles.

**II.** - Multiple (10) of Sol, monetary unit of **Peru.**


## LIBRA PORTUGAL

Early money of **Portugal.** Divided into 20 Soldos, and 240 Dinheiros.

Origin of name - See *Livre.*

Predecessor - See *Portugal.*

**12th Century** - Independent Portugal maintained accounts in Libras of 20 Soldos or 240 Dinheiros, according to Carolingian monetary system.

**1499** - Emanuel I minted silver Libras of 1.9 grams.


## *LIBYA*

**Prior to 250 B.C.** - Specie monies of Carthage, then Greece.

**250 B.C. to 431 A.D.** - Roman specie monies.

**500 A.D.** - Part of Byzantine Empire. Monetary system under Byzantine influence.

**1510** - Spanish specie monies on coast.

**1551** - Turkish rule established. Monetary system influenced by Ottoman system. - See *Turkey.*

**18th Century** - Unit of account: Piastre of 13 Grimellini or 52 Aspers. Specie monies: most Mediterranean types and gold Sequin (Sultanine). - See *Sequin.*

**19th Century** - Turkish monies: Piastre of 40 Para. Use of silver Mathbu (Mahbub) worth 8 Qurush or 800 Para.

**1912** (October 18th) - Ceded to Italy. Introduction of Italian monetary system with banknotes from Bank of Italy. - See *Lira Italy.*

**1927** (December) - U.S. Dollar rate fixed at:
     1 U.S. Dollar = 19.00 Lire
In Tripolitania, British Pounds and French Francs used for commercial transactions.

**1930** (October 1st) - Foreign exchange controls introduced.

**1934** (December 10th) - Tightening of foreign exchange controls.

**1935** (September) - Further tightening of controls on foreign exchange transactions.

**1939** (September 11th) - U.S. Dollar rate adjusted:
1 U.S. Dollar = 19.80 Lire

**1942** - British Occupation of Tripolitania and Cyrenaica. French Occupation of Fezzan.

**1943-1952** - Circulation of Occupation currencies. French Administration introduced Algerian Francs. British Military Authority created Military Authority Lira (BMA Lira). Egyptian Pound allowed to circulate in Tripolitania and Cyrenaica.

**1952** (March 24th) - Creation of independent monetary unit to replace Occupation currencies. - See *Pound Libya.*

## LIECHTENSTEIN

**18th Century** - Austrian monies. Accounts maintained in Gulden (Florins).

**1857** - German Monetary Union: Liechtenstein used Austrian Gulden of 60 Kreuzer.

**1862** - Minting of Thaler by agreement.

**1898** - Gold coins of 20 Kronen, conforming to new Austrian monetary system. Use of Krone of 100 Heller.

**1921** (February) - Adoption of Swiss Franc as monetary unit. - See *Franc Switzerland.*

**1924** ( January) - Included in Swiss Customs Union.

**1936** (October) - Principality followed monetary measures adopted by Switzerland.

## LIKUTA

Submultiple (1/100) of Zaire, monetary unit of **Congo Democratic Republic.** Plural - Makuta.

## LION

Name given to various coins bearing the imprint of lion.

**I.** - Gold money issued in **France** by Philip VI of Valois in 1338. Weight: 4.89 grams of fine gold. Also called fine gold Denier with Lion.

**II.** - Gold money in **Netherlands.**

**14th Century** - Issued in Flanders (1364). - See *Heaume.*

**15th Century** - Issued in Brabant (1409: worth 60 Grooten); in Netherlands unified under Philip the Good (1453: worth 60 Grooten).

**III.** - Silver money in **Netherlands,** also called Helmeted Lion, or Botdrager (issued in Flanders in 1364 for 2 Grooten, in 1384 by Philip the Bold; in Holland by William V in 1346-89).

**IV.** - Gold money minted in **Scotland** in 15th and 16th Centuries. Also called Saint Andrew. Weight: 3.89 grams. Large coin of nearly twice the size called Demy.

**16th Century** - Minted in silver/copper and called Hard Head.

# LIRA

Money of most of Italian States, later of unified Italy. Based upon Carolingian monetary system. Was equal to 20 Soldi or 240 Denari. In 19th Century, divided into 100 Centesimi (singular: Centesimo).

Origin of name - From As Libralis (As of one Livre), former monetary unit of Rome. Called Litra by Southern Italians. - See *Litra*. Cf. *Livre*.  *

Plural - Lire.

**I.** - Unit of account of numerous **Italian** States before unification: Bassano, Bergamo, Bologna, Genoa, Leghorn, Lucca, Mantua, Milan, Modena, Padua, Parma, Piedmont, Sardinia, Savoy, Tuscany, Trieste, Venice. . .

Equal to 20 Soldi or 240 Denari everywhere.

Other submultiples - 2 Paoli or 120 Quattrini in Bologna; 4 Reali in Sardinia; 12 Crazie in Trieste; 1.5 Paoli (or Giuli), 12 Crazie, 20 Soldi di Lira or 60 Quattrini in Florence.

Multiples - Scudo (7 Lire) in Bergamo; Pezza (6 Lire) and Testone (2 Lire) in Leghorn; Scudo (6 Lire) in Mantua; Fiorino or Guilder (5 Lire) in Trieste; Testone (2 Lire), Pezza or Livornino (5.75 Lire), Ducato or Piastra (7 Lire) and gold Scudo (7.5 Lire) in Florence.

**II.** - Specie money of numerous Italian states before unification.

**1474** - In Milan, silver coin of 9.78 grams 963 fine, or 9.42 grams fine. Called Grossone, or Testone.

Minted in **Florence** in 1252 (gold Guilder, or Fiorino, of 3.5 grams) and in 1534 (silver Lira).

**18th Century** - Small silver coin.

**19th Century** - From 1826 to 1859, Lira della Moneta Buona. Before unification of Italy, Lira and its multiples minted in gold and silver, copying French types, in various Italian states: Naples, Parma, Lucca, Piedmont, Papal States.

**III.** - In **Venice,** under name Lira di Grossi, unit of account from 13th to 16th Century. Divided into 20 Soldi or 240 Denari, or Grossi.

**1192** - Lira de Grossi worth 26 Lira di Piccioli.

**1278** - Lira de Grossi worth 28 Lira di Piccioli.

**1282** - Lira de Grossi worth 32 Lira di Piccioli.

**1373** - Lira de Grossi worth 48 Lira di Piccioli.

**1472** - Lira de Grossi worth 62 Lira di Piccioli. Relationship then remained constant.

**18th Century** - Bank of Venice kept its records in Lire Grossi (singular: Lira Grossa) of 20 Soldi Grossi or 240 Denari Grossi.

Lira Grossa worth 10 Ducati, 62 Lire, 240 Denari, 1,240 Soldi (or Marchetti), 2,880 Grossetti, or 14,880 Denari di Lira.

**IV.** - In **Venice,** under name of Lira di Piccioli, silver, then silver/copper money.

Based on Carolingian monetary system, Lira di Piccioli of 20 Soldi or 240 Piccioli (Denari) became silver specie money in 1472; silver/copper money in 18th Century.

In its relationship to other monies (Grosso, silver Ducato, gold Zecchino. . .) exchange value of Lira evolved as follows:

|  | In Grams of Silver | In Milligrams of Gold |
|---|---|---|
| 1192 | 20.0 | – |
| 1278 | 19.0 | – |
| 1282 | 16.0 | – |
| 1284 | – | 1,451 |
| 1324 | – | 1,126 |
| 1350 | 11.0 | 726 |
| 1379 | 10.0 | – |
| 1399 | 9.1 | – |
| 1429 | 7.7 | – |
| 1443 | – | 612 |
| 1472 | 6.6 | 563 |
| 1527 | 5.4 | – |
| 1562 | – | 435 |
| 1578 | 4.6 | – |
| 1599 | – | 325 |
| 1608 | 3.8 | – |
| 1630 | 3.5 | – |
| 1687 | – | 206 |
| 1702 | 3.3 | – |
| 1704 | 2.9 | – |
| 1739 | 2.7 | 160 |
| 1797 | 2.5 | – |

**V.** - Money of unified **Italy.** - See *Lira Italy.*

**VI.** - In **Greek Islands** under domination of Republic of Venice, unit of account in 18th Century: worth 1/10 Reali or 10 Soldi, or Aspers.

**VII.** - Money of **Turkey.** - See *Lira Turkey.*


# LIRA AUSTRIACA

**I.** - Monetary unit of **Lombard-Venetian Kingdom,** under administration of Austria from 1815 to 1848. Divided into 100 Centesimi. Defined as being equal to 1/3 Austrian Gulden. Lira Austriaca corresponded to 0.85 Italian Lira.

**II.** - **Milan,** in 1848, minted gold and silver coins conforming to French monetary system. - See *Milan.*

## LIRA ITALY

Monetary unit of modern **Italy.**Divided into 100 Centesimi.

Bank of issue - First by State, Banca Nazionale del Regno d'Italia, and five local banks (Banco di Roma, Banca Nazionale Toscana, Banca Toscana di Credito, Banco di Napoli, Banco di Sicilia). Then, after 1893, by Banca d'Italia (created by union of Banca Nazionale del Regno d'Italia and two Tuscan Banks) and by Banco di Napoli and Banco di Sicilia. After June 1926, only by Banca d'Italia (Bank of Italy); nationalized in March 1936.

Origin of name - See *Lira.*

Predecessors - See *Lira* and *Italy.*

Plural - Lire.

**1816 and 1820** - Piedmont, which became accustomed to accounting in Francs as result of French Occupation (from 1800 to 1814), minted gold coins of 10, 20, 40 and 80 Lire, and silver coins of 1, 2 and 5 Lire in conformance with French monetary system.

**1862** (August 24th) - Adoption of Lira as monetary unit of Italy headed by House of Savoy:

    1 Lira = 4.5 grams of fine silver
    1 Lira = 290.322 milligrams of fine gold
    1 Lira = 1 Franc

**1865** (November 20th) - Adherence of Italy to Latin Monetary Union.

**1866** (May 1st) - Suspension of convertibility. Forced legal tender (corso forzoso). Depreciation of from 5% to 20%.

**1874** - Law limiting fiduciary issue of banks to 755 million Lire (450 for Banca Nazionale del Regno d'Italia, 45 for Banco di Roma, 63 for Banca Nazionale Toscana, 15 for Banca Toscana di Credito, 146 for Banco di Napoli, 36 for Banco di Sicilia).

**1878** - Complete suspension of free minting of silver.

**1881** (July 1st) - Law for abolition of forced parity.

**1883** (March 1st) - Law fixing restoration of convertibility for April 12th.

**1883** (April 12th) - Lifting of forced parity.

**1884** (January) - Resumption of specie payments in both gold and silver at par.

**1887** - Forced parity. New depreciation of from 8% to 10%.

**1893** - Banking reform. With creation of Banca d'Italia, strict rules for banknote issue. Lira remained incovertible, with exchange rate maintained near parity.

**1914** (August) - Lifting of ceiling on amount of banknote issue.

**1915** - Loans to government from banks of issue resulted in monetary inflation. Depreciation of from 42% in June 1918 to 82% in 1920.

**1925** (August 29th) - Law establishing foreign exchange controls.

**1926** (September 12th) - Royal decree calling for repayment of loans to government.

**1927** (December 21st) - Stabilization of Lira, recognizing devaluation of 72.47%:

    1 Lira = 79.19 milligrams of fine gold
    1 U.S. Dollar = 19.00 Lire

**1928** (June 7th) - Law confirming stabilization.

**1930** (March 12th) - Lifting of foreign exchange controls.

**1931** (September 29th) - Restoration of some foreign exchange controls.

**1934** (May 26th) - Controls on the exportation of banknotes, checks and securities. De facto suspension of convertibility.

**1935** (June 18th) - Withdrawal of silver coins from circulation.

**1935** (July 22nd) - Abolition of rule fixing minimum cover for demand liabilities at 40%. Official abandonment of convertibility.

**1935** (November 27th) - Gold purchased by State at price carrying premium of 18.53%.

**1936** (March 29th) - Creation of Tourist Lira. Depreciation of 31%:
    1 U.S. Dollar = 24.89 Lire

**1936** (October 5th) - Devaluation of 40.94% in line with that of U.S. Dollar, without return to convertibility:
    1 Lira = 46.77 milligrams of fine gold
    1 U.S. Dollar = 19.00 Lire
Moreover, possibility of additional devaluation of 10% permitting lowering of Lira to 42.10 milligrams of fine gold.
In addition to official Lira, existence of Tourist Lira and several categories of blocked Lire.

**1939** (September) - U.S. Dollar parity lowered to 19.80 Lire.

**1940** (October) - Creation of Special Account Lira for regulation of transport fees. Initial depreciation in relation to official Lira was 56%.

**1941** (May) - U.S. Dollar parity restored to 19.00 Lire.

**1943** (June) - With invasion of Italy by Allies, new official exchange rate (first in Sicily):
    1 U.S. Dollar = 120.00 Lire

**1943** (July) - Amended rate of exchange:
    1 U.S. Dollar = 100.00 Lire
In Allied-occupied Italy, issue of banknotes called Amlire.

**1943** (September-November) - In part of Italy occupied by Germans, issues of Reichs-kreditkassen vouchers at rate of:
    1 Reichsmark = 10.00 Lire

**1943** (November 16th) - Exchange rate for clearing between Germany and Italy raised from 7.60 to 10.00 Lire per Reichsmark.

**1946** (January 4th) - New exchange rate for commercial payments as result of premiums and surcharges:
    1 U.S. Dollar = 225.00 Lire

**1946** (March 26th) - Authorization of fluctuating free market, on which exporters could sell 50% of their foreign exchange to importers at profit. Average rate of exchange on free market (May-December 1946):
    1 U.S. Dollar = 509.00 Lire

**1947** (May) - Black market rate of Lire hit record 800.00 per U.S. Dollar.

**1947** (July) - New official exchange rate:
    1 U.S. Dollar = 350.00 Lire

**1948** (November 28th) - Linking of official rate of exchange to free market exchange rate with monthly revisions within limits of 350 to 650 Lire per U.S. Dollar:
1 U.S. Dollar = 575.00 Lire

**1949** (September 21st) - After devaluation of Pound Sterling, stabilization of Lira, but with daily fixings:
1 U.S. Dollar = 625.00 Lire
Export receipts subject to surrender on basis of "50% retention system" at official fixing. Remainder credited to exchange account negotiable at fluctuating free market. Due to stability of latter, effective rates for export and import transactions virtually identical.

**1949** (September 21st) - **1958** (December) - During this period numerous additional Lira Accounts existed. Among more important varieties were Non-Resident Lira Accounts encompassing Convertible Accounts, E.P.U. Accounts and Bilateral Accounts; Foreign Exchange Accounts encompassing Convertible Accounts and E.P.U. Accounts; Financial Accounts entailing Dollar Area Accounts, E.P.U. Area Accounts and Other Country Accounts.

**1952** - Receipts from current account transactions deposited in exchange account could be held for only 60 days, then surrendered at official rate.

**1955** (July 28th) - The "50% retention system" abolished. Full amount of exchange receipts retained for certain period. Such balances used for approved transactions or sold to other residents or to authorized banks.

**1957** (February) - Transferable Lira governed multilateral accounts, which began to reduce need for bilateral clearing system.

**1958** (December 29th) - Exchange system simplified to Non-Resident Lira Commercial Account, including Foreign and Bilateral Accounts, and Non-Resident Capital Account.

**1959** (June 1st) - Bilateral Lira Accounts abolished.

**1960** (March 30th) - Par value registered with International Monetary Fund:
1 Lira = 1.4218736 milligrams of fine gold
1 U.S. Dollar = 625.00 Lire

**1969-1970** - Renewed capital flight. Lira on unofficial market after years of relative stability weakened, hitting 661.00 per U.S. Dollar in June 1970. Subsequently improved to near 630.00 per U.S. Dollar level at end of 1970.


# LIRA TURKEY

Monetary unit of **Turkey** from 1881. Divided into 100 Piastres (then Kurus from 1929) or 4,000 Paras.

Bank of issue - By Imperial Ottoman Bank (founded in 1863); by State from 1915; by Banque Centrale de la République de Turquie (Central Bank of Turkish Republic) since October 1931.

Variation of name - Turkish Pound.

Predecessor - See *Turkey.*

**1881** (January 6th) - Theoretical adoption of gold standard:

1 Turkish Lira = 6,615.183 milligrams of fine gold

**1884** - Suspension of free minting of silver.

**1914** (August 3rd) - Suspension of gold standard.

**1915** (March 30th) - Law authorized first government issue of Turkish paper Liras theoretically redeemable in gold within six months after World War I:
1 Turkish paper Lira = 1 Turkish gold Lira

**1915** (August 18th) to **1917** (March 28th) - Six subsequent issues of Turkish paper Liras backed by German Treasury Notes.

**1916** (April 17th) - Currency reform law established Turkish gold Lira of 100 Piastres or 4,000 Paras. Authorized gold coins in denominations of from 25 to 500 Piastres, silver coins of from 2 to 20 Piastres and nickel coins of 1 Piastre and fractions thereof:
1 Turkish Lira = 6,615.183 milligrams of fine gold
1 Turkish Lira = 4.3965 U.S. Dollars
Silver was legal tender up to 300 Piastres, and nickel up to 50 Piastres.

**1916** - Erosion of Turkish paper Lira:
1 Turkish gold Lira = 2 Turkish paper Liras

**1917-1929** - After Armistice, precipitous decline in value of Turkish paper Lira from average of $3.18 in 1917 to $0.48 in 1929.

**1930** (February 26th) - Foreign exchange controls introduced. Exportation of capital forbidden. First appearance of blocked accounts.

**1930** (September) - Stabilization of Turkish paper Lira on basis of Pound Sterling:
1 Pound Sterling = 10.30 Turkish Liras

**1931** (September) - Following devaluation of Pound Sterling, Turkish Lira pegged to French Franc:
1 Turkish Lira = 12.06 Francs Poincaré
1 U.S. Dollar = 2.11 Turkish Liras

**1932** (January 1st) - Exchange control authority transferred to Central Bank.

**1933** - Adoption of Kurus as submultiple of Turkish Lira to replace Piastre:
1 Turkish Lira = 100 Kurus = 100 Piastres

**1936** (September 26th) - After devaluation of French Franc, Turkish Lira linked to Pound Sterling:
1 Pound Sterling = 6.365 Turkish Liras

**1936-1939** - U.S. Dollar cross rate fluctuated around 1.26-1.28 Turkish Liras per U.S. Dollar.

**1939** (November 28th) - Introduction of multiple rate system of variable import and export premiums according to currency involved. Based on fluctuating official rate which ranged from 1.378 to 1.320 Turkish Liras per U.S. Dollar.

**1942** (May 25th) - Cancellation of export premiums for U.S. Dollars and Belgian Francs.

**1944** (November 15th) - Export premium reestablished for U.S. Dollars.

**1945** (April 4th) - Export premium reestablished for Belgian Francs.

**1946** (September 9th) - Premium rate system abolished, and Turkish Lira devalued 54%:
1 U.S. Dollar = 2.80 Turkish Liras (for all transactions)

**1947** (June 19th) - Parity registered with International Monetary Fund:

1 Turkish Lira = 317.383 milligrams of fine gold
1 U.S. Dollar = 2.80 Turkish Liras

**1950** (September 1st) - "Takas System" became effective. Allowed use of proceeds of certain marginal exports to pay for some less essential imports for which exchange not readily available. Created export and import premiums for EPU currencies and U.S. Dollar.

**1953** (September 3rd) - Takas System abolished. Replaced by multiple rate system of variable premiums that depended solely (except in case of raisins) upon whether proceeds were U.S. Dollars, EPU currencies, or clearing agreement currencies. Premiums were 50%, 40% and 25%, respectively, of value of exchange earned. Raisin rate further modified by volume of export.
All luxury and nonessential imports subject to surcharges of 25%, 50% or 75%.

**1954** (December 28th) - Premiums on proceeds from a few specified items raised to 100% for U.S. Dollars, 75% for EPU currencies and 40% for clearing currencies.

**1955** (August 29th) - Variable premium system revised and regrouped. Premiums on export proceeds varied according to nature of both commodity and currency involved:
U.S. Dollar and EPU currencies: Premiums of 40%, 50% and 75%.
Clearing currencies: Premiums of 20%, 40% and 50%.
Raisin rate further modified by volume of export.

**1956** (September 15th) - Premiums revised and regrouped:
U.S. Dollars: 50%-85%
EPU currencies: 40%-75%
Clearing currencies: 25%-50%

**1956** (October 8th) - Special exchange rate established for specified secondary imports, exports and invisibles transactions:
1 U.S. Dollar = 5.25/5.75 Turkish Liras (buying/selling)

**1957** (March 1st) - Introduction of uniform exchange tax of 40% for imports (20% for rubber) creating principal import rate:
1 U.S. Dollar = 3.955 Turkish Liras
Surcharges of 35%-75% on luxury and nonessential goods created selling rates of from 4.944 to 6.922 Turkish Liras per U.S. Dollar.

**1957** (July 27th) - Preferential treatment for Dollar Area exports abolished. Modification of premiums for exports against U.S. Dollars and EPU currencies as group. New buying rates:
1 U.S. Dollar = 3.92-5.60 Turkish Liras (official rate plus
                40%-100% premium for exports of certain goods
                paid for in U.S. Dollars or EPU currencies)
1 U.S. Dollar = 3.50-4.90 Turkish Liras (official rate plus
                25%-75% premium for exports of certain goods
                paid in clearing currencies)

**1958** (July) - Turkish Lira hit record low of 21.50 per U.S. Dollar on black market, premium of 668% for Greenback. Subsequent improvement, Turkish Lira fluctuating between 12.50-17.00 per U.S. Dollar on black market.

**1958** (August 4th) - Major revision in exchange rate system. Complex rates replaced by simplified structure consisting of three effective buying rates (based upon nature of exports) and one effective selling rate:

Buying Rates:
  1 U.S. Dollar = 4.90 Turkish Liras (official rate plus premium of 2.10 Turkish Liras for Category A exports)
  1 U.S. Dollar = 5.60 Turkish Liras (official rate plus premium of 2.80 Turkish Liras for Category B exports)
  1 U.S. Dollar = 9.00 Turkish Liras (official rate plus premium of 6.20 Turkish Liras for Category C exports)
Selling Rate:
  1 U.S. Dollar = 9.0252 Turkish Liras (official rate plus surcharge of 6.20 Turkish Liras)

**1958** (December 27th) - Uniform exchange tax of 40% for imports abolished.

**1959** (August 15th) - Further modification of export premiums resulting in two effective rates:
  1 U.S. Dollar = 5.60 Turkish Liras (official rate plus premium of 2.80 Turkish Liras for tobacco and opium)
  1 U.S. Dollar = 9.00 Turkish Liras (official rate plus premium of 6.20 Turkish Liras for all other exports)

**1960** (August 20th) - De jure devaluation, and abolition of multiple rate structure:
  1 Turkish Lira = 98.7412 milligrams of fine gold
  1 U.S. Dollar = 9.00 Turkish Liras (official rate)
  1 U.S. Dollar = 9.00/9.045 Turkish Liras (buying/selling)

**1961** (June 6th) - Special tax of 4.50 Turkish Liras per U.S. Dollar on exchange purchased for foreign travel, creating a resident tourist rate of:
  1 U.S. Dollar = 13.50 Turkish Liras

**1964** (January 2nd) - Selling rate adjusted:
  1 U.S. Dollar = 9.08 Turkish Liras

**1968** (March 4th) - Tourist rate created through system of advanced tax refunds:
  1 U.S. Dollar = 12.00 Turkish Liras
Rate also applied to remittances by Turkish workers abroad.

**1969** (October 26th) - Special export premium rate created for proceeds from certain invisibles:
  1 U.S. Dollar = 11.25 Turkish Liras (official rate plus 25% premium)

**1970** (August 9th) - Devaluation, and unfication of rate structure:
  1 Turkish Lira = 59.2447 milligrams of fine gold
  1 U.S. Dollar = 15.00 Turkish Liras

## LIRA VATICAN

Monetary unit of **Vatican City.** Divided into 100 Centesimi.

Note-issuing authority - Istituto Per le Opere di Religione, and later Prefecture of Economic Affairs.

Predecessors - See *Rome* and *Papal States.*

**1929** (June 7th) - Monetary autonomy for Vatican City. Creation of Vatican Lira equal to Italian Lira. - See *Lira Italy.*

**1930** (December 31st) - Minting of Vatican coins:
In gold - 100 Lire of 8.799 grams 900 fine
In silver - 5 and 10 Lire
In nickel - 1 and 2 Lire
In bronze - 3 and 10 Centesimi

**1950** - Minting of Holy Year coins in gold (100 Lire of 5.19 grams 900 fine) and in mixed metals (1 and 10 Lire).

## LIRAZZA

Silver/copper money of **Venice,** having 1 Lira 10 Soldi as its exchange rate in 18th Century.

Origin of name - Diminutive of Lira.

## LIS

**I.** - Gold and silver monies minted in **France** under Louis XIV.

Origin of name - From imprint of fleur de lis (lily of the valley).

Variation of name - Lys.

**1655** (December) - Minting of gold Lis (4.01 grams 968 fine, or 3.88 grams fine). Exchange rate: 7 Livres.
Silver Lis (7.90 grams 958 fine, or 7.57 grams fine). Exchange rate: 20 Sols.

**1656** (April) - Debasement of silver Lis.

**1679** (March) - Debasement of gold Lis.
For monies minted in 16th Century, see *Fleur de Lis.*

**II.** - Silver money minted in **Savoy** in 18th Century.

## LISBONINO

**I.** - Early gold money of **Portugal** and **Brazil.** Weight: 10.75 grams 916 fine. Exchange rate: 4,000-4,800 Reis. Also called Double Moeda de Ouro or more commonly Moidore.

**II.** - Multiple of Cruzado, early money of **Portugal.**

# LITAS

Monetary unit of **Lithuania** from 1922 to 1941. Divided into 100 Centu.

Origin of name - Root of word Lithuania.

Bank of issue - By Lietuvos Bankas (Bank of Lithuania).

Predecessor - See *Lithuania.*

Plural - Litai.

**1922** (August 9th) - Substitution of Litas for Mark and Ruble in circulation:
1 Litas = 150.462 milligrams of fine gold
1 U.S. Dollar = 10.00 Litai

**1922** (August 11th) - Creation of Bank of Lithuania.

**1935** (October) - Foreign exchange controls. Foreign currency transactions monopoly of Bank of Lithuania.

**1939** - In territory of Memel, substitution of Reichsmark for Litas:
1 Reichsmark = 2.50 Litai

**1939** (October) - Annexation of territory of Vilnyus where Litas replaced Zloty:
1 Litas = 5.00 Zlote

**1940** (November 25th) - Annexation by U.S.S.R. Introduction of Ruble circulating simultaneously with Litas:
1 Ruble = 1.11 Litai

**1941** (April) - Abolition of Litas. Ruble remained only legal money.

**1941** (July) - German Occupation. Issue of banknotes denominated in Reichsmark by Reichskreditkassen. Gradually substituted for Ruble.

**1942** (July 30th) - Creation of Central Bank of Ostland. Authorized to issue banknotes denominated in Ostland Marks. - See *Mark Ostland.*

# *LITHUANIA*

**After 14th Century** - Polish monies. Minting of local silver Denier.

**15th Century** - Circulation of cut bars of gold called Rubles.

**1535** - Minting of silver Gros following example of Poland.

**1547** - Minting of gold Ducats following example of Poland.

**1564** - Neopolitan Scudi, brought as dowry by nobleman, were countermarked and became Thaler. Exchange rate: 30 Gros.

**1575** - Adoption of Polish monetary system.

**19th Century** - Russian monies.

**1917** - Mixed circulation of Mark and Ruble. Mark called Auksinas. Divided into 100 Statiku.

**1922** - Creation of Litas of 100 Centu. - See *Litas.*

## LITRA

Money of **Sicily** and southern **Italy** in ancient times. Equal to Roman As (12 ounces). Divided into 2 Hemilitra (6 Ounces), 3 Tetras (4 Ounces), 4 Trias (3 Ounces), 6 Hexas (2 Ounces).

Origin of name - Greek *litra* (weight of 12 ounces). Corresponded to Roman *libra*.

**6th Century B.C.** - In Sicily and Campania, minting of silver coin called Litra, akin to Greek Obol (0.70 to 0.80 grams) and used for domestic transactions.

**5th Century B.C.** - In Sicily, minting of bronze Litra of 107 grams.

**4th Century B.C.** - Disappearance of silver Litra. Bronze coinage in abundance in Sicily and in southern Italy. Progressive reduction of Litra to about 13 grams of bronze.

**1st Century B.C.** - In Sicily, which became Roman province, Litra, bronze coin of 6.7 grams, still used as simple divisionary coinage.


## LIVONESE

Silver money, circulating in **Livonia** and **Estonia** in 18th Century (after October 25, 1756).

Weight: 20.2 grams fine (minted in 1757). Exchange rate: 96 Kopeks. Also ½ and ¼ Livonese coins.

Variations of name - Livonaise, Livonina, Livonine.


## *LIVONIA*

See *Latvia* and *Estonia.*


## LIVORNINO

**I.** - Silver coin struck in 1656 for **Leghorn** by Grand Duke of Tuscany and by his successors.

Also called Livornina delle Torre.

**II.** - Money of **Tuscany** (18th Century). Synonym for Pezza. - See *Pezza.*


## LIVRE

Unit of account of several countries.

Origin of name - Unit of weight (12 ounces). From Latin *libra,* Greek *litra.* - See *Litra.* Cf. *Lira.*

**I.** - In **Rome**, 6th Century B.C., use of large bars of bronze (copper, with alloy of lead and tin). Theoretical weight of 327 grams (1 pound of bronze).

**4th Century B.C.** - This pound (Libra) was used as basis for weight of As (As Libralis). Progressively reduced in weight. - See *As.*

**II.** - In **Carolingian** monetary system in 8th Century, Roman pound gave rise to Carolingian Livre (436 to 491 grams). Unit of weight and unit of account. In principle, pound of silver was to yield 240 Deniers:

> 1 Carolingian Livre = 20 Sous = 240 Deniers

See *Sou* and *Denier.*

**III.** - In **France,** during 12th Century, Carolingian Livre gave rise to various systems of weights and accounts: French Livre (489 to 506 grams) and its local variations (Tournois and Parisis). - See *Livre Parisis* and *Livre Tournois.* For Colonies, see *Livre Coloniale.*

**IV.** - For **Italy,** see *Lira and Lira Italy.*

**V.** - In **Netherlands,** unit of account inherited from Carolingian monetary system. Called Livre de Gros (Pondt Vlaams):

> 1 Livre = 20 Schelling = 240 Grooten

**1355** - Introduction of new system of accounting, based on Guilder (1/6 Livre) and Stuyver (1/120 Livre). Two systems of accounting existed simultaneously until 19th Century, with Livre system predominating in Belgian provinces, and Guilder system predominating in Northern provinces.

**18th Century** - Livre de Gros equalled 2.5 Rijksdaalder, 6 Guilders, 20 Schelling, 120 Stuyver, 240 Grooten, 1,920 Penning, and in Brabant, 5,760 Myten.

**VI.** - For **England,** see *Pound,* followed by other varieties of Pound, and those monies linked to Pound.

**VII.** - In **German** states, Carolingian monetary system gave rise to Livre of 20 Schilling or 240 Pfennig. - See *Schilling* and *Pfennig.*

The 1/2 Livre, or Marc (Mark of Cologne of 233.845 grams), gave rise to Mark, divided into 12 Schilling or 144 Pfennig. - See *Mark.*

**18th Century** - Livre (Pfund), divided into 30 Groschen or 360 Pfennig, used as unit of account by Brandenburg Bank. Corresponding to 5.85 Gulden and divided into 41 Schillings, 164 Groschen, 492 Regensburgers, 1,230 Pfennig, or 2,460 Heller. Used as unit of account (called "black money") in Bavaria (Regensburg) for payment of taxes and fines.

**VIII.** - In certain **Swiss** cantons until 1850, unit of account divided into 20 Sols (Sous) or 240 Deniers (in Basel, Berne, Geneva), 10 Batzen or 40 Kreuzer (in Berne).

**IX.** - For **Spain,** see *Libra.*

**X.** - For **Portugal,** see *Libra Portugal.*

## LIVRE COLONIALE

Unit of account of **French Colonies** (Canada, Antilles, Guiana, Ile de France-Mauritius, Ile de Bourbon-Réunion, Senegal) from 17th Century to beginning of 19th Century. Also called "Livre des Iles".

In order to keep specie monies circulating in Colonies, their exchange rate in Livres Coloniales was higher than their exchange rate in Livres Tournois.

**1654** (July 18th) - Decision of Council of Quebec giving French specie monies accounting value in Livres Coloniales, 20% higher than their value in France:
100 Livres Tournois = 120 Livres Coloniales

**1661** (October 7th) - Premium raised to 33⅓%:
100 Livres Tournois = 133 Livres Coloniales

**1662** (March 2nd) - Premium raised to 50%:
100 Livres Tournois = 150 Livres Coloniales
This parity later extended to Mauritius and Réunion, and maintained during entire 18th Century.

**1820** (February 2nd) - Linking of Colonial monetary system to that of Metropolitan France.
Abolition of Livre des Iles, and introdution of Franc. - See *Franc.*

## LIVRE PARISIS

Unit of account in early **France** (in royal domain). Gradually eclipsed by Livre Tournois. Divided into 20 Sous Parisis or 240 Deniers Parisis.
Relationship of two systems:
1 Livre Parisis = 25 Sous Parisis = 300 Deniers Tournois
1 Livre Tournois = 4/5 Livre Parisis

Origin of name - See *Livre.*

Predecessors - See *Livre I* (Roman Libra or Pound) and *Livre II* (Carolingian Livre).

**10th Century** - From Carolingian Livre (491.179 grams) French Livre, or Livre Parisis (489.506 grams), was derived. Became official unit of weight (divided into 2 marcs) under Louis VI.
Livre Parisis, according to Carolingian rule, divided into 240 silver Deniers (Deniers Parisis).
Progressive debasement of Denier separated its multiple, Livre Parisis (unit of account), from French livre (unit of weight).
Weights of Livre Parisis in grams of fine silver:

| | |
|---|---|
| Hugh Capet (987-996) ............... | 305 |
| Philip I (1060-1108) .............. | 223 |
| Philip I (1060-1108) .............. | 189 |
| Louis VI (1108-1137) ............ | 153 |
| Philip Augustus II (1179-1223) ...... | 115 |
| Louis VIII (1223-1226) ............ | 106 |

**13th Century** - Under Saint Louis, adoption of Tournois monetary system (from Tours) for accounting purposes of Kingdom. Livre Parisis gradually eliminated. - See *Parisis, Denier Parisis, Sou* and *Livre Tournois.*

**1329** - Under Philip VI, minting of gold Parisis (7.41 grams). Worth 1 Livre Parisis or 25 Sous Tournois.

**1336** - Livre Parisis demonetized.

## LIVRE TOURNOIS

Unit of account of **French** monetary system from 13th to 18th Century. Divided into 20 Sous Tournois or 240 Deniers Tournois.

Origin of name - See *Livre.*

Predecessors - See *Livre I* (Roman Libra or Pound), *Livre II* (Carolingian Livre) and *Livre Parisis.*

**10th Century** - French Livre, or Livre Parisis (489.506 grams), substituted for Carolingian Livre (491.179) grams). Livre Parisis was unit of weight which yielded 240 silver Deniers.

Many local variations: Livre of Tours (Livre Tournois) represented only 455.2 grams.

**1204** - Extension of Tournois monetary system to Normandy.

**13th Century** - Under Saint Louis, adoption of Livre Tournois monetary system as basic unit of account in Kingdom.

Weights of Livre Tournois:

| | In Grams of Fine Gold | In Grams of Fine Silver |
|---|---|---|
| Philip Augustus II (1179-1223) .... | 84.00 | – |
| Saint Louis (1266) | 80.84 | 8.271 |
| Philip III (1270-85) | 80.84 | 7.840 |
| Philip IV the Fair (1305) | 24.64 | 2.270 |
| Philip IV the Fair (1313) | 80.84 | 5.600 |
| Louis X (1316) | 80.84 | 6.720 |
| Philip V (1318) | 63.36 | 5.510 |
| Charles IV (1326) | 39.00 | 3.370 |
| Philip VI (1342) | 15.63 | 1.550 |
| Philip VI (1349) | 26.05 | 3.170 |
| John II the Good (1360) | 1.98 | – |
| John II the Good (1361) | 44.64 | 3.880 |
| Charles V (1365) | 39.00 | 3.820 |
| Charles VI (1422) | 1.30 | – |
| Charles VII (1461) | 26.05 | 2.420 |
| Louis XI (1478) | 23.68 | 2.040 |
| Charles VIII (1494) | 21.71 | 1.860 |
| Louis XII (1513) | 18.00 | – |
| Francis I (1541) | 16.01 | 1.460 |
| Francis II (1550) | 15.55 | 1.400 |
| Charles IX (1573) | 13.55 | 1.190 |
| Henry III (1577) | 11.70 | 1.080 |
| Henry IV (1602) | 11.06 | 0.990 |
| Louis XIII (1640-41) | 8.68 | 0.620 |
| Louis XIV (1709) | 5.86 | 0.380 |
| Louis XV (1720) | 2.61 | 0.170 |
| Louis XV (1726) | 4.50 | 0.310 |
| Louis XVI (1785) | 4.50 | 0.290 |

Principal metallic monies:

| | In Gold | In Silver | In Silver/Copper and Copper |
|---|---|---|---|
| 13th Century: | Denier à l'Ecu Agnel | Gros | |
| 14th Century: | Royal Masse d'Or Chaise Agnel Ecu Franc | Chatel Etoile Fleur de Lis | Denier Maille Bourgeois |
| 15th Century | Ecu Mouton | Florette Carolus | Denier |
| 16th Century: | Ecu Henri d'Or | Teston Franc | Denier |
| 17th Century: | Louis Lis | Ecu | Liard Sou |
| 18th Century: | Louis | Ecu | Liard Sou |

Various paper issues:

**1701** (September 19th) - Issue of banknotes in exchange for coins called in for smelting.

**1703** (May 29th) - Second issue of banknotes. Redeemed in 1704.

**1704** - Third issue of banknotes. Not redeemable, they soon depreciated. Reabsorbed from 1709 to 1712.

**1716** (May 2nd) - Authorization for Bank of John Law to issue banknotes.

**1718** (December 4th) - Declaration changing Bank of John Law into Royal Bank.

**1719** (April 22nd) - Decree protecting banknotes "from depreciations which could arise against specie monies".

**1720** (February 22nd) - Merger of Royal Bank and East India Company. Inflation of banknotes (up to 3 billion Livres).

**1720** (February 27th) - Use of metallic monies for payments of more than 100 Livres forbidden. Also forbidden was holding of more than 500 Livres in gold or silver.

**1720** (March 11th) - Announcement of total demonetization of metals.

**1720** (April 6th) - Contractual stipulations in metallic monies forbidden.

**1720** (May 21st) - Decree of Council ordering reduction of banknotes by 50% of their face value. Revoked May 27th.

**1720** (June 1st) - Convertibility into specie monies limited to denominations of 100 and 10 Livres. Collapse in value of large denomination banknotes.

**1720** (July 13th) - Convertibility into specie monies limited to denominations of 10 Livres.

**1720** (August 15th) - Withdrawal of legal tender status for 1,000 and 10,000 Livre banknotes October 1st) and for small banknotes May 1, 1721).

**1720** (October 10th) - Abrupt demonetization of all banknotes as of November 1, 1720.

**1759** (October 26th) - Issue of banknotes with proper redemption.

**1776** (March 24th) - Creation of Caisse d'Escompte authorized to issue banknotes in Paris. Payable at sight.

**1783** (September 27th) - Suspension of convertibility of banknotes of Caisse d'Escompte.

**1783** (November 9th and 23rd) - Decrees restoring convertibility.

**1788** (August 18th) - New suspension of convertibility. Actually, banknotes of Caisse were convertible in limited amounts.

**1789** (December 19th) - Demand of Treasury on Caisse d'Escompte for 80 million Livres.

**1790** (April 16th-17th) - Decree ordering exchange of banknotes of Caisse d'Escompte for Assignats. - See *Assignats.*

**1793** (August 24th) - Dissolution of Caisse d'Escompte. - See *France* and *Franc.*


## LOCHA

In **Venezuela,** popular name for Cuartillo, coin of cupro-nickel worth ¼ Real or 0.125 Bolívar.


## *LOMBARDY*

See *Milan.*


## LOSO

Early silver money of **Madagascar** corresponding to ½ Mexican Piaster (13.5 grams). Equal to ½ Ariary, or 2 Kirobo, 4 Sikajy, 6 Roavoamena, 24 Ilavoamena, 36 Eranambatry, 48 Varifitoventy, 72 Varidimoventy.


## LOTT

Submultiple (¹⁄₁₂₈) of **Siamese** Tical. Minted in bronze at end of 19th Century.


## LOUIS

I. - **French** gold money from 17th to 19th Century.

Origin of name - From Louis XIII (and from his successors named Louis), whose image was on coin.

**1640** (March 31st) - Edict ordering minting of Louis weighing 6.69 grams 917 fine, or

613 grams fine gold. Exchange rate: 10 Livres. Minting of ½ Louis, Double Louis, and of coins of 4, 6, 8 and 10 Louis.

**1670 to 1709** - Exchange rate of Louis varied between 11 Livres 10 Sols (1693) and 15 Livres (1704).

**1709** (May) - Minting of Louis au Soleil weighing 8.16 grams 917 fine, or 7.48 grams fine. Exchange rate: 20 Livres. Lowered to 14 Livres between 1713 and 1715. Minting of Double Louis.

**1715** - Minting of Louis aux Armes weighing 8.16 grams 917 fine, or 7.48 grams fine. Exchange rate: 15 Livres 10 Sous. Minting of Double Louis.

**1716** (November) - Minting of Louis de Noailles weighing 12.24 grams 917 fine, or 11.22 grams fine. Exchange rate: 30 Livres. Minting of Double Louis.

**1718** (May) - Minting of Louis à la Croix de Malte weighing 9.79 grams 917 fine, or 8.98 grams fine. Exchange rate: 36 Livres. Raised by John Law to 72 Livres. Minting of Double Louis.

**1720** (September) - Minting of Louis aux L of same type. Exchange rate: 54 Livres. Minting of Double Louis.

**1723** (August) - Minting of Louis Mirlitons weighing 6.53 grams 917 fine, or 5.98 grams fine. Exchange rate: 27 Livres, then 20, then 14. Minting of Double Louis.

**1726** (January) - Minting of Louis à Lunettes weighing 8.16 grams 917 fine, or 7.48 grams fine. Exchange rate: 20 Livres, raised to 24 Livres on May 26, 1726. Minting of Double Louis.

**1786** - Minting of Louis aux Armes weighing 7.65 grams 917 fine, or 7.01 grams fine. Exchange rate: 24 Livres. Minting of Double Louis.

**1791** - Minting of Louis Constitutionnel with same weight, fineness and exchange rate as its predecessor.

**1793** (April 11th) - Payments in Louis forbidden.

**1796** - Rise of Louis against Assignats and Mandats (up to 17,950 Livres).

**1796** (July 23rd) - Legal tender status of Louis restored.

**1803** - Minting of gold coins of 20 Francs weighing 6.45 grams 900 fine, or 5.80 grams fine. Called Napoléons under Empire, and Louis from 1814 to 1840. - See *Napoléon*.

**1810** - Legal tender value of earlier Louis of 24 Livres fixed at 23.55 Francs.

**1829** (June 14th) - Demonetization of old Louis fixed on April 1, 1834 (then December 31, 1834).
Later, name Louis remained on gold coin of 20 Francs, and in wider sense used as unit of account to designate all sums of 20 Francs.

**II.** - Silver monies of **France**, minted with image of Louis XIII, Louis XIV, or Louis XV.

**1641** (December 23rd) - Minting of coins of 5, 15, 30 and 60 Sous. Called Louis d'Argent, then Ecus Blancs (see *Ecu*). Coins of 5 Sous were in demand in Levant under name Timmin in Turkey and Luigino in Italy. - See *Timmin*.

**Under Louis XIV** - Minting of silver Louis of 5 and 15 Sous. Destined for commerce with Canada.

**1720** (May) - Issue of silver Louis weighing 8.16 grams 917 fine, or 7.48 grams fine. Initial exchange rate: 60 Sous. Lowered to 55 Sous in May, 50 in June, 45 in July,

40 in August, 35 in September, 30 in October, 25 in November, 20 in December.

**1726** - Repudiation of Louis.


# LOUISDOR

Monetary unit of **Bremen** and **Oldenburg**. Also called gold Louis, or gold Louis Thaler or Pistole. Divided into 72 Groten or 360 Schwaren.

**1871** - 10 Mark equal to 3$^{1}$/93 gold Louis.


# LUBSK

Former system of accounting in **Hamburg** and several other **German** cities.

Lübsk, or Sol Lübsk (Shilling Lübsk), worth $^{1}$/48 Reichsthaler, $^{1}$/32 Thaler, $^{1}$/16 Mark, or 12 Deniers Lübsk (Pfennig Lübsk). Later developed into accounting system in connection with Banco monetary system (bank money). - See *Banco* and *Hamburg*.


# *LUXEMBOURG*

Roman monies, then Carolingian monetary system. - See *Holy Roman Empire* and *Netherlands*.

**13th Century** - Luxembourg Denier contained 0.73 grams of silver.

**Early 14th Century** - Minting of silver Gros, then under John the Blind (1309-1346), first gold monies: Gulden (Guilder), Chaise, Royal.

Other silver monies: Plak, Esterlin (imitating English Esterlin). Numerous Luxembourg mintings. Spread as far as England where coins were called Lushburgers.

**15th Century** - Gold Gulden (Guilder) and silver Groschen (Gros) of $^{1}$/22 Guilder in 1424. Lewekin worth $^{1}$/12 Groschen.

**17th Century** - Guilder was monetary unit of Luxembourg. - See *Netherlands*.

**1848** (December 20th) - Adoption of Franc as unit of account, in place of Netherlands Guilder. - See *Franc Luxembourg*.

Until 1918, German monies also circulated. - See *Germany*.

## MACAO

Mixed circulation of Chinese, Mexican and Portuguese (Reis and Milreis) monies.

**1894** - Monetary unit: Pataca of 100 Avos.
Simultaneous circulation of Hong Kong Dollar and subsidiary coins. - See *Pataca Macao.*

## MACE

Term used by foreigners to designate Chinese Tsien.

**I.** - Unit of weight and unit of account in **China** representing ¹/₁₀ Tael. Equal to 10 Candareens and 1,000, or 1,600 Cash. Minted in early 20th Century in the form of silver coin 3.75 grams 850 fine. - See *Tael.*

Variation of name - Mas.

**II.** - In **Japan** until 19th Century, unit of account representing ¹/₁₀ Tael and worth 100 Candareens.

**III.** - For Kingdom of Achin in **Sumatra** and for **Java,** see *Mas.*

## MACUTA

**I.** - Early unit of account on West Coast of Africa, particulary in **Portuguese Angola.** Macuta represented the number 10. - See *Cowrie.*

Origin of name - From Makua, or Makuana, one of the tribes of Mozambique.

**1762** - Minting of silver coins (2 to 12 Macutas) and of copper coins (1 Macuta and submultiples).

**1814** - Minting of copper coins of 1 and 2 Macutas:
1 Macuta = 50 Reis

**1928** - Name Macuta used to refer to 5 Centavo coin.

**II.** - Basis of monetary system of **Sierra Leone** in late 18th Century:
1 Macuta = 2,000 Zembi

## MADAGASCAR

Before arrival of Europeans, transactions on barter basis.

**17th Century** - East India Company struck coins for local use with silver brought by natives.

**18th Century** - Circulation of copper and gold bracelets made with metal from European coins or introduced by the French established in the Bays of Antongil and Saint Augustin. See - *Manilla.*

**19th Century** - Native silver monies: Ariary, imitating Mexican Piaster. - See *Ariary.*

Circulation of French coins of 5 Francs (22.50 grams fine silver), cut into pieces for subsidiary coinage.

**1896** (August 6th) - Island became French protectorate.

**1900** (January 12th) - Decree withdrawing coin fragments. Exchange rate:
    5 Francs = 30 grams of cut coins
Legal tender status given French specie money and banknotes of Banque de France. - See *Franc.*

**1920** - All money of Metropolitan France, including divisionary coinage, became legal tender.

**1925** (July 1st) - Regular account opened by French Treasury with Banque de Madagascar. Permitted alignment of exchange between Metropolitan France and Madagascar.

**1925** (December 22nd) - Privilege of note-issue granted to Banque de Madagascar et des Comores. Banknotes from Banque de France completely replaced by December 1928.

**1939** (September 8th) - Exchange controls within Franc-Zone.

**1940** (May 20th) - Decree established exchange control between Metropolitan France and Overseas Territories.

**1942** (May) - Incorporated within Sterling Area.

**1944** (February 8th) - Franco-British agreement fixed rate of exchange of free territories:
    1 Pound Sterling = 200.00 Francs

**1944** (June) - Franco-American agreement fixed rate of exchange:
    1 U.S. Dollar = 50.00 Francs

**1944** (December 6th) - Returned to Franc-Zone. Parities confirmed and made precise:
    1 Pound Sterling = 200.00 Francs
    1 U.S. Dollar = 49.625 Francs

**1945** (December 26th) - Creation of Franc of French Colonies of Africa, and incorporation of Madagascar into group of French African Colonies. - See *Franc CFA.*

**1958** (September 28th) - Became autonomous republic under name of Malagasy Republic. Monetary unit unchanged - See *Franc CFA* and *Malagasy.*


## MADEIRA

Monetary system of Portugal. - See *Portugal.*


## MADONNINA

**I.** - In **Bologna,** in 16th Century, silver coin equal to 6 Bolognini.

**II.** - In **Genoa,** in 18th and 19th Centuries, silver coin with image of Madonna. Worth 20 Soldi. Doppia Madonnina (9.1 grams 835 fine, or 7.6 grams fine) had 40 Soldi exchange rate.

III. - **Papal** copper coin in 18th Century, equal to 5 Baiocci. The $1/2$ Madonnina was called Sampietrino.


## MAHMUDI

I. - Unit of account and specie money in **Persia** in 18th Century. Mahmudi worth $1/100$ Toman, $1/10$ Hor(Kran), $1/2$ Abbasi, or 2 Shahis, 5 Bisti, 20 Kazbegi, 100 Dinars.
Specie money: Mahmudi, or Khodabandi, was a silver/copper coin.

II. - Unit of account in **Arabia** (Basra, Persian Gulf), worth $1/100$ Toman, 10 Danims, or 100 Flusch.

III. - Former copper coin of **Muscat** equal to $1/20$ Spanish Piaster. Subdivided into 20 Gass.


## MAILLE

In principle, money worth 1 Obol or $1/2$ Denier.

Origin of name - From Vulgar Latin *medalia* (medal) according to Littré; from *medius* (half) according to Grandsaignes d'Hauterive, and Bloch von Wartburg; Dauzat discarded these two etymologies.

I. - Silver/copper money, then unit of account of early **France,** worth 1 Obol or $1/2$ Denier. Equal to 2 Pites or 4 Half Pites.

**12th Century** - Maille equal to $1/2$ Denier.

**1315** - Minting of silver/copper Maille, called Maille Noire, in two types: Maille Tournois, Maille Bourgeoise, or Bourgeois ($1/2$ Denier Tournois); Maille Parisis ($1/2$ Denier Parisis or $5/8$ Denier Tournois).

**1373** (October 12th) - Minting of silver/copper Maille of $1/2$ Denier Tournois (0.81 gram 100 fine, or 0.08 grams fine silver).

**1389** - Last minting of Maille Tournois.

**1411** - Last minting of Maille Parisis. However, Maille remained unit of account with value of $1/2$ Denier.

**17th Century** - Maille identical with Obol.
Name Maille kept in general use. To "have a Maille to share" was to have neither a Sou, nor a Maille.

II. - Silver money in early **France** often called Maille Blanche in order to distinguish it from Maille Noire.

**1295** - Issue of Maille Blanche, or Petit Tournois. Weight: 2.11 grams of silver $12/12$ fine. Exchange rate: $71/2$ Deniers.

**1308** - New Mailles (1.40 grams $12/12$ fine). Had exchange rate of $43/8$ Deniers. Exchange rate of earlier Mailles: $69/16$ Deniers.

**1313** - Exchange rate lowered to 4 Deniers, then raised to 6 Deniers.

**1326** - Creation of Maille (1.73 grams 750 fine, or 1.30 grams fine silver) with exchange rate of 8 Deniers.

**1329-1330** - Exchange rate of these Mailles lowered to 6 Deniers, then to 4 Deniers.

**1351** - Last minting of silver Maille. Exchange rate: 7½ Deniers.

**III.** - Silver and silver/copper money, equivalent to ½ Denier or 1 Obol, in various **Western European** countries:
  - In **Portugal** during 12th and 13th Centuries.
  - In **Catalonia** called Malla.
  - In **Genoa** called Medaglia. - See *Medaglia.*
  - In **Geneva** during 14th Century.

## MAKUTA

See *Likuta.*

## *MALACCA*

Primitive monies of India and Java.

**1511-1640** - Domination by Portugal and use of Portuguese monies. Introduction of Mexican Piaster of 24.4356 grams fine silver. - See *Piaster Mexico.*

**1641-1794** - Dutch domination and use of Dutch monies. Accounts kept in Rijksdaalder of 8 Schelling, 64 Stuyver, or 192 Duiten.

**1795-1818** - British control and use of monies of British East India Company. - See *Dollar East India Company.*

**1818-1823** - Return to Dutch control.

**1824** - Control given to British East India Company. - See *Straits Settlements.*

## *MALAGASY*

Early history - See *Madagascar.*

**1958** (September 28th) - Malagasy Republic formed from French Colony of Madagascar. For money in circulation, see *Franc CFA.*

**1960** (June 26th) - Independence.

**1962** (March 8th) - Banque de Madagascar et des Comores replaced as bank of issue by Institut d'Emission Malgache.

**1963** (July 1st) - Malagasy Franc established as legal tender. - See *Franc Malagasy.*

## MALAWI

Predecessor - See *Federation of Rhodesia and Nyasaland.*

**1964** (July 6th) - Nyasaland renamed Malawi.

**1964** (July 23rd) - Reserve Bank of Malawi created as Central Bank with note-issuing authority.

**1964** (November 16th) - First issue of Malawi Pound. - See *Pound Malawi.*

**1971** (February 15th) - Decimalization and new currency. - See *Kwacha Malawi.*

## MALAYSIA

Predecessor - See *Federation of Malaya.*

**1963** (September 16th) - Federation of Malaysia formed from Federation of Malaya, State of Singapore, North Borneo (renamed Sabah) and Sarawak. Currency in circulation, see *Dollar Malaya.*

**1965** (August 9th) - Singapore seceded from Federation.

**1967** (June 12th) - Issue of new currency. - See *Dollar Malaysia.*

## MALDIVE ISLANDS

Primary source for cowrie shells. - See *Cowrie.*

**16th Century** - Use of Persian Larin for trade transactions. - See *Larin.*
Simultaneous circulation of specie monies of several European trading nations (i.e., Portugal, Spain, Holland and Venice).

**Early 18th Century** - Minting of copper coins for local transactions. - See *Lari.*

**19th Century** - Principal media of exchange became Indian silver Rupee and Ceylonese 50 cent piece. Paper currency generally not accepted. Exchange rate with local coins:
1 Indian Rupee = 120 Laree
1 Indian Rupee = 30 Bodularee

**1960** - Maldivian Rupee banknotes issued by Central Bank of Ceylon. - See *Rupee Maldive Islands.*

## MALI

Predecessor - See *French Sudan.*

**1960** (September 22nd) - Republic created from French Sudan. Monetary unit unchanged. - See *Franc CFA.*

**1962** (July 2nd) - Mali Franc created to replace CFA Franc at par. - See *Franc Mali.*

## MALTA

Carthaginian monies until 216 B.C.; Roman monies until 454 A.D.; Byzantine monies until 870; Arab monies until 1090; 1090 to 1284 (Germanic and Angevin domination), mixed money circulation; Spanish monies from 1284 to 1530.

**1530** - Cession of Island to Knights of Saint John of Jerusalem (Knights of Malta). Monetary system stemming from Naples and Sicily: Taro equal to 2 Carlini, 4 Cinquini, 20 Grani or 120 Piccioli.

Specie monies:
>  In gold - Zecchino copied after coin of Venice
>  In silver - Taro, Carlino, and Cinquino
>  In copper - Grano, Picciolo

**1730** - New monetary system: Scudo of 12 Tari, 24 Carlini, 144 Piccioli, 240 Grani, 1,440 Denari. System of accounting "in silver" valued 50% higher than system of accounting "in copper".

Specie monies: silver coins of 8 to 1½ Tari; other coins of 15 to ½ Grani.

Parallel circulation of Spanish and Italian monies.

**1798** - French Occupation. Monetary system unchanged.

**1802** - English Occupation. Monetary system unchanged.

**1815** - Cession of Island to England. Introduction of British monies.

**1886** (September 24th) - British coins declared only legal tender.

**1915** (June 16th) - British treasury notes made legal tender.

**1949** (July) - Currency Note Ordinancy making Government of Malta banknotes legal tender. - See *Pound Malta*.


## MAME GIN

Small, bean-shaped piece of silver 640 fine. Cast in **Japan** from 1695. Submultiple of Cho gin.


## MANCHURIA

Predecessor - See *China.*

**Early 20th Century** - For small payments, use of copper Sapèque. Called Tzan in Manchurian, Tchok in Russian, Cash in English. Pierced with square hole and strung together as beads, called Tiao. - See *Sapèque.*

For larger payments, use of silver bars in form of shoes. - See *Sycee.*

In seaports and large commercial centers, use of Dollar and Mexican Piaster.

**1932 to 1944** - Under Japanese Occupation, called Manchukuo. Issue of Manchukuo Yuan. - See *Yuan Manchukuo.*

**1945** - Returned to China. - See *China.*

## MANCOSO

Name given in West to **Arabian** Dinar introduced in 9th Century. - See *Dinar I.*

Origin of name - Various explanations: From *monca,* corruption of *marca* (marc weight); from *mann cusus* (imprint of a hand); from Latin *mancus* (incomplete). More probably from Arabic *manqous* (weakened, diminished); or from *mancoush,* past participle of verb *nacasha* (engrave, mint money).

Variations of Name - Mancosus, Mancuser, Mancusus, Mancus, Mancuso.

**815** - Charter of Louis the Pious:
     1 Mancoso = 30 Deniers

**9th and 10th Centuries** - Italian documents:
     1 Mancoso = 30 Denari

## MANDAT

Paper money issued in **France** from 1796 to 1797.

Predecessor - See *Assignat.*

**1796** (March 18th) - Law creating Mandat Territorial as legal money. Assignats exchanged for Mandats at 30 for 1.

**1796** (March 27th) - Contracts stipulated in anything other than Mandats forbidden, as were payments in metal. Consistent rise in price of gold and other prices. Black market. Clandestine payments made with specie money.

**1796** (July 23rd) - Return of freedom for contracts to be stipulated in specie money.

**1797** (February 4th) - Withdrawal of Mandats. Accepted by public payments offices at 100 to 1. - See *Franc.*

## MANILLA

Copper or bronze bracelets first worn as manacles on wrists and ankles of slaves and then used as money by natives of **Ivory Coast, Nigeria (Grand Bassam),** and **Madagascar.**

Origin of Name - Portuguese *manellio* (bracelet), Spanish *manilla* (bracelet), Latin *manicula* (little hand). Root *manus* (hand).

Variation of name - Manille.

Types - Flat bracelet without engraving; thick bracelet, round, embossed, and decorated in relief with leaves. Two types were interchangeable in weight and number. In Madagascar, wealthy people wore gold Manillas formed from European gold coins.

Uses - Worn on arm above elbow or at ankle. Introduced by Egyptian, Portuguese, or Dutch traders (by French in Madagascar) in exchange for slaves or goods.

**18th - 19th Century** - Abundant circulation of Manillas. Value in 1892: 20 Centimes.

**1895** (August 23rd) - Monetary use of Manillas forbidden in Ivory Coast.

**1899** - Manilla continued to serve as money in French Ivory Coast.

**1902** - Importing of Manilla in British Protectorates prohibited.

**1948** (November 11th) - Monetary use of Manillas in Nigeria outlawed:
1 Shilling = 7 to 18 Manillas
Circulation: from 15 to 40 million.

**1949** (March) - Withdrawal of Manillas completed in Southwest Nigeria.


## MANTELET D'OR

In **France,** gold coin (3.50 grams fine) minted by Philip III (1270-1285). Also called Petit Royal d'Or. - See *Royal d'Or.*


## *MANTUA*

Monies of Rome (see *Rome*). Later Carolingian monetary system (see *Lira*).

**16th Century** - Austrian monies (see *Austria*).

**19th Century** - After unification, Italian monetary system (see *Italy*).


## MARABOTIN

**I.** - Name given in **Spain** (since 1084) and in **France** (12th Century) to gold coins of Spanish and Arabic origin copied after Marabet-Maravedi type (see *Maravedi*), which circulated principally in provinces near Pyrenees. Accepted throughout France in 12th and 13th Centuries. Exchange rate in France: 8 Sous 1 Denier.

Origin of name - See *Maravedi.*

Variations of name - Marbotin, Maurabotin, Morabitin.

**II.** - Used as unit of account in **Papal States.**


## MARAVEDI

**I.** - **Arabic,** then **Spanish** money. Gold, silver, silver/copper, then copper coin and unit of account.

Origin of name - Arabic Dinar took name Marabet (Latin translation: *marabotinus*), from Arabic *marabout* (saint, hermit: root - *morâbit,* frontier guard), by allusion to Koranic inscriptions on imprint. Also, from Arabic *marâbitî* (money) of Al-moravides. Derived through Almorabitini, Morabitini, Marabitini, Marevedi.

**8th to 11th Century** - Dinar, or Marabet, a gold Arabic coin. First Spanish minting under Abd-er-Rahman III (912-961). - See *Marabotin.*

**1085** - After conquest of Toledo, Marabet, or Marabotin, became Maravedi.

**12th Century** - Alphonso VIII in León (1126), and Ferdinand II in Castille minted gold Maravedi of about 4 grams imitating Arabic coins.

**About 1250** - Maravedi became silver Marabet, gradually Marabotin, in weight: 23 grams in 1252, 16 grams in 1258, 3 grams in 1263, 1.35 grams in 1303, 1.08 grams in 1391.

Maravedi equal to 48 Denarios, then 96, then 180 (in 1222), 90 (in 1252), 60 (in 1258), 15 (in 1263), 10 (in 1303).

**1537** - Adoption by Charles V of Maravedi as unit of account along with Ducat:

    1 Ducat = 375 Maravedis

Thereafter, Maravedi was inferior unit of account in Spanish monetary system.

**1558** - As specie money, Maravedi fell to level of silver/copper money.

**1599** - Increase in number of silver/copper Maravedis at exchange rate higher than their intrinsic value.

**1627** - Unsuccessful attempts at deflation.

**1642** (August 31st) - Decree reducing silver/copper money to ⅙ its issued value. 12 Maravedi coin lowered to 2 Maravedis.

**1680** (May 22nd) - Maravedi became copper coin. General evolution of equivalent of Maravedi in grams of silver: 52 in 1200; 23 in 1252; 1.08 in 1391; 0.30 in 1451; 0.11 in 1479; 0.076 in 1550; 0.031 in 1808.

Future multiples of Maravedi (in copper): Ochota (8 Maravedis), Quarto (4 Maravedis), Ochavo (2 Maravedis).

**1847** - Maravedi no longer unit of account. Submultiple of Maravedi in Navarra called Cornado (½ Maravedi).

**II. - Spanish** variations of Maravedi (unit of account):
- In Aragon: 1 Livre = 10 Reales = 640 Maravedis
- In Navarra: 1 Livre = 60 Maravedis
- In Catalonia: 1 Livre = 480 Maravedis = 960 Mallas (Mailles)
- In Valencia: 1 Piaster = 8 Reales = 512 Maravedis
- In Majorca: 1 Livre = 453 Maravedis
- In Canary Islands: 1 Piaster = 80 Maravedis

**III.** - First independent money of **Portugal:** gold Maravedi (3.88 grams at first) minted by Alphonso I (1152-1185) imitating Arabic coins. Subsequent minting of silver Maravedi.

**IV.** - Gold coin circulating in **France** under Philip Augustus. - See *Marabotin.*

**V.** - Early submultiple of **Mexican** Piaster (see *Piaster Mexico*):

    1 Piaster = 8 Reales = 272 Maravedis

## MARCHETTO

Unit of account in **Venice,** corresponding to Soldo. Also copper coin in early 17th Century.

Origin of name - From figure of St. Mark on coin.

Plural - Marchetti.

**18th Century** - 5,166 Marchetti were equal to 1 Grosso, 20 to 1 Lira, 124 to 1 Ducato,

1,240 to 1 Lira Grossa. Marchetto corresponded to 2.3 Grossetti or to 12 Denari di Lira.

## MARENGO

**I.** - Gold coin of 20 Francs minted in **Turin** in 1800. Also called Marenghino.

**II.** - In wider sense, name also given to **Italian** 20 Lire gold coins similar to Latin Monetary Union type (6.45 grams 900 fine).

## MARIA

**Spanish** silver coin worth 1 Real. Issued in 1684 with the monogram of the Virgin Mary. Minting of multiples (2, 4 and 8 Maria).

## MARIA THERESIA THALER

Silver coin minted in Vienna by various mints. Became traditional money of numerous **Arab** countries and **Ethiopia.**

Origin of name - From effigy of Maria Theresia of Austria, who reigned from 1740 to 1780, and from Thaler.

Variations of name - Levantine in Austria, Ber, or Bep, in Ethiopia, Imadi in Yemen.

**1751** - Struck by Mints of Vienna and Hall:

1 Maria Theresia Thaler = 28.0668 grams of silver 833 fine, or 23.83 grams fine silver

**1764-1820** - Struck by Mints of Vienna, Hall, Gunzburg, Kremnitz.

**1765** (August 15th) - Death of Francis I, husband of Maria Theresia. New type of Thaler destined for wide circulation: Empress wore widow's veil with her hair styled in the manner of an Arab woman.

**1780** - Minting date preferred by Arabs. Maria Theresia Thaler, type of 1765 dated 1780 and worn as pendant, was said to have magic powers. It was to appeal more to Arab populations than to Austria, which did not have colonial aspirations. Circulation of Maria Theresia Thaler observed in Arabia by traveller Niebuhr (exploring on behalf of Denmark).

**1820-1857** - Minting by Austrian Mints of Vienna, Milan and Venice, always with imprint of Empress Maria Theresia, imitating earlier mintings in 18th Century. Progressive distribution in Arabia, in countries bordering on Red Sea and Indian Ocean (Yemen, Hejaz, Eritrea, Somalia, Ethiopia), on routes to Sudan up to Oasis of Touareg, as far as Moslem communities of the Niger and Nigeria, and toward the Congo.

**1857-1866** - Mintings by Vienna, Prague and Italian Mints of Milan and Venice. Mints liberated from Austria started to mint Austrian coin.

**1865-1889** - Vain attempts by British to supplant Maria Theresia Thaler on Upper Nile and in Ethiopia.

**1890** - Vain attempts by Italians to supplant Maria Theresia Thaler in Eritrea.

**1893** (February 9th) - Ethiopia adopted Talari as national money: same definition as Maria Theresia Thaler. - See *Talari.*

**1894** - At request of Menelik II, Paris Mint struck Talari. Way opened for minting of Maria Theresia Thaler.

**20th Century** - Mintings of Maria Theresia Thaler by Mints of Vienna, Paris, London, Rome, Brussels, Bombay for use by Arab populations; 320 million Thalers minted during two centuries. Type remained constant.

**1924** - Minting of Yemen Thaler for Arabia, having same weight, size and fineness as Maria Theresia Thaler but with Arabic inscription.

**1935** - Last mintings of Maria Theresia Thaler by most mints. Mint in Vienna continued to strike Maria Theresia Thaler coins (restrikes).

**1964** - Yemen Thaler withdrawn from circulation. Replaced by Yemen Riyal.

## *MARIANA ISLANDS*

For Guam, see *Guam.*

**19th Century** - Use of special monies for trade transactions.

**1899** (October 12th) - German control. Introduction of German monetary system. - See *Mark.*

**1919** - Japanese control. Monetary system of Japan. - See *Yen.*

**1947** - United States trusteeship. Introduction of United States monetary system. - See *Dollar.*

## MARIENGROSCHEN

**German** silver money and unit of account.

Origin of name - German for Gros of Marie. - See *Gros.*

Variation of name - Mariengros.

Predecessor - See *Groschen.*

**1555** - Northern states of Germany adopted Thaler as unit of account, divided into 24 Silbergroschen or 32 Mariengroschen. Mariengroschen equal to $2/3$ Groschen.

**1623** - Saxony replaced Mariengroschen with Gute Groschen.

**1667** - Conference of Zinna (electoral Saxony, Brandenburg, Brunswick, Lüneburg), silver coin of $2/3$ Thaler corresponded to 24 Mariengroschen.

**18th Century** - Unit of account Mariengroschen equivalent to $1/36$ Thaler or 8 Pfennig in Brunswick, Hanover, Westphalia, and Lüneburg. Issued in same states as a silver/copper money.

**19th Century** - In Brunswick and Hanover equal to $1/36$ Thaler or 8 Pfennig.

## MARK

Monies of countries of **Northern Europe.**

**I. - German** weight, unit of account, then specie money.

Origin of name - From Frankish *marka,* meaning, as does French *marc,* weight of half a pound. Probably from same root as *marque,* German *marke,* Germanic *merk.* The marc weight was designated by a mark.

Bank of issue - By Bank of Hamburg in 18th Century; by 17 local banks until 1875; then by Reichsbank and 4 local banks.

Predecessors - See *Germany, Holy Roman Empire.*

Plural - Mark.

**11th Century -** Pound-weight of Charlemagne divided into two marcs gave rise to Marc of Cologne (233.856) from which Mark was created as unit of account, divided into 12 Schilling or 144 Pfennig. General use of system of accounting in Mark in German states.

**13th Century -** Feudal dislocation of systems of accounting. Southern regions accounted in Guilders (Gulden). Mark sometimes divided into 10 Schilling (Oldenburg and Netherlands) or 16 Schilling (Hamburg). Debasement of Mark (of 16 Schilling or 192 Pfennig) in Hamburg in grams of fine silver: 109 in 1226; 77 in 1325; 64 in 1375; 40 in 1430; 24 in 1450; 19 in 1461; 17 in 1506.

**18th Century -** Mark (used as well in Rostock) equal to 16 Schilling, 32 Groschen, 96 Dreiling, or 192 Pfennig. 3 Mark equal to 1 Thaler. Mark-Lübsk, later called Mark-Banco, designated an unvarying weight of metal in coffers of Bank of Hamburg. - See *Banco.* In Westphalia (Aachen), Mark equal to $1/54$ Reichsthaler, $1/72$ Speciesthaler, or 6 Buschen. Unit of account, and minted in silver/copper.

**1871** (December 4th) - Law creating new gold coins of 10 and 20 Mark for all of Germany. 10 Mark replaced 3.33 Thaler, 5.50 Guilder, 8 Mark 5.33 Schilling of Hamburg:

$$1 \text{ Mark} = 358.422919 \text{ milligrams of fine gold}$$

**1873** (July 12th) - Law establishing gold standard. Progressive withdrawal from circulation of earlier coins.

**1875** (March 14th) - Right of note-issue granted to Reichsbank and to 4 State Banks (Bavaria, Saxony, Württemberg, Baden) whose small denomination banknotes enjoyed full legal tender status.

**1876** (January 1st) - Activation of new system of accounting. All accounts maintained in Mark of 100 Pfennig.

**1914** (August 4th) - Forced parity of banknotes. Progressive depreciation of Mark.

**1919** (September 12th) - Foreign exchange controls.

**1923** Galloping inflation swelled currency circulation to 496 quintillion Mark and exchange rate of U.S. Dollar to 4,200 billion Mark.

**1923** (October 15th) - Creation of Rentenmark "guaranteed by gold mortgage on all German lands, by gold obligations of industry, commerce and banks". - See *Rentenmark.*

**1923** (November 30th) - Allied Commission for Reparations invited Committee of Experts (Dawes Committee) to "seek measures for stabilizing currency".

**1924** (April 9th) - Dawes Plan for restoration of convertible currency.

**1924** (August 30th) - Law creating Reichsmark, new monitary unit of Germany, equal to Rentenmark and to gold Mark. - See *Reichsmark*. For later varieties, see *Mark Coupon, Mark German Federal Republic, Mark German Democratic Republic.*

**II. - Danish** silver money and unit of account.

**10th Century** - Scandinavian Marc, unit of weight (216 grams), divided into 8 Oere, or 24 Oertug. Gave rise to Mark, unit of account, which quickly changed from marc-weight.

**1534** - Under Christian III, minting of silver Mark.

**1618** - Under Christian IV, new system of accounting. Mark worth no more than 1/8 Krone or 16 Skilling.

**18th Century** - As unit of account, Mark represented 1/6 Rigsdaler and equalled 16 Skilling, 32 Fyrk, 48 Hvid, 192 Penning.

**III. -** Unit of account in **Sweden.**

**10th Century** - Scandinavian unit of account (see above under II).

**1560** - Under Erik XIV, system of accounting in Daler divided into 4 Mark. Mark thus represented 1/4 Daler and equalled 8 Oere or 192 Penning.

**1509** - Multiples of Mark minted in gold (from 3 to 48).

**18th Century** - In system of accounting in Silver Mynt (silver money), Mark represented 1/24 Riksdaler (specie money), 1/4 Daler, and equalled 2 Skilling, 8 Oere, or 32 Oerlein. In system of accounting in Kopper Mynt (copper money), used in certain provinces, Mark represented 1/72 Riksdaler (specie money), 1/12 Daler, 2/3 Skilling, 2.66 Oere, or 10.66 Oerlein. Silver Mynt Mark equalled 3 Kopper Mynt Mark.

**1812 to 1875** - In Norway, under Swedish domination, Mark was 1/5 Speciesdaler and equalled 24 Skilling.

## MARK COUPON

Name given to **East German** Mark in its first format.

**1948** (June 24th) - After monetary reform of Western Zone, which substituted Deutsche Mark for Reichsmark (see *Mark German Federal Republic*), creation of new money in Eastern Zone by attaching special coupon to Reichsmark in circulation. Conversion of banknotes:

    1 Reichsmark = 1 Coupon Mark (per capita allocation up to 70 Reichsmark)

    10 Reichsmark = 1 Coupon Mark (all other banknotes up to 5,000 Reichsmark per family with excess deposited in blocked account until proven that money was rightfully earned)

    10 Reichsmark = 1 Coupon Mark (without limitation for business enterprises)

Conversion of deposits:

    1 Reichsmark = 1 Coupon Mark (savings deposits up to 100 Reichsmark)

    5 Reichsmark = 1 Coupon Mark (savings deposits in ex-

cess above 100 Reichsmark but not more than
1,000)

10 Reichsmark = 1 Coupon Mark (for    remainder    with
reservation for amounts exceeding 5,000 Reichsmark as above)

10 Reichsmark = 1 Coupon Mark (other deposits with financial institutions, with same reservation for
amounts exceeding 5,000 Reichsmark as above)

Prices, salaries, taxes:

1 Reichsmark = 1 Coupon Mark

For money in Berlin, see *Berlin.*

**1948** (July 20th) - Coupon Mark replaced by Ostmark. - See *Mark German Democratic Republic.*


## MARK ESTONIA

Monetary unit of **Estonia** from 1918 to 1928. Divided into 100 Penni.

Bank of issue - By Bank of Estonia and State.

Predecessor - See *Estonia.*

**1918** - In new Estonia, issue of Estonian Mark, which replaced Rubles and Finnish
Markkaa in circulation:

1 Estonian Mark = 1 German Mark

Progressive depreciation of currency.

**1921** (March) - Issue of banknotes by Bank of Estonia, parallel to issue by State.

**1924** (June) - Adoption of Estonian Kroon as unit of account.

**1928** (January 1st) - Effective creation of Estonian Kroon:

1 Estonian Kroon = 100 Estonian Mark

- See *Kroon.*


## MARK GERMAN DEMOCRATIC REPUBLIC

Monetary unit of **German Democratic Republic (East Germany)** since 1948. Divided
into 100 Pfennig.

Bank of issue - By Deutsche Notenbank created on July 20, 1948. On January 1, 1968,
reorganized and name changed to Staatsbank der Deutschen Demokratischen
Republik (State Bank of German Democratic Republic).

Variation of name - Ostmark, East Mark.

Predecessor - See *Reichsmark, Mark Coupon.*

**1948** (July 20th) - Exchange of banknotes. Coupon Mark replaced by Ostmark:

1 Deutsche Mark = 1.25 Ostmark

1 U.S. Dollar = 3.75 Ostmark (theoretical cross rate)

In West Berlin, money changers were asking for 4.50 Ostmark against 1 Deutsche
Mark.

**1949** (February) - On black market, Ostmark hit record 105.00 per U.S. Dollar, premium of 2,700% for Greenback. Subsequent improvement of Ostmark on black market.

**1953** (October 29th) - Ostmark linked to Russian Ruble:
  1 Ruble = 0.55 Ostmark
  1 Ostmark = 399.902 milligrams of fine gold
  1 U.S. Dollar = 2.22 Ostmark

**1956** (August-September) - Creation of "Messe-Mark" by doubling official exchange value of all foreign currencies spent by nonresidents during this two month period at Leipzig Fall Fair.

**1957** (October 13th) - "Shock" currency exchange designed to punish hoarders of banknotes. Up to 300 old Ostmark exchanged for one new Ostmark. Excess amounts blocked for six days, and sums not considered "legitimate" confiscated. Some 20 million Ostmark notes in West German possession made worthless, and about 600 million Ostmark confiscated domestically.

**1958** (January 7th) - Partial devaluation by creation of a Capitalistic tourist and/or support rate:
  1 U.S. Dollar = 4.20 Ostmark

**1961** (January 1st) - Soviet monetary reform:
  1 New Ruble = 2.47 Ostmark (official)
  1 New Ruble = 3.88 Ostmark (Ruble Area noncommercial,
       tourist and/or support rate)

**1961** - Appearance of Valuta Mark governing all foreign trade and Capitalistic tourist and/or support payments:
  1 U.S. Dollar = 4.20 Ostmark
Official rate of 2.22 Ostmark per U.S. Dollar practically inoperative.

**1963** (April 1st) - U.S.S.R. revalued Ruble in relation to other Socialist lands for noncommercial transactions only:
  1 Ruble = 3.19 Ostmark

**1964** (August) - On black market Ostmark improved to 8.75 per U.S. Dollar, premium of "only" 294% for Greenback. From this point, Ostmark fluctuated within range of 11.00 - 17.50 per U.S. Dollar.


## MARK GERMAN FEDERAL REPUBLIC

Monetary unit (also called Deutsche Mark) of **West Germany** created in 1948. Divided into 100 Deutsche Pfennig.

Origin of name - German *Deutsche* (German) and *Mark.* - See *Mark.*

Variation of name - West Mark, as opposed to East Mark (Ostmark).

Bank of issue - By Bank Deutscher Länder, founded on March 1st, 1948; renamed Deutsche Bundesbank (Central Bank of Federal Republic of Germany) on July 26, 1957.

Predecessors - See *Mark* and *Reichsmark.*

**1948** (June 20th) - In three Western zones of Germany, because of collapse of purchasing power of Reichsmark, creation of Deutsche Mark with exchange of banknotes on general basis of:

1 Deutsche Mark = 10 Reichsmark

Allocation of 40 Deutsche Mark per person in June, and 20 Deutsche Mark in September in exchange for 60 Reichsmark in banknotes.

Allocation per business establishment of 60 Deutsche Mark in exchange for 600 Reichsmark.

Accounts credited with 1 Deutsche Mark for 10 Reichsmark: 50% free, 35% cancelled, 10% unblocked in October, 5% consolidated into securities.

Credits in Reichsmark reduced 10 to 1.

Salaries, wages, pensions, rents, converted 1 for 1.

For circulation in Berlin and exchange relationship with Ostmark, see *Berlin*.

Provisional parity of Deutsche Mark:

1 U.S. Dollar = 3.33 Deutsche Mark

**1949** (September 18th) - Devaluation of 20.6% following that of Pound Sterling:

1 U.S. Dollar = 4.20 Deutsche Mark

**1951** (March 31st) - Creation of Sperrmark (negotiable blocked Deutsche Mark accounts for purchase of German securities by foreigners).

**1951** (December) - Sperrmark hit low of 8.06 Deutsche Mark per U.S. Dollar. Subsequent improvement.

**1954** (April 1st) - Creation of Freely Convertible Deutsche Mark accounts (Freie Konvertierbare Deutsche Mark) for hard currencies and Partly Convertible Deutsche Mark accounts (Beschränkte Konvertierbare Deutsche Mark-Bekomark) for all other payments.

**1954** (September 16th) - Sperrmark accounts consolidated into new Liberalized Capital Accounts (Liberalisierte Kapital Deutsche Mark-Libkamark) used by nonresidents for local investments.

**1954** (October 19th) - Ownership and dealings in gold coins authorized.

**1954** (November) - Bekomark hit low of 4.35 Deutsche Mark per U.S. Dollar. Subsequent improvement.

**1955** - Progressive dismantling of foreign exchange controls.

**1956** (June 12th) - Free import of gold coins.

**1957** (April 1st) - Import and domestic dealings in gold bullion authorized.

**1958** (July 1st) - Libkamark abolished.

**1958** (December 29th) - Bekomark abolished. Deutsche Mark made fully convertible.

**1959** (January 29th) - Free import and export of gold and precious metals.

**1961** (March 6th) - Upvaluation of Deutsche Mark by 5%:

1 Deutsche Mark = 222.168 milligrams of fine gold

1 U.S. Dollar = 4.00 Deutsche Mark

**1968** (June 18th) - Free gold market established.

**1969** (September 30th) - De facto upvaluation. Deutsche Mark set free to float.

**1969** (October 29th) - De jure upvaluation of Deutsche Mark by 9.3%:

1 Deutsche Mark = 242.806 milligrams of fine gold

1 U.S. Dollar = 3.66 Deutsche Mark

## MARK OSTLAND

Monetary unit of Ostland (**Estonia, Latvia, Lithuania,** and **White Russia**) from 1942 to 1944.

Bank of issue - By Central Bank of Ostland.

Variation of name - Ostland Mark.

Predecessors - See *Estonia, Latvia, Lithuania* and *Kroon, Lat Latvia, Litas.*

**1942** (July 30th) - German Occupation authorities created Central Bank of Ostland (in Riga), authorized to issue banknotes secured by general mortgage on all landed property:
1 Ostland Mark = 1 Reichsmark

**1943** (April 1st) - Beginning of Central Bank operations. Issue of Ostland Mark delayed and never materialized. Banknotes of Reichskreditkassen, denominated in Reichsmark, continued to circulate.

**1944** - Russian Occupation. - See *Ruble.*

## MARK SAAR

Monetary unit of **Saar** in 1947. Divided into 100 Pfennig.

Variation of name - Saarmark.

Predecessor - See *Saar.*

**1947** (July 16th) - Exchange of banknotes denominated in Reichsmark against banknotes denominated in Saarmark:
1 Saarmark = 1 Reichsmark

**1947** (November 15th) - Exchange of banknotes denominated in Saarmark against banknotes denominated in French Francs:
1 Saarmark = 20.00 French Francs
Temporary blocking of 40% of deposits above 8,000 Francs.
Incorporation of Saar into Franc-Zone. - See *Franc.*

**1957** (January 1st) - Return to West Germany. - See *Mark German Federal Republic.*

## MARKA

Monetary unit of **Poland** from 1919 to 1924. Divided into 100 Fennigy.

Bank of issue - By Polska Krajowa Kasa Pozyezkowa (Polish State Loan Bank).

Origin of name - From German Mark, forerunner of Polish Marka.

Predecessor - See *Poland.*

**1916** - Creation of Polish Marka by Germans in Warsaw:
1 Polish Marka = 1 German Mark

**1918** (December 7th) - Legal tender status given to Polish Marka. In Austrian section of Poland, circulation of Austrian Krone until 1919, then exchanged at:
100 Kronen = 70 Marka

German Mark in Poland deprived of legal tender status.

**1919** - Adoption of Zloty as unit of account, equal to gold Franc Germinal.

**1920** - Inflation and depreciation of currency.

**1923** - Galloping inflation. Depreciation of Polish Marka (1 U.S. Dollar = 15 million Polish Marka at end of year).

**1924** (January 11th) - Full power accorded to government by the Diet to establish new monetary system. - See *Zloty*.


## MARKKA

Monetary unit of **Finland**. Divided into 100 Pennia (singular: Penni).

Origin of name - See *Mark*.

Bank of issue - By Suomen Pankki (Bank of Finland), which had monopoly òn note-issue since 1886.

Predecessor - See *Ruble*.

Plural - Markkaa.

**1860** (April 4th) - Monetary independence acquired before political independence. Imperial manifesto assigning silver standard to Finnish Markka, linked to Franc at 1 Markka = 25 grams of silver 900 fine = 22.50 grams fine silver.

**1877** (August 9th) - Adoption of gold standard and link to parity of Franc:
>           1 Markka = 290.3225 milligrams of fine gold = 1 Franc
>                     Germinal

Minting of gold coins (10 and 20 Markka) similar to French type. Finnish Markka minted in silver at 5.18 grams 868 fine.

**1915** (April 11th) - Forced parity and suspension of gold payments.

**1925** - Maximum depreciation of banknotes (90%).

**1925** (December 21st) - Stabilization law approving devaluation of 86.9%:
>           1 Markka = 37.895 milligrams of fine gold
>           1 Pound Sterling = 193.23 Markkaa
>           1 U.S. Dollar = 39.70 Markkaa

Minting of 100 and 200 Markka gold coins.

**1931** (October 12th) - Suspension of gold convertibility.

**1933** (March) - Adherence to Sterling Area on basis of:
>           1 Pound Sterling = 193.75 Markkaa

**1938** (December 22nd) - Valuation of gold on basis of:
>           1 Markka = 20 milligrams of fine gold

**1939** (October 26th) - Foreign exchange controls.

**1940** - Adoption of fixed exchange rate (in principle) in relation to U.S. Dollar:
>           1 U.S. Dollar = 49.35 Markkaa

**1945** (June 1st) - Modification of this relationship:
>           1 U.S. Dollar = 86.30 Markka

**1945** (July 28th) - Modification of this relationship:
>           1 U.S. Dollar = 120.80 Markkaa

**1945** (October 17th) - Modification of this relationship:
　　　　1 U.S. Dollar = 136.00 Markkaa

**1949** (February) - Markka on black market hit record 580.00 per U.S. Dollar, premium of 327% for Greenback.

**1949** (July 5th) - Another modification in relationship to U.S. Dollar:
　　　　1 U.S. Dollar = 160.00 Markkaa

**1949** (September 19th) - Following devaluation of Pound Sterling:
　　　　1 U.S. Dollar = 230.00 Markkaa

**1951** (June 11th) - Travel Markka introduced, based on 30% tax on foreign exchange purchased:
　　　　1 U.S. Dollar = 299.00 Markkaa

**1951** (June 27th) - Parity registered with International Monetary Fund:
　　　　1 Markka = 3.86379 milligrams of fine gold
　　　　1 U.S. Dollar = 230.00 Markkaa

**1951** (December 31st) - Travel Markka abolished.

**1952** (June 3rd) - Reinstitution of Travel Markkaa at premium (50%) over official rate:
　　　　1 U.S. Dollar = 345.00 Markkaa

**1953** (March 13th) - System of export subsidies financed by import taxes through Ulkomaankaupan Clearingkunta.

**1957** (September 15th) - Devaluation of Markka. Travel rate and other multiple currency practices abolished:
　　　　1 Markka = 2.777 milligrams of fine gold
　　　　1 U.S. Dollar = 320.00 Markkaa
Most exports subject (for one year) to special levy designed to absorb part of increased export revenue resulting from devaluation. Bilateral payments agreements governed trade transaction. Gradually evolved to multilateral system and then phased out.

**1962** - Cancellation of obligation to redeem banknotes in gold.

**1963** (January 1st) - Exchange of banknotes:
　　　　1 New Markka = 100 Old Markkaa
　　　　1 New Markka = 277.7 milligrams of fine gold
　　　　1 U.S. Dollar = 3.20 New Markkaa
All prices and wages converted into new currency at same ratio. Black market virtually disappeared, and unofficial trading of Markka held remarkably stable, the U.S. Dollar at times being at discount.

**1967** (October 12th) - Devaluation of 23.8% in terms of gold and 31.25% in terms of foreign currency:
　　　　1 Markka = 211.59 milligrams of fine gold
　　　　1 U.S. Dollar = 4.20 Markkaa
Temporary export duty of 14% levied on most products. Lowered gradually and abolished at end of 1969.


## MARQUE

**I.** - Silver/copper coins used from 1738 to 1844 in **French Antilles** and **French Guiana**.

Called "Marqués" in contrast to worn out coins.

**1738** (October) - Minting of coins of 2 Sols with low silver content (thus often called "Marqués Noirs"). Exchange rate in Antilles: 2 Sols (Sous) 6 Deniers.

**1763** (January) - Stamping of these coins at Paris Mint; Marqué became Tampé (for "Estampé"). - See *Tampé*.

**1818** (October 4th) - Minting of silver/copper coins of 10 Centimes (called "Marqués Blancs" because of better alloy) worth 10 Centimes in colonial money (or 6 coins for 1 Livre Coloniale). Circulated in rolls of 30, then 60 coins.

**1820** (February 2nd) - With abolition of Livre Coloniale, followed by link to Franc of Metropolitan France, Marqué Blanc worth 10 Centimes. Marqué Noir worth 7 1/2 Centimes.

**1828** (February 24th) - Withdrawal from circulation of Tampés and Marqués Noirs.

**1844** (June 8th) - Withdrawal from circulation of Marqués Blancs.

**II.** - Silver/copper coin of **Mauritius** and **Réunion**, worth 3 Sols (1769 and 1781). Exchange rate in France was one-half less (1 Sol 6 Deniers). Demonetization through decree of February 24, 1828.


## MARSHALL ISLANDS

**19th Century** - Spanish control. Use of Spanish monies for trade transactions.

**1885** - German control. Introduction of German monetary system. - See *Mark*.

**1919** - Japanese control. Monetary system of Japan. - See *Yen*.

**1947** - United States trusteeship. Monetary system of United States. - See *Dollar*.


## MARTINIQUE

See *French West Indies*.


## MAS

**I.** - In the Kingdom of Achin in **Sumatra**, unit of account: 1/16 Tayell, or 1/4 Pardaw. Mas worth 4 Koupans or 1,300 Cash.

Specie money containing 0.48 grams of gold.

Variations of name - Massi, Massia, Mace.

**II.** - In **Java**, unit of account: 2,500,000 Mas equal to one Bahar, 250,000 to 1 Uta, 25,000 to 1 Catty, 2,500 to 1 Laxsan, 250 to 1 Pecco, 10 to 1 Tayell, 2 to 1 Sata. Mas of Batavia valued at 4 Cash or 40 Candareens. The 6 Mas coin called Pataca.

## MASSAMUTINO

Gold coin minted in **Spain** at end of 12th Century and during 13th Century. Weight: 2.30 to 2.40 grams. Exchange rate in France in 1268: 5 Sous.
Multiple - Double Masmodina of 4.70 grams.
Origin of name - From Berber Tribe Mazmuda.
Variations of name - Marmutina, Masmodina.

## MASSE D'OR

Gold money of **France** in 14th Century.
Origin of name - From imprint showing king holding gold mace.
**1308** (January 18th) - Philip the Fair minted Masse d'Or (7 grams 915 fine, or 6.4 grams fine gold). Exchange rate: 22 Sous 6 Deniers.
**1310** (August 4th) - Minting of identical Masse d'Or, with exchange rate raised to 30 Sous.
**1313** (July 22nd) - Demonetization of Masse d'Or.

## MATAPAN

Name given to Grosso of **Venice,** silver money issued after 1192. - See *Grosso.*
Variations of name - Matopan, Matagan.

## MATHBU

**I.** - Gold coin of **Morocco** in latter part of 17th Century. Valued at 1.50 Rials or 20.25 Ukkias.
Variations of name - Metbuo, Mahbub.
**II.** - Silver money of **Tripoli,** used toward end of 19th Century. Worth 8 Qurush or 800 Para.

## *MAURITANIA*

Predecessor - See *Senegal.*
**1920** - Became separate colony within French West Africa. - See *French West Africa.*
**1945** (December 26th) - Creation and use of CFA Franc. - See *Franc CFA.*
**1960** (November 28th) - Became independent republic. Monetary unit unchanged.

## *MAURITIUS*

**16th to 17th Century** - Simultaneous use of Indian Rupee and Dutch monies.

**18th Century** - Barter trade of East India Company. Introduction of copper coins of 1 and 2 Sols (minted at Pondicherry), copper coins of 9 Deniers (minted in France), then coins of 24 Deniers in silver / copper. Exchange rate 50% higher than exchange rate in Franc:

          100 Livres Tournois = 150 Livres    de    Ile    de    France
                           (Mauritius)

- See *Livre Coloniale.*

Some issues of banknotes of 5 Sols to 1,000 Livres.

**1719-1729** - Receipt vouchers of East India Company.

**1736** - Business vouchers.

**1737-1761** - Countinghouse vouchers.

**1766** (December) - Withdrawal of paper money of East India Company. Issue of royal banknotes of 10 Sols to 3 Livres.

**1768** - New issue of banknotes of 2 to 120 Livres (then to 1,000 Livres).

**1779** (August) - Edict stipulating minting of silver / copper coins of 3 Sols, called Marqués, worth 1 Sol 6 Deniers in France. - See *Marqué.*

**1793** - Henceforth, issue of paper money continued (confidence money, Mandats ). Removed from circulation during Napoleonic Empire at exchange rate of 1 Piastre for 10,000 Livres.

**1810** - After seizure of Portuguese ship carrying metal, local minting of silver coins of 20 Livres, called "Piastres Decaen" (after name of governor).

**1811** - British Occupation. Issue of banknotes of 1 Piastre.

**1816** - Issue of nickel coins still denominated in Sous (25 and 50 Sous), minted by English in Calcutta.

**1820-1821** - British authorities minted silver Dollars and copper Cents.

**1826-1831** - Issue of Treasury Bonds by Caisse d'Escompte.

**19th Century** - Under British domination, introduction of English monetary system. - See *Pound.*

**1878** - Rupee became official money. Circulation of Rupee notes issued locally and in India. Bronze and silver submultiples in Cents minted by Mauritius Government, and silver Indian Rupees and submultiples from British India.
Accounts kept in Indian Rupees. - See *Rupee India.*

**1934** - Creation of independent monetary unit. - See *Rupee Mauritius.*


## MAXIMILIAN D'OR

Gold money (5 grams fine) of **Bavaria** in 18th Century. Exchange rate: 428 Kreuzer. There were ¼ , ½ and 2 Maximilian d'Or coins.

Origin of name - From Elector Maximilian.

Variations of name - Max, Maxdor.

## MAYON

See *Salung.*


## MEDAGLIA

I. - In **Naples,** silver/copper money in 13th Century.
II. - In **Genoa,** silver money in 14th Century worth ½ Denaro or ½₄ Soldo.
Also called Mezzo Denaro, or Pitta Genovese.
Cf. *Maille* and *Pite.*


## MEDALLA

Popular name for **Spanish** gold coin called Quadruple, or gold Onza (Ounce). - See
*Quadruple.*


## MEDIAN

Gold money of Kingdom of **Tlemcen,** then of Kingdom of **Algeria.** Value: ½ Zian (see
*Zian*), or 50 Aspers.


## MEDINO

I. - Name sometimes given to Para, silver money of **Turkey** in 19th Century. - See *Para.*
Variations of name - Medin, Maidine, Medine, Meiden.
Plural - Medini.
II. - Copper coin in **Egypt** in 19th Century. Equal to ½₄₀ Ghrush, ½₂₀ Yigirmlik and
⅕ Beshlik.


## MEDIO

In **Spain** and **Spanish America,** term referring to one-half the monetary unit.


## MEDJIDIE

I. - Turkish gold coin, minted in 1845. Weight: 7.2166 grams 916 ⅔ fine, or 6.6152
grams fine gold. Value: 1 Turkish Lira or 100 Piastres. - See *Lira Turkey.*
Origin of name - After Sultan Abdul-Mejid.

**II.** - **Turkish** silver coin in late 19th Century. Weight: 0.601 grams 830 fine. Value: 20 Piastres or 80 Metalliks.

**III.** - Also circulated in **Saudi Arabia** until 1932.


## *MEMEL*

Predecessor - See *Germany.*

**1919** - Mark called Marku-arkès.

**1923** - In territory of Memel, use of Litas of Lithuania. - See *Litas.*

**1939** (March) - Replacement of Litas by Reichsmark at rate of:
1 Reichsmark = 2.50 Litai


## MERIGAL

Gold coin in 18th Century, having exchange rate in Sofala and in Kingdom of Monomotapa (**Mozambique**). Weight: about 7 grams.


## METALLIK

Name given to variety of low grade silver coins in **Turkey** during late 19th Century. Largest of these coins called Altiliks or Beshliks depending on silver content.


## *MEXICO*

Before arrival of Spaniards, Aztecs used following as money: for small payments, grains of cocoa and small squares of cloth; for medium payments, T or hatchet-shaped pieces of copper or tin; for large payments, gold powder encased in tubes made from animal bones. With Spanish conquest, introduction of Piasters of Dolera type. - See *Duro.*

**1535** (May 11th) - Decree for construction of a mint in Mexico. Minting of Mexican Piaster of Spanish type (8 Reales) and of its submultiples: silver coins of 4 Reales (Toston), 3 Reales, 2 Reales, 1 Real, ½ Real, ¼ Real (Quarto).
- See *Piaster Mexico* and *Spanish America.*

**1535** (May 31st) - Unit of account: Real of 34 Maravedis.

**1675** (February 25th) - Mint in Mexico authorized to strike gold monies: Doblon (8 Escudos), Escudo.

**1822** - Independence. Mexico continued Spanish monetary system: Piaster of 8 Reales.

**1857** (February 5th) - Law revoking right of Mexican states to mint coins and issue banknotes.

**1905** - Adoption of gold standard. Minting of gold coins called Centenarios, Aztecas, Hidalgos. Gold Piaster called Peso. - See *Peso Mexico.*

**1913** - Suspension of gold standard. Government required private banks to issue nonconvertible banknotes in excess of legal limitations.

**1914** - By August, practically all metallic currency disappeared from circulation. Complete monetary confusion owing to flood of revolutionary paper money.

**1916-1917** - Monetary recovery. Circulation limited to Mexican gold Pesos, Mexican silver Piasters and paper and metallic currency of United States. No attempt made to reintroduce paper currency.

**1918** (November 13th) - Mexican Peso officially adopted as monetary unit with fixed legal value of 750 milligrams of fine gold.

**1919** - American gold coins declared legal tender:
    1 U.S. Dollar = 2.00 Mexican gold Pesos

**1925-1926** - Reintroduction of banknotes denominated in Mexican gold Pesos. - See *Peso Mexico.* Continued use of Mexican silver Piaster coins. - See *Piaster Mexico.*

**1931-1934** - Issue of Mexican Peso banknotes denominated in Mexican silver Pesos. Subsequently replaced Mexican silver Piasters.


## MIDDLE CONGO

See *French Equatorial* and *Congo People's Republic (Brazzaville).*


## MIL

**I.** - Submultiple ($^1$/1.000) of **Cyprus** Pound since August 1955. - See *Pound Cyprus.*
**II.** - Word meaning a division by 1,000.


## MILAN

Roman monies, then monies of Carolingian monetary system. - See *Livre* and *Lira.*
**10th to 12th Century** - Use of silver Denier (Denaro).
**End of 13th Century** - Minting of gold Guilder (Fiorino) and of silver Grosso.
**14th Century** - Minting of gold Cavalier.
**1474** - First minting of silver Lira. Later called Grossono or Testone.
    Other specie monies:
        In gold - Ducato
        In silver - Grosso, Soldino
        In silver/copper - Trillina, Denaro
**1500-1512** - Louis XII added silver Ducatone, Bissona, and silver/copper Sesino.
**16th Century** - Spanish and Austrian monies.

**18th Century** - Systems of accounting: Lira of 20 Soldi or 240 Denari, and Imperial Scudo.
Specie monies:
        In gold - Doppia, Zecchino, Ducato
        In silver - Scudo, Ducatone, Filippo
        In silver/copper - Lira, Parpagliola
        In bronze - Soldo, Quattrino, Quirino, Sesino.

**1800** - Minting of Ecu of 6 Lire and coin of 30 Soldi.

**1815** - Lombardy-Venice (Austrian) used Fiorino of 100 Soldi (also called Gulden of 100 Kreuzer), and Lira Austriaca (Austrian Lira) of 100 Centesimi, (but corresponding only to 87 Italian Centesimi). Lira Austriaca equivalent to ⅓ Austrian Gulden.

**1848** - Milan minted gold coins of 20 and 40 Italian Lire conforming to Napoléon and Double Napoléon, and silver coins of 5 Lire similar to French coins of 5 Francs.

**1865** - After unification, Italian monetary system linked to Latin Monetary Union. - See *Italy.*

## MILESIMO

**I.** - Submultiple (¹/₁.₀₀₀) of monies of **Spanish** origin.

**II.** - Former copper denomination in the **Philippine Islands.**

## MILIARENSIS

Silver coin of **Roman Empire** and **Byzantium.**

Origin of name - Miliarensis equivalent to ¹/₁.₀₀₀ gold Livre.

Variations of name - Miliares (French), Miliaresion (Greek).

**312** - Monetary reform of Constantine: Miliarensis of 4.54 grams silver and worth ¹/₁₄ Solidus.

**Mid-4th Century** - Appearance of lighter silver coin, Siliqua of 2.63 grams. Miliarensis was worth 1.75 Siliquae. - See *Siliqua.*

**6th Century** - Minting of new Miliarensis of 5.26 grams, worth 2 Siliquae (or Keratia), or ½ Solidus (or Benzant). Submultiples in copper: Follis, Nummus.

**7th Century** - Under Heraclius, Miliarensis reduced to 3.41 grams.

**10th Century** - Silver Miliarensis (¹/₁₂ Bezant) equal to 2 Keratia, 12 Follis, 24 Obols. Relationship maintained until end of Eastern Empire. According to certain etymologists, Miliarensis gave rise to Liard. - See *Liard.*

## MILLIEME

**I.** - Submultiple of **Libyan** Pound (¹/₁.₀₀₀) and of earlier Piastre (¹/₁₀). - See *Pound Libya.*

**II.** - Submultiple of **Egyptian** Pound (¹/₁.₀₀₀), Talari (¹/₂₀₀) and Egyptian Piastre (¹/₁₀). - See *Pound Egypt.* Also a nickel coin valued at 4 Para or ¹/₁₀ Piastre.

**III.** - Submultiple of **Sudanese** Pound (¹/₁.₀₀₀) and Piastre (¹/₁₀) - See *Pound Sudan.*

**IV.** - Submultiple of **Tunisian** Dinar (¹/₁.₀₀₀). - See *Dinar Tunisia.*


# MILREIS

Money of **Portugal** and **Brazil** representing 1,000 Reis.

Origin of name - From mil (1,000) and Reis (plural of Real, Portuguese unit of account).

Bank of issue - Banco de Portugal (Bank of Portugal) established 1846.

**I.** - Unit of account, then monetary unit of **Portugal.**

Predecessor - See *Real.*

**18th Century** - Milreis used as multiple of Real. Minted in form of gold coin. Also called Saint Stephen, from name of Saint pictured thereon.

**1854** (July 29th) - Adoption of gold standard, and designation of Milreis as unit of account:

> 1 Milreis = 1,000 Reis
> 1 Milreis = 1,625.85 milligrams fine gold

Minting of gold coins on basis of 1.77 grams 916 fine per Milreis.

Circulation of coins in gold (Crowns of 10, 5, 2 and 1 Milreis), in silver (Tostao or Teston of 500, 200, 100 and 50 Reis) and in copper (20, 10, 5 and 3 Reis).

Legal circulation of British gold coins (Sovereigns and ½ Sovereigns).

**1882** (June 2nd) - Minting of gold Milreis (1,774 milligrams 916 fine).

**1887** - Monopoly of paper money issue to Banco de Portugal.

**1891** (July 19th) - Suspension of gold standard. Progressive raising of ceiling on banknote issue.

**1898** - Maximum depreciation of paper Milreis of 37%. Milreis minted in form of silver coin (25 grams 916 fine).

**1911** - After advent of Republic, repudiation of name "Milreis" as vestige of royalty. Creation of Escudo at par with Milreis. - See *Escudo.*

**II.** - Monetary unit of **Brazil** until 1942. Divided into 1,000 Reis.

Bank of issue - Banco do Brasil (Bank of Brazil), founded in 1808, reorganized in 1906; Caixa de Estabilzaçãs (Stabilization Bureau) and Caixa de Conversão (Conversion Office). After 1831, also by Federal Treasury.

Predecessor - See *Brazil.*

**18th Century** - Use of Milreis as multiple of Real, unit of account.

**1821** - Forced parity of banknotes denominated in Milreis.

**1822** - Independent Brazil retained Portuguese monies denominated in Reis with gold Oitava, which had exchange rate of 1,600 Reis, then 1,777. - See *Oitava.*

Minting of gold coins analogous to those of Portugal: Lisbonino of 4,800 Reis (8.05 grams), Portuguez of 6,400 Reis (14.03 grams), Dobrao of 12,800 Reis (28.06 grams), all 916 fine.

**1846** (September 11th) - Adoption of Milreis as legal monetary unit:

1 Milreis = 822.076 milligrams of fine gold
Thereafter, Oitava had exchange rate of 4 Milreis.

**1867** (September 26th) - Law modifying silver money: 2 Milreis silver coin corresponded to 5 Franc gold coin of 25 grams 900 fine, or 22.50 grams fine gold.

**1889** - After revolution, State inflation and depreciation of Milreis (44% in 1891). Recovery of exchange rate between 1898 and 1905.

**1906** (December 6th) - 1 Milreis = 15 Pence (against a 27 Pence initial parity and 5 $\frac{1}{2}$ Pence at lowest point). Note-issue entrusted to Caixa de Conversão (Conversion Office).

**1910** (December 30th) - 1 Milreis = 16 Pence.

**1914** (December 12th) - Suspension of convertibility. Progressive depreciation to at least 5 Pence (November 1923).

**1923** - Monopoly of note-issue given to Banco do Brasil.

**1926** (December 18th) - Stabilization with devaluation of 78.1%:
    1 Milreis = 180 milligrams of fine gold
    1 Milreis = 5 $\frac{58}{64}$ Pence
Maintenance of earlier gold Milreis value of 1846 for payment of customs duties.

**1929** (December) - Following collapse of coffee market, depreciation of Milreis.

**1931** (May 18th) - Foreign exchange controls.

**1931** (September 28th) - Monopoly of foreign exchange dealings given to Banco do Brasil.

**1933** (November 21st) - Abolition of gold Milreis value of 1846 for payment of customs duties.
Devaluation of Milreis:
    For State expenses:
        1 Milreis = $\frac{1}{10}$ gold Milreis
        1 Milreis = 82.2076 milligrams of fine gold
    For State purchases:
        1 Milreis = $\frac{1}{8}$ gold Milreis
        1 Milreis = 102.76 milligrams of fine gold
    Official exchange rate:
        1 Milreis = 4 Pence (if Pound Sterling worth more than 1
            U.S. Dollar)
        1 Milreis = 8.33 U.S. Cents (if Pound Sterling fell below U.S.
            Dollar)
De facto definition of currency in terms of Sterling, with eventual substitution of definition in terms of U.S. Dollars.

**1934** (May 19th) - Authorization for free dealings in foreign exchange not derived from exports.

**1934** (September) - Free foreign exchange dealings expanded to exports (except coffee).

**1935** (February 11th) - Free foreign exchange dealings on 65% of proceeds derived from exports.

**1937** - Tax of 3% on all foreign exchange transactions.

**1939** (April) - Tax raised to 5% with establishment of three exchange rates.

1 U.S. Dollar = 16.64 Milreis (official rate for 30% of export proceeds)

1 U.S. Dollar = 19.22 Milreis and 20.18 Milreis with tax (free market rates for balance of export proceeds and for all imports)

1 U.S. Dollar = 21.54 Milreis and 22.62 Milreis with tax (special free market rate for commercial transactions).

**1942** (November 1st) - Milreis changed to Cruzeiro of 100 Centavos. - See *Cruzeiro.*

## MINA

**I.** - Unit of account in ancient **Greece.** Borrowed from Sumerian (505 grams) and Phoenician unit of weight.

Origin of name - Greek *mna,* Hebrew *manah* (to count).

**Late 10th Century B.C.** - Phoenicians spread their system of weights in area of Mediterranean. Phoenician Mina represented 364 grams.
Babylon devised another Mina of 425 grams.

**6th Century B.C.** - In Aegina, Phoenician Mina became unit of account. Silver Mina (364 grams) consisted of 60 Drachmae (6 grams). This monetary system spread to Corinth in Pelopponesus, to Delphi and as far as Thessaly.
Euboea proposed another system of accounting: Mina of Euboea (of Babylonian origin) corresponded to 425 grams of silver, 1/60 Talent (25.50 kilos), 100 Drachmae (4.25 grams) or 600 Obols (0.7 gram).
In Thrace, Mina equal to 90 Drachmae. Monetary system adopted in Macedonia.

**595 B.C.** - In Athens, Solon substituted monetary system of Euboea for system of Aegina. Spread of Euboean system to Thrace, Magna Graecia, Sicily.

**3rd Century B.C.** - Adoption by Ptolemies in Egypt, then in Rhodes, of new division of Mina of 364 grams. Was equal to 100 Drachmae of 364 grams.

**II.** - Unit of account in **Turkey** from the 17th to 19th Century. Mina represented 1/100.000 Juk, 1/50.000 Beutel, 1/100 Piastre or 2/5 Para. Was equivalent to 1.2 Aspers.

## *MINICOY ISLANDS*

**19th Century -** British control. Introduction of monetary system of India. - See *Rupee India.*

## MISCAL

**I.** - Weight of gold powder (about 4.5 grams) used in **Sudan** from 14th Century. Originally equivalent in weight to 4 carb tree seeds or 96 grains of wheat.

**II.** - In **Morocco,** gold coin, later silver coin. Divided into 10 Ukkias, 40 Muzunas or 240 Falus.

Variations of name - Mitkal, Metikal, Mitsqal, Metskal, Miskal, Misqual, Misqali, Mithgal.

**Early 8th Century** - Name given to Arabian gold Dinar weighing 4.25 grams. Weight reduced gradually to 3 grams.

**1760** - Minting of silver Miscal weighing 25 grams. Silver content gradually reduced to 206 fineness.

**1881** - Monetary reform of Moulay-Hassan. Name Miscal carried over to silver Rial Hassani. - See *Hassani.*

**III.** - In **Turkestan,** Chinese struck silver Miscals in denominations of 5, 3, 2 and 1.

**IV.** - In 19th Century **Persia,** standard of bullion weight equal to 71.04 grains.


# MITE

See *Myte.*


# MOCO

Coin obtained by cutting another coin in **French Antilles.** Edges of new money were jagged, and bore a counter-mark.

Origin of name - From Creole *moco* for *morceau* (piece).

Variations of name - Guiotin, Guillotinacorta (in the British and Dutch Antilles), Moso.

**1781** - First minting of Mocos in Santo Domingo, from Spanish coins of 1 Real and ½ Real.

**1797** - In Martinique, cutting of Spanish Piaster Gourdes (silver), ½ Gourdes and ¼ Gourdes into 4 parts, each worth 45 Sols. Later, these same coins cut in shape of heart.

**1802** - In Guadeloupe, cutting of Spanish Piaster Gourdes (silver) into 9 parts: octagon representing ⅓ Gourde and worth 3 Livres, 8 other segments of circle around octagon each representing 1/12 Gourde and worth 15 Sols. All these Mocos had legal tender status.

**1803** and **1805** - Nailed Moedas of Portugal verified and marked in French Antilles. - See *Moeda.*

**1811** - By order of British Occupation in Guadeloupe, new cutting of Piaster Gourdes into 2 or 5 parts: square taken out of center worth 1 Livre, rest worth 2 Livres 5 Sols, or divided into 4 segments often unequal.
Introduction of various Mocos cut in British Antilles:
In Martinique, Gourdes cut in form of heart. In Saint Lucia, in vertical strips. In Tobago, in octagons. In Haiti, in circles.

**1812** - In Saint Lucia, occupied by British, legal tender status reserved for Mocos stamped with letters S.L.

**1813** - In Saint Lucia, new cutting of Gourdes, ½ Gourdes, and ¼ Gourdes into 3 pieces, separated by 2 parallel lines.

**1817** - General demonetization of Mocos. Replaced by coins denominated in Francs.


## MOEDA

Gold money of Portugal and Brazil.

Origin of name - Portuguese *moeda* (money).

Variations of name - Moidore, Lisbonino, Portuguez.

**I.** - Gold coin of **Portugal** from 16th to 19th Century.

**1557 to 1578** - Cruzado of 500 Reis took name Moeda.

**1722 to 1835** - The ½ Dobra (Meia-Dobra) took name Moeda. Exchange rate: 6,400 Reis.

**II.** - Coins introduced into **Brazil** after 1694 (coins of 1,000, 2,000 and 4,000 Reis). Local variation minted from 1752 to 1774 for mining regions: Moeda Miniera of 75, 150, 300 and 600 Reis.

**III.** - Favorite coins of **French Antilles.** At beginning of 19th Century, clipped Moedas pierced in a way to open the metal. Hole filled by gold of varying purity. These coins called "nailed Moedas". Certified and marked with a G in Guadeloupe after 1803; in Martinique after 1805.


## MOHAR

Name commonly used in reference to early gold and silver coins in **Nepal.** Gold Mohar called Patla Ashrafi (5.8319 grams 995 fine). Silver Mohar was 2 Suka coin 5.5403 grams 800 fine. Currently, cupro-nickel submultiple (½) of Nepalese Rupee.


## MOHUR

**I.** - Gold coin of **India** in Moslem monetary system. Fluctuating exchange rate in Rupees (from 14 to 16) according to price of gold. Minted in 1835 (11.664 grams 916 fine). Fineness equal to that of silver Rupee. Issued for 15 Rupees. Also minted in coins of 2 Mohur worth 30 Rupees.

Variation of name - Mohar.

**II.** - British East India Company minted gold Mohur in **Java** in 18th Century.

**19th Century** - English regal coinage of Mohurs when government of India transferred to the Crown.

**1899** - Mohur replaced by Sovereign when gold standard superseded silver standard of India.

**III.** - In **Hyderabad,** minting of Mohur (or Ashrafi) in multiples and submultiples (up to ¹⁄₁₆).

**IV.** - In **Nepal,** minting of Mohar and submultiples. - See *Mohar.*

## *MOLUCCAS*

**Prior to 17th Century** - Barter economy. Monetary use of small pieces of iron and tin in odd shapes.

**1612** - Dutch introduced copper monies on Island of Batjan. - See *Netherlands East Indies.*

## MON

See *Moun.*

## *MONACO*

**1505 and 1523** - Minting of gold Ecu copying French Ecu.

**18th Century** - Minting of silver money called Monaco. - See *Monaco.*

**1815** - Treaty of Vienna established Sardinian control of Principality. - See *Piedmont.*

**1837** (March 7th) - Minting of silver coins of 5 Francs and of 5 and 10 Centimes in copper.

**1861** (February 2nd) - Treaty ending Sardinian control of Principality.

**1865** (November 9th) - Customs union agreement between France and Monaco.

**1878** - Minting of gold coins of 20 and 100 Francs.

**1891, 1895, 1896** - Gold coins of 100 Francs.

**1925** - Decree giving legal tender status only to French and Monégasque monies. Princes, by virtue of royal prerogative, had divisionary coins minted by Paris Mint, denominated in Francs, on same order as French coinage. Banknotes of Banque de France, in fact only paper money circulating in Monaco, were legally only an auxiliary currency to banknotes of Principality, which were never issued.

**1939** (September 8th) - Foreign exchange controls placing Monaco in Franc-Zone. - See *Franc.*

## MONACO

**I.** - Silver money minted for Prince of **Monaco** in 18th Century. Value: 58 French Sous. Also, all coins minted in Principality generally called Monacos.

**II.** - In 19th Century, copper coins minted by Prince Honoré V for **Monaco.** Inferior in weight to corresponding coins of France, were refused for French payments, until minting of new coins of copper alloy during Second Empire.

## MONGO

Submultiple ($^1/_{100}$) of Tughrik, monetary unit of **Mongolia.**
Variations of name - Mungo, Mong, Mung.

## *MONGOLIA*

Modern Mongolia loosely dependent upon China until Tannu Tuva became republic
   in 1911, and Outer Mongolia declared its independence. - See *China, Tuva, Mangolia, Inner* and *Outer.*

## *MONGOLIA, INNER*

For currency in circulation, see *China.*
**1936** - Portions of Inner Mongolia under influence of Japenese used Yuan of Central
   Bank of Inner Mongolia, at par with Japanese Yen. - See *Yuan Mongolia.*
   Remainder of area continued to use Chinese monies.
**1945** - All provinces again Chinese.

## *MONGOLIA, OUTER*

For earlier history and money in circulation, see *China.*
**1911** - Outer Mongolia, under Russian auspices, declared independence.
**1915** - Adoption of Tughrik as monetary unit. - See *Tughrik.*
**1919** - Brief reincorporation with China.
**1924** - Under Russian control, establishment of Mongolian People's Revolutionary
   Government. Commercial and Industrial Bank of Mongolia created as monetary
   authority.
**1936** - Independence guaranteed by Soviet Union.
**1945** - Declared independence by plebiscite as Mongolian People's Republic. Name of
   note-issuing authority changed to State Bank of Mongolian People's Republic.

## *MONTENEGRO*

**19th Century** - Use of Gulden (Guilder) of 100 Novtchitcha.
**1902** - Use of Krone of 100 Heller or 100 Para. Local minting of coins of 20 Para in
   nickel and of 1 and 2 Para in bronze.
**1910** - Independent kingdom. Monetary unit the Perper of 100 Para. - See *Perper.*
**1919** - See *Yugoslavia* and *Dinar Yugoslavia.*
**1941** - Italian occupation. Italian monetary system. - See *Lira Italy.*

**1944** - Return to Yugoslavia. - See *Dinar Yugoslavia.*

# *MOROCCO*

Monies of Carthage, Rome, the Vandals, then Byzantines.

**788 A.D.** - Beginning of Moorish rule. Arabic monies: gold Dinar (see *Dinar*) and silver Dirhem (see *Dirhem*), sustained and fixed according to Koranic Law, for settlements of dowries, divorces, fines, tithes. . .
Varieties issued by feudal lords.

**11th Century** - Dinar no longer minted, but remained unit of account. Random introduction of Portuguese, Spanish, English, French, Turkish coins, and of Maria Theresia Thaler.
Spanish influence predominant.

**18th Century** - Monies in use: Ashrafi, Sherify, or Xeraphin (variations of Sultanine or Turkish Sequin); Ducat (gold) worth 48 Blanquillos (silver) and 960 Falus (copper).

**19th Century** - Local minting of coins whose nominal value largely exceeded their intrinsic metal value:
> In gold - Benduqi
> In silver - Ukkia
> In copper - Muzuna (Fels)

**1881** - Monetary reform of Moulay-Hassan. Minting of silver coinage. - See *Hassani.*
Minting in Fez of copper Centimos, or Grammos.
Persistence of payments made with Muzunas.
French, British, Spanish gold and silver specie monies were legal tender.

**1906** (April 7th) - Act of Algeciras created Banque d'Etat du Maroc (State Bank of Morocco) with right of banknote issue.
De facto introduction of French subsidiary coinage and banknotes of Banque de l'Algérie.

**1909** - Issue of Treasury Bonds by Banque d'Etat du Maroc.

**1910** (December 2nd) - First issue of banknotes (100 Peseta Hassani) by Banque d'Etat du Maroc. Exchange rate of silver coins varied with fluctuations in silver bullion price.

**1920** (March 19th) - Demonetization of Hassani money in French Morocco.

**1920** (June 21st) - Decree made Moroccan Franc legal money of Morocco. - See *Franc Morocco.* Dominance of Spanish money in Spanish Morocco. - See *Spain* and *Peseta.*
French and Spanish monies were legal tender in Tangier.

**1956** (October 29th) - French Morocco, Spanish Morocco and Tangier incorporated into independent Moroccan nation. Official monetary unit, Moroccan Franc.
Spanish banknotes exchanged for Moroccan Francs:
> 1 Spanish Peseta = 10 Moroccan Francs

**1959** (October 17th) - Devaluation and creation of new monetary unit to replace Moroccan Franc. - See *Dirham.*

# MOUN

**I.** - Submultiple of **Japanese** Yen ($1/10.000$), Sen ($1/100$) and Rin ($1/10$). - See *Yen.*

**II.** - Submultiple ($1/100$) of **Korean** Hwan, then Won, generally called Chon. - See *Hwan* and *Won.*

Variations of name - Mun, Mon.

# MOUTON

**I.** - **French** gold money, also called Agnel. - See *Agnel.*

**II.** - Gold money of **Netherlands.** Issued in Flanders, Holland and Brabant during 14th Century, and again in Brabant during 15th Century.

# *MOZAMBIQUE*

Introduction of Portuguese monetary system in 18th Century. Copper coins of 15 and 30 Reis (1725), silver coins (1735-1743), and gold money (1755-56). - See *Merigal* and *Pardo.*

**1922** (September 1st) - Creation of separate monetary unit. - See *Escudo Mozambique.* In Laurenço Marques and in Beira, Libra Esterlina (Sterling) notes continued to be issued by local banks.

**1939** (July 22nd) - Decree making Escudo sole legal tender in Mozambique.

# *MUSCAT AND OMAN*

Money in circulation - See *Maria Theresia Thaler* (interior); *Rupee India* (coastal region and official currency); *Baiza* (general use).

**1959** - Indian Rupee replaced by Persian Gulf Rupee. - See *Rupee Persian Gulf.*

**1970** (May 7th) - New currency, Rial Saidi, replaced Persian Gulf Rupee. - See *Rial Saidi.*

**1970** (July 25th) - Country renamed. - See *Oman.*

# MUZUNA

**I.** - Small copper coin of **Algeria** prior to French conquest. Equal to $1/24$ Budschu.

**II.** - In **Morocco,** money of copper used in the 19th Century and worth $1/100$ Piastre, $1/40$ Miscal, or $1/4$ Ukkia. Was equal to 6 Falus. Minted in coins of 1 to 10 Muzuna.

Variations of name - Mouzonnat, Mouzouna, Mazuna

**1881** - Monetary reform of Moulay-Hassan, and creation of Hassani monetary system.

- See *Hassani.* New bronze coins, modeled after Spanish prototype, called Centimos or Grammos. But, outside cities, natives still used old Muzunas.

**1920** - Monetary reform making Franc monetary unit of Morocco. - See *Franc Morocco.*

**1922** - Minting of bronze coins of 5 and 10 Centimes, which preserved Muzuna format.


# MYTE

Silver/copper money and unit of account in **Netherlands** from 14th to 18 Century.

Origin of name - From Flemish *mijt* or *mitje* (little thing). From this money old French Mite derived, designating small copper money, *Mitaille,* which became *Mitraille* (small money, then small scrap iron, root of words *mitrailler, mitrailleuse.* . .).

Variations of name - Mite, Mijt.

Plural - Myten, Mites or Mijten.

**14th Century** - Silver/copper money in Flanders worth 1/48 Groot.

**15th Century** - Silver/copper money in Flanders and in Brabant.

**1433** - In unified Netherlands under Philip the Good, Mijt (Myte) of Flanders worth 1/24 Groot. Later called Denier Noir.

**1467** - Same exchange rate under Charles the Bold. Coin of 2 Myten (1/12 Groot) called Korten.

**1520** - Monetary system of Charles V. All monies of Netherlands were multiples of Myte of Flanders and Myte of Brabant. Units of account: 2 Myten of Flanders were worth 3 Myten of Brabant.

**17th and 18th Centuries -** Myte remained inferior unit of account in records of Austrian Netherlands (Belgian provinces: Brussels, Antwerp) equivalent to 1/3 Penning. 24 Myten needed for 1 Groot, 48 for 1 Stuyver, 288 for 1 Schelling, 960 for 1 Gulden, 2,340 for 1 Rixdale, 5,760 for 1 Pondt Vlaams.

## *NAPLES*

Greek monies (see *Greece*), then Roman (see *Rome*).

**5th to 6th Century** - Cf. *Sicily.*

**9th Century** - Minting of silver Carolingian Denier (Northern influence) and of Follaro (Eastern influence).

**13th Century** - Gold monies: Augustalis, which became Reale.
Silver monies: Carlino or Saluto, Taro, Gigliato.
Silver/copper monies: Denaro, Medaglia.

**14th Century** - Gold and silver monies: Saluto, Gigliato.
Silver or silver/copper monies: Cella, Tornesello, Quattrino.

**15th Century** - Appearance of silver Taro, or Double Carlino. Minting of gold Ducato.

**16th Century** - Minting of silver Ducato. - See *Ducato.*

**18th Century** - Unit of account: Ducato of 5 Tari, or Tarini, 10 Carlini, 40 Cinquini, 100 Grani, 200 Tornesi, 300 Quartini, 600 Piccioli, 1,200 Cavalli or Denari.
Gold monies: Doppia, Oncia.
Silver monies: Ducato, Scudo, Taro, Carlino, Grano. - See *Two Sicilies.*

**1808 to 1815** - Murat began his reign by minting Scudo, then introduced French monetary system in 1810. Minted gold coins of 40 Franchi, then of 20 and 40 Lire, and silver coins of 1, 2 and 5 Lire.

**1816** - Return to old Neapolitan monetary system.

**1818** (April 20th) - Unification of monies of Naples and Sicily:
Unit of account - silver Ducato of 100 Grani or 1,000 Cavalli.
Gold coins - Oncette (3 Ducati) and its multiples (2, 5 and 10).
Silver coins - Scudo (120 Grani), Ducato (100), Carlino (10).

**1865** - After unification, Italian monetary system linked to that of Latin Monetary Union. - See *Italy* and *Lira Italy.*

## NAPOLEON

**French** gold coin worth 20 Francs. Minted in 19th Century.

Origin of name - From Napoléon I and Napoléon III, represented on coin.

Predecessor - See *Louis.*

**1803** (April 7th) - Law authorizing minting of 20 Franc gold coins weighing 6.4516 grams 900 fine, or 5.80 grams fine. - See *Franc.* Coins called Napoléons during Empire and under Louis from 1815 to 1840. Minting of coins of 40 Francs (Double Napoléons), then of 10 Francs (½ Napoléons).

**1854** (January 12th) - Decree authorizing minting of gold 5 Franc coins (¼ Napoléons).

**1865** (December 23rd) - Convention of Paris, called Latin Monetary Union, provided for minting of uniform gold coins of 100, 50, 20, 10 and 5 Francs 900 fine by the signatory countries (France, Belgium, Italy, Switzerland). - See *Union Latine.*

**1870 to 1914** - Name Napoléon (or Louis) remained attached to 20 Franc coins, even when minted by Republic. Types: Grand Coq, Petit Coq. . .

**1914** (August 5th) - Forced parity, which implied demonetization of Napoléon.

**1951** (May) - Minting of gold coins of 20 Francs of Coq type, bearing dates prior to 1914, (restrikes) on behalf of Banque de France.

## NASARA

Silver money of **Tunis** having square shape. Used in 18th and 19th Centuries. Exchange rate: 52 Aspers.

## *NAURU*

**1888** - Annexed by Germany. Use of German monetary system. - See *Mark.*

**1914** - Surrendered to Australia. Use of Australian monies. - See *Australia.*

**1920** - British mandate. Use of British monetary system. - See *Pound.*

**1942-1945** - Japanese Occupation. Use of military Yen. - See *Gumpyo.*

**1945** - Returned to status of British mandate.

**1947** - Joint trusteeship (Australia, New Zealand, United Kingdom). Use of Australian monetary system. - See *Pound Australia.*

## NEGENMENNEKE

Silver coin of **Brabant** in 1480. Originally equal to 9 Myten.

**1520** (February 4th) - Value reduced to 6 Myten. - See *Seskin.*

## NEGRO

Silver/copper money issued in **Spain** by Alphonso X in 1258. Equal to 1 Denier, like Pépion of Ferdinand II: 8.53 grams 333 fine, or 2,84 grams fine silver. So named to contrast with Blanco of 2 Deniers issued from 1252 to 1258.

Origin of name - Spanish *negro* (black).

Variation of name - *Prieto* (Spanish for very brown).

## *NEPAL*

Prior to Gurkha unification, limited use of locally minted metallic coinage. Simultaneous circulation of specie monies of India. - See *India.*

**1768** - Establishment of modern kingdom with introduction of silver monetary system. - See *Suka.*
Basic gold coin: Mohar (Patla Ashrafi).

**1870** - Gold Mohar divided into 15 silver Dabals. - See *Dabal.*

**19th and early 20th Centuries** - Scarcity of domestic metallic currency led to dominance of Indian specie money.

**1945** - Issue by His Majesty's Government of first paper money. Denominated in Mohar Rupaiya (Nepalese Rupees). - See *Rupee Nepal.*

## *NETHERLANDS*

**6th to 8th Century** - Frisians used Merovingian Triens derived from Roman Sou, and Anglo-Saxon Sceattae.

**9th Century** - Carolingian unit of account: Livre of 20 Sous or 240 Deniers. Sou was to become Schelling; Denier was to become Groot.

**10th to 13th Century** - Minting of silver Deniers and Obols, then silver Esterlin (4 Deniers).

**13th Century** - Use in Netherlands and in Oldenburg of system of accounting of German and English origin; Marc or Esterlin, composed of 10 Schilling or 120 Pfennig.

**14th Century to 1433** - Counter-marking of Gros of Prague. Supplemented by various feudal issues:
In Hainaut: gold Guilder, Crown, Ange d'Or; silver Plaisant.
In Flanders: gold Royal d'Or, Guilder, Ange d'Or, Chaise, Noble, Mouton, Franc, Lion d'Or, Heaume. . .; silver Groot, Esterlin, Lion or Botdrager, Roosebeker; silver/copper Myte.
In Brabant: gold Guilder, Chaise, Mouton, Ecu, Angel d'Or, Cavalier d'Or, Lion d'Or, Noble, Peter; silver Plak, Peter; silver/copper Myte.
In Holland: gold Mouton, Chaise, Franc, Guilder, Crown; silver Gros.
- See also *Luxembourg.*

**1336** - Attempt at common money in Hainaut and Brabant: Denier Blanc.

**1344** - Attempt at monetary union of Flanders with England (minting of gold Noble).

**1355** - Introduction of Stuyver within framework of system of accounting:
1 Livre = 6 Guilders = 120 Stuyver = 240 Grooten

**1384** - Attempt at common monies for five years between Flanders and Brabant: gold Denier, Roosebeker, Groot, Double Myte.

**1420** - Attempt at money common among three countries, Hainaut, Holland and Brabant: Dreilander.

**1433** (October 21st) - Decree of Philip the Good, unifying monetary system of Netherlands (Flanders, Hainaut, Luxembourg, Namur, Brabant, Holland, Zeeland):
Gold coins - Cavalier or Rijder (and submultiples)
Silver coins - Vierlander (and submultiples)
Silver/copper coins - Double Myte and Myte
Subsequent additions - Lion and Lion d'Or (1453); Guilder of Burgundy and silver Groot (1466); Briquet or Double Groot (1474).
Progressive reduction in weight of monies (1453, 1454, 1466, 1467, 1477).

**1487** (March 15th) - Ordinance of Maximilian of Austria restoring hard monies, with accounting in Reales:
Gold coins - Grand Real of Austria (24 Reales), Noble of Burgundy (12 Reales), Guilder (6 Reales)
Silver coins - Grand Real, Griffon (¼ Real)
Independent coinage in Ghent, Brussels, Louvain, Mechelin

**1489** (December 14th) - Decree of Breda, by which House of Austria made Gulden (Guilder or Florin) monetary unit of Netherlands.

**1496** (April 10th) - Monetary system of Philip the Fair:
Gold coins - Vlies (Toison), Guilder
Silver coins - Vlies, Patard

**1520** (February 4th) - Monetary reform of Charles V:
Gold coins - Guilder, Crown, Real d'Or
Silver coins - Vlieguyt, Real, Groot
Silver / copper coins - Sixain, Korten

**1542** (February 22nd) - Minting of silver Carolus, analagous to Thaler and worth 1 Guilder.

**1606** (May 21st) and **1610** (July 6th) - Adoption of two gold monies (Ducat and Rijder) computed in Guilders. Limitation of legal tender status of small silver coins. Silver / copper coins forbidden.

**1622-1659** - Minting of silver Rijksdaalder, or Rix Daler.

**1686** - Minting of silver Guilders.

**1694** (March 17th) and **1699** (December 31st) - Resolution of Estates-General for adoption of independent Guilder as monetary unit, with minting of 3 Guilder coins. - See *Guilder Netherlands.*

**1749** (March 31st) - Minting of Gouden (gold) Rijders (14 Guilders).
Unit of account: Livre de Gros (Pondt Vlaams) of 2.5 Rijksdaalder. 6 Guilders, 20 Schelling, 120 Stuyver, 240 Groot, or 1,920 Penning.
Specie monies:
In gold - Gouden Rijder (14 Guilders), Dukat or Ducat (5.25 Guilders)
In silver - Ducaton (63 Stuyver), Rijksdaalder (50 Stuyver, 53 in Zeeland), Daalder (30 Stuyver), Guilder (20 Stuyver)
In silver / copper - Schelling (6 Stuyver), Stuyver (16 Penning)
In copper - Duit (2 Penning)

**1806** - Louis Bonaparte provided for minting of coins of 10 and 20 Guilders (in gold), of 1, 2 and 5 Guilders (in silver). Actual minting of Ducats and coins of 50 Stuyver.

**1810** - Introduction of French monetary system.

**1816** - Restoration of Netherlands monetary system, on bimetallic basis. - See *Guilder Netherlands.*

## *NETHERLANDS ANTILLES*

Consisting of Leeward Islands (Curaçao, Aruba and Bonaire) and Windward Islands

(St. Maarten, St. Eustatius and Saba).

**18th Century** - Unit of account: Piaster of 8 Reaals (Schelling) or 48 Stuyver. Specie money - Coins of Spain and Portugal.

**1794** - Circulation of silver 3 Guilder coins.

**Beginning of 19th Century** - Puncturing and counter-marking of Spanish Piasters.

**1821** - First coins struck especially for Netherlands Antilles: silver Reaal (worth 6 Stuyver).

**1822** - Minting of silver Stuyvers

**19th Century** - Introduction of Dutch monetary system. - See *Guilder Netherlands.*

**1940** (May 10th) - After German Occupation of Netherlands, break with Metropolitan Unit. - See *Guilder Netherlands Antilles.*

# NETHERLANDS EAST INDIES

**Early monies** - Chinese porcelain vases, Chinese bronze knives, Tibetan bricks of pressed tea. Glass pearls on Palan Islands. - See also *Java, Sumatra, Moluccas.*

**1601** (March 1st) - Van Verre Company of Amsterdam authorized to mint silver Piastres of 8 Reales and submultiples.

**1645** - Dutch East India Company issued silver Crowns (48 Stuyver). Withdrawn in 1647.

**1686** - Introduction of Dutch counter-marked Ducats.

**1690** - Use of Japanese gold Coban and Ichi Bu ban, counterstamped with Dutch lion, for 20 Rijksdaalder and 20 Schelling.

**18th Century** - Dominance of Dutch monies: silver Ducatons and Duiten in 1726; silver Guilders, Stuyver and Duiten in 1786.

**1796-1799** - Minting of "bonks", pieces of copper rods marked 1S (1 Stuyver) and 2S (2 Stuyver).

**1814-1938** - Periodic minting of gold Ducats struck exclusively for use in Netherlands East Indies.

**1817** (January 14th) - Official adoption of Netherlands Guilder as monetary unit. - See *Guilder Netherlands East Indies.*

**1949** (December 28th) - Became independent Republic of United States of Indonesia (excluding Netherlands New Guinea). - See *Indonesia* and *New Guinea.*

**1961** (May 1st) - Netherlands New Guinea transferred to Indonesia, and name changed to West Irian. - See *West Irian.*

## *NEW CALEDONIA*

**Before French control** - Introduction of Peruvian and Chilean Piasters by seafaring traders.

**1853** - French domination. Introduction of French monetary system. Treasury issued vouchers denominated in Francs. - See *Franc.*

**1871** (February 7th) - Company of New Caledonia granted authority to form bank of issue.

**1874** (July 14th) - Creation of Banque de la Nouvelle-Calédonie (Bank of New Caledonia) as note-issuing authority.

**1877** - Bankruptcy of Banque de la Nouvelle-Calédonie. Issue of banknotes taken over by Treasury.

**1888** (February 20th) - Banknote issuing authority granted to Banque de l'Indochine.

**1918** (November 14th) - Issue of Treasury vouchers as divisionary money.

**1920** (August 8th) - Legal tender status declared for all banknotes and divisionary coinage of Metropolitan France.

**1939** (September 9th)'- Foreign exchange controls within framework of Franc-Zone.

**1940** (May 20th) - Decree establishing foreign exchange controls between Metropolitan France and Overseas Territories.

**1941** - Incorporation into Sterling Area.

**1944** (February 8th) - Franco-British Agreement fixed rate of exchange of Free French Territories:
    1 Pound Sterling = 200.00 Francs

**1944** (June) - Franco-American Agreement confirmed February 8th exchange rate and fixed exchange rate for U.S. Dollar:
    1 U.S. Dollar = 50.00 Francs

**1944** (December 6th) - Parities confirmed and specified:
    1 Pound Sterling = 200.00 Francs
    1 U.S. Dollar = 49.625 Francs
Return to Franc-Zone.

**1945** (December 26th) - Creation of CFP Franc. Consolidation of earlier parities with Pound Sterling and U.S. Dollar. Lowering of parity with Metropolitan Franc. - See *Franc CFP.*

## NEW CEDI

See *Cedi.*

## *NEW GUINEA*

Primitive monies - Human skulls, dogs' teeth.

**I.** - Eastern territory (i.e., Papua and N.E. New Guinea): British monies (in Papua) and

German monies (N.E. New Guinea) around 1894; gold, silver and bronze coins denominated in Mark and Pfennig, issued by New Guinea Co. Replaced by Australian monies (September 1, 1906, in Papua and September 12, 1914, in N.E. New Guinea). - See *Australia, Pound Australia.*

**II.** - In Western Territory (i.e., Netherlands New Guinea or West Irian) before 1950, see *Netherlands East Indies.*

**1950** (March 30th) - Creation of New Guinea Guilder equal to Netherlands Guilder. - See *Guilder New Guinea.*

**1963** (May 1st) - Netherlands New Guinea transferred to Indonesia, and name changed to West Irian. - See *West Irian.*

## NEW HEBRIDES

**18th and 19th Centuries** - Barter between Europeans and natives. Then, introduction by first colonists of local money: vouchers signed by plantation owners and zinc tokens minted in France in Saint-Etienne (3 to 6 Pence, 1 and 2 Shillings, 5 Francs), convertible into merchandise. Issuance of bearer banknotes by Compagnie Calédonienne.

**1888** - Right of banknote issue granted to Banque de l'Indochine (Noumea Branch).

**1894** - End of issuance of banknotes by Compagnie Calédonienne reorganized into Société Francaise des Nouvelles-Hébrides.

**1906** (October 20th) - Franco-British Agreement prohibited issuance and circulation of zinc tokens (continued to circulate until 1914).

**1908** - Decision of General Assembly of Société des Etablissements Ballande at Noumea to create bearer banknotes to facilitate payments in New Hebrides. Banknotes redeemable in specie at Port-Villa and Noumea. Printed in Paris by Chaix, these banknotes circulated successfully until 1930.

**1914** (August 6th) - Franco-British Protocol on Statute of Condominium, giving legal tender status to French and British coins and banknotes (see *Franc* and *Pound*). De facto circulation of Australian coins and paper money of small denomination: silver coins of 1 and 2 Shillings and banknotes of Commonwealth Bank of Australia. - See *Pound Australia.*

**1935** - Exchange of Franco-British banknotes. Legal tender status given Australian currency for all payments in Sterling.

**1940** - Importation of British banknotes banned.

**1941** (August 31st) - Creation of New Hebrides Franc. - See *Franc New Hebrides.*

## NEW PENCE

See *New Penny.*

## NEW PENNY

Submultiple (1/100) since February 15, 1971, of Pound Sterling, monetary unit of **Great Britain** and countries whose currencies derived from Pound Sterling. Malta, Nigeria and Gambia retained old Pound, Shilling, Pence system. New 1/2 Penny, New Penny and 2 New Penny coins minted in copper; 5, 10 and 50 New Penny coins were 75% copper and 25% nickel.

Predecessor - See *Penny.*

Plural - New Pence.

## *NEW ZEALAND*

**18th Century** - Issue of a copper Token, denominated in Pennies, by merchants.

**19th Century** - British monies. - See *Pound.*

**1907** - With transformation of Colony into Dominion, creation of New Zealand Pound of 20 Shillings and 240 Pence. - See *Pound New Zealand.*

## NGWEE

Submultiple (1/100) of Kwacha, monetary unit of **Zambia.**

## NI SHU GIN

Rectangular silver piece struck in **Japan** beginning in 1772, worth 2 Shu. Gold Ni Shu struck in 1697.

Variation of name - Nanryo gin.

## *NICARAGUA*

Primitive money of Niquirans: Cacao beans and coconuts, having stipulated and unchanging value.

**16th to 19th Century** - Circulation of Spanish and Mexican silver Piasters, as well as heterogeneous mixture of coins. Coins not of uniform character, many being crudely minted as irregular pieces of silver cut to proper weight and bearing official stamp.

**1821** - Revolted from Spain.

**1823-1838** - Loosely grouped into United Provinces of Central America. - See *Peso Central America.*

**1838** - Independence. Peso of Central America gave rise to Nicaraguan Peso. - See *Peso Nicaragua.*

Coins of other countries had legal tender status in Nicaragua.

**1875** - Government paper money, "billetes del Tesoro", issued in moderate amounts. Redeemable in gold or silver but not legal tender until 1885.

**1887** - Bank of Nicaragua granted exclusive right of note issue. However, notes were not legal tender.

**1893** - New government issued "billetes del Tesoro Nacional". Continued depreciation of banknotes.

**1912** - Adoption of gold standard, with creation of Córdoba. - See *Córdoba*.


## NIGER

**Early native monies** - Flat bars of iron (2.92 x 0.009 meters), divided into 12 Pattes or 36 Dialots. Dialot was large enough to form into spade. Monetary use of iron bars discontinued toward end of 19th Century. Iron arrowheads used by Bornbou people; molded copper forms in region of Air Mountains.

**Early 20th Century** - French military presence and introduction of French Franc. - See *Franc*.

**1922** (October 13th) - Became part of French West Africa. - See *French West Africa*.

**1945** (December 26th) - Creation and use of CFA Franc. - See *Franc CFA*.

**1960** (August 3rd) - Became independent republic. Monetary unit unchanged.


## NIGERIA

**Early native monies** - See *Gold Coast*. In Southwest Nigeria, use of ring money known as Manilla. - See *Manilla*.

**19th Century** - Gradual extension of British influence and introduction of British specie monies. Introduction of Maria Theresia Thalers dated 1870. - See *Maria Theresia Thaler*.

**End of 19th Century** - British domination and use of British monetary system. - See *Pound*.

**1913** - Newly formed West African Currency Board minted special coinage for British West Africa. - See *Pound West Africa*.

**1959** (July 1st) - Creation of new monetary unit to replace West African Pound at par. - See *Pound Nigeria*.

**1968** (January 10th) - Secessionist Biafra created independent monetary unit. - See *Pound Biafra*.


## NIL

Unit of account in **Mogul Empire** and in **Bengal**. Equivalent of 100 Badams, 10,000 Crores, 1 million Lakhs, or 1 hundred billion Rupees.

## NIQUET

Silver/copper coin minted in **France** by English (Henry V) in 15th Century.
Variation of name - Nique.
**1421** (August 11th) - Minting of Niquet: 2.18 grams 123 fine, or 0.27 grams fine silver.
Exchange rate: 2 Denier Tournois.

## *NIUE*

**1900** - British protectorate annexed to New Zealand (1901). Use of monetary system of New Zealand. - See *New Zealand.*

## NOBLE

Name given to various early monies of Northern Europe.
Origin of name - From adjective noble, Latin *nobilis.*
  Cf. *Ducat.*
**I. -** In **England,** gold money.
**1344** (July 9th) - After failure of issue of gold Florins (see *Florin)* at exchange rate that was too high, minting of gold Nobles (9.4 grams) having an exchange rate of 6 Shillings 8 Pence.
**1346** - Weight of Noble lowered to 8.3 grams.
**1353** - Weight of Noble lowered to 7.8 grams.
**1411** - Weight of Noble lowered to 7 grams.
**1464** - Exchange rate of Noble raised to 8 Shillings 6 Pence by Edward IV.
**1465** - Edward IV issued new Noble, called Noble à la Rose (from Rose of York), or Rose Noble, weighing 7.8 grams, and worth 10 Shillings. Other name of Rose Noble: Real (see *Real).* Sometimes also called Raymond Noble because of assurance that Raymond Lulle had enough gold in the Tower of London for minting.
**1489** - Sovereign corresponded to ½ Noble.
**1526** (October 30th) - Exchange rate of Rose Noble raised to 11 Shillings 3 Pence by Henry VIII. Minting of new type of Noble, called George Noble, weighing 4.6 grams and having an exchange rate of 6 Shillings 8 Pence.
**1552** - Exchange rate of Noble (Real) raised to 15 Shillings.
**1611** - Exchange rate of Noble (Real) raised to 33 Shillings.
**II. -** In **Denmark,** gold coin minted after 1496 on style of English Sovereign created by Henry VII (16.59 grams 965 fine, or 16 grams fine). Rate of exchange: 6 Guilders.
**III. -** Gold money of **Netherlands.** Derived from English coin.
**1344** - Flanders used same money as England from whom she adopted the Noble.
**1388** - Philip the Bold minted gold Noble in Flanders. Identical to English Noble.
**1410** - Gold Noble issued in Flanders by John the Fearless.

**1417** - Gold Noble issued in Brabant. The ½ Noble called Peter.

**1419** - Gold Noble issued in Flanders by Philip the Good.

**1487** (March 13th) - In unified Netherlands, Maximilian of Austria minted Noble of Bourgogne (Flemish: *Schuithen*) worth 12 Reales.

**IV.** - In **Scotland,** gold money issued in 1358. Gold and silver monies issued by James VI (1567-1603).


# NOMOS

Term used in the ancient world under **Greek** influence to designate most common monetary unit of the monetary system in local use: Litra in Sicily (6th to 4th Century B.C.); Tetradrachm of Athens; Tridrachm of Corinth (4th Century B.C.); Sestertius of Rome (2nd Century B.C.). Word Stater often used in a similar sense.

Origin of name - Greek *nomos,* the law; from which comes *nomisma,* legal money (corresponds to the Latin *nummus*).


# *NORFOLK ISLAND*

**19th Century** - Limited use of British monies.

**1914** - Australian dependency. Use of Australian monetary system. - See *Pound Australia.*


# *NORWAY*

**10th and 11th Centuries** - Introduction and imitation of English Penny (Denier) which gave rise to silver Pfennig. - See *Pfennig.*

**13th and 14th Centuries** - Bracteates.

**1450 to 1814** - Norway was part of Kingdom of Denmark. Danish monetary system subject to some variations in unit of account: Bergen and Copenhagen accounted in Riksdaler of 6 Mark or 96 Skilling; Christiania, Trondheim, Romsdal. . ., divided Riksdaler into 4 Ort or 96 Skilling. - See *Denmark.*

**1814 to 1905** - Norway was part of Kingdom of Sweden. Swedish monetary system. - See *Sweden.*

Unit of account: Speciesdaler of 5 Ort or Mark, or 120 Skilling.

Minting of silver Speciesdaler. No gold coins.

**1875** (March 8th) - Norway became member of Scandinavian Monetary Union.

**1905** - Creation of Norwegian Krone, patterned after Swedish Krona. - See *Krone Norway.*

# NUMMUS

Smallest bronze money in **Eastern Empire** from 4th to 9th Century.
Multiple - Follis of 20 Nummi.
Origin of name - Latin *nummus* (money), Greek *nomos* (law).
Plural - Nummi.

# NOVENO

Silver money issued in **Spain** in second half of 13th Century. Equal to 3 Deniers or $1/60$ gold Maravedi.
Variations of name - Noven, Novene.

# NOVTCHITCHA

Submultiple ($1/100$) of Austrian Gulden used in **Bosnia** from 1879 to 1900, in **Montenegro** from 1874 to 1902. - See *Gulden Austria*.

# *NYASALAND*

See *Federation of Rhodesia and Nyasaland.*

# OBAN

Gold elliptical piece used as money in **Japan** from 16th to 19th Century. Equivalent to 10 Coban, 40 Ichi Bu ban or 160 Shu Kin.

Variation of name - Obang.

**1586** - First known appearance of Obans. Weighed 166 grams and imitated Portuguese who used gold coins made from gold plaques.

**1601** - Weight of Oban: 164.40 grams 661 fine.

**1695** - Weight of Oban: 165.23 grams 523 fine.

**1725** - Weight of Oban: 165.00 grams 681 fine.

**1837** - Weight of Oban: 164.70 grams 677 fine.

**1860** - Weight of Oban: 111.83 grams 567 fine.

**1871** - Monetary reform abolishing earlier coins. - See *Yen*.

# OBOL

**I.** - For **Hebrews,** submultiple of Shekel ($\frac{1}{20}$), a weight, then silver money. - See *Shekel*.

**II.** - Bar, then coin money of ancient **Greece** and Greek world.

Origin of name - Greek *obolos,* corruption of *obelos,* a skewer, or pole. Root of word obelisk.

**6th Century B.C.** - Originally, Obol was small bar in form of iron or copper nail. Later became small silver coin of 0.7 grams. Imitated in Sicily under name Litra and scattered throughout Gaul via Marseilles.

In accounting system of Euboea, adopted in Athens in 595 B.C., 6 Obols equalled 1 Drachma; 600 Obols, 1 Mina; 36,000 Obols, 1 Talent. Obol equivalent of 4 Dichalcoi, 8 Chalcoi, 56 Lepta. Coin of $1\frac{1}{2}$ Obols called Trihemiobolian; 2 Obols, Diobolon; 3 Obols, Triobolon; 4 Obols, Tetraobolon; 5 Obols, Pentobolon. Coin of $\frac{1}{2}$ Obol called Hemiobol. Coin of $\frac{1}{4}$ Obol called Tetartemorion.

**4th Century B.C.** - In Southern Italy, minting of bronze Obols of 8 grams.

**4th to 3rd Century B.C.** - Marseilles minted silver Obols of 0.5 to 0.7 grams.

**III.** - Bronze money of **Eastern Empire** from 9th to 15th Century. With end of Nummus ($\frac{1}{20}$ Follis, successor to Roman Denarius), Obol represented $\frac{1}{2}$ Follis, $\frac{1}{12}$ Keration, $\frac{1}{24}$ Miliarensis, $\frac{1}{288}$ Bezant.

**IV.** - In **France,** copper monies, then unit of account.

**9th Century** - In Carolingian monetary system, copper money equal to $\frac{1}{2}$ Denier or $\frac{1}{24}$ Sou. Consequently, Obol corresponded to $\frac{1}{2}$ Denier Tournois and in this sense became unit of account.

**17th Century** - Obol identical with Maille. - See *Maille*.

**V.** - In **France,** silver coin often called Obol Blanche. Minted under Philip the Fair (exchange rate in 1306: 4 Deniers), and under Charles IV (weight: 2.08 grams 832 fine, or 1.73 grams fine silver; exchange rate: $7\frac{1}{2}$ Deniers).

**VI.** - In all **Western European** countries, Obol, under various names, corresponded during Feudal Age to $\frac{1}{2}$ Carolingian Denier.

In feudal Germany, name given to 1/2 Pfennig (or Halbling).
In Genoa, name given to 1/2 Denaro (Medaglia, or Pitta).
Minting of Obols (1/2 Denier) in Italy, Spain, Portugal, Hungary, Netherlands, Swiss Canton of Vaud, and Geneva.
For Latvia and Estonia (Archbishopric of Riga and Livonia), see *Artig*.

**VII.** - In **Levant,** silver/copper Obol and copper Obol issued by Crusaders.

## OCHAVO

**I.** - Copper coin in **Spain** dating from early 16th Century and worth 1/8 Real. Same as 1/2 Quarto.

**1808-1814** - Issued during French Occupation of Barcelona and Catalonia.

**II.** - In the **Philippines,** copper coin minted in 1823.

## OCHOTA

**Spanish** copper coin of 18th Century. Worth 2 Quartos or 8 Maravedis.

## OCTAVO

A copper coin of **Mexico** in early 19th Century. Valued at 1/8 Real.

## OERE

Money of Scandinavian countries. More exactly Oera, Oere being plural form.
Variations of name - Ore, Ort.

**I.** - In **Sweden,** certain silver money had name Oertug in 14th and 15th Centuries. - See *Oertug*.

**16th Century** - As unit of account, Oere worth 1/32 Daler, 1/8 Mark, or 24 Penning.

**18th Century** - In Sweden, Oere was unit of account according to two systems: Silver Oere worth 1/192 Species Riksdaler, 1/32 Daler, 1/8 Mark, 1/4 Skilling, or 4 Oerlein. Copper Oere worth 1/576 Species Riksdaler, 1/32 copper Daler, 1/12 Skilling, 1/8 copper Mark, or 4 copper Oerlein. Silver Oere corresponded to 3 copper Oere; silver Oerlein to 3 copper Oerlein.
Oere also silver specie coin, and under name of Rundsteycken (round coin), a copper coin. - See *Rundstycken*.
Submultiple - 1/2 Oere.

**1855** (February 3rd) - Division of Riksdaler into 48 Skilling replaced by division into 100 Oere.

**II.** - Unit of account in **Denmark** and silver/copper money worth 24 Skilling and called Riksoere.

**18th Century** - Oere as unit of account worth ¼ Rigsdaler, 1.5 Mark, 12 Stuyver, 24 Skilling, 48 Fyrk, 72 Hvid, or 288 Penning.

**III.** - In **Norway,** Oere was submultiple (⅕) of Speciesdaler, equal to 24 Skilling in 1812. Also called Mark.

**IV.** - Under Scandinavian Monetary Union of December 18, 1872, Oere became sub-multiple (¹⁄₁₀₀) of Danish Krone, Norwegian Krone and Swedish Krona.

## OERTERER

Silver money created by Charles V in 1524 as money of **Holy Roman Empire.** Worth ¼ Gulden.

## OERTUG

Silver money minted in **Sweden** in 14th and 15th Centuries. Equivalent to Pfennig. The ½ Oertug called Fyrk, or Fyrkar. Gave rise to Oere. - See *Oere.*

## OITAVA

Gold money in **Brazil** minted in 19th Century: 3.585 grams 917 fine, or 3.29 grams fine gold.

**1822** - Exchange rate of Oitava raised from 1,600 to 1,777 Reis.

**1833** (October 8th) - Exchange rate: 2,500 Reis.

**1846** (September 11th) - Exchange rate: 4,000 Reis or 4 Milreis.

## OKINAWA

See *Ryukyu Islands.*

## OMAN

Predecessor - See *Muscat and Oman.*

**1970** (July 25th) - Oman became new name for Muscat and Oman. For currency unit, see *Rial Saidi.*

## ONCIA

Old unit of weight which became money.

Origin of name - From Greek *oine,* name for ace in game of dice; Latin *unica,* 12th part of a unit.

Variations of name - Unica, Onza.

**I.** - In **Sicily** and in southern **Italy,** bronze bar worth 1/12 Litra. - See *Litra.*

**18th and 19th Centuries** - Until unification of Italy, unit of account. Equivalent to 2.5 Scudi, 5 Fiorini, 30 Tari, 60 Carlini, 450 Ponti, 600 Grani or 3,600 Piccioli.

**II.** - Gold coin of **Naples** and **Sicily** in 1793. Weight: 4.4 grams 909 fine, or 4 grams fine gold. Exchange rate: 30 Tari. Originally equal to Oncetta of Naples.

**1818** - Value reduced to 1/2 Oncetta.

**III.** - Silver coin of **Malta** in early 18th Century. Equal to 30 Tari or 2 Scudi.

**IV.** - For **Spain** and **Spanish Colonies,** see *Onza.*

**V.** - For Rome, see *Uncia.*

**VI.** - For Morocco, see *Ukkia.*

## ONLIK

**I.** - Silver coin of **Turkey** minted in 19th Century: 12.027 grams 830 fine, or 9.98 grams fine silver. Value: 10 Para.

**II.** - In **Egypt,** copper coin of late 16th Century. Valued at 10 Aspers.

**1845-1877** - Silver/copper coin.

**1877-1899** - Silver coin valued at 10 Paras.

**III.** - In **Tripoli,** silver/copper coin equal to 1/4 Ghrush in early 19th Century.

## ONZA

**I.** - Gold coin in **Spain.** Also called Quadruple. Worth 4 Doubloons or 8 Escudos. Issued under Philip III (1598-1621).

**II.** - Gold coin of **Spanish America.** Also called Doubloon.

**III.** - Gold coin of **Mexico.** Also called Quadruple. Exchange rate: 16 Piasters.

**IV.** - In **Argentina,** gold coin used at end of 19th Century. Weight: 27.06 grams 875 fine, or 23.68 grams fine gold. Exchange rate: 16 Pesos.

**V.** - Same coin used in **Uruguay** until 1854. Called Once de la Plata.

**VI.** - In **Bolivia,** gold coin minted in small quantities after 1863. Weight: 23 grams 900 fine, or 20.7 grams fine gold. Exchange rate varied according to price of gold. Worth 4 Doubloons or 8 Escudos.

## ORT

See *Oere.*

## OSELLA

Money of **Venice**, first silver, occasionally gold, finally silver/copper.

Variation of name - Oselle.

**1521 -** Minted for first time to replace gift of wild ducks (uccelli) usually offered by Doge to nobles of Republic at Christmas.

**18th Century -** Exchange rate: 3 Lire 18 Soldi.

## OSTMARK

Monetary unit of **East Germany.** - See *Mark German Democratic Republic.*

# PA'ANGA

Monetary unit of **Tonga.** Divided into 100 Seniti. Australian Dollar subsidiary coinage circulates beside Tonga coinage.

Note-issuing authority - Tonga Treasury.

Variation of name - Tonga Dollar.

Predecessors - See *Tonga* and *Pound Tonga.*

**1966** (February 14th) - Adoption of decimal currency system following similar move by Australia. Creation of new monetary unit:
>1 Pa'anga = 1 Australian Dollar
>1 Pa'anga = 1.12 U.S. Dollars

# PACHA

In **India,** particularly in Mogul Empire and Kingdom of Gujarat, copper money.

Variation of name - Pecha, Pessa. - Cf. *Pice.*

Multiple - Indian Rupee, with exchange relationship varying according to location.

Submultiples - Cowrie shells of Maldive·Islands. - See *Cowrie:*
>1 Pacha = 50 to 60 Cowries

Badam, almond imported from Asia Minor and Persia. - See *Badam:*
>1 Pacha = 40, 44 or 68 Badams

# PACHANO

In **Venezuela,** gold coin worth 100 Bolívares. Pachano never circulated.

# PAGODA

**I.** - In **India** (Southern States, Hindu monetary system), gold money containing average of 2.66 grams fine gold. It had, in general, exchange rate of 3.6 Rupees.

Origin of name - First Portuguese explorers called all gold coins with image of a god, Pagoda.

Variation of name - Hun, a native term.

Minting of Pagodas in India by several European nations: by English at Fort Saint George; by Dutch at Pulicat; by French, from 1705 to 1789 at Mint of Pondicherry.

**II.** - Unit of account and copper coin in **Madras** equal to 36 Fanams. Value constantly changed.

**III.** - Silver money in some **Indian** kingdoms.

## PAHLEVI

**I.** - Multiple (100) of Rial, monetary unit of **Persia** then **Iran.**
Origin of name - From Mohammed Reza Shah Pahlevi, founder of ruling dynasty of Iran.
Variation of name - Pahlavi.
**II.** - Gold coin in **Persia** then **Iran,** minted in 5, 2, 1, 1/2 and 1/4 denominations.
**1927-1930** - 1 Pahlevi = 1.90 grams 900 fine, or 1.71 grams fine gold.
**1932-1955** - 1 Pahlevi = 8.10 grams 900 fine, or 7.27 grams fine gold.
　　Did not constitute legal tender.

## PAI

Early unit of account in **Siam.** Corresponded to 2 Clam, 1/2 Song Pai, 1/4 Fuang, 1/8 Salung, 1/32 Tical, 1/128 Tael, 1/2,500 Catty.
Variation of name - Paye, Phai, Pynung, Paje.
**End of 19th Century** - Minted in bronze.

## *PAKISTAN*

Predecessors - See *India, Rupee India.*
**1948** (April 1st) - Adoption of independent money. - See *Rupee Pakistan.*

## *PALESTINE*

Persian, Greek, Roman, Byzantine, then Arabic monies.
**11th to 13th Century** - Circulation of Bezants, Arabic Dinars, and Draham (Singular: Dirham).
　　Adopted and copied by Crusaders. Introduction of Western specie monies: Denier, Obol, Pite, silver Gros.
**16th Century to 1918** - Turkish domination and use of Turkish monies. - See *Turkey.*
**1918** - Egyptian Pound replaced Turkish currency. Simultaneous circulation of British subsidiary coinage. - See *Pound Egypt.*
**1927** (November 1st) - Creation of independent monetary system for Palestine and Transjordan. - See *Pound Palestine.*
**1928** (March 31st) - Egyptian Pound ceased to be legal tender.
**1948** (May 14) - Following expiration of British Mandate, part of Palestine became independent Israel. - See *Israel.*
**1950** (April 24th) - Arab Palestine became part of Jordan. - See *Jordan.*

# PANAMA

**16th to 19th Century** - Circulation of Spanish and Mexican silver Piasters.

**Before 1904** - Under rule of Colombia. - See *Peso Colombia.*

**Since 1904** - Independent republic. Simultaneous circulation of U.S. Dollars and silver Balboas. - See *Balboa.*

# PANAMA CANAL ZONE

Circulation of U.S. Dollars of 100 Cents.

# PAO CH'AO

Paper money of value issued in **China** several times.

**650** - First issue by T'angs of rectangular paper notes, worth 10,000 copper Yuan Pao. Exact name: Ta T'ang Pao Ch'ao (paper money of value of the Great T'angs).

**841 and 846** - Second issue of banknotes, worth 1,000 and 9,000 copper Yuan Pao. Exact name: Ta T'ang Pang-hing Pao Ch'ao (paper money of value issued for general circulation by the Great T'angs).

**1287** - New issue. Exact name: Che Yuan Pao Ch'ao. Small paper money of 5 Wen to 2 Kwan.

**1374** - Issue of banknotes by Mings, in paper made from mulberry tree. Exact name: Ta Ming t'ong Pao Ch'ao (paper money issued by the Great Mings). From 100 Wen to 1 Kuan.

**1394** - In order to support value of these banknotes, use of copper Tsien forbidden.

**1403** - Monetary usage of gold and silver bars forbidden.

**1436** - Depreciation of paper accelerated. Partial return to use of silver.

**1488** - Elimination of Pao Ch'ao.

# PAOLO

Unit of account and money in **Italy** before unification.

Origin of name - Pope Paul.

Variations of name - Paul, Paule.

Plural - Paoli.

**I.** - In **Papal States** (Rome), unit of account worth 1/16 Ducato di Camera, 1/10 Scudo Romano, 1/3 Testone, 10 Baiocchi, 50 Quattrini, 100 Mezzi Quattrini. Minted in silver/copper.

**II.** - In Grand Duchy of **Tuscany,** unit of account worth 1/3 Testone, 2/3 Lira, 8 Crazie, 13.33 Soldi di Lira, 40 Quattrini, 160 Denari di Lira. Minted in silver/copper until 1859. In Leghorn called Reale.

**III.** - Early unit of account in **Ancona**. Worth 1/10 Scudo, 2 Soldi, 8 Bolognini, 10 Baiocchi, 24 Denari.

**IV.** - Early unit of account and silver/copper money in **Bologna**. Worth 1/2 Lira, 10 Soldi, 60 Quattrini, or 120 Denari.

## PAPAL STATES

**Before 8th Century** - See *Rome*.

**9th Century** - Minting of silver Carolingian Denier. Carolingian system gave rise to Lira of 20 Soldi or 240 Denari. - See *Lira*.

**13th and 14th Centuries** - Senate of Rome minted silver Grosso, then Fiorino, or gold Zecchino, copying those of Venice.

**15th Century** - Popes reminted these coins plus Giulio and Carlino. Fiorino, or Zecchino, generally called Ducato di Camera.

**End of 15th Century** - Appearance of copper Quattrino.

**Beginning of 16th Century** - Minting of silver Testone. Circulation of gold Ducato.

**17th Century** - Minting of Quadruple Ducati.

**18th Century** - Units of account: Scudo Romano of 10 Paoli or Giuli, 100 Baiocchi, 500 Quattrini, 1,000 Mezzi Quattrini; Scudo de Stampa d'Oro; Ducato di Camera. Specie monies:

> In gold - Doppia or Pistole, Scudo d'Oro, Zecchino
> In silver - Piastra Vecchia, Scudo Romano, Testone, Papetto
> In silver/copper - Paolo or Giulio, Carlino, Baiochella
> In copper - Baiocco, Quattrino

**1798 to 1801** - Roman Republic minted silver Scudo, Baiocco, Quattrino.

**1835 (January 11th)** - Adoption of decimal system. Minting of gold 10, 5 and 2.5 Scudi (later 1 Scudo) and silver Scudo (100 Baiocchi), Testone (30 Baiocchi), Papetto (20), Paolo (10), Grosso (5).

**1866** - Pius IX minted gold Lira coins of 100, 50, 20 and 10 and silver Lira coins of 5, 2½, 2 and 1; copper Soldo coins of 4, 2 and 1 and copper Centesimo and Baioccone.

**1867 (February)** - Link to Latin Monetary Union. - See *Union Latine*.

**1870** - After unification, Italian monetary system. - See *Italy*.

**1929** - Agreement between Italy and Holy See creating Vatican City. - See *Vatican* and *Lira Vatican*.

## PAPETTO

In **Rome**, in Papal States, silver money as legal tender worth 2 Paoli or 20 Baiocci. Weight: 5.3 grams 906 fine, or 4.8 grams fine silver.

Origin of name - From Italian *papa* (Pope).

Variations of name - Papeta, Papet.

Plural - Papetti.


# PARA

**I.** - Unit of account and specie money in **Turkey**.

Variations of name - Parat, Parasi, Parales.

**18th Century** - Unit of account Para represented $1/40.000$ Juik, $1/20.000$ Beutel, $1/40$ Piastre, $3/10$ Timmin. Was equal to 2.5 Minas, or 3 Aspers.
As specie money, Para was light silver coin. Also called Medino. Exchange rate: 3 Piastres.

**1881** - Monetary reform. Para, equal to $1/40$ Piastre, became $1/4.000$ Turkish Lira, new monetary unit.

**1929** - With Piastre becoming Kurus, Para worth $1/40$ Kurus, and $1/4.000$ Turkish Lira. - See *Lira Turkey.*

**II.** - Unit of account in **Egypt** in 18th Century. Generally called Medino. Valued at $1/25.000$ Beutel, $1/33$ Piastre, 3 Aspers, 6 Forlis, 8 Burbes, or 12 Falle.

**III.** - In **Cyprus**, former submultiple of Cyprus Pound ($1/7.200$) and of Cyprus Piastre ($1/40$).

**IV.** - In **Serbia** in 1867, submultiple ($1/100$) of Serbian Dinar.

**1883** - Nickel coins of 5 and 10 Paras minted.

**V.** - In **Montenegro**, from 1902 to 1910, submultiple ($1/100$) of Krone. Also called Heller. Local minting of coins of 10 and 20 Para in nickel, of 1 and 2 Para in bronze.

**1910-1919** - Submultiple ($1/100$) of Perper.

**VI.** - In **Yugoslavia**, submultiple ($1/100$) of Yugoslav Dinar. - See *Dinar Yugoslavia.*

**VII.** - In **Tripoli (Libya)**, Para worth $1/800$ Mahbub, or $1/100$ Qurush.

**VIII.** - In **Russia**, copper coin issued in 1771 and 1772 for Moldavia and Wallachia. Equal to 3 Dengi. Double Para equal to 3 Kopeks.


# *PARAGUAY*

**16th and 19th Century** - Circulation of Spanish and Mexican silver Piasters. - See *Spanish America.*
In Jesuit community of Paraguay, moneyless economy.

**19th Century** - Use of Argentine Peso, which had full power of legal tender, and of silver Paraguayan Peso, derived from Piaster and sometimes called Patagon. - See *Peso Paraguay.*

**1943** (November) - Elimination of Argentine Peso and substitution of Guaraní for Peso at rate of 1 Guaraní for 100 Pesos. - See *Guaraní.*

## PARALI

Subdivision ($^1/_{28}$) of silver Leu of **Romania** before adoption of decimal system, when it was replaced by Banu ($^1/_{100}$ Leu).


## PARDAO

**I.** - In **Goa** (Portuguese India), unit of account used in 18th Century. Pardao equalled 4 Good Tangas, or 5 Bad Tangas, 16 Good Vintems or 20 Bad Vintems, 240 Reis, 300 Good Bazaruccos or 360 Bad Bazaruccos.
Silver coin, also called Pardao, Pardao-Serafin, or Pardao-Xeraphin. Circulated in Goa and on Malabar coast.
Multiples of Pardao (12, 8, 4, and 2) minted in gold in 1818 under name of Saint Thomas (Santo Thomé).

**II.** - **Spanish** Piaster, called Pardo Real or Pardao de Reales, in Goa.

**III.** - Silver money having legal tender status in **Mozambique** in 18th Century. Value: 200 Reis.


## PARDAW

Unit of account in the Kingdom of Achin in **Sumatra.** Worth ¼ Tayell, 4 Mas, 16 Koupan or 6,400 Cash.


## PARISIS

In **France,** system of accounting used in royal domains, then supplanted by Tournois system. Coins minted on basis of this system. - See *Livre Parisis, Sous, Denier.*
1 Livre Parisis = 20 Sous Parisis = 240 Deniers Parisis =
25 Sous Tournois = 300 Deniers Tournois

Origin of name - From Paris.

**1311** - Denier Parisis put into concrete form under name Bourgeois. - See *Bourgeois.*

**1315-1411**· - Issue of Mailles Parisis. - See *Maille.*

**1329** - Minting of gold Parisis (7.41 grams) worth 1 Livre Parisis or 25 Sous Tournois. Repudiated in 1336.

**1346** - Minting of Double Parisis in silver/copper. Worth 2 Deniers Parisis.

**1360** - Denier Parisis in silver called Petit Parisis (1.27 grams 165 fine, or 0.21 grams fine silver).

**1361** - Sou Parisis took form of pure silver Gros.

**Under Charles VIII** - Last minting of Denier Parisis.

**Under Charles IX** - Last minting of Sou Parisis.

**Under Louis XIV** - Definitive demonetization of Parisis specie money.

# PARPAGLIOLA

In Duchy of **Milan,** silver/copper money worth 2.5 Soldi.

Variations of name - Parbayolle, Parbajollo.


# PATACA

Silver and copper money as well as unit of account in **Portugal** similar to Spanish Piaster. Used also in Colonies.

Origin of name - From Arabic *ba taca,* for *bon ataca* "father of the window," because Arabs regarded Pillars of Hercules appearing on Spanish Piasters as a window frame.

Variations of name - Patacon, Patagon, Pattacon, Patacao, Pataga, Pataque.

**I. - Portuguese** silver coins valued at 320 Reis in 17th Century. Coins of 2 Patacas and ½ Pataca also existed.

**II. -** In **Portuguese Colonies,** silver coin referred to as Patachine. Worth 6 good Tangas or 360 Reyes (Reis).

**III. -** In **Java,** specie money worth 6 Mas or 24 Cash.

**IV. -** In **Brazil,** silver coin worth 320 Reis in 18th and 19th Centuries. Coins of ¼, ½ and 2 Patacas also existed.

**V. -** In **Algiers** and **Barbary,** units of account in 18th Century called Pataca Chica and Pataca Gourda. Former equal to 8 Muzunas or 320 Aspers; latter worth 24 Muzunas or 696 Aspers.

**VI. -** For **Macao** and **Timor,** see *Pataca Macao.*


# PATACA MACAO

Monetary unit of **Macao.** Divided into 100 Avos. Circulated in Timor from 1895.

Bank of issue - Banco Nacional Ultramarino, established in 1864.

Predecessor - See *Portugal.*

**1894 -** Special monetary unit created for Portuguese Colony of Macao. Linked to Portuguese Milreis:

    1 Pataca = 450 Reis

See *Milreis.*

**1911** (May 22nd) - Following adoption by Portugal of Escudo, Pataca linked to Escudo:

    1 Pataca = 5.60 Portuguese Escudos

- See *Escudo Portugal.*

Silver Pataca coin corresponded to Mexican silver Piaster: 26.95 grams 900 fine.

**1967** (November 27th) - Following Hong Kong Dollar devaluation, Macao devalued Pataca:

    1 Pataca = 4.75 Portuguese Escudos

    1 U.S. Dollar = 6.0527 Patacas

# PATAGON

**I.** - In **Netherlands,** unit of account in 18th Century. Worth $\frac{1}{20}$ Guilder or 16 Penning. Origin of name - Like Piefort, means heavy. Variation of name - Patacon.
- In Brabant, silver coin (22.2 grams fine) worth 50 Stuyver in 17th Century.
- In Flanders, identical with Rijksdaalder.
- In Liege and Westphalia, unit of account consisting of 4 Guilders, 8 Schelling, 80 Stuyver, 320 Ortje (Oord), 1,280 Penning. Also, silver coin of 22.1 grams fine. Cf. *Patard.*

**II.** - In **Switzerland,** silver coin of certain cantons from 18th to mid-19th Century.
- In Berne, exchange rate: 33 Batzen.
- In Geneva, where it was also called Ecu (27 grams 840 fine), exchange rate: 3 Livres.

**III.** - Name sometimes given to **Paraguayan** Peso at end of 19th Century. Coin of 4 Patagons (called Escudo) contained 6.73 grams of gold 875 fine. Coin of 1 Patagon ($\frac{1}{4}$ Escudo) contained 1.68 gram of gold 775 fine.

**IV.** - Name sometimes given to **Uruguayan** Peso minted in 1854. The Patagon (1 Peso or 5 Reales) contained 13.014 grams of silver 833 fine. Gold Patagon (Escudo) weighed 1.07 grams 875 fine.

# PATAQUE

Largest silver coin of **Turkey** (Ottoman Empire).

# PATARD

Monies of **Netherlands** and some fiefs of **Western Europe.**
Origin of name - From Peter (Pieter), coin bearing image of St. Peter with keys. - Cf. *Peter.*
Variations of name - Patar (Netherlands), Patac (Dauphiné and Avignon, probably influenced by Pataca).

**I.** - In **Netherlands,** silver money minted by Philip the Fair in 1496. Exchange rate: 2 Grooten.

**II.** - In **French Flanders** in 18th Century, Patard was small copper money equivalent to Liard.

**III.** - Money of **Dauphiné.** Worth $\frac{1}{2}$ Liard Dauphinois or 3 local Deniers.

**IV.** - Money of Popes of **Avignon.** Worth 2 French Deniers.
In France during 15th Century, words Patard and Patart designated money of small value.

# PATRICK

Copper money of **Ireland** issued in 1460. Equal to ½ Farthing.
Origin of name - From imprint of Apostle of Ireland.

# PATTE D'OIE

Silver coin minted in **France** under John II (the Good) in 1354. Exchange rate: 5 Deniers.

# PAVILLON D'OR

Gold money (5 grams fine) minted in **France** in 1329 by Philip VI and debased in 1330.
Origin of name - From canopy or tent under which King is seated.

# PECA

Gold coin of **Portugal.** Weighed 14.34 grams 916 fine. Equal to 6,400 Reis or 4 Escudos. Introduced in 1750 as reduced form of Dobra. Circulated in Brazil.

# PECCO

Early unit of account in **Java:** 1/10,000 Bahar, 1/1,000 Uta, 1/100 Catty, 1/10 Laxsan, or 25 Tayells, 50 Satas, 250 Mas, 1,000 Cash or 10,000 Candareens.
Plural - Peccoes.

# PECUNIA NUNDINATIONUM

Semi-official money in **Rome,** designed to remedy monetary instability. Used either in form of pure metal bars weighed for payments, or as unit of account for contracts.
Use of this "money of the marketplace" tolerated, along with official money. It circulated largely in Gaul, where it persisted after Germanic invasions.

# PENCE

I. - Submultiple of Pound Sterling (1/240), monetary unit of **Great Britain,** and of Shilling (1/12). After February 15, 1971, submultiple (1/100) of Pound Sterling and called New Pence.

**II.** - Submultiple ($1/240$) of Pounds of **Gambia, Malta** and **Nigeria,** and of Pound varieties no longer in existence. - See *Pound* currencies.

## PENGOE

Former monetary unit of **Hungary.** Divided into 100 Fillér.

Bank of issue - National Bank of Hungary.

Predecessors - Austrian monetary system from 1892 to 1919, Hungarian Korona from 1920 to 1924.

**1925** (November 4th) - Adoption of new monetary system:
    1 Pengoe = 12,500 Paper Koronas
    1 Pengoe = 263.1579 milligrams of fine gold

**1926** (December 27th) - Pengoe placed in circulation.

**1931** (July 17th) - Foreign exchange controls.

**1935** (March 7th) - Ban on private gold dealings. Confiscation of hoarded metal at rate of:
    6,000 Pengoe = 1 kilo of gold
    1 Pengoe = 166.66 milligrams of fine gold

**1935** (December 4th) - Purchases of foreign exchange by National Bank at premium of 38% or 50%, according to currency involved. Sales of foreign exchange by National Bank at surcharge of 41% or 53%.

**1936** (April 8th) - Consolidation of depreciation of Pengoe at 33.3%.

**1939** (January 15th) - Revaluation of gold:
    1 Pengoe = 175.44 milligrams of fine gold

**1941** (September 30th) - Second revaluation:
    1 Pengoe = 217.49 milligrams of fine gold
    1 U.S. Dollar = 3.46 Pengoe

**1944** (November) - Circulation rose tenfold to 11 billion Pengoe during war years.

**1944** (December) - Seige of Budapest. Start of wild inflation.

**1945** (January) - Russian Occupation. Issue of Red Army Pengoe and Russian Rubles:
    1 Ruble = 2.50 Pengoe

**1945** (April 1st) - 1 U.S. Dollar = 250 Pengoe in black market.

**1945** (September) - In territories regained by Yugoslavia, exchange of banknotes:
    1 Yugoslavian Dinar = 1 Pengoe

**1945** (October) - National Bank of Hungary began to set daily quotations for U.S. Dollar.

**1945** (December 31st) - 1 U.S. Dollar = 104,000 Pengoe (Official Rate)
    1 U.S. Dollar = 265,000 Pengoe (Black Rate)

**1946** (March 3rd) - 1 U.S. Dollar = 10.3 million Pengoe (Official Rate)

**1946** (May 31st) - 1 U.S. Dollar = 52.0 billion Pengoe (Black Rate)

**1945-1946** - As note circulation expanded (see table), denomination of banknotes increased accordingly. Printing of "Milpengoe" (for one million), "Bilpengoe" (for one billion) notes.

Finally, overprinting to create Pengoe notes denominated in trillions, called "blues" or "browns".

## PENGOE IN CIRCULATION

| At end of month | In millions of Pengoe |
|---|---|
| 1944, December | 11,000 |
| 1945, December | 765,400 |
| 1946, January | 1,646,000 |
| February | 5,238,000 |
| March | 34,000,000 |
| April | 434,000,000 |
| May | 65,589,000,000 |
| June | 6,277,000,000,000,000 |
| July 15 | 76,047,000,000,000,000,000 |

**1946** (July) - Creation of Adó-Pengoe (Tax-Pengoe or Index-Pengoe) worth 2 billion Bilpengoe.

**1946** (July 13th) - Demonetization of Pengoe. Adó-Pengoe provisionally retained for accounting purposes.

**1946** (July 26th) - Decree instituted new monetary unit to replace Pengoe. - See *Forint.*

## PENNI

Submultiple (¹⁄₁₀₀) of **Finnish** Markka and **Estonian** Mark.
Origin of name - See *Penny.*
Plural - Pennia (Finnish), Penni (Estonian).

## PENNING

**I.** - Early money of **Netherlands** equivalent to Denier. As unit of account, 1,920 Penning equal to 1 Livre, 768 to 1 Rijksdaalder, 320 to 1 Guilder, 96 to 1 Schelling, 16 to 1 Stuyver, 8 to 1 Groot, and 2 to 1 Duit. In Brabant, Penning divided into 3 Myten.

**II.** - Money of **Scandinavian** countries in 10th Century imitating English Penny.

**11th Century** - Depletion of silver Pennies in England by Danish. Minting of Scandinavian Penning of 0.9 grams silver. Progressive lightening with seasonal mintings (every year on September 29th at Saint-Michel).

**12th Century** - In **Norway,** Penning assumed form of Bracteate, thin leaf of metal inscribed only on one side.

**13th Century** - Penning was coin of poor quality silver/copper in Denmark. In Sweden it was a Bracteate.

**14th Century** - Danish Penning was copper, sometimes a Bracteate. In Sweden, minting of white Penning, Oertug, then (end of 15th Century), minting of its half, called Fyrkar.

**16th Century** - As unit of account in Sweden, Penning was 1/768 Daler, 1/192 Mark, 1/24 Oere.

**18th Century** - Unit of account Penning identical with copper Oere in Sweden. Was worth 1/576 Speciesdaler, 1/96 silver Daler, 1.32 copper Daler, 1/24 silver Mark, 1/12 Skilling, 1/8 copper Mark, 1/3 silver Oere. Computed as 1.33 silver Oerlein, or 4 copper Oerlein.

In Denmark and in Norway under Danish domination, Penning of account represented 1/1.152 Riksdaler, 1/288 Oere, 1/192 Mark, 1/24 Stuyver, 1/12 Skilling, 1/6 Fyrk, 1/4 Hvid.

# PENNY

Unit of account and coin in **Great Britain** and in countries whose currencies came from Pound Sterling: 1/12 Shilling, 1/240 Pound Sterling (until Febraury 15, 1971).

Origin of name - From Saxon *penig,* which gave rise to Dutch *Penning,* German *Pfennig.* Indo-European root *pet* (idea opening, unfolding) from which came Greek *patina* (bowl), English *pan* (earthen dish), German *Pfanne* (pot), Spanish *padilla,* Italian *padella,* French *poêle.* Allusion to round form of coins.

Plural - Pennies (several coins of one Penny); Pence (Penny multiples). Cf. *Pfennig, Penni, Penning, Fennigy.*

**10th Century** - Introduction into Saxon England by Normans of Carolingian system of accounting: Livre of 20 Sols or 240 Deniers.

**11th Century** - Minting of silver Pennies, which Danish invaders spread through Scandinavian countries.
Weight: 24 grains (or 1 Pennyweight) = 1.55 grams.

**13th Century** - Minting of Penny called Esterlin on Continent. - See *Esterlin.*

**14th to 16th Century** - Progressive reduction in weight of silver Penny, from 1,458 milligrams to 1,438 (in 1299, under Edward I), 1,315 (in 1343, under Edward III), 1,296 (in 1346), 1,166 (in 1351), 972 (in 1411, under Henry IV), 778 (in 1464, under Edward IV), 687 (in 1526, under Henry VIII), 648 (in 1523), 518 (in 1552, under Edward VI).

**End of 18th Century** - Silver coins: Crown of 60 Pence; 1/2 Crown of 30 Pence; Shilling of 12 Pence; Groat of 4 Pence; coins of 3 and 2 Pence, and of 1 Penny.
Copper coins: Halfpenny (1/2 Pence); Farthing (1/4 Pence).

**1774-1816** - Series of laws putting England on way toward gold standard at expense of silver coinage. - See *Shilling.*

**19th Century** - Penny was silver/copper coin.

**20th Century** - Penny was bronze coin (9.45 grams).

**1948** - Last minting of special Penny (of bronze) with coat of arms of Guernsey.

**1971** (February 15th) - Decimalization of Pound Sterling, and introduction of New Penny. - See *New Penny.*
As of this date, Malta, Nigeria and Gambia retained old Pound, Shilling and Pence (Penny).

# PENZA MONEY

Monetary tokens of **Soviet Union,** minted at Penza in June 1918 and circulated until 1921.

# PENZOZARI

Gold coin of **Persia** at end of 19th and beginning of 20th Century. Weight: 1.436 grams 900 fine, or 1.292 grams fine. Value: ½ Toman.

# PEPION

Silver money created in **Spain** by Ferdinand III (1230-1252). Valued at 1 Dinero, ¹/₁₂ Sueldo, or ¹/₁₈₀ gold Maravedi. Minting stopped in 1252 by Alphonso X, started again in 1258 under name Negro, or Prieto. - See *Negro.*
Variations of name - Papione, Pepione.

# PERPER

**I.** - Money of Republic of **Ragusa** issued in 1692 and in 1801. Equal to 12 Grossetti.
Variation of name - Perpero (Italian).
Plural - Perpera.
**II.** - Monetary unit of **Montenegro** from 1910 to 1919. Equal to Franc Germinal. Divided into 100 Para.
Minted in form of gold coins of 100, 20, and 10 Perpera:
　　　1 Perper = 322.9 milligrams of gold 900 fine, or 290.61 grams fine

# *PERSIA*

Originally, barter economy. Salaries payed in mutton and wine.
**6th Century B.C.** - Darius I organized coherent monetary system, with gold coin (Daric of 8.40 grams) and silver coin (Median Shekel of 5.60 grams):
　　　1 Daric = 20 Median Shekels
　　See *Daric* and *Shekel.*
**5th Century B.C.** - In order to impose payments in money in place of payments in barter, Darius I proposed following equivalents:
　　　1 sheep = 3 Shekels
　　　1 jar of wine = 1 Shekel
(This was Hebrew Shekel of 8.4 grams, which supplanted Median Shekel of 5.60 grams.)

**4th Century B.C.** - After conquest of Alexander, introduction of gold Macedonian Staters and Greek Drachmae. Latter remained money in circulation under Seleucidae and Parthian Kings until 30 B.C.

**1st Century A.D.** - Reduction in weight of silver coins, probably aligning to Roman Denarius.

**3rd to 7th Century** - Minting of silver Drachma by Sassanidae.

**7th to 13th Century** - Arab domination. - See *Arabia.*

**13th to 15th Century** - Mongol invasion and domination.

**16th to 17th Century** - Issue of gold Toman. Originally valued at 10,000 Dinars (unit of account money) and equal to 50 Abbasis.

**18th Century** - Unit of account: Toman of 10 Hor, 50 Abbasis, 100 Mahmudis, 200 Shahis, 1,000 Dinars-Bisti, 2,000 Kazbegi, or 10,000 Dinars.
Sometimes, Larin ($1/80$ Toman).
Specie monies:
      In gold - Cherassi, or Tola (20 Mahmudis), minted only at accession of princes
      In silver - Hasaer Denarie (10 Mahmudis), Daazajie (5 Mahmudis), Larin or Paenzajie
      In silver/copper - Abbasis (2 Mahmudis), Chodabende or Mahmudi, Shahi ($1/2$ Mahmudi)
      In copper - Kazbegi (5 Dinars)

**19th Century** - Toman, linked to $1/2$ Napoléon (10 Francs), worth 10 Kran, 200 Shahis or 10,000 Dinars.
Gold coins - Toman or Ashraffi
Silver coins - Kran, Shahi

**1877** - Adoption of silver standard. - See *Kran.*

**1932** (March 13th) - Adoption of gold standard and substitution of Rial for Kran. - See *Rial.*

**1935** (March 22nd) - Official name of modern Persia changed to Iran.


## *PERSIAN GULF STATES*

See *Bahrain, Qatar, Kuwait,* and *Trucial States.*


## *PERU*

Inca civilization. Economy without monetary system.

**16th Century** - Introduction of Spanish and Mexican silver Piasters.

**1598** - Opening of Mint of Lima which struck Peruvian Piasters copying Spanish and Mexican types. - See *Piaster Peru.*

**1675** (February 25th) - Mint of Lima authorized to mint gold monies: Doubloon (of 8 Escudos), Escudo. - See *Spanish America.*

**1821** - Independent Peru retained Spanish monetary system: Piaster (Peso) of 8 Reales, 5 Pesetas or 10 Dineros, and Toston of 4 Reales.

**1863** (February 14th) - Peruvian Piaster renamed Sol, and divided into 10 Dineros and 100 Centavos. - See *Sol Peru.*


## PESETA

I. - In **Ecuador,** coin worth 1/5 Sucre, 2 Decimos or 20 Centavos. Minted in silver (5 grams 900 fine, or 4.50 grams fine silver) at end of 19th Century. Equal to Franc Germinal.

II. - In **Zanzibar,** bronze coin worth about 1/4 Anna. Used at beginning of 20th Century.

III. - In **Costa Rica** before the monetary reform of 1896, Peseta corresponded to 1/4 Peso.

IV. - In **Peru,** silver coin equal to 1/5 Sol, 2 Dineros or 20 Centavos.

V. - For **Spain,** see *Peseta Spain.*


## PESETA GUINEANA

Monetary unit of **Equatorial Guinea.** Divided into 100 Centimos.

Origin of name - See *Peseta Spain.*

Bank of issue - Banco Central de Guinea Equatorial.

**1969** (October 12th) - Peseta Guineana replaced Spanish Peseta at par:
    1 Peseta Guineana = 12.6953 milligrams of fine gold
    1 U.S. Dollar = 70.00 Pesetas Guineanas


## PESETA HASSANI

Unit of account, then silver money in **Morocco** under Sultan Moulay-Hassan.

Bank of issue - Banque d'Etat du Maroc (State Bank of Morocco), created April 7, 1906.

**1881** - After introduction of Rial Hassani, general confusion with Spanish monetary system resulted in custom of accounting in Spanish Duro and Peseta Hassani:
    1 Duro = 5 Pesetas Hassani
See *Rial Hassani.*

**1900** - General debasement of Hassani coinage, establishing direct link to Spanish types. First minting of Peseta Hassani as basic monetary unit. Minted in Paris, Berlin and Birmingham, Peseta Hassani was 4.50 grams of fine silver:
    1 Peseta Hassani = 1/5 Duro Azizi = 1/4 Rial Hassani

**1906** (April 7th) - In Spanish Zone, Hassani silver currency became legal tender concurrently with Spanish money under Act of Algeciras.

**1910** - Issue of banknotes denominated in Peseta Hassani. Exchange rates of coins varied according to fluctuations in silver price.

**1914** - Exchange rate with French Franc given at:
　　　1 French Franc = 1.25 Pesetas Hassani

**1915** - Arnauné Commission proposed adoption of Algerian money, currently circulating in French Morocco.

**1917** (October 8th) - Rising silver prices. Decree fixed Peseta Hassani at par with French Franc:
　　　1 French Franc = 1 Peseta Hassani

**1917** (October 15th) - Continued rise in silver prices gave Peseta Hassani greater value than French Franc and caused former's disappearance from circulation. Resulted in declaration of freedom of exchange rate for silver money. French authorities began repurchasing silver coins at rates between 1.30 and 1.90 Francs per Peseta Hassani.

**1920** (March 19th) - Demonetization of Peseta Hassani to take place over following two months. Replaced by Metropolitan and Algerian Franc banknotes:
　　　1 Peseta Hassani = 2.50 French Francs
See *Franc Morocco*.
Peseta Hassani continued to circulate in Tangiers and Spanish Morocco, but gradually disappeared.
Exchange rate allowed to fluctuate with price of silver. Stabilized at about 10 Peseta Hassani = 1 U.S. Dollar by late 1920's in Spanish Morocco.

## PESETA SPAIN

Silver money, then monetary unit of **Spain.** Divided at first into 4 Reales, then 100 Centimes.

Origin of name - Diminutive of Spanish *peso* (weight).

Bank of issue - Before 1856, by Banco da Isabel and Banco Español de San Fernando. After 1856, by Banco de España (Bank of Spain) which absorbed provincial banks of issue in 1874.

Predecessor - See *Spain*.

**1772** (May 29th) - Ordinance of Aranjuez, lowering fineness of monies. Peseta was silver/copper coin of about 4.5 grams fine silver, worth 4 Reales. Corresponded to 1 French Livre Tournois; 5 Pesetas needed for 1 silver Duro.

**1808-1814** - Joseph Bonaparte retained Peseta of 4 Reales.

**1847** - In framework of reform of Isabella II, Peseta remained silver coin of 4 Reales.

**1859** (January 1st) - Adoption of Franc Germinal monetary system:
　　　1 Peseta = 4.50 grams fine silver
　　　1 Peseta = 290.322 grams fine gold
　　　1 Peseta = 1 Franc Germinal

**1864-1868** - In temporary monetary system with Escudo as monetary unit, Peseta circulated in form of silver coin(5.192 grams 810 fine) equal to 4 Reales.

**1868** (October 19th) - Peseta again became equal to Franc Germinal. Confirmation of bimetalism, without specific adherence to Latin Monetary Union. Depreciation of Peseta in wake of decline in price of silver bullion.

**1871** (March 21st) - Creation of gold coin of 25 Pesetas: 8.065 grams 900 fine.

**1877** (July 11th) - Suspension of free minting of silver, but silver retained full power of legal tender with banknotes convertible into silver. Silver Peseta (5 grams 835 fine) became worth more than its metal content.

**1884** - Forced parity. Inflation, and depreciation of Peseta.

**1914** (August 5th) - Banco de España authorized to issue banknotes above legal ceiling for sum corresponding to increase of metallic cover.

**1924** (March 6th) - Foreign exchange futures contracts forbidden.

**1930** - Creation of Foreign Exchange Office at Banco de España.

**1931** (May 18th) - Foreign exchange controls.

**1931** (November) - After advent of Republic, nationalization of Banco de España.

**1932** (January) - Overstamping of banknotes with motto "Spanish Republic."

**1936** (March 16th) - Foreign exchange controls tightened.

**1936** (May 29th) - Creation of Foreign Exchange Controls Fund.

**1936** (November 13th) - Creation of Nationalist Peseta by Government of Burgos.

**1937** (January 4th) - Peseta-Franco outlawed by Government of Valencia.

**1939** (September) - Official exchange rate:
    1 U.S. Dollar = 9.90 Pesetas

**1940** (April) - Official exchange rate:
    1 U.S. Dollar = 11.22 Pesetas

**1941** - Official exchange rate:
    1 U.S. Dollar = 11.085 Pesetas

**1942** (March 13th) - Law verifying accounts of National Bank and repudiating Republican banknotes.

**1946** (August 25th) - Preferential exchange rate for tourists:
    1 U.S. Dollar = 16.605 Pesetas

**1948** (December 3rd) - According to nature of merchandise:
    1 U.S. Dollar = 12.59-21.190 Pesetas (14 special export rates)
    1 U.S. Dollar = 13.14-27.375 Pesetas (8 special import rates)

**1949** (January) - Preferential exchange rate for tourists raised:
    1 U.S. Dollar = 25.00 Pesetas

**1949** (October 7th) - Revision of trade rates:
    1 U.S. Dollar = 13.14-28.47 Pesetas (11 special export rates)
    1 U.S. Dollar = 15.76-39.40 Pesetas (10 special import rates)

Official exchange rate applied to transactions and countries not entitled to special exchange rates:
    1 U.S. Dollar = 10.95/11.22 Pesetas (buying/selling)

**1950** (February) - Peseta on black market hit low of 60.00 per U.S. Dollar. Subsequent minor improvement.

**1950** (August 1st) - Institution of official free market, for financial transactions, tourism and for percentage of certain export proceeds:

    1 U.S. Dollar = 39.60 Pesetas

**1950** (October 18th) - Regrouping of exchange rates:

    1 U.S. Dollar = 13.14-32.85 Pesetas (12 special export rates)

    1 U.S. Dollar = 16.425-32.664 Pesetas (6 special import rates)

    1 U.S. Dollar = 39.84/40.11 Pesetas (official free rate for remaining percentages of specified exports, other authorized imports, invisibles and capital)

According to merchandise, percentages of exchange for imports obtained in official free market.

**1951** (November 1st) - Revision of exchange rate system. Official buying and selling rates applied only to government transactions. Right to retain portion of export proceeds for imports revoked:

    1 U.S. Dollar = 21.90 Pesetas (exports not listed in any special group and exchange receipts in currencies not specified)

    1 U.S. Dollar = 23.673-37.875 Pesetas (Group 1-5 export rates)

    1 U.S. Dollar = 16.425-32.55 Pesetas (Group A-E import rates)

    1 U.S. Dollar = 39.63/39.65 Pesetas (invisibles, capital and for all other imports)

Export rates based on percentages of 90%, 70%, 50%, 30%, and 10% at 21.90 Pesetas and the remainder at official free rate.

**1953** (September) - Official free rate reduced:

    1 U.S. Dollar = 38.95 Pesetas

**1956** (March) - For collection of customs duties, exchange rate changed from 35.77 to 71.54 Pesetas per U.S. Dollar.

**1957** (April 5th) - Revision of exchange system:

    1 U.S. Dollar = 10.95/11.22 Pesetas (official basic buying and selling rates for government transactions)

    1 U.S. Dollar = 42.00/42.27 Pesetas (official buying and selling rates for all transactions not subject to other rates)

    1 U.S. Dollar = 31.00-45.00 Pesetas (export rates based on official rate less taxes of 6 and 11 Pesetas, or plus premium of 3 Pesetas)

    1 U.S. Dollar = 46.00 Pesetas (noncommercial Dollar remittances from the U.S.)

**1958** (April 18th) - New revisions as range of export rates widened:

    1 U.S. Dollar = 31.00-50.00 Pesetas (resulting from official

rate less taxes of 6 and 11 Pesetas, or plus premiums of 3, 6, and 8 Pesetas)

1 U.S. Dollar = 52.00 Pesetas (official rate plus 10 Pesetas premium for certain noncommercial Dollar remittances from U.S.)

1 U.S. Dollar = 52.77-126.27 Pesetas (official rate plus taxes and commissions of 25%, 30%, 40%, 50%, or 200%)

**1958** (September 24th) - Temporary tax (fondo de retorno) imposed on certain imports in addition to existing taxes.

**1959** (January) - Peseta on black market hit low of 62.50 per U.S. Dollar.

**1959** (April 10th) - Rate for certain noncommercial Dollar remittances from U.S. changed to 56.00 Pesetas per U.S. Dollar.

**1959** (July 17th) - Devaluation and revision of exchange rates. Multiple rate system abolished. New official rate registered with International Monetary Fund, applied to all transactions:

1 Peseta = 14.8112 milligrams of fine gold

1 U.S. Dollar = 60.00 Pesetas

**1967** (November 20th) - New devaluation following Pound Sterling:

1 Peseta = 12.6953 milligrams of fine gold

1 U.S. Dollar = 70.00 Pesetas

**1970** (March) - Peseta hit record low of 74.50 per U.S. Dollar on black market.


## PESEWA

Submultiple (¹⁄₁₀₀) of Cedi, monetary unit of **Ghana.**


## PESO

**I.** - Early **Spanish** unit of account: 10 Pesos = 12 Ducats.

**II.** - Name given to Piasters of **Spain** and **Spanish America.**

**III.** - Silver coin of **Spain** and various countries under Spanish control. - See following varieties.


## PESO ARGENTINA

Monetary unit of **Argentina,** also called Piaster. Divided into 8 Reales, then (after 1875) into 100 Centavos.

Bank of issue - Since 1935, by Banco Central de la República Argentina (Central Bank of Republic of Argentina).

Predecessors - See *Spanish America* and *Argentina.*

**1813** - Independent Argentina retained Spanish monetary system with Peso of 8 Reales (27.06 grams silver 902 fine, or 24.43 grams fine silver).

**1821** - Circulation of disks of tin plate, marked with name of issuer.

**1826** - Issue of banknotes of Banco de Descuentos, accepted by Government offices. Increase of paper money at forced parity.

**1854** - Minting of copper Centavos.

**1875** - Reduction in price of silver bullion, which resulted in depreciation of silver coins. Adoption of gold standard (law of September 29, 1875):

> 1 Peso Fuerte = 1.666 grams gold 900 fine, or 1.499 grams
> fine gold

Peso Fuerte divided into 10 Decimos, 100 Centavos, or 1,000 Milesimos. Minting foreseen for gold coins (Colón of 10 Pesos Fuertes) and silver (Peso de Plata of 27.11 grams 900 fine) with legal tender status limited to 20 Pesos. Forced parity maintained for depreciated banknotes.

**1881** (November 5th) - Argentine Peso linked to 5 Franc coin:

> 1 Argentine Peso = 1,451.61 milligrams fine gold
> 1 Argentine Peso = 22.50 grams fine silver

Minting of silver Argentine Peso (25 grams 900 fine) and of gold Argentine Peso (1.6916 grams 875 fine). Minting of multiples of Argentine Peso: Medio (2.5 Pesos), Argentino (5 Pesos), Onza (16 Pesos).

- See *Medio, Argentino, Onza.*

**1885** - Forced parity. Depreciation of currency.

**1887** - Inflation, and depreciation of currency.

**1891** - Creation of Caja de Conversion (Conversion Office) for exchanging paper Argentine Pesos (Moneda Nacional) for gold (Peso Oro).

**1899** - Conversion law creating a new monetary unit:

> 1 paper Argentine Peso = 0.44 gold Argentine Peso
> 1 Argentine Peso = 638.7084 milligrams fine gold

Coexistence of two units of account: gold Peso and paper Peso. Issue entrusted to Caja de Conversion. New depreciation of currency.

**1914** (August 9th and September 30th) - Suspension of gold standard.

**1927** (April 25th) - Restoration of gold standard:

> 1 U.S. Dollar = 2.36 gold Argentine Pesos

**1929** (December 16th) - Suspension of convertibility. Depreciation of currency.

**1931** (October 10th) - Foreign exchange controls. De facto stabilization:

> 1 U.S. Dollar = 1.71 gold Argentine Pesos

**1933** - After devaluation of U.S. Dollar, de facto stabilization in relation to Franc:

> 1 gold Argentine Pesos = 14.84 Francs Poincaré

**1933** (November 29th) - Stabilization on a new devalued base:

> 1 gold Argentine Peso = 12.36 Francs Poincaré
> 1 U.S. Dollar = 3.00 gold Argentine Pesos

Sale of foreign exchange to importers at auction.

**1934** (January 20th) - Adherence to Sterling Area:

1 Pound Sterling = 15.00 paper Argentine Pesos (buying rate)

Sale of currency by Exchange Control Commission at rates varying between 17.00 and 17.50 Argentine Pesos per Pound Sterling.

Fluctuating rates of exchange on free market.

**1935** (March) - Creation of Exchange Stabilization Fund.

**1935** (May 30th) - Creation of Banco Central de la República Argentina. Abolishment of sales of foreign exchange at auction. Revaluation of monetary gold stock:

1 gold Argentine Peso = 292.6 milligrams of fine gold

1 paper Argentine Peso = 0.201773 gold Argentine Peso

**1936** (December 10th) - Official price for surrender of foreign exchange reduced from 17.00 to 16.00 paper Argentine Pesos per Pound Sterling.

**1938** (November) - Official selling rate raised from 16.00 to 17.00 Argentine Pesos per Pound Sterling.

**1939** (August) - Stabilization on basis of U.S. Dollar:

1 U.S. Dollar = 3.36/4.22 Argentine Pesos (buying/selling)

Multiple exchange rates of 3.98 to 5.00 Argentine Pesos buying and 3.73 to 4.81 Argentine Pesos selling. Sale of foreign exchange at auction for nonessential imports.

**1943** (April) - Official selling rate lowered from 4.22 to 3.97 Argentine Pesos per U.S. Dollar.

**1948** (June) - Three buying rates and five selling rates, varying between 3.35 to 5.00 Argentine Pesos per U.S. Dollar.

**1949** (October 3rd) - New official rates of exchange after devaluation:

1 U.S. Dollar = 3.36/6.07 Argentine Pesos (buying/selling)

1 U.S. Dollar = 4.83/9.00 Argentine Pesos (multiple export rates)

1 U.S. Dollar = 3.73/13.22 Argentine Pesos (multiple import rates)

**1950** (July 19th) - Fluctuating rates of auction system for certain nonessential import payments replaced by fixed selling rate of 12.53 Argentine Pesos per U.S. Dollar. Revised periodically.

**1950** (August 28th) - Simplification of exchange rate system:

1 U.S. Dollar = 5.00 Argentine Pesos (for basic exports and essential imports)

1 U.S. Dollar = 7.50 Argentine Pesos (minor exports and most other imports)

Auction market terminated, and free market established for some marginal exports, luxury imports, invisible and capital transactions:

1 U.S. Dollar = 14.60 Argentine Pesos

**1952** (February 20th-November 25th) - Various mixed export rates created, ranging from 5.00 to 10.73 Argentine Pesos per U.S. Dollar. Fluctuating free market rate adjusted to 13.95 Argentine Pesos per U.S. Dollar.

**1953** - Additional export rates created, bringing range to 12.16 Argentine Pesos per

U.S. Dollar. Fluctuating free market changed to a controlled "free" market at level of 13.95 Argentine Pesos per U.S. Dollar.

**1955** (October 28th) - Three previous rates abolished. Devaluation to:

> 1 Argentine Peso = 49.371 milligrams of fine gold
> 1 U.S. Dollar = 18.00 Argentine Pesos

Four Export Peso rates maintained, ranging from 13.50 to 16.20 per U.S. Dollar. Import Peso rate at 18.00 per U.S. Dollar. Special Import Peso at Import Peso rate plus 20.00 Pesos (38.00) also operative. Later raised to fluctuating free market Peso plus surcharge of 20.00 and 40.00 Pesos.

Fluctuating free market Peso in existence for all other exports, imports, invisible and capital transactions.

Black markets, prevalent since 1931, practically disappeared.

**1957** (January 10th) - Par value of October 28, 1955 registered with International Monetary Fund.

**1958** (December 30th) - Currency reform abolished official rate and created free fluctuating rate as basis for all operations. Blocked Account (Cuenta Existente) also abolished.

**1959** (January 2nd) - Fluctuating free rate became operative at:

> 1 U.S. Dollar = 64.59 Argentine Pesos

Numerous changes in official peg followed. Export rates based on free rate plus taxes of 10% and 15%, and import rates based on free rate plus duty of 0%, 20%, 40% and 300%. Rates constantly revised by changing tax or duty percentage.

**1962** (March 19th-April 4th) - Exchange markets closed. Central Bank support for Argentine Peso withdrawn. De facto devaluation of fluctuating free rate to near 114.50 Argentine Pesos per U.S. Dollar. Official peg periodically lowered as currency depreciated.

**1964** (April) - Reintroduction of widespread exchange control regulations. Rebirth of parallel (black) market.

**1967** (March 13th) - Fluctuating free rate abolished, and exchange controls largely eliminated. New basic rate set at:

> 1 U.S. Dollar = 350.00 Argentine Pesos

Export and import taxes and duties reduced or removed. Parallel (black) market declined in importance.

**1970** (January 1st) - Creation of "heavy" Peso:

> 1 heavy Peso (Peso Fuerte) = 100 old Argentine Pesos
> 1 U.S. Dollar = 3.50 Argentine Pesos

De facto multiple rate structure still existed as result of export taxes and import surcharges according to category of commodity.

**1970** (June 18th) - Argentine Peso devalued:

> 1 U.S. Dollar = 4.00 Argentine Pesos

**1970** (October) - Adoption of inflationary policies. Introduction of exchange controls. Rebirth of black market dealings.

**1970** (December) - Argentine Peso hit historic low of 4.38 per U.S. Dollar in black market.

## PESO BOLIVIA

Monetary unit of **Bolivia.** Divided into 100 Centavos.

Bank of issue - See *Boliviano.*

Predecessor - See *Bolivia.*

**1963** (January 1st) - Creation of Peso at rate of:
    1,000 Bolivianos = 1 Peso
Official fluctuating free market divided into three operative rates:
    1 U.S. Dollar = 11.25/11.885 Pesos (public sector)
    1 U.S. Dollar = 11.865/11.910 Pesos (private sector)
    1 U.S. Dollar = 12.112 Pesos (commercial bank)

**1969** (October) - All export proceeds subject to surrender to Central Bank.

**1970** (December) - Unofficial Peso note dropped to low of 20.00 (20,000 Bolivianos) per U.S. Dollar.

## PESO CENTRAL AMERICA

Monetary unit of **United Provinces of Central America** (Guatemala, Costa Rica, Honduras, Nicaragua, El Salvador) from 1821 to 1847: 27.064 grams silver 902 fine, or 24.42 grams fine silver. Divided into 8 Reales.

Derived from Mexican Piaster.

Gave rise to Pesos of Guatemala, Costa Rica, Honduras, Nicaragua and El Salvador.

## PESO CHILE

Monetary unit of **Chile** until 1960. Divided into 8 Reales, then into 100 Centavos.

Bank of issue - Formerly by the State. Since January 11, 1926, by Banco Central de Chile (Central Bank of Chile).

Predecessor - See *Chile.*

**Beginning of 19th Century -** Circulation of Spanish and Mexican Piasters (24.42 grams of fine silver).

**1811 -** Forced parity for banknotes.

**1817 -** Independent Chile retained Spanish monetary system with Piaster, or Peso, of 8 Reales.

**1851** (January 9th) - Law creating silver Chilean Peso divided into 10 Decimos or 100 Centavos:
    1 Chilean Peso = 5.00 French Francs
    1 Chilean Peso = 25 grams of silver 900 fine, or 22.5 grams
                  fine silver

**1860 -** Reduction of 8% in weight of divisionary coins.

**1865 -** Forced parity under pressure. Banknotes accepted in payment of taxes.

**1876 -** Reduction in price of silver bullion forced depreciation of Chilean Peso.

**1878-1879** - War with Peru. Banknotes at forced parity, guaranteed by duties levied on export of nitrates. Depreciation of currency.

**1885** (February 11th) - Adoption of gold standard:
    1 Chilean Peso = 548.785 milligrams of fine gold
    1 Chilean Peso = 18 Pence
On this basis, minting of gold coins: 20 Chilean Pesos (see *Condor*), 10 Chilean Pesos (see *Doubloon*), 5 Chilean Pesos (see *Escudo*).
Peso minted in form of a silver coin of 20 grams 835 fine.

**1898** - Suspension of gold standard. Progressive lowering in value of Chilean Peso until 1915 (from 18 to 8 Pence). Recovery of Chilean Peso during war (to nearly 18 Pence).

**1910** - Fineness of gold coins lowered from 916 to 900 (Condor, Doubloon, Escudo).

**1925** (September 16th) - Stabilization of Chilean Peso with devaluation of 66.6%:
    1 Chilean Peso = 183.057 milligrams of fine gold
    1 Chilean Peso = 6 Pence

**1931** (July 30th) - Foreign exchange controls.

**1932** (April 20th) - Suspension of gold standard. Devaluation of 50%:
    1 Chilean Peso = 91.528 milligrams of fine gold
    1 Chilean Peso = 3 Pence

**1935** (January 1st) - New devaluation of 50%:
    1 Chilean Peso = 45.764 milligrams of fine gold
    1 Chilean Peso = 1½ Pence
Sharper depreciation of free exchange rates used for noncommercial transactions.

**1937** - Introduction of multiple exchange rates:
    1 U.S. Dollar = 19.37 Chilean Pesos (government transactions)
    1 U.S. Dollar = 25.38 Chilean Pesos (perferential exports)
    1 U.S. Dollar = 27.95 Chilean Pesos (official rate for all other exports)
    1 U.S. Dollar = 26.37 Chilean Pesos (free rate for noncommercial transactions)

**1939** - Exchange rates revised:
    1 U.S. Dollar = 19.37 Chilean Pesos (government transactions)
    1 U.S. Dollar = 25.00 Chilean Pesos (essential imports and exports)
    1 U.S. Dollar = 31.00 Chilean Pesos (nonessential and luxury imports)
    1 U.S. Dollar = 32.47 Chilean Pesos (free rate for noncommercial transactions)

**1946** (December 18th) - Parity registered with International Monetary Fund:
    1 Chilean Peso = 28.6668 milligrams of fine gold
    1 U.S. Dollar = 31.00 Chilean Pesos

**1948** (February) - Exchange rates revised:
    1 U.S. Dollar = 19.37 Chilean Pesos (government rate for receipts from principal mining companies)

       1 U.S. Dollar = 25.00 Chilean Pesos (preferential rate for imports of certain primary materials)

       1 U.S. Dollar = 31.00 Chilean Pesos (official rate for essential imports, nitrate exports, certain mining, agricultural and industrial exports)

       1 U.S. Dollar = 43.00 Chilean Pesos (bank rate for majority of imports)

       1 U.S. Dollar = 60.48 Chilean Pesos (free rate for noncommercial transactions)

**1950** (January 17th) - Exchange rates revised:

       1 U.S. Dollar = 31.10-50.10 Chilean Pesos (official rate for most imports)

       1 U.S. Dollar = 49.85-54.28 Chilean Pesos (for most exports)

       1 U.S. Dollar = 60.00-60.10 Chilean Pesos (commercial rate)

       1 U.S. Dollar = 75.82 Chilean Pesos (free rate for noncommercial transactions)

       1 U.S. Dollar = 150.00 Chilean Pesos (fluctuating gold market rate for sales of newly-minted gold and authorized luxury imports)

**1951-1952** - Periodic changes and additions to multiple rate structure.

**1953** (October 2nd) - Devaluation and new par value registered with International Monetary Fund:

       1 Chilean Peso = 8.07883 milligrams of fine gold

       1 U.S. Dollar = 110.00 Chilean Pesos

Numerous accessory or multiple rates existed based on par value. Among such rates were Mining Peso, Consular Peso, Copper Peso, Wool and Hide Peso, Seaweed Peso, Lentil Peso, and Wine Peso.

**1954** (March-May) - Most multiple rates abolished. A few special rates, such as for wine (170.00 Chilean Pesos) and iron ore (19.37 Chilean Pesos) exports remained in effect as did fluctuating free brokers' rate (220.00 Chilean Pesos) initially for travel receipts. Rate of 110.00 Chilean Pesos per U.S. Dollar remained for government payments and minor imports. Rates subsequently devalued (de facto) periodically.

**1954** (November 12th) - Banking rate changed from 110 to 200 Chilean Pesos per U.S. Dollar for most imports and exports.

**1955** (August) - Free market Chilean Peso rate reached all-time low of more than 800 per U.S. Dollar. By this time, Chile had experienced 3,000% increase in cost of living since 1940.

**1956** (April 16th) - New monetary constitution became effective, with dual official exchange rate system. Former official rate of 110 Chilean Pesos per U.S. Dollar inoperative.

Fluctuating free bank rate:

       1 U.S. Dollar = 490 Chilean Pesos (commodity transactions)

Fluctuating free brokers' rate:

1 U.S. Dollar = 535 Chilean Pesos (private capital dealings and some invisibles)

**1957** (January 19th) - All foreign exchange sales became subject to a tax.

**1958** (June) - Fluctuating rates deteriorated to 1,200 Chilean Pesos per U.S. Dollar, but improved near end of year.

**1958** (November 29th) - Exchange operations suspended.

**1959** (December 10th) - Banking free market rate now set by Central Bank and lowered from 837 Chilean Pesos to 989 Chilean Pesos per U.S. Dollar.

**1959** (January 20th) - Devaluation making banking rate 1,005 Chilean Pesos per U.S. Dollar.

**1959** (January 27th) - Banking and brokers' rates merged at 1,050 Chilean Pesos per U.S. Dollar.

**1960** (January 1st) - New "hard" currency unit created. - See *Escudo Chile.*


## PESO COLOMBIA

Monetary unit of **Colombia.** Divided into 100 Centavos.

Bank of issue - Banco de la República (Bank of the Republic) and the State (national banknotes).

Predecessor - See *Colombia.*

**1819** - Republic of Colombia retained Spanish monetary system with silver Peso of 8 Reales equal to Mexican Piaster (23.4356 grams of fine silver).

**1847** - Colombian Peso divided into 10 Reales or 100 Centavos.

**1871** (June 9th) - Silver standard linked to French 5 Franc coin:
1 Colombian Peso = 22.5 grams fine silver

**1880** - After decline in price of silver bullion, adoption of gold standard:
1 Colombian Peso = 5.00 French Francs
1 Colombian Peso = 1,451.61 milligrams of fine gold
Minting of gold coins on this monetary base: Double Condor (20 Colombian Pesos), Condor (10 Pesos), Doubloon (5 Pesos), Escudo (2 Pesos). - See *Condor, Doubloon, Escudo.*

**1886** (December 20th) - Suspension of convertibility.

**1899** - Revolution, inflation and depreciation of currency.

**1903** - Excess of banknotes absorbed by selling gold at auction. Temporary adoption of U.S. Dollar as monetary unit. Banknote issue by State.

**1905** - Convertion of paper Colombian Pesos into gold Pesos:
1 gold Colombian Peso = 100 paper Colombian Pesos

**1907** (June 12th) - Effective return to gold standard, with link to Pound Sterling:
1 Colombian Peso = 4 Shillings
1 Colombian Peso = 1,464.48 milligrams of fine gold
On this monetary base, minting of new gold coins 916 fine: 10 Pesos, 5 Pesos (Colombian Pound similar to English Sovereign).

**1909** - Creation of Junta de Conversion (Conversion Board), which began operations in January 1910.

**1910** - British gold coins made legal tender.

**1913** - Junta de Conversion directed by law to replace all paper money in circulation with gold Pesos at rate of 100 to 1.

**1914** - Suspension of gold standard.

**1923** - Restoration of gold standard at former parity. Currency issued by Banco de la República and State. Junta de Conversion ceased to operate.

**1931** (September 25th) - Suspension of gold standard. Foreign exchange controls introduced. Colombian Peso linked to U.S. Dollar:
　　　　1 U.S. Dollar = 1.05 Colombian Pesos

**1932** (January) - Tax of 1% levied on foreign exchange transactions.

**1933** - After de facto devaluation of U.S. Dollar, exchange rate modified several times.

**1935** - 1 U.S. Dollar = 1.75 Colombian Pesos.

**1935** (January) - Free market of Colombian Peso began operation for most transactions.

**1937** (April) - Creation of Exchange Stabilization Fund.

**1937** - Abandonment of fixed exchange rate. Free exchange rate maintained close to former official exchange rate.

**1940** (February) - System of preferential exchange rates for imports ranging from 1.782-1.98 Colombian Pesos per U.S. Dollar.

**1940** (November) - Tax on foreign exchange transactions raised to 3.85%.

**1944** (April) - Unification of preferential exchange rates:
　　　　1 U.S. Dollar = 1.817 Colombian Pesos
Official exchange rate remained
　　　　1 U.S. Dollar = 1.75 Colombian Pesos

**1946** (December 18th) - Parity registered with International Monetary Fund:
　　　　1 Colombian Peso = 507.816 milligrams of fine gold
　　　　1 U.S. Dollar = 1.75 Colombian Pesos

**1947** (July) - Tax on foreign exchange transactions raised to 4%.

**1948** (January and June) - Introduction of system of mixed rates for imports of nonessential products, resulting in variable exchange rates of from 2.001-2.282 Colombian Pesos per U.S. Dollar. Fluctuating Certificate Market rate of 2.738 Colombian Pesos per U.S. Dollar existed also.

**1948** (December 17th) - New parity registered with International Monetary Fund:
　　　　1 Colombian Peso = 455.733 milligrams of fine gold
　　　　1 U.S. Dollar = 1.95 Colombian Pesos

**1949** - Maintenance of basic exchange rate at 1.95 Colombian Pesos per U.S. Dollar, and of system of certificates for nonessential imports. Unified tax of 4% on all imports permitted at official exchange rate:
　　　　1 U.S. Dollar = 2.038 Colombian Pesos
In addition, remittance tax (6% to 30%) created mixture of rates ranging between 2.156 and 2.872 Colombian Pesos per U.S. Dollar. Latter (Fluctuating Exchange Certificate rate) applied to all exports not covered by official rate of 1.95 Colombian Pesos per U.S. Dollar.

**1950** (February 2nd-July 10th) - Revisions in multiple rate system. Official exchange for various imports obtained at 80%, 70% and 60% at 1.95 rate, remainder at Fluctuating Certificate rate. Remittance taxes of 6%, 12% and 26% were abolished; 4% stamp tax remained. In addition, some other transactions still subject to 6% or 30% remittance tax. Import rates ranged from 2.038 to 3.236 Colombian Pesos per U.S. Dollar. Export rates, also on mixing system, ranged from 2.1815 to 3.58 Colombian Pesos per U.S. Dollar, latter being Fluctuating Exchange Certificate rate. Noncommercial transactions took place at rates of 2.0185 Colombian Pesos per U.S. Dollar (certain foreign banking services), 3.158 Colombian Pesos (foreign diplomat payments) and 3.821 Colombian Pesos (certain invisibles such as foreign travel and emigrant remittances).

**1951** (March 20th) - Complete revision of exchange and import control system. Basic buying/selling rate depreciated to 2.50/2.51 per U.S. Dollar. Exchange taxes simplified, and basis for computation changed to 3% tax on rate of 2.50 Colombian Pesos per U.S. Dollar. Coffee rate of 2.09 Colombian Pesos per U.S. Dollar existed based on 25% at 2.50 rate and remainder at 1.95 rate.

**1951** (October 29th) - Revision of percentage of exchange proceeds from coffee exports raised from 25% to 40% at 2.50 rate, then by 1½% a month until rate of 2.50 Pesos applied to total proceeds.

**1953** (July 22nd) - Free trading in gold established. Fluctuating rate for gold exports initially at 3.16 Colombian Pesos per U.S. Dollar. Also applied to nontrade payments.

**1954** (February 19th) - Free importation of gold.

**1955** (May 13th) - Fluctuating Free Market rate (4.17 Colombian Pesos per U.S. Dollar) created for most import categories and nontrade payments. Taxes of 10% to 100% based on 2.50 Colombian Pesos per U.S. Dollar applied depending on category. Periodically changed.

**1956** (May) - Revaluation of monetary gold stock of Banco de la República at 2.50 Colombian Pesos per U.S. Dollar.

**1956** (November 30th) - Free Market changed to Free Certificate Market (Titulo de Divisas), with fluctuating rate initially set at 6.50 Colombian Pesos per U.S. Dollar.

**1957** (June 17th) - Monetary reform. Former basic rate of 2.50 Colombian Pesos per U.S. Dollar abolished. Certificate Market rate (5.42 Colombian Pesos per U.S. Dollar) revamped and based on already existing Titulo de Divisas. Fluctuating Free Market rate (6.20 Colombian Pesos per U.S. Dollar) instituted for unregistered capital and invisibles.

**1958-1964** - Fixed Certificate rate de facto devalued numerous times: 6.10 to 7.30 Colombian Pesos per U.S. Dollar. Auction Certificate rate and other rates, based on Fixed Certificate rate, existed.

**1965** (September 2nd) - Official exchange market modified. Banco de la República sold foreign exchange at:

　　　　1 U.S. Dollar = 9.00 Colombian Pesos (preferential rate for certain imports and certain government payments)

　　　　1 U.S. Dollar = 13.50 Colombian Pesos (intermediate rate

for export proceeds other than coffee, registered
foreign investment and foreign loans)
In addition, petroleum rate (7.67 Colombian Pesos), coffee rate (8.50 Colombian Pesos and gradually depreciated) and Free Market rate (18.27 Colombian Pesos) for invisibles and other capital existed.

**1965** (September 8th) - Auction system for sale of official exchange abolished.

**1966** (August 21st) - Payments for imports shifted from preferential rate to intermediate rate.

**1966** (December 1st) - Capital Market, fixed at 16.25/16.30 Colombian Pesos per U.S. Dollar, replaced Free Market. Transactions made only through Banco de la República or authorized banks.

**1967** - Institution of exchange controls and creation of black market with U.S. Dollar rising to 21.00 Colombian Pesos in February.

**1967** (March 22nd) - Revision of currency system. Fluctuating Certificate Market rate (15.76/15.82 Colombian Pesos) replaced Intermediate rate and governed some exports and imports other than into free ports. Fixed rate of 9.00 Colombian Pesos per U.S. Dollar applied to crude oil purchases. Coffee exports based on Certificate Market rate less 23%, with percentage gradually reduced. Capital Market rate used for exports from free ports, imports into free ports and most capital transactions. All other exports subject to average Certificate Market rate for previous month plus 15% tax.

**1968** (June 1st) - Capital Market abolished, all exchange transactions conducted through Certificate Market (16.18/16.95 Colombian Pesos). The 9.00 Colombian Peso per U.S. Dollar rate still applied to crude oil purchases.

**1969-1970** - Slow, but constant deterioration of Certificate Market rate to 19.15 Colombian Pesos per U.S. Dollar in December 1970, when black market rate hit record low of 24.50 Colombian Pesos per U.S. Dollar.

## PESO COSTA RICA

Monetary unit of **Costa Rica** from 1847 to 1896. Divided into 8 Reales, then into 100 Centavos (after 1864).

Predecessors - See *Costa Rica, Piaster Mexico,* and *Peso Central America.*

**1847** - With separation from United Provinces of Central America, Costa Rican Peso remained similar to Peso of Central America: 27.064 grams 902 fine, or 24.42 grams fine silver. Double Peso called Escudo; quarter Peso called Peseta. Minting of some gold Escudos.

**1864** - Minting of silver coins (5 to 50 Centavos) and coins of copper/nickel alloy.

**1870** - Linking of Peso to French coin of 5 Francs and to new Spanish Duro: 25 grams 900 fine, or 22.50 grams fine silver. Subsequent depreciation according to fluctuations in price of silver bullion.

**1885** (October 31st) - Fiscal Code confirmed definition of Peso.

**1896** - Adoption of gold standard with Colón of 100 Centavos as monetary unit.
 - See *Colón Costa Rica.*

## PESO CUBA

Silver money, then monetary unit of **Cuba.** Divided into 100 Centesimos and 1,000 Milesimos from 1881 to 1899, then into 100 Centavos.

Bank of issue - Since April 1950 by Banco Nacional de Cuba, reorganized in 1961. Until 1951, coins and banknotes of United States circulated simultaneously with Cuban Peso. All deposits and checks were payable in U.S. Dollars or Cuban Pesos.

Predecessor - See *Cuba.*

**1881** - Adoption of silver Peso as monetary unit.

**1899** - Introduction of American monies, which circulated simultaneously with Cuban Peso.

**1914** (November 7th) - Cuban Peso linked to U.S. Dollar:
1 Cuban Peso = 1,504.6 milligrams of fine gold
1 U.S. Dollar = 1 Cuban Peso
Gold Peso minted in denominations of 20, 10, 5, 4, 2 and 1.

**1934** (May 22nd) - Cuban Peso linked to devalued U.S. Dollar:
1 Cuban Peso = 888.67 milligrams of fine gold
1 U.S. Dollar = 1 Cuban Peso

**1935-1936** - Printing of first Pesos in paper.

**1937** - Cuban Government levied tax of 2% on all external payments.

**1939** (June) - Creation of Stabilization Fund.

**1946** (December 18th) - Previous parity registered with International Monetary Fund.

**1951** (June 30th) - National currency system replaced dual system under which U.S. Dollar and Cuban Peso both had been legal tender.

**1959** - With establishment of Fidel Castro regime, foreign exchange controls instituted. Black market activity flourished.

**1960** (October 18th) - Membership in Dollar Area ceased. Became part of Ruble sphere of influence.

**1965** (January-May) - Black market rate hit record 25.00 Cuban Pesos per U.S. Dollar.

**1968-1970** - Black market rate improved in very limited dealings.


## PESO DOMINICAN REPUBLIC

Monetary unit of **Dominican Republic.** Divided into 8 Reales, then 100 Centavos. At first called Piaster.

Bank of issue - By Banco Reserva de la República Dominicana, then by Banco Central de la República Dominicana (Central Bank of Dominican Republic) since 1947.

Predecessors - See *Haiti, Dominicano, Piaster Gourde.*

**1846** - After separation of Haiti and Dominican Republic, use of Piaster Gourde modeled after Mexican Piaster (24.4356 grams of fine silver), then modeled after French coin of 5 Francs (25 grams 900 fine, or 22.5 grams fine silver). Circulation of U.S. Dollars.

**1883** - Peso linked to Haitian Gourde. Adoption of gold standard:

1 Peso = 5 Francs
1 Peso = 1,451.61 milligrams of fine gold

**1889** - Theoretical creation of Dominicano did not prevent continuance of Peso as actual money.

**1897** (July 1st) - Introduction of U.S. Dollar.

**1905** (June 21st) - Formal adoption of U.S. gold Dollar as monetary unit. National silver money given arbitrary value of:
1 U.S. Dollar = 5.00 Pesos

**1918** - Silver Pesos exported to realize their bullion value, then in excess of legal parity. U.S. Dollar became principal circulating medium.

**1942** (July 29th) - Foreign exchange controls.

**1945** - Exchange controls all but eliminated, except for some minor restrictions based on import, export and exchange licensing.

**1947** (October) - Linking of Peso-Oro to U.S. Dollar:
1 U.S. Dollar = 1 Peso-Oro
Central bank began operations, and Peso banknotes issued.

**1948** (February 1st) - Peso declared only legal tender, but U.S. Dollars still circulated.

**1948** (April 23rd) - Parity registered with International Monetary Fund:
1 Peso = 888.671 milligrams of fine gold
1 U.S. Dollar = 1 Peso

**1960** - Foreign exchange controls. Dominican Peso became subject to black market transactions.

**1961** (November) - Peso on black market hit record of 1.75 per U.S. Dollar. Subsequent improvement.

## PESO ECUADOR

Monetary unit of **Ecuador** until 1884. Divided originally into 8 Reales, then (after 1871) into 5 Francos, 10 Reales or 100 Centavos.

Predecessor - See *Ecuador.*

**1836** - Independent Ecuador retained Spanish Piaster (or Peso): 27.064 grams of silver 902 fine, or 24.42 grams fine silver.

**1856** (December 5th) - Custom of accounting in Pesos of 8 Reales (and Testons of 4 Reales) continued despite temporary official adoption of Franco as monetary unit. - See *Franco.*

**1871** (November 21st) - Silver Peso became monetary unit of Ecuador:
1 Peso = 5 Francos = 25 grams of silver 900 fine = 22.50 grams fine silver

**1874** (May 1st) - Sucre, monetary unit based on bimetallic standard, was substituted for Peso, monetary unit based on silver standard. - See *Sucre.*

## PESO EL SALVADOR

Monetary unit of **El Salvador** from 1847 to 1919. Divided into 8 Reales, then 100 Centavos.

Predecessors - See *El Salvador, Piaster Mexico,* and *Peso Central America.*

**1847** - After separation from United Provinces of Central America, El Salvador Peso remained similar to Central American Peso: 27.064 grams 902 fine, or 24.42 grams fine silver.

**1870** - Linking of Peso to French coin of 5 Francs and new Spanish Duro: 25 grams 900 fine, or 22.50 grams fine silver. Depreciation according to fluctuations in price of silver bullion.

**1897** - Adoption of gold definition:
1 Peso = 5 Francs = 1,451.61 milligrams fine gold
Convertibility into silver retained.

**1914** - Suspension of silver standard.

**1919** (September 11th) - Monetary reform, with adoption of gold standard and creation of Colón.
- See *Colón El Salvador.*

## PESO GUATEMALA

Monetary unit of **Guatemala** from 1847 to 1925. Divided into 4 Reales, then into 8 Reales, finally into 100 Centavos.

Bank of issue - By six private banks (Banco Internacional, Banco Colombiano, Banco Occidente, Banco Agricola-Hipotecario, Banco de Guatemala, Banco Americano).

Predecessors - See *Guatemala, Peso Central America.*

**1847** - After separation from United Provinces of Central America, Peso of Central America gave rise to Guatemalan Peso of 4 Reales: 27.064 grams 902 fine, then 875 fine (24.42 grams fine silver, then 23.68 grams).

**1870** - Guatemalan Peso, divided into 8 Reales, linked to French coin of 5 Francs:
1 Peso = 25 grams 900 fine = 22.50 grams fine silver = 5 Francs
Issue of banknotes by private banks.
Minting of gold coins from 1 Peso (1.61 grams 900 fine) to 20 Pesos.

**1895** - Suspension of convertibility confirmed by decree of June 9, 1899. Depreciation of currency.

**1903** (June 25th) - Unsuccessful attempt at limiting issue of banknotes.

**1923** (September) - Creation of Caja Reguladora to stabilize exchange rate.

**1925** (May 7th) - Substitution of new money for Peso. - See *Quetzal.*

## PESO HONDURAS

Monetary unit of **Honduras** from 1847 to 1926. Divided into 8 Reales, then into 100 Centavos.

Predecessors - See *Honduras, Piaster Mexico,* and *Peso Central America.*

**1847** - With separation from United Provinces of Central America, Peso of Honduras remained similar to Peso Central America: 27.064 grams 902 fine, or 24.42 grams fine silver.

**1870** - Linking of Peso to French coin of 5 Francs and new Spanish Duro: 25 grams 900 fine, or 22.50 grams fine silver. Subsequent depreciation according to price of silver bullion.

**1918** - Introduction of American monetary system:
    1 U.S. Dollar = 2.00 Pesos

**1926** (April 3rd) - Creation of new monetary unit. - See *Lempira.*


## PESO MEXICO

Monetary unit of **Mexico.** Divided into 100 Centavos. Often referred to as Mexican Piaster or Mexican Dollar.

Bank of issue - Under Law of 1897, 20 private banks of issue until September 15, 1916. From September 1, 1925, by Banco de Mexico (Bank of Mexico), which was granted monopoly on banknote issue September 11, 1937.

Predecessors - See *Mexico* and *Piaster Mexico.*

**1905** (March 25th) - Adoption of gold standard. Mexican Peso, defined in terms of gold, replaced Mexican Piaster, defined in terms of silver:
    1 Mexican Peso = 750 milligrams of fine gold
    1 Mexican Peso = 0.4985 U.S. Dollar
Minting of gold 5 and 10 Peso coins (Hidalgos), 20 Peso coins (Aztecas) and 50 Peso coins (Centenarios). Mexican silver Piaster continued to circulate. - See *Piaster Mexico.*

**1918** (November 13th) - Official adoption of Mexican Peso as monetary unit of Mexico.

**1925** (April 29th) - Decree reaffirming Mexican gold Peso of 750 milligrams fine gold as monetary unit of Mexico.

**1925-1926** - Issue by Banco de Mexico of Mexican Peso banknotes denominated in gold Pesos, although not actually redeemable in gold.

**1931** (July 25th) - Monetary reform. Irregular bimetallic system adopted:
Gold standard - Mexican Peso maintained at 750 milligrams of fine gold. No embargo on gold exports.
Silver standard - Unlimited legal tender status given to silver coins.

**1931-1934** - Issue of Mexican Peso banknotes denominated in silver Pesos, although not actually convertible into silver.

**1933** (July) - De facto stabilization of exchange rate in relation to U.S. Dollar:
    1 U.S. Dollar = 3.55 Mexican Pesos

**1933** (November) - De facto stabilization on following basis:

1 U.S. Dollar = 3.60 Mexican Pesos

**1935** (April 26th) - Demonetization of Mexican silver Pesos. Replaced by banknote issue. Suspension of theoretical convertibility of banknotes.

**1938** (Januray 1st) - Conclusion of a monetary agreement with United States.
Mexico obliged to maintain Mexican Peso on basis of:
1 U.S. Dollar = 3.60 Mexican Pesos

**1938** (March 19th) - Following expropriation of petroleum companies, depreciation of Mexican Peso:
1 U.S. Dollar = 4.92 Mexican Pesos (average Dec. 1938)
1 U.S. Dollar = 5.52 Mexican Pesos (average Dec. 1939)

**1940** - New parity established:
1 U.S. Dollar = 4.855 Mexican Pesos

**1941** (November 19th) - Agreement with United States for stabilization of exchange rate.

**1946** (December 18th) - Parity established in 1940 registered with International Monetary Fund:
1 Mexican Peso = 183.042 milligrams of fine gold
1 U.S. Dollar = 4.855 Mexican Pesos

**1948** (July 22nd) - Banco de Mexico ceased supporting exchange rate of 4.855 Mexican Pesos per U.S. Dollar. Rate subsequently fell to 6.88 Mexican Pesos per U.S. Dollar.

**1949** (June 17th) - Exchange rate stabilized. Devaluation of 43.9% registered with International Monetary Fund:
1 Mexican Peso = 102.737 milligrams of fine gold
1 U.S. Dollar = 8.65 Mexican Pesos

**1954** (April 19th) - Devaluation of 31% registered with International Monetary Fund:
1 Mexican Peso = 71.0937 milligrams of fine gold
1 U.S. Dollar = 12.50 Mexican Pesos

## PESO NICARAGUA

Monetary unit of **Nicaragua** from 1847 to 1912. Divided into 8 Reales, then into 100 Centavos.

Predecessors - See *Nicaragua, Piaster Mexico,* and *Peso Central America.*

**1847** - With separation from United Provinces of Central America, Nicaraguan Peso remained similar to Peso Central America: 27.064 grams 902 fine, or 24.42 grams fine silver.

**1870** - Linking of Peso to French coin of 5 Francs and new Spanish Duro: 25 grams 900 fine, or 22.5 grams fine silver. Depreciation according to fluctuations in price of silver bullion.

**1893** - Suspension of silver standard. Depreciation of banknotes.

**1912** - Adoption of gold standard, and creation of new monetary unit. - See *Córdoba.*

# PESO PARAGUAY

Monetary unit of **Paraguay** until 1943. Originally divided into 8 Reales, 16 Medios or 32 Cuartillos, from 1870, into 100 Centesimos, and after 1881, into 10 Reales or 100 Centavos.

Bank of issue - Banco de la República Paraguay (Bank of Republic of Paraguay) since February 22, 1936, after abolition of Officina de Cambios (Exchange Office).

Predecessor - See *Paraguay.*

**19th Century** - Use of silver Peso derived from Mexican silver Piaster.

**1845** - First minting of local coins: copper monies worth $1/12$ Medio or $1/192$ Peso.

**1864** - Minting of a silver Peso.

**1868** - Affixing of countermarks on foreign specie monies.

**1903** - Linking of Paraguayan Peso to gold Argentine Peso:
1 Paraguayan Peso = 1 Argentine Peso = 5 Francs Germinal
1 Paraguayan Peso = 1,451.61 milligrams of fine gold
Minting of coins of 4 Pesos, or Patagons, called Escudos (6.73 grams gold 875 fine) and of coins of 1 Peso, or Patagon, equal to $1/4$ Escudo (1.68 grams of gold 0.875 fine).

**1914** - 1 Paraguayan Peso = $1/16$ gold Peso.

**1923** (March) - Law of stabilization and devaluation:
1 Argentine paper Peso = 18.75 Paraguyan Pesos
1 Paraguayan Peso = 34.07 milligrams of fine gold

**1929** (November) - Depreciation of currency.

**1932** (June 20th) - Introduction of foreign exchange controls.

**1935** (August 17th) - After war with Bolivia, new exchange rate:
1 Argentine paper Peso = 25.00 Paraguayan Pesos

**1936** (February 1st) - New exchange rate:
1 Argentine paper Peso = 35.00 Paraguayan Pesos

**1936** - New exchange rate:
1 Argentine paper Peso = 61.50 Paraguayan Pesos

**1943** (November) - Paraguayan Peso depreciated to $1/100$ Argentine paper Peso and replaced by Guaraní. - See *Guaraní.*

# PESO PHILIPPINES

Monetary unit of the **Philippines.** Divided into 100 Centavos and 1,000 Milesimos.

Bank of issue - From 1903 to 1948, by Treasury with 100% cover in U.S. Dollars; also by two commercial banks, one of which was National Bank of the Philippines (since May 2, 1916). Since January 1949, by Central Bank of the Philippines, created June 15, 1948.

Predecessor - See *Philippines.*

**1903** (March 2nd) - Creation of silver Philippine Pesos:

1 Philippine Peso = 20 grams of silver 800 fine, or 16 grams
            fine silver
1 U.S. Dollar = 2.00 Philippine Pesos

**1922** (June 13th) - Gold Standard Fund Act, for maintenance of U.S. Dollar parity:
1 Philippine Peso = 752.3 milligrams of fine gold
1 U.S. Dollar = 2.00 Philippine Pesos

**1934** (February 1st) - Philippine Peso linked to devalued U.S. Dollar:
1 Philippine Peso = 444.335 milligrams of fine gold
1 U.S. Dollar = 2.00 Phillipine Pesos

**1942** - Japanese Occupation. Circulation of Philippine Pesos and U.S. Dollars maintained at previous parity. Introduction of Japanese military Yen, called Gumpyo, denominated in Philippine Pesos.

**1942** (April) - Tokyo decided to eliminate U.S. Dollars, Philippine Pesos and Gumpyo, and to issue new banknotes. Circulation of U.S. Dollar banned.

**1943** (April) - Issue of banknotes in Philippine Pesos by Bank for Development of South Seas. Philippine Peso linked to Yen, implying devaluation of 53%.

**1945** - Demonetization of banknotes issued by Japanese. Restoration of Philippine Peso:
1 U.S. Dollar = 2.00 Philippine Pesos

**1946** - Agreement between United States and Philippines making (until July 3, 1974) all suspension of convertibility of Philippine Peso into U.S. Dollars and all restrictions on transfers between Philippines and United States contingent upon approval by President of United States.

**1946** (December 18th) - Parity of 1934 confirmed by registration with International Monetary Fund.

**1948** (June 15th) - Legistlation reorganizing monetary system on same parity, with flexible rules for banknote cover.

**1949** (December 9th) - Foreign exchange controls, with import licenses.

**1951** (March 29th) - Tax of 17% levied on sales of foreign exchange for most imports, invisibles and capital:
1 U.S. Dollar = 2.00375/2.015 Philippine Pesos (buying-
                                    /selling)
1 U.S. Dollar = 2.34 Philippine Pesos (with 17% tax)

**1954** (June) - New rate approved by International Monetary Fund.

**1956** (January 1st) - Tax of 17% abolished. Replaced by special 17% levy on imports.

**1958** (October 22nd) - Blocked fiduciary accounts established with limited domestic use:
1 U.S. Dollar = 3.20 Philippine Pesos

**1959** (July 17th) - Margin fee of 25% on sales of most foreign exchange. Subject to periodic reductions.

**1959** (July) - Philippine Peso dropped to 4.65 per U.S. Dollar in black market.

**1960** (April 25th) - Controlled free market established. Set at 3.20 Philippine Pesos per U.S. Dollar. Multiple rates created. Subject to revisions.

**1962** (January 22nd) - Philippine Peso unpegged. Most margin fees abolished. Restrictions on foreign trade and payments, including capital movements, withdrawn.

Freely fluctuating rate (3.49 Philippine Pesos) applied to all exchange payments and receipts, except that par value of 2.00 Philippine Pesos per U.S. Dollar continued to apply to 20% of proceeds from merchandise exports. Blocked nonresident fiduciary accounts dissolved.

**1965** (November 7th) - Basic official rate abolished. Free rate registered with International Monetary Fund as official par value:
> 1 Philippine Peso = 227.864 milligrams of fine gold
> 1 U.S. Dollar = 3.90 Philippine Pesos

Mixed export rates and free exchange market eliminated.

**1968** (December) - Philippine Peso fell to low on black market, being offered at discount of 45.4%.

**1970** (February 1st) - De facto devaluation of Philippine Peso, with establishment of an Official Fluctuating Free Market rate for all international transactions:
> 1 U.S. Dollar = 4.22 Philippine Pesos (mixed rate of 80% at Basic rate and 20% at Free rate for major exports)
> 1 U.S. Dollar = 5.50 Philippine Pesos (Fluctating Free rate for all other transactions)

**1970** (May 1st) - Surrender requirement of 80% at Basic rate removed. Replaced by 10% tax at Fluctuating Free rate:
> 1 U.S. Dollar = 5.49 Philippine Pesos

**1970** (December) - Philippine Peso on black market hit a record low of 7.10 per U.S. Dollar.


# PESO URUGUAY

Monetary unit of **Uruguay.** Divided into 100 Centesimos. Originally divided into 10 Reales or 100 Centavos, then in 1859 into 1,000 Milesimos.

Bank of issue - Banco de la República Oriental del Uruguay, established 1896. Replaced March 1, 1967, by Banco Central del Uruguay (Central Bank of Uruguay).

Predecessor - See *Uruguay.*

**19th Century** - Circulation of Mexican Piasters (23.4356 grams of fine silver) and of derivative Peso.

**1854** - Minting of silver Peso (27.086 grams 875 fine) and ½ Peso (13.094 grams of silver 833 fine) equal to ½ Patagon and valued at 5 Reales.

**1862** (June 23rd) - Creation of Uruguayan Peso based upon gold standard:
> 1 Uruguayan Peso = 1,556.149 milligrams of fine gold

However, no minting of gold (except perhaps from 1870 to 1877: Doubloons of 10 Pesos).

**1873** - Minting of silver 1 Peso coins, linked to French 5 Franc coin and Spanish Duro: 25 grams 900 fine, or 22.50 grams fine silver.

**1875** - Issue of banknotes at forced parity, and ban on monetary use of gold. Collapse of Uruguayan Peso.

**1914** - New suspension of gold standard. Gold exports prohibited. Depreciation, then return to former gold parity.

**1929** (December) - New suspension of gold standard. Depreciation of currency (60%).

**1931** - Official selling exchange rate for commercial transactions:
1 Pound Sterling = 9.50 Uruguayan Pesos (average)

**1941** (January 10th) - Official exchange rate:
1 U.S. Dollar = 1.90 Uruguayan Pesos

**1944** (July) - "Free" exchange rate for noncommercial transactions:
1 U.S. Dollar = 1.785 Uruguayan Pesos
"Free" exchange for nonessential imports:
1 U.S. Dollar = 1.90 Uruguayan Pesos

**1947** (July) - Abolition of "Free" exchange rate of 1.785. All transactions executed at official rate of 1.90 Uruguayan Pesos per U.S. Dollar.

**1948** (September) - Exchange rate of 1.90 maintained for nonessential imports; "Free" exchange rate (2.38) applied to noncommercial transactions.
Other exchange rates: 1.519 and 1.70 (exports), 2.45 (essential imports). Limited use of buying rates of 1.78 and 1.88 for certain export proceeds.

**1948** (December) - "Free official" exchange rate for noncommercial transactions:
1 U.S. Dollar = 2.25 Uruguayan Pesos

**1949** (October 6th) - New system of multiple exchange rates introduced.
Three official buying rates per U.S. Dollar: 1.519 (basic exports); 1.78 (oils, hides and rice); 2.35 (wool, leather, sheep and other farm products, bricks).
Three official selling rates per U.S. Dollar: 1.519 (government payments, newsprint and printing supplies); 1.90 (essential imports); 2.45 (nonessential and luxury imports).
Fluctuating free market rate:
1. U.S. Dollar = 3.10 Uruguayan Pesos (for noncommercial transactions)
A 1% exchange tax applied to purchases of export proceeds.

**1950** (February 24th) - Temporary supplementary premium of 0.60 Uruguayan Peso per U.S. Dollar established for leather exports.

**1950** (March 9th) - Temporary supplementary premium of 0.35 Uruguayan Peso per U.S. Dollar established for beef exports.

**1950** (May 23rd) - Temporary supplementary premium of 0.57 Uruguayan Peso per U.S. Dollar established for certain rice exports.

**1950** (November 1st) - Temporary surcharge of 0.80 Uruguayan Peso per U.S. Dollar applied to certain luxury imports creating effective rate of 3.25 Uruguayan Pesos per U.S. Dollar.

**1950** (November 29th) - Temporary premium of 0.35 Uruguayan Peso per U.S. Dollar established for exports of shoes and leather.

**1951** (January 31st) - Temporary premium of 0.25 Uruguayan Peso per U.S. Dollar established for exports of shoes and leather.

**1952** (June 6th) - Proceeds from exports of canned meat exchanged 75% at 2.35 Uruguayan Peso rate and 25% at original rate of 1.519 Uruguayan Pesos per U.S. Dollar. Created effective rate of 2.143 Uruguayan Pesos per U.S. Dollar.

**1953** (February 10th) - Rate of 1.60 Uruguayan Pesos per U.S. Dollar applied to exports of washed wool.

**1953** (April 17th) - Exchange tax of 6% introduced for all imports except a few essentials.

**1953** (April 22nd) - Rate of 1.90 Uruguayan Pesos applied to exports of rice.

**1953** (May 19th) - Rate of 2.15 Uruguayan Pesos applied to exports of wheat gluten.

**1953** (June 25th) - Rate of 2.05 Uruguayan Pesos applied to exports of canned meat.

**1953** (July 23rd) - Rate of 2.06 Uruguayan Pesos per U.S. Dollar applied to exports of combed wool tops.

**1953** (September 1st) - Rate of 2.15 Uruguayan Pesos per U.S. Dollar applied to native sandals and rayon fabrics.

**1953** (November 10th) - Rate of 2.10 Uruguayan Pesos per U.S. Dollar applied to exports of crushed dolomite.

**1954** (January 22nd) - Rate of 1.967 Uruguayan Pesos per U.S. Dollar applied to exports of combed wool tops.

**1954** (February 9th) - Rate of 2.20 Uruguayan Pesos applied to exports of canned meat.

**1954** (February 23rd) - Rate of 2.10 Uruguayan Pesos per U.S. Dollar applied to exports of linseed oil.

**1954** (February 26th) - Import rate of 2.45 Uruguayan Pesos plus 1.35 Uruguayan Peso per U.S. Dollar surcharge applied to most nonessential and luxury imports. Effective rate (including 6% exchange tax): 2.597 Uruguayan Pesos per U.S. Dollar.

**1954** (April 1st) - Rate of 2.10 Uruguayan Pesos per U.S. Dollar applied to export of brown paper.

**1954** (June 24th) - Rate of 2.80 Uruguayan Pesos applied to woolen textile exports. Rate of 2.60 Uruguayan Pesos applied to leather exports. Both rates subject to 2 million Uruguayan Pesos quota.

**1954** (August 2nd) - Rate of 2.45 Uruguayan Pesos plus surcharge of 0.90 Uruguayan Peso per U.S. Dollar applied to imports of automobiles. Subject to 4 million Uruguayan Pesos quota. Preferential rate of 2.35 Uruguayan Pesos per U.S. Dollar applied to exports of rice and linseed oil. Transactions subject to exchange subsidies, quotas and time periods.

**1954** (September 21st) - Rate of 2.35 Uruguayan Pesos per U.S. Dollar applied to fresh fruits.

**1954** (December 10th) - Exchange surcharge of 1.05 Uruguay Pesos attached to rate of 2.45 Uruguayan Pesos per U.S. Dollar applied to certain nonessential and luxury imports subject to quotas. Effective rate (including 6% exchange tax): 3.65 Uruguayan Pesos per U.S. Dollar.

**1955** (January 1st) - Rate of 2.45 Uruguayan Pesos plus 1.05 Uruguayan Pesos per U.S. Dollar surcharge applied to imports of olive oil, whiskey, cigarettes, watches, buttons, furs, worsteds, automobiles, pottery, porcelain and textiles. Other nonessential and luxury imports transacted at 1.90 and 2.45 Uruguayan Pesos per U.S. Dollar.

**1955** (February 8th) - Rate of 2.026 Uruguayan Pesos per U.S. Dollar applied to exports of wool tops, broken tops and by-products.

**1955** (July 1st) - Rate of 2.35 Uruguayan Pesos applied to exports of canned meat.

**1955** (August 23rd) - Rate of 2.35 Uruguayan Pesos per U.S. Dollar applied to exports of liver powder.

**1955** (September 15th) - Schedule of premiums for wool exports introduced, based upon date of export. Premiums ranged from 0.21 to 0.07 Uruguayan Peso per U.S. Dollar and subject to revision. Selling rates of 1.90 Uruguayan Pesos (essential imports) and 2.45 Uruguayan Pesos (nonessentials and luxury good) changed to 2.10 Uruguayan Pesos and 2.80 Uruguayan Pesos, respectively.

**1955** (September 22nd) - Three rates applied to linseed products: 1.78 Uruguayan Pesos (linseed cake and flour); 2.126 Uruguayan Pesos (linseed oil exported prior to September 15, 1955); 1.90 Uruguayan Pesos per U.S. Dollar (other linseed oil).

**1955** (November 25th) - Rate of 2.35 Uruguayan Pesos per U.S. Dollar applied to exports of frozen mutton.

**1955** (December 28th) - Premiums for exports of wool tops and broken tops introduced, based upon date of export: 0.14 and 0.047 Uruguyan Peso per U.S. Dollar.

**1956** (January 10th) - Rate of 2.25 Uruguayan Pesos per U.S. Dollar established for exports of dried cattle hides.

**1956** (February 1st) - Single rate of 1.78 Uruguayan Pesos per U.S. Dollar established for exports of linseed oil and its by-products.

**1956** (April 30th) - Premium of 0.07 Uruguayan Peso per U.S. Dollar established for exports of raw wool.

**1956** (July 12th) - Temporary export rates established for frozen and canned meats: 2.35 Uruguayan Pesos (frozen mutton and pork); 3.21 Uruguayan Pesos (frozen beef); 3.80 Uruguayan Pesos (canned beef).

**1956** (August 20th) - Exchange reform and introduction of mixed rate system. Freely fluctuating certificate market established for imports and exports. More than 30 different effective exchange rates resulted from various combinations of 1.519 Uruguayan Pesos per U.S. Dollar rate, 2.10 Uruguayan Pesos per U.S. Dollar rate, and fluctuating certificate rate. Special effective rate of 3.00 Uruguayan Pesos per U.S. Dollar applied to a few specified imports. Subsequent shifts in category and applicable exchange rates for many imports and exports. Rates ranged from 1.519 to 6.10 Uruguayan Pesos per U.S. Dollar.

**1956** (November 30th) - Exchange surcharge (0.50, 1.50, and 2.00 Uruguayan Pesos per U.S. Dollar) applied to all but essential import payments.

**1957** (October 15th) - Reclassification of large numbers of manufactured export goods, reducing number of effective export rates for manufactured goods from 35 to 6. Unmanufactured exports were classified under 11 different exchange rates.

**1957** (October 17th) - Certificate market temporarily closed to all but exporters.

**1957** (November 11th) - Special import rate of 3.00 Uruguayan Pesos per U.S. Dollar abolished. Depreciation of exchange rates for wool and wool products resulted from major shifts of exports into categories with inferior exchange rates. Commodities inported at 2.10 Uruguayan Peso rate for the most part shifted to certificate market rate.

**1958** (February 6th) - New mixed rate created for exports of wool tops and by-products. Half of proceeds given access to official rate (1.519 Uruguayan Pesos per U.S. Dollar and half used free commercial market rate (4.1025 Uruguayan Pesos per U.S. Dollar).

**1958** (April 8th) - Number of export groups reduced to six, ranging in exchange rates from 4.1025 Uruguayan Pesos to 1.519 Uruguayan Pesos per U.S. Dollar.

**1958** (June 3rd) - Government announced that premiums on exports were granted on a case-by-case basis.

**1958** (September 11th) - Number of export rate groups reduced to four, ranging from 4.1025 Uruguayan Pesos to 2.81075 Uruguayan Pesos per U.S. Dollar. Subsequent shifting of items within framework of four groups. Temporary additional premium of 0.10 Uruguayan Peso per U.S. Dollar applied to all export proceeds.

**1958** (September 11th) - Additional import surcharges introduced on nonessential and luxury imports. Several imports subject to 2.10 Uruguayan Peso rate, shifted to 4.11 Pesos per U.S. Dollar.

**1959** (April 22nd) - Exchange surcharges on imports doubled on nonessential and luxury imports.

**1959** (April 25th) - Substantial recategorizations of imports resulted in several changes in applicable exchange rates.

**1959** (June 30th) - Proceeds of all but certain major export commodities were given access to free financial market rate. Subsequently, proceeds from major exports were given partial or full access to free financial market.

**1959** (December 17th) - Exchange and monetary reform. Official exchange rates abolished. Freely fluctuating exchange rate for all financial and commercial transactions. Gold parity of Uruguayan Peso reduced 76.6%:
1 Uruguayan Peso = 136.719 milligrams of fine gold
Imports and exports controlled by use of elaborate system of taxes, surcharges and advanced deposits.

**1960** (October 7th) - Initial par value established with International Monetary Fund:
1 Uruguayan Peso = 120.091 milligrams of fine gold
1 U.S. Dollar = 7.40 Uruguayan Pesos
Fluctuating free rate continued to apply to all financial and commercial transactions (about 11.00 Uruguayan Pesos per U.S. Dollar).

**1963** (May 9th) - De facto devaluation. Banco de la República withdrew from exchange market. Unofficial quotations rose to 16.80 Uruguayan Pesos per U.S. Dollar.

**1963** (May 31st) - Banco de la República reentered exchange market. Initial rates:
1 U.S. Dollar = 16.15/16.55 Uruguayan Pesos
New gold parity and official rate created:
1 Uruguayan Peso = 85.00 milligrams of fine gold
1 U.S. Dollar = 10.40 Uruguayan Pesos

**1963** (July 19th) - Emergence of second exchange market mainly for certain invisibles. Exchange bought and sold at more depreciated rates.

**1963** (November 11th) - Banco de la República announced new buying and selling rates:
1 U.S. Dollar = 16.30/16.40 Uruguayan Pesos

**1964** (Januray 16th) - Official buying rate revised from 16.20 to 16.30 Uruguayan Pesos per U.S. Dollar.

**1964** (November 24th) - Uruguyan Peso buying and selling rates reduced:
1 U.S. Dollar = 18.20/18.70 Uruguayan Pesos

**1964** (December 28th) - Official gold parity changed:
1 Uruguayan Peso = 59.245 milligrams of fine gold
1 U.S. Dollar = 14.99 Uruguayan Pesos

**1965** (January 11th) - Interbank exchange market temporarily closed.

**1965** (March) - Uruguayan Peso fell to low of 34.00 per U.S. Dollar in black market.

**1965** (March 18th) - Devaluation:
    1 U.S. Dollar = 23.00/24.00 Uruguyan Pesos
Interbank exchange market reopened. Rates applied to exports and imports with surcharges of 30% or less. All other imports and invisible transactions used fluctuating free rate (about 68.50 Uruguayan Pesos per U.S. Dollar in June 1965).

**1965** (October) - Uruguayan Peso dropped to low of 80.00 per U.S. Dollar on black market.

**1965** (October 18th) - Devaluation of Banco de la República exchange rates, bringing dual rate system into closer alignment:
    1 U.S. Dollar = 58.90/59.90 Uruguyan Pesos

**1965** (May 12th) - Devaluation. Banco de la República initiated policy of maintaining buying and selling rates in interbank market within 1% of freely fluctuating market. Thus, official rate was dropped:
    1 U.S. Dollar = 64.00/65.00 Uruguyan Pesos

**1966** (September 29th) - Devaluation:
    1 U.S. Dollar = 68.00/68.30 Uruguayan Pesos

**1966** (November 28th) - Devaluation:
    1 U.S. Dollar = 75.00/75.50 Uruguayan Pesos

**1967** (March 1st) - Banco Central del Uruguay began operating as Central Bank.

**1967** (March 16th) - Devaluation:
    1 U.S. Dollar = 85.50/85.90 Uruguayan Pesos

**1967** (May 30th) - Devaluation:
    1 U.S. Dollar = 87.70/88.30 Uruguayan Pesos

**1967** (July 6th) - Exchange market closed.

**1967** (July 17th) - Exchange market reopened.

**1967** (August) - Uruguayan Peso fell to black market low of 128.00 per U.S. Dollar.

**1967** (August 11th) - Devaluation:
    1 U.S. Dollar = 98.00/99.00 Uruguayan Pesos

**1967** (November 6th) - Devaluation:
    1 U.S. Dollar = 198.00/200.00 Uruguayan Pesos

**1968** (April 29th) - Devaluation:
    1 U.S. Dollar = 248.00/250.00 Uruguayan Pesos

**1971** (January) - Uruguayan Peso fell to record low of 310.00 per U.S. Dollar in black market dealings.


## PETER

Gold, then silver coin of **Brabant** in 15th Century bearing image of Saint Peter.

**1417** - Minting of gold Peter worth ½ Noble.

**1429** - Minting of silver Peter.
    Cf. *Patard.*

## PETERMENGER

Early small money of **German** countries.

Variations of name - Petremenne, Petermännchen.

**17th Century** - Petermenger was unit of account and silver/copper money in Trier. Worth 1/54 Thaler and equal to Albus. Coin of 3 Petermenger called Dreier.

## PETRONO

Name given to silver Testone in **Bologna.**

## PEZZA

**I.** - Money of **Tuscany** and **Leghorn** (16th to 18th Century).

Origin of name - Italian *pezza* (coin), from Vulgar Latin *pettia* (coin).
  - In Tuscany, Pezza (or Livornino) equal to 5.75 Lire, 20 Soldi de Pezza, 69 Crazie, or 240 Denari di Pezza.
  - In Leghorn, Pezza (Pezza da Otto Reali) divided into 20 Soldi (or 240 Denari). Was equivalent to 6 Lire.
  - In Bologna, Pezza (Pezza da Otto Reali) or Scudo, consisted of 85 Soldi. Pezza della Rosa was silver money minted by Cosimo III: 26 grams 919 fine, or 23.9 grams fine silver. Pezza delle Torre (or Livornino) was silver money minted by Ferdinand II: 27.1 grams 923 fine, or 25 grams fine silver.

**II.** - In **Genoa,** unit of account, also called Piastra. Divided into 20 Soldi or 240 Denari di Pezza. Equal to 5 Lire 15 Soldi.

**III.** - In **Florence** in 1716, gold coin called Pezza d'Oro della Rosa. Double Zecchino of this series popularly called Rosina.

## PFENNIG

**I.** - Money of **German** states. First a unit of account and silver money, then copper money.

Origin of name. - See *Penny.* Cf. *Penni, Fennigy, Penning.*

**10th Century** - In accounting system of Livres inherited from Carolingian monetary system, Pfennig (equivalent to Denier) was 1/240 Livre, or 1/12 Schilling (Sol). In system of accounting in Mark, derived from Marc of Cologne (weighing 233.856 grams), Pfennig (1.624 grams) was 1/144 Mark or 1/12 Schilling. As specie money, Pfennig was silver coin of 1.8 grams in beginning of 9th Century. Progressively reduced in weight to about 1.5 grams in 11th Century.

**12th Century** - Diversification of Pfennig with breakup of feudalism. In West, minting

of Deniers varied between 1.4 and 0.8 grams. In East, minting of Braceteates (thin silver sheets imprinted on one side only). - See *Bracteate.*
Annual exchange of Deniers (12 new against 13 to 16 old).

**13th Century** - End of annual exchange, except in East (Brandenburg, Silesia, Brunswick). Collapse of Pfennig. According to region: 0.7 to 0.3 gram.
Submultiple - Obol or Hälbling (1/2 Pfennig), Vierling (1/4 Pfennig).
Variation - Heller, minted in Hall in 1228. - See *Heller.*

**14th Century** - Reduction in weight of Pfennig to 0.5 gram of silver. End of annual exchange in Silesia and Brandenburg.

**1412** - End of annual exchange in Brunswick.

**15th Century** - Heller, even more depreciated, was no longer identical with Pfennig. In 1420, represented only 1/2 Pfennig. - See *Heller.*
Appearance of another variation of Pfennig, marked with cross (*kreuz*), and called Kreuzer to distinguish it from Pfennig. Minted in Tyrol in 1490. - See *Kreuzer.*

**1524** - Decree of Essling of Charles V attempted to create monies of Holy Roman Empire, and allowed states to coin Pfennig.

**1559** - Same authorization.

**16th Century** - Left to states, Pfennig became copper money.
In accounting system of Empire, Pfennig worth 1/240 Guilder (Gulden) and 1/4 Kreuzer. System used especially in South and West (Austria, Bavaria, Swabia, Franconia, Rhineland).

**1690** (January) - Decisions of Conference of Leipzig (electoral Saxony, Brandenburg, Brunswick-Lüneburg): Pfennig corresponded to 1/12 Gute Groschen, or 1/288 Thaler (unit of account).

**18th Century** - Pfennig was unit of account on basis of 1/192 Mark, 1/12 Schilling in Hamburg and Rostock; 1/540 Guilder, 1/18 Groschen in Prussia; 1/240 Guilder, 1/4 Kreuzer in Austria, Bavaria, Franconia, Upper Palatinate, Frankfurt; 1/168 Guilder, 1/6 Schilling in Swabia; 1/288 Thaler, 1/12 Gute Groschen in Brandenburg, Saxony, Thuringia; 1/288 Thaler, 1/4 Groot in Bremen, Oldenburg; 1/288 Thaler, 1/8 Mariengroschen in Brunswick, Hanover, Lüneburg; 1/366 Thaler, 1/42 Blamüser, 1/12 Schilling in Münster; 1/576 Thaler, 1/12 Schilling in Mecklenburg; 1/960 Thaler, 1/12 Albus in Cologne; 1/252 Thaler, 1/12 Schilling in Osnabrück; 1/480 Reichsthaler, 1/8 Stuyver in Lower Westphalia; 1/360 Livre, 1/12 Groschen in Brandenburg (bank money); 1/1.230 Livre, 1/30 Schilling in Regensburg (for payment of taxes and fines).
In Stettin, Pfennig called Fierkien. In Silesia, called Denare. As specie money of silver/copper or copper, Pfennig issued in Bavaria, Brandenburg, Saxony, Trier, Austria, Westphalia, Osnabrück.
Multiples - Drier in Brandenburg (4 Pfennig), Schware in Bremen (4 Pfennig), Mathieu in Hildesheim (4 Pfennig), Goesgen in Osnabrück (5.25 Pfennig), Fricks in Cleve (2 Pfennig).

**1871-1876** - Monetary reform, with adoption of Mark of 100 Pfennig as monetary unit. - See *Mark.*

**20th Century** - Pfennig was submultiple of monies derived from Mark: Rentenmark, Reichsmark (Reichspfennig), Deutsche Mark (Deutsche Pfennig), Ostmark, Saarmark, Danzig Gulden.

**II.** - Unit of account in certain **Swiss** cantons until 1850. In Basel, 1/300 Guilder, 1/540 Thaler, 1/5 Kreuzer, 1/2 Rappe.

**III.** - In **Livonia,** in 15th Century, minting of concave Pfennig.


# PFUND

**German** name for Pound or Livre. - See *Pound, Livre.*


# PFUNDNER

Silver money of **Holy Roman Empire** according to monetary system of July 28, 1551. Exchange rate: 12 Kreuzer or 1/6 Reichsguldiner.

Variation of name - Zwölfer.


# PHILIPPI

**I.** - Gold money minted by Philip of **Macedonia** in 356 B.C., also called Stater. - See *Stater.*

**II.** - Gold money of **Brabant** in 1435, also called Philippus. Not to be confused with Filips Gulden, later gold coin.


# *PHILIPPINES*

Primitive money - Rice.

**16th Century** - Introduction by Spanish merchants of Spanish and Mexican Piasters of 24.4356 grams fine silver. - See *Piaster Mexico.*

**1823** - Minting of Quartos and Ochavos of copper.

**1828** - Overstamping of Mexican and Peruvian Piasters.

**1833-1868** - Under Isabella II, gold coins (Pesos), silver coins (10 to 50 Centimos de Peso), and copper coins (4 Quartos).

**Before 1876** - Spanish monetary system: Real of 20 Quartos until 1864; Escudo from 1864 to 1868; Peseta after 1868. Impromptu use of Peso Fuerte of 100 Centimos or 8 Reales.

**1876 to 1900** - Use of Peso of 100 Centavos or 1,000 Milesimos.

**1900** - Substitution of U.S. Dollar for Mexican Piaster at rate of:
    1 U.S. Dollar = 2.00 Mexican Piasters

**1903** (March 2nd) - Creation of Philippine Peso. - See *Peso Philippines.*

# PHOENIX

Monetary unit of **Greece** from 1828 to 1833. Divided into 100 Lepta. Defined in silver as being equal to ⅙ Spanish Piaster, or 4.07 grams of fine silver.

Origin of name - From imprint of a phoenix on a pyre, symbolizing resurrection of Greece.

**1833** (February 8th) - Phoenix replaced at par by Drachma. - See *Drachma.*

# P'I PI

Money made of skin in **China** under Emperor Wu Ti (140 - 87 B.C.). Issued during first experiments with money inflation. P'i Pi was piece of white kid 36 cm square. Official seal marked it as having exchange rate of 40,000 copper coins.

Variation of name - Li Fu.

# PIASTER, PIASTRE

Because of prestige of Spanish Piaster, Piaster became classic money of Mediterranean (Spain, Middle East, Turkey, Egypt. . .), then spread to Latin America (Mexico, South America) and to Far East (Indochina).

Origin of name - From Italian *Piastra* (metal blade) coming from Greek root meaning "to fashion" from which came words plaster, plastic, etc. Also, from Spanish *Piastra* (metal coin).

Variation of name - In Spanish and Italian: Piastra.

**I.** - For **Spain,** see *Piaster Spain.*

**II.** - In **Latin America,** common name given all Pesos, for as long as they were made of silver.
- See *Piaster Mexico, Piaster Peru* and *Peso.*
- In **Ecuador,** Piaster Fuerte called Sucre. - See *Sucre.*
- In **United States** (South) and in **Canada,** name sometimes given to Dollar.

**III.** - In **Morocco:** Piaster Hassani, Piaster Azizi. - See *Hassani* and *Duro (III).*

**IV.** - For **Turkey, Egypt, Tunisia,** see *Piastres Turkey, Egypt, Tunisia.*

**V.** - In **Cyprus,** submultiple (¹/₁₈₀) of Cyprus Pound prior to August 1955. Divided into 40 Para. - See *Pound Cyprus.*

**VI.** - In **Libya,** submultiple (¹/₁₀₀) of Libyan Pound. Divided into 20 Centimes. - See *Pound Libya.*

**VII.** - In **Lebanon,** submultiple (¹/₁₀₀) of Lebanese Pound. Divided into 20 Centimes. - See *Pound Lebanon.*

**VIII.** - In **China,** name sometimes given to Chinese Dollar from local mintings: in Canton, Piaster with dragon (29.95 grams of silver 900 fine); in Pei-Hang, Piaster with dragon (28.20 grams of silver 820 fine).

**IX.** - For **Indochina,** see *Piastre Indochina.*

**X.** - In **Thailand (Siam),** name given to Double Tical (30.58 grams of silver 903 fine) at end of 19th Century.

**XI.** - Silver money minted in 1810 in **Ile-de-France (Mauritius),** called "Piastre Decaen" (from name of Governor). Value: 20 Livres Coloniales.

**1811** - Under British Occupation, issue of banknotes of one Piastre.

**XII.** - Unit of account in **Réunion** in 1810 under British Occupation. Piastre for accounting derived from Spanish Piaster worth 10 Livres Coloniales, 66 Marqués or 2 Indian Rupees.

**XIII.** - Silver money and unit of account in several **Italian** states in 18th Century:
- In Florence, name given to Ducat. - See *Ducato.*
- In Genoa, name given to Pezza of 20 Soldi or 240 Denari di Pezza. Equivalent to 5 Lire 15 Soldi.
- In Rome (Papal States), silver money called Piastra Vecchia. Exchange rate: 10.5 Paoli.
- In Leghorn, unit of account, also called Scudo Corrente, Ducato or Ducatone.
- In Bologna, silver coin, worth 1/5 Scudo.

**XIV.** - Unit of account introduced in **Java** by Europeans. Corresponded to 20,000 or 35,000 Cash:
$$1 \text{ Piastre } = 60 \text{ Stuyver}$$

**XV.** - Silver coin minted for **Netherlands East Indies** by Van Verre Company (March 1, 1601).

**XVI.** - For **Viet Nam,** see *Piastre Viet Nam, Piastre Dong Viet.*

**XVII.** - Submultiple (1/100 ) of **Sudanese** Pound. - See *Pound Sudan.*

**XVIII.** - Submultiple (1/100 ) of **Syrian** Pound. - See *Pound Syria.*

## PIASTER GOURDE

Early monetary unit of **Santo Domingo** (Dominican Republic) and **Saint-Domingue** (Haiti).

Submultiples - Half Gourde (1/2 Piaster), Gourdin (1/4 Piaster), Escalin (1 Real, though originally 1/8 Piaster, but actually 1/11 ). Subsequently divided into 100 Centièmes, or Centimes de Gourde, or Cobs in Saint-Domingue. - See *Cob.*

**18th Century** - Piaster Gourde was equal to Mexican Piaster: 24.4356 grams of fine silver. In Santo Domingo, equal to 8 Livres Coloniales 5 Sols of Saint-Domingue.

**1808** (May 4th) - Exchange rate for Piaster Gourde raised to 9 Livres Coloniales.

**1811** (June 28th) - Law calling for puncturing of Piaster Gourde called Piastre Gourde in French portion of Island . Punctured coins retained their former value. Discs stamped out of center of coin were used as coins, called pièces d'Haiti, whose exchange rate was arbitrarily raised to 2 Escalins. Counterfeits multiplied rapidly.

**1813** (May 8th) - Withdrawal of pièces d'Haiti, accepted for half their value. Minting of silver/copper coins (1/3 silver, 2/3 copper), of 6, 12 and 25 Centimes of Piaster Gourde. Issue of paper money in large denominations, secured by government lands of Port-au-Prince.

**1814** (June 30th) - Withdrawal of punctured Piaster Gourde of 1811. Minting of new silver Gourde.
- See *Gourde Haiti.*


# PIASTER MEXICO

Former silver money and monetary unit of **Mexico**. First divided into 8 Reales, 32 Cuartillas (Granos), 272 Maravedis, then divided into 100 Centavos. Also known as Mexican Peso or Mexican Dollar.

Variation of name - Piastra.

**1535** (May 11th) - Decree calling for opening of a mint in Mexico. Minting of Mexican Piaster imitating Spanish Piaster or Dolera (see *Duro* ):

 1 Mexican Piaster = 27.0695 grams of silver 9027 fine, or
   24.4356 grams fine silver

Successor types - Perulera (with Pillars of Hercules) also reminted from 1650-1732, Macquina (Spanish type with cross) from 1570 to 1650, Columnaria (two hemispheres with Pillars of Hercules) from 1732 to 1771, Busto from 1772 to 1821, Iturbide from 1822 to 1823, Republic from 1824 to 1893.

Submultiples - Coins of 4 Reales (Toston), 3 Reales, 2 Reales, 1 Real, ½ Real, ¼ Real (Quarto).

Minted in Mexico, then in Lima (1598), Potosí (1650), Santa Fe de Bogotá (1665), Guatemala (1701).

During four centuries (16th to 19th), 3.320 million Piasters minted by Mexico, world's first silver producer.

Spread of Piaster coins throughout Latin America and into countries bordering on Pacific and Indian Oceans: North America, Central and South America, Antilles, Pacific Islands, Japan and large parts of Asia. Imitations in China, Indochina and United States (whose Dollar in 1792 and later Trade Dollar copied Mexican Piaster). In China, punctured Mexican Piasters called Chopped Dollars. Mexican Piasters not punctured called Clean Dollars.

**1732** - Coins of ancient mintage called soft Piasters or Piasters by weight, because they were accepted in trade only by weight. Coins of new mintage called hard Piasters or Peso Gordo (Gourde) and accepted at face value.

**1822** - Independent Mexico retained Spanish monetary system with Piaster of 8 Reales.

**1861** (March 15th) - Law confirming Mexican Piaster (27.073 grams of silver 90277 fine) as monetary unit. Henceforth, divided into 10 Decimos or 100 Centavos. Minting of Piaster in silver and gold (1.692 grams 875 fine).

**1890** - Gold Piaster raised to 900 fine to maintain ratio between gold and silver of 1 to 16.

**1905** (March 25th) - Adoption of gold standard. Monetary unit took name Peso. Word Piaster reserved for silver coins. - See *Peso Mexico.*

**1918** (November 13th) - Increase in world silver bullion price resulted in hoarding of silver coins.
Substitution of new Mexican silver Piasters of lower fineness (800).

**1919** (October 27th) - Continuation of rising price trend for silver resulted in issue of Mexican silver Piaster with further reduced fineness (720).
Subsequent fall in world silver bullion prices.

**1925** (December 31st) - Unification of silver coinage to eliminate confusion caused by four different types in circulation. Mexican silver Piaster coins and submultiples of 720 fineness remained legal tender.
Coins of 2 Mexican Piasters were 900 fine silver.

**1935** (April 26th) - New pressure on Mexican silver Piaster from rising world silver bullion prices resulted in demonetization of coins. Replaced by Mexican Peso banknotes denominated in terms of silver.
Theoretical convertibility of banknotes into bullion suspended. - See *Peso Mexico.*

## PIASTER PERU

Monetary unit of **Peru** until 1863. Divided into 8 Reales, then into 5 Pesetas or 10 Dineros.

Predecessor - See *Peru.*

**1598** - Minting in Lima of Peruvian Piaster, similar to Mexican Piaster and imitating Spanish Piaster:
> 1 Piaster = 27.0695 grams of silver 902 fine, or 24.4356 grams fine silver

This coin was frequently called Perulero.

**1821** - Independent Peru retained Spanish monetary system, with Piaster (or Peso) of 8 Reales, and Toston of 4 Reales.

**1863** (February 14th) - Susbstitution of silver Sol linked to French coin of 5 Francs and to new Spanish Duro. - See *Sol Peru.*

## PIASTER SPAIN

**I.** - Silver money, minted in **Spain** after 1497 (Ordinance of 1497), under name Duro of 8 Reales. Imitated in Mexico after 1535, in Peru after 1598. - See *Duro, Piaster Mexico, Piaster Peru.*

Variations of name - Peso, Peso Fuerte, Real of Eight, Duro, Piaster Gourde, Pataca.

**II.** - Gold **Spanish** money, called Coronilla in 18th Century, worth 21 Reales 8.5 Maravedis.

**III.** - Common unit of account in **Spain:**
> 1 Piaster Forte = 20 silver/copper Reales = 680 silver/copper Maravedis = 10 silver Reales = 340 silver Maravedis

## PIASTRE DONG VIET

Early monetary unit of **Viet Nam** controlled by Viet Minh. Divided into 100 Xu.

Variations of name - Piastre Ho Chi Minh (named after former Viet chief of state whose portrait is on banknotes) and People's Piastre.

Predecessors - See *Indochina* and *Piastre Indochina.*

**1946** (November 3rd) - In areas of Viet Nam under control of Viet Minh, banknotes of Banque de l'Indochine ceased to be legal tender. Issue of banknotes denominated in Piastres Dong Viet. Subsequent inflation and currency depreciation.

**1951** - Monetary reform and exchange of banknotes:
1 Piastre Dong Viet (1951) = 10 Piastres Dong Viet (1946)

**1953** - After continued depreciation, second exchange of banknotes:
1 Piastre Dong Viet (1953) = 10 Piastres Dong Viet (1951)
Piastre Dong Viet was legal tender only in "liberated" areas. Circulation of Indochinese Piastre along with Piastre Dong Viet tolerated by Viet Minh in border areas.

**1954** (July 20th) - Partition of Indochina. Viet Nam separated into North and South. For monetary unit of South, see *Piastre Viet Nam,* for North, see *Dong.*


## PIASTRE EGYPT

Early monetary unit of **Egypt.** Divided into 40 Para.

Variations of name - Piastre-Tarif, Grouch.

**Before 1834** - Monetary anarchy. - See *Egypt.*

**1834** - Reform of Mohammed Ali:
1 Piastre = 40 Para = 23.4 grams of fine silver
Minting of gold coins on basis of 85.44 milligrams per Piastre.

**1885** (November 14th) - Adoption of gold standard. Piastre divided into 10 Millièmes as submultiple of Egyptian Pound ($1/100$) and Talari ($1/20$):
1 Egyptian Pound = 100.00 Piastres = 1,000 Millièmes
1 Pound Sterling = 97.50 Piastres
Minting of silver Egyptian Piastre of from 20 Piastres (28 grams 833 fine), called Talari, to 1 Piastre (1.4 grams 833 fine). - See *Pound Egypt.*


## PIASTRE INDOCHINA

Monetary unit of **Indochina** since 1895, and of **Associated States** since their creation and until their independence following Geneva Accord. Divided into 100 Cents.

Bank of issue - By Banque de l'Indochine, priviledged January 21, 1875, replaced December 31, 1951, by Institut d'Emission Quadripartite.

Predecessor - See *Indochina.*

**1885** (December 22nd) - Indochinese refused acceptance of all coins which did not resemble Mexican Piaster (27.0695 grams of silver 903 fine, or 24.4356 grams fine).

Issue of French Piastres, called "Piastres de Commerce", based on Trade Dollar type (27.215 grams of silver 900 fine, or 24.493 grams fine), itself copied from Mexican Piaster. - See *Piaster Mexico* and *Trade Dollar.*

**1895** (July 8th) - Decree reducing weight of Piastre de Commerce, which became Indochinese Piastre (or Piastre Congai):
> 1 Indochinese Piastre = 27 grams of silver 900 fine = 24.3
> grams fine silver

**1905** (January 3rd) - As result of foreign demand for silver money, export of Indochinese Piastres forbidden.
Indochina on silver standard (free minting, free convertibility, full power of legal tender for Indochinese Piastre).
Fluctuating exchange rates for Indochinese Piastre in terms of French Francs, according to price of silver bullion (from 2.50 Francs in 1914 to 16.50 in February 1920).

**1917** (January 1st) - Decree forbidding sale of Indochinese specie monies at prices surpassing their nominal legal value.

**1920** (March 27th) - As result of increase in silver bullion prices, suspension of convertibility of banknotes into silver. Periodic fixing of exchange rate of Indochinese Piastre. French Treasury opened an account with Banque de l'Indochine, which permitted stabilization of exchange rate.

**1921** (December 30th) - As result of decline in price of silver bullion, which lowered Indochinese Piastre to 6.75 French Francs, restoration of convertibility into silver.

**1926** (July) - Indochinese Piastre raised to 27.50 French Francs.

**1930** (May 31st) - Abandonment of silver standard, adoption of gold standard (convertibility from 50,000 Indochinese Piastres and more):
> 1 Indochinese Piastre = 589.5 milligrams of fine gold
> 1 Indochinese Piastre = 10 Francs Poincaré

**1930** (August 20th - Weight of one Indochinese Piastre silver coin reduced to 20 grams 900 fine, or 18 grams fine.

**1931** (December 31st) - Withdrawal from circulation of silver monies issued before 1930.

**1932** (April 14th) - Same measure for area called Laos.

**1936** (October 2nd) - Decree substituting French Franc standard for gold standard:
> 1 Indochinese Piastre = 10.00 French Francs

**1939** (September 9th) - Foreign exchange controls within framework of Franc-Zone.

**1940** (May 20th) - Decree establishing foreign exchange controls between Metropolitan France and Overseas Territories.

**1943** (January) - Adoption of exchange ratio between Indochinese Piastre and Japanese Yen:
> 1 Indochinese Piastre = 0.976 Japanese Yen

**1945** - Japanese occupiers increased volume of banknotes of 500 Indochinese Piastres.

**1945** (November 17th) - Demonetization without compensation for banknotes of 500 Indochinese Piastres issued by Japanese from March 9th to September 23rd 1945. Deposit of other banknotes, which remained blocked until September 20, 1946.

**1945** (December 26th) - Revision of Franc-Indochinese Piastre ratio, resulting from devaluation of French Franc:
1 Indochinese Piastre = 17.00 French Francs

**1946** (March 4th and August 10th) - Franco-Vietnamese Conference of Dalat on status of Indochinese Piastre.

**1946** (November 3rd) - Demonetization of banknotes of Banque de l'Indochine in zones controlled by Viet Minh, where "popular" Piastre issued. - See *Piastre Dong Viet.*

**1951** (December 31st) - Conforming to decisions of Dalat and specified by Conference of Pau (December 1950), transfer of right of banknote issue from Banque de l'Indochine to Institut d'Emission Quadripartite, which took over (and progressively replaced) banknotes of Banque de l'Indochine.

**1953** (May 11th) - Decree of Paris devaluing Indochinese Piastre by 41%:
1 Indochinese Piastre = 10.00 French Francs
1 Indochinese Piastre = 25.391 milligrams of fine gold
1 U.S. Dollar = 35.00 Indochinese Piastres

**1954** (July 20th) - Geneva Accord partitioned Indochina. - See *Cambodia* and *Riel, Laos* and *Kip, Viet Nam* and *Piastre Viet Nam.*


# PIASTRE LAOS

See *Kip.*


# PIASTRE TARIF

See *Piastre Egypt.*


# PIASTRE TUNISIA

Early monetary unit of **Tunisia.**

Predecessor - See *Tunisia.*

**18th Century** - Piastre, inherited from Ottoman monetary system, was unit of account divided into 52 Aspers or 624 Burbes.

**1864** - Minting in Paris of 100, 50, 25, 10 and 5 Piastre gold coins 900 fine.
1 Piastre = 175.5 milligrams of fine gold
Silver coins of 2 and 1 Piastre 900 fine.
1 Piastre = 2.787 grams of fine silver
Bronze coin (Kharub) worth 1/16 Piaster.

**1881** - French Occupation and introduction of French Franc:
1 Piastre = 0.60 Franc

**1884-1890** - Minting of 25 Piastre gold coins worth 15 Francs.

**1890** - Minting of gold coins worth 100, 50, 25, 10 and 5 Piastres. Called Boumia, Boukhamsin, Boukoufa, Bouachera, Boukhama, respectively.

**1891** (July 1st) - Decree of Bey made Franc official monetary unit of Tunisia. Withdrawal of Piastres. - See *Franc Tunisia.*


# PIASTRE TURKEY

**I.** - Unit of account and specie money of **Turkey.** Divided into 40 Para. Also called Grouch, Kurus, Qurush.

Bank of issue - During 19th Century, by Banque Ottomane.

**18th Century** - Unit of account Piastre represented 1/1.000 Juik, or 1/500 Beutel. It equaled 12 Timmins, 40 Para, 100 Minas or 120 Aspers. As silver specie money, Piastre also called Grouch. Dutch, English and Swedes in Smyrna gave it name of Leeuwendaalder (Thaler with a Lion). Weight: 26.5 grams 585 fine, or 15.5 grams fine. Reduced in 1760 to 19.2 grams 651 fine, or 12.5 grams fine; in 1771 to 19.2 grams 552 fine, or 10.6 grams fine; in 1780 to 17.9 grams 503 fine, or 9 grams fine.

Coin of 1/2 Piastre called Yigirmlik, 1/4 Piastre called Rebia or Onlik.

**1811** - Minting of gold coin of 30,000 Piastres, called Kitze and weighing 36.08 grams 916 fine.

**1828** - Minting of silver coins of 5 and 6 Piastres: Altilik, Beshlik.

**1844** - Adoption of silver Piastre of 40 Para as monetary unit.

**1845** - Minting of gold coin (7.216 grams 916 fine) of 100 Piastres called Medjidie.

**1870** - Progressive reduction in weight to 0.8 grams.

**1881** - Monetary reform and theoretical adoption of gold standard.
Piastre of 40 Para became 1/100 Turkish Pound. Continued to be minted in silver of 1.2 grams 830 fine, or 1 gram fine. Multiples of 2 to 20 Piastres minted in silver (called Ikilik, Beshlik, Onlik, Yigirmlik).

**1929** - Piastre renamed Kurus (1/100 Turkish Lira). - See *Kurus* and *Lira Turkey.*

**II.** - Unit of account in various countries under control or influence of Turkey before disintegration of Ottoman Empire:
 - In **Syria,** Piastre equal to 24 Siani or 80 Aspers.
 - In **Greece,** Piastre equal to 80 Aspers.
 - In **Arabia,** Piastre equal to 80 Kabir or Bugsha.
 - In **Tripoli,** Piastre equal to 13 Grimellini or 52 Aspers.
 - In **Tunis,** Piastre equal to 52 Aspers or 624 Burbes.
 - In **Egypt,** Piastre equal to 33 Medinos (or Paras), 99 Aspers, 198 Forles, or 264 Burbes.
 - In **Georgia,** Piastre equal to 2.625 Abbasis, 5.25 Usaltons, 10.5 Chaouris, or 105 Aspers.


# PIASTRE VIET NAM

Monetary unit of **South Viet Nam.** Divided into 100 Centimes. For **North Viet Nam,** see *Piastre Dong Viet* and *Dong.*

Bank of issue - Banque Nationale du Viet Nam (National Bank of Viet Nam).

Predecessor - See *Piastre Indochina.*

**1955** (October) - Viet Nam Piastre replaced Indochinese Piastre as national currency at par:

1 Viet Nam Piastre = 10 French Francs
1 Viet Nam Piastre = 25.391 milligrams of fine gold
1 U.S. Dollar = 35.00 Viet Nam Piastres

Special EFAC (Exportations-Frais Accessories) Account existed, resulting from retention of varying percentages of export receipts and used for certain payments abroad.

Exchange controls, established in September 1939, resulted in blocked Piastre variety.

**1955** (December) - Piastre on black market fell to 115.00 per U.S. Dollar, premium of 230% for Greenback.

**1956** (July 2nd) - Controlled free rate for authorized transfers of nonresident profits and dividends, travel expenses and other specified financial transactions:

1 U.S. Dollar = 74.00 Piastres

**1956** (September 1st) - Viet Nam became member of International Monetary Fund. No par value established.

**1957** (October 1st) - EFAC system discontinued. New export rates established:

1 U.S. Dollar = 47.92 Piastres (66% official rate and 34% at
free market rate for exports of rice)
1 U.S. Dollar = 48.30 Piastres (65% at official rate and 35%
at free market for exports other than rice, tea
and goods sold in compensation transactions)

In addition, there where various export subsidies in Piastres.

**1957** (October 21st) - Stabilization tax of 87.00 Piastres on imports not financed by U.S. aid. Ten days later, reduced to 75.00 Piastres or:

1 U.S. Dollar = 110.00 Piastres

Official rate of 35.00 Piastres per U.S. Dollar applicable only to government transactions, imports financed by U.S. aid and certain invisibles.

**1958** (January 1st) - Rice exports shifted to 48.30 Piastres per U.S. Dollar.

**1958** (January 18th) - Exchange rate in terms of Francs changed:

1 Piastre = 12.00 French Francs

**1958** (June 2nd) - Stabilization tax reduced to 60.00 Piastres per U.S. Dollar.

**1959** (January 1st) - Exchange rate in terms of Francs changed:

1 Piastre = 14.1088 French Francs

**1959** (May 5th) - Stabilization tax reduced to 50.00 Piastres per U.S. Dollar.

**1960** (June 1st) - Mixed rates for exports abolished, and fixed export premium of 13.48 Piastres per U.S. Dollar established:

1 U.S. Dollar = 48.13 Piastres

**1960** (September 19th) - New rate for certain imports financed with Viet Namese resources established, based on stabilization tax of 39.00 Piastres:

1 U.S. Dollar = 74.35 Piastres

**1961** (January 3rd) - Stabilization on tax of 50.00 Piastres reduced to 39.00 Piastres.

**1962** (January 1st) - Import taxes and export premiums abolished. Reform of rate structure:

> 1 U.S. Dollar = 34.65/35.35 Piastres (official buying and selling rates practically inoperative

> 1 U.S. Dollar = 59.65/60.35 Piastres (effective rate resulting from premium or tax of 5/7 of 35 Piastres for exports not receiving subsidy, all imports, government transactions and some private invisibles)

> 1 U.S. Dollar = 62.15/74.65 Piastres (official rate plus premium of 5/7 of 35 Piastres and supplementary exchange subsidy for certain secondary exports)

> 1 U.S. Dollar = 72.765/74.235 Piastres (controlled free rate for other invisibles)

**1964** - Supplementary export subsidies on various products raised, bringing export rates to range of 64.65-99.65 Piastres per U.S. Dollar.

**1965** (September 1st) - For expenses of nonresident physical persons during their stay in Viet Nam and for most private invisible payments, special subsidy of 44.50 Piastres per U.S. Dollar established, resulting in rate of:

> 1 U.S. Dollar = 117.265/118.735 Piastres

Foreign troops serving in Viet Nam paid in scrip (military payment certificates) which could be exchanged for Piastres at 118 Piastres per U.S. Dollar (mid-rate).

**1966** (June 18th) - Controlled free market abolished, and rate structure revised:

> 1 U.S. Dollar = 80.00 Piastres (official rate for foreign governments, international organizations and foreign contractors)

> 1 U.S. Dollar = 118.00 Piastres (official rate plus subsidy or tax of 38 Piastres for exports, expenses of nonresident physical persons during their stay, military scrip, all other exchange receipts, and imports, invisibles and authorized capital repatriation)

Additional import subsidies and equalization taxes, as well as export taxes and premiums, still existed. Piastre on black market fell to 220.00 per U.S. Dollar.

**1968** - Changes in equalization taxes on imports and consolidation premiums and subsidies for exports, created various new rates:

> 1 U.S. Dollar = 116.03 Piastres (official rate plus consolidation premium less 1% tax for rubber exports)

> 1 U.S. Dollar = 205.10 Piastres (official rate plus consolidation premium plus subsidy of 75% for handicraft exports)

> 1 U.S. Dollar = 128.80-333.80 Piastres (official rate plus consolidation tax plus 21 equalization taxes of from 10 to 215 Piastres for imports subject to equalization tax)

**1969** (June 12th) - Number of equalization tax rates increased from 21 to 35 with a range of from 7 to 460 Piastres. Range later reduced to 7-235 Piastres.

**1970** (October 3rd) - Partial devaluation:

> 1 U.S. Dollar = 80.00 Piastres (official rate practically inoperative, used only for calculation of duties)
>
> 1 U.S. Dollar = 118.00 Piastres (80% of imports, government transactions)
>
> 1 U.S. Dollar = 275.00 Piastres (military scrip, all exports, 20% of imports, transfers of capital abroad)

Export subsidies abolished, while duties on luxury imports raised. Piastre on black market fell to 430.00 per U.S. Dollar.


## PIASTRINO

Silver/copper money of Grand Duchy of **Tuscany**, having an exchange rate in 18th Century of 17 Crazie 1 Quattrino. Exchange rate in Leghorn: 1 Lira 10 Soldi (in "long" money) or 1 Lira 8 Soldi Denari (in "good" money).

Origin of name - Diminutive of Piastra.


## PIATAK

A copper coin issued in **Russia** and **Siberia** in 1758. Worth 5 Kopeks. Circulated at end of 19th Century and beginning of 20th Century under name Piatatchenk.


## PIATALTININCK

Coin in circulation in **Russia** at end of 19th and beginning of 20th Century. Valued at 15 Kopeks.


## PICAILLON

Copper money used in **Piedmont** and in states controlled by King of Sardinia in 18th Century. Worth 2 Denari.

Origin of name - From Italian *picarre* (to ring), or Italian *piccolo* (small).


## PICCIOLO

Small money of various **Italian** states.

Origin of name - From Italian *piccolo* (small).

Plural - Piccioli.

**I.** - Money of **Venice**. First in silver, then in copper.

**12th Century** - Issue of Denier of Charlemagne, $1/12$ Sol and $1/240$ Livre. Denaro of Venice progressively reduced in weight to 8.3 milligrams of silver in 1192. Usually called Picciolo. Silver Grosso (Matapan) of 2.1 grams was worth 26 Piccioli.

**1278** - Picciolo worth $1/28$ Grosso.

**1282** - Picciolo worth $1/32$ Grosso.

**1350** - Picciolo worth $1/48$ Grosso.

**1462** - Minting of copper Picciolo.
Lower level of accounting retained name Picciolo to designate Lira di Piccioli, as opposed to Lira di Grossi.

**II.** - Money of **Florence**. Originally equivalent to Denaro, $1/12$ Soldo or $1/240$ Lira, derived from Livre of Charlemagne.

**1531** - When Medicis created Duchy of Tuscany, name Picciolo given to Soldo. Gold Fiorino (Guilder), which became Ducato, had exchange rate at that time of 150 Piccioli.

**III.** - Copper money of Grand Duchy of **Tuscany**. Worth 1 Denaro from 1826-1829.

**IV.** - In **Sicily**, unit of account representing $1/3.600$ Oncia, $1/1.440$ Scudo, $1/720$ Fiorino (Guilder), $1/120$ Tarin (Taro), $1/60$ Carlino, $1/8$ Ponto, $1/6$ Grano.

**V.** - In **Bergamo, Bassano,** and **Padua,** Picciolo was unit of account worth $1/288$ Ducato, $1/12$ Grosso.

**VI.** - Unit of account in **Naples** until 19th Century. Worth $1/600$ Ducato, $1/120$ Tarin or Taro, $1/60$ Carlino, $1/15$ Cinquina, $1/6$ Grano, $1/3$ Tornese, $1/2$ Quartino, or 2 Cavalli or Denari.

**VII.** - Unit of account in **Malta** during domination by Knights of Malta (1530-1798) and in 19th Century. Minted in copper since 16th Century.

**Before 1730** - Worth $1/120$ Tarin or Taro, $1/60$ Carlino, $1/30$ Cinquina, $1/6$ Grano.

**After 1730** - Worth $1/44$ Scudo, $1/12$ Tarin or Taro, $1/6$ Carlino.


# PICE

**I.** - Small copper money of States of **Grand Mogul** (particularly in Amadabath). Still used in 19th Century in State of Jhalawar. Value: $1/54$ Rupee.

Variations of name - Peyse, Passa, Paissah, Paisa, Paise.

**II.** - In **Afghanistan,** submultiple of Afghanistan Rupee ($1/60$), Kran ($1/30$) and Abbasi ($1/20$), former monetary units. - See *Rupee Afghanistan.*

**III.** - Submultiple ($1/100$) of **Pakistan** Rupee since 1961.

**IV.** - Early submultiple of **Indian** Rupee ($1/64$) and Anna ($1/4$). Appeared as bronze coin of 1 Pice or $1/2$ Pice. Submultiple: Pie (1 Pice = 3 Pie). After 1955, worth $1/100$ Rupee and called Naysa Paisa, then Paisa in 1964. - See *Rupee India.*

**V.** - Submultiple ($1/100$) of **Nepalese** Rupee. Minted in bronze. Formerly minted in silver and in copper.

## PIE

**I.** - Until 1955, submultiple of **Indian** Rupee ($^1/_{192}$), Anna ($^1/_{12}$) and Pice ($^1/_3$). Minted in bronze.

**II.** - Submultiple of **French** Rupee ($^1/_{192}$) and early **Pakistan** Rupee ($^1/_{192}$).

**III.** - Submultiple of **Burmese** Rupee ($^1/_{192}$) and Burmese Anna ($^1/_{12}$), early monetary units.

## *PIEDMONT*

Monies of Rome (see *Rome* ), then Carolingian system (see *Livre* and *Lira* ).

**14th Century** - Minting of silver Denier. Analagous first to Denier Tournois, then to gold Fiorino (Guilder).

**15th to 18th Century** - Monies of France, Holy Roman Empire and Savoy. - See *Savoy.*

**1798** - Minting of $^1/_2$ Ecu in silver, $^1/_4$ Ecu in silver, and copper coins of 2 Soldi.

**1800** - Minting of gold coin of 20 Francs, called Marengo, and of silver coin of 5 Francs.

**1802** - French monetary system.

**1814** - Return to French monetary system before French Occupation: gold Doppia of 24 Lira; silver coins of 2 Soldi 6 Denari.
Continued computations in Francs and Centimes.

**1816** - Minting of coins of 10 and 20 Lire conforming to French monetary system.

**1820** - Minting of gold coins of 40 and 80 Lire, and silver coins of 1, 2 and 5 Lire.

**1825** - Minting of copper Centesimo.

**1865** - Italy, unified by House of Savoy, adhered to Latin Monetary Union. - See *Lira Italy.*

## PILARTE

Silver **Portuguese** money issued under Ferdinand I (1367-1383). Equal to 3 Dinheiros.

## PISTOLE

**I.** - Popular name for early money of **Spain.** Officially called Double Escudo. - See *Doubloon.*

Origin of name - Spanish *pistola* (small gun or pistol). Also from piastrulola, diminutive of Piaster.

Predecessor - See *Spain.*

**1537** - Charles V created gold Escudo of 3.10 grams fine, and gold Double Escudo of 6.20 grams fine. Latter became famous under name Pistole. For successive exchange rates of Escudo as unit of account (Maravedi), see *Escudo.*
Successive fineness of Pistole: 917 (in 1537); then 909; 893 (in 1722); 872 (in 1785).

Multiples and submultiples - See *Doubloon* (1772), *Quadruple.*

**1847** - Pistole disappeared under monetary system of Isabella II.

**II.** - In **France,** unit of account popularly designating sum of 10 Livres.

**1577** - Edict of Henry III repudiating foreign monies, but exempting Spanish Pistoles from decree.

**1640** - First minting of Louis, imitating Spanish Pistole. - See *Louis.*

**1652** (March 23rd) - Declaration fixing exchange rate of Spanish Pistole at 10 Livres.

**1660** - After marriage of Louis XIV and Maria-Theresia, Spanish Pistoles circulated largely in France, especially in South, and had exchange rate of 10 Livres Tournois (like primitive Louis). Until 19th Century, sums of 10 Livres expressed in terms of Pistoles.

**III.** - In **Papal States,** gold coin corresponding to Double Ecu (Doppia Scudo) or Doppia: at first 6.6 grams 900 fine (old Pistole); then 5.4 grams 900 fine in 1778 (new Pistole).

**IV.** - In **German** states, name sometimes given in 18th Century to Friedrichsdor, gold Prussian money of 6.6 grams 894 fine, or 5.9 grams fine.

**19th Century** - Name given to gold Louis in Bremen, to coin of 5 Thaler in Brunswick, to coin of 4.66 Thaler in Hanover, and to coin of 10 Thaler in Westphalia.

**V.** - In canton of **Geneva,** gold coin circulating in 18th and 19th Centuries until 1850. Old Pistole (minted before 1752), equal to Pistole of Spain and to old Louis of France, had exchange rate of 11 Livres 10 Sols. New Pistole (minted since 1752; 5.65 grams 920 fine, or 5.2 grams fine) had exchange rate of 10 Livres.

**VI.** - Gold coin of **Mexico** before 1861. Exchange rate: 4 Piasters.

**VII.** - Name given to gold Christian d'Or of **Denmark.** - See *Christian d'Or.*


# PITE

Silver/copper money, then unit of account from 13th to 15th Century **France.** Equal to ½ Maille or Obol, ¼ Denier, or ¹⁄₄₈ Sou. Also called Pogesia or Pougeoise.

Origin of name - *Pictavium,* Latin city of Poitiers, where early coin was minted.

Variations of name - Pitta, Picta.

Cf. *Pitta.*


# PITJE

Tin coin of **Java** in 18th Century, 4,000 of which equalled 1 Spanish Real. Sewn in bags or on mats to facilitate use. 1,000 Pitjes equal to 1 Soekoe.

Variations of name - Pitji, Pitis.

## PITTA

Silver money of Republic of **Genoa** issued in 14th Century for 1 Obol or ½ Denaro. Also called Medaglia or Mezzo Denaro.
Cf. *Pite.*

## PLAISANT

Silver money of **Hainanut** issued in 1387 for 15 Deniers. The ⅓ Plaisant was called Tiercelin.

## PLAK

I. - Silver money of various **Flemish** lands:
- In Luxembourg (minted by Jean the Blind: 1309-1346)
- In Brabant (15th Century), also called Botdrager
  Cf. *Plaquette.*
Variation of name - Plaque (French).
Plural - Plakken.
II. - Silver/copper money in **Scotland** from 15th to 17th Centruy. Exchange rate under James VI: 18 Pence.

## PLAQUETTE

Early money of silver/copper in **Brabant** with exchange rate of 3½ Sols in 18th Century. Diminutive of Plak.
Cf. *Plak.*

## PLATE MONEY

See *Plätmynt.*

## PLATMYNT

Copper plaques issued as money in **Sweden** in 17th and 18th Centuries.
Origin of name - "Flat money" usually called "plate" or "Swedish money".
Variations of name - Plate Money, Kopparplätmynt, Toler.
**1625** - Minting of divisionary monies of pure copper by Gustavus Adolphus II.
**1633-1654** - During reign of Christina, issue of square plaques of copper (Plätmynt),

marked with stamp of Sweden. Plaques used metal from Swedish mines and had exchange rate based on their intrinsic value. Weighed from 160 to 20,000 grams.

**1697-1718** - Under Charles XII, increase in circulation of copper plaques. From 1715 to 1719, issue of copper coins (Myntteken) with exchange rate much higher than their intrinsic value. - See *Daler.*

**1776** - End of issue of Plätmynt.


# POGESIA

Name sometimes given to Pite (½ Maille or Obol) in **France** and in **Levant**. Variation of name - Pougeoise.


# POLAND

**10th Century** - First national money, Denier. Simultaneous circulation of numerous Saxon and other coins.

**12th and 13th Centuries** - Minting of thin silver sheets (Bracteates).

**14th Century** - Counter-marked Gros of Prague. Issue of silver Grosz by Casimir the Great. - See *Grosz.*
Submultiple - Kwartnik, which depreciated from ½ Grosz to ⅙ .

**15th Century** - Jagellons minted gold Ducat and new submultiple of Grosz called the Coronat.

**1526** - Strengthening of Grosze and Deniers of silver by Sigismund I. Minting of Ducats imitating Ducat of Hungary (3.53 grams 979 fine, or 3.45 grams fine gold).

**1580 and 1601** - Successive reductions in weight of coins among which were Thaler and Orty of silver, Szelong and Denier of silver/copper. Gold coins of 5 and 10 Ducats were called Portugaloeser.

**1614** - Reform of Sigismund III Vasa, creating gold Thaler or Taler Zloty. Florin Zloty, divided into 30 Grosze of 12 Deniers (or 360 Deniers), was to become unit of account.
- See *Florin Zloty.*

**1623** - Reduction in fineness of silver Grosze.

**1631** - Raising of exchange rate of gold Ducat to 165 Grosze in terms of unit of account.

**1650-1656** - Minting of new silver coins (Thaler, Orty, Grosz).

**1659-1666** - Inflation of copper Szelong at forced parity.
- See *Szelong.*

**1785** - After First Partition:
Unit of account - Florin Zloty of 30 Grosze or 360 Deniers
Gold money - Ducat (3.39 grams fine) worth 9 Florins Zloty
Silver money - Thaler (27.45 grams fine), worth 4 Florins Zloty
Silver/copper monies - Tympf, worth 1 Florin Zloty 6 Grosze; Szostak (18 Grosze); Trojak (3 Grosze); Póltora (1½ Grosze)
Copper money - Grosz (4 Szelong); Szelong

All these coins exchangeable in Florins Zloty and Grosze for twice the value in Greater Poland.

**1793** - After Second Partition, breakup of Poland. Monetary systems of occupying countries: Prussia (Mark), Russia (Ruble) and Austria (Korona).

**1794** - In Russian Kingdom of Poland, temporary minting of Stanislas and ½ Stanislas of gold. Heavier than Ducat.

**1810-1813** - Grand Duchy of Warsaw minted gold Ducats, silver Thalers, copper Grosze.

**1815** (November 19th) - Russian Kingdom of Poland minted:
In gold - Royal Florin or Zloty Krolewskic
In silver - Florin or Zloty
In copper - Coins of 3 Grosze

**1830-1831** - Polish Republic minted gold Ducats (similar to Ducats of Holland) and silver coins of 5 Zlote.

**1833** (January 27th) - On becoming Russian province, Poland again mixed national and Russian monies:
1 Florin or Zloty = 0.15 Ruble

**1835** - In Republic of Cracow, independent since 1815, minting of silver Zloty and of copper coins of 5 and 10 Grosze.

**1846** - Cracow annexed by Austria.

**1847** (April) - Withdrawal from circulation of Zloty in Russian Poland. Russian monies only legal tender.

**1914** - German invasion, followed by introduction of German Mark.

**1916** - Marka succeeded German Mark.
- See *Marka.*

**1922** - Creation of new Zloty as unit of account.

**1924** - Issue of Zloty of 100 Grosze as national currency.
- See *Zloty.*

# POLPOLTIN

**Russian** coin worth ¼ Ruble.

# POLTINA

**Russian** coin worth ½ Ruble. First appeared in 1655 as cut pieces of silver Thaler, called Jafimske.
- See *Jafimske.*

Variation of name - Poltinink.

**1701-1725** - Appeared as copper plaques.
Circulated until beginning of 20th Century.

# POLTORA

**I.** - In **Austria,** coin worth ½ Groschen (18th Century).

**II.** - In **Poland,** between Partitions of 1785 and 1793, silver/copper coin worth 1.5 Grosze.

Origin of name - From Polish *pol* (half) and *twory* (the other).

Variations of name - Polturac, Pultura, Poltorak.

**III.** - Copied in **Germany** and **Sweden** and called Dreipölker and Trepölcher, respectively.

# POLUSCHKA

**Russian** copper coin worth ¼ Denga, then ⅛ Kopek. Minted in late 14th and early 15th Centuries in Novgorod, Tver and Moscow (also called Pulo), then under Peter the Great.

Smallest divisionary coin according to law of December 17, 1885.

# PONDT VLAAMS

**Dutch** name for Pound, unit of account representing 6 Guilders.
- See *Livre* and *Netherlands.*

# *PONDICHERRY*

See *French India.*

# PONI

In ancient **Mogul** Empire and in **Bengal,** coin worth ½ Anna, ⅙ Cawne, 1/32 Rupee.
- See *Rupee India.*

Submultiple of Burrie (¼), Gunda (1/20), Cowrie (1/80).

# PONT

In **Sicily** until unification of Italy, unit of account worth 1/450 Oncia (Ounce), 1/180 Scudo, 1/90 Fiorino (Guilder), 1/15 Taro, or 8 Piccioli.

## POON

**I.** - Submultiple of **Korean** Won (1/500) and Chon (1/5). Consisted of 2 Rin.
  - See *Won.*

**II.** - Money of account in **Maldive Islands,** equal to 80 Cowries.

## *PORTUGAL*

**3rd Century B.C.** - Appearance of Carthaginian and Greek monies.

**10th Century** - Before independence, see *Spain.*

**11th Century** - Portugal retained Spanish monies.

**12th Century** - First independent monies imitated Arab and Carolingian monetary systems.
  System of accounting: Livre of 20 Soldos or 240 Dinheiros.
  Gold coin - Maravedi (see *Maravedi* ).
  Silver coins - Dinheiro (Denier) and 1/2 Dinheiro (Maille).

**1279-1325** - Monetary reform of Diniz. Minting of Esterlin. Soldo became specie money of silver with name Forte.
  - See *Forte.*

**13th and 15th Centuries** - Types of coins multiplied:
      In gold - Cruzado (see *Cruzado* ).
      In silver - Tornez, Sou, Alfonsino, Gentil, Barbuda, Grave,
              Pilarte, Real (see *Real* ).

**15th Century** - New specie monies:
      In gold - Escudo, Cruzado, Espadim, Justo
      In silver - Grosso, Chimfram, Vintem, Espadim
      In silver/copper - Royal, Cotrim
      In copper - Royal, Ceitil

**1499** - With influx of metals, minting of new coins:
      In gold - Portuguez of 10 Cruzados (see *Portuguez* ), Cruzado
      In silver - Tostao worth 1/4 Portuguez (see Tostao), Indio
              (33), Vintem (20), Cinquinho (10), silver Real of
              5 copper Reis
      In copper - Real of 6 Ceitil, Ceitil
      (Later variations of Portuguez: Esphera, Calvario.)
Lowering of fineness, raising of exchange rate in terms of unit of account (Reis).

**1556** - New gold coin: San Vicente.

**1584-1589** - Issue of Francs, minted in Holland, imitating French money.

**1651** (October 9th) - Minting of new gold Cruzado and silver Conception.

**1722** (April 4th) - Creation of gold Escudo, worth 16 silver Tostaos. Progressive restoration of Real (Reis). Monetary system was as follows:
  Unit of account: Milreis of 1,000 Reis.
  Specie monies:
      In gold - Dobra (12,800 Reis), 1/2 Dobra or Moeda (6,400
              Reis), Escudo (1,600 Reis)

In copper - coins of 5, 3 and 1½ Reis.

**1835** (April 24th) - Edict fixing monetary system: gold Corôa of 5,000 Reis, gold Escudo of 2,000 Reis; silver Corôa of 1,000 Reis, silver Tostao of 100 Reis.

**1854** (July 29th) - Adoption of gold standard, and designation of Milreis of 1,000 Reis as unit of account. Demonetization of all early coins. Legal circulation of British gold Sovereigns and ½ Sovereigns.
  - See *Milreis.*

**1911** (May 22nd) - Replacement of Milreis by Escudo.
  - See *Escudo.*

**1931** (June 9th) - Creation of Conto of 1,000 Escudos as unit of account.
  - See *Conto.*


## PORTUGALOESER

**I.** - Gold money of **Hamburg** in 18th Century. Weight equal to 10 times that of Dukat (Ducat), or 34.9 grams 980 fine. Varying rates of exchange between 60 and 75 Mark.
Submultiple - Half Portugaloeser.

**II.** - In **Poland,** gold coins of 5 and 10 Ducats, minted after 16th Century.


## *PORTUGUESE GUINEA*

**16th to late 19th Century** - Trading posts under auspices of Cape Verde. Introduction of Cowries and Portuguese specie money.
  - See *Cape Verde Islands.*

**1879** - Became separate Colony. Monetary unit, Portuguese Escudo, issued by Banco Nacional Ultramarino.
  - See *Escudo Portugal.*


## *PORTUGUESE INDIA*

Predecessor - See *India.*

**1500** - Portuguese introduced gold coins (½ Cruzado) and copper coins.

**1521** - First minting of gold Saint Thomas (Santo Thomé).

**1557** - Use of first silver coins.

**18th Century** - In Goa, unit of account was Pardao of 4 Good Tangas, 5 Bad Tangas, 16 Good Vintem, 20 Bad Vintem, 240 Reis, 300 Good Bazaruccos or 360 Bad Bazaruccos.
Specie monies:
      In gold - Saint Thomas (Santo Thomé)
      In silver - Xeraphin, Pardao
      In silver/copper - Conodis

In tin and in copper - Bazarucco

**End of 18th Century** - Use of tin coins for minor trade.

**1818** (October 10th) - Minting of gold monies (Santo Thomé), silver monies (Rupia, Pardao, Tanga) and copper monies (Tanga, Vintem of 20 Reis), multiples of Real.

**1881** - Adoption of monetary unit: Rupia divided into 16 Tanga or 192 Reis. - See *Rupia.*

**20th Century** - Retention of same monetary unit. Rupia divided into 16 Tanga or 192 Reis, with same value as Indian Rupee.

1 Rupia = 11.06 grams silver 916 fine, or 10.13 grams fine

**1962** - Annexed by India. - See *India* and *Rupee India.*


# PORTUGUEZ

Early money of **Portugal.**

Origin of name - From name of country.

Predecessor - See *Portugal.*

**1499** - Influx of precious metals. Creation by Emanuel I of gold Portuguez (38.40 grams, 989 ½ fine, or 38 grams fine) equal to 4,000 Reis or 10 gold Cruzados. - See *Cruzado.*

**1504** - Minting of silver Portuguez (Portuguez de Prato) with exchange rate of 400 copper Reis.

**1538** (November 26th) - Decree suspending minting of gold Portuguez.

**1543** (October 18th) - Minting of new gold Portuguez (36.2 grams fine).

**1722-1835** - Minting of gold Portuguez. Most widely used denomination was the Peca. - See *Peca.*

**Before 1854** - Prior to monetary reform, gold Portuguez equal to 7,500 Reis.

**1854** - Demonetization.


# POUND

Monetary unit (full name, Pound Sterling) of **England,** then (from 1707) of **Scotland** and (from 1804 to 1921) of **Ireland.** Divided into 20 Shillings and 240 Pence. Decimalized into 100 New Pence on February 15, 1971.

Bank of issue - By Bank of England created on July 27, 1694 and given monopoly of banknote issue for England and Wales in 1708. Private bank until March 1, 1946, when nationalized. By State (Currency Notes) from August 1914 to November 1928.

Origin of name - From word livre, unit of weight. - See *Livre.* Word Sterling (in old French, Esterlin or Estrelin) came from Anglo-Saxon *Easterling,* which referred to men from East, i.e., merchants of Hanseatic League and Netherlands who worked in Mint in London. Cf. *Esterlin.*

**10th Century** - Introduction of Carolingian system of accounting into Saxon England

by way of Normans, but before conquest of William: 1 Livre of 20 Sols or 240 Deniers. Livre (Pound) remained as England's unit of account.
Evolution of metallic equivalent of Pound:

|  | In grams of fine silver | In grams of fine gold |
|---|---|---|
| William I (1066) | 350 | – |
| Edward I (1300) | 342 | – |
| Edward III (1344) | – | 23.6 |
| Edward III (1351) | 280 | – |
| Henry IV (1412) | 233 | 21.3 |
| Edward IV (1464) | 187 | – |
| Henry VIII (1543) | 129 | 7.5 |
| Edward VI (1551-52) | 26 | – |
| Elizabeth (1601) | 111 | – |
| James I (1603) | – | 8.3 |
| George III (1816) | 104 | 7.3 |

**1666** - Free minting of gold.

**1695** - First experiment with forced parity (depreciation of 12%).

**1774** - Decline in value of silver bullion. Creditors authorized to weigh silver coins for payments greater than 25 Pounds.
Prinicpal metallic monies:
In gold - Florin (Edward III), Noble (Edward III), Angel (Edward IV), Sovereign (Henry VIII), Crown (Henry VIII), Guinea (Charles II)
In silver - Esterlin, Groat (Edward I), Shilling (Henry VII), Testoon (Henry VIII), Crown (Edward VI).

**1797** (May 3rd) - Forced parity voted by Parliament for 52 days, and then extended (two more times in 1797, then in 1802, twice in 1803, in 1815, 1816, 1818, 1819 and 1820). Maximum depreciation of 29% in 1813.

**1816** (June 22nd) - Adoption of principle of gold standard. - See *Shilling*.

**1821** (May 1st) - Restoration of convertibility on basis of gold definition of Pound adopted in 1816:
1 Pound = 123.2745 troy grains of gold of 22 carats =
7.322382 grams of fine gold
1 fine ounce of gold = 85 Shillings

**1844** - Bank Act, fixing rules of banknote issue (circulation limited to cummulative amount of monetary gold stock and to "fiduciary issue" latter being limited originally to 14 million Pounds).

**1914** (August 6th) - Forced parity through suspension of rules relative to ceiling on banknote issue. Maximum depreciation of 34% in 1920.

**1925** (April 28th) - Restoration of gold standard at former parity:
1 Pound Sterling = 4.86653 U.S. Dollars

**1931** (September 21st) - Abandonment of gold standard. Depreciation of 43% in 1935.

**1932** (April 25th) - Creation of Exchange Equalization Fund.

**1939** (August 25th) - Foreign exchange controls.

**1939** (September) - Transfer of all gold from Bank of England to Exchange Equalization Fund. Depreciation of Pound.

**1940** (March) - Pound pegged at 4.03 U.S. Dollars.

**1946** (December 18th) - Previous parity registered with International Monetary Fund:
1 Pound = 3,581.34 milligrams of fine gold

**1947** (February 27th) - Adoption of system of "Transferable Sterling".

**1947** (July 15th) - Convertibility of Pound into U.S. Dollars.

**1947** (August 21st) - Suspension of convertibility.

**1949** (September 18th) - Devaluation of 30.52%:
1 Pound = 2,488.28 milligrams of fine gold
1 Pound = 2.80 U.S. Dollars

**1950** (September) - Three categories of negotiable blocked Sterling Accounts grouped into single Security (Switch) Sterling, used by nonresidents for purchase of British securities. Security Pound dropped to low of 1.92 U.S. Dollars. Subsequent improvement.

**1954** (March 22nd) - Reopening of free gold market (purchases limited to nonresidents of Sterling Area, residents of American Account Area and Canada). Registered Account created for other nonresidents dealing in London gold market. Reduction from 89 varieties of Pound Sterling to 10 varieties.

**1958** (December 29th) - Nonresident Sterling accounts made convertible for commercial purposes and named External Accounts.

**1962** (May 17th) - Creation of Investment Dollar through merger of "soft" and "hard" Dollars. Used by residents for purchase, at premium, of foreign securities.

**1964** (April 6th) - Property Dollar, used by residents for purchase, at premium, of properties outside Sterling Area, abolished.

**1965** (April 7th) - Property Dollar reestablished.

**1966** (April 27th) - Approval required for gold coin ownership of more than 4 gold coins minted after 1837.

**1967** (April 11th) - Security (Switch) Sterling abolished.

**1967** (November 18th) - Devaluation of 14.3%:
1 Pound = 2,132.81 milligrams of fine gold
1 Pound = 2.40 U.S. Dollars

**1968** (March 15th) - London gold market closed.

**1968** (April 1st) - London gold market reopened.

**1968** (May) - Property Dollar premium hit 60%, resulting in rate of:
1 Pound = 1.50 U.S. Dollars

**1969** (April) - Investment Dollar premium hit 60%, resulting in rate of:
1 Pound = 1.50 U.S. Dollars

**1970** (August 19th) - Property Dollar abolished.

**1971** (February 15th) - Decimalization of Pound with division into 100 New Pence.

## POUND AUSTRALIA

Former monetary unit of **Australia.** Divided into 20 Shillings and 240 Pence. Circulated also in Bismarck Archipelago, New Guinea, and New Hebrides.

Bank of issue - Initially by private banks, then in 1910 by Commonwealth Treasury. Finally entrusted to Commonwealth Bank of Australia in December 1920. Renamed Reserve Bank of Australia on January 14, 1960.

Predecessor - See *Australia.*

**1909** (September 4th) - Australian Pound officially defined at par with Pound Sterling:
1 Australian Pound = 7,322.38 milligrams of fine gold
1 Australian Pound = 4.866 U.S. Dollars

**1915** (July 14th) - Embargo on gold shipments.

**1925** (April 25th) - Gold embargo lifted. Restoration of Australian Pound to earlier parity.

**1929** (December 17th) - Suspension of gold standard. Progressive depreciation in relation to Pound Sterling to rate of:
1.30 Australian Pounds = 1.00 Pound Sterling

**1932** (January) - Depreciation of 20% in official relationship to Pound Sterling. Adherence to Sterling Area at rate of:
1.25 Australian Pounds = 1.00 Pound Sterling

**1939** (August 28th) - Foreign exchange controls introduced.

**1940** - Australian Pound fixed at:
1.25 Australian Pounds = 1.00 Pound Sterling
1 Australian Pound = 3.20 U.S. Dollars

**1947** (November 17th) - Parity registered with International Monetary Fund:
1.25 Australian Pounds = 1.00 Pound Sterling
1 Australian Pound = 2,865.07 milligrams of fine gold
1 Australian Pound = 3.224 U.S. Dollars

**1949** (September 18th) - Official devaluation of 30.5%, parallel to Pound Sterling:
1 Australian Pound = 1,990.062 milligrams of fine gold
1 Australian Pound = 2.24 U.S. Dollars

**1951** (November) - Australian Pound fell to low of U.S. $1.84 in black market dealings. Subsequently recovered.

**1966** (February 14th) - Decimalization, and creation of Australian Dollar.
- See *Dollar Australia.*


## POUND BAHAMA ISLANDS

Former monetary unit of **Bahama Islands.** Divided into 20 Shillings and 240 Pence.

Note-issuing authority - Government Treasury, then Bahama Monetary Authority.

Predecessor - See *Pound.*

**19th Century** - Bahama Pound notes issued by Treasury began circulating at par with British notes.

**1946** (December 18th) - Parity of Bahama Pound, equal to Pound Sterling, registered with International Monetary Fund:

  1 Bahama Pound = 3,581.34 milligrams of fine gold

  1 Bahama Pound = 4.03 U.S. Dollars

**1949** (September 18th) - Devalued along with Pound Sterling:

  1 Bahama Pound = 2,488.28 milligrams of fine gold

  1 Bahama Pound = 2.80 U.S. Dollars

**1966** (May 25th) - Decimal system introduced. Creation of Bahama Dollar.

 - See *Dollar Bahama Islands.*

Sterling currency withdrawn, while American and Canadian currency continued to circulate freely.


## POUND BERMUDA

Former monetary unit of **Bermuda.** Divided into 20 Shillings and 240 Pence.

Note-issuing authority - Bermuda Government, then Currency and Exchange Board of Bermuda.

Predecessor - See *Bermuda.*

**19th Century** - Subsequent to adoption of British monetary system, Colonial Government issued Pound banknotes in 1 Pound denominations. Linked at par with Pound Sterling.

 - See *Pound.*

**1946** (December 18th) - Parity of Bermuda Pound, equal to that of Metropolitan unit, registered with International Monetary Fund:

  1 Bermuda Pound = 1 Pound Sterling

  1 Bermuda Pound = 3,581.34 milligrams of fine gold

  1 Bermuda Pound = 4.03 U.S. Dollars

**1949** (September 18th) - Devaluation parallel to Pound Sterling:

  1 Bermuda Pound = 2,488.28 milligrams of fine gold

  1 Bermuda Pound = 2.80 U.S. Dollars

**1967** (November 18th) - Devaluation parallel to Pound Sterling:

  1 Bermuda Pound = 2,132.81 milligrams of fine gold

  1 Bermuda Pound = 2.40 U.S. Dollars

**1970** (February 6th) - Decimalization, and creation of Bermuda Dollar to replace Bermuda Pound.

 - See *Dollar Bermuda.*


## POUND BIAFRA

Monetary unit of secessionist **Biafra.** Divided into 20 Shillings and 240 Pence.

Bank of issue - Bank of Biafra.

Predecessor - See *Pound Nigeria.*

**1968** (January 10th) - Biafran Pound created in show of sovereignty. Served domestic monetary function, but had no real international value. Issue of notes and aluminum subsidiary coinage.

**1969** (December 31st) - Bank note circulation reached 135 million Biafran Pounds.

**1970** (January 9th) - Collapse of Biafra and return to Nigeria.
  - See *Pound Nigeria.*

**1970** (January-May) - Monetary confusion. Banknotes ordered surrendered by March 11, 1970, then by April 20, 1970. Exchange transactions recorded at:
  1 Nigerian Pound = 50 to 130 Biafran Pounds
Coins were used to purchase staples.

**1970** (May 17th) - Nigerian Government declared Biafran currency "worthless and useless " and demonetized Biafran Pounds with no exchange. Aluminum coinage ordered destroyed on sight.


# POUND COLOMBIA

Early gold money of **Colombia** from 1907 to 1914. Equal to British Sovereign.
  Weight: 7.98 grams 916 fine, or 7.32 grams fine gold. Value: 5 Colombian Pesos.


# POUND CYPRUS

Monetary unit of **Cyprus.** Divided into 1,000 Mils. Before August 1955, divided into 20 Shillings, 180 Piasters or 7,200 Para.

Bank of issue - At first by Treasury, then in 1963, by Central Bank of Cyprus.

Predecessor - See *Cyprus.*

**1917** (September 5th) - Treasury began issuing Cyprus Pound notes linked to Pound Sterling.
  - See *Pound.*

**1940** (March) - Fixed parity in relation to Pound Sterling:
  1 Cyprus Pound = 1 Pound Sterling
  1 Cyprus Pound = 3,581.34 milligrams of fine gold
  1 Cyprus Pound = 4.03 U.S. Dollars

**1949** (September 18th) - Devaluation along with Pound Sterling:
  1 Cyprus Pound = 1 Pound Sterling
  1 Cyprus Pound = 2,488.28 milligrams of fine gold
  1 Cyprus Pound = 2.80 U.S. Dollars

**1962** (July 25th) - Previous par value registered with International Monetary Fund.

**1967** (November 20th) - Change in parity following devaluation of Pound Sterling:
  1 Cyprus Pound = 1 Pound Sterling
  1 Cyprus Pound = 2,132.81 milligrams of fine gold
  1 Cyprus Pound = 2.40 U.S. Dollars

**1969** (October) - Cyprus Pound fell to low of U.S. $2.22 on black market. Subsequent improvement to level of U.S. $2.36.

## POUND EAST AFRICA

Multiple of East African Shilling, former monetary unit of **British East Africa**. Equivalent to 20 Shillings or 2,000 Cents.
- See *Shilling East Africa.*

## POUND EGYPT

Monetary unit of **Egypt**. Divided into 5 Talari, 100 Piastres (Piastres-Tarif) or 1,000 Millièmes (Qurush or Och'r el Guerche). Formerly circulated in Sudan.

Bank of issue - National Bank of Egypt(private bank),whose banknotes did not become legal tender until 1914 with note-issue privilege since 1898. Nationalized in 1950. Issue of small denominations by Ministry of Finance. Central Bank of Egypt became bank of issue in 1961. National Bank became commercial bank.

Predecessor - See *Piastre Egypt.*

**1834** - Under reform of Mohammed, minting of 100 Piastre coins (8.544 grams 875 fine, or 7.476 grams fine gold) referred to as Pounds.

**1885** (November 14th) - Adoption of gold standard. Egyptian Pound established as official monetary unit:
  1 Egyptian Pound = 100 Piastres
  1 Egyptian Pound = 7,437.5 milligrams of fine gold
  1 Pound Sterling = 0.975 Egyptian Pound
  1 Egyptian Pound = 4.87 U.S. Dollars
Gold Pounds minted, based upon 8.544 grams 875 fine. Simultaneous minting of silver Piastres.

**1914** (August 2nd) - Suspension of gold standard. Increased banknote issue. Continuous depreciation of currency to maximum of 30%.

**1916** (October 30th) - Decree authorizing use of British Government Bonds as monetary reserves.

**1926** (January 1st) - Restoration of convertibility at previous parity.

**1931** (September 26th) - Suspension of convertibility and adherence to Sterling Area:
  1 Pound Sterling = 0.975 Egyptian Pound

**1939** (September 28th) - Foreign exchange controls.

**1946** (December 18th) - New parity registered with International Monetary Fund:
  1 Egyptian Pound = 3,672.88 milligrams of fine gold
  1 Egyptian Pound = 4.133 U.S. Dollars

**1947** (July 14th) - Egypt abandoned Sterling Area, but maintained traditional exchange ratio:
  1 Pound Sterling = 0.975 Egyptian Pound

**1949** (September 21st) - Devaluation following Pound Sterling:
  1 Egyptian Pound = 2,551.87 milligrams of fine gold
  1 Egyptian Pound = 2.87156 U.S. Dollars

**1950** - Export Pound variety created for payment of approved imports from various

"hard currency" countries and for payment to residents in settlement of exports to certain "soft currency" countries. Exchange rate:
1 Egyptian Pound = 2.58 U.S. Dollars

**1952** (August) - Creation of Travel and Maintenance Pound resulting from 10% tax on exchange allocated for travel, maintenance remittances to Egyptians, and revenue remitted to Egyptian nationals residing abroad permanently:
1 Egyptian Pound = 2.58 U.S. Dollars

**1953** (February 28th) - Import Entitlement Account gave rise to additional multiple rates ranging from U.S. $2.56 to U.S. $2.73 per Egyptian Pound. Rates fluctuated constantly since based on discounts from Egyptian Pound.

**1955** (September 1st and 28th) - Import Entitlement Account abolished.

**1957** - Various premiums granted on exchange earned from cotton exports. Percentage differed according to purchasing nation and date of shipment.

**1957** (October 24th) - Import surcharges imposed. Subsequent periodic changes. Import payments in certain currencies subject to fee of 10% for private imports, 20% for government imports.

**1958** (February 10th) - Transferable Export Account Pound replaced Export Pound. Applied to all trade transactions (except rice exports) and import financing:
1 Egyptian Pound = 2.27 U.S. Dollars

**1958** (March 1st) - National Bank of Egypt began to stabilize Transferable Export Pound.

**1958** (March 5th) - Tourist rate created for nonresident travelers in Egypt. Based on 25% premium:
1 Egyptian Pound = 2.30 U.S. Dollars

**1958** (March 10th) - Transferable Export Pound premium fixed at 25% buying, 27% selling.

**1958** (September 1st) - Premium changed to 17.6% buying and selling.

**1959** (September 1st) - Transferable Export Pound system abolished. Replaced by premiums on Egyptian Pound for receipts and payments in convertible currencies. Variable premium applied to exports of raw cotton and certain other goods. Most other exports received 17.5% premium. A 27.5% premium applied to most invisibles and all imports.

**1960** (January 5th) - Premium on most invisibles and all imports reduced to 20%. Rate structure as follows:
1 Egyptian Pound = 2.87156 U.S. Dollars (par value)
1 Egyptian Pound = 2.866/2.8375 U.S. Dollars (commercial banks' rate for certain specified exports and invisibles, Suez Canal dues, all receipts in bilateral agreement and inconvertible currencies; payments for some invisibles and all payments in bilateral agreement currencies)
1 Egyptian Pound = 2.439 U.S. Dollar ($2.866 plus 17.5% premium on par value for exports, except cotton, silk and items not entitled to a premium)
1 Egyptian Pound = 2.379 U.S. Dollar ($2.866 plus 20.48% premium on par value for exports of cotton and

silk - premium gradually reduced throughout 1960 to 6.38% at year's end)

1 Egyptian Pound = 2.364 U.S. Dollars ($2.8375 plus 20% premium on par value for all imports and other invisibles)

1 Egyptian Pound = 2.248 U.S. Dollars ($2.866 plus 27.5% premium on par value for invisibles)

1 Egyptian Pound = 2.208 U.S. Dollars ($2.8375 plus 20% premium and 10% tax on par value for travel and remittances to nationals abroad)

Special rate of 1 Egyptian Pound = 7.75 Lebanon Pounds applied to transactions with Lebanon.

**1960** (July 4th) - Premium applicable to payments for all imports and most invisibles reduced to 10%.

**1960** (November 1st) - Premium of 20% applied to capital payments to nonresidents leaving Egypt permanently.

**1961** (August 1st) - Variable premium for exports of cotton and silk removed.

**1961** (December 31st) - Premium of 20% on par value replaced all other existing premiums. Applied to all payments and receipts. Special Dollar banknote rate of U.S. $1.65 per Egyptian Pound applied to banknotes credited to U.S. Dollar accounts for settlement of nonresident obligations toward residents. Not applied to Canal dues.

**1962** (May 7th) - Multiple rates virtually abolished:

1 Egyptian Pound = 2.30 U.S. Dollars (almost all transactions)

1 Egyptian Pound = 2.87156 U.S. Dollars (Suez Canal dues)

Special rate of 1 Egyptian Pound = 8.00 Lebanese Pounds applied to travel allocations by Egyptians to Lebanon.

**1963** (January 1st) - Uniform exchange rate:

1 Egyptian Pound = 2.30 U.S. Dollars

**1963** (September 30th) - Special rate with Lebanon expired.

**1964** (April 10th) - Exchange tax of 5% applied to payments for most invisibles and capital transfers.

**1967** (June) - Egyptian Pound on black market fell to record low of U.S. $0.90. Minor recovery followed.

**1969** (January 4th) - Development tax of 10% imposed on c.i.f. value of imports (5% for highly essential imports).


## POUND FALKLAND ISLANDS

Monetary unit of **Falkland Islands.** Formerly divided into 20 Shillings and 240 Pence. Following decimalization (February 15, 1971), divided into 100 New Pence.

Note-issuing authority - Commissioner of Currency.

Predecessor - See *Pound.*

**1946** (December 18th) - Parity registered with International Monetary Fund:
    1 Pound Sterling = 1 Falkland Pound
    1 Falkland Pound = 3,581.34 milligrams of fine gold
    1 Falkland Pound = 4.03 U.S. Dollars

**1949** (September 18th) - Devaluation parallel to Pound Sterling:
    1 Falkland Pound = 2,488.28 milligrams of fine gold
    1 Falkland Pound = 2.80 U.S. Dollars

**1967** (November 18th) - Devaluation parallel to Pound Sterling:
    1 Falkland Pound = 2,132.81 milligrams of fine gold
    1 Falkland Pound = 2.40 U.S. Dollars

**1971** (February 15th) - Decimalization of Falkland Pound, with subdivision of 100 New Pence.

## POUND FIJI ISLANDS

Former monetary unit of **Fiji Islands.** Divided into 20 Shillings and 240 Pence.
Note-issuing authority - Commissioner of Currency.
Predecessor - See *Fiji Islands.*

**1946** (December 18th) - Parity registered with International Monetary Fund:
    1 Pound Sterling = 1.11 Fiji Pounds
    1 Fiji Pound = 3,226.44 milligrams of fine gold
    1 Fiji Pound = 3.63 U.S. Dollars

**1949** (September 18th) - Devaluation parallel to Pound Sterling:
    1 Fiji Pound = 2,241.69 milligrams of fine gold
    1 Fiji Pound = 2.52 U.S. Dollars

**1967** (November 18th) - Devaluation parallel to Pound Sterling:
    1 Fiji Pound = 1,921.45 milligrams of fine gold
    1 Fiji Pound = 2.16 U.S. Dollars

**1967** (November 26th) - Revaluation created new relationship to Pound Sterling:
    1 Pound Sterling = 1.045 Fiji Pounds
    1 Fiji Pound = 2,040.96 milligrams of fine gold
    1 Fiji Pound = 2.30 U.S. Dollars

**1969** (January 13th) - Introduction of decimal currency system, and creation of new unit.
    - See *Dollar Fiji.*

## POUND GAMBIA

Monetary unit of **Gambia.** Divided into 20 Shillings and 240 Pence.
Note-issuing authority - Gambia Currency Board established May 13, 1964 to take over activities of West African Currency Board.
Predecessors - See *Pound West Africa* and *Gambia.*

**1964** (May 13th) - New monetary unit repaced West African Pound at par.

1 Gambia Pound = 2,488.28 milligrams of fine gold
1 Gambia Pound = 2.80 U.S. Dollars

**1964** (October 5th) - First issue of Gambia Pound banknotes.

**1967** (November 20th) - Devaluation of 14.3% parallel to Pound Sterling:
1 Gambian Pound = 2,132.81 milligrams of fine gold
1 Gambian Pound = 2.40 U.S. Dollars

**1968** (July 8th) - Par value of Gambian Pound registered with International Monetary Fund.

**1971** (July 1st) - Gambian Pound replaced. - See *Dalasy.*


## POUND GHANA

Former monetary unit of **Ghana.** Divided into 20 Shillings and 240 Pence.

Bank of issue - Bank of Ghana established March 1957.

Predecessors - See *Ghana* and *Pound West Africa.*

**1958** (July 14th) - First issue of Ghana Pound to replace West African Pound at par:
1 Ghana Pound = 2,488.28 milligrams of fine gold
1 Ghana Pound = 2.80 U.S. Dollars

**1959** (July 1st) - Ghana Pound became sole legal tender.

**1965** (July) - Ghana Pound hit low of U.S. $0.90 in black market dealings.

**1965** (July 17th) - De facto devaluation. Introduction of new monetary unit.
- See *Cedi.*


## POUND IRELAND

Monetary unit of **Ireland.** Divided into 20 Shillings or 240 Pence (formerly Irish).
Decimalized into 100 New Pence on February 15, 1971.
Also called Saorstát Pound.

Bank of issue - Eight private banks, then (1934) Currency Commission. Replaced February 1, 1943 by Central Bank of Ireland.

Predecessor - See *Ireland.*

**18th Century** - English monies were legal tender in Ireland at value higher than their accounting value in England: Guinea (21 Shillings in London) worth 22 Shillings 9 Pence in Dublin. Crown (5 Shillings in London) worth 5 Shillings 5 Pence. Shilling (12 Pence in London) worth 13 Pence, or Irish.

**1804** - 31 Irish Shillings were equal to 9 English Shillings.

**1825** - Introduction of English monetary system.

**1845** - Irish Bankers Act: privilege of unlimited banknote issue given to private banks.

**1927** (August 20th) - Reinstatement of Irish Pound:
1 Irish Pound = 1 Pound Sterling
1 Irish Pound = 7,322.38 milligrams of fine gold

Currency Act established Currency Commission charged with preparing system of banknote issue.

**1931** (September 26th) - Gold standard abandoned. Adherence to Sterling Area with maintenance of Irish Pound at par with Pound Sterling.
- See *Pound.*

**1939** (September 3rd) - Foreign exchange controls within framework of Sterling Area.

**1949** (September 18th) - Devaluation (30.52%) parallel to Pound Sterling:
1 Irish Pound = 2,488.28 milligrams of fine gold
1 Irish Pound = 2.80 U.S. Dollars

**1951** (October) - Irish Pound hit low of 2.40 U.S. Dollars in black market. Subsequently strengthened.

**1967** (November 18th) - Devaluation parallel to Pound Sterling:
1 Irish Pound = 2,132.81 milligrams of fine gold
1 Irish Pound = 2.40 U.S. Dollars

**1971** (February 15th) - Decimalization of Irish Pound into 100 New Pence.


## POUND ISRAEL

Monetary unit of **Israel.** Divided into 100 Agorot. Prior to January 1, 1960, divided into 1,000 Prutot.

Bank of issue - Issue Department of Anglo-Palestine Bank (created in England, January 27, 1902), Issue Department of Israel National Bank (from June 1952 to December 1, 1954), then Bank of Israel.

Precedessor - See *Pound Palestine, Palestine* and *Israel.*

**1948** (August 16th) - Creation of Israel Pound to replace Palestinian Pound. Law required complete changeover at fixed 1 to 1 rate before September 30, 1948:
1 Israel Pound = 1 Pound Sterling
1 Israel Pound = 3,581.34 milligrams of fine gold
1 Israel Pound = 4.03 U.S. Dollars
Rate for approved imports and financial transactions with hard currency areas:
1 Israel Pound = 3.015/2.986 U.S. Dollars (buying/sell-
ing)

**1949** (September 18th) - Devaluation parallel to Pound Sterling:
1 Israel Pound = 2,488.28 milligrams of fine gold
1 Israel Pound = 2.80 U.S. Dollars

**1951** (March 26th) - Unauthorized gold dealings prohibited. Black market activity increased considerably.

**1951-1952** (February) - Precipitous decline of Israel Pound in black market dealings. Pound listed at 87.2% discount from official rate by February 1952.

**1952** (February 17th) - Partial devaluation. Introduction of multiple rate system:
1 Israel Pound = 2.80 U.S. Dollars (government transac-
tions, essential imports, diamond exports)
1 Israel Pound = 1.40 U.S. Dollars (contributions from
abroad, tourism, certain exports, semi-essential
imports, authorized service payments)

1 Israel Pound = 1.00 U.S. Dollar (investment remittances, all other exports)

Subsequent modifications through regrouping of categories in favor of 1.00 U.S. Dollar rate.

**1952** (June 9th-June 23rd) - Currency changeover and forced loan. Small denominations exchanged at face value. Large denominations exchanged at 90% of face value, remaining 10% in bonds.

**1953** (April-July) - Introduction of premiums (80%) and surcharges (80%) created additional effective rates.

**1954** (January 1st) - Partial devaluation. Single official rate established:

1 Israel Pound = 1 U.S. Dollar

Surcharge of 80% applied to certain payments and premium of 30% and 80% applied to certain receipts created additional effective rates.

**1954** (January-September 2nd) - Premium and surcharge rate of 80% gradually expanded to cover all foreign exchange transactions, except contributions from abroad (30% premium).

**1955** (July 1st) - Basic effective rate became new official rate:

1 U.S. Dollar = 1.80 Israel Pounds

**1955** (October 2nd) - Buying rate for receipts from foreign contributions changed:

1 U.S. Dollar = 1.50 Israel Pounds

**1956** (February) - System of premiums introduced for specified exports to particular countries.

Premiums and subsidies increased and given expanded coverage throughout 1956. Year-end effective rates:

1 U.S. Dollar = 1.26-1.62 Israel Pounds (exports to certain countries)

1 U.S. Dollar = 0.45-1.45 Israel Pounds

**1957** (March 13th) - Par value registered with International Monetary Fund:

1 Israel Pound = 493.706 milligrams of fine gold

1 U.S. Dollar = 1.80 Israel Pounds

**1957-1958** (January 1st) - All exchange subsidies on imports reduced, then abolished with exception of imports under Information Media Guaranty program (i.e., books, etc.). Rate:

1 U.S. Dollar = 1.40 Israel Pounds

Periodic increases and expansion of export premium program to cover additional currencies.

**1958** (April 1st) - Special rate for foreign contributions abolished.

**1959** (March 13th) - Partial devaluation. Creation of tourist rate:

1 U.S. Dollar = 2.16 Israel Pounds (official rate plus 20% premium)

**1959** (August 18th) - Special Information Media rate abolished.

**1960** (January 1st) - Creation of new submultiple of Israel Pound:

1 Israel Pound = 100 Agorot

1 Agora = 10 Prutot

**1960** (November 28th) - Israel citizens given freedom to own and trade in gold, both within Israel and abroad.

**1962** (February 9th) - Devaluation and elimination of multiple rate practices except in case of certain small premiums for foreign security transactions:
    1 Israel Pound = 296.224 milligrams of fine gold
    1 U.S. Dollar = 3.00 Israel Pounds

**1967** (November 19th) - Following devaluation of Pound Sterling, Israel Pound devalued:
    1 Israel Pound = 253.906 milligrams of fine gold
    1 U.S. Dollar = 3.50 Israel Pounds

**1970** (March) - Israel Pound fell to historic low of 4.55 per U.S. Dollar, premium of 30% for Greenback.

## POUND JAMAICA

Former monetary unit of **Jamaica, Turks** and **Caicos Islands,** and **Cayman Islands.** Divided into 20 Shillings and 240 Pence.

Bank of issue - Barclay's Bank, Bank of Nova Scotia, Royal Canadian Bank, Canadian Bank of Commerce and Jamaican Treasury, then from 1958 by Jamaican Treasury, and since 1961 by Bank of Jamaica.

Predecessor - See *Jamaica.*

**18th Century** - Unit of account: Jamaican Pound, 40% inferior to Pound Sterling:
    1 Pound Sterling = 1.40 Jamaican Pounds

**19th Century** - Accounting value of Jamaica Pound adjusted to equal Pound Sterling.
    - See *Pound.*

**1920** (March) - First issue of local currency notes by Jamaican Treasury. Denominations of 2½. 5 and 10 Shillings. Simultaneous circulation of banknotes of several private banks.

**1946** (December 18th) - Parity of Jamaican Pound, along with Pound Sterling, registered with International Monetary Fund:
    1 Jamaican Pound = 3,581.34 milligrams of fine gold
    1 Jamaican Pound = 4.03 U.S. Dollars

**1949** (September 18th) - Devalued with Pound Sterling:
    1 Jamaican Pound = 2,488.28 milligrams of fine gold
    1 Jamaican Pound = 2.80 U.S. Dollars

**1961** (May 1st) - Bank of Jamaica became note-issuing authority for Jamaican Pound.

**1963** (March 8th) - Par value of Jamaican Pound registered with International Monetary Fund.

**1967** (November 21st) - Devalued with Pound Sterling:
    1 Jamaican Pound = 2,132.81 milligrams of fine gold
    1 Jamaican Pound = 2.40 U.S. Dollars

**1969** (September 8th) - Jamaican Pound replaced by Jamaican Dollar.
    - See *Dollar Jamaica.*

## POUND LEBANON

Monetary unit of **Lebanon.** Divided into 100 Piastres.

Bank of issue - Banque de Syrie et du Liban, then Banque du Liban (Bank of Lebanon) from April 1, 1964.

Predecessor - See *Pound Lebanon-Syria.*

**1948** (January 1st) - Franco-Lebanese financial agreement. Breakup of common exchange control and monetary system for Syria and Lebanon. Creation of separate and distinct monetary unit in Lebanon:
>1 Lebanese Pound = 1 Lebanese-Syrian Pound
>1 Lebanese Pound = 405.512 milligrams of fine gold
>1 U.S. Dollar = 2.19148 Lebanese Pounds

**1948** (February 3rd) - Syrian currency withdrawn from circulation in Lebanon. Introduction of independent foreign exchange controls.

**1948** (November) - Fluctuating free market rate recognized and made applicable to 90% of foreign exchange proceeds. Remaining 10% transacted at official rate. Fluctuating free rate averaged 3.55 Lebanese Pounds per U.S. Dollar.

**1949** (February) - Appearance of free market premium of Lebanese Pound over Syrian Pound. Averaged 7% in 1949. Reached record high of 15% in early 1950, before settling back to 7% level.

**1949** (July) - Lebanon abandoned Franc-Zone.

**1949** (September 26th) - Requirement for surrender of 10% of exchange proceeds at official rate limited to nonexport proceeds. Official rate also applied to government transactions and to 80% of local expenditures of foreign concessions.

**1950** (March 14th) - Customs union between Lebanon and Syria dissolved. Exchange transactions between two countries made subject to same controls and restrictions applicable to third countries.

**1951** (November) - Free rate of Lebanese Pound hit 3.86 per U.S. Dollar. Subsequent improvement to below 3.00 per U.S. Dollar in 1962.

**1952** (January 26th) - All non-export proceeds given complete access to fluctuating free market.

**1952** (May 24th) - All local expenditures of foreign concessions given access to fluctuating free market. Official rate remained applicable only to government transactions.

**1954** - Government intervention in free market preventing rate from falling below 3.20 Lebanese Pounds per U.S. Dollar.

**1965** (January 1st) - Provisional legal parity established and applied to government transactions, to valuation of official assets and to customs valuation:
>1 Lebanese Pound = 288.529 milligrams of fine gold
>1 U.S. Dollar = 3.08 Lebanese Pounds

**1967** (June) - Free rate of Lebanese Pound fell to 3.40 per U.S. Dollar, improving to 3.13 in early 1968, before leveling at range of 3.21-3.30 per U.S. Dollar in 1970.

## POUND LEBANON-SYRIA

Former monetary unit of **Lebanon** and **Syria.** Divided into 100 Piastres or 2,000 Centimes.

Bank of issue - Banque de Syrie, established 1919 under French Treasury control; renamed Banque de Syrie et du Gran Liban in 1924; renamed Banque de Syrie et du Liban (Bank of Syria and Lebanon) in 1939.

Variation of name - Often called Syrian Pound or Lebanese Pound.

Predecessor - See *Syria*.

**1920** (May 1st) - Introduction of Lebanese-Syrian monetary system by decree of French Commissioner:

> 1 Lebanese-Syrian Pound = 20 French Francs

**1926** - Wide fluctuations in French Franc value resulted in adoption of Syrian-Lebanese gold Piastre for accounting purposes.

**1928** (June 24th) - Following stabilization of French Franc, adoption of gold exchange standard:

> 1 Lebanese-Syrian Pound = 20 Francs (Poincaré)
> 1 Lebanese-Syrian Pound = 1.179 milligrams of fine gold

**1929** (January 1st) - French High Commissioner abolished Syrian-Lebanese gold Piastre. Had been abolished for certain purposes on September 1, 1928.

**1935** (May 23rd) - Demonetization of Turkish silver coins.

**1936** (October 1st) - Suspension of gold exchange standard, following devaluation of French Franc.

**1939** (December 3rd) - Foreign exchange controls. Exchange rate maintained at:

> 1 Lebanese-Syrian Pound = 20 French Francs
> 1 Lebanese-Syrian Pound = 2.20 U.S. Dollars

**1944** (February) - Anglo-French financial agreement fixed exchange rate in terms of Pound Sterling:

> 1 Pound Sterling = 8.83 Lebanese-Syrian Pounds

**1946** (October) - Appearance of free exchange market. Used for large portion of exchange transactions, but not officially recognized. Average rate:

> 1 U.S. Dollar = 3.33 Lebanese-Syrian Pounds

**1947** (July 29th) - Parity registered with International Monetary Fund:

> 1 Lebanese-Syrian Pound = 405.512 milligrams   of   fine
> gold
> 1 U.S. Dollar = 2.19148 Lebanese-Syrian Pounds

**1948** (January 1st) - Franco-Lebanese financial agreement. Breakup of common exchange control and monetary system for Syria and Lebanon. Creation of two separate and distinct monetary systems.

- See *Pound Lebanon* and *Pound Syria*.


# POUND LIBYA

Monetary unit of **Libya**. Divided into 100 Piastres or 1,000 Millièmes.

Note-issuing authority - Libyan Currency Commission, then National Bank of Libya (April 26, 1955). Name changed to Bank of Libya in 1963.

Predecessor - See *Libya.*

**1952** (March 24th) - Creation of independent monetary unit, at par with Pound Sterling, to replace Occupation currencies:
>  1 Libyan Pound = 97.50 Eygptian Piastres
>  1 Libyan Pound = 480.00 BMA Lire
>  1 Libyan Pound = 980.00 Algerian Francs

**1959** (August 12th) - Par value registered with International Monetary Fund:
>  1 Libyan Pound = 2,488.28 milligrams of fine gold
>  1 Libyan Pound = 2.80 U.S. Dollars

**1969** (September) - Black market rate of Libyan Pound fell to low of U.S. $1.85-U.S. $2.00.


# POUND MALAWI

Former monetary unit of **Malawi.** Created in 1964 and divided into 20 Shillings and 240 Pence.

Bank of issue - Reserve Bank of Malawi.

Predecessor - See *Pound Rhodesia* and *Nyasaland, Pound Southern Rhodesia, Pound.*

**1964** (July 6th) - Nyasaland became independent of Federation of Rhodesia and Nyasaland and changed name to Malawi.

**1964** (July 23rd) - Reserve Bank of Malawi created as Central Bank with note-issuing authority.

**1964** (November 16th) - First issue of Malawi Pound at par with Pound of former Federation and Pound Sterling:
>  1 Malawi Pound = 2,488.28 milligrams of fine gold
>  1 Malawi Pound = 2.80 U.S. Dollars

**1965** (June 1st) - Pound notes of former Rhodesian Federation demonetized.
Exchange controls imposed on transactions with Rhodesia and Zambia.

**1966** (May 27th) - Par value of Malawi Pound established with International Monetary Fund.

**1967** (November 20th) - Devaluation of 14.3% in line with Pound Sterling devaluation:
>  1 Malawi Pound = 2,132.81 milligrams of fine gold
>  1 Malawi Pound = 2.40 U.S. Dollars

**1969** (March) - Malawi Pound offered at 17% discount in black market.

**1971** (February 15th) - decimalization, and name of currency changed.
>  - See *Kwacha Malawi.*

## POUND MALTA

Monetary unit of **Malta**. Divided into 20 Shillings and 240 Pence.

Note-issuing authority - Government, then Central Bank of Malta.

Predecessor - See *Malta.*

**1949** (July) - Maltese Pound created as legal tender by Currency Note Ordinancy.
　　1 Maltese Pound = 1 Pound Sterling
　　1 Maltese Pound = 3,581.34 milligrams of fine gold
　　1 Maltese Pound = 4.03 U.S. Dollars

**1949** (September 18th) - Devaluation parallel to Pound Sterling:
　　1 Maltese Pound = 2,488.28 milligrams of fine gold
　　1 Maltese Pound = 2.80 U.S. Dollars

**1949** (September 20th) - Banknotes of Bank of England no longer legal tender. Coins kept legal tender status.

**1964** - Independent republic within British Commonwealth.

**1967** (November 20th) - Devaluation parallel to Pound Sterling:
　　1 Malta Pound = 2,132.81 milligrams of fine gold
　　1 Malta Pound = 2.40 U.S. Dollars

**1968** (June 7th) - Central Bank of Malta began operations with note-issuing authority.

**1969** (June 27th) - Parity of 1967 registered with International Monetary Fund.


## POUND NEW ZEALAND

Monetary unit of **New Zealand** from 1907 to 1967. Divided into 20 Shillings and 240 Pence.

Bank of issue - At first by six private banks (Bank of New Zealand, National Bank of New Zealand, Commercial Bank of Australia, Union Bank of Australia, Bank of New South Wales, Bank of Australia), then by Reserve Bank of New Zealand, created by Act of November 27, 1933, activated on August 1, 1934, nationalized on April 8, 1936.

Predecessor - See *New Zealand.*

**1907** - At transformation of Colony into Dominion, creation of New Zealand Pound:
　　1 New Zealand Pound = 1 Pound Sterling
　　1 New Zealand Pound = 7,322.38 milligrams of fine gold
　　1 New Zealand Pound = 4.8665 U.S. Dollars
Banknote issue entrusted to six private banks.

**1915** - Abandonment of gold standard. Depreciation of currency.

**1929** (December) - De facto up valuation of New Zealand Pound to gold parity.

**1930** (April) - New depreciation of about 10%.

**1931** (September 21st) - Adherence to Sterling Area.

**1933** (February) - 1 Pound Sterling = 1.25 New Zealand Pounds.

**1936** (April 8th) - Banknote issue entrusted to Reserve Bank of New Zealand, which became government institution.

**1938** (December 5th) - Reserve Bank authorized not to convert banknotes into Pound Sterling at officially quoted rate of exchange.

**1938** (December 7th) - Foreign exchange controls.

**1948** (August 19th) - Revaluation at par with Pound Sterling:
      1 New Zealand Pound = 1 Pound Sterling
      1 New Zealand Pound = 3,581.24 milligrams of fine gold
      1 New Zealand Pound = 4.03 U.S. Dollars

**1949** (September 19th) - Devaluation parallel to Pound Sterling:
      1 New Zealand Pound = 1 Pound Sterling
      1 New Zealand Pound = 2,488.28 milligrams of fine gold
      1 New Zealand Pound = 2.80 U.S. Dollars

**1961** (October 27th) - Par value registered with International Monetary Fund:
      1 New Zealand Pound = 2,471.3 milligrams of fine gold
      1 New Zealand Pound = 2.7809 U.S. Dollars

**1966** (September) - New Zealand Pound hit record low of U.S. $1.90 on black market.

**1967** (July 10th) - Decimalization, and creation of new unit.
  - See *Dollar New Zealand.*


## POUND NIGERIA

Monetary unit of **Nigeria.** Divided into 20 Shillings and 240 Pence.

Bank of issue - Central Bank of Nigeria, established July 1, 1959.

Predecessor - See *Pound West Africa.*

**1959** (July 1st) - Creation of Nigerian Pound to replace West African Pound at par:
      1 Nigerian Pound = 2,488.28 milligrams of fine gold
      1 Nigerian Pound = 2.80 U.S. Dollars

**1962** (July 16th) - All currencies, except Nigerian Pounds, designated as foreign currencies under Exchange Control Act of 1962.
Notes and coins issued by West African Currency Board ceased to be legal tender.

**1963** (April 17th) - Par value established with International Monetary Fund.

**1967** (July) - Secessionist Biafra, controlling 25%-33% of Nigerian Pounds in circulation, exported vast amounts of currency to purchase war material.

**1967** (October 20th) - Private imports of gold and silver subject to customs duty of 100%, ad valorem.

**1967** (December) - Dumping of banknotes by Biafra through local smuggling and overseas purchases.
Discount for Pound fell to 40% on black market.

**1968** (January 3rd) - To halt illegal dealings, Central Government decreed currency changeover.
New banknotes issued to replace old issues, 30% of which were in Biafran hands.

**1968** (January 10th) - Secessionist Biafra issued independent currency.
  - See *Pound Biafra.*

**1968** (January 23rd) - All old Nigerian banknotes decreed null and void.

**1968** (July) - Black market rate of currency continued dramatic decline (40% below par), despite temporary positive effects of new banknote issue.

**1970** (December) - Nigerian Pound hit new low of U.S. $1.50 on black market, discount of 46% from official rate.


## POUND PALESTINE

Monetary unit **Palestine** and **Transjordan.** Divided into 100 Piastres and 1,000 Mils.

Note-issuing authority - Palestine Currency Board.

Predecessor - See *Palestine.*

**1927** (November 1st) - Creation of Palestinian Pound at par with Pound Sterling:
   1 Palestinian Pound = 7,322.38 milligrams of fine gold
   1 Palestinian Pound = 4.8665 U.S. Dollars
   Replaced Egyptian Piastre at:
   1 Palestinian Pound = 97.50 Egyptian Piastres

**1931** (September 21st) - Suspension of gold standard. Linked to Pound Sterling at par.

**1939** (September 21st) - Foreign exchange controls.

**1948** (August 16th) - In Israel, replaced at par by Israel Pound.
   - See *Israel* and *Pound Israel.*

**1949** (September 18th) - Devaluation parallel to Pound Sterling:
   1 Palestinian Pound = 2,488.28 milligrams of fine gold
   1 Palestinian Pound = 2.80 U.S. Dollars

**1950** (July 1st) - In Jordan, replaced at par by Jordan Dinar.
   - See *Jordan* and *Dinar Jordan.*


## POUND RHODESIA

Former monetary unit of **Rhodesia.** Divided into 20 Shillings and 240 Pence.

Bank of issue - Reserve Bank of Rhodesia.

Predecessor - See *Pound Rhodesia and Nyasaland, Pound Southern Rhodesia, Pound.*

**1963** (December 31st) - Southern Rhodesia reverted to status of self-governing Colony within Commonwealth.

**1964** (November 16th) - Bank of Rhodesia and Nyasaland issued Rhodesian Pound at par with Pound of former Federation and Pound Sterling:
   1 Rhodesian Pound = 2,488.28 milligrams of fine gold
   1 Rhodesian Pound = 2.80 U.S. Dollars

**1965** (June 1st) - Reserve Bank of Rhodesia replaced Bank of Rhodesia and Nyasaland. Pound of former Rhodesian Federation demonetized.

**1965** (November) - Rhodesian currency listed on black market at average discount of 50%. Some sporatic transactions at a discount of 82%.

**1965** (November-December) - Rash of domestic controls and foreign exchange restrictions on Rhodesian funds decreed and extended.

Rhodesia subject to United Nations economic sanctions.
Government announced that Rhodesian Pound would be linked to gold, but not to Sterling.

**1968** (March) - Rhodesian Pound recovered in black market dealings, being offered at discount of 10%.

**1970** (February 17th) - Decimalization of currency and new unit created.
- See *Dollar Rhodesia.*

## POUND RHODESIA AND NYASALAND

Monetary unit of **Federation of Rhodesia** and **Nyasaland.** Divided into 20 Shillings and 240 Pence.

Variation of name - Federal Pound.

Bank of issue - Bank of Rhodesia and Nyasaland.

Predecessors - See *Pound Southern Rhodesia, Pound.*

**1956** (April 1st) - Bank of Rhodesia and Nyasaland created. First issue of new currency replacing Southern Rhodesian Pound at par:
1 Rhodesia and Nyasaland Pound = 2,488.28 milligrams
of fine gold
1 Rhodesia and Nyasaland Pound = 2.80 U.S. Dollars

**1962** (December) - Pound, weaken by political strife, fell to low of U.S. $2.30 in black market.

**1963** (December 31st) - Federation formally dissolved.

**1964** (November 16th) - Each of former Federation partners began issuing their own currency notes.
- See *Pound Rhodesia, Pound Malawi, Pound Zambia.*

**1965** (June 1st) - Rhodesia and Nyasaland Pound demonetized.

## POUND SOUTH AFRICA

Former monetary unit of **Southwest Africa, Basutoland, Bechuanaland, Swaziland,** and **South Africa.** Divided into 20 Shillings and 240 Pence.

Bank of issue - South African Reserve Bank.

Predecessor - See *South Africa.*

**1920** - Monetary independence of South Africa. Creation of South African Pound at par with Pound Sterling:
1 South African Pound = 1 Pound Sterling
1 South African Pound = 7,322.38 milligrams of fine gold
South African Reserve Bank established as note-issuing authority.

**1922** (September 15th) - Suspension of convertibility into gold.

**1922** (June 30th) - Embargo on gold lifted.

**1925** (July 1st) - Convertibility into gold reestablished on basis of former parity.

**1932** (December 28th) - Gold standard abandoned. Depreciation of currency and adherence to Sterling Area on basis of:
    1 South African Pound = 1 Pound Sterling

**1934** - Foreign exchange holdings of South African Reserve Bank valued at rate of:
    100 Pounds Sterling = 100.375 South African Pounds

**1939** (September 9th) - Foreign exchange controls covering Union of South Africa and territories under mandate, i.e., Southwest Africa, Basutoland, Swaziland, Bechuanaland.

**1944** - Reestablishment of gold convertibility of banknotes with proviso "temporarily suspended ".

**1946** (December 8th) - Parity registered with International Monetary Fund:
    1 South African Pound = 3,581.34 milligrams of fine gold
    1 South African Pound = 4.03 U.S. Dollars

**1949** (September 18th) - Devaluation parallel to Pound Sterling. New parity registered with International Monetary Fund:
    1 South African Pound = 2,488.28 milligrams of fine gold
    1 South African Pound = 2.80 U.S. Dollars

**1951** (November) - South African Pound fell to U.S. $2.42 on black market with subsequent improvement to level of U.S. $2.60-U.S. $2.74.

**1961** (February 14th) - Decimalization of South African Pound, and creation of new monetary unit. - See *Rand.*


## POUND SOUTHERN RHODESIA

Monetary unit of **Northern** and **Southern Rhodesia** and **Nyasaland.** Divided into 20 Shillings and 240 Pence.

Note-issuing authority - Southern Rhodesian Currency Board.

Predecessor - See *Pound.*

**1940** - Southern Rhodesian Pound created and kept at par with Pound Sterling, which it replaced as legal tender:
    1 Southern Rhodesian Pound = 4.03 U.S. Dollars

**1940** - Northern Rhodesia adopted Southern Rhodesian Pound as its currency, replacing Pound Sterling.

**1941** - Nyasaland adopted the unit as its own, replacing Pound Sterling.

**1947** - Northern Rhodesia and Nyasaland adopted Southern Rhodesian coins, though British coins remained legal tender in these territories.

**1949** - Currency changed in line with Pound Sterling devaluation:
    1 Southern Rhodesian Pound = 2,488.28 milligrams of fine
        gold
    1 Southern Rhodesian Pound = 2.80 U.S. Dollars

**1953** (August 1st) - Federation of Rhodesia and Nyasaland created. Southern Rhodesian Pound adopted as legal tender.

**1956** (April 1st) - Bank of Rhodesia and Nyasaland established, replacing Southern

Rhodesian Currency Board as note-issuing authority. Southern Rhodesian Pound replaced by Rhodesia and Nyasaland Pound.
- See *Pound Rhodesia and Nyasaland.*


# POUND SUDAN

Monetary unit of **Sudan.** Divided into 10 Riyals, 100 Piastres, or 1,000 Millièmes.

Note-issuing authority - Sudan Currency Board created by Currency Act of 1956, then Bank of Sudan established February 1960.

Predecessor - See *Sudan* and *Pound Egypt.*

**1957** (April 8th) - Creation of independent monetary unit in Sudan to replace Egyptian Pound at par:

> 1 Sudanese Pound = 1 Egyptian Pound
> 1 Sudanese Pound = 2,551.87 milligrams of fine gold
> 1 Sudanese Pound = 2.87156 U.S. Dollars

**1960** (February 22nd) - Bank of Sudan, established on December 1, 1959, began operations.

**1966** (March 1st) - Stamp duties of 1%-3% levied on foreign exchange remittances and bills of exchange.

**1966** (September 20th) - Import surcharge of 5% ad valorem introduced on all goods. Customs duties on certain commodities raised.

**1966** (October 15th) - Stamp duties of March 1st abolished and replaced by new stamp duties on application forms for remittances. Ranged from 0.25 to 5.00 Sudanese Pounds, depending on type of transaction.

**1968** (March 3rd) - Special export levies imposed on certain goods.

**1968** (August 21st) - Import surcharge increased to 8% of c.i.f. value.

**1968** (October 14th) - Import surcharge increased to 10%.

**1968** (October 15th) - Stamp duties raised to range of 0.25 to 10.00 Sudanese Pounds.

**1969** (July 1st) - Import surcharge raised to 15%.

**1969** (September) - Sudanese Pound hit record low of U.S. $1.59 in black market dealings.

**1969** (December 30th) - Surcharge of 19.65% on exchange for foreign currency used for travel abroad. Resulted in partial devaluation and special rate:

> 1 Sudanese Pound = 2.40 U.S. Dollars

**1970** (June) - Second travel rate established for travel to Egypt:

> 1 Sudanese Pound = 2.30 U.S. Dollars

**1970** (October) - Sudanese Pound fell to low of U.S. $1.35 in black market dealings, discount of 53% from official rate.


# POUND SYRIA

Monetary unit of **Syria.** Divided into 100 Piastres.

Bank of issue - Banque de Syrie et du Liban, replaced August 1, 1956 by Banque Centrale de Syrie (Central Bank of Syria).

Variation of name - Syrian Lira.

Predecessor - See *Pound Lebanon-Syria.*

**1948** (January 1st) - Breakup of common exchange control and monetary system for Lebanon and Syria. Creation of separate and distinct monetary unit in Syria:
   1 Syrian Pound = 1 Lebanese-Syrian Pound
   1 Syrian Pound = 405.512 milligrams of fine gold
   1 U.S. Dollar = 2.19148 Syrian Pounds

**1948** (August 12th) - Multiple rate system. Official recognition of fluctuating free market. Applied to all imports and nontrade remittances, 80% of export proceeds, and 20% of local currency requirements of foreign oil concessions in Syria. Balance of transactions, including those of government, used official rate.

**1948** (November) - Fluctuating free rate made applicable to 90% of foreign exchange proceeds. Remaining 10% transacted at official rate. Fluctuating free rate averaged 3.55 Syrian Pounds per U.S. Dollar in 1948.

**1949** (September 26th) - Requirement for surrender of 10% of exchange proceeds at official rate limited to certain nonexport proceeds.

**1950** (March 14th) - Customs union between Lebanon and Syria dissolved. Exchange transactions between two countries made subject to same controls and restrictions that applied to third countries.

**1950** (May) - Additional fluctuating "exportation exchange" market rate established. Applied to specified imports and certain exports. Authorized arbitrage between this and fluctuating free rate resulted in practically equal relationship between two markets.

**1951** (April 15th) - Local expenditures of foreign concessions came completely under official rate.

**1951** (June 4th) - Syrian gold Pounds (6.75 grams 900 fine) issued by l'Institut d'Emission de Syrie and put into circulation by Banque de Syrie et du Liban.

**1951** (September 10th) - Mixed rate for certain nonexport proceeds eliminated. Shifted to fluctuating free market rate.

**1952** (April 26th) - Recodification and significant liberalization of exchange controls.

**1953** (January 23rd) - Exchange Office quoted single rates without discrimination between free and export exchange.

**1953** (February 14th) - Exchange Office required banks to charge single rate for all transactions that were not at official rate.

**1953** (March 2nd) - Legal distinction between exportation exchange rate and free market rate abolished.

**1953** (July 1st) - Government transactions completely shifted to fluctuating free market rate, leaving only local currency purchases of petroleum companies and petroleum imports at official rate.

**1955** (November 29th) - Shift of petroleum company currency purchases to free market.

**1956** (December) - Exchange Office initiated control of free market. Most exchange transactions took place at buying and selling rates maintained at 2.565/3.585

Syrian Pounds per U.S. Dollar. Invisibles, capital transfers and certain authorized imports negotiated in uncontrolled fluctuating free market.

**1961** (February 4th) - Presidential decree imposed comprehensive exchange control system.
Authorized exchange transactions took place at official buying and selling rates maintained by Exchange Office for banks and authorized brokers:
1 U.S. Dollar = 3.565/3.585 Syrian Pounds
Uncontrolled free market abolished.

**1962** (July 10th) - Official buying and selling rates devalued:
1 U.S. Dollar = 3.80/3.82 Syrian Pounds
Free market reinstated and applied to all imports and most exports to neighboring countries, certain luxury imports, most invisibles and capital transactions.

**1963** (May 3rd) - Free exchange market abolished. Most exchange transactions took place through official market. Import payments, which had access to free market, transacted at selling rate of 4.10 Syrian Pounds per U.S. Dollar.

**1963** (December 31st) - Special import selling rate quoted at 3.90 Syrian Pounds per U.S. Dollar.

**1964** (January 7th) - Limited free market established. Applied to all imports and most exports of neighboring countries, most invisibles and capital imports. Quoted at 3.93/3.95 Syrian Pounds per U.S. Dollar. Later pegged at 4.17 Syrian Pounds per U.S. Dollar.

**1965** (July 1st) - Free market rate unpegged.

**1965** (September 1st) - Free market rate repegged at about 4.03 Syrian Pounds per U.S. Dollar.

**1965** (December) - Syrian Pound on unofficial market in Beirut hit 5.00 per U.S. Dollar.

**1966** (March 15th) - Decree limiting access to official selling rate, retroactive to January 11, 1965.

**1966** (November 10th) - Complete reorganization of exchange market. Access to official or free market based entirely upon commodity. Official rate applied to major exports, essential imports, most invisibles, government transactions. All other transactions used fluctuating free market.

**1967** (January) - Free market rate came under control of Commercial Bank of Syria.

**1967** (June) - Syrian Pound on unofficial market in Beirut hit over 6.00 per U.S. Dollar. Subsequently improved to more normal levels of about 4.18-4.26 per U.S. Dollar, maintaining that range through 1969.

**1967** (September 20th) - Allocation of official exchange limited to 300 specified commodities. All other exchange available only through free market.

**1967** (September 24th) - Certain exports free from repatriation commitment. New access lists to official and free market export proceeds. Subsequently revised.

**1970** - Unofficial rate of Syrian Pound weakened to over 4.50 per U.S. Dollar.


# POUND TONGA

Former monetary unit of **Tonga.** Divided into 20 Shillings and 240 Pence. Use of

British, then Australian subsidiary coinage.

Note-issuing authority - Tonga Treasury.

Predecessor - See *Tonga.*

**1900** - Introduction of British monetary system with subsequent issue by Tonga Treasury of currency notes denominated in Tonga Pounds. Currency linked at par to Pound Sterling. - See *Pound.*

**1936** - Depreciation in official relationship to Pound Sterling. Adoption of exchange standard system based upon Australian Pound:
  1 Australian Pound = 1 Tonga Pound
  1 Pound Sterling = 0.2525 Tonga Pounds

**1946** (December 18th) - Parity registered with International Monetary Fund:
  1 Pound Sterling = 1.2525 Tonga Pounds
  1 Tonga Pound = 2,859.36 milligrams of fine gold
  1 Tonga Pound = 3.217565 U.S. Dollars

**1949** (September 18th) - Devaluation parallel to Pound Sterling:
  1 Tonga Pound = 1,990.62 milligrams of fine gold
  1 Tonga Pound = 2.239997 U.S. Dollars

**1950** (August 2nd) - Parity between Tonga Pound and Pound Sterling adjusted:
  1 Pound Sterling = 1.25 Tonga Pounds

**1966** (February 14th) - Decimalization and adoption of new currency.
  - See *Pa'anga.*


# POUND TURKEY

See *Lira Turkey.*


# POUND WEST AFRICA

Former monetary unit of **British West Africa** (Nigeria, Gambia, Gold Coast and Sierra Leone). Divided into 20 Shillings and 240 Pence.

Note-issuing authority - West African Currency Board, established in 1913.

Predecessor - See *Gold Coast* and *Nigeria.*

**1913** - Special silver coinage introduced in British West Africa. Weight and fineness corresponded to coins of United Kingdom.

**1916** - First issue of local currency notes denominated in West African Pounds and Shillings. At par with British monetary unit, moved parallel to Pound Sterling.
  - See *Pound.*

**1920** - Alloy coinage issued in same denominations as silver coinage in circulation. Gradual withdrawal of silver coins.

**1946** and **1949** - Parity of West African Pound, along with Pound Sterling, registered with International Monetary Fund.

**1958** (July 14th) - In Ghana, creation of Ghana Pound to replace West African Pound at par.
- See *Pound Ghana.*

**1959** (July 1st) - In Nigeria, creation of Nigerian Pound to replace West African Pound at par.
- See *Pound Nigeria.*

**1964** (May 13th) - In Gambia, creation of Gambia Pound to replace West African Pound at par.
- See *Pound Gambia.*

**1964** (August 4th) - In Sierra Leone, creation of Leone to replace West African Pound.
- See *Leone.*


## POUND WESTERN SAMOA

Former monetary unit of **Western Samoa.** Divided into 20 Shillings and 240 Pence. Use of New Zealand subsidiary coinage.

Note-issuing authority - Samoan Treasury under direction of New Zealand Government, then from February 1961, Bank of Western Samoa.

Predecessor - See *Western Samoa.*

**1920** (December 17th) - Samoan Pound directly linked at par to New Zealand Pound and experienced similar monetary history.
- See *Pound New Zealand.*

**1967** (July 10th) - Decimalization along with New Zealand Pound. Creation of new monetary unit.
- See *Tala.*


## POUND ZAMBIA

Former monetary unit of **Zambia.** Divided into 20 Shillings and 240 Pence.

Bank of issue - Bank of Zambia established August 1, 1964.

Predecessor - See *Pound Rhodesia* and *Nyasaland, Pound Southern Rhodesia, Pound.*

**1964** (October 24th) - Northern Rhodesia became independent and changed name to Zambia.
Foreign exchange controls imposed.

**1964** (November 16th) - First issue of Zambian Pound at par with Pound of former Federation and Pound Sterling:
1 Zambian Pound = 2,488.28 milligrams of fine gold
1 Zambian Pound = 2.80 U.S. Dollars

**1965** (June 1st) - Pound of former Rhodesian Federation demonetized.
Exchange controls imposed on transactions with Malawi and Rhodesia.

**1966** (March 7th) - Par value of Zambian Pound established with International Monetary Fund.

**1968** (January 16th) - Zambian Pound replaced by Kwacha.
 - See *Kwacha Zambia.*

**1968** (December 15th) - Zambian Pound demonetized.


## PRIETO

Silver/copper money issued in **Spain** in 1258.
 - See *Negro.*


## *PRUSSIA*

See *Holy Roman Empire.*

**12th to 14th Century** - Minting in Brandenburg of silver Pfennig with annual remintings and reductions (refunding of 12 new Pfennig for 16 old ones).
 - See *Pfennig.*

**14th Century** - Teutonic Order minted own monies: Denier or Pfennig, and its multiples: Vierchen (4 Pfennig), Schilling (12 Pfennig), Halbskoter (16 Pfennig).

**15th Century** - In Brandenburg, gold Gulden and silver Gros. In Pomerania, gold Gulden, Schilling and Witten.
In Prussia, Teutonic Order minted gold Dukat or Ducat (in 1410), patterned on model of Ducat of Hungary.
Depreciation of Schilling. Minting of Gros, worth 3 Schilling or 36 Pfennig.

**About 1520** - Teutonic Order minted gold Gulden.

**18th Century** - In Brandenburg, unit of account: Thaler of 24 Gute Groschen or 240 Pfennig.
Specie monies:
       In gold - Friedrichsdor, Dukat
       In silver - Reichsthaler, Gute Groschen
       In copper - Pfennig and its multiples
In East Prussia (Königesberg), unit of account: Guilder (Gulden) of 30 Groschen. Same specie monies as in Brandenburg, plus Zwei Drittel (coin of 2/3 Thaler) and smaller silver coins: Tympf (18 Groschen), Sechser (6), Duytke (3).

**1751** - Thaler of 24 Groschen or 288 Pfennig defined at 16.7 grams of fine silver.

**1821** - Thaler of 30 Silbergroschen or 360 Pfennig kept same definition. Minting of gold coin (Friedrichsdor) containing 6.68 grams and worth 5 Thaler.

**1838** (July 20th) - Agreement with Bavaria, Sàxony, Württemberg, Baden, Hesse
. . .fixing relationship between Thaler and Gulden:
       1 Thaler = 1.75 Gulden
Minting of a silver coin common to all (Vereinsmünze) containing 33.4 grams and worth 2 Thaler or 3.50 Gulden.

**1857** (January 24th) - Germanic monetary convention: 1 Thaler = 1.50 Austrian

Gulden = 1.75 Gulden of South German States. Minting of common silver money (Vereinsthaler) of 16.7 grams.

**1871** (December 4th) - Monetary unification of Germany: 10 Mark replaced 3.33 Thaler.
   - See *Mark.*

## PRUTOT

Submultiple (¹/₁.₀₀₀) of **Israel** Pound until January 1, 1960. Minted in aluminum.
   - See *Pound Israel.*

Variations of name - Prutoth, Proutha, Pruta, Prutah.

## *PUERTO RICO*

**16th to 19th Centuries** - Circulation of Spanish and Mexican Piastres.

**19th Century** - Spanish monetary system based on Peso of 8 Reales until 1859, from 1859 to 1864 on Peseta, from 1864 to 1868 on Escudo, after 1868 on Peseta.
   - See *Spain.*

**1881** - Use of silver Peso of 100 Centavos or 1,000 Milesimos.

**1895** - Minting of silver Peso of 5 Pesetas and of silver coins from 5 to 40 Centavos.

**1899** - Introduction of U.S. monetary system.
   - See *Dollar.*

## PUL

**I.** - Submultiple (¹/₁₀₀) of Afghani, monetary unit of **Afghanistan.** Minted as copper coins.
   - See *Afghani.*

Variations of name - Poul, Pool.

Plural - Puli.

**II.** - Submultiple (¹/₅₀) of Tanga, monetary unit of **Turkestan.** Minted in copper.

**III.** - Copper coin in **Russia** from 15th to 17th Century.

**IV.** - In **Georgia,** 10 Puli equalled 1 Kopek.

**1810** - Coinage ceased.

**V.** - In **Persia (Iran),** insignificant copper coin equal to ¹/₄₀ Kran.

## PYA

Submultiple (¹/₁₀₀) of Kyat, monetary unit of **Burma** since 1952.
   - See *Kyat.*

# QATAR

**19th Century** - Under Turkish protection. For money in circulation, see *Lira Turkey.*

**1916** (November 3rd) - Sheikdom entered into treaty with Britain to become protectorate. For money in circulation, see *Rupee India.*

**1959** - Persian Gulf Rupee replaced Indian Rupee as principal currency. - See *Rupee Persian Gulf.*

**1966** (June) - Gulf Rupee replaced by Saudi Riyal. - See *Riyal Saudi.*

**1966** (September) - New Qatar/Dubai Riyal replaced Saudi Riyal.
- See *Riyal Qatar/Dubai*

**1969** (October 22nd) - Qatar became part of Federation of Arab Emirates. - See *Federation of Arab Emirates.*


# QINDAR

**I.** - Submultiple ($\frac{1}{100}$) of Franka, monetary unit of **Albania** from 1925 to 1947, equal to Albanian Centime.

**II.** - Submultiple ($\frac{1}{100}$) of Lek, monetary unit of **Albania.**

Variations of name - Quindar, Qintar, Qinter, Quintar.


# QUADRANS

**I.** - **Roman** money worth $\frac{1}{4}$ As or 3 Ounces. - See *As.*

Origin of name - Derived from *quatuor* (four).

**II.** - Money of **Franks,** equal to $\frac{1}{4}$ gold Sou. - See *Sou.*


# QUADRIGATUS

Silver coin minted in 3rd Century B.C. (after 269 B.C.) by Capua on behalf of **Rome.** Destined for trade with Southern Italy, which demanded silver money. Was first Roman minting of silver.

Origin of name - Coin marked with quadriga (*quater,* four; *jugum,* yoke). - Cf. *Bigatus.*

Plural - Quadrigati.

**269 B.C.** - First minting of Quadrigatus of 6.82 grams of silver. Value in bronze monies (As and Libella) increased in proportion to debasement of these coins.

**217 B.C.** - During second Punic War, debasement of Quadrigatus to 5 grams of silver, then to 4.5 grams. Weight equal to that of original Denarius, which became basic silver coin in Roman monetary system. - See *Denarius.*

# QUADRUPLE

**I.** - Gold coin issued in **France** under Louis XIII; equal to 20 Livres.

**II.** - **Spanish** gold coin, worth 4 Pistoles or Doubloons, or 320 Reales. Weighing 27.06 grams, fineness progressively reduced (910 - 917 in 1730 to 893 - 896 in 1772, 860 - 875 in 1786 and until 1848).
Also called gold (Onza de Oro), or Doubloon de Ocho, commonly called Medalla. - See *Doubloon.*

# QUADRUSSIS

In **Rome,** piece of bronze worth 4 Libra or 4 As. - See *As.*
Origin of name - Derived from *quatuor* (four) and from *assis* (As).

# QUARANTIEME

Silver coin minted in Island of **Chios** in 5th Century B.C. Weighed about 9 grams, or 1/40 Mina, hence its name.
Circulated widely in Peloponnesus.
Variation of name - Tessarakostón (Greek).

# QUARTAROLA

Gold money (0.89 grams fine) of **Genoa.** Issued in 12th Century for 1/4 Genovino or 2 Soldi.

# QUARTAROLO

Copper coin of **Venice** in early 13th Century.

# QUARTER

**I.** - In **United States,** silver coin of 25 Cents (1/4 Dollar) created April 10, 1792 at 900 fine.

**1853** - Weight reduced from 103.12 to 87.5 grams.

**1965** - Coinage Act of 1965 authorized minting of three layer clad coin; two outer layers of 75% copper and 25% nickel and an inner core of pure copper.

**II.** - In **Canada,** silver coin of 25 Cents created May 4, 1910 at 925 fine.

**1920** (May 11th) - Fineness reduced to 800.
**1967** (August 17th) - Fineness reduced to 500.


## QUARTINHO

Gold coin of **Portugal** issued by Joseph (1750-1777). Succeeded Moeda. Valued at 1,000 Reis. Quartinhos of 1,200 Reis periodically minted.
Origin of name - From being 1/4 Moeda.
**1792** - Coin abolished.


## QUARTINO

**I.** - Early unit of account in **Naples:** valued at 1/300 Ducat, 1/60 Taro, 1/30 Carlino, 1/3 Grano, 2 Piccioli, 4 Cavalli.
**II.** - In **Papal States,** gold coin equal to 1/4 Doppia or 1/2 Scudo. Weight: 1.7 grams 900 fine.


## QUARTO

**I.** - **Spanish** silver money worth 1/4 Real, according to monetary system prevailing in 1497. Same Spanish coin, worth 4 Maravedis, minted in copper in 18th and 19th Centuries.
Variation of name - Cuarto.
**II.** - In **Spanish America,** small copper coin minted at beginning of 16th Century at Mint of Santo Domingo, Haiti. Oldest metallic money of New World. Subsequently became silver coin worth 1/2 Real.
**III.** - In **Philippines,** copper coin from 1823 to 1864, worth 1/20 Real.
**IV.** - In **Gibraltar** in 1802, private firms issued tokens of 1 and 2 Quartos valued at 1/2 Penny and 1 Penny, respectively.
**1842** - Regal coinage, called Quart, minted by British in denominations of 1/2, 1, 2. Quart was equal to 1/2 Penny.


## QUATTRINO

Monies of various **Italian** States before unification.
Origin of name - From quatro, because Quattrino was worth 4 Denari (Deniers).
Variations of name - Quatrin, Quatrino.
Plural - Quattrini.
**I.** - In **Papal States,** unit of account worth 1/500 Scudo, 1/150 Testone, 1/50 Paolo, 1/5 Baiocco, or 2 Mezzi Quattrini.

Minted in copper after 15th Century. Subsequent minting of Mezzo Quattrino.

**II.** - In **Bologna,** unit of account worth $^1/120$ Lira, $^1/6$ Soldo, or 2 Denari. Minted in copper.

**III.** - In **Milan,** copper money worth 3 Denari.

**IV.** - In Grand Duchy of **Tuscany** and in **Leghorn,** unit of account worth $^1/120$ Testone, $^1/60$ Lira, $^1/40$ Paolo, $^1/5$ Crazia, $^1/3$ Soldo, or 4 Denari. Minted in copper until 1859. Coin of 5 Quattrini called Grâce.

**V.** - In **Naples,** silver/copper money issued in 15th Century.


# QUETZAL

Monetary unit of **Guatemala** since 1925. Divided into 100 Centavos.

Origin of name - From Quetzal, sacred bird of Mayan kings, and national emblem.

Bank of issue - Banco Central de Guatemala, organized in 1925, from 1946 by Banco de Guatemala. (Bank of Guatemala).

Predecessor - See *Guatemala, Peso Guatemala.*

Plural - Quetzales.

**1925** (May 7th) - Peso replaced by Quetzal, linked to U.S. Dollar in accordance with law of November 26, 1924:

　　　1Quetzal = 1,504.6 milligrams of fine gold
　　　1 U.S. Dollar = 1 Quetzal

**1926** - Minting in Philadelphia of gold coins of 5, 10 and 20 Quetzales (8.35, 16.71 and 33.43 grams 900 fine).

**1933** (April) - Depreciation parallel to that of U.S. Dollar.

**1933** (July) - Embargo on gold shipments.

**1934** (February) - Devaluation conforming to that of U.S. Dollar:

　　　1 Quetzal = 888.671 milligrams of fine gold
　　　1 U.S. Dollar = 1 Quetzal

Collection by Banco Central of commission of 1% on foreign exchange transactions.

**1946** (December 18th) - Parity registered with International Monetary Fund.

**1954** - During insurrection, temporary black market pushed exchange rate to 2.50 Quetzales per U.S. Dollar.

**1963** (October 13th) - Foreign exchange controls decreed. Multiple rates established, and black market of Quetzal became operative. Three separate exchange markets established for specified transactions:

a) Official Market for obligatory surrender of exchange proceeds and for essential imports, specified invisibles and capital.

b) Auction Market for exchange licenses and for payments of nonessential imports and specified nonessential remittances.

c) Free Market derived from salaries and expenses of foreign diplomats, foreign investment capital not eligible for Official Market, repatriation of Guatemalan capital invested abroad, tourist expenditure and for foreign payments.

Quetzal on black market quoted at 1.50 per U.S. Dollar.

**1962** (November 13th) - Inoperative Auction Market replaced. New rate structure announced:

> 1 U.S. Dollar = 1.00/1.01 Quetzales (official rate for most exports, imports, government transactions some invisibles)
>
> 1 U.S. Dollar = 1.03 Quetzales (official rate plus 2% tax for nonessential imports and remittances)
>
> 1 U.S. Dollar = 1.03/1.04 Quetzales (free market rate for other exports and transactions listed previously under "C")

**1963** (May 25th) - Multiple rate structure abolished. All transactions took place at par value. Black market of Quetzal disappeared, but unit still traded at discount of from 8% to 11% in limited dealings abroad.

## QUILO

Small silver money of Grand Duchy of **Tuscany** (Florence) in 18th Century.

## QUINARIUS

**I.** - Silver money of **Rome** about 187 B.C. Submultiple of Denarius of 4.89 grams: 1 Quinarius equalled ½ Denarius, 2 Sestertii, 5 bronze Asses. See *Denarius.*

**II.** - In **Rome,** gold Quinarius referred to ½ Aureus, and was minted during 1st to 3rd Century A.D.

Origin of name - Latin *quinarius,* from *quini* (5 times 5). Coin carried the mark V.

## QUINCUSSIS

In **Rome,** large rectangular copper coin of 5 Libra or 5 Asses. - See *As.*

Origin of name - Derived from *quinque* (five) and from *assis* (As).

## QUINZAIN

**French** gold coin minted in 1719 by John Law. Exchange rate: 15 Livres.

## QURUSH

Variations of name - Kurus, Guerche, Miri, Saudi Piaster, Qursh, Quirsh.

**I.** - Submultiple of Riyal ($\frac{1}{11}$), monetary unit of **Saudi Arabia.** Minted in nickel. Equal to 2 Darij (Qurush Darij) or 8 Halalas.

**1954** - Riyal subdivided into 22 Qurush, but 11 Qurush per Riyal still used for certain official payments and customs duties.

**1960** (January 8th) - Riyal subdivided into 20 Qurush or 100 Halalas.

**II.** - Early submultiple of **Egyptian** Pound ($\frac{1}{1,000}$) and Egyptian Piastre ($\frac{1}{10}$). Also called Ochrel Qurush. Minted in form of coin of 1.75 grams (25% nickel, 75% copper). The $\frac{1}{2}$ and $\frac{1}{4}$ Qurush were bronze.

**III.** - Submultiple ($\frac{1}{16}$) of **Ethiopian** Talari, according to law of February 9, 1893. Minted in copper.

**1896** - Replaced by decimal submultiples, but circulated until 1908.

**IV.** - In **Tripoli (Libya),** submultiple of Mahbub ($\frac{1}{8}$), worth 100 Para.

## *RAGUSA*

Roman, Byzantine and Hungarian monies.

**Until 13th Century** - Copper Follaro imitating Byzantine Follis.

**13th to 16th Century** - Silver Gros and ½ Gros, imitating Venetian Grosso.

**16th Century** - Monetary system patterned on Venetian system, with Grosseto (silver money and unit of account) as basic unit. No gold money.

**1627** - Minting of Artilucco (3 Grosseti).

**1692** - Minting of Perpero (12 Grosseti).

**1729** - Issue of Scudo (36 Grosseti).

**18th Century** - Other silver monies: Ducato (40 Grosseti), Vislino (60 Grosseti).

**1791** - Minting of Libertina (80 Grosseti).
Then see *Turkey, Austria, Yugoslavia.*


## RAND

Monetary unit of **Southwest Africa, Lesotho, Botswana, Swaziland** and **South Africa.** Divided into 100 Cents.

Bank of issue - South African Reserve Bank.

Predecessor - See *Pound South Africa.*

**1961** (February 14th) - Adoption of decimal system. Creation of Rand equivalent to one-half the former South African Pound:
> 1 Rand = 1,244.14 milligrams of fine gold
> 1 Rand = 1.40 U.S. Dollars

**1961** (May) - Exchange controls tightened.

**1961** (May 3rd) - South Africa proclaimed Republic.

**1961** (June) - Creation of Security (Switch) Rand, resulting from sales by nonresidents of South African securities to residents, and usable for purchase of South African securities by nonresidents. Security Rand hit low of 1.05 U.S. Dollars.

**1961** (June) - Rand in black market hit low of 1.10 U.S. Dollars. Subsequent recovery.

**1968** (March) - Security Rand hit high of 1.41 U.S. Dollars.

**1969** (July) - Security Rand dropped to 1.07 U.S. Dollars.


## RAPPE

Silver, then copper money and unit of account in **Swiss** cantons.

Origin of name - From *Rabe* (raven).

Plural - Rappen (German).

**14th Century** - Minted in silver in various Swiss states. Formation of Rappenbund (1387) for issue of identical Rappen.

**15th Century** - Basel minted coins of 4 Rappen.

**18th Century** - In Basel, 1/150 Guilder or 1/270 Thaler; and silver/copper coin worth 1/10 Good Batz.

- In Lucerne, copper coin worth 1/3 Schilling.

- In canton of Schwyz, copper coin worth 4 Deniers or 2 Angster.

- In canton of Zug, copper coin.

**1799** (March 17th) - Helvetic Republic made Rappe 1/100 Swiss Franc, and 1/10 Batz. Minting of Rappen in silver/copper.

**1850** (May 7th) - Rappe, also called Centime, became 1/100 Swiss Franc, linked to French Franc. Minting of multiples of Rappe in argentan (alloy of silver, copper, nickel, zinc), then in nickel (after 1879).


## RATRE

Small silver/copper money of certain **Swiss** cantons in 18th Century (Montbéliard, Lucerne, Fribourg, Neuchâtel, Solothurn).


## REAL

Money of Spanish and Portuguese origin, circulating in overseas territories of Spain and Portugal.

Origin of name - Spanish *real* (royal).

Predecessors - See *Spain* and *Portugal.*

Plural - Reales (Spanish), Reis (Portuguese).

**I.** - Money of **Spain.** Successively, silver coin and unit of account.

**About 1350** - Peter I minted silver Real of 3.48 grams. Fineness progressively altered under Henry II (1369-1379). Weight in fine silver fell to 0.20 grams.

**1391** (January 21st) - Henry III reestablished Real at 3.24 grams fine silver. Exchange rate in units of account (Maravedis) raised in stages and fineness reduced under Henry IV (1454-1474).

**1471** (April 10th) - Minting of new Real of 3.2 grams fine silver. The 1/4 Real became popular under names Cuartillo and Cuartino.

**1497** (June 13th) - Ordinance of Medina del Campo fixing Real at 3.24 grams fine silver with exchange rate of 34 Maravedis. Minting of multiples of Real, among which was Duro, or Spanish Piaster of 8 Reales. - See *Duro.* Minting of submultiples (Medio, Quarto, Ochavo. . .). System persisted for 145 years.

**1642** (December 23rd) - Demonetization of earlier Reales and minting of Real of 2.60 grams fine silver.

**1643** (March 12th) - Restoration of Real to its former weight of 3.24 grams.

**1684** - Minting of silver Maria worth 1 Real, but reduced in weight.

**1686** (October 14th) - Real reduced in weight to 2.58 grams, under name silver Ecu (Escudo de Plata) - See *Escudo.* At same time, use of silver/copper Real authorized. Progressive raising of exchange rate of silver Escudo in terms of silver/copper Reales.

**1742** (June 22nd) - Silver/copper Real (Real de Villon) became unit of account with Maravedi, along with silver Real (Real de Plata).

**1772** (May 29th) - Ordinance of Aranjuez, lowering fineness of monies. Silver coin called Realito corresponded to Real.

**1808-1814** - Joseph Bonaparte retained two systems of accounting: silver/copper Reales, and silver Reales.

**1847** (May 31st) - Monetary reform of Isabella II instituting silver Real of 1.25 grams 900 fine, or 1.125 grams fine, as monetary unit.
Submultiples - Decimo, Cuartillo.

**1859** (January 1st) - Link to French monetary system, with Peseta of 4 Reales as monetary unit. - See *Peseta*.

**1864-1868** - Real was silver coin of 1.298 grams 810 fine.

**1868** - After Spain adhered to system of Latin Monetary Union (Peseta of 100 Centimos), custom of accounting in Reales persisted in retail trade:
    1 Real = 25 Centimos
    4 Reales = 1 Peseta

**II.** - In **Spanish America** (Mexico, Central America, South America, Antilles), submultiple (1/8) of silver Piasters (Pesos). Equal to 34 Maravedis, according to decree of May 31, 1535. The 1/4 Real called Quarto.
  - In **Ecuador,** 1/8. then 1/10 Ecuadorean Peso. After 1884, 1/10 Sucre, 1 Decimo or 10 Centavos. Minted in silver at end of 19th Century (2.5 grams 900 fine, or 2.25 grams fine silver), then in nickel.
  - In **Venezuela,** submultiple (1/2) of Bolívar. Consisted of 50 Centavos. Circulated in 20th Century in form of silver coin.
  - In **Colombia,** from 1847 to 1871, Real was 1/8 Grenadino, and 1/10 silver Peso.
  - In **Paraguay,** Real was 1/8 Peso until 1870, equal to 2 Medios and 4 Cuartillos. After 1870, became 1/10 Peso.

**III.** - In **Morocco,** Real, or Real Hassani, was created by Sultan Moulay-Hassan based on Spanish type. - See *Hassani*.

**IV.** - In **Netherlands,** Maximilian of Austria on March 13, 1387 made Real, called Reaal, unit of account. Minted Gouden Reaal of Austria in fine gold (exchange rate: 24 Reales) and silver Reaal (1 Real).

**1505** - Philip the Fair minted silver Reaal.

**1520** - Charles V followed with minting of gold Reaal (120 Grooten) and silver Reaal ˙(16 Grooten).

**V.** - In **England,** gold money (English Royal), generally called Noble à la Rose. - See *Noble*.
Double Real corresponded to Sovereign. - See *Sovereign*.

**VI.** - In **Italy,** Spanish Real called Reale. - See *Reale*.

**VII.** - In **Portugal,** silver money, then copper money and unit of account.

**1279-1325** - Under Diniz, minting of coins of 40 Reis.

**1367-1383** - Under Ferdinand I, minting of silver Real.

**1383-1433** - Under John I, minting of silver Real of 2.42 grams then about 1.20 grams, with exchange rate of 9 Dinheiros (Deniers).

**1433-1438** - Under Edward, minting of white Real with exchange rate of 1 Sou, and of black Real worth ¹⁄₁₀ white Real.

**1438-1481** - Under Alphonso V, three reductions in weight of white Real.

**1473** - The Cortes decided that these coins would be accepted only at their intrinsic metal value.

**1499** - In monetary system of Emanuel I, silver Real (1.99 grams) worth 5 copper Reis, or 30 copper Ceitil. Copper Real worth 6 Ceitil. Progressive reduction in weight. Henceforth, Real played role of small divisionary coin and was authorized as unit of account. Succeeding equivalents of Real in milligrams of gold: 36 around 1200; 31 around 1360; 5.8 in 1580; 2.2 in 1688; 2 in 1722; 1.7 in 1835.

**1835** (April 24th) - Gold Corôa of 8.757 grams fine gold represented 5,000 Reis; silver Tostao was 100 Reis.

**1864** - Forced parity of banknotes of Banco de Portugal (Bank of Portugal). Depreciation of currency.

**1854** (July 29th) - Designation of Milreis: 1,000 Reis = 1,625.85 milligrams of fine gold, as unit of account. - See *Milreis*.

**VIII.** - In **Goa** (Portuguese India), unit of account worth ¹⁄₂₄₀ Pardao, ¹⁄₆₀ Good Tanga. In 1818, minting in copper of multiples of Real (3 to 15) and of Vintem (20 Reis).

**After 1881** - Subdivision of Rupia (Rupee). 192 Reis equal to 1 Rupia, and 12 Reis to 1 Tanga.

**IX.** - In **Brazil,** use of Portuguese Real as unit of account after 17th Century. Exchange rate of local monies in Reis higher by 50% (silver Patagon) and by 100% (copper coins), in relation to exchange rate for same monies in Portugal.

**18th Century** - Use of Milreis (for 1,000 Reis) as multiple of Real, unit of account. - See *Milreis*.

# REALE

**I.** - Money in **Sardinia**. Derived from Spanish Real.

Plural - Reali.

**14th Century** - Sardinia, attached to Kingdom of Aragon, given Spanish monies. Introduction of Real, which became Reale in 1324.

**18th Century** - Substitution of monetary system of Savoy with Lira. Reale remained unit of account equal to ¹⁄₄ Lira, 5 Soldi or 60 Denari.

**1814** - Minting of silver/copper Reale.

**II.** - Unit of account in **Greek** islands under Venetian control in 18th Century. Divided into 10 Lire, or 100 Soldi (Aspers).

**III.** - Gold money of **Naples.** Formerly named Augustalis. Called Reale by Charles of Anjou (13th Century).

**IV.** - Silver money in **Sicily.** Issued in 15th Century.

# REBAH

Coin equal to ¼ Shekel under monetary system of **Hebrews,** during reign of Simon Maccabaeus (143-135 B.C.).

# REICHSGULDINER

Silver money of the **Holy Roman Empire** (Reich). Worth 1 Gulden.

**1524** - Monetary Ordinance of Essling. Charles V created money for Holy Roman Empire, called Reichsguldiner (292 grams 930 fine, or 27.3 grams fine). Exchange rate: 1 gold Gulden.

**1551** (July 28th) - Debasement of Reichsguldiner. Maintained as principal coin of monetary system of Holy Roman Empire. Exchange rate: 72 Kreuzer.

**1559** - Decree of Ferdinand I, confirming silver Reichsguldiner (24.62 grams 930 fine, or 22.9 grams fine) as major coin of monetary system of Holy Roman Empire. Exchange rate: 60 Kreuzer.

**1566** - Reichsguldiner became known as Guldenthaler. Supplanted by Reichsthaler. - See *Guldenthaler.*

# REICHSMARK

Monetary unit of **Germany** from 1924 to 1948. Divided into 100 Reichspfennig.

Origin of name - From German *Reich* (Empire) and Mark. - See *Mark.*

Bank of issue - By Reichsbank, created in 1875 (see *Mark),* and reorganized in 1924. By Rentenbank for small banknotes.

Predecessors - See *Mark* and *Rentenmark.*

**1923** (November 30th) - Because of galloping inflation which annihiliated Mark, Commission of Reparations invited Committee of Experts (Dawes Committee) to "research measures to take in order to stabilize money."

**1924** (April 9th) - Completion of Dawes Plan.

**1924** (August 30th) - Signing of Protocols of London, securing a loan for Germany and voting for monetary reform:

> 1 Reichsmark = 1 trillion paper Marks = 1 Rentenmark =
> 1 old gold Mark = 358.422939 milligrams of
> fine gold

Gold convertibility written into law, but subordinate to unanimous decision of Reichsbank.

**1931** (July 13th) - Following banking crisis originating in Austria (Kreditanstalt), creation of foreign exchange controls.

**1931** (July) - Increasing categories of blocked Mark: *Altguthaben,* derived from private credits; *Kreditsperrmark,* arising from domestic reimbursement of these credits or resulting from sale of property owned by foreigners.

**1931** (August) - Creation of *Auswanderersperrmark*, resulting from deposits of emigrants leaving Germany.

**1931** (November) - Creation of *Effektensperrmark*, resulting from sale or redemption of securities.

**1932** (February) - Creation of *Notensperrmark*, resulting from ban on redemption into foreign exchange of banknotes held by foreigners.

**1933** (February) - Creation of *Registermark*, resulting from assets of foreign banks and used by tourists. Special category: *Reisemark.*

**1933** (June) - Creation of *Konversionsperrmark* or *Scrips*, debt vouchers issued by Konversionskasse to represent credits blocked by new moratorium on transfers abroad.

**1934** (July 1st) - General moratorium on transfers abroad.

**1936** (December 1st) - Death penalty for capital flight. Depreciation of different categories of Reichsmark.

**1938** (March) - Introduction of Reichsmark in Austria:
1 Reichsmark = 1.50 Schillings

**1939** (March) - Introduction of Reichsmark in Czechoslovakia:
1 Reichsmark = 10 Czechoslavakian Koruny

**1939** (September) - Introduction of Reichsmark in Danzig and Poland:
0.70 Reichsmark = 1 Danzig Florin
'1 Reichsmark = 2.00 Zlote

**1940** (June) - Introduction of Reichsmark in France, Belgium and Netherlands:
1 Reichsmark = 20.00 French Francs
1 Reichsmark = 12.50 Belgian Francs
1 Reichsmark = 0.66 Netherlands Guilder
Reichskreditkassen issued banknotes denominated in Reichsmark for territories occupied by Germany.

**1942** - Creation of satellite monies. - See *Carbovanez, Mark Ostland.*

**1944** (September) - Introduction by Allied Military Government of Military Mark, worth 10.00 Reichsmark.

**1945** (April) - With German defeat, collapse of purchasing power of Reichsmark.

**1948** (May 1st) - Official parity:
1 U.S. Dollar = 3.33 Reichsmark

**1948** (June 20th) - Monetary reform in West Germany, with demonetization of Reichsmark and creation of Deutsche Mark:
1 Deutsche Mark = 10.00 Reichsmark
For West Germany, see *Mark German Federal Republic.* For East Germany, see *Mark German Democratic Republic.*


## REICHSTHALER

**I. - German** money from 16th to 19th Century.
Origin of name - From *Reich* (Empire) and Thaler (silver coin). - See *Thaler.*
Variations of name - Reichsthale, Richedale, Rixdale, Risdale.

Predecessor - See *Thaler.*

**1566-** Along with Guldenthaler worth 60 Kreuzer, creation of slightly heavier silver coin called Reichsthaler worth 68 Kreuzer.

**1585** - Value of Reichsthaler raised to 74 Kreuzer by tradesmen assembled in Frankfurt.

**1587** - Exchange rate of Reichsthaler: 69 Kreuzer.

**1604** - Exchange rate of Reichsthaler: 74 Kreuzer.

**1608** - Exchange rate of Reichsthaler: 80 Kreuzer.

**1609** - Exchange rate of Reichsthaler: 84 Kreuzer.

**1614** - Exchange rate of Reichsthaler: 88 Kreuzer.

**1615** - Exchange rate of Reichsthaler: 90 Kreuzer.

**1619** - During Thirty Years War, exchange rate raised to 124 Kreuzer in 1619, 140 in 1620, 360 in 1621, 600 in March 1622.

**1623** (December 14th) - Exchange rate of Reichsthaler lowered to 90 Kreuzer by imperial decree.

**1667** - Exchange rate of Reichsthaler raised to 96 Kreuzer in Bavaria, Swabia and Franconia by Diet of Regensburg. Extended to entire Empire in 1681.

**1690** - Decisions of Conference of Leipzig (electoral Saxony, Brandenburg, Brunswick-Lüneburg), completed in Torgau and extended in 1693 to entire Holy Roman Empire (except Hamburg and Lübeck). Reichsthaler became Speciesthaler with exchange rate of 120 Kreuzer. - See *Speciesthaler.*

**18th Century** - As unit of account, Reichsthaler divided into 24 Groschen, 32 Albus or 384 Heller in Hesse-Kassel; 54 Mark or 324 Buschen in Aachen; 60 Stuyver, 480 Pfennig, or 960 Heller in Cleve and Lower Westphalia; 54 Stuyver or 540 Witten in Prussian Frisia (Emden).
As specie money in silver, Reichsthaler (conventional Ecu) issued in Holy Roman Empire (28.1 grams 832 3/4 fine, or 23.4 grams fine silver, conventional weight). Reichsthaler minted in Bavaria (sometimes under name of Gros Ecu), in Brandenburg, Cologne, Frankfurt, Hamburg, Bremen, Lübeck, Austria, Swabia, Hanover, Saxony, Franconia and Prussia. Fineness varied between 25.2 and 20.6 grams of silver.

**19th Century** - Reichsthaler was unit of account in Austria and Mecklenburg-Strelitz.

**1857** (January 24th) - Monetary agreement suppressing all varieties of Thaler, and making Thaler uniform (18.52 grams of silver 900 fine, or 16.67 grams fine). - See *Thaler.*

**II.** - Money of various **Swiss** cantons in 17th and 18th Centuries. Minted in Saint Gall from 1621 to 1624, in Schaffhausen from 1621 to 1623, in Zurich from 1661 to 1727, in Basel (Species Reichsthaler) from 1624 to 1669. Fine silver content varied, according to types, from 24.7 to 23.7 grams.

# RENGUI

In **Siam,** money of lead circulating in 18th Century. Equal to 1/36 Tical or 1/9 Salung (Mayon).

## RENMINBI

Since June 1969, new name for currency of **Communist China.** Divided into 10 Tsjao and 100 Fyng.

Predecessor - See *Jen Min Piao.*

**1970** (June) - Black market rate of Renminbi reached high of 3.08 per U.S. Dollar, premium of 25¼% for Greenback.


## RENTENMARK

**German** money used during period of transition between Mark and Reichsmark after galloping inflation of 1923. Divided into 100 Rentenpfennig.

Origin of name - From German *Rente* (revenue) and *Mark* (Mark). - See *Mark.*

Bank of issue - Rentenbank, created in November 1923.

Predecessor - See *Mark.*

**1923** (October 15th) - Communiqué from Reich Government announcing creation of the Rentenmark, legal money along with paper Mark, "guaranteed by gold mortgage on all German properties and by gold obligations of industry, commerce and banks."

**1923** (November) - Issue by Rentenbank of banknotes in Rentenmark secured by Rentenbriefe (mortgage bonds), the latter secured by mortgage on German economy.

**1923** (December 14th) - Rentenmark fixed at parity with old paper Mark, equal to 1 trillion paper Mark.

**1924** (August 30th) - Law creating Reichsmark equal to Rentenmark and to gold Mark. - See *Reichsmark.* Withdrawal from circulation of banknotes of Rentenbank delayed until 1934.

**1930** - Withdrawal from circulation of banknotes of Rentenbank postponed until 1942.

**1939** (September) - Suspension of withdrawal of banknotes of Rentenbank. Note issue accrued until 1943.


## RESELLADO

Early French Ecu of 3 Livres circulating in North of **Spain.** Withdrawn from circulation in 1821 by Spanish authorities, and counter-marked (*resellado*) without being reminted. Exchange rate: ½ Duro or 10 Reales.


## RESHID

In **Turkey,** gold coin of 7.21657 grams 916 ⅔ fine, equal to Turkish Lira.
Origin of name - From effigy of Sultan Reshid.

## *REUNION*

**18th Century** - In Ile Bourbon (Réunion), barter trade of East India Company. Introduction of copper coins of 1 and 2 Sols (minted at Pondicherry) and of copper coins of 9 Deniers (minted in France), then coins of 24 Deniers in silver/copper. Exchange rate 50% higher than rate in France (100 Livres Tournois = 150 Livres of Ile Bourbon). - See *Livre Coloniale.*
Some issues of banknotes by East India Company (from 5 Sols to 1,000 Livres).

**1719-1729** - Receipt vouchers of East India Company.

**1736** - Vouchers of commercial enterprises.

**1737-1761** - Cash vouchers.

**1766** (December) - Withdrawal from circulation of paper money of East India Company and issue of royal banknotes of from 10 Sols to 3 Livres.

**1768** - New issue of banknotes of from 2 to 120 Livres (then to 1,000).

**1779** (August) - Edict calling for minting of silver/copper coins of 3 Sols, called Marqués (worth 1 Sol 6 Deniers in France). - See *Marqué.*

**1793** - Henceforth, continuous issue of paper money (confidence currency, Mandats Territoriaux. . .).

**1810** - British Occupation. Introduction of Indian Rupee. Spanish Piaster became unit of account worth 10 Livres Coloniales, 66 Marqués, or 2 Rupees.

**1816** - Minting and circulation of coins denominated in Francs and Centimes. De facto continued use of Rupee (prevailing exchange rate: 2.50 French Francs).

**1820** (February 2nd) - Abolition of Livre Coloniale.

**1823** - Issue of Treasury vouchers by discount bank.

**1828** - Demonetization of Marqué.

**1839** (July 16th) - Decree introducing, in principle, monetary system of Metropolitan France. Indian Rupee continued to circulate.

**1851** (July 11th) - After abolition of slavery, which implied birth of wage-earning class and which required new means of payment, creation of Banque de la Réunion, privileged with banknote issue. Withdrawal of Treasury vouchers issued since 1823.

**1859** - In order to remedy scarcity of small coinage, introduction of coins of 20 Kreuzer demonetized by Austria in 1857. Circulation of these coins until 1879 for 1 Franc under name Kervéguen.

**1879** - General demonetization of foreign monies, notably Rupees and Kervéguen. On the other hand, issue of Treasury paper authorized.

**1884** - Depreciation of Réunion currency (by 17% at maximum). Issue of Treasury paper denominated from 1 to 100 Francs, then from 0.50 to 50,000 Francs.

**1897** - Replacement of Treasury paper of ½ and 1 Franc by tokens of nickel/silver.

**1920** (August 8th) - Legal tender status for all monies of Metropolitan France, including metallic divisionary coinage.

**1928 and 1936** - Stabilization, and devaluation of French Franc. - See *Franc.*

**1939** (September 9th) - Exchange controls within framework of Franc-Zone.

**1940** (May 20th) - Decree instituting exhange controls between Metropolitan France and Overseas Territories.

**1941** (March 19th) - Franco-British agreement fixing exchange rate of Pound at 176.625 French Francs.

**1943** (February 2nd) - Allied agreement fixing Pound at 200.00 French Francs, U.S. Dollar at 50.00 French Francs.

**1944** (June 27th) - Ordinance transferring right of banknote issue to Caisse Centrale de la France d'Outre-Mer, renamed Caisse Centrale de Coopération Economique on December 30, 1958. Replaced on January 7, 1959, by Institut d'Emission des Départements d'Outre-Mer. - See *Franc CFA.*

## *RHODESIA*

Predecessors - See *Federation of Rhodesia and Nyasaland, Southern Rhodesia.*

**1965** (November 11th) - Southern Rhodesia issued Unilateral Declaration of Independence (UDI). Name changed to Rhodesia. Expelled from Sterling area and abandoned membership in International Monetary Fund. - See *Pound Rhodesia.*

## RIAL

I. - In **Zanzibar,** a silver coin with Arabic inscriptions issued in 19th Century.

II. - For **Morocco,** see *Rial Hassani.*

III. - For **Saudi Arabia,** see *Riyal Saudi Arabia.*

IV. - For **Iraq,** see *Riyal.*

## RIAL HASSANI

Silver coin of **Morocco** under Sultan Moulay-Hassan.

Variation of name - Piasre Hassani, Duro Azizi.

Other name - Sometimes called Ducat.

**1881-1892** - Rial Hassani minted in Paris. Weight: 29.216 grams of silver 900 fine, or 26.29 grams fine silver. Value: 10 Ukkias or Draham (plural of Dirhem). Minting of ¼ Rial weighing 7.30 grams 847 fine, or 6.10 grams fine silver and ¹⁄₁₀ Rial (Shraia or Shahi) weighing 2.911 grams 835 fine.
Confusion with Spanish monetary system resulted in custom of accounting in Duro and Peseta Hassani (¹⁄₅) rather than Rial Hassani and ¼ Rial Hassani. - See *Peseta Hassani.*
Rial Hassani interchangeable at par with Spanish Duro (22.50 grams fine silver).

**1900** - General debasement of Hassani coinage establishing direct link to Spanish types. Minting of Peseta Hassani as basic monetary unit. - See *Peseta Hassani.*

**1903** - Minting in Paris, Berlin and Birmingham of new silver Rials Hassani (Piastres), called Duro Azizi, and weighing 25 grams 900 fine, or 22.50 grams fine silver.

Term "Hassani Gros" generally applied to silver coins of 1, ½ and ¼ Duro. "Hassani Petit" referred to silver 50 and 25 Centime pieces.

> 1 Duro Azizi = 5 Pesetas Hassani

Followed developments of Peseta Hassani.

**1906** (April 7th) - In Spanish Zone, Hassani silver currency became legal tender concurrently with Spanish money under Act of Algeciras.

**1920** (March 19th) - Rial Hassani demonetized in French Morocco and exchanged for Metropolitan Francs and Algerian Francs at rate of:

> 1 Rial Hassani = 10 Francs

See *Franc Morocco.*


# RIAL IRAN (PERSIA)

Monetary unit of **Iran (Persia)** since 1932. Divided into 100 Dinars. Multiple: Pahlevi of 100 Rials.

Origin of name - Cf. *Real.*

Bank of issue - Imperial Bank of Persia from 1889 to 1926, then National Bank of Persia which became Bank Melli Iran. In May 1960, Bank Markazi Iran took over Central Bank activities.

Predecessors - See *Persia* and *Kran.*

**1930** (February 25th) - Foreign exchange controls.

**1932** (March 13th) - Kran replaced by Rial. Adoption of principle of gold standard:

> 1 Rial = 73.22382 milligrams of fine gold

De facto maintenance of silver standard with convertibility of banknotes into silver:

> 1 Rial = 1 Kran = 4.14 grams of fine silver

**1933** (May 30th) - Lifting of foreign exchange controls. Replaced by controls on imports:

> 1 U.S. Dollar = 16.35 Rials

**1933** (March 1st) - Abandonment of silver standard. Reestablishment of foreign exchange controls:

> 1 Pound Sterling = 80.00 Rials

Exchange rate carried premiums bringing it to as high as 174.00 Rials per Pound Sterling.

**1936** (November 16th) - Crown jewels were deposited in order to complement monetary stock of precious metals.

**1940-1941** (September) - 1 U.S. Dollar = 17.11 Rials.

**1941** (October 1st) - New exchange rate:

> 1 Pound Sterling = 140.00 Rials

**1942** (May 14th) - New revaluation permitted by accumulation of holdings of Pound Sterling:

> 1 Pound Sterling = 129.00 Rials
> 1 U.S. Dollar = 32.25 Rials

**1942** (November 19th) - New theoretical gold definition:

         1 Rial = 27.41 milligrams of fine gold
         1 U.S. Dollar = 32.25 Rials

**1945** - New rate structure:
         1 U.S. Dollar = 32.25 Rials (official)
         1 U.S. Dollar = 49.34 Rials (certificate rate for 90% of ex-
                port receipts and nonessential imports)
Certificate rate allowed to fluctuate.

**1946** (December 18th) - Parity registered with International Monetary Fund:
         1 Rial = 27.5557 milligrams of fine gold
         1 U.S. Dollar = 32.25 Rials

**1948** (February) - Certificate rate raised to 60.00 Rials for all export receipts.

**1948** (August 14th) - Imports of machines and sugar at official selling rate of 32.50 Rials. Other imports payable at 30% or 60% of official exchange rate. All other transactions at certificate rate.

**1949** (January 16th) - New rate structure:
         1 U.S. Dollar = 32.50 Rials (official selling rate for govern-
                ment transactions, imports of machines and
                sugar and local sales of Anglo-Iranian Oil Com-
                pany)
         1 U.S. Dollar = 54.50 Rials (certificate rate for all other im-
                ports and receipts of exchange)
Average exchange rate existed for essential imports.

**1949** (September 17th) - Revision of exchange rates:
         1 U.S. Dollar = 32.50 Rials (official selling rate for imports
                of commodities, government imports, exchange
                for Iranian students studying abroad and local
                sales of Anglo-Iranian Oil Company)
         1 U.S. Dollar = 40.00 Rials (official rate with certificate
                stabilized at 7.50 Rials per Dollar for all other
                transactions)

**1950** (January 8th) - Extension of official exchange rate on imports of sugar.

**1950** (July 24th) - Fluctuating exchange rate introduced for all export proceeds except oil and for authorized nonessential imports.

**1950** (November 8th) - Fluctuating rate fixed at 16.25 Rials per U.S. Dollar above official rate:
         1 U.S. Dollar = 32.00/32.50 Rials (official buying and sell-
                ing rate of local currency requirements of the oil
                company, invisibles, government payments,
                medical and educational expenses of Iranians
                abroad)
         1 U.S. Dollar = 40.00 Rials (official rate plus 7.50 Rials for
                essential imports and some invisibles)
         1 U.S. Dollar = 48.25/48.75 Rials (official rate plus 16.25
                Rials for all other exports, authorized imports
                and invisibles)

**1951** (December 4th) - Fixed certificate rates abolished and replaced by fluctuating rate. At end of December all exports and authorized imports conducted at rates of

64.25/64.75 Rials per U.S. Dollar. Special rate of 41.00 Rials per U.S. Dollar introduced for Dollar invisibles and capital earnings.

**1952** (November 11th) - New import and export rates:

> 1 U.S. Dollar = 83.5375 Rials (official rate plus 95% at fluctuating certificate rate for Category I exports)
>
> 1 U.S. Dollar = 84.0125 Rials (official rate plus 95% at fluctuating second certificate rate for Category II exports)
>
> 1 U.S. Dollar = 86.75 Rials (official rate plus fluctuating certificate rate for Category I imports)
>
> 1 U.S. Dollar = 87.25 Rials (official rate plus fluctuating second certificate rate for Category II imports)

Rates for Category I and II imports and exports changed continuously.

**1953** (March 21st) - Category III for exports and imports announced at 88.05 and 91.50 Rials per U.S. Dollar, respectively.

**1953** (April 23rd) - All noncommercial foreign exchange proceeds governed by rate equal to official rate plus 88% of average Category I certificate rate for previous quarter. Rate fluctuated widely, up to as high as 125.00 Rials per U.S. Dollar.

**1953** (June) - Rial on black market hit record low of 125.00 per U.S. Dollar with subsequent improvement to range of 80-95 Rials per Greenback.

**1954** (March 21st) - Category III imports and exports shifted to Category II.

**1955** (February 6th) - Official rate virtually inoperative. Practically all transactions conducted at trade rate of 75.00/76.50 Rials per U.S. Dollar. The 41.00 Rial rate remained for student expenses, as did Category II rate of 78.00/78.50 Rials per U.S. Dollar for small amount of exports and imports.

**1957** (May 22nd) - Multiple rates abolished. New par value established with International Monetary Fund:

> 1 Rial = 11.7316 milligrams of fine gold
>
> 1 U.S. Dollar = 75.75 Rials

Minor tax on imports.

**1963** (September 1st) - System of export subsidies introduced ranging from 9% to 20%.

**1967** (October 29th) - Bank Markazi's selling rate for U.S. Dollar reduced from 76.50 to 75.50 Rials.

**1968** (February 15th) - Bank Markazi's selling rate for U.S. Dollar reduced to 75.175 Rials.

**1968** (March 20th) - Registration fee of 3.00 Rials per U.S. Dollar, applied to all imports, replaced by fee of 4% on import amount.

**1968** - Black market for Rial all but ceased, and Rial fluctuated at only small discount from official rate.

**1969** (October 4th) - Official buying and selling rates for U.S. Dollar increased to 76.25 and 76.50 Rials, respectively.

## RIAL SAIDI

Monetary unit of **Oman.** Divided into 1,000 Baizas.

Currency issuing authority - Muscat Currency Authority administered by British Bank of the Middle East under supervision of Sultanate Secretary for Financial Affairs.

Predecessors - See *Rupee Persian Gulf* and *Muscat and Oman.*

**1970** (May 7th) - Creation of Rial Saidi to replace Persian Gulf Rupee:

      1 Rial Saidi = 1 Pound Sterling

      1 Rial Saidi = 2,132.81 milligrams of fine gold

      1 Rial Saidi = 2.40 U.S. Dollars

## *RIAU ARCHIPELAGO*

For earlier history, see *Indonesia.*

**1963** (October 15th) - Kepulauan Riau Rupiah created as separate monetary unit. Adoption of exclusive foreign exchange regulations. - See *Rupiah Kepulauan Riau.*

**1963** (December 1st) - Malayan Dollar circulating in Riau Archipelago ceased to be legal tender.

**1964** (July 1st) - Indonesian Rupiah replaced Kepulauan Riau Rupiah as monetary unit. - See *Rupiah Indonesia.*

## RIDER

Gold coin of **Scotland** in 1475. Divisions of ¼, ⅓, and ⅔ minted also.

Origin of name - See *Rijder.*

## RIEL

Monetary unit of **Cambodia.** Divided into 100 Sen.

Origin of name - From Real, recalling Portuguese navigators of 16th Century.

Bank of issue - Banque Nationale du Cambodge (National Bank of Cambodia).

Predecessor - See *Piastre Indochina.*

**1955** (October 28th) - Riel replaced Piastre as national currency:

      1 Riel = 10 French Francs

      1 U.S. Dollar = 35.00 Riels

Official free market rate of 75.00 Riels per U.S. Dollar applied to some nonessential imports requiring license and to transactions with French Currency Area. Special EFAC (Exportations-Frais Accessories) Account, resulting from retention in varying percentages of export receipts. Used for certain payments abroad. Exchange controls also led to blocked Riel variety.

**1955** (December) - Dollar premium on black market rose to 214%.

**1956** (March 26th) - Riel defined in terms of gold:
    1 Riel = 25.3905 milligrams of fine gold

**1960** (January 1st) - Creation of Nouveau Franc:
    1 Riel = 10 N Francs

**1960** (October 15th) - Premium of 25 Riels per U.S. Dollar given to tourists staying at accredited hotels:
    1 U.S. Dollar = 60.00 Riels

**1961** (April) - Dollar premium on black market fell to 65%.

**1964** (January 1st) - All special exchange facilities, such as EFAC account for exporters, abolished. Balances usable until July 1st. Foreign trade transferred to a state-trading basis.

**1965** (January 1st) - Tourist rate abolished.

**1965** (July) - Black market rate of Riel fell to low of 116.00 per U.S. Dollar, premium of 254% for Greenback.

**1966** (Feburuary 4th) - Tourist rate officially reinstated until end of year, but continued thereafter. System of multiple import rates created, resulting from compensation charges of from 35 to 46 Riels to 10% to 50% of c.i.f. price, according to category of commodity.

**1969** (May) - Improvement in black market rate of Riel to 57.95 per U.S. Dollar.

**1969** (August 18th) - Following French Franc devaluation, value of Riel aligned:
    1 Riel = 16 milligrams of fine gold
    1 Riel = 0.10 Francs
    1 U.S. Dollar = 55.5419 Riels
Tourist rate and compensation charges on imports abolished.

**1970** - New weakening of Riel on the black market, hitting 108.00 per U.S. Dollar in May. By end of year improved to 89.00 per U.S. Dollar.

## RIGSDALER

**Danis** silver money and unit of account.

Origin of name - Derived from *Daler* (Thaler). Variation of Reichsthaler (Thaler of Holy Roman Empire). - See *Reichsthaler.*

Predecessors - See *Denmark* and *Daler.*

**18th Century** - Minting of Rigsdaler and Speciesdaler (as opposed to Rigsdaler of account) worth 1.5 Dalers.
In Copenhagen and Bergen, accounts in Rigsdaler divided into 6 Mark, 96 Skilling, 192 Fyrk, 288 Hvid, or 1,152 Penning.
In various parts of Norway under Danish control (in Christiania, Trondheim, Romsdal. . .) accounts in Rigsdaler, divided into 4 Oere or Ort, 48 Stuyver, or 96 Skilling.

**1776** - New Speciesdaler minted containing 29.1 grams 804 fine, or 23.4 grams fine silver. Circulation of banknotes denominated in Rigsbankdaler from 1 to 100.

**1812** - In Norway, control of which passed from Denmark to Sweden, Speciesdaler became unit of account.

**1813** (January 5th) - Silver (12.5 grams) Rigsbankdaler, the double Rigsdaler, became monetary unit, equal to 6 Mark or 96 Skilling.

**1873** - Monetary reform and demonetization of Rigsdaler.

## RIJDER

Early gold money of **United Provinces,** which later became Netherlands.

Origin of name - From Dutch *rijder* (cavalier), German *Reiter* (cavalier). Armored knight on horseback depicted on coin.

Variation of name - Ryder.

**1433** (October 21st) - Philip the Good minted Cavalier, or Gouden Rijder, worth 45 Gros.

**1581** - Minting of gold Rijder of Gelderland.

**1583** - Minting of gold Rijder of Friesland.

**1606** (May 21st) and **1610** (July 6th) - Minting of gold Rijder worth 10.2 Guilders.

**1749** (March 31st) - Minting of gold Rijder (8.3 grams fine) with exchange rate of 14 Guilders.

## RIJDERDAALDER

Early silver money of **United Provinces,** which became **the Netherlands.**

**1581** - Minting of Rijderdaalder, also called Ducaton. Value: 40 Stuyver.

## RIJKSDAALDER

**I.** - Early silver money and unit of account of **the Netherlands.**

Origin of name - See *Reichsthaler.*

Variations of name - Rijcksdaler, Rixdale, Richedale, Risdale, Rix Dollar, Rix Daler.

Types - Specie Rijksdaalder, 23.05 grams of fine silver, minted from 1622 to 1659. Rijksdaalder in use (22.07 grams of fine silver). As unit of account, Rijksdaalder worth 2.4 Guilders, 8 Schelling, 48 Stuyver, or 96 Grooten.

- In Zeeland, Rijksdaalder had exchange rate of 53 Stuyver.
- In Brabant, Rijksdaalder called Patacon.
- In Malacca, Rijksdaalder equal to 8 Schelling, 64 Stuyver or 192 Duiten.

**20th Century** - The 2.5 Guilder coin still called Rijksdaalder (25 grams of silver 700 fine, or 17.5 grams fine silver).

**II.** - In **Ceylon** (Dutch until 1802), Rijksdaalder equal to 48 Stuyver or 12 Fanams. Minted in silver by English from 1803 until 1821 and called Rix Dollar.

**III.** - In **Cape Colony,** first Dutch settlers introduced Rijksdaalder.

## RIKSDALER

**Swedish** silver money and unit of account.

Predecessors - See *Sweden* and *Daler.*

**1598** - Riksdaler equal to 4 Mark, 32 Oere or 768 Penning.

**1664** - Riksdaler, silver money worth 6 silver Daler or 18 copper Daler. Weighed 29.2 grams 880 fine, or 25.7 grams fine silver.

**18th Century** - Two systems of accounting, depending upon province.
Silver Mynt (silver money): Species Riksdaler equal to 6 Daler, 24 Mark, 48 Skilling, 191 Oere, 768 Oerlein.
Kopper Mynt (copper money): Species Riksdaler equal to 18 Kopper Mynt Daler, 72 Kopper Mynt Mark, 576 Kopper Mynt Oere, 2,304 Kopper Mynt Oerlein.

**1776** (November 27th) - Under Gustavus III, unification of system of accounting on basis of system in silver money.
Riksdaler of type of 1664 had exchange rate of 6 silver Daler, 48 Skilling, or 192 Oere.

**1830** (June 25th) - Lowering of fineness of silver monies. Riksdaler represented 25.2 grams of fine silver; Speciesdaler, 25.1 grams. Inflation of banknotes denominated in Riksdaler. Paper Riksdaler fell to 1/4 Speciesdaler in exchange value.

**1855** (February 3rd) - Monetary reform. Adoption of paper Riksdaler as monetary unit, Riksdaler Riksmynt, divided into 100 Oere. Minting of silver coins. Earlier gold monies were legal tender based on their intrinsic metal value.

**1868** (July 31st) - Minting of gold Carolins by King Charles XV. Based on 1/2 Napoléon (coin of 10 Francs). Exchange rate: 7 Riksdaler 40 Oere.

**1873** - Demonetization of earlier silver monies.

## RIN

**I.** - Copper submultiple of **Japanese** Yen (1/1.000) and Sen (1/10). Consisted of 10 Moun. - See *Yen* and *Sen.*

**II.** - Submultiple of **Korean** Won (1/1.000), Chon (1/10) and Poon (1/2). - See *Won.*

## *RIO MUNI*

See *Spanish Guinea.*

## RIYAL IRAQ

Submultiple (1/5) of **Iraqi** Dinar. Equal to 4 Dirhams or 200 Fils. Minted in silver, 20 grams 900 fine.

## RIYAL QATAR/DUBAI

Monetary unit of **Qatar** and **Trucial States** (except Abu Dhabi) since 1966. Divided into 100 Dirhams.

Origin of name - See *Real.*

Note-issuing authority - Qatar/Dubai Currency Board.

Predecessors - See *Saudi Riyal, Rupee Persian Gulf* and *Indian Rupee.*

**1966** (September) - Trucial States (except Abu Dhabi) and Qatar replaced Saudi Riyal with Qatar/Dubai Riyal:

> 1 Qatar/Dubai Riyal = 186.621 milligrams of fine gold
> 1 U.S. Dollar = 4.76 Qatar/Dubai Riyals

## RIYAL SAUDI ARABIA

Monetary unit of **Saudi Arabia.** Originally subdivided into 11 Qurush Miri, 22 Qurush Darij or 88 Halalas. Then in January 1960, divided into 20 Qurush or 100 Halalas (except for certain official transactions, including customs duties, where 11 Qurush remained equal to 1 Saudi Riyal).

Variations of name - Rial, Reyal.

Note-issuing authority - Saudi Arabian Monetary Authority, established 1952.

Predecessor - See *Arabia.*

**1928** (January 22nd) - Creation of new silver currency based in practice on British gold Sovereign:

> 1 Saudi Riyal = 24.005 grams of silver 830 fine
> 1 British gold Sovereign = 10.00 Saudi Riyals (official par
> > value)

**1935** (December) - 1 British gold Sovereign = 22.00 Saudi Riyals (free market).

**1936** - Issue of new coinage debased to same weight and fineness as Indian Rupee:

> 1 Saudi Riyal = 11.664 grams of silver 916 2/3 fine
> 1 British gold Sovereign = 20.00 Saudi Riyals

Steady weakening of exchange ratio in following years.

**1948** (July) - Exchange rate of British gold Sovereign fixed at 65 Saudi Riyals.

**1948** (September 4th) - Exchange rate of British Sovereign amended to 62 Saudi Riyals. Sovereign given legal tender status, and value allowed to fluctuate relative to Saudi Riyal.

**1952** (October 22nd) - Saudi Arabian monetary authority issued gold Saudi Guineas equal in weight and fineness to British gold Sovereign. - See *Saudi Guinea.* Official rates fixed at:

> 1 Saudi Riyal = 236.979 milligrams of fine gold
> 1 U.S. Dollar = 3.75 Saudi Riyals

**1953** - Saudi Arabian Monetary Authority created special paper currency called "pilgrims' receipts" in denominations of 5 and 10 Riyals. Fully backed by gold coin reserves. Generally accepted into circulation beside silver Riyal and nickel Qurush.

Widespread counterfeiting of gold Guineas resulted in their virtual disappearance from circulation.

**1955** - Rapid increase in international silver price drove silver Riyals out of circulation.

**1956-1957** - Foreign exchange controls.

**1958** (March) - Saudi Riyal fell to low of 7.25 per U.S. Dollar in unofficial dealings.

**1958** (June 4th) - Controlled free market for all but a few specified imports and government transactions initially set at:
> 1 U.S. Dollar = 5.50 Saudi Riyals

**1959** (July 22nd) - Free market rate set at 4.75 Saudi Riyals per U.S. Dollar.

**1959** (December 31st) - New decimal submultiple system:
> 1 Saudi Riyal = 20 Qurush or 100 Halalas

**1960** (January) - Issue of paper Riyals to replace "pilgrims' receipts." Gold coins ceased to be legal tender.

**1960** (January 8th) - Controlled free market abolished. Par value established with International Monetary Fund:
> 1 Saudi Riyal = 197.482 milligrams of fine gold
> 1 U.S. Dollar = 4.50 Saudi Riyals

Removal of all import restrictions and controls on gold and silver movements.

**1966** (June 16th) - Qatar and Trucial States (except Abu Dhabi) temporarily adopted Saudi Riyal to replace External Gulf Rupee issued by India. - See *Riyal Qatar/-Dubai.*

**1966** (September) - Saudi Riyal replaced in Qatar and Trucial States.

## RIYAL YEMEN

Monetary unit of **Yemen Arab Republic.** Divided into 40 Bugshas.

Note-issuing authority - Yemen Currency Board.

Predecessor - See *Yemen.*

**1964** (February) - Creation of Yemen Riyal as monetary unit of Yemen Arab Republic:
> 1 Yemen Riyal = 829.427 miligrams of fine gold
> 1 U.S. Dollar = 1.07526 Yemen Riyals
> 1 U.S. Dollar = 4.00 Yemen Riyals (official tourist rate)

## ROAVOAMENA

In **Madagascar,** early native submultiple ($^1/_{12}$) of Ariary. - See *Ariary.*

## *ROMANIA*

Roman, Byzantine, Turkish monetary systems.

**14th Century** - Walachia minted Gros.

**19th Century** - Turkish monies: Piastre of 40 Paralis.

**1867** (April 14th) - Introduction of bimetallic monetary system of Latin Monetary Union linked to Franc.

**1890** (April 14th) - Linking of Leu of 100 Bani to gold standard on basis of gold definition of Franc. - See *Leu*.

## *ROME*

Primitive money - Cattle (pecus).

For first monies of Southern Italy, see *Italy* and *Sicily*.

**6th Century B.C.** - Use of large bars of bronze (copper with alloy of lead and tin) with theoretical weight of 327 grams (1 Livre).

**5th Century B.C.** - For payments made in cattle, Rome legally substituted payments in bronze (law of Julia Papiria, 430 B.C.):

1 bull = 100 Asses
1 sheep = 10 Asses

- See *As*.

**269 B.C.** - Minting in Capua of silver Quadrigatus (6.82 grams), used as medium of exchange with Southern Italy.

**241 B.C.** - Unusual minting of gold money (4.50 grams), worth 30 bronze Asses.

**End of 3rd Century B.C.** - Minting of new silver coin: Victoriatus (3.40 grams) in Illyria; Bigatus (3.89 grams) in Spain.

**Between 249 and 217 B.C.** - Minting of gold coins (10.91 grams) called Denarius Aureus, or, more commonly, Aureus. - See *Aureus*.

**187 B.C.** - Victories in Carthage and East permitted stabilization and alteration of monetary system: gold Aureus; bronze As; silver Denarius worth 1/25 Aureus or 10 Asses. - See *Denarius*.

**89 B.C.** - Relationship of silver Denarius to bronze As changed from 10 to 16; and Sestertius, or 1/4 Denarius, became unit of account instead of As. - See *Sestertius*. Monetary uncertainty caused widespread use of semi-official money, called Pecunia Nundationum (money of marketplace), in addition to official money.

**312 A.D.** - Reform of Constantine. Basic coins were:

In gold - Solidus, from Aureus (see *Solidus*)
In silver - Miliarensis (see *Miliarensis)*
In bronze - Denarius, which became Follis

**476** - With fall of Western Empire, Rome left as a memento the Solidus (which became Sol for Barbarians, Bezant in Byzantium, Dinar for Arabs), and the Denarius or Denier (which became natural submultiple of Sol and its equivalents). - See *Byzantium* and *Bezant, Arabia* and *Dinar, Denier*.

**9th Century** - Carolingian monetary system (Livre of 20 Sols or 240 Deniers) gave rise to Lira of 20 Soldi or 240 Denari.

For later history of money of Rome, see *Papal States* and *Italy*.

# ROOB

Silver coin of **Ethiopia** (Abyssinia) equal to ¼ Ber, Ber being Amharic word for Talari or Maria Theresia Thaler. Primarily means silver.
Variations of name - Rub, Yaber Roob.


# ROOSEBEKER

Silver money common to **Flanders** and **Brabant** in 14th Century (1384-1389). Corresponded to Double Groot.
Origin of name - Crown of roses.


# ROULEAU

I. - Small metal wheel (of gold or bronze) probably used in **Gaul** as money.
Plural - Rouleaux.
II. - In **France,** roll of coins equal to a fixed unit.
III. - In **French Guiana,** rolls (rouleaux) of 30 silver/copper 10 Centime pieces, called Marqué Blanc, were equal to 3 Francs in 1819.


# ROYAL

Gold money of France, then of various European states, which sometimes minted it of silver or silver/copper.
Origin of name - To differentiate money of King from money of vassals. - Cf. *Real.*
I. - In **France,** gold money of 13th and 14th Centuries.
**1266** (August 15th) - Minting of gold coin, called Denier à l'Agnel, and sometimes Royal à l'Agnel. - See *Agnel.*
**1295** (April 15th) - Creation of Royal d'Or, weighing 6.99 grams fine. Exchange rate: 25 Sous.
**1303** (August 22nd) - Minting of new Royal, called à la Chaise, weighing 7.09 grams. Exchange rate: 62 Sous 6 Deniers. Exchange rate of first Royal raised to 51 Sous 3 Deniers.
**1305** (May 7th) - Exchange rate of Royal à la Chaise: 40 Sous 3 Deniers.
**1305** (July 22nd) - Creation of Petit Royal (or Mantelet), weighing 3.50 grams of fine gold. Exchange rate: 13 Sous 9 Deniers.
**1308** (January 18th) - Exchange rate of Royal à la Chaise lowered to 25 Sous and exchange rate of Petit Royal lowered to 12 Sous 6 Deniers. Minting of new Royal weighing 6.99 grams 917 fine, or 6.41 grams fine gold, with exchange rate of 22 Sous 6 Deniers.
**1313** (June) - Demonetization of all Royals.

**1326** (February 16th) - Creation of new Royal, weighing 4.22 grams of fine gold. Exchange rate: 25 Sous.

**1330** (April 8th) - Exchange rate of Royal reduced to 15 Sous.

**1358** (August 31st) - Minting of gold Royal of 3.71 grams 916½ fine, or 3.4 grams fine gold. Exchange rate: 25 Sous.

**1359** (April 15th) - Minting of Royal of 3.5 grams fine gold. Exchange rate: 25 Sous, raised to 30 Sous (June 3, 1359), then to 40 Sous (November 22, 1359). Lowered to 25 Sous on May 28, 1360.

**1360** (December 5th) - Exchange rate of Royal lowered to 16 Sous 8 Deniers. Repurchased by Mints for 17 Sous 4½ Deniers, Royal disappeared.

**1361** (April 10th) - Demonetization of Royals.

**1429** (October 9th) - Charles VII created Royal of 3.82 grams fine gold worth 25 Sous.

**II.** - Gold money of various **Flemish** countries:
 - In Luxemburg and Bohemia, minted by John the Blind (1306-1349).
 - In Flanders (14th Century).

**III.** - In **England**, gold money minted under Elizabeth I (1558-1603).

**IV.** - In **Scotland**, gold, then silver money, issued in 16th Century.

**V.** - For **Spain** and **Portugal**, see *Real*.

**VI.** - For **Italy**, see *Reale*.

**VII.** - In **Portugal** (independent from Real), silver/copper money minted under Ferdinand I (1367-83). Under Alphonso V (1438-81), white Royal was of silver/copper, and black Royal was of copper.


## *RUANDA-URUNDI*

Note: Included territory of Burundi.

**1890** - Territory of German East Africa. - See *German East Africa*.

**1919** - Became Belgian territory as part of Belgian Congo. - See *Belgian Congo*.

**1960** (August 31st) - Separate Central Bank created for Ruanda-Urundi, Banque d'Emission de Ruanda-Urundi (Bank of Issue of Ruanda-Urundi).

**1960** (September 22nd) - Central Bank issued currency to replace Congo Franc. - See *Franc Ruanda-Burundi*.

**1962** (April) - Ruanda and Burundi formed monetary and customs union.

**1962** (July 1st) - Ruanda-Urundi territory dissolved. Ruanda became independent Republic of Rwanda. Burundi became independent state. - See *Rwanda* and *Burundi*.


## RUBA

Silver coin of **Egypt** in 1839. Equal to 5 Piastres.

# RUBIE

Gold money of Kingdom of **Tlemcen,** later **Algiers.** Value: 35 Aspers.

# RUBLE

Monetary unit of **Russia,** then **U.S.S.R.** Divided into 100 Kopeks. Multiple of Ruble: Chervonetz of 10 Rubles.

Origin of name - From Russian verb *rubit* (to cut). Primitive bar was notched for rapid cutting.

Bank of issue - Imperial Bank of Russia, created in 1860. Renamed Gosbank after 1917 Revolution.

Predecessor - See *Russia.*

**1547** - With accession of Ivan IV, Ruble used as unit of account. Existed in form of gold bar.

**1613-1645** - First minting of gold Rubles under Michael Romanoff.

**1654-1655** - Silver Thaler circulated for 1/2 Ruble, gold Ducat for 1 Ruble. Affixing of imprint on Thaler, which circulated under name Jafimske. - See *Jafimske.*

**1655** - Issue of submultiples of Ruble in copper at forced parity:
1/2 Ruble, Altyn (3 Kopeks), Grochevik (2 Kopeks), Kopek. Depreciation to 1/4 of issue value in 1662, to 1/15 in 1663.

**1663** - Withdrawal from circulation of copper coins. Minting of silver coins by Corporation of Minters.

**1704** - Peter the Great minted silver Ruble of 27.30 grams 854 fine, or 23.31 grams fine silver. Monetary system of Peter the Great (unit of account Rûble of 100 Kopeks) consisted of following coins:
> In gold - Ducat, Double Ducat, Double Ruble
> In silver - Ruble, Poltina (1/2Ruble), Polpoltin (1/4Ruble),
> > Grivna (10 Kopeks), Altyn (3 Kopeks), Kopek
> In copper - Denga (1/2Kopek), Poluschka (1/4Denga)

**1725** - Issue of copper monies in form of large plaques analagous to Platmynt of Sweden: plaques of 1 Ruble to 1 Kopek.

**1755** (November 23rd) - Ukase of Elizabeth II defined Ruble in gold:
> 1 Ruble = 1.6695 grams of fine gold
Minting of gold Imperials of 10 and 5 Rubles. - See *Imperial.*

**1756** - Minting of gold coïns of 1 and 2 Rubles. Monetary system was as follows:
Gold coins - Imperial (10 Rubles), 1/2 Imperial (5 Rubles), Ducat (21/4 Rubles)
Silver coins - Ruble (100 Kopeks), Poltina (50 Kopeks), Polpoltin (25 Kopeks)
Silver/copper coins - Grivna (10 Kopeks), Piatak (5 Kopeks)
Copper coins - Kopek, Denga (1/2 Kopek), Poluschka (1/4 Denga)

**1768** (December 29th) - Ukase of Catherine II diminishing fineness of Imperials. Introduction of paper money called Assignatzia, or Ruble-Banco, exchangeable for copper money. - See *Assignatzia.*

**1770** (February 16th) - Creation of giant copper Ruble weighing 1.024 kilos. Abandoned after one year.

**1796** (December 2nd) - Temporary reform of Paul I attempted to raise fineness and weight of gold and silver monies. Minting of Ducats like those of Holland and of silver Rubles equal to 50 Stuyver.

**1797** (October 3rd) - Repeal of reform.

**1828** (April 24th) - Ukase of Nicolas I, creating coins of platinum with impurities of irridium (3 Rubles, weighing 10.3 grams). Circulated from 1829 to 1845.

**1829 and 1830** - Minting of 6 and 12 Ruble platinum coins.

**1839** (July 1st) - Consolidation of depreciated paper money:
1 silver Ruble = 3.50 Ruble Assignatzia
Silver Ruble became official unit of account.

**1843** (June 1st) - Withdrawal of Assignatzia. Replaced by credit banknotes:
1 Credit Ruble banknote = 3.50 Ruble Assignatzia
Credit Ruble banknotes guaranteed by public domains, then by fund of metals.

**1858** - Forced parity. New depreciation of currency.

**1862** (May 1st) **to 1863** (November 19th) - Unsuccessful attempts at exchanging banknotes for metal on a diminishing scale.

**1885** (December 17th) - Law making silver Ruble official monetary unit:
1 Ruble = 20 grams of silver 900 fine
1 Ruble = 4.00 French Francs
In gold - Imperial, linked to double Napoléon (10 Rubles of 12.903 grams 900 fine), 1/2 Imperial (5 Rubles)
In silver - Ruble coins of 5 to 50 Kopeks
In copper - Kopek, multiples and submultiples

**1893** - Suspension of free minting of silver. Banknotes still inconvertible.

**1897** (January 3rd-15th) - After accumulation of gold in Imperial Bank, devaluation of Credit Ruble. Adoption of gold standard:
1 Ruble = 774.234 milligrams of fine gold
1 U.S. Dollar = 1.94 Rubles
Exchange rate of Imperial raised from 10 to 15 Rubles. Minting of new gold coin of 10 Rubles, 8.602 grams 900 fine.
Minting of silver coins: Ruble of 20 grams 900 fine and submultiples: Poltina, Tschetwertak, Dvougrivenik, Piataltininck, Grivna, Piatak or Piatatchenk.

**1914** (July) - Suspension of convertibility into gold. Inflation, raising currency in circulation from 1.7 billion Rubles (January 1914) to 10 billion (March 1917, fall of Czarist regime) and 19 billion (October 1917).

**1917** (August 22nd) - Issue of Treasury banknotes, called "Kerenskies". Depreciated in relation to Czarist paper money.

**1917** (October) **to 1924** (February) - After October Revolution, inflation progressively accelerated, raising circulation to 829 quadrillion Rubles.
Parallel issue of local monies (2,181 types of monetary signs were counted). Progressive depreciation of ruble, up to 200 billionths of its gold value (March 10, 1924).

**1917** (December 14th) - Confiscation of gold in all forms.

**1918** (August) - Decision of Council of People's Commissars abolishing money.

**1918** (October 3rd) - Confiscation of all foreign exchange.

**1919** - Soviet Ruble took name Sovnazki (monetary sign for payment).

**1920** - Attempt at economic system without money. Organization of barter trade entrusted to Central Union of Consumer Cooperatives. In Moscow (1920), salt was price standard. In Ukraine (1922), rye was price standard.

**1921** (January 26th) - Decision of Council placing limits on People's Commissars in view of adoption of labor standard.

**1921** (October 26th) - Decision of Council of People's Commissars putting an end to obligatory barter.

**1921** (November 3rd) - First exchange of Rubles fixed for January 1, 1922:
1 Ruble of 1922 = 10,000 Rubles of 1921

**1921** (November 5th) - Adoption of "Prewar Ruble"as budgetary unit of account.

**1921** (November 16th) - Gosbank (State Bank) began operations.

**1921** (December) - The 9th Soviet Congress recognized necessity of stable money and ordered People's Commissariat of Finance to prepare "reestablishment of money on basis of gold currency".

**1922** (January 18th-February 25th) - "Prewar Ruble"used as basis for calculating taxes and railroad tickets.

**1922** (March 30th) - Abandonment of "Prewar Ruble"as unit of account.

**1922** (April 4th) - Abolition of State monopoly on holding of gold. Reappearance in foreign exchange markets of hoarded gold.

**1922** (October 22nd) - Second exchange of Rubles decided for January 1, 1923:
1 Ruble of 1923 = 100 Rubles of 1922 $\doteq$ 1,000,000 earlier
Rubles

**1922** (November 27th) - State Bank issued banknotes called Chervonets, covered 25% by precious metals and hard currencies. "The date on which banknotes could be exchanged for gold would be fixed later", but never materialized. - See *Chervonets*. Until April 1923, Chervonets reserved for large industrial and commercial State enterprises. Issue of Rubles Sovnazki continued.

**1923** - Increasing substitution of Ruble Chervonets for Ruble Sovnazki.

**1924** (February 6th) - Treasury issued Ruble banknotes of $1/10$ Chervonets.

**1924** (February 14th) - Issue of old Rubles stopped.

**1924** (March 7th) - Exchange of old Rubles for new $1/10$ Chervonets Rubles:
1 new Ruble = 50,000 Rubles of 1923 = 5 million Rubles
of 1922 = 50 billion old Rubles = 774.23 milligrams of fine gold

**1926** (July 31st) - Decree specifying foreign exchange controls and limiting capital transfers abroad.

**1935** (November 14th) - Decree authorizing State Bank to buy foreign exchange from tourists, on basis of French Franc definition, after devaluation of 77.15%:
1 Ruble = 3.00 French Francs = 0.2284 Prewar Rubles
1 Ruble = 1.7685 milligrams of fine gold
1 U.S. Dollar = 5.025 Rubles

**1936** (February) - Extention of this exchange rate to all foreign exchange operations.

**1936** (October 26th) - After devaluation of French Franc:
    1 Ruble = 4.25 French Francs
    1 Ruble = 187.425 milligrams of fine gold

**1937** (July 17th) - Adoption of U.S. Dollar definition:
    1 Ruble = 167.673 milligrams of fine gold
    1 U.S. Dollar = 5.30 Rubles

**1941** - In territories occupied by Germans, issue of banknotes in Reichsmark by Reichskreditkassen.
In Ukraine, issue of Carbovanez. - See *Carbovanez.*

**1947** (November) - Ruble on black market hit record 135.00 per U.S. Dollar, premium of 2,400% for Greenback. Subsequent improvement.

**1947** (December 16th-29th) - Exchange of banknotes:
    1 new Ruble = 10 old Rubles
Conversion of State loans prior to 1947 at rate of 1 new Ruble for 3 old; and of deposits in savings banks at rate of 1 new for 1 old (up to 3,000 Rubles), 2 new for 3 old(from 3,000 to 10,000 Rubles), 1 new for 2 old (above 10,000 Rubles). Exchange of amounts deposited by cooperatives and kolkhozy at rate of 4 new Rubles for 5 old. Maintenance of 1 new for 1 old relationship for salaries, pensions, allowances, taxes, contracts.
Diplomatic exchange rate, in favor of small number of privileged foreigners residing in U.S.S.R., lowered from 12.00 to 8.00 Rubles per U.S. Dollar.

**1950** (February 28th) - Abandonment of U.S. Dollar definition. Adoption of gold definition, with revaluation of 32.5%:
    1 Ruble = 222.168 milligrams of fine gold
    1 U.S. Dollar = 4.00 Rubles
Diplomatic exchange rate lowered from 8.00 to 6.00 Rubles per U.S. Dollar.

**1950** (July 1st) - Abolition of diplomatic exchange rate.

**1957** (April 1st) - Creation of tourist rate. Extension to noncommercial transactions on basis of 150% premium:
    1 U.S. Dollar = 10.00 Rubles

**1957** (April 10th) - Repudiation of government internal debts of about 253 billion Rubles. Russian wage earner deprived of service payment as well as maturity.

**1960** (November) - Ruble on black market reached 57.50 per U.S. Dollar, premium of 1,338% for Greenback.

**1961** (January 1st) - Creation of hard Ruble:
    10 old Rubles = 1 new Ruble
    1 new Ruble = 987.412 milligrams of fine gold
    1 U.S. Dollar = 0.90 Ruble
De facto devaluation of 55½%. Tourist rate abolished, and all Satellite official and noncommercial rates realigned.

**1961** (September) - Ruble on black market listed at 1.50 per U.S. Dollar, premium of 67% for Greenback.

**1967** - Appearance of Daro-Ruble created by payments of Western hard currencies to Soviet authorities abroad for benefit of residents to purchase luxury goods otherwise not available. Resulted in rate of 3.00-4.50 Rubles per U.S. Dollar.

**1970** (January) - Ruble on black market reached 6.60 per U.S. Dollar, premium of 633% for Greenback. Daro-Ruble rose to 6.25-7.00 per U.S. Dollar.

## RUBLE LATVIA

Former monetary unit of **Latvia.**

Predecessor - See *Latvia.*

**1918** - At time of independence, Russian monies in circulation.

**1918** (November) - Issue of Latvian Rubles on basis of: 1 Latvian Ruble = 1 Russian Ruble. Inflation, and depreciation of currency.

**1922** (August 3rd) - Creation of new monetary unit. - See *Lat Latvia.*

## RUNDSTYCKEN

**Swedish** copper money in 18th Century. Worth 1 copper Oere.

Origin of name - Round coin.

Variation of name - Rundstücke.

## RUPEE AFGHANISTAN

Monetary unit of **Afghanistan** until 1927. Divided into 2 Kran, 3 Abbasis, 12 Shahis or 60 Pice. Since 1927, name sometimes given to Afghani of 100 Pul. - See *Afghani.*

## RUPEE BURMA

Former monetary unit of **Burma.** Divided into 16 Annas or 192 Pie.

Bank of issue - Reserve Bank of India, then Burma Currency Board, then Union Bank of Burma established on February 3, 1948, as Central Bank.

Predecessors - See *India* and *Burma.*

**1937** (April 1st) - Overprint placed on banknotes from Reserve Bank of India destined for Burma reading "Legal tender in Burma only." Convertible into silver Rupees. Creation of Burmese Rupee:
    1 Burmese Rupee = 1 Indian Rupee
    1 U.S. Dollar = 2.65 Burmese Rupees

**1939** (April 1st) - Demonetization of Indian Rupee in Burma.

**1940** (February) - Exchange controls introduced.

**1940** (March) - After pegging of Pound Sterling, new exchange rate:
    1 U.S. Dollar = 3.32 Burmese Rupees

**1943** - Linking of Burmese Rupee to Yen, with devaluation of 22%:
    1 Burmese Rupee = 1 Yen

**1945** (August) - Demonetization of banknotes issued by Japanese and return to old parity. Direct link to Pound Sterling, and introduction of B.M.A. notes issued by British Military Administration.

**1948** (April 1st) - Monetary system detached from Indian monetary system.

**1949** (September 22nd) - Following Pound Sterling devaluation, new official exchange rate:

       1 Burmese Rupee = 18 Pence
       1 U.S. Dollar = 4.7619 Burmese Rupees

**1952** (July 1st) - Union Bank of Burma, established in 1948, began operations as successor to Burma Currency Board in London. Creation of new money. - See *Kyat*.


## RUPEE CEYLON

Monetary unit of **Ceylon**. Divided into 100 Cents.

Origin of name - See *Rupee India.*

Bank of issue - By Ceylon Currency Board until July 31, 1950, then by Central Bank of Ceylon.

Predecessor - See *Ceylon.*

**1949** (December 16th) - Law decreeing independent monetary system:

       1 Ceylonese Rupee = 1 Indian Rupee
       1 Ceylonese Rupee = 186.621 milligrams of fine gold
       1 U.S. Dollar = 4.7619 Ceylonese Rupees

Parity maintained at 18 Pence:

**1950** (August 28th) - Central Bank of Ceylon began functioning.

**1952** (January 16th) - Earlier parity registered with International Monetary Fund.

**1957** (August 15th) - Tightening of exchange controls. Blocked Rupee originated.

**1959 - 1965** - Nationalization of economy. Dollar premium on Colombo's black market rose to 224%.

**1966** (February) - Dollar premium on black market cut almost in half, to 128%.

**1966** (June 6th) - India devalued Rupee. Parity with Ceylon no longer 1 to 1.

**1967** (November 22nd) - Following Pound Sterling devaluation, Ceylonese rupee cut 20% in value:

       1 Ceylonese Rupee = 149.297 milligrams of fine gold
       1 U.S. Dollar = 5.95 Ceylonese Rupees

**1968** (May 6th) - Currency reform established multiple rate structure. Official rate for essential imports and exports and government capital transactions only. Foreign Exchange Entitlement Certificates applicable to all other exports, most imports and earnings from invisibles, including tourism. Weekly tenders held by Central Bank. Initial rate set at 8.00 Ceylonese Rupees per U.S. Dollar, but allowed to fluctuate.

**1968** (June) - Weekly auction for Certificates eliminated. Sold at fixed price periodically set by Central Bank. Initial rate under new system was 8.57 Ceylonese Rupees per U.S. Dollar.

**1969** (June 18th) - Certificate rate devalued to 9.23 Ceylonese Rupees per U.S. Dollar.

**1970** (May) - Certificate system suspended for trade transactions.

**1970** (October) - Exchange of banknotes with signing of income tax declaration. High denomination banknotes of 50 and 100 Ceylonese Rupees demonetized and withdrawn from circulation at 1 to 1, up to 1,000 Ceylonese Rupees. Amounts in excess of limit taxed up to maximum of 50%.

**1971** (January) - Ceylonese Rupee on black market fell to record low of 17.25 per U.S. Dollar, a premium of 190% for the Greenback.


## RUPEE EAST AFRICA

Monetary unit in **East Africa** during 18th and early 19th Centuries. Variation of British Indian Rupee - See *Rupee India.*

**I.** - In **British East Africa,** Imperial British East Africa Company minted silver coins denominated in 1, ½, ¼ Rupees and 2 Annas, as well as bronze 1 Pice.

**1899** - Minting of bronze Cents.

**1906** - Indian Rupee system dropped. New submultiple became Cent:
   1 East African Rupee = 100 Cents
Minting of 50 and 25 Cent silver coins and cupro-nickel coins of 10, 5, 1 and ½ Cents.

**1920** - British Colonialists referred to Rupee as Florin.

**1922** (January 1st) - East African Rupee replaced by East African Shilling. - See *Shilling East Africa.*

**II.** - In **Zanzibar,** Rupees circulated with·French gold Napoléons and British gold Sovereigns from early 19th Century:
   1 British Sovereign = 15 Rupees
   1 French Napoléon = 12 Rupees
Rupee, divided into 16 Annas or 192 Pie, became unit of account. Local minting of bronze Pesetas worth ¼ Anna.

**1908** - Government accounts kept in Rupees divided into 100 Cents.

**1936** (January 1st) - Rupee replaced by East African Shilling. - See *Shilling East Africa.*

**III.** - In **German East Africa** (1890), German East Africa Company issued paper Rupees (Rupien) divided into 64 Pesas.

**1905** - Issuing authority transferred to German East African Bank in Dar-es-Salaam. East African Rupee then divided into 100 Heller.

**1916** - Local minting of 15 Rupee gold coin.

**1918** - British control of German East Africa. Monetary unit replaced by British East African Rupee.


## RUPEE FRENCH

Monetary unit of **French Settlements of India.** Formerly divided into 8 Fanams (Fanons), 24 Duddus and 96 Cache. From 1871 divided into 16 Annas, 64 Pice and 192 Pie.

Origin of name - See *Rupee India.*

Bank of issue - Branch of Banque de l'Indochine authorized to be opened in Pondicherry, according to decree of January 21, 1875, for issuance of banknotes for India. Simultaneous circulation of Indian banknotes (issued by Treasury, then after 1934 by Reserve Bank of India).

Predecessor - See *French India.*

**1736** - Dumas obtained, from Mogul Mohammed Shah, right of perpetuity for minting at Pondicherry of silver Rupees like Arcate type: 11.4 grams 956 fine, or 10.9 grams fine.
Minting of these coins until 1840, last type being issued in name of Shah Alam II, 1221 A.H. (1806).
Minting in Pondicherry of silver coins (½, 1 and 2 Fanams) and of copper coins (1 Duddu of 4 Cache, 1 Cache), Copied from French model with fleur de lis or rooster.

**1793** - Closing of mint at Pondicherry.

**1871** (June 7th) - Decree demonetizing Pondicherry coins. Only those coins current in India circulated. Custom of accounting in Fanams (2 Annas) and in Cache (2 Pie) continued in Pondicherry.

**1875** (January 21st) - Authorization given to Banque de l'Indochine, Pondicherry branch, to issue banknotes expressed in French, English and Tamil, denominated in Rupees and convertible into Indian Rupees. Exchange rate varied with rate of Indian Rupee and price of silver bullion. - See *Rupee India.*

**1884** (September 13th) - For needs of public accounting, decree calling for annual decree of Governor in September that would fix exchange rate between French Franc and French Rupee for 12 months, according to average exchange rate of 12 preceding months: 2.40 French Francs per Rupee in 1884; 2.06 from 1885 to 1888; 1.74 in 1889; 2.05 in 1890.

**1890** (September 22nd) - Decree prescribing trimester fixing of exchange rate between Rupee and French Franc. Annual average rate: 1.90 in 1891; 1.84 in 1892; 1.63 in 1893; 1.56 in 1894; 1.44 in 1895.

**1895** (October 17th) - Because of fluctuations in price of silver bullion, decree prescribing monthly fixing (more frequently in case of marked differences between official and commercial exchange rates) of exchange rate between Rupee and French Franc. Annual average rates varied between 1.49 (at lowest in 1896) and 13.23 (highest in 1939).

**1918** (November 14th) - Issue of Treasury paper.

**1924** (March 1st) - Withdrawal from circulation of Treasury paper. Replaced by metal coins used in Metropolitan France.

**1939** (September 8th) - Foreign exchange controls.

**1940** (May 20th) - Decrees establishing foreign exchange controls between Metropolitan France and Overseas Territories.

**1941** (January 28th) - Agreement realizing custom's union between French Settlements and British India, and incorporating French Settlements into Sterling Area.

**1944** (February 26th) - Official exchange rate:
1 French Rupee = 15.00 French Francs

**1945** (March 27th) - Franco-British Agreements withdrawing French Settlements from Sterling Area and linking them to Franc-Zone, subject to "foreign exchange controls for certain purposes".

**1945** (December 26th) - After devaluation of French Franc, official exchange rate:
1 French Rupee = 36.00 French Francs

**1946** (December 18th) - Parity registered with International Monetary Fund:
1 French Rupee = 268.61 milligrams of fine gold
1 U.S. Dollar = 3.30852 French Rupees

**1948** (January 26th) - Following French Franc devaluation, decision of Foreign Exchange Office fixing new parity not agreed upon by International Monetary Fund:
1 French Rupee = 64.80 French Francs

**1948** (October 17th) - 1 French Rupee = 79.70 French Francs.

**1949** (April 1st) - 1 French Rupee = 79.65 French Francs.

**1949** (April 27th) - 1 French Rupee = 82.275 French Francs.

**1949** (September 20th) - 1 French Rupee = 73.50 French Francs.
Exchange rate could be modified each month according to U.S. Dollar-Indian Rupee exchange ratio.
Corresponding parity registered with International Monetary Fund:
1 French Rupee = 186.621 milligrams of fine gold
1 French Rupee = 1 Indian Rupee
1 U.S. Dollar = 4.7619 French Rupees

**1950** (May 2nd) - In Chandernagor, ceded to India, Indian Rupee became only legal tender.

**1954** (November 1st) - French Rupee eliminated from Pondicherry, Yanaon, Karikal and Mahé. French Settlements, annexed by India, became part of Sterling Area.
- See *Rupee India*.


# RUPEE INDIA

Monetary unit of **India**. First divided into 16 Annas, 64 Pice and 192 Pie, then into 100 Nayse Paise (1955-1964), and then into 100 Paise. Circulated outside India on shores of Indian Ocean and in Arabia. Early submultiples in Mogul Empire and in Bengal: 2 Came, 16 Annas, 32 Poni, 128 Burrie, 640 Gunda, 2,560 Cowries. Multiples (units of account): Lakh (100,000 Rupees), Areb (2,500,000 Rupees), Crore (100 Lakh or 10 million Rupees).
In Surat: Nil (100 Badams, 10,000 Crore, or 100 billion Rupees).

Origin of name - Sanscrit *Rûpya* (gold, silver), from Indo-European *Rûpa* (cattle).

Bank of issue - First by private and Presidency banks, then by Treasury (1861). Since April 1, 1935, by Reserve Bank of India.

Predecessor - See *India*.

**16th Century** - In Moslem monetary system (Central and Northern States of India), monetary unit was silver Rupee of 16 Annas.

**1671** - East India Company minted Rupees based on native type.

**18th Century** - Type of Rupee varied according to minters (Benares, Bombay, Calcutta, Madras East India Company. . .).
In Golconda, minting of gold Rupee equal to 14 silver Rupees.
In Bombay, minting of copper Rupee by English ($1/24$ silver Rupee).

**1835** (August 17th) - Law unifying Indian Rupee:
> 1 Indian Rupee = 11.664 grams of silver 916 fine, or 10.684
> > grams fine silver

Minting of gold coins of 15 and 30 Indian Rupees with same weight and fineness as Indian silver Rupee. - See *Mohur.*

**1861** - First issue of banknotes by government. Called Currency Notes.

**1870** - Indian Coinage Act, adopting silver standard for paper issue on basis of same equivalence:
> 1 Indian Rupee = 27 Pence

**After 1875** - Depreciation of price of silver bullion made Indian Rupee drop below its Pound Sterling parity.

**1893** (June 26th) - Suspension of free minting of silver. Duty of 5% on silver imports. New parity:
> 1 Indian Rupee = 16 Pence

In actuality, Indian Rupee continued to decline to $14^{1}/2$ Pence.

**1898** - Withdrawal from circulation of silver coins. Officially, Indian Rupee maintained at 16 Pence. Sovereign exchangeable in India for 15 Indian Rupees.

**1910** - Duty on imports of silver raised to 20%.

**1914** (August) - Suspension of convertibility into Sterling. Later modification of parity in relation to Sterling according to fluctuations of price of silver bullion.

**1920** (February) - Record exchange rate in London:
> 1 Indian Rupee = 32 Pence

Because of increase in price of silver bullion, abolishment of duty on silver imports.

**1920** (September 8th) - Legal parity raised to:
> 1 Indian Rupee = 24 Pence

**1927** (March 22nd) - Adoption of gold standard (convertibility into bullion):
> 1 Indian Rupee = 549.1786 milligrams of fine gold
> 1 Indian Rupee = 18 Pence

**1931** (September 24th) - Suspension of gold standard and adherence to Sterling Area at old parity:
> 1 Indian Rupee = 18 Pence

**1939** (September 3rd) - Foreign exchange controls. Exchange rate pegged at:
> 1 Indian Rupee = 18 Pence
> 1 U.S. Dollar = 3.31 Indian Rupees

**1940** (February) - Fineness of silver coins lowered from 916 to 500. Indian Rupee minted in silver with weight of 11.66 grams 500 fine.

**1946** (December 18th) - Parity registered with International Monetary Fund:
> 1 Indian Rupee = 268.601 milligrams of fine gold

1 U.S. Dollar = 3.30852 Indian Rupees

**1948** (April 1st) - In Pakistan, creation of independent money. - See *Rupee Pakistan.*

**1949** (September 18th) - Devaluation following Pound Sterling:
1 Indian Rupee = 186.621 milligrams of fine gold
1 U.S. Dollar = 4.7619 Indian Rupees

**1950** (August 20th) - In Ceylon, creation of independent money. - See *Rupee Ceylon.*

**1965** (February 17th) - Customs surcharge of 10% ad valorem introduced on most imports.

**1965** (October 1st) - Tax Credit Certificate (Exports) Scheme introduced. Issued to exporters for 2, 5, 10 or 15% of Indian Rupee equivalent of foreign exchange value of specified exports.

**1966** (April) - Indian Rupee fell to record low of 11.25 per U.S. Dollar, premium of 136% for Greenback.

**1966** (June 6th) - Devaluation of Indian Rupee:
1 Indian Rupee = 118.489 milligrams of fine gold
1 U.S. Dollar = 7.50 Indian Rupees

Tax Credit Certificate (Exports) Scheme and various export promotion schemes eliminated, as was 10% customs surcharge.

**1970** (June) - Indian Rupee hit record low of 13.15 per U.S. Dollar, premium of 75% for the Greenback.


## RUPEE MALDIVE ISLANDS

Monetary unit of **Maldive Islands.** Divided into 100 Laree (singular: Lari).

Bank of issue - Central Bank of Ceylon.

**1960 -** Issue of Maldivian Rupee banknotes linked at par to Ceylonese Rupee:
1 Ceylonese Rupee = 1 Maldivian Rupee
1 Maldivian Rupee = 186.621 milligrams of fine gold
1 U.S. Dollar = 4.7619 Maldivian Rupees

**1967** (November 22nd) - Ceylon devaluation established new relationship between two units:
1 Ceylonese Rupee = 0.798 Maldivian Rupee


## RUPEE MAURITIUS

Monetary unit of **Mauritius.** Divided into 100 Cents.

Note-issuing authority - Mauritius Currency Board; then from September 4, 1967, Bank of Mauritius.

Predecessor - See *Mauritius.*

**1934 -** Mauritius Rupee linked directly to Pound Sterling:
1 Mauritius Rupee = 1 Shilling 6 Pence

**1946** (December 18th) - Parity along with Pound Sterling registered with International Monetary Fund:

1 Mauritius Rupee = 26.601 milligrams of fine gold
1 Mauritius Rupee = 0.30225 U.S. Dollar

**1949** (September 18th) - Devaluation along with Pound Sterling:
1 Mauritius Rupee = 786.621 milligrams of fine gold
1 Mauritius Rupee = 0.21 U.S. Dollar

**1967** (September 4th) - Bank of Mauritius began issuing new Rupee notes to replace Rupees of Currency Board at par.

**1967** (November 21st) - Devaluation of 14.3%, parallel to Pound Sterling:
1 Mauritius Rupee = 159.961 milligrams of fine gold
1 Mauritius Rupee = 0.18 U.S. Dollar
Introduction of 5% surcharge on 15% stamp tax on outward capital transfers, creating effective tax of 15.75% on capital outflows.

**1968** (April 24th) - Stamp tax increased to 25%, creating new effective tax of 26.25% on capital outflows.

**1969** (June 21st) - Stamp tax increased to 34%, creating new effective tax of 35.7% on capital outflows.


## RUPEE NEPAL

Official monetary unit of **Nepal.** Divided into 100 Pice. Circulated beside Indian Rupee in Nepal until October 1966.

Note-issuing authority - Government Treasury; from 1960 by Nepal Rastra Bank, established April 26, 1956.

Variations of name - Mohar Rupee, Mohar Rupaiya.

Predecessors - See *Nepal* and *Debal.*

**1945** - First issue of paper Rupee. Theoretically defined as 171 grains of silver 800 fine. Circulation generally limited to Kathmandu Valley. Exchange rate fluctuated vis-à-vis Indian Rupee.

**1956** (April 26th) - Nepal Rastra Bank established to function as sole monetary authority. Attempted to stabilize exchange rate of Rupee and secure countrywide circulation of Nepalese currency.

**1956 and 1958** - Regulations requiring that monetary payments to government be made in Nepalese currency only.

**1958** (August) - Official exchange rates fixed:
100 Indian Rupees = 150 Nepalese Rupees
1 U.S. Dollar = 7.143 Nepalese Rupees

**1960** - Nepal Rastra Bank began issuing banknotes. Assumed liability for previously issued government banknotes.

**1960** (April 13th) - Exchange rate adjusted:
100 Indian Rupees = 160 Nepalese Rupees
1 U.S. Dollar = 7.619 Nepalese Rupees
Nepalese Rupee declared fully convertible. Subsequent attempt to encourage circulation of Nepalese Rupees and abolish dual currency system in Nepal.

**1966** (June 6th) - Following Indian Rupee devaluation of 36.5%, new exchange rate established:
> 100 Indian Rupees = 101.55 Nepalese Rupees
> 1 U.S. Dollar = 7.616 Nepalese Rupees

**1966** (October 17th) - Final push toward monetary unification. According to Foreign Exchange Regulation Act 1962, circulation of other than Nepalese currencies made illegal throughout Nepal.

**1967** (December 11th) - Devaluation of 24.78%. Exchange rate with Indian Rupee adjusted:
> 100 Indian Rupees = 135 Nepalese Rupees

Par value established with International Monetary Fund:
> 1 Nepalese Rupee = 87.770 milligrams of fine gold
> 1 U.S. Dollar = 10.1250 Nepalese Rupees

**1968** (February) - Nepalese Rupee hit low of 20.00 per U.S. Dollar on black market. Subsequent improvement to range of 14.25 - 17.50 per U.S. Dollar by end of 1970.

## RUPEE PAKISTAN

Monetary unit of **Pakistan.** Divided into 16 Annas and 192 Pie until 1961, then into 100 Paisa.

Bank of issue - State Bank of Pakistan and Government.

Predecessor - See *Pakistan.*

**1947** (August) - Foreign exchange controls similar to those in India continued by Pakistan.

**1948** (April 1st) - Creation of Pakistan Rupee at par with Indian Rupee:
> 1 Pakistan Rupee = 268.601 milligrams of fine gold
> 1 U.S. Dollar = 3.30852 Pakistan Rupees

**1949** (September 20th) - Pakistan refused to devalue. Pakistan Rupee ceased to be at par with Indian Rupee.

**1951** (March 19th) - Parity registered with International Monetary Fund.

**1954** (June) - Pakistan Rupee hit record low of 6.72 per U.S. Dollar on the black market, a premium of 103% for the Greenback.

**1955** (July 31st) - Devaluation of Pakistan Rupee:
> 1 Pakistan Rupee = 1 Indian Rupee
> 1 Pakistan Rupee = 186.621 milligrams of fine gold
> 1 U.S. Dollar = 4.7619 Pakistan Rupees

**1959** (January 15th) - Export bonus vouchers introduced. Equal to 20% or 40% of surrendered exchange receipts depending on commodity. Freely negotiable at fluctuating rate and useable to import specified commodities.

**1961** (January 1st) - Decimal coinage introduced based on subsidiary unit, Paisa:
> 1 Pakistan Rupee = 100 Paisa

**1962** (August 21st and November 27th) - Export bonuses of 10% and 35% added to two previous bonuses.

**1963** - New export bonuses of 15% and 30%.

**1963** (September 1st) - Bonus scheme of 30% became applicable to incoming remittances from Pakistanis working abroad.

**1964** (June 12th) - Export bonus scheme simplified to 20% and 30%.

**1965** (November 22nd) - A 25% surcharge on existing rates of customs duties applied to all imports except machinery. Other surcharges of 5%, 7½% and 10% of c.i.f. value also applicable to certain commodities on free list.

**1967** - Export bonus of 40% added to previous ones. Bonus for home remittances of Pakistani nationals residing abroad raised from 30% to 40%.

**1969** (March) - Pakistan Rupee hit record low of 12.50 per U.S. Dollar on the black market, a premium of 163% for the Greenback.

**1969** (June) - Bonus voucher quoted in Karachi at record high of 212% above official parity.

**1970** (July 22nd) - Fluctuating tourist rate introduced based upon 45% bonus voucher plus its saleable premium.


## RUPEE PERSIAN GULF

Monetary unit of **Persian Gulf** region, created in 1959. Divided into 16 Annas, 64 Pice, 192 Pie.

Origin of name - See *Rupee.*

Variations of name - External Rupee, Gulf Rupee, External Gulf Rupee.

Bank of issue - Reserve Bank of India.

Predecessor - See *Rupee India.*

**1959** - India issued external Rupee for use in Persian Gulf region:
1 U.S. Dollar = 4.76 External Gulf Rupees

**1966** (January 28th) - Rupee withdrawn from circulation in Bahrain. - See *Bahrain.*

**1966** (June 16th) - Most other Persian Gulf communities halted the circulation of Gulf Rupee after the devaluation of the Indian Rupee. - See *Trucial States, Qatar* and *Kuwait.*

**1969** - Gulf Rupee used only in Muscat and Oman.

**1970** (May 7th) - Rial Saidi replaced Persian Gulf Rupee. - See *Rial Saidi.*


## RUPEE SEYCHELLES

Monetary unit of **Seychelles.** Divided into 100 Cents.

Note-issuing authority - Government Currency Commission.

Predecessor - See *Seychelles.*

**1934** - Seychelles Rupee linked directly to Pound Sterling:
1 Seychelles Rupee = 1 Shilling 6 Pence

**1946** (December 18th) - Parity of Seychelles Rupee along with Pound Sterling registered with International Monetary Fund:
1 Seychelles Rupee = 268.601 milligrams of fine gold

1 Seychelles Rupee = 0.30225 U.S. Dollar

**1949** (September 18th) - Devaluation parallel to Pound Sterling:
1 Seychelles Rupee = 186.621 milligrams of fine gold
1 Seychelles Rupee = 0.21 U.S. Dollar

**1967** (November 21st) - Devaluation parallel to Pound Sterling:
1 Seychelles Rupee = 159.961 milligrams of fine gold
1 Seychelles Rupee = 0.18 U.S. Dollar

## RUPIA

Monetary unit of **Portuguese Settlements of India** (Goa, Damao, Diu). Divided into 16 Tanga or 192 Reis.

Origin of name - See *Rupee India.*

Variation of name - Portuguese Rupee.

Bank of issue - Banco Nacional Ultramarino.

Predecessor - See *Portuguese India.*

**1725** - Silver coin valued at 600 Reis.

**1881** - Legally adopted and minted in silver, Portuguese Rupia linked to British Indian Rupee (11.06 grams of silver 916 fine). - See *Rupee India.*

**1962** - Portuguese territories on Indian Coast annexed by India.

## RUPIAH INDONESIA

Monetary unit of **Indonesia.** Divided into 100 Sen or Cents.

Bank of issue - Bank Indonesia, established 1928; succeeding Javasche Bank (Bank of Java) on July 1, 1928; Reorganization of Central Banking functions with Bank Indonesia renamed Bank Negara Indonesia Unit No. 1 on August 17, 1965. Reconstituted as Central Bank on December 31, 1968. Name reverted to Bank Indonesia.

Predecessors - See *Netherlands East Indies* and *Guilder Netherlands East Indies.*

**1949** (November 2nd) - Indonesian Guilder became Indonesian Rupiah.

**1950** (March 13th) - Revision of exchange rate structure with introduction of Exchange (Dollar) Certificate:
1 U.S. Dollar = 3.79/3.81 Indonesian Rupiahs (official)
1 U.S. Dollar = 7.54/7.62 Indonesian Rupiahs (Exchange
Certificate rate)
1 U.S. Dollar = 7.56 Indonesian Rupiahs (official rate plus
50% at Exchange Certificate rate for surrender
of all foreign exchange proceeds)
Banknotes of Javasche Bank and Treasury of more than 5 Indonesian Guilders reduced in value by 50%.

**1950** (August 15th) - Promulgation of provisional Constitution of Republic of Indonesia; Articles 109 and 110 affirmed independence of monetary unit and bank of issue.

**1951** (March 5th) - Additional exchange rates:

>1 U.S. Dollar = 7.62 Indonesian   Rupiahs   (Inducement Certificate rate)
>
>1 U.S. Dollar = 11.43 Indonesian Rupiahs (for approved capital investments)
>
>1 U.S. Dollar = 19.00 Indonesian Rupiahs (for imports with Inducement Certificates)

**1952** (February 4th) - Devaluation with abolition of Exchange Certificate:

>1 U.S. Dollar = 11.40 Indonesian Rupiahs (official rate applicable to most transactions)

Creation of negotiable export certificates for Dollar transactions. Also, levies via Inducement Certificates of 100%-200% of value on certain imports.

**1953** (January 23rd) - TPI Certificate for import levies of 33 1/3%, 100% and 200% on special imports. At end of 1953:

>1 U.S. Dollar = 22.30 Indonesian Rupiahs

**1953** (October 12th) - Certificates for export of certain native products with premiums between 5% and 10%. At end of 1953:

>1 U.S. Dollar = 11.90-12.45 Indonesian Rupiahs

**1954** (January 1st) - Dollar export certificates abolished

**1954** (March 2nd) - Introduction of TPT Certificate for 66 2/3% tax on foreign exchange payments for most invisibles:

>1 U.S. Dollar = 19.125 Indonesian Rupiahs

**1955** (June 1st) - Inducement Certificate system abolished.

**1955** (September 1st) - Import and exchange structure revised. Imports classified into four categories with additional import levies (TPI) from 50% - 400%:

>1 U.S. Dollar = 17.203-57.40 Indonesian Rupiahs

**1955** (October 24th) - Introduction of 5% - 10% export premiums.

**1956** (August 6th) - Introduction of negotiable Export Incentive Certificates (BPE) ranging between 2% and 20% of export proceeds. BPE Certificates also used to finance certain imports and invisibles.

**1956** (September 3rd) - Imports reclassified into nine categories: levies of 25%-400%.

**1956** (December) - Existence of nine effective export rates:

>1 U.S. Dollar = 11.35-57.35 Indonesian Rupiahs

**1957** (June 20th) - New exchange rate system. Introduction of negotiable Export Certificate (BE) equivalent to 100% of foreign exchange proceeds surrendered and subject to 20% exchange tax. BE Certificates also used for invisibles, capital transfers and imports reclassified into six categories with surcharges ranging from 20% to 175%:

>1 U.S. Dollar = 23.251 Indonesian Rupiahs (BE rate less 20% for all exports)
>
>1 U.S. Dollar = 29.00 Indonesian Rupiahs (BE rate for capital and invisibles)
>
>1 U.S. Dollar = 34.904-79.952 Indonesian Rupiahs (BE rate plus surcharges of 20%-175% for imports)

**1958** (April 19th) - BE Certificate rate fixed at:
1 U.S. Dollar = 37.85 Indonesian Rupiahs

**1959** (August 25th) - Devaluation and revision of exchange structure:
1 U.S. Dollar = 45.00 Indonesian Rupiahs (official rate)
Exchange tax of 20% extended to all exports, capital and invisibles. Surcharges of 25%-200% levied on six import categories:
1 U.S. Dollar = 35.865 Indonesian Rupiahs (official rate
plus 20% exchange tax)
1 U.S. Dollar = 56.60-135.85 Indonesian Rupiahs (for imports)
Reduction in value by 90% of 500 Indonesian Rupiah and 1,000 Indonesian Rupiah banknotes and withdrawal from circulation. Bank deposits over 25,000 Rupiahs frozen to 90% and usable only to purchase government bonds.

**1960** (August 29th) - Exchange tax of 20% replaced by 10% export tax. Imports reclassified into two groups subject to special Komponen Harga (price component) levies of 25% and 60%. Special import rate created. Transfer tax of 100% applicable to certain invisibles and capital transactions.
1 U.S. Dollar = 56.55-200.00 Indonesian Rupiahs (for imports)
1 U.S. Dollar = 90.00 Indonesian Rupiahs (for invisibles, capital)

**1961** (May 2nd) - Creation of tourist rate with subsidy of 45.00 Indonesian Rupiahs per U.S. Dollar:
1 U.S. Dollar = 89.85 Indonesian Rupiahs

**1962** (March 5th) - Revision of exchange structure. Retention of 15% of foreign exchange proceeds to be exchanged for freely negotiable SIVA certificates for payment of imports and services.
One-half of SIVA certificates subject to general fluctuating rate. Remaining half subject to regional rate authorizing imports for specific areas. Imports regrouped into five categories with Komponen Harga levies set at 100%-500%, or subject to special tax:
1 U.S. Dollar = 44.85-173.10 Indonesian Rupiahs (for foreign exchange proceeds)
1 U.S. Dollar = 45.30-1,170.00 Indonesian Rupiahs (for imports and invisibles)

**1962** (July 16th) - New tourist rate:
1 U.S. Dollar = 179.85 Indonesian Rupiahs

**1963** (May 27th) - Revision of exchange rate structure. Retention of foreign exchange proceeds reduced to 5%. Exchange subsidy of 270.00 Indonesian Rupiahs added to official rate. Imports regrouped into three categories with exchange surcharge on official rate plus exchange taxes of 225.00 and 495.00 Indonesian Rupiahs and duties of 50%-100%:
1 U.S. Dollar = 315.00 Indonesian Rupiahs (basic rate)
1 U.S. Dollar = 315.00-379.00 Indonesian Rupiahs (for foreign exchange receipts)
1 U.S. Dollar = 315.00-1,620.00 Indonesian Rupiahs (for imports)

**1964** (April 17th) - Devaluation and exchange rate revision:
> 1 U.S. Dollar = 250.00 Indonesian Rupiahs (basic transactions rate)

Exchange taxes abolished. System of freely negotiable SPP Certificates (Production-Inducement) introduced. Exporters provided with automatic foreign exchange allocation equivalent to 20% of exchange proceeds. Imports reclassified into five categories with additional duty of 50%-800%. Levy of 5% exchange fee (LAAPLN) on basic transactions rate imposed on payments used for invisibles and most imports.

**1964** (December) - Three effective rates for export proceeds and foreign exchange receipts:
> 1 U.S. Dollar = 520.00-2,237.00 Indonesian Rupiahs

Seven effective rates for imports and foreign payments:
> 1 U.S. Dollar = 250.00-6,887.00 Indonesian Rupiahs

SPP Certificate Rates:
> 1 U.S. Dollar = 3,350.00 Indonesian Rupiahs (special rate)
> 1 U.S. Dollar = 6,625.00 Indonesian Rupiahs (free rate)

Enactment of Foreign Exchange Law of 1964 reorganizing foreign exchange operations.

**1965** (August 17th) - Indonesia withdrew from International Monetary Fund.

**1965** (December 13th) - Currency reform and banknote exchange with 10% levy:
> 1 Indonesian Rupiah (new) = 1,000.00 Indonesian Rupiahs (old)
> 1 U.S. Dollar = 10.00 Indonesian Rupiahs (new transaction rate)

**1965** (December 22nd) - Revision of basic transaction rate, renamed transaction rate. Subsidy for exports and surcharge for imports of 9.75 Indonesian Rupiahs (new) added to basic transaction rate of 0.25 Indonesian Rupiahs (new). Resulted in transaction rate of:
> 1 U.S. Dollar = 10.00 Indonesian Rupiahs (new)

**1966** (February 11th) - Exports regrouped into three categories. Introduction of freely negotiable Export Bonus BE Certificate permitting retention of 10%-50% of export proceeds. Imports also financed with BE Certificates. Freely fluctuating market for DP (Devisa Pelengkap) Complementary Foreign Exchange created for invisibles.

**1966** (May 20th) - Percentage of BE export proceeds for retention raised to 20%-100%.

**1966** (October 3rd) - Percentage of BE export proceeds for retention revised to 50%-90%. Surrender of 10% of export proceeds to regional authorities called ADO (Alokesi Devisa Otomatis) exchange.

**1966** (December) - 1 U.S. Dollar = 10.00 Indonesian Rupiahs (transaction rate)
> 1 U.S. Dollar = 85.00 Indonesian Rupiahs (fluctuating BE rate)
> 1 U.S. Dollar = 105.00 Indonesian Rupiahs (fluctuating DP rate)

**1967** (February 21st) - Indonesia rejoined International Monetary Fund.

**1967** (July 28th) - Regrouping of exports into two categories. Percentage of BE export proceeds for retention revised to 75% and 90%. Creation of special Credit BE for imports financed by foreign aid.

**1967** (September 6th) - Creation of blocked Rupiah accounts (DICS Rupiah), negotiable at discount from BE rate and used for local investment.

**1967** (December) - 1 U.S. Dollar = 235.00 Indonesian Rupiahs (BE rate)
  1 U.S. Dollar = 260.00 Indonesian Rupiahs (DP rate)

**1968** (February 21st) - Exchange rate for oil transactions depreciated from 85.00 to 240.00 Indonesian Rupiahs per U.S. Dollar. Periodically adjusted.

**1968** (October) - Indonesian Rupiah hit historic low in black market of 500.00 per U.S. Dollar (500,000 old Rupiahs). Subsequent improvement and stabilization.

**1968** (December) - 1 U.S. Dollar = 326.00 Indonesian Rupiahs (BE rate)
  1 U.S. Dollar = 414.00 Indonesian Rupiahs (DP rate)
  1 U.S. Dollar = 300.00 Indonesian Rupiahs (for oil transactions)

**1969** (December) - 1 U.S. Dollar = 327.00 Indonesian Rupiahs (BE rate)
  1 U.S. Dollar = 378.00 Indonesian Rupiahs (DP rate)
  1 U.S. Dollar = 300.000 Indonesian Rupiahs (for oil transactions)

**1970** (April 17th) - Devaluation and revision of exchange rate structure:
  1 U.S. Dollar = 378.00 Indonesian Rupiahs (flexible general foreign exchange rate or Devisa Umum-DU, used for all transactions except foreign aid)
  1 U.S. Dollar = 326.00 Indonesian Rupiahs (flexible credit foreign exchange rate or Devisa Kredit-DK, applicable to imports and services financed by foreign aid)

**1970** (December 10th) - Exchange rate unified:
  1 U.S. Dollar = 378.00 Indonesian Rupiahs (official rate for all transactions)

## RUPIAH IRIAN BARAT

Monetary unit of **West Irian.** Divided into 100 Sen.

Bank of issue - Bank Indonesia.

Predecessor - See *Guilder New Guinea.*

**1963** (May 1st) - Creation of Irian Barat Rupiah to repl..ce New Guinea Guilder:
  1 Irian Barat Rupiah = 12.43 Indonesian Rupiahs
  1 U.S. Dollar = 3.62 Irian Barat Rupiahs
Indonesia decreed exchange subsidy or surcharge of 74.58 Indonesian Rupiahs per Irian Barat Rupiah, resulting in effective rate of:
  1 Irian Barat Rupiah = 87.01 Indonesian Rupiahs

**1963** (October 1st) - Indonesian exporters to West Irian received additional 53.11 Indonesian Rupiahs per Irian Barat Rupiah, resulting in effective rate of:
  1 Irian Barat Rupiah = 140.12 Indonesian Rupiahs

**1967** (April 3rd) - New official exchange rate:

1 Irian Barat Rupiah = 10.00 Indonesian Rupiahs

1 U.S. Dollar = 10.00 Irian Barat Rupiahs

**1970** (April 17th) - Exchange reform simplifying rate structure and establishing new rate:

1 Irian Barat Rupiah = 18.90 Indonesian Rupiahs

1 U.S. Dollar = 20.00 Irian Barat Rupiahs

**1971** (February 18th) - Indonesian Rupiah replaced Irian Barat Rupiah as monetary unit. - See *Rupiah Indonesia.*

## RUPIAH KEPULAUAN RIAU

Monetary unit of **Riau Archipelago.** Divided into 100 Sen.

Bank of issue - Bank Indonesia.

Predecessor - See *Indonesia.*

**1963** (October 15th) - Kepulauan Riau Rupiah created:

1 Kepulauan Riau Rupiah = 14.70 Indonesian Rupiahs

1 U.S. Dollar = 3.06 Kepulauan Riau Rupiahs

Indonesia decreed exchange subsidy or surcharge of 88.20 Indonesian Rupiahs per Kepulauan Riau Rupiah, resulting in effective rate of:

1 Kepulauan Riau Rupiah = 102.90 Indonesian Rupiahs

Exporters to Riau Archipelago received additional 61.27 Indonesian Rupiahs per Kepulauan Riau Rupiah, resulting in effective rate of:

1 Kepulauan Riau Rupiah = 164.17 Indonesian Rupiahs

**1964** (July 1st) - Indonesian Rupiah replaced Kepulauan Riau Rupiah as monetary unit. - See *Rupiah Indonesia.*

## RUSPONE

Gold money of Grand Duchy of **Tuscany.** Legal tender during 18th and 19th Centuries (until 1859), having value of 24 Guilders, 60 Paoli, 2,400 Quattrini or 9,600 Denari. It retained fleur de lis imprint of old Guilder.

Variations of name - Ruspono, Triple Zecchino.

## *RUSSIA*

First medium of exchange - Animal furs. First coins, imitating those of Byzantines and Arabs, minted by private individuals, as well as State after 11th Century. Initially circulated in Kiev.

**Until 15th Century -** General circulation of foreign coins (Swedish, Lithuanian, Tartar . . .).

**1420 -** First minting of local monies in Novgorod (then in Moscow, Pskov, Tver). Used for private accounts: silver Denga, and silver, then copper Poluschka.

**End of 15th Century** - First State issues by Ivan III. Hungarian minters in Russia issued gold Ducats.

**16th Century** - Introduction of Western monies: English Nobles, gold Ducats, silver Thaler. Payments to foreigners made in Dutch and German monies. Thalers cut into pieces (see *Jafimske*).
Ruble of 100 Kopeks used as unit of account.
Ducat exchanged for 1 Ruble, Thaler for 1/2 Ruble.
For subsequent Russian monetary history, see *Ruble.*

**1768** - Introduction of paper money. - See *Assignatzia.*

**1922** - In disaster of inflation, creation of Chervonets of 10 gold Rubles.
- See *Chervonets.*


## RWANDA

Formerly part of Ruanda-Urundi. - See *Ruanda-Urundi.*

**1962** (July 1st) - Independence, Ruanda changed name to Rwanda.

**1964** (September 30th) - Monetary and customs union with Burundi dissolved.

**1964** - Banque Nationale du Rwanda (National Bank of Rwanda) established as Central Bank. Issued Rwanda Franc to replace Ruanda-Burundi Franc at par.
- See *Franc Rwanda.*


## RYO

**Japanese** unit of weight. Equal to Chinese Ounce (37.5 grams), and used to designate unit of account in Japan.

**16th Century** - Coban, gold bar, used as unit of account under name Ryo, equal to 17.8 grams. - See *Coban.*


## RYUKYU ISLANDS

**Prior to 19th Century** - Use of Chinese monies - See *China.*

**1871** - Annexed by Japan. Introduction of Japanese monetary system. - See *Yen.*

**1945** (June 21st) - American Occupation. Provisional American military government established. Use of military script denominated in U.S. Dollars.

**1950** (December 5th) - United States Civil Administration established. U.S. Dollar, subsequently given sole legal tender status. - See *Dollar.*

**1953** (December 25th) - Amami Islands returned to Japan. Reintroduction of Japanese monetary system. - See *Yen.*

**1968** (June 26th) - Bonin, Marcus, Rosario, Volcano and Parce Vela Islands returned to Japan. Reintroduction of Japanese monetary system. - See *Yen.*

## SAAR

**1793** - French monetary system. Subsequent introduction of Franc. - See *France* and Franc.

**1815** - Prussian and Bavarian monetary systems, then German system (1871). - See *Prussia* and *Mark*.

**1921** - French monetary system. - See *Franc*.

**1935** (February 18th) - Introduction of Reichsmark. - See *Reichsmark*.

**1947** (June 16th) - Creation of Saarmark. - See *Mark Saar*.

**1947** (November 20th) - Legal tender status given to French Franc, which replaced Saarmark:
> 1 Saarmark = 20.00 French Francs

**1954** (July 7th) - Law authorizing issue of divisionary coinage for Saar. Denominated in Francs and circulated simultaneously with French coins. Minting at Paris Mint of 10, 20 and 50 Franc coins (November 1954) and 100 Franc coins (September 1955).

**1957** (January 1st) - Returned to West Germany by plebiscite. - See *Mark German Federal Republic*. Was to remain in Franc-Zone until December 31, 1959.

**1959** (July 5th) - Left Franc-Zone. Economic union with West Germany completed.


## SABAH

Predecessor - See *Borneo*.

Member state of Federation of Malaysia (September 16, 1963). Formerly called British North Borneo. - See *Dollar Malaysia*.


## SAIME

Unit of account in **Algeria** during 18th Century, equal to 50 Aspers.


## SAINT ANDREW

Gold money (3.89 grams) of **Scotland** from 14th to 16th Century.

Origin of name - From Saint Andrew, patron saint of Scotland.

Variation of name - Lion d'Or.


## SAINT-DOMINGUE

Predecessors - See *Haiti* and *French Antilles*.

**1670** (March 24th) - Decree of King's Council establishing monetary system for overseas possessions. - See *Livre Coloniale.*

**1697** - Treaty of Rijswijk separating Saint-Domingue from rest of Island of Hispaniola. French monies circulated at premium simultaneously with Piaster Gourde, Gourdin and Escalin.

**18th Century** - Gourde had exchange rate of 8 Livres Coloniales 5 Sols.

**1773** - Paper money experiment. Plantation owners paid for imported commodities with "billets de sucre" used during War of Spanish Succession. Fixed value, independent of price of sugar, was given to these notes.

**1720** (March) - Minting in France for Saint-Domingue of copper coins of 12 Deniers.

**1721** (June) - Minting in France for Saint-Domingue of copper coins of 9 Deniers.

**1730** (December) - Decree calling for minting of silver coins of 6 and 12 Sols for Lesser Antilles. These coins circulated in Saint-Domingue and in British Antilles.

**1738** (June) - Circulation of Double Sol of France (24 Deniers) for 2 Sols 6 Deniers under name of Marqué Noir. - See *Marqué.*

**1766** (October) - Minting of coin of 1 Sol.

**1801** (November 11th) - Decree of Toussaint L'Ouverture. - See *Haiti.*


## SAINT HELENA

**17th Century** - Introduction of British specie money by British East India Company.

**19th Century** - Following British colonization, adoption of British monetary system. - See *Pound.*


## SAINT PIERRE AND MIQUELON

English monetary system 1713-1763, 1778-1783, 1793-1802, 1802-1816. - See *Pound.*

French monetary system in intervening years. - See *Franc.*

**19th Century** - Simultaneous circulation of English, French, American and Spanish specie monies.

**1839** (July 17th) - Decree promulgated Law of July 4, 1837. Franc made sole legal tender as of July 1, 1840.

**1866** (October 14th) - Decree extended agreement of Latin Monetary Union to Saint Pierre and Miquelon.

**1873** (June 16th) - Decree authorized government agencies to receive and to make payments in foreign gold and silver monies with legal tender status. The U.S. Dollar exchanged for 5.40 Francs, then for 5.20 (from 1875); British Sovereign exchanged for 26 Francs; Spanish Doubloon exchanged for 86.40 Francs, then for 84.00 Francs (from 1892), and for 82.00 (from 1899).

**1880** (October 16th) - Payment of wages and salaries to be made in Francs.

**1889** (February 16th) - Mexican and Colombian Doubloons placed in same category as Spanish Doubloons.

**1920** (August 8th) - Legal tender status given all monetary units of Metropolitan France, including subsidiary metal coinage.

**1939** (September 9th) - Foreign exchange controls within framework of Franc-Zone.

**1940** (May 20th) - Decree establishing foreign exchange controls between Metropolitan France and Overseas Territories.

**1942** (December 4th) - Decree revoking legal tender status for banknotes of Banque de France that circulated in Saint Pierre and Miquelon.

**1943** (January 26th) - Legal tender status given to banknotes issued by Caisse Centrale de France Libre (Caisse Centrale de la France d'Outre-Mer after February 2, 1944).

**1944** (February 8th) - Franco-British Agreement fixed exchange rate of Free French Territories:
   1 Pound Sterling = 200.00 Francs

**1944** (June) - Franco-American Agreement ratified Pound exchange rate and fixed U.S. Dollar at 50.00 Francs.

**1944** (December 6th) - Parities confirmed and specified:
   1 Pound Sterling = 200.00 Francs
   1 U.S. Dollar = 49.625 Francs
Return to Franc-Zone.

**1945** (December 26th) - Creation of CFA Franc. Incorporation of Saint Pierre and Miquelon into CFA group. - See *Franc CFA*.


## SALUNG

Coin of **Siam,** worth 1/4 Tical or Baht, minted in silver. As unit of account called Mayon. Corresponded to 16 Clam, 8 Pais, 4 Song Pais, 2 Fuang, 1/4 Tical, 1/16 Tael, or 1/320 Catty. Also minted as silver coin.

**End of 19th Century** - Salung minted in three forms: silver coin of 3.95 grams 928 fine; 3.87 grams 903 fine and 3.75 grams 900 fine.

**20th Century** - Silver coin of 3.75 grams 650 fine.


## SALUTE

**I.** - Gold coin (3.88 grams) minted in **France** by British Occupation in 15th Century.

Origin of name - From imprint showing Annunciation to Virgin Mary.

**1421** (August 11th) - Minting of Salute in fine gold (3.88 grams). Exchange rate: 25 Sous.

**1423** (September 6th) - Henry VI debased Salute to 3.50 grams fine gold. Exchange rate: 22 Sous 6 Deniers.

**II.** - Gold money of **Naples,** minted in 1266 by Charles of Anjou, then by Charles II. Also called Carlino.

## *SAN MARINO*

Predecessors - See *Rome* and *Italy*.

Italian monetary system - See *Lira*.

Money of Vatican City also had legal tender status. Minting and circulation of local coins (10 and 20 Lire in gold, later demonetized; 1, 2 and 5 Lire in silver, later demonetized; 5 and 10 Centesimi in bronze).

Mintings in 1861 of local coins (5 and 10 Centesimi in bronze), in 1898 (50 Centesimi in bronze; 1, 2 and 5 Lire in silver), in 1925 (10 and 20 Lire in gold), and in 1932 (5, 10 and 20 Lire in silver, 5 and 10 Centesimi in bronze).

## SAN VICENTE

**Portuguese** gold money issued in 1556 and worth 1,000 Reis. Also, a ½ San Vicente.

Origin of name - From full length figure of St. Vincent.

## SANTIM

Submultiple ($1/100$) of Lat, monetary unit of **Latvia.**

Plural - Santimi.

## *SANTO DOMINGO*

See *Dominican Republic*.

## SANTO THOME

Gold money introduced into **Portuguese India** by Portuguese after 1521. Valued at 2 Piasters.

Origin of name - From image of Saint Thomas, Apostle of India.

Variation of name - In English, Saint Thomas.

**1818** (October 10th) - Minting of gold Santo Thomé of several types worth 12, 8, 4, 2 and 1 Pardao.

## *SAO TOME AND PRINCIPE*

For monetary developments, see *Cape Verde Islands*.

## SAPEQUE

**I.** - In **Indochina**, zinc coin, later of copper (after 19th Century), punctured in center with square hole. A bundle of Sapèques consisted of 600 coins. Crude use also of Chinese copper Tsien (Sapèque).

**541** - Minting of Annamite Sapèques by Ly-Nam-Dé. Henceforth, Sapèque was basic money of exchange.
Minting of Sapèques by government.
In Annam, zinc Sapèques and Chinese copper Tsien (Sapèques).
In Tonkin and in Cochin China, zinc Sapèques.

**1814** - Sapèque of Gia-Long: 3.375 grams of copper.

**1859** - Arrival of French. Closing of official Sapèque mints.

**1863** (March 5th) - Attempt at fixing exchange ratio between Sapèque and other monies, on basis of:
          5 bundles = 1 Mexican silver Piaster

**1863** (June 3rd) - Decree fixing bundle at 1 French Franc. In fact, variable exchange rates. Limitations placed on local trade and small paymements made with bundle.

**1878** - Attempt at issuing coins of 1 Centime punctured with square hole in center, in manner of Sapèque. Method failed and was terminated.

**1886** - Sapèque of Dong-Khank: 5.285 grams.

**1894** - Establishment of French Sapèque Mint in Ben-thuy, near Vinh.

**1904** (December 29th) - Zinc Sapèque had legal tender status in Tonkin for 1/600 Indochinese Piastre. Sapèque of copper (4 grams, 95% copper, 4% tin, 1% bronze) equaled 1/500 Indochinese Piastre.

**20th Century** - Native mintings of Sapèques until middle of 20th Century.

**II.** - Unit of account in **Java.** - See *Soekoe.*

**III.** - For **China,** see *Tsien.*

## SARAWAK

Currency in circulation before 1946, see *Dollar Straits Settlements.*

**1946** (May 17th) - Became Crown Colony after Straits settlements dissolved.
Money in circulation, see *Dollar Malaya.*

**1963** (September 16th) - Became part of Federation of Malaysia. - See *Federation of Malaysia.*

## SARDINIA

**Until 240 B.C.** - Carthaginian monies. - See *Carthage.*
**From 240 B.C. to 5th Century** - Roman monies. - See *Rome.*
**8th Century** - Arabic monies.

**9th Century** - Pisans and Genoans adopted Carolingian monetary system: Lira of 20 Soldi or 240 Denari. - See *Lira.*

**End of 13th Century** - Minting of silver Grosso.

**14th Century** - Returned to Kingdom of Aragon, Sardinia used Spanish monies. - See *Reale.*

**15th to 18th Century** - Money of Savoy. - See *Savoy.*

**18th Century** - System of accounting: Lira of 4 Reali, 20 Soldi or 240 Denari.

**1755** - Gold monies: Carlino (12 Lire), Doppia (24 Lire). Silver money: Scudo (6 Lire).

**1812** - Minting of silver/copper Reale and coins of 3 Cagliaresi.

**1814** - Piedmont monetary system. - See *Piedmont.*

**1865** - Italian monetary system. - See *Italy* and *Lira Italy.*

## SATA

Early unit of account in **Java,** sometimes called Santa: 500,000 Sata equal to 1 Bahar, 50,000 to 1 Uta, 5,000 to 1 Catty, 500 to 1 Laxsan, 50 to 1 Pecco, 2 to 1 Tayell. Sata was the equivalent of 5 Mas, 20 Cash or 200 Candareens. 200 Caixa (coins of copper and lead) threaded on cord of straw equalled 1 Sata; 5 Sata of 200 Caixa equalled 1 Soekoe. - See *Caixa* and *Soekoe.*

## SATANG

Submultiple ($1/100$) of **Baht,** formerly Tical, monetary unit of **Thailand (Siam).** Minted in bronze (5 grams). - See *Tical* and *Baht.*

## *SAUDI ARABIA*

Predecessor - See *Arabia.*

**Early 20th Century** - Simultaneous circulation of Maria Theresia Thalers and British gold Sovereigns.

**1928** - Adoption of independent monetary system based upon British gold Sovereign. Creation of Saudi Riyal. - See *Riyal Saudi Arabia.*

## SAUDI GUINEA

Gold coin of **Saudi Arabia** issued in 1952. Equal in weight and fineness to the British Sovereign:

      1 Saudi Guinea = 7.32238 grams of fine gold

      1 Saudi Guinea = 40 Saudi Riyals

# SAUDI RIYAL

See *Riyal Saudi Arabia.*

# SAVOY

Monies of Rome (see *Rome*), then Carolingian monetary system (see *Livre* and *Lira*) with minting of silver Denier.

**End of 13th Century** - Amadeus V adopted monetary system of Saint Louis and minted Gros.

**14th Century** - First gold monies: Fiorino (Florin), Agnel, Ecu, then Cavalier and Ducat.

**1483** - Minting of silver Testone (8 Gros).

**1553** - Minting of silver Tallero imitating Thaler (42 Gros).

**1562** - New monetary system:
Specie monies:
>In gold - Filiberto (9 Lire), Scudo (3 Lire)
>In silver - Filiberto (5 Soldi), Soldo, Denero

**17th Century** - Many units of account: Fiorino (Florin), equal to 1/2 Livre Tournois; Scudo; Lira.

**1717** - Adoption of single unit of account, Piedmont Lira of 20 Soldi or 240 Denari.

**18th Century** - Specie monies:
>In gold - Doppia, Pistole, Zecchino, Carlino
>In silver - Scudo, Ducaton
>In copper - Soldo, Picaillon

**1811** - Creation of Bank of Savoy for issue of banknotes.

**1860** - Introduction of French monetary system - See *Franc.*

**1865** - Absorption of Bank of Savoy by Banque de France.
Other areas of Italy unified themselves around House of Savoy with Lira as monetary unit. - See *Italy* and *Lira Italy.*

# SAXONY

Predecessor - See *Holy Roman Empire.*

**10th Century** - Minting of silver Denier (Pfennig), copied from Carolingian Denier.

**12th Century** - Denier, reduced in weight and thickness, became Bracteate.

**14th Century** - Gros, Pfennig, Heller and Bracteates.

**18th Century** - Unit of account: Thaler of 24 Gute Groschen or 288 Pfennig.
Specie monies:
>In gold - August d'Or, Ducat, Guilder (Gulden)
>In silver - Speciesthaler, Reichsthaler, Zwei Drittel (coin of
>>2/3 Thaler), Gute Groschen

In silver/copper - Pfennig and its multiples, Heller

**1838** (July 30th) - Agreement among Prussia, Bavaria, Württemberg, Baden, Hesse
. . .fixing Thaler-Guilder (Gulden) relationship:
　　　1 Thaler = 1.75 Guilders (Gulden)
Minting of common silver coin (Vereinsmünze of 33.4 grams) worth 2 Thaler or
3.50 Guilders (Gulden).

**1840** - Saxony minted Thaler based on Prussian Thaler (16.7 grams fine silver). Thaler
divided into 30 Neugroschen or 300 Pfennig.

**1840** - Minting of August d'Or.

**1857** (January 24th) - Germanic Monetary Agreement: 1 Thaler = 1.50 Austrian
Gulden = 1.75 Guilders (Gulden) of South German states.
Minting of common silver money (Vereinsthaler of 16.7 grams).

**1871** (December 4th) - Monetary unification of Germany. Mark replaced Thaler:
　　　10 Mark = 3.33 Thaler
　- See *Mark*.


# SCEAT

Silver coin minted by Anglo-Saxons in **England** between 5th and 9th Century. Corresponded to Denarius. Also circulated from 6th to 8th Century in **Frisia** located
in Low Countries.

Origin of name - From Frisian *sceat* (silver, value, cattle), German *Schatz* (treasure).

Variation of name - Skeat.

Plural - Sceattae.


# SCHERIF

Corruption of Ashrafi, gold money of **Persia.** - See *Ashrafi.*

Other variations - Seraphin, Sherify.


# SCHILLING, SCHELLING

Money of numerous countries of Anglo-Saxon and Northern Europe.

Origin of name - English *shield,* German *Schild;* from Germanic *Skilling;* Indo-
European root *Skel.* By virture of shield of arms pictured on first impressions.

Variations of name - English, Shilling; German, Schilling; Flemish, Schelling; Scandinavian, Skilling; Polish, Szelong; French, Escalin, Chelin; Italian, Scellino.

**I. - Carolingian** monetary system, unit of account: 1 Livre = 20 Sols or Shillings =
240 Deniers.

**II. - In England,** Carolingian monetary system was spread by Normans, even before
conquest by William: 1 Livre = 20 Shillings = 240 Pence. - See *Shilling.*

**III.** - In **Netherlands,** adoption of Carolingian unit of account: 1 Livre = 20 Sols or Schellings = 240 Grooten.
This system of accounting persisted until 19th Century, although after 1355 it competed in Northern provinces with Guilder (Florin) system.

**18th Century** - Livre de Gros (Pondt Vlaams) equivalent to 6 Guilders, or 20 Schelling. Each Schelling worth 6 Stuyver, 12 Grooten, or 96 Penning and in Brabant, 288 Myten.
Schelling was then silver/copper coin having exchange rate of 6 Sols, or 3 Duiten. - See *Netherlands.*
In Brabant, after 1749, there was Nieuwe Schelling and heavier Oude Schelling (new and old Schelling).

**IV.** - For **Austria,** see *Schilling Austria.*

**V.** - For **Poland,** see *Szelong.*

**VI.** - In **Liege, Maestricht** and **Westphalia** in 18th Century, silver money and unit of account worth 1/8 Patagon, 1/2 Gulden (Guilder), 10 Stuyver, 40 Ortje (Oord), 160 Penning. The 1/2 Schelling, called Blamuse, was worth 5 Sols.

**VIII.** - In **German** states, Livre, inherited from Carolingian monetary system, was equal to 20 Schillings; Marc (Marc of Cologne of 233.856 grams) gave rise to Mark, divided into 12 Schillings. In each system of accounting, Schilling computed as 12 Deniers or Pfennig:
    1 gold Schilling = 4.6 grams
    1 silver Schilling = 18.4 grams
    1 gold Schilling = 3 silver Shillings
Third system of accounting based on gold Gulden (Guilder). Replaced system of Schillings, especially in Southern countries.

**14th Century** - First mintings of silver Schilling (Lübeck in 1365, Teutonic Order in 1370).

**15th Century** - Minting of Schilling by various German states: Pomerania, Hamburg.
In Hamburg, Schilling contained 6.8 grams fine silver in 1226; 4.8 in 1325; 4 in 1375; 2.5 in 1430; 1.5 in 1450; 1.2 in 1461; 1.1 in 1506.
North German states with Hamburg continued to keep accounts in Mark (until 1667) divided into 16 Schillings. Each Schilling counted as 12 Deniers.

**End of 17th Century** - Hamburg returned to system of accounting in Mark of 16 Schillings (or Sols Lübsk). Each Schilling worth 2 Groschen, 6 Dreiling or 12 Pfennig.

**18th Century** - Schilling also unit of account in Münster (1/28 Thaler or 12 Pfennig), in Osnabrück (1/21 Thaler or 12 Pfennig), in Württemberg (1/28 Gulden or 6 Pfennig), in Mecklenburg (1/48 Thaler or 12 Pfennig), in Bavaria for payments of taxes and fines (1/41 Livre, 12 Regensburger, 30 Pfennig or 60 Heller).

**1873** - Adoption of new German Mark. Substituted for Mark in Hamburg, Bremen and Lübeck at rate of 1 new Mark for 12.83 Schilling.

**VIII.** - In certain **Swiss** cantons until 1850, unit of account and silver/copper money. In Lucerne and Zurich, 1/40 Guilder (Gulden) or 12 Heller. Zurich minted Schilling in 1751.
In Saint Gall, 1/10 Guilder (Gulden) or 1.5 Batzen.
Silver/copper coin in Lucerne, Zurich, Zug.

IX. - Order of **Livonia** and Archbishop of Riga **(Latvia)** minted silver Schilling and submultiples (Pfennig, Artig) in 15th Century.

X. - For **Scandinavian** countries, see *Skilling.*

## SCHILLING AUSTRIA

Monetary unit of **Austria.** Divided into 100 Groschen.

Origin of name - See *Schilling.*

Bank of issue - By Oesterreichische Nationalbank (National Bank of Austria), created November 4, 1922, liquidated in April 1938 and absorbed by Reichsbank. Reconstituted in 1945.

Predecessor - See *Krone Austria.*

**1923** (December) - Creation of Schilling, at rate of:
1 Schilling = 10,000 paper Kronen

**1924** (December 20th) - Definition of Schilling in gold:
1 Schilling = 211.72 milligrams of fine gold

**1925** (March) - Return to freedom of foreign exchange dealings.

**1931** (October 9th) - Foreign exchange controls. Progressive depreciation of Schilling.

**1934** (October 30th) - Revaluation of monetary reserves of Nationalbank, implying devaluation of 21.3%:
1 Schilling = 166.67 milligrams of fine gold
Parity revised annually according to average price of kilogram of gold at Banque de France (until October 1936), in London and in New York (after October 1936).

**1936** (December) - Parity according to revaluation of monetary gold stock:
1 Schilling = 167.33 milligrams of fine gold

**1938** (March 17th) - Anschluss with Germany. Introduction of Reichsmark:
1 Reichsmark = 1.50 Schillings

**1938** (April 25th) - Abolition of legal tender status of Schilling. Accepted until May 15th at government offices.

**1945** - Allied and Russian Occupation. Issue of Military Schillings. Military rate of exchange:
1 U.S. Dollar = 10.00 Schillings
1 Ruble = 2.00 Schillings

**1945** (December) - Restoration of Austrian Schilling, substituted for Reichsmark and Military Schilling. Exchange limited to 150 Reichsmark or Schillings per person. Excess balances blocked (Sperrschilling):
1 Schilling = 1 Reichsmark

**1946** (July 25th) - Exchange controls tightened.

**1946** (October 28th) - Adoption of military exchange rate for commercial transactions. De facto, numerous transactions at higher exchange rates. No parity registered with International Monetary Fund.

**1947** (December 4th) - New exchange of banknotes:
1 new Schilling = 3 old Schillings

Exchange of 1 for 1 up to 150 Schillings; exchange for farmers up to amount of their delivered crops.

Large amounts of previously blocked Schillings (1945) invalidated and rendered worthless.

Temporary blockage of 50% of deposits.

Debts in Schillings left untouched by law.

**1949** (November 25th) - Devaluation by 53.2% and adoption of three exchange rates:

1 U.S. Dollar = 14.23/14.57 Schillings (basic buying and selling rate for essential imports and 40% of export proceeds)

1 U.S. Dollar = 21.19/21.53 Schillings (effective rate at 40% of basic and 60% premium for all exports)

1 U.S. Dollar = 25.83/26.17 Schillings (premium rate for luxury imports and invisibles)

**1950** (January 25th) - Uniform 60% retention quota applicable to export proceeds replaced by general surrender requirement with individual retention quotas for each exporter to meet his authorized expenses.

**1950** (October 6th) - Exchange rates revised. Basic rate of 14.40 Schillings per U.S. Dollar abolished:

1 U.S. Dollar = 21.23/21.49 Schillings (for commercial operations)

1 U.S. Dollar = 25.87/26.13 Schillings (premium rate for other transactions)

Purchase of gold by Nationalbank on basis of:

1 Schilling = 43.8 milligrams of fine gold

**1952** (January 1st) - Export retention quota system abolished.

**1953** (May 4th) - Unification of exchange rates. Parity registered with International Monetary Fund:

1 Schilling = 34.1796 milligrams of fine gold

1 U.S. Dollar = 26.00 Schillings

**1958** (December 28th) - Currency reform based on liquidation of European Payments Union and its replacement by European Monetary Agreement. Accounts of non-residents became completely convertible and called Free Schilling Accounts.

**1959** (January 12th) - Blocked Schilling Accounts (Sperrschilling) became freely convertible.

**1959** (February 17th) - Foreign exchange rates for convertible currencies no longer fixed by Nationalbank. Black market dealings came to an end.

**1970** (August) - Free market rate of Austrian Schilling hit record high of 25.71 per U.S. Dollar.

# SCHOCK

Unit of account of Kingdom of **Bohemia.** Divided into 60 Gros of Bohemia (Kopy-Grossuw-Czeskich). Was equivalent to 2 Thaler or 3 Guilders (Gulden). Simple Schock (Kopy-Missenky) divided into 30 white Gros (Bili-Gross).

Origin of name - From old German word meaning sixty.

## SCHWAREN

**I.** - In **Bremen,** copper coin used until 1870 and submultiple of gold Thaler-Louis ($1/360$) and Grote ($1/5$).

Origin of name - German *schwer* (heavy).

**II.** - In **Oldenburg,** submultiple of gold Thaler-Louis ($1/360$) and Grote ($1/5$), then after 1857, of Thaler ($1/360$) and Groschen ($1/30$).

## *SCOTLAND*

Predecessor - See *England.*

**12th Century** - Autonomous silver coinage: English Penny. Simultaneous circulation of Edwardian Penny. Unit of account: Scottish Pound of 20 Shillings or 240 Pence.

**13th Century** - Use of Esterlin. Progressively debased during 14th Century. - See *Esterlin.*

**1280** - Minting of silver Penny and Farthing as divisionary coinage.

**Until 1355** - Common money with England.

**1358** - Appearance of hard monies: gold Noble, silver Groat (4 Penny coin) copying English money.

**15th Century** - New gold monies: Lion or Saint Andrew, Rider, Unicorn. Use of silver/copper coin called Plack. Debasement of coins.

**16th Century** - Variety of monies circulated:
> Gold coins - Ecu, Lion, Royal, Bonnet, Ducat, Noble, Rider
> Silver coins - Teston, Royal, Noble,. . .
> Silver/copper coins - Bawbee, Penny, Lion, Plack. . .

**1576** - Maximum depreciation of Scottish Pound (unit of account).

**1603** - James I minted a type of Sovereign called Unite to celebrate reunion of England with Scotland.

**1695** - Establishment of Bank of Scotland for issue of banknotes.

**1707** - Act of Union assimilating two monetary systems - See *England* and *Pound.*

**1727** - Creation of Royal Bank of Scotland for issue of banknotes.

**1746** - Establishment of British Linen Bank with privilege of banknote issue. Subsequent extensions of banknote issue privilege to National Bank of Scotland and Commercial Bank of Scotland, which merged into National Commercial Bank of Scotland; then into Royal Bank of Scotland, to North of Scotland Bank and to Clydesdale Bank, which merged into Clydesdale and North of Scotland Bank (name later changed back to Clydesdale Bank); to Aberdeen Town and Banking Co., to Caledonian Banking Co., and to Union Bank of Scotland, which later merged with Bank of Scotland.

## SCUDO

Gold, then silver money, and unit of account of Italian states (16th to 19th Century). Origin of name - From Italian *Scudo* (crown). - Cf. *Ecu, Shilling, Schilling, Skilling*. Plural - Scudi.

**I.** - In **Venice,** gold money (1535), then silver (1561). Weighed 33 grams 933 fine, and circulated under name Ducato. Became Scudo in 1578. Exchange rate raised from 6 Lire 4 Soldi in 1561 to 7 Lire in 1578; 8 Lire 8 Soldi in 1608; 9 Lire in 1630; 10 Lire in 1702; 11 Lire in 1704; 12 Lire 8 Soldi in 1739 and during 19th Century. Submultiples - In silver: 1/2 and 1/4 Scudo.

Variations of name - Scudo della Croce (Crown with Cross, according to imprint) or Scudo Veneto.

**II.** - In **Florence,** unit of account in two systems:
- *Scudo d'Oro* (gold Crown) equal to 7.5 Lire, 20 Soldi d'Oro, 90 Crazie, or 240 Denari d'Oro. In 1534, all payments and contracts had to be made in Scudi d'Oro, minted in gold.
- *Scudo Corrente* (common crown), also called Ducato or Ducatone or Piastra, equal to 7 Lire, 20 Soldi di Ducato, 84 Crazie or 240 Denari di Ducato.

**III.** - In **Turin** (Piedmont, Savoy, Sardinia), silver coin:
- Old Scudo, with exchange rate after 1755 of 4 Lire 10 Soldi.
  Mintings from 1733 to 1735: 29.8 grams 913 fine, or 27.2 grams fine silver. Exchange rate after 1755: 5 Lire.
- New Scudo with exchange rate after 1755 of 35 grams 908 fine, or 31.8 grams fine silver. Exchange rate: 6 Lire.

**IV.** - In **Genoa,** unit of account divided into 20 Soldi or 240 Denari. In records of Banco di San Giorgio (until 1746):
> Scudo d'Oro equal to 9 Lire 8 Soldi
> Scudo d'Oro Marche equal to 9 Lire 6$^{72/125}$ Soldi
> Scudo d'Argento equal to 7 Lire 12 Soldi
> Scudo di Cambio equal to 4 Lire

Gold money, Scudo d'Oro had exchange rate outside bank of 11 Lire 16 Soldi. Silver money, Scudo d'Argento (38.4 grams 932, then 35.30 grams 952 fine) had exchange rate outside bank of 9 Lire 10 Soldi. Scudo di Cambio, or San Giovannino (20.8 grams 918 fine, or 19.1 grams fine) had exchange rate outside bank of 5 Lire 10 Soldi.

Other names of Scudo d'Argento: Genovino, Genoite, Croisat, Croizat.

**V.** - In **Bologna,** unit of account, also called Pezza da Otto Reale, worth 85 Soldi. Minted in silver, 1/5 Scudo called Piastra.

**VI.** - In **Bergamo,** unit of account worth 7 Lire, 140 Soldi, or 1,680 Denari.

**VII.** - In **Ancona,** unit of account divided into 10 Paoli, 20 Soldi, 30 Bolognini, 100 Baiocci, or 240 Denari.

**VIII.** - In **Rome** (Papal States), unit of account:
> Scudo Romano equalled 3.33 Testoni, 10 Paoli, 100 Baiocci, 500 Quattrini, or 1,000 Mezzi Quattrini.
> Scudo da Stampa d'Oro equalled 20 Soldi, 240 Denari, or 1,525 Mezzi Quattrini.

In silver, Scudo Romano (minted since 1753) weighed 26.4 grams 917 fine, or 24.2 grams fine. Exchange rate: 10 Paoli or 100 Baiocci.
In gold, Scudo d'Oro worth ½ Doppia: 3.3 grams in 16th and 17th Century. Reduced to 1.73 grams in 1818. - See *Corsini.*

**1835** - Pope Gregory XV adopted decimal system with Scudo as monetary unit. Coin of 5 Scudi called Gregorina.

**IX.** - In **Leghorn** and **Lucca,** unit of account: Scudo d'Oro equalled 7.5 Lire; Scudo Corrente (or Ducato, Ducatone, Piastra) equalled 7 Lire.

**X.** - In **Mantua,** unit of account equal to 6 Lire.

**XI.** - In **Milan,** unit of account: Scudo Imperiale, or Scudo di Cambio, worth 117 Soldi; Scudo Corrente, 115 Soldi. Minted in silver.

**XII.** - In **Modena,** silver coin worth 3.75 Lire.

**XIII.** - In **Sicily** and **Naples,** silver coin minted by Charles V in 1525 (34 grams). Exchange rate: 12 Tari.
In Sciliy, unit of account worth 2 Fiorini, 12 Tari, 24 Carlini, 180 Ponti, 240 Grani or 1,440 Piccioli.

**XIV.** - In **Sardinia,** silver coin issued in 1755 and equal to 6 Lire.

**XV.** - In **Malta,** unit of account during domination of Island by Knights of Malta (1530-1798) and in 19th Century. Divided into 12 Tari, 24 Carlini, or 240 Grani.

**18th Century** - Scudo of "silver value" (in 18th Century equal to 1.2 grams of fine gold, or 16.6 grams of fine silver) worth 50% more than Scudo of "copper value".

**XVI.** - In **Ragusa,** silver coin worth 36 Grossetti in 18th Century.

## SECHSER

Silver money of **Holy Roman Empire,** according to monetary system of July 28, 1551. Exchange rate: 6 Kreuzer or ¹/12 Reichsguldiner.
Origin of name - German *sechs* (six).

## SECURITY RAND

See *Rand.*

## SECURITY STERLING

See *Pound.*

## SEMIS

**I.** - Half of **Roman** As of bronze. - See *As.*

Variations of name - Semissis from *semis* (half) and *Assis* (As), Sexcunx.

**180 A.D.** - Ceased being coined.

**II.** - Gold coin of **Late Roman Empire** worth ½ Solidus in monetary system of Constantine. - See *Solidus.*

**III.** - Gold coin of **Byzantium** worth ½ Bezant. - See *Bezant.*


# SEN


**I.** - Round, copper coins (sometimes of iron), pierced with square hole.Used in **Japan** until 19th Century.

Variation of name - Zeni.

**708** - Imitation of Chinese Tsien. Minting of coins made of copper, weighing 7.9 grams (weight reduced in 907 and 958), under name Wado Kaiho. Used for small payments during centuries following.

**10th to 16th Century** - Importation of Chinese Tsien, called Eiraku Sen.

**1636** - Minting of Sen, or Zeni, coin derived from earlier issues. Alloy of copper (0.621), tin (0.372) and lead (0.007).

**17th and 18th Centuries** - Various issues of Sen. Unit was Mon or Moun; bundle of 1,000 Mon was Kwammon (3.75 kilos). Various alloys used, with iron predominating during 18th Century. Fixed parity in relation to gold.

**1871** (June) - After monetary reform and adoption of Yen as monetary unit, Sen of 10 Rin or 100 Mon became ¹/100 Yen.

**II.** - In **Indonesia,** submultiple (¹/100) of Rupiah.

**III.** - In **Cambodia,** submultiple (¹/100) of Riel.


# SENE


Submultiple (¹/100) of Tala, monetary unit of **Western Samoa.**


# *SENEGAL*


**17th and 18th Centuries** - Slave and gum trade with European nations resulted in irregular circulation of French, British and Portuguese specie monies, and Maria Theresia Thalers. Unit of account: Livre Coloniale. - See *Livre Coloniale.*

**19th Century** - French domination, and introduction of French monetary system.

**1825** (August 17th) - France minted bronze coins (5 and 10 Centimes) especially for Senegal.

**1826** (June 15th) - Government required all accounts be kept in Francs.

**1840** - Silver and gold coins of Metropolitan France entered circulation.

**1851** (July 11th) - Creation of Banque du Senegal (Bank of Senegal) to issue Franc banknotes for circulation in French West African territories.

**1853** (December 21st) - Banque du Senegal began to issue banknotes. - See *Franc.*

**1902** - Became part of French West Africa. - See *French West Africa.*

**1945** (December 26th) - Creation of CFA Franc. - See *Franc CFA.*

**1960** (August 20th) - After brief federation with French Sudan, became independent republic. Monetary unit unchanged.

## SENGI

Submultiple (¹/₁.₀₀₀) of Zaire, monetary unit of **Congo Democratic Republic.** - See *Zaire.*

## SENITI

Submultiple (¹/₁₀₀) of Pa'anga, monetary unit of **Tonga.** - See *Pa'anga.*

## SENT

Submultiple (¹/₁₀₀) of Kroon, monetary unit of **Estonia.** - See *Kroon.*

## SENTI

Submultiple (¹/₁₀₀) of Shilling, monetary unit of **Tanzania.** - See *Shilling Tanzania.*

## SEQUIN

**I.** - Gold money of **Turkey, Egypt** and **Barbary States.** Similar to Funduk. - See *Funduk.*

Origin of name - From Arabic, *sikka* (coining die).

Variations of name - Chequin, Chekin, Chickino.

**II.** - Gold money of **Tunis** and **Tripoli** in 18th and 19th Centuries. Fine gold content ¹/₃ greater than that of Funduk. Exchange rate in Tunis: 100 Aspers.

**III.** - For **Venice** and various **Italian** states, see *Zecchino.*

## SERAFIN

See *Xeraphin.*

## *SERBIA*

**Before 13th Century** - Monies of Byzantium. - See *Byzantium.*

**13th and 14th Centuries** - Independent Serbia minted silver Gros, imitating Bulgarian Gros, then Venetian Gros.

**15th to 19th Century** - See *Turkey.*

**1868** (June 10th) - Decree authorizing minting of bronze Serbian coins of 10 Para.

**1873** - Adoption of Dinar, linked to Franc, as monetary unit. - See *Dinar Serbia.*

**1918** - See *Yugoslavia.*

**1941 to 1944** - Division of Yugoslavia between Serbia (Serbian Dinar) and Croatia (Kuna).
Then see *Yugoslavia.*


## SESKIN

Silver coin of 6 Myten (or ¼ Groot) used in **Netherlands** under Charles V (monetary system of 1520).

Variations of name - Sixain, Sesken, Negenmenneke.


## SESTERTIUS

Silver money of **Rome,** submultiple of Denarius, then Roman unit of account: 1 Sestertius = ¼ Denarius = ½ Quinarius

Origin of name - Latin, from *Semi Tertius,* because coin was marked IIS (unum, unum semis: i.e., one As, one As, ½ As). In this inscription, letter S (*Semis*) was in third position (Tertius).

Variation of name - Sesterce.

Plural - Sestertii.

**187 B.C.** - Appearance of silver Sestertius, ¼ Denarius of 3.89 grams, worth 2½ bronze Asses.

**89 B.C.** - Exchange rate of Sestertius rose to 4 Asses of depased bronze. New unit of account no longer bronze As, but silver Sestertius.

**About 43 B.C.** - Silver Sestertius replaced by bronze Sestertius (popularly called Grand Bronze), which was used as unit of account for more than three centuries. Worth ¼ Denarius, or ¹⁄₁₀₀ Aureus.
Augustus minted Sestertius in brass (copper and zinc alloy).

**217 A.D.** - After end of coinage of As, rare mintings of Sestertius.


## SEXTANS

**Roman** money worth ⅙ As or 2 Uncias.

## *SEYCHELLES*

**Mid-18th Century** - French colonization with introduction of French specie monies.

**1794** - British Occupation followed by incorporation as dependency of Mauritius (1814). - See *Mauritius.*

**1903** - Break with Mauritius. Circulation of Rupee banknotes issued in India and locally. - See *Rupee India.*

**1934** - Seychelles Rupee linked directly to Pound Sterling. - See *Rupee Seychelles.*

## SHAHI

**I.** - **Persian** money in 18th and 19th Centuries.

Variations of name - Zaejier, Chaye, Chahi, Schali, Shahy.

**18th Century** - Unit of account Shahi equal to $1/200$ Toman, $1/20$ Hor, $1/4$ Abbasi, $1/2$ Mahmudi, 10 Kazbeqi, or 50 Dinars. Shahi also minted in silver/copper.

**19th Century** - Submultiple ($1/20$) of Kran minted in silver (coins of 1.125 grams of which 1.09 grams were fine silver), then of metal coins of 3 grams (75% nickel and 25% copper).

**II.** - Submultiple of **Afghanistan** Rupee ($1/12$) and Abbasi ($1/4$). - See *Rupee Afghanistan.*

## SHEKEL

Originally a weight, this piece was adopted into monetary system of **Hebrews** under Simon Maccabaeus (143-135 B.C.).
 1 Shekel = 4 Drachmae
 1 Shekel = 4 Denarii
Submultiples - Bekah ($1/2$ Shekel), Rebah ($1/4$ Shekel) and Gerah ($1/20$ Shekel). - See also *Siglos.*

## SHILLING

In **Great Britain,** unit of account and silver money. Later $1/20$ of Pound Sterling and of monies derived from Pound Sterling.
 Submultiples - Shilling equal to 12 Pence (see *Penny*) or 48 Farthing.
 In Guernsey, Shilling equal to 96 Doubles.

Origin of name - See *Schilling.*

Predecessor - See *England.*

**10th Century** - Carolingian system of accounting introduced into Saxon England by Normans: 1 Livre of 20 Sols or 240 Deniers.
 Successive weights of Shilling in grams of fine silver:

| | | | | |
|---|---|---|---|---|
| 1066 - William I. | 16.2 | 1546 - Henry VIII. | 2.6 |
| 1300 - Edward I. | 15.8 | 1551 - Edward VI. | 1.3 |
| 1344 - Edward III. | 14.6 | 1552 - Edward VI. | 5.8 |
| 1351 - Edward III. | 12.9 | 1553 - Mary Tudor | 5.7 |
| 1412 - Henry IV. | 11.1 | 1601 - Elizabeth I. | 5.6 |
| 1461 - Edward IV. | 8.6 | 1816 - George III. | 5.2 |
| 1527 - Henry VIII. | 7.5 | | |

**1485-1509** - Under Henry VII, first minting of silver coin corresponding to 1 Shilling.

**1601** - In defining Shilling at weight of 5.6 grams silver, Elizabeth I made it basic unit of monetary system.

**1696** - General demonetization of Shillings (worn out or cut, thereby having lost much of their value), and minting of new coins with original definition of silver content.

**1774** (May 10th) - Limitation of legal tender status of silver coins to 25 Pounds. Above this amount, obligatory weighing of coins which implied advance (unconscious) toward gold standard.

**1798** (June 21st) - Law suspending free minting of silver, another step toward gold standard.

**1816** (June 22nd) - Adoption of gold standard. Free minting of silver theoretically restored, but never materialized. Demonetization of old coins; substitution of new coins lightened in weight. Limitation of legal tender status to 40 Shillings.

**19th Century** - Shilling, divisionary money, was silver coin of 5.655 grams 925 fine, or 5.23 grams fine.
Silver coins of 2 Shillings were called Florins, while silver coins of 5 Shillings were called Crowns.

**1920** - Fineness of Shilling lowered to 500, with an unchanged weight of 5.655 grams, or 2.82 grams fine.

**1946** - Law calling for issue of Shilling in cupro-nickel.

**1971** (February 15th) - Decimalization of Pound Sterling, and demonetization of Shilling. Replaced by New Penny.

## SHILLING EAST AFRICA

Monetary unit of **British East Africa**. Also circulated in Aden, Ethiopia, Italian Somaliland, British Somaliland. Equal to English Shilling and divided into 100 Cents.

Note-issuing authority - East African Currency Board of Nairobi.

**1922** (January 1st) - Adoption of East African Shilling, equal to English Shilling.

**1936** (January 1st) - Zanzibar adopted East African Shilling.

**1940** - In British Somaliland, East African Shilling circulated beside Indian Rupee.

**1941** (April) - Introduction of East African Shilling in British-occupied Ethiopia:
1 Talari = 1 Shilling 10½ Pence

**1941** (May) - Use of East African Shilling in British-occupied Italian Somaliland.

**1945** (July 23rd) - In Ethiopia, substitution of East African Shilling at rate of:
1 Ethiopian Dollar = 2 East African Shillings

**1946** (December 18th) - Parity registered with International Monetary Fund:
1 Pound Sterling = 20 East African Shillings
1 East African Shilling = 223.834 milligrams of fine gold
1 U.S. Dollar = 4.96278 East African Shillings

**1949** (September 18th) - Devaluation parallel to Pound Sterling:
1 Pound Sterling = 20 East African Shillings
1 East African Shilling = 155.517 milligrams of fine gold
1 U.S. Dollar = 7.14286 East African Shillings

**1950** (May) - East African Shilling replaced in Italian Somaliland by newly created Somalo. - See *Somalo.*

**1951** - East African Shilling became sole legal tender in British Somaliland.

**1951** (October 1st) - East African Shilling given legal tender status in Aden.

**1960** (July 1st) - Somali Shilling replaced East African Schilling at par in newly formed Somali Republic. - See *Shilling Somalia.*

**1961** (June 26th) - East African Shilling ceased to be legal tender in Somali Republic.

**1965** (April 1st) - East African Shilling replaced by South Arabian Dinar in Aden. - See *Dinar South Arabia.*

**1966** (June 14th) - East African Shilling replaced by Tanzanian Shilling at par in Tanzania. - See *Shilling Tanzania.*

**1966** (August 15th) - Uganda Shilling replaced East African Shilling at par in Uganda. - See *Shilling Uganda.*

**1966** (September 14th) - Kenya Shilling replaced East African Shilling at par in Kenya. - See *Shilling Kenya.*

**1967** (September 14th) - East African Shilling ceased to be legal tender in Tanzania, Kenya and Uganda.


## SHILLING KENYA

Monetary Unit of **Kenya.** Divided into 100 Cents.

Bank of issue - Bank of Kenya, established May 23, 1966. Began operations September 14, 1966.

Predecessor - See *Kenya, Shilling East Africa.*

**1966** (September 14th) - Kenya Shilling replaced East African Shilling at par:
1 Kenya Shilling = 1 East African Shilling
1 Kenya Shilling = 124.414 milligrams of fine gold
1 U.S. Dollar = 7.14286 Kenya Shillings

**1970** (September) - Kenya Shilling fell to low of 9.85 per U.S. Dollar on black market.

## SHILLING SOMALI

Monetary unit of Republic of **Somali.** Divided into 100 Cents.

Bank of issue - Banca Nazionale Somala (Somali National Bank), established July 1, 1960.

Predecessors - See *Somalo, Shilling East Africa.*

**1960** (July 1st) - Newly formed Republic of Somali adopted Somali Shilling to replace East African Shilling at par in Northern Region ( British Somaliland) and Somalo in Southern Region (Italian Somaliland).

1 Somali Shilling = 1 East African Shilling = 1 Somalo
1 Somali Shilling = 124.414 milligrams of fine gold
1 U.S. Dollar = 7.14286 Somali Shillings

**1965** (December 30th) - Introduction of "statistical and administrative" tax (5%) on imports and exports and exchange tax (3%) on purchases of foreign exchange.

**1967** (January 1st) - Exchange tax reduced to 1.5%, and new import tax of 1.5% applied to imports for which no official exchange was made available. "Statistical" tax raised to 8%.

**1968** (January 1st) - Exchange and import taxes removed. Statistical tax raised to 10%.

**1969** (January 1st) - "Administrative and statistical" tax of 5% on exports eliminated.


## SHILLING TANZANIA

Monetary unit of **Tanzania.** Divided into 100 Senti (Cent).

Variation of name - Shilingi.

Bank of issue - Bank of Tanzania, established December 1965. Began operations June 14, 1966.

Predecessor - See *Tanzania, Shilling East Africa.*

**1966** (June 14th) - Tanzania Shilling replaced East African Shilling at par:
1 Tanzania Shilling = 1 East African Shilling
1 Tanzania Shilling = 124.414 milligrams of fine gold
1 U.S. Dollar = 7.14286 Tanzania Shillings

**1970** (December) - Tanzanian Shilling fell to low of 10.45 per U.S. Dollar on black market.


## SHILLING UGANDA

Monetary unit of **Uganda.** Divided into 100 Cents.

Bank of issue - Bank of Uganda, established May 28, 1966. Began operations August 15, 1966.

Predecessor - See *Uganda, Shilling East Africa.*

**1966** (August 15th) - Uganda Shilling replaced East Africa Shilling at par:
1 Uganda Shilling = 1 East African Shilling

1 Uganda Shilling = 124.414 milligrams of fine gold
1 U.S. Dollar = 7.14286 Uganda Shillings

**1971** (January) - Uganda Shilling fell to low of 11.00 per U.S. Dollar on black market.

## SHIN PLASTER

Name used to designate depreciated Continental Dollar of **United States** after Revolutionary War.

**1837** - Name given to small notes for fractional parts of U.S. Dollar. Issued by private banks during period of financial stress.

**1862** - Revived to designate fractional currency issued when specie payments were suspended.

## SHO KANG

Money of early **Tibet** in form of silver piece containing a considerable quantity of alloy. Nominally valued at 4 Annas.

**20th Century** - Called Srang, and minted in form of silver, then gold coins. Also issued in paper form. Srang fell to $1/16$ of its value in November 1950, after Communist Chinese invasion.

## SHRAIA

**Moroccan** silver coin minted between 1891 and French Occupation. Weight: 2.91 grams 835 fine. Equivalent to $1/10$ Piastre Hassani or $1/2$ Peseta Hassani.

## SHU

See *Shu gin, Shu kin.*

## SHU GIN

Small silver piece minted in **Japan** in 1824, 1854 and 1868. Equal to $1/4$ Bu or $1/16$ Ryo. Coin of 1 Shu gin called Ichi Shu gin, 2 Shu gin being Ni Shu gin. Latter also minted in gold as early as 1697 (Ni Shu kin).

## SHU KIN

Small rectangular gold coin used in **Japan** in 19th Century (after 1824). Equivalent to 1/160 Oban, 1/16 Coban, 1/4 Ichi Bu ban.

## *SIAM*

See *Thailand.*

## *SICILY*

**7th Century B.C.** - Implantation of system of accounting of Euboea. - See *Mina.*

**6th Century B.C.** - Mintings imitating Greeks: silver Drachma of 6 grams, Tetradrachm of 17.5 grams. - See *Drachma.*
Native coinage: silver Litra from 0.70 to 0.80 grams, similar to Greek Obol. - See *Litra.*

**5th Century B.C.** - Unusual minting of gold coins (1.32 grams) in Agrigento. Generalized minting of bronze Litra of 107 grams.

**4th Century B.C.** - Agathocles had following coins minted: gold (4.30, then 5.20 grams), silver (8.73 then 7 grams) and bronze (often 8.73 grams).
Bronze Litra declined in weight to 13 grams.

**3rd Century B.C.** - Sicily under control of Carthage (see *Carthage*). Syracuse, still independent, minted gold coins (8.50 grams); silver coins (Drachmae of 5.5 then 3.5 grams; Tetradrachm of 13.5 grams) and bronze coins (up to 35 grams).

**210 B.C.** - Sicily became Roman province. Retained only bronze money (in 1st Century B.C., Litra of 6.7 grams). - See *Rome.*

**6th Century** - Monies of Byzantium. - See *Byzantium.*

**9th Century** - Arabic monies. Naples minted silver Carolingian Denier, and bronze Follaro.

**10th and 11th Centuries.** - Salerno copied gold Taro from Arabs and copper Follaro from Byzantines.

**1140** - Issue of silver Ducato.

**1231** - Frederick II minted gold Augustalis.

**About 1285** - Minting of gold Ducato.

**13th to 16th Century** - Alternating, or simultaneous, use of monies from Holy Roman Empire, France and Spain.

**15th Century** - Minting of silver Reale.

**16th to 19th Century** - Monies of Kingdom of Two Sicilies.
Unit of account: Oncia of 2.5 Scudi, 5 Fiorini, 30 Tari, 60 Carlini, 450 Ponti, 600 Grani, or 3,600 Piccioli.
Specie Monies:
      In gold - Oncia
      In silver - Scudo de Sicilia, Carlino, Taro

In copper - Grano and multiples

**1818** - Unification of monies of Sicily and Naples. - See *Naples.*

**1865** - In unified Italy, link to French monetary system. - See *Italy* and *Lira Italy.*

## SIERRA LEONE

Early native monies - See *Gold Coast.*

**1791** - Introduction of silver Dollars and copper Pennies (Pence). Minted in England especially for Sierra Leone Colony.

**Late 18th Century** - Macuta basis of monetary system. - See *Macuta.*

**19th Century** - Dominant use of British specie monies.

**1896** - Became British Protectorate. Monetary system of United Kingdom. - See *Pound.*

**1913** - Newly formed West African Currency Board minted special coinage for British West Africa. - See *Pound West Africa.*

**1964** (August 4th) - Creation of new monetary unit to replace West African Pound. - See *Leone.*

## SIGLOS

Early **Persian** weight and money.

Origin of name - From Hebrew *sagala* (to weigh).

Variations of name - Sekel, Shekel, Sicle.

Plural - Sigloi.

**I.** - In **Mesopotamia,** ca 2,000 B.C., weight of silver about 8 or 8.4 grams. Used as measure of prices. Sumerians used silver Sigloi for payments.

**II.** - Silver money of **Persian** Empire, minted by Darius about 515 B.C. Weight equal to $1/100$ Mina:

1 Siglos of Media $= 5.60$ grams of silver $= 1/20$ gold Daric

Introduced in India in 5th Century B.C. Siglos of Media scarely used.

Persia continued using Semitic Shekel (Siglos) of 8.4 grams.

**About 493 B.C.** - In order to enforce payments in money in place of payments in kind, Darius proposed following equivalents:

1 sheep $= 3$ Semitic Shekels (Sigloi)

1 jug of wine $= 1$ Semitic Shekel (Siglos)

Persian multiple of Semitic Shekel (Siglos): Karba of 10 Sigloi (84 grams).

## SIKAJY

In **Madagascar,** early native submultiple ($1/8$) of Ariary. - See *Ariary.*

## *SIKKIM*

**19th Century** - Strong British influence. Use of Indian specie monies.

**1890** - Became complete British Protectorate. Monetary system of India. - See *Rupee India.*

## SILBERGROSCHEN

Early money of **German** states.

Origin of name - From German *Silber* (silver) and *Groschen* (Gros). - See *Gros.*

**1555** - Northern States adopted Thaler as unit of account divided into 24 Silbergroschen or 32 Mariengroschen.

**18th Century** - Silbergroschen, equal to ¹/30 Thaler or 12 Pfennig, was unit of account and silver/copper money in Silesia.

**19th Century** - Specie money in Brunswick, Prussia, Oldenburg, Bavaria, Bremen, Lübeck and Luxembourg. Copied in Saxony and Hanover and called Neugroschen. Valued at 10 Pfennig.

**1857** (January 24th) - Silbergroschen of 12 Pfennig or 2 Kreuzer remained ¹/30 uniform Thaler adopted by North German Confederation.

**1873** - Monetary system based on Mark eliminated Silbergroschen.

## SILIQUA

Silver coin of **Late Roman Empire** and **Eastern Roman Empire.**

Origin of name - From Latin *Siliqua,* seed of a fruit. Weight corresponding to a seed.

Plural - Siliquae.

**4th Century** - Creation of Siliqua of 2.63 grams silver. Coin of ¹/2 Siliqua (1.30 grams) gave rise to Denier (Denarius) of Franks. - See *Denier.*

**6th Century** - Coin of ¹/2 Siliqua was the common silver money. Siliqua, or Keration, worth ¹/2 Miliarensis or ¹/24 Solidus (gold Bezant); or, according to the exchange value for copper and silver, from 7 to 9 Follis, from 240 to 300 Nummi.

**7th Century** - Weight of Siliqua reduced under Heraclius to 1.70 grams.

**10th Century** - Siliqua or Keration (¹/24 Bezant, ¹/2 Miliarensis) worth 60 Follis or 120 Obol.

**15th Century** - Siliqua disappeared with collapse of Byzantine Empire.

## *SINGAPORE*

Currency in circulation before 1946, see *Dollar Straits Settlements.*

**1946** (April 1st) - Singapore became separate Crown Colony when Straits Settlements dissolved. Money in circulation, see *Dollar Malaya.*

**1963** (September 16th) - Singapore became part of Federation of Malaysia. - See *Malaysia.*

**1965** (August 9th) - Singapore seceded from Malaysia to become independent state.

**1967** (May 19th) - Board of Commissioners of Currency set up as note-issuing authority. Singapore Dollar issued. - See *Dollar Singapore.*


## SIXAIN

**I.** - Silver coin of 6 Deniers, used principally in **Geneva** in 14th Century.
Variation of name - Sizain.

**II.** - Silver/copper coin of **France** equal to $\frac{1}{6}$ Franc or Ecu in 15th and 16th Centuries.

**III.** - Obsidional copper coin used by French during occupation of **Barcelona** (1640-1652) and **Gerona** (1648).


## SKAR

In **Tibet,** copper coins of 20th Century.


## SKILLING

Scandinavian unit of account, silver and copper money. Derived from Carolingian Sol (Shilling).

Origin of name - See *Schilling.*

**I.** - Money of **Denmark** and **Norway** under control of Denmark.

**About 1445** - Minting of silver Skilling, which became principal specie money.

**16th Century** - Submultiple ($\frac{1}{24}$) of Florin, unit of account.

**1513** - Hvid was equal to $\frac{1}{3}$ Skilling.

**17th Century** - Progressive debasement of silver Skilling.

**1618** - As unit of account, Skilling worth $\frac{1}{16}$ Mark or $\frac{1}{128}$ Krone.

**18th Century** - As specie money, Skilling was a copper coin only.
As unit of account, Skilling worth $\frac{1}{16}$ Mark or $\frac{1}{96}$ Rigsdaler in Copenhagen and Bergen.
In various areas of Norway (Christiana, Trondheim. . .), represented $\frac{1}{2}$ Stuyver, $\frac{1}{24}$ Oere, $\frac{1}{96}$ Rigsdaler. Equal to 2 Fyrk, 3 Hvid or 12 Penning.

**1814** - In Norway, ceded by Denmark to Sweden, Skilling represented $\frac{1}{120}$ Speciesthaler or $\frac{1}{24}$ Oere.

**II.** - **Swedish** money.

**18th Century** - As unit of account, Skilling represented $\frac{1}{48}$ Species Riksdaler.
In system of keeping records in silver money (Silver Mynt), Skilling worth $\frac{1}{8}$ Daler, $\frac{1}{2}$ Mark, 4 Oere or 16 Oerlein.

In system of keeping records in copper money (Kopper Mynt), same Skilling worth ³/₈ Daler, 1.5 Mark, 12 Oere or 48 Oerlein.

**1776** - Unification of accounting system on basis of system in silver money.

**1855** (February 3rd) - Division of Riksdaler into 48 Skilling replaced by its division into 100 Oere.

## SOEKOE

Unit of account used in **Java** and on some neighboring islands. Valued at ¼ Real. Represented 5 Sata, each of which was worth 200 Caixa (coins of copper and lead) threaded on cord of straw, or 1,000 Caixa. - See *Caixa* and *Sata.*

Origin of name - Derived from Sapèque.

## SOL

Unit of account and specie money in numerous countries. Derived from Roman Solidus by way of Carolingian monetary system.

Origin of name - See *Solidus.*

Variations of name - Sou, Soldo, Sueldo.

**I.** - For **France,** see *Sou.*

**II.** - For **Spain,** see *Sueldo.*

**III.** - For **Italy, Venice** and **Portugal,** see *Soldo.*

**IV.** - For **Netherlands,** see *Stuyver.*

**V.** - For **Northern countries,** see *Schilling, Shilling, Skilling, Szelong.*

**VI.** - Until 1850, unit of account in certain **Swiss** cantons: in Basel, Berne and Geneva, ¹/₂₀ Livre, or 12 Deniers; in Basel, ¹/₆₀ Ecu; in Geneva (in government records and for minor trade), ¹/₁₂ Guilder, or 4 Quarts.

## SOL PERU

Monetary unit of **Peru** since 1930. Divided into 10 Dineros or 100 Centavos. Multiple called Libra, which was official monetary unit divided into 10 Soles from 1901-1930.

Bank of issue - Banco de Reserva del Peru (Reserve Bank of Peru), established in 1922; reconstituted as Banco Central de Reserva del Peru (Central Reserve Bank of Peru) in 1931.

Predecessor - See *Peru, Piaster Peru.*

Plural - Soles.

**1863** (February 14th) - Silver Sol substituted for silver Pisater, with decimal division. Linked to French coin of 5 Francs and new Spanish Duro:

1 Sol = 25 grams silver 900 fine = 22.5 grams fine silver = 5 Francs Germinal

Minting of 1 Sol gold coins (1.163 gram 900 fine, or 1.45 grams fine gold) and of multiples of Sol (2, 5, 10, 20).

**1867** - Gold monies accepted only according to bullion price of gold.

**1881** - "Incas" and "Soles" banknotes at forced parity.

**1897** (April) - Suspension of free minting of silver.

**1901** (December 14th) - Adoption of gold standard, with link to Pound Sterling:
1 Sol = 2 Shillings
1 Sol = 732.23817 milligrams of fine gold

Minting of gold coins of 10 Soles, called Peruvian Libras, equal to Sovereign. Libra officially adopted as monetary unit.

Sol remained a silver coin of 25 grams 900 fine.

Issue of banknotes forbidden.

**1922** (March 8th) - Paper issue entrusted to Reserve Bank of Peru.

**1930** (February) - Stabilization of Sol on gold standard base:
1 U.S. Dollar = 2.50 Soles

**1930** (March 21st) - Sol officially replaced Libra as monetary unit.

**1931** (April 18th) - Devaluation:
1 Sol = 421.264 milligrams of fine gold
1 U.S. Dollar = 3.57 Soles

**1932** (May 18th) - Suspension of gold standard. Depreciation of currency.

**1934** - Stabilization on basis of:
1 U.S. Dollar = 2.50 Soles

**1941** - New official exchange rate, sanctioning de facto exchange rate effective since May 1940:
1 U.S. Dollar = 6.50 Soles

**1945** (January 23rd) - Foreign exchange controls.

**1946** (June) - Opening of free market.

**1946** (December 18th) - Parity registered with International Monetary Fund:
1 Sol = 136.72 milligrams of fine gold
1 U.S. Dollar = 6.50 Soles

**1947** (March 7th) - Issue of negotiable gold certificates, denominated in weight of fine gold. Given to producers and holders of gold against obligatory surrender of gold at Central Bank.

**1948** (September 7th) - System of multiple exchange rates: Official rate, Free Market rate, Certificates rate (applying to 35% of export receipts).

**1948** (December 4th) - Certificate rate applied to 55% of export receipts, with remainder at Official rate.

**1949** (August 5th) - Export receipts from Sterling Area surrendered 100% at Certificate rate.

**1949** (November 11th) - Abandonment of Official rate (6.50 per U.S. Dollar), without any parity being proposed to International Monetary Fund. New system of exchange rates:
1 U.S. Dollar = 14.81 Soles (fluctuating Exchange Certifi-

cate rate for exports, imports and certain invisibles)
<br>1 U.S. Dollar = 16.34 Soles (fluctuating Free Market rate
for invisibles and capital)

**1953** - On free market, U.S. Dollar rose to nearly 20.00 Soles.

**1959** (June) - Sol fell to low of 30.00 per U.S. Dollar in free market.

**1960** (May 17th) - Exchange reform abolished Exchange Certificate system. Single offically controlled rate introduced and maintained close to:
<br>1 U.S. Dollar = 26.80 Soles

**1967** (September 1st) - Central Reserve Bank suspended operations in foreign exchange market, changing status from controlled free market to free market. Sol dropped from 27.40 to 38.50 per U.S. Dollar by month's end.

**1967** (October 5th) - Reintroduction of dual exchange market with two fluctuating rates: Exchange Certificate Market rate, applying to all trade and specified non-trade transactions; Free Draft Market rate, for services and most other nontrade transactions. Latter closely paralleled unofficial free market rate.

**1967** (October 9th) - Central Reserve Bank sold Exchange Certificates at 38.70 per U.S. Dollar.
<br>Obligatory surrender of all export proceeds for Exchange Certificates.
<br>Free Draft rate was:
<br>1 U.S. Dollar = 39.30 Soles

**1968** (May 29th) - Surcharge of 15% levied on imports using Exchange Certificate. Created an Import Certificate rate of:
<br>1 U.S. Dollar = 44.50 Soles

**1968** (June 24th) - Surcharge on imports reduced to 10%, or:
<br>1 U.S. Dollar = 42.68 Soles

**1968** (December 31st) - Certificate Market rate fell to 38.70 Soles per U.S. Dollar, and Free Draft rate hit 44.08/44.54 Soles per U.S. Dollar, buying and selling.

**1969** (May 27th) - Surcharge of 10% on imports, constituting an exchange tax, replaced by a 10% tariff surcharge, in effect abolishing Import Certificate rate.

**1969** (December 31st) - Free Draft rate listed at 43.40/43.60 Soles per U.S. Dollar, buying and selling.

**1970** (May 16th) - With imposition of confiscatory exchange controls, black market operations increased.

**1970** (September) - Taxes levied on foreign exchange purchased by residents for travel abroad. A 10% tax up to 8,000 Soles limit and 50% over this amount, created two Resident travel rates of
<br>1 U.S. Dollar = 47.85 Soles
<br>1 U.S. Dollar = 65.25 Soles
<br>Sol hit a record low of 80.00 per U. S. Dollar on black market.

## SOLDINO

**I.** - Silver coin issued in **Venice** in 1329 by Francesco Dandolo.

**II.** - Silver coin issued in **Milan** in 1468 for 1/20 Testone.

# SOLDO

**I.** - Early money of **Portugal.** Subdivision of Livre. Divided into 12 Deniers.

Origin of name - Latin *solidus* (solid). - See *Solidus.*

Predecessor - See *Portugal.*

**12th Century** - Independent Portugal kept accounts in Livres, divided into 20 white Soldos of 12 Deniers or Dinheiros (silver Sous) and into black Soldos (silver/copper Sous).

**1279-1325** - During reign of Diniz, minting of silver Soldo coin of 12 Dinheiros, called Forte.

**1325-1357** - Under Alphonso IV, lightening of weight of Soldo by one-quarter.

**1433-1438** - Under Edward, Soldo used as unit of account: white Real exchangeable for 1 Soldo.

**15th Century** - Real confirmed as unit of account. - See *Real.*

**II.** - Unit of account and specie money of **Venice:** 20th part of Lira, derived from Carolingian Livre.

**18th Century** - Soldo (or Marchetto) equal to 2.3 Grossetti or 12 Denari di Lira (Deniers); 5.166 Soldi needed for 1 Grosso, 20 for 1 Lira, 124 for 1 Ducato, 1,240 for 1 Lira Grossa. Also, copper coin divided into 2 Bagattini.

In Greek Islands belonging to Republic of Venice, unit of account, also called Asper. Worth $1/10$ Livre or $1/100$ Reale.

**III.** - Unit of account and specie money of **Florence:** $1/20$ Lira (or Fiorino), derived from Carolingian Livre. Silver Fiorino (Guilder), minted in 1252 at 2.1 grams, originally worth 1 Soldo.

**18th Century** - Soldo was 20th part of each of units of account in four concurrent systems: Scudo d'Oro, Scudo Corrente (or Ducato or Piastra), Pezza (or Livornino), and Lira. In each system computed as 12 Denari (Denari d'Oro, Denari di Ducato, Denari di Pezza, Denari di Lira). Soldo d'Oro worth 1.71 Soldi di Ducato, 1.3 Soldi di Pezza, 7.5 Soldi di Lira.

Struck in form of copper coin until 1859 (Grand Duchy of Tuscany).

Submultiples: $2/3$ Soldo equalled 1 Duetto, $1/3$ Soldo equalled 1 Quattrino.

**IV.** - Unit of account, worth $1/20$ Lira or 12 Denari in numeroua **Italian** states before unification; in Bassano, Bergamo, Bologna, Genoa, Lucca, Mantua, Milan, Modena, Padua, Parma, Trieste, Turin (Piedmont, Savoy, Sardinia).

Local variations - Soldo was $1/20$ Scudo de Stampa d'Oro in Rome, $1/20$ Scudo in Ancona, Nova; $1/120$ Pezza in Leghorn; $1/140$ Scudo in Bergamo; $1/85$ Scudo in Bologna.

Minted in silver/copper or copper.

# SOLIDUS

Money of **Roman Empire** derived from Aureus.

Origin of name - Latin *Solidus* (firm, massive), Indo-European root *Sol* (entire, intact).

Predecessor - See *Aureus*.

**312** - Monetary reform of Constantine: Aureus became Nummus Solidus (hard money), shortened to Solidus: gold coin of 4.54 grams (compared to original 10.91 grams of Aureus five centuries earlier).

**367** - Weight of Solidus in gold lowered (for West) to 3.89 grams by Valentinian.

**5th Century** - With fall of Western Empire, Rome bequeathed Solidus to Byzantium, which created Solidus Byzantius, or Bezant; to Barbarian invaders who prolonged Solidus through Sol (Sou, Soldo, Sueldo, Shilling. . .); to Arabs, who created Dinar. - See *Bezant, Sol, Dinar*.

## *SOLOMON ISLANDS*

See *British Solomon Islands* (East) and *Bismarck Archipelago* (West).

## *SOMALI*

From early 10th Century to 19th Century, use of Arab specie monies in coastal settlements.

**Early 19th Century** - Gradual, introduction of Indian Rupee of 16 Annas. - See *Rupee India*.

**1875-1884** - During Egyptian Occupation of Northern Region, use of Egyptian Piastres. - See *Piastre Egypt*.

**1884-1886** - Reintroduction of Indian Rupee in newly formed British Protectorate of Northern Region (British Somaliland).

**1909** (January 28th) - Copper coins of 1, 2 and 4 Bese struck in Rome for Italian Somaliland, - See *Besa*.

**1925** (July 1st) - In Southern Region (Italian Somaliland) under Italian control, Indian Rupee was replaced as legal tender by Italian Lira. General circulation of silver coins and notes issued by Banca d'Italia (Bank of Italy) branch in Mogadiscio. - See *Lira Italy*.

**1940** - In British Somaliland, East African Shilling began to circulate beside Indian Rupee. - See *Shilling East Africa*.

**1941** (May) - In Italian Somaliland, during British military administration, use of East African Shilling. - See *Shilling East Africa*.

**1950** (May) - In Italian Somaliland, East African currency replaced by newly created Somalo. - See *Somalo*.

**1951** - In British Somaliland, East African Shilling became sole legal tender.

**1960** (July 1st) - Newly formed Republic of Somali adopted Somali Shilling as official monetary unit.
Replaced East African Shilling in Northern Region (Somaliland) and Somalo in Southern Region (Italian Somaliland). - See *Shilling Somali.*


## SOMALO

Monetary unit of **Italian Somaliland.** Divided into 100 Centesimi.

Note-issuing authority - Cassa per la Circolazione Monetaria della Somalia (Somaliland Monetary Agency), established in 1950.

Predecessor - See *Somalia.*

Plural - Somali.

**1950** (May 22nd) - Following return to Italian control, creation of Somalo as independent monetary unit in Italian Somaliland to replace East African Shilling at par:
 1 Somalo = 1 East African Shilling
 1 Somalo = 124.414 milligrams of fine gold
 1 Somalo = 87.49 Italian Lira
 1 U.S. Dollar = 7.14286 Somali

**1950** (July 22nd) - Somalo acquired legal tender status.

**1960** (July 1st) - Somalo replaced at par in Southern Region (Italian Somaliland) of newly formed Republic of Somali. - See *Shilling Somali.*


## SONG PAI

Early unit of account and silver coin **Thailand (Siam).** Corresponded to 4 Clam, 2 Pais, $1/2$ Fuang, $1/4$ Salung, $1/16$ Tical, $1/64$ Tael, $1/1.280$ Catty.

Variations of name - Sompaye, Sompaje.


## SOU

**I.** - In **France,** gold, silver, then bronze money, and unit of account, derived from Roman Solidus.

Origin of name - See *Solidus.*

Variation of name - Sol. Old custom was to write Sol and pronounce Sou.

**5th to 8th Century** - From Roman Solidus (4.55 grams of gold under Constantine, 3.89 under Valentinian), Franks created gold Sou (3.78 grams in 7th Century), divided into $1/2$ Sou (Semissis), $1/3$ Sou (Triens), $1/4$ Sou (Quadrans).

**8th Century** - Scarcity of gold made Sou unit of account worth 40 silver Deniers.

**755** - Decree of Pepin the Short: 1 Livre = 22 Sous.

**About 779** - Carolingian system of accounting: 1 Livre = 20 Sous = 240 Deniers.

Application of this system in regions of royal domain (Sou Parisis and Sou Tournois) and in feudal domains.

**801** - Decree establishing system of accounting: 1 Sou = 12 Deniers.

**12th Century** - Minting of Sou in silver and copper alloy (about 6 grams, of which 3 were fine silver).

**1266** - Saint Louis minted Sou Tournois in silver, called Gros. - See *Gros.*

**1361** (April 10th) - Minting of Gros of 2.79 grams of pure silver worth 1 Sou Parisis.

**Under Charles IX** - Last minting of Sou Parisis.

**1674** - Minting of numerous coins of 4 Sous (1.63 grams, of which 1.36 were fine silver).

**1679** - Exchange rate lowered to 3 Sous 6 Deniers.

**Under Louis XV** - Minting of Sou in copper.

**1796** - Name commonly given to 5 Centime coin minted in copper.

**1852** (May 6th) - Demonetization of copper coins. Minting of 5 Centime coins in bronze (5 grams).

**1928** (June 25th) - Issue of coins of 5 Centimes in bronze/nickel.

**1935** (February 1st) - Demonetization of bronze coins.

**1938** (February 24th) - Decree calling for substitution of zinc for bronze/nickel.

**1940** (November 24th) - Law demonetizing Sou as of January 1, 1941.

**II.** - In **Canada**, name given by French Canadians to Cent ($1/100$ Canadian Dollar).


## SOUTH AFRICA

**17th and 18th Centuries** - Dutch monies. - See *Rijksdaalder.*

**19th Century** - British monetary system. - See *Pound.*

**1920** - Monetary autonomy, and creation of South African Pound. - See *Pound South Africa.*

**1961** (February 14th) - Creation of new monetary unit. - See *Rand.*


## SOUTHERN RHODESIA

Predecessor - See *Federation of Rhodesia and Nyasaland.*

**1963** (December 31st) - Federation of Rhodesia and Nyasaland dissolved. Monetary unit unchanged. - See *Pound Rhodesia and Nyasaland.*

**1964** (November 16th) - Bank of Rhodesia and Nyasaland issued Rhodesian Pound. - See *Pound Rhodesia.*

**1965** (June 1st) - Reserve Bank of Rhodesia replaced Bank of Rhodesia and Nyasaland as Central Bank.

**1965** (November 11th) - Southern Rhodesia issued Unilateral Declaration of Independence. Name changed to Rhodesia. - See *Rhodesia.*

## SOUTHERN YEMEN

Predecessor - See *Federation of South Arabia.*

**1967** (November 30th) - Southern Yemen established as People's Republic. Monetary unit unchanged. - See *Dinar South Arabia.*

**1968** - Name of currency changed to Southern Yemen Dinar.


## SOUTHWEST AFRICA

**1884** - Annexed by Germany. Introduction of German specie monies. - See *Mark.*

**1915** (July 9th) - Surrendered to Union of South Africa. Monetary development parallel to South Africa. - See *South Africa.*


## SOVEREIGN

**I.** - **English** gold money.

Origin of name - Early coin carried effigy of Sovereign (Henry VII) with scepter in hand seated on throne.

**1489** - Under Henry VII, creation of gold coin, weighing 16.59 grams 964½ fine, or 16 grams fine gold, called Sovereign or Double Royal (Ryal), issued for 20 Shillings. The ½ Sovereign, or Royal, bore name Noble à la Rose. - See *Noble.*

**1509-1547** - Under Henry VIII, minting of Double Sovereign (44 or 45 Shillings) and of ¼ Sovereign, or Crown.

**1544** - Henry VIII reduced weight of Sovereign to 12.44 grams 900 fine, or 11.40 grams fine gold.

**1545** - Fineness lowered to 833, or 10.36 grams fine gold.

**1550** - Under Edward VI, weight of Sovereign reduced to 10.97 grams 833 fine, or 9.14 grams fine gold. Exchange rate: 24 Shillings.

**1552** - Accounting value of Sovereign raised to 30 Shillings. Minting of Sovereign 916 fine, issued for 20 Shillings. Abolished in 1553 by Mary Tudor.

**1558-1603** - Elizabeth I minted Sovereign of fine gold (30 Shillings) and Sovereign 916 fine.

**1603** (November 11th) - James I minted Sovereign of 10.04 grams 833 fine, or 8.36 grams fine gold, having exchange rate of 20 Shillings. This Sovereign called Unite upon occasion of Anglo-Scotch unity.

**1611** (November 22nd) - Value of Sovereign raised to 22 Shillings.

**17th and 18th Centuries** - Guinea replaced Sovereign.

**1816** (June 22nd) - Law establishing gold standard. Basic metallic coin again became Sovereign, worth 1 Pound Sterling or 20 Shillings and weighing 7.988 grams 916 fine, or 7.32 grams fine gold.
Minting of ½ Sovereign.

**1823-1826** - Minting of Double Sovereigns.

**1887** - Appearance of 5 Sovereign or 5 Pound coin.

**1914** - With forced parity, minting of Sovereigns ceased. Did not begin again until 1925, with return to gold parity.

**1950** - Minting of Sovereigns by British Royal Mint for Middle East, where Sovereign (with head of King) used as ordinary currency. In Saudi Arabia, Sovereign had exchange rate of 62 Riyals.

**1952** - Minting of Sovereigns by Italian counterfeiters, with exact weight and fineness. Swiss court recognized these mintings by refusing to extradite counterfeiters.

**1957** - Minting of Elizabeth II Sovereigns by British Royal Mint.

**II.** - Early gold money of **Brabant** (4.6 grams of fine gold), with exchange rate of 8 Guilders 18½ Sols in 18th Century.
Double Sovereigns and ½ Sovereigns also minted.

Variation of name - Severin.

**III.** - Gold money of **Austria** (5.5 grams 945 fine, or 5.2 grams fine), with exchange rate of 760 Kreuzer in 18th Century.
Multiple - Double Sovereign.

**IV.** - Standard gold coin of **India** since 1899. Equal to 15 Rupees, 240 Annas, 960 Pice or 2,880 Pie.


## SOVNAZKI

Name given to paper Ruble issued in **U.S.S.R.** by Soviets. Circulated from 1919 to 1924. Progressively replaced by Chervonets Ruble.

Origin of name - In Russian, monetary sign for payment.

- See *Ruble.*


## SPAIN

Carthaginian (see *Carthage*), Greek, Iberian, Roman (see *Rome*) monies.

**5th to 8th Century** - Monies of Suevi (Triens, or ⅓ Sou), and of Visigoths along lines of Roman monetary system:
Gold coin - Sueldo (Sou). - See *Sueldo.*
Silver coin - Denario or Dinero (Denier) of 3.6 grams. - See
*Denario, Dinero.*
Copper coin - Fels. - See *Fels.*

**11th Century** - Castile and León minted silver Denier and Obol. Kings of Castile minted a gold Dinar with Arabic inscriptions under name of Alfonsino.

**12th Century** - After conquest of Toledo, use of Arabic Marabotin, Maravedi (see *Maravedi*), gold, then silver coin. Progressively debased. Other gold coins: Massamutino and Double Massamutino.

**13th Century** - New silver coins: Pépion (1 Denier), Blanco (2 Deniers), Negro (1

Denier), Noveno (3 Deniers), Cornado (1.5 Deniers).

**1303** - Minting of new gold coins: Dobla Castellana. - See *Doubloon.*

**About 1350** - Minting of new silver coin, Real (see *Real*), which depreciated in stages.

**About 1370** - Minting of Cavalier d'Or by Henry II, then John II.

**1391** - Due to extreme monetary confusion (simultaneous circulation of 132 types of coins), restoration of a more regular monetary system:
> Gold coin - Dobla (Doblon)
> Silver coin - Real of 3.24 grams fine

**1471** - After new depreciation of monies, monetary reform:
> Gold coin - Enrique (Henry)
> Silver coin - Real, of 3.20 grams fine. Its quarter became
> popular under name Cuartillo.

**1497** (June 13th) - In unified Spain, general demonetization of earlier gold, silver and copper monies.
New monetary system:
> Gold coin - Excelente de Granada
> Silver coin - Duro (25.92 grams) of 8 Reales (see *Duro*), Real
> (3.24 grams) and its submultiples
> Silver/copper coin - Blanco (0.35 grams of silver)

**1537** - Because of influx of metals from America, creation by Charles V of new gold coins, Escudo or Corona, or Double Escudo (usually called Pistole) worth 20 silver Reales.
See *Pistole, Doubloon* and *Escudo.*
Adoption of Ducat of 375 Maravedis as unit of account. - See *Ducado.*

**1625** - Inflation of silver/copper money.

**1642** (August 31st) - Reduction of silver/copper money to ⅙ issued value.

**1642** (December 23rd) - After vain attempts at deflation of silver/copper monies (Maravedis of pure copper and Calderillas of silver alloy), monetary reform raising exchange rate of gold Escudo. Silver coins demonetized and new lighter weight coins created.

**1686** (October 14th) - New monetary reform with creation of silver Escudo. - See *Escudo.*

**1742** (June 22nd) - Creation of gold Ventein. Silver/copper Real (equivalent to silver ½ Real), became unit of account with Maravedi.

**1772** (May 29th) - Decree of Aranjuez lowering fineness of gold from 909-915 to 885-893 and of silver from 906 to 892-896.
Monetary system as follows:
Units of account: heavy Piaster worth 20 silver/copper Reales (Reales de Vellon), or 680 silver/copper Maravedis or 10 silver Reales (Reales de Plata), or 340 silver Maravedis; Ducado of 375 Maravedis.
Local variations:
- In Alicante, Catalonia, Mallorca, Valencia, Libra (Livre) equal to Peso of 10 Reales. Divided into 20 Sueldos (Sous), 240 Dineros (Deniers), or 480 Mallas in Catalonia.
- In Aragon, Libra divided into 10 Reales, 20 Sueldos, or 320 Dineros.
- In Castile, Escudo equalled 10 Reales or 340 Maravedis.

- In Malaga, Real worth 8.50 Quartos, 17 Ochavos, 34 Maravedis, 64 Blancos, 136 Cornados, or 340 Dineros.
- In Navarre, Ducado (Ducat) of 49 Tarjas, 65⅓ Gruesos, 196 Ochavos, 392 Maravedis, or 784 Cornados.

Specie monies:
>           In gold - Quadruple (worth 4 Pistoles, or 320 Reales), Pistole
>                     (or Doubloon, worth 80 Reales), Escudo (½
>                     Pistole, worth 40 Reales), Piaster (or Coronilla,
>                     worth 21 Reales and 8.50 Maravedis)
>           In silver - Piaster (Peso Fuerte or Duro) of 20 Reales
>           In silver/copper - Peseta (⅕ Piaster or 4 Reales)
>           In copper - Ochota (8 Maravedis), Quarto (4), Ochavo (2)

Specie monies of Navarre in copper: Maravedi, Cornado (½ Maravedi)

**1808 to 1814** - Joseph Bonaparte maintained two systems of accounting: in silver/copper Reales and in silver Reales.
Specie monies: gold Onza; silver Duro, or Piaster; Peseta.
In same period Catalonia minted gold Doubloons, silver Duros and Pesetas, and copper Quartos.

**1814** - Ferdinand VII minted same coins in gold: Onza, Escudo, Escudillo d'Oro.

**1821** - Demonetization of French Ecus of 3 Livres. Formerly legal tender in North Spain. Minted in excess; issued for 1/2 Duro or 10 Reales. - See *Resellado.*

**1847** (May 31st) - Monetary reform of Isabella II created new silver Real (1 gram 125 fine) as monetary unit.
Other specie monies: gold Doubloon (100 Reales); silver Duro (20), Escudo (10), Peseta (4); copper Decimo de Real.

**1859** (January 1st) - Link to French monetary system, with Peseta as monetary unit: 1 Peseta = 1 Franc = 4.50 grams of fine silver

**1864** (June 21st) - New monetary unit, silver Escudo (12.98 grams 900 fine) of 10 Reales.

**1868** (October 19th) - Link to system of Latin Monetary Union. Peseta, equal to Franc, adopted as monetary unit. - See *Peseta Spain.*


## SPANISH AMERICA

**1531** (May 11th) - Ordinance for construction of mint in Mexico. Minting of Piasters of 8 Reales, imitating Spanish Dolera (see *Duro* ), and of coins of 4 Reales (Toston), 3, 2, 1, ½ and ¼ Real. - See *Piaster Mexico.*

**1535** (May 31st) - Unit of account: Real equal to 34 Maravedis.

**1542** (June 28th) - Minting of coins worth 2 and 4 Maravedis. Stopped soon thereafter.

**1598** - Opening of mint in Lima.

**1650** - Opening of mint in Potosí. Piaster struck at these mints.

**1665** - Opening of mint in Santa Fe de Bogotá.

**1675** (February 25th) - Mints in Mexico and Lima authorized to strike gold coins: Doblon (or Onza), Escudo, Durillo (½ Escudo).

**1701 -** Opening of mint in Guatemala. Circulation of silver Piasters throughout Spanish America. - See *Argentina, Bolivia, Central America, Chile, Colombia, Cuba, Ecuador, Mexico, Paraguay, Peru, Puerto Rico, Uruguay, Venezuela.*

## SPANISH GUINEA

For types of monies prior to 19th Century, see *French Guinea.*

**1844 -** Settlers of Rio Muni introduced Spanish specie money.

**1885 -** Spanish colonization. Monetary system of Spain. - See *Peseta Spain.*

**1968** (October 12th) - Became independent nation. Monetary unit unchanged. - See *Equatorial Guinea.*

## SPANISH SAHARA

Also called Rio de Oro.

Part of Morocco prior to 1860. - See *Morocco.*

**1860 -** Ceded to Spain. Introduction of Spanish monetary system. - See *Spain* and *Peseta Spain.*

## SPARKRONE

Because of hyper-inflation, unit of account created in **Hungary** in 1924 to provide more stable unit for commercial purposes. Number of paper Korona equivalent to Sparkrone fixed daily by State Note Institute.

## SPECIESDALER

Unit of account of **Norway** from 1812 to 1875. Derived from Riksdaler and divided into 5 Oere or Mark, or 120 Skilling. Also minted in silver (25.2 grams fine).

Origin of name - From *Species* (money) and *Daler* (see Thaler).

## SPECIESTHALER

Silver money and unit of account in **German** states.

Origin of name - See *Thaler.*

Predecessor - See *Reichsthaler.*

**1690 -** Reichsthaler became Speciesthaler, with exchange rate in Holy Roman Empire of 120 Kreuzer. Weight: 29.2 grams of silver 887 fine, or 25.9 grams fine.

**18th Century -** Speciesthaler was simultaneously unit of account and specie money. As unit of account, divided into 80 Albus or 960 Heller in Cologne. Divided into 72 Mark in Aachen. As silver specie money, issued in Cologne (for 80 Albus), in Saxony (for 32 Groschen).

**1753** - Convention of Vienna: Speciethaler (28 grams of silver 828½ fine, or 23.2 grams fine) had exchange rate of 1.33 Thaler or 2 Gulden (Florins). In Hungary, called Egisthaler.

**19th Century** - Speciesthaler, worth 1.33 Thaler, was used in Anhalt, Austria, Bavaria, Frankfurt, Hesse, Saxony and Saxe-Cobourg, Hohenzollern, Lippe-Detmold, Nassau. Divided into 32 Groschen.
Another Speciesthaler, slightly heavier, used in Hanover.

**1857** (January 24th) - Agreement making Thaler uniform (18.52 grams of silver 900 fine, or 16.07 grams fine). Speciesthaler disappeared from Germany, but persisted in Austria. - See *Thaler*.

## SPERRMARK

See *Mark German Federal Republic.*

## SPERRSCHILLING

See *Schilling Austria.*

## SRANG

See *Sho Kang.*

## SSEU CH'AO

Banknotes (Ch'ao) backed by raw silk (Sseu). Used in **China** in 13th Century.

**1260** - Issue by Kublai Khan of Sseu Ch'ao at value fixed in silver metal.

## STANISLAS

Gold money minted in **Poland** in 1794. Also in form of ½ Stanislas.
Origin of name - From Stanislas II.

# STATER

Earliest of **Greek** monies. First in electrum, then in gold and sometimes in silver.
Multiple - Double Stater.
Submultiples - Hemistater (1/2), Trite (1/3), Tetarte (1/4), Hecte (1/6), Hemihecte (1/12).

Origin of name - From Greek *stao* (I am fixed).

**7th Century B.C.** - Minting of Stater in electrum, of 14.5 grams (70% gold and 30% silver): in Lydia by Gyges; in Ionia (Miletus, Ephesus).
Stater of Miletus circulated on shores of Black Sea.
Other primitive Staters in electrum: from Phocaea (16 to 17 grams), Samos, Chios, Cyzicus, Lampsacus.
Minting of silver Staters in Aegina, by King Phidon of Argos.

**6th Century B.C.** - In Lydia, minting by Croesus of Staters called Kroiseioi, of gold (10.7 grams and 8 grams) and silver (10.7 grams).
$$1 \text{ Stater of 14 grams electrum} = 1 \text{ Stater of } 10.7 \text{ grams gold}$$
$$1 \text{ Stater of 8 grams gold} = 1 \text{ Stater of 10.7 grams silver}$$
Term Stater sometimes applied to silver coins which became base of each monetary system: coins of 8 Drachmae in Thrace, 4 Drachmae in Athens and in Sicily, 3 Drachmae in Corinth and in Magna Graecia, 2 Drachmae in Aegina and Phocaea; 1/40 Mina in Chios.

**356 B.C.** - In Macedonia, exploiting mines of Mount Pangaeus, Philip minted gold Stater of 7.27 grams. Circulated also in Greece and in the East:
$$1 \text{ gold Stater} = 20 \text{ silver Drachmae}$$

# STATI

Silver coin minted in **Morocco** (19th Century).

# STATIKU

Submultiple (1/100) of Auksinas, monetary unit of **Lithuania** in 1917.

# STERLING

**I.** - **English** system of accounting and name given to silver monetary standard under Henry II (1154-1189). - See *Pound.*

**II.** - **English** silver Penny issued in 13th Century by Henry III, then by Edward I. Copied in Ireland, Scotland, Brabant, German states, Luxembourg, Netherlands. Equal to 4 Deniers.
Luxembourg type, having circulated widely, appeared within England where it was called Lushburger. Term eventually applied all monetary imitations. - See *Esterlin.*

## STOTINKI

Submultiple ($^1/_{100}$) of Lev, monetary unit of **Bulgaria.** - See *Lev.*
Pural - Stotinka.

## *STRAITS SETTLEMENTS*

Predecessor - See *Malacca.*
**1824** - British control, with monies of British East India Company. - See *Dollar East India Company.*
**1835** - Minting of 1 and 2 Kapang coins in copper.
**1903** (June 25th) - Minting of Straits Settlements Dollar. - See *Dollar Straits Settlements.*
**1946** (April 1st) - Straits Settlements dissolved and succeeded by Malayan Union and later (February 1, 1948) by Federation of Malaya. - See *Dollar Malaya.*

## STUYVER

Money of Netherlands, copied and circulated about surrounding areas (Germany and Denmark) and in Netherlands possessions.
Variation of name - Stuiver.
**I.** - Money of **Netherlands,** corresponding to common Sou.
In first accounting system of Netherlands, derived from Carolingian system, Livre consisted of 20 Schelling or Sols; each Sol worth 12 Grooten or Gros. This Sol called Sol de Gros.
In second accounting system of Netherlands, introduced in 1355, Livre worth 6 Guilders (Florins), 120 Stuyver or 250 Grooten. This Stuyver, or common Sol, equivalent to $^1/_{20}$ Guilder and worth 2 Grooten.
This system persisted until 19th Century as Livre de Gros (Pondt Vlaams), divided into 6 Guilders, 20 Schelling, 120 Stuyver, 240 Grooten or 1,920 Penning.
Stuyver, silver/copper money, then worth $^1/_6$ Schelling, 2 Grooten, 8 Duiten, or 16 Penning and, in Brabant, 48 Myten.
**20th Century** - In Netherlands and Dutch possessions, name remained linked with 5 Cent coin, or $^1/_{20}$ Guilder.
Minted in nickel/bronze.
**II.** - In **Java** and **Indonesia,** unit of account introduced by Dutch: $^1/_{60}$ Piastre in 18th Century.
**After 1817** - Submultiple ($^1/_{30}$) of Netherlands East Indies Guilder. 30 Netherlands East Indies Stuyver worth 20 Dutch Stuyver. Each Stuyver counted as 4 Duiten. Minted in copper in Java.
**1854** (May 1st) - Division of Guilder into 100 Cents replaced division into Stuyver.
**III.** - In **Ceylon,** Dutch until 1802, submultiple of Rijksdaalder ($^1/_{48}$). Minted in 1815 by English.

**IV.** - In **Brazil**, in 1654, Dutch West Indies Company minted square coins of 10, 20 and 40 Stuyver in silver.

**V.** - Money of various **German** states near to Netherlands.

**18th Century** - Stuyver was unit of account in Lower Westphalia (1/60 Reichsthaler, 8 Pfenning, or 16 Heller) and in Prussian Frisia (1/54 Reichsthaler, 1/20 Gulden, or 10 Witten). Was silver/copper money in Cologne (16 Heller). Multiples minted in silver/copper and in silver in Prussian Frisia.

**VI.** - Unit of account in **Denmark** in 18th Century. Stuyver worth 1/48 Rigsdaler, 1/64 Daler, 1/12 Oere, 1/8 Mark, or 2 Skilling, 4 Fyrk, 6 Hvid or 24 Penning.


## STYCA

Copper coin minted by Anglo-Saxons in **England** between 5th and 9th Centuries.

Origin of name - Saxon *styca* (coin). - Cf. German *Stück* (coin).


## SUCRE

Monetary unit of **Ecudor.** Divided into 100 Decimos or 100 Centavos. Sometimes called Piaster fuerte.

Origin of name - From General Antonio-José de Sucre.

Bank of issue - Before 1927, by six private banks. Since March 4, 1927, by Banco Central del Ecuador (Central Bank of Ecuador), granted exclusive privilege of banknote issue in 1937.

Predecessors - See *Ecuador* and *Peso Ecuador.*

**1884** (April 1st) - Sucre substituted for Ecuadorean Peso, which was on silver standard. Sucre defined as equal to 5 French Francs, with bimetallic standard:
>    1 Sucre = 1 Peso
>    1 Sucre = 22.5 grams of fine silver
>    1 Sucre = 1,451.6125 milligrams of fine gold

Sucre minted in silver at 25 grams 900 fine, or 22.5 grams fine silver.

**1898** - Adoption of gold standard:
>    1 Sucre = 732.24 milligrams of fine gold
>    1 Sucre = 2 Shillings

On this basis, minting of gold coins (10 Sucres or 1 Condor) equal to Sovereign. Silver coins, conforming to earlier definition: Peseta (2 Decimos), Real or Decimo (10 Centavos), Medio (5 Centavos).

**1914** - Suspension of gold standard.

**1918** - Progressive depreciation of currency.

**1922** - Foreign exchange controls.

**1927** (March 4th) - Stabilization, with devaluation of 58.8%:
>    1 Sucre = 300.933 milligrams of fine gold
>    1 U.S. Dollar = 5.00 Sucres

Real and Medio no longer minted, except in nickel.

Gold coins in denominations of 25 Sucres (1 Condor) and 50 Sucres (2 Condors).

**1932** (February 9th) - Suspension of gold standard.

**1932** (April 30th) - Foreign exchange controls reinstituted. Official rate:
    1 U.S. Dollar = 5.95 Sucres

**1934** - Free exchange rate depreciated by 75%.

**1935** (October 7th) - Lifting of foreign exchange controls.

**1935** (December 19th) - New devaluation of 63.9%:
    1 Sucre = 103.52 milligrams of fine gold
    1 U.S. Dollar = 8.58 Sucres

**1936** (June 13th) - New valuation of monetary gold stock:
    1 Sucre = 85.86 milligrams of fine gold
    1 U.S. Dollar = 10.35 Sucres

**1936** (July 31st) - Foreign exchange controls reimposed. Monopoly on foreign exchange transactions given to Central Bank.

**1937** (July 31st) - Lifting of foreign exchange controls.

**1937** (September) - New exchange rates:
    1 U.S. Dollar = 11.67 Sucres (official rate)
    1 U.S. Dollar = 13.50 Sucres (free rate)
Official rate progressively changed: 14.13 Sucres (1938), 14.83 Sucres (1939).

**1940** (June 4th) - Foreign exchange control reinstituted. New gold definition:
    1 Sucre = 60.17 milligrams of fine gold
Official rate changed many times.

**1942** (April 28th) - Adoption of exchange rate fixed against U.S. Dollar:
    1 U.S. Dollar = 14.00 Sucres

**1943** (March) - Levy of 1% tax on foreign exchange.

**1944** (November) - New official exchange rate:
    1 U.S. Dollar = 13.50 Sucres
Tax on exchange raised to 2%, creating effective rate of 13.77 Sucres per U.S. Dollar.

**1946** (February) - Additional tax of 2%, making effective exchange rate:
    1 U.S. Dollar = 14.04 Sucres

**1946** (May 5th) - Effective exchange rate increased to:
    1 U.S. Dollar = 15.04 Sucres

**1946** (December 18th) - Official parity registered with International Monetary Fund:
    1 Sucre = 65.82751 milligrams of fine gold
    1 U.S. Dollar = 13.50 Sucres

**1947** (February) - Abolition of all taxes on foreign exchange, and de facto confirmation of effective exchange rate:
    1 U.S. Dollar = 15.04 Sucres

**1947** (June 6th) - Reorganization of exchange rate system:
    1 U.S. Dollar = 13.40/13.50 Sucres (official buying and
                      selling rates for certain invisibles and govern-
                      ment transactions)
    1 U.S. Dollar = 13.13 Sucres (export rate)

1 U.S. Dollar = 15.04 Sucres (effective rate for essential imports)

1 U.S. Dollar = 18.07 Sucres (free market rate for noncommercial transactions)

1 U.S. Dollar = 20.04 Sucres (effective rate plus surcharge of 5 Sucres for semi-essential imports)

1 U.S. Dollar = 24.74 Sucres (free market rate plus tax and surcharge of 5 Sucres for luxury imports)

**1949** (December 2nd) - Exchange rate system revised:

1 U.S. Dollar = 13.40/13.50 Sucres (official rates for registered capital, certain invisibles and government transactions)

1 U.S. Dollar = 15.00-18.33 Sucres (multiple export rates, latter also for other invisibles and nonregistered capital, resulting from tax of 2% and subsidies of 1.87 and 3.87 Sucres as well as mixing official and free market rate at 40% and 60%)

1 U.S. Dollar = 15.175 Sucres (official rate plus 5% tax plus 1 Sucre surcharge for essential imports and special invisibles)

1 U.S. Dollar = 20.175 Sucres (official rate plus 5% tax plus 6 Sucres surcharge for useful imports)

1 U.S. Dollar = 25.00 Sucres (free market rate plus 5% tax plus 6 Sucres surcharge for luxury imports)

Fluctuating compensation rate system for prohibited imports also existed at rates of 19.00-23.00 Sucres per U.S. Dollar.

**1950** (December 1st) - New par value registered with International Monetary Fund, and simplification of exchange rate system:

1 Sucre = 59.2447 milligrams of fine gold

1 U.S. Dollar = 15.00/15.15 Sucres (official buying and selling rates for most exports and essential imports)

1 U.S. Dollar = 18.37 Sucres (free rate for invisibles)

1 U.S. Dollar = 20.15 Sucres (effective rate for semi-essential imports)

Central Bank entered free market by establishing buying rate of 17.30 Sucres per U.S. Dollar.

**1951** - Mixed export rates ranging from 15.00 - 17.80 Sucres per U.S. Dollar again in force.

**1952** (February 28th) - Compensation and mixed rate systems abolished:

1 U.S. Dollar = 15.00/15.15 Sucres (official buying and selling rates for most exports, essential and semi-essential imports, government transactions and certain invisibles)

1 U.S. Dollar = 17.30/17.40 Sucres (fluctuating free market for invisibles, unregistered capital, certain exports and luxury imports)

**1952** (June) - Central Bank selling in free market at 17.40 Sucres per U.S. Dollar.

**1952** (July) - Export receipts from chemical products and medicines surrendered at mixed rate of 15.92 Sucres per U.S. Dollar. Various other rates for bananas, shrimp and shellfish result from surrender requirements.

**1955** - Free market divided into controlled free market for minor and marginal exports and List 2 (luxury) imports at 17.30/17.40 Sucres per U.S. Dollar, and uncontrolled free market for invisibles, unregistered capital and optional for List 2 imports at about 17.38/17.43 Sucres per U.S. Dollar.

**1955** (December 21st) - Taxes of 5% and 10% established on List 1 and 2 imports, respectively.

**1957** (March 12th) - Controlled and uncontrolled free market unified at uncontrolled free market rate.

**1961** (July 24th) - New par value registered with International Monetary Fund, and rate system simplified:

    1 Sucre = 49.3706 milligrams of fine gold

    1 U.S. Dollar = 17.82/18.18 Sucres (official buying and selling rate for all trade and related transactions, official transactions, essential invisibles, registered capital)

    1 U.S. Dollar = 21.60 Sucres (free market for all other transactions)

Tax on List 2 imports raised to 15%.

**1966** (May 20th) - Monetary stabilization surcharge established at 20% for List 2 imports, in addition to another tax of 10% or 15%.

**1970** (June 22nd) - Uncontrolled free market abolished.

**1970** (July 1st) - Controlled free market introduced initially at 21.54 Sucres per U.S. Dollar. Foreign exchange holdings surrendered at latter rate and exchange controls instituted, resulting in appearance of Sucre on black market.

**1970** (August 31st) - Devaluation and unification of exchange rate. New par value registered with International Monetary Fund:

    1 Sucre = 35.5468 milligrams of fine gold

    1 U.S. Dollar = 25.00 Sucres

**1971** (January) - Sucre fell to low of 29.50 per U.S. Dollar in unofficial dealings.


## *SUDAN*

**Early history** - Monies of ancient Egypt, Rome, Byzantium, Moslem and Turkish Empires.

**1889** (January 19th) - Anglo-Egyptian Condominium established. Simultaneous use of Egyptian and British monies, with eventual preponderance of Egyptian Pounds. - See *Pound Egypt.*

**1957** (April 8th) - Newly independent Sudan (January 1, 1956) introduced Sudanese Pound to replace Egyptian Pound at par. - See *Pound Sudan.*

**1958** (January 1st) - British and Egyptian monies ceased to be legal tender.

## SUELDO

**I.** - Early **Spanish** money derived from Roman Sou (Solidus).

Origin of name - Spanish *Sueldo* (Sou); Latin *Solidus*.

Predecessor - See *Solidus*.

**5th to 8th Century** - Among monies of Visigoths, Sueldo, derived from Solidus, took form of gold coin (4.6 grams, then 4 grams).

**8th Century** - With Arabs, Sueldo combined with Arabic Dinar and became Marabotin (see *Marabotin*), which gave rise to Maravedi.

**13th Century** - Sueldo was silver coin (2.13 grams fine in 1222; 1.33 grams in 1252; raised to 3.6 grams in 1258; 2.4 grams in 1263; 1.6 grams under Sancho IV (1284-1295); 1.07 grams in 1303; 0.86 grams in 1391).
Sueldo, 1/20 Libra (Livre), equal to Peso of 10 Reales, also used as unit of account (divided into 12 Dineros) in Alicante, Catalonia, Mallorca, Valencia; and unit of account (divided into 16 Dineros) in Aragon.

**II.** - Silver coin of early **Boliva**. Equal to Real or 1/8 Peso.

**III.** - Silver/copper coin at **Perpignan** in the Pyrenees during French Occupation (1642-1655).

## SUKA

Basic silver coin of **Nepal** after Gurkha unification (1768).

**1870** - Silver submultiple (1/4) of Dabal.

**1945** - Submultiple (1/4) in cupro-nickel of Nepalese Rupee.

## SULTANINE

Another name for Sequin, gold coin of **Turkey, Egypt** and **Barbary States.** - See *Sequin*.

## *SUMATRA*

In Kingdom of Achin, unit of account: Tayell (Tael) of 4 Pardaws, 16 Mas, 64 Koupans, or 25,600 Cash.
Specie monies: gold dust
Ordinary coins: gold Mace or Mas (0.48 grams), tin Cash

**1786** - Minting of copper coins of 1, 2, and 3 Kapang, by British India Company.

**1824** - Cession to Netherlands. Subsequent introduction of Dutch monetary system.
- See *Netherlands East Indies, Guilder Netherlands East Indies*.

## *SURINAM*

**1667** - Became Dutch Colony. Use of cut and counter-marked Spanish and Portuguese silver coinage. Gradual use of silver Guilders.

**1670** - Minting of copper Duiten in denominations of 1, 2 and 4 Stuyver.

**18th Century** - Unit of account: Guilder of 20 Stuyver or 240 Penning. Specie money - coins of Netherlands.

**1799-1815** - Dominant British influence.

**1815** (November 20th) - Treaty of Paris. Reestablished as Dutch Colony. Introduction of Dutch monetary system. - See *Guilder Netherlands.*

**1940** (May 10th) - After German Occupation of Netherlands, break with Metropolitan unit. - See *Guilder Surinam.*

## SWARE

Money of **Bremen** in 15th Century. - Cf. *Schwaren.*

## *SWAZILAND*

Use of South African currency. - See *South Africa.*

## *SWEDEN*

**10th and 11th Centuries** - Introduction and imitation of English Penny (Denier), which gave rise to silver Penning. - See *Penning.*

**14th Century** - Minting of silver Oertug and its half, Fyrkar. In Gotland minting of Hvid.

**16th Century** - After attempt to restore heavier silver monies (in 1512), issue of Klippe of deteriorated silver during war between Sweden and Denmark (1540-1557).

**1534** - Minting of Daler.

**1560** - Under Eric XIV, unit of account: Daler of 4 Mark, 32 Oere or 768 Penning. - See *Daler, Mark, Oere.*

**1509** - Minting of gold Ducat.

**1598** - Riksdaler succeeded Daler.

**1625** - Issue of divisionary monies of pure copper.

**1633-1654** - Under Christina, issue of Platmynt, heavy copper placques. Increased in number under Charles XII. - See *Platmynt.*

**1661** - Stockholms Banco (Bank of Stockholm) issued banknotes in Daler.

**1715-1719** - Issue of Myntteken, copper coins whose intrinsic metal value was 100 times inferior to official exchange rate.

**18th Century** - Two systems of accounting according to province. Accounts in silver money (Silver Mynt) and copper money (Kopper Mynt), based on Riksdaler of 48 Skilling and divided into Daler of 4 Mark, 32 Oere or 128 Oerlein. - See *Riksdaler*.

Specie monies:
> In gold - Ducat
> In silver - Riksdaler, Oere
> In copper - Taler, Oere (called Rundstücke), ½ Oere

**1776** (November 27th) - Monetary reform of Gustavus III, unifying systems of accounting on basis of silver money. Monetary unit was Riksdaler of 48 Skilling or 192 Oere.

**1830** - Reduction of fineness of silver money. Inflation of paper money denominated in Riksdaler. Paper Riksdaler fell to ¼ silver Riksdaler.

**1855** (February 3rd) - Adoption of paper Riksdaler, under name of Riksdaler Riksmynt, as monetary unit. Substitution of Oere for Skilling as submultiple (¹/₁₀₀) of Riksdaler.

**1968** (July 31st) - Issue of gold Carolins based on coin of 10 French Francs.

**1872** (December 18th) - Scandinavian Monetary Union.

**1873** (May 27th) - Adoption of gold standard, with Swedish Krona as basic unit. - See *Krona Sweden*.

**1905** - Separation of Norway. Norwegian Krone created based on Swedish Krona. - See *Krone Norway*.


## SWITCH RAND

See *Rand*.


## SWITCH STERLING

See *Pound*.


## *SWITZERLAND*

Roman money, then Carolingian monetary system (Livre of 20 Sols, 240 Deniers).

**12th Century** - Local mintings of silver Denier.

**13th Century** - In Basel, issue of Bracteates, first round, then square.

**14th Century** - Return to minting of silver Denier, with submultiples (Obol or Maille) and multiples (Tresel of 3 Deniers in Lausanne; Sixain of 6 Deniers in Geneva, Gros Tournois in Vaud.) Continued circulation of Bracteates in Basel and Berne. Geneva issued gold Guilder (Florin) imitating the one of Savoy.

**15th Century** - Berne, Lucerne, Zurich, Saint Gall, issued Blaffert of silver/copper (15 Heller). Berne minted Batz of silver/copper (4 Kreuzer or 24 Heller). Basel minted coins of 4 Rappen. Local monetary agreements for minting of identical coins (Rappenbund Agreement of 1424 among Schaffhausen, Saint Gall and Zurich).

**16th Century** - Minting of gold Guilders and Ducats, silver Thalers and Testons.

**18th Century** - Systems of accounting varied according to canton;

Livre of 20 sols or 240 Deniers in Basel, Berne, Geneva (bank and large business transactions).

Livre of 20 Batzen or 40 Kreuzer in Berne.

Guilder of 60 Kreuzer in Basel (divided into 15 Batzen, 25 Blaffert, 150 Rappen, or 300 Pfennig), in Neuchatel (divided into 15 Batz), in Zurich (240 Angster or 480 Heller), in Saint Gall (480 Heller).

Guilder of 12 Sols, 48 Quarts or 144 Deniers in Geneva (for government or small trade).

Guilder of 40 Schillings in Lucerne and Zurich.

Guilder of 10 Schillings or 15 Batzen in Saint Gall.

Crown of 25 Batzen or 100 Kreuzer in Berne.

Ecu of 60 Sols or 720 Deniers in Basel.

Specie monies:

In gold - Ducat, Pistole in Geneva

In silver - Reichsthaler (or Ecu), Guilder in Basel and Lucerne, Patagón in Berne and Geneva, Bajoire in Geneva

In silver/copper - Batz, Schilling, Kreuzer and their multiples

In copper - Angster, Rappen

**1799** (March 17th) - Helvetic Republic adopted Swiss Franc as monetary unit (6.66 grams of fine silver), divided into 10 Batzen or 100 Rappen. Minting of gold coins (16 and 32 Francs), of silver coins (4 Francs, 5, 10 and 20 Batzen), of silver/copper coins (Batzen, Kreuzer, Rappen).

**1803** (August 11th) - Law defining Swiss Franc equal to 1.5 French Francs (6.75 grams of fine silver). This system superimposed on cantonal systems. As for Neuchatel, canton adopted French monetary system in 1806, while minting Batz and Kreuzer.

**1815** - Right to mint money restored to Swiss cantons alone. Monetary anarchy.

**1819** (July 14th) - Agreement of 19 Cantons adopting Swiss Franc as monetary unit, equal to 1.5 Livre Tournois (6.66 grams of silver). Only minor specie money issued on this basis.

**1838** (February 7th) - Geneva adopted French monetary system: Franc of 4.50 grams of silver divided into 100 Centimes.

**1848** (September 12th) - Federal constitution reserved monetary privilege to Confederation and ended mintings of cantons.

**1850** (May 7th) - Monetary unification on monometallic-silver basis, with adoption of Swiss Franc equal to French Franc.

- See *Franc Switzerland.*


# SYCEE

Silver tablet in form of shoe used as money in **China.**

Weight and fineness varied: from 1 to 50 Tael.

Origin of name - Cantonese expression *Hsi Ssu* (fine floss silk), because silver could be stretched into very fine threads, or because polished silver shined like silk.

Variations of name - Ting, Pao. In English, Shoe.

**11th Century** - Under Sung dynasty, monetary use of silver in form of tablets called Ting. Weight: 1,865 kilos.

**End of 12th Century** - Ting worth 100,000 copper Tsien. Weight lowered to 1.8 kilos by Mongols.

**13th Century** - Transactions in Ting forbidden.

**1311** - Removal of ban. Growing use of silver tablets because of decay of paper money.

**About 1550** - Silver bars occupied first place among monetary instruments.

**17th Century** - Sycees continued to be used in spite of simultaneous use of Mexican Piasters and imitations.

**20th Century** - Minting of Sycees by numerous private organizations, called "Loofangs" which, in principle, bore their name, city where they were minted and number of smelter on bar.
Controls by official Assay Bureau (Kung-Ku-Chu) created by Chinese banks and Shanghai Chamber of Commerce. Bureau weighed bars, estimated fineness, and inscribed weight and fineness in Chinese ink on Sycees. Average weight close to 1.8 kilos.

**1933** (March 8th) - Monetary reform calling for minting of silver Dollars in Mint of Shanghai. Elimination of Sycees.

**1933** (September 14th) - To put an end to continuous manufacture of Sycees by "Lootangs", closing of official Assay Bureau whereby Sycees lost character of a controlled and certified money.

## *SYRIA*

**6th Century B.C.** - Monetary system of Persians. - See *Persia.*

**4th Century B.C.** - Following conquest by Alexander, money of Seleucidae.

**1st Century B.C.** - Roman domination and use of Roman money. - See *Rome.*

**638** - Arab conquest. Abd-al-Malik (685-705) minted gold Dinar. - See *Arabia.*

**11th to 13th Century** - Crusaders in Syria encountered Bezant, Dinar and Dirhem coinage which they adopted and copied. Simultaneous introduction of European specie monies: Denier, Obol, Pite, silver Gros.

**1516** - Incorporated into Ottoman Empire. Turkish monetary system. - See *Turkey.*

**18th Century** - Unit of account: Piastre of 80 Aspers.

**19th Century** - Turkish monetary system (Piastre of 40 Paras). - See *Pound Turkey.*

**1918** - British Occupation. Use of Egyptian Pound. - See *Pound Egypt.*

**1920** (May 1st) - Establishment of French Mandate of Lebanon-Syria. Creation of Lebanese-Syrian Pound equal to 20 Francs. - See *Pound Lebanon-Syria.*

**1948** (January 1st) - Break up of common exchange control and monetary system for

Lebanon and Syria. Creation of separate and distinct monetary unit in Syria. - See *Pound Syria*.

## SZELONG

Silver/copper money, then copper money in early **Poland.** Originally equal to 12 Denarii or 1 Gros.

Origin of name - See *Schilling*.

**1578** - Szelong, Polish form of Denier, minted in silver/copper.

**1659 to 1668** - Inflation of copper Szelong at forced parity.

**1785** - Szelong (0.48 gram) worth 1/4 Grosz; 1/120 Florin Zloty, or 3 Deniers.

# TAEL

Unit of weight and unit of account in Far East.

**I.** - In **China,** unit of weight equivalent to about 1⅓ ounces. Varied according to region. Sometimes designated silver bars functioning as money.

Origin of name - From Hindu *tola* through Malayan word *tahil.*

Variations of name - Lyang, Liang, Leam, Telle, Tayell.

Submultiples - 1 Tael equalled 10 Mas, 100 Candareens, 1,000 (or 1,600) Cash. These units used as both units of weight and money. Equivalents in copper Tsien: 1 Tael = 1,000 Tsien (official) and from 800 to 1,800 Tsien (actual).

Multiple - Sycee of from 1 to 50 Tael.

Weights of official Tael:

In Shanghai = 36.48 grams 9354 fine, or 34.123 grams fine silver

In Tientsin = 35.95 grams 996 fine, or 35.806 grams fine silver

In Hankow = 35.57 grams 967 fine, or 34.396 grams fine silver

Hai Kwan (Customs) Tael fixed by international agreement at 37.72 grams

Other Taels: Canton, Peking.

Tael of "tribute in grains" recalled earlier provincial taxes.

Hai Kwan Tael designated Mexican Piaster.

**1908** (October) - Imperial decree defining uniform Tael: 1 Tael = 37.80 grams of silver 980 fine, or 34.044 grams fine silver.

**1930** (February 1st) - Hai Kwan Tael abandoned as customs unit of account. Adoption of Gold Unit. - See *Gold Unit.*

**1933** (March 3rd) - Tael abandoned as monetary unit. Adoption of Chinese Dollar. - See *Dollar China.*

**1933** (April 6th) - Ban on contractual agreements in Tael.

**II.** - Unit of account in **Siam** in 18th Century, also called Tamling: 1 Tael equalled ⅟₂₀ Catty, 4 Tical, 16 Mayon, 32 Fuang, 25,000 Cowries, or 64 Song Pais, 128 Pais, 256 Clam.

10 Tael of Siam made 8 Chinese Tael.

**III.** - Early unit of account of Kingdom of Achin in **Sumatra:** Tayell (Tael) counted as 4 Pardaw, 16 Mace, 64 Koupang or 25,600 Cash.

**IV.** - Early unit of account in **Java:** ⅟₂₅,₀₀₀ Bahar, ⅟₂₅,₀₀₀ Uta, ⅟₂,₅₀₀ Catty, ⅟₂₅₀ Laxsan, ⅟₂₅ Pecco. Tael of Batavia counted as 2 Sata, 10 Mas, 40 Cash or 400 Candareens.

**V.** - Unit of account in **Japan** in 18th Century. Also minted in form of small bars, grouped into rolls.

# TAHEGAN

**I.** - Silver money issued in **Armenia** under reign of Leon II (1185-1218). Copied from

Grosso of Venice. Coin of ½ Tahégan called Tram.

II. - Gold coin of **Armenia** issued from 12th to 14th Century. Value varied, being equal to approximately 30 Drachmae of silver or 40 Poghs of copper.

## TAIWAN (FORMOSA)

**Prior to 1895** - Chinese monetary system. - See *China.*

**1895 to 1945** - Japanese monetary system with issue of Yen of Bank of Formosa (Taiwan), linked to Yen of Japan.

**1945 to 1949** - Chinese monetary system.

**1949** - Communist victory on Chinese Mainland. Creation of separate monetary unit for Taiwan. - See *Dollar Taiwan.*

## TALA

Monetary unit of **Western Samoa.** Divided into 100 Sene.

Bank of issue - Bank of Western Samoa.

Variation of name - West Samoan Dollar.

Predecessor - See *Pound Western Samoa.*

**1967** (July 10th) - Decimalization of currency system, following move of New Zealand. Adoption of Tala to replace Samoan Pound:

      1 Samoan Pound = 2.00 Talas

      1 Tala = 1.40 U.S. Dollars (approximate airmail buying
           rate)

## TALAR

**Polish** name for Thaler. Also coin of Frederick August (1807-1815). - See *Thaler IV.*

## TALARI

I. - Early monetary unit of **Ethiopia,** divided into 16 Qurush (until 1908), 16 Piastres (from 1908 to 1928), 16 Mehalek or 100 Bese (from 1928 to 1936), 100 Centimes (from 1936 to 1945).

Other traditional submultiples - Amolés, small bars of white salt (1 Talari worth from 5 to 6 Amolés in Addis Ababa, from 7 to 8 Amolés in Harar). - See *Amolé.*

Origin of name - From Maria Theresia Thaler, traditional instrument for hoarding and medium of exchange. - See *Maria Theresia Thaler.*

Variations of name - Menelik (series of King Menelik), Ber in Amharic language, Argenteus.

Bank of issue - Bank of Abyssinia, private until 1931, then by Bank of Ethiopia, state institution, from 1931 to 1936; by Italian Bank of Ethiopia from 1936 to 1941; then by State Bank.

Predecessors - See *Ethiopia* and *Maria Theresia Thaler.*

**1893** (February 9th) - Adoption of Talari as national unit of Ethiopia.

**1894** - Minting by Paris Mint of Talari with effigy of Menelik II, sometimes called Menelik. Weight and fineness very close to that of Maria Theresia Thaler: 1 Talari = 28.075 grams of silver 835 fine or = 23.44 grams fine silver.
Simultaneous circulation of Talari and Thaler.
In Menelik series, 1/2 Talari called Agod; 1/4 Talari, Yaber Rub; 1/8 Talari; Tenan.

**1936** (July 15th) - After Italian conquest, control of circulation of silver by Rome, and attempt to develop circulation of paper money on basis of:
1 Talari = 3 Lire
Official exchange rate raised at that time to 4.50 Lire, then progressively higher to 13.50 Lire.

**1938** (January) - Designation of Lira as only official money. But circulation of Thaler and Talari at rising exchange rates persisted.

**1941** (April) - After British conquest, introduction of East African Shilling:
1 Talari = 1 Shilling 10 1/2 Pence

**1942** (October 31st) - Foreign exchange controls.

**1945** (July 23rd) - Creation of new monetary unit replacing Talari and Shilling. - See *Dollar Ethiopia.*

**II.** - Submultiple (1/5) of **Egyptian** Pound since October 10, 1916. Consisted of 20 Piastres, or 200 Millièmes. Minted in silver (28 grams 833 fine).

Variation of name - Tallari.

## TALARO

Name given in **Trieste** (18th and 19th Centuries) to Reichsthaler minted in silver by Holy Roman Empire.

Origin of name - Derived from Thaler. - See *Thaler.*

## TALENT

**I.** - In Ancient **Syria,** major unit of weight and unit of account representing value of quantity of silver weighing one Talent.

Origin of name - From Greek *talanton* (level of balance), Sancrit *Tula* (balance), Indo-European root *tel* (to raise). From Talent (money) is derived the word talent (aptitude).

**6th Century B.C.** - In Euboea, then Athens, silver Talent (25.50 kilos) worth 60 Minas (425 grams), 6,000 Drachmae (4.25 grams) or 36,000 Obols (0.7 grams).

Expression gold Talent designated weight in gold corresponding to value of Talent of copper, or 8.5 grams.

Expression copper Talent first meant weight of one copper Talent, then weight of copper, very debased.

**II.** - In **Sicily** during 1st Century B.C., copper Talent weighed 1.6 kilos and corresponded to 3 silver Denarii.

**III.** - In **Egypt,** Talent of copper of Alexandria, worth 12 silver Denarii.


## TALLARO

Silver money of Grand Duchy of **Tuscany,** circulating under name of Tallaro delle Tore (or Lanternina) with exchange rate of 6 Lire.


## TALLERO

**I.** - Silver coin issued in Duchy of **Savoy** in 16th Century (after 1553) for 42 Grossi. Also called Tallaro, modeled after Thaler.

**II.** - In Republic of **Ragusa,** silver coin issued in 18th Century.

**1725** - Tallero Vecchio, or Vislino, worth 60 Grosseti or 1.50 Ducati.

**1795** - Tallero, or Libertina (with bust of Liberty), worth 80 Grossetti was of Maria Theresia Thaler type.

**III.** - Money issued by Italians in **Eritrea** in 1890. Minted in silver (28.125 grams 800 fine) in effort to supplant Maria Theresia Thaler. - See *Maria Theresia Thaler.*


## TAMBALA

Submultiple ($^1$/100) of **Malawi** Kwacha since February 15, 1971.


## TAMPE

Silver/copper money of **French West Indies** and **French Guiana** in 18th and 19th Centuries.

Origin of name - Shortening of French word meaning stamp, Etampé (coins counterstamped with a "C" for Colonies).

Variation of name - Etampé.

Predecessors - See *French West Indies* and *French Guiana.*

**1763** (January) - Prestamping of Marqué of 1738 worth 2 Sous and having low silver content. Resulted in renaming of coin to Tampé.

**1765** - Exchange rate of Tampé in French West Indies raised to 3 Sous 9 Deniers.

**1774** - Minting of Tampé using new dies.

**1779** - In Guiana, exchange rate of Tampé raised to 2 Sous 6 Deniers.

**1797** - British Occupation. Because of extensive counterfeiting. Tampé temporarily suspended. Restoration of legal tender status at value of 10 Deniers. Usually circulated in rolls of 60 coins.

**1828** (February 24th) - Withdrawal of Tampé in French West Indies.

**1844** (June 8th) - Withdrawal of Tampé in Guiana.


## TANG KA

**I.** - Silver coin of early **Tibet,** containing considerable amount of alloy. Valued at 6 Annas, though 3 Tang Ka were equal to Indian Rupee (16 Annas). Basis of coinage system. Subdivisions arose by cutting Tang Ka: Sho Kang (2/3, or 4 Annas), Chhi Ke (1/2, or 3 Annas), Kar Ma Nga (1/3, or 2 Annas), Kha Kang (1/6, or 1 Anna), Khap Chhe (1/12, or 1/2 Anna).

**II.** - In 20th Century, submultiple (1/6) of **Tibetan** Rupee. - See *Tibet.*

Variations of name - Trangkas, Trangkaz.


## TANGA

**I.** - In **Goa** (Portuguese India) and on **Malabar** Coast (India), unit of account used in 18th Century. Tanga of good alloy worth 1/4 Pardao, 4 Good Vintems, 60 Reis, 75 Good Bazaruccos. Tanga of bad alloy worth 1/5 Pardao, 4 Bad Vintems, 48 Reis, 72 Bad Bazaruccos.

**1818** - Minting of silver and copper Tanga in Portuguese Indies.

**1881** - In Portuguese India, submultiple of Rupia; 16 Tanga needed for 1 Rupia, and 12 Reis made 1 Tanga.
Cf. *Tankah.*

**II.** - Monetary unit of **Turkestan.** Divided into 50 Pul. Minted in silver.


## *TANGANYIKA*

**1st to 8th Century** - Coastal trade centers. Likely introduction of specie monies of Greece, Arabia, Persia, India and possibly China.

**8th to 16th Century** - Dominant use of Arab and Persian monies in coastal area.

**16th Century** - Introduction of Portuguese specie monies.

**Late 17th Century** - Dominance of Arabic monies. Interior trade for ivory and slaves based on cowrie shells.

**Early 19th Century** - Free trade with India resulted in gradual importance of Indian Rupee.

**1890** - German East Africa Company given authority to issue Rupee banknotes, divided into 64 Pesa. - See *Rupee East Africa.*

**1905** - German East Africa Bank established in Dar-es-Salaam to issue German East African Rupees (Rupien) divided into 100 Heller.

**1918** - German East African Rupee replaced by British East African Rupee divided into 100 Cents.

**1920** - British Colonists referred to Rupee as Florin, silver coin worth two Shillings and divided into 100 Cents.

**1922** (January 1st) - Adoption of East African Shilling to replace Florin. - See *Shilling East Africa.*

**1964** (October 29th) - Newly formed Republic of Tanganyika and Zanzibar (April 26th) renamed Tanzania. Monetary unit unchanged. - See *Tanzania.*

## *TANGIER*

Predecessor - See *Morocco.*

**1906** - Act of Algeciras (Article 37): Spanish money used as legal tender in Tangier.

**1912** - Granting of special status to Tangier. De facto monies in use: Franc and Peseta.

**1923** (December 18th) - International agreement. Moroccan Franc became sole legal tender. Spanish Peseta circulated as well with status of legal tender.

**1940** - Spanish Occupation. Peseta only legal money.

**1945** - Restoration of Free City. Moroccan Franc was only legal tender (banknotes of State Bank of Morocco). Peseta also continued to be used as legal tender. Free currency markets. - See *Peseta Spain* and *Franc Morocco.*

**1958** (February) - Peseta replaced by Moroccan Franc.

**1960** (April 17th) - All dealings in gold and foreign exchange ceased. Free City status all but terminated, and Tangier became part of Moroccan Franc Area.

**1961** (January 1st) - New unit replaced Moroccan Franc. - See *Dirham.*

## TANKAH

Silver coin (11.3 grams), minted in **East Indies** after Moslem invasions. Divided into 4 Shashkani, 24 Jettal, 48 Adli, or 96 Bikh. Minted in copper in 1329 by Sultan of Delhi (for the value of one silver Tankah), coin was quickly victim of inflation. Return to silver Tankah.
Cf. *Tanga.*

## *TANNU TUVA*

See *Tuva.*

## TANZANIA

For early history see *Tanganyika* and *Zanzibar.*

**1964** (October 29th) - Tanganyika and Zanzibar renamed Tanzania.

**1966** (June 14th) - Termination of common currency arrangements of Tanzania, Uganda and Kenya. Introduction of Tanzanian Shilling to gradually replace East African Shilling. - See *Shilling Tanzania.*

**1967** (September 14th) - East African Shilling ceased to be legal tender.

## TAO PI

Bronze knives used in **China** for small money payments during period of Hwan (about 650 B.C.).

Variations of name - Tao, Tao Ch'ien.

## TARIN

**I.** - Unit of account and specie money of **Malta,** from domination of Island by Knights of Malta (1530-1798) and into 19th Century. Until 1730, worth 2 Carlini, 4 Cinquini, 20 Grani, or 120 Piccioli. After 1730, 1/12 Scudo, or 2 Carlini, 12 Piccioli, 20 Grani.

Specie monies from 8 to 1½ Tarini in silver, minted from 16th Century.

Variation of name - Taro.

Plural - Tarini or Tari.

**II.** - Gold money minted in **Sicily** and **Salerno** in 10th and 11th Centuries, derived from 1/4 Arabic Dinar, about 1 gram.

As unit of account, Tarin worth 1/30 Oncia, 1/12 Scudo, 1/6 Fiorino, or 2 Carlini, 15 Ponti, 20 Grani, 120 Piccioli.

**III.** - In **Naples,** gold money minted during 13th Century by Charles of Anjou. Silver money minted after 15th Century (7.20 grams).

As unit of account Tarin worth 1/2 Ducato, or 2 Carlini, 8 Cinquini, 20 Grani, 40 Tornesi, 60 Quartini, 120 Piccioli, or 240 Cavalli or Denari.

## TARTEMORION

Small silver money of **Ancient Greece.** Worth 1/4 Obol or 1/24 Drachma.

Variation of name - Tetartemorion.

## TCH'A YIN

Tea vouchers used as money in **China** in 10th Century.
Origin of name - Goods for withdrawal (*Yin* ) of tea ( *Tch'a* ).

## TEGATA

Voucher issued in **Japan** as representing copper coins (Sen) or rice, and often taking
the place of money.
**13th Century -** First issue of Tegata for private accounts.
**18th Century -** Wider use of Tegata (issued for one day validity).

## TENAR

Gold coin issued in **Armenia** in 14th Century. Corresponded to Dinar.

## TERNAR

Silver coin of 3 Denarii (Pfennig) minted in 16th Century in **Poland.**
Variations of name - Ternare, Ternarius.

## TERZAROLA

**I. -** Gold coin of **Genoa** issued in 14th Century for ⅓ Genovino.
**II. -** Silver/copper coin of **Milan** in 14th Century. Equal to ⅓ Denaro.

## TESTON

Early silver money, or unit of account in several countries.
Origin of name - From early French *teste* (head). Head of King pictured on these coins.
**I. -** In **France,** coin created by Louis XII on April 6, 1513. Heavier (9.6 grams) than
earlier coins. Exchange rate: 10 Sous, raised to 10 Sous 6 Deniers (March 5, 1532),
10 Sous 8 Deniers (May 18, 1540), 12 Sous (August 30, 1561), 13 Sous (June 9,
1573), 14 Sous 6 Deniers (June 17, 1575), 15 Sous (September 16, 1602).
**II. -** In **England,** silver coin issued by Henry VIII. Fine metal content progressively
reduced (in 1546, in 1550).
**III. -** In **Scotland,** silver coin issued in 16th Century.
**IV. -** For **Portugal,** see *Tostao.*
**V. -** For **Italy,** see *Testone.*

## TESTONE

Unit of account and silver or silver/copper money in several **Italian** states before unification in 19th Century.
Origin of name - See *Teston.*
Variation of name - Testano.
Plural - Testoni.
**I.** - In **Florence**, silver Testone appeared in 1533. In Grand Duchy of **Tuscany**, unit of account worth 2 Lire, 3 Paoli, 24 Crazie, 40 Soldi di Lira, 120 Quattrini, or 480 Denari di Lira. Silver/copper money worth 3 Paoli.
**II.** - In **Rome** (Papal States), first Testone issued at beginning of 16th Century. Weight: 9.2 grams 902 fine, or 8.3 grams fine silver.
**18th Century** - Silver money worth 3 Paoli. Weight: 8.4 grams 917 fine, or 7.7 grams fine. Unit of account worth 1/3 Scudo Romano, 3 Paoli, 30 Baiocci, 150 Quattrini, or 300 Mezzi Quattrini.
**1835** - Silver Testone worth 30 Baiocci.
**III.** - In **Bologna**, silver money, also called Petrono, worth 3 Paoli or 30 Soldi.
**IV.** - In **Leghorn**, unit of account worth 2 Lire, 3 Paoli, 24 Crazie, 40 Soldi, 120 Quattrini, 480 Denari.
**V.** - In Duchy of **Savoy**, silver coin issued in 1483 for 8 Grosso.
**VI.** - In **Milan**, silver coin minted for first time in 1474 (Testone, Grossone or Lira): 9.78 grams 963 fine, or 9.42 grams fine silver.
**1500-1512** - Louis XII raised exchange rate of Testone from 20 to 22 Soldi. Charles V issued Testone.
**VII.** - In **Naples** and **Sicily**, Charles V issued Testone equal to 2 Carlini.
**VIII.** - In **Venice**, in 1471, minting of Lira under name Testone.
**IX.** - In **Ferrara**, Alfonso II (1559-1597) issued Testone equal to 18 Paoli.

## *THAILAND*

Primitive money - Cowrie, shell of Maldive Islands, called Bia by Siamese. - See *Cowrie.*
**7th to 9th Century** - Silver bracelets used as money as were silver Ka'Kim, conical in shape but with a hole. Silver bars or Lats, with stamps on the upper surface, also used as currency.
**16th Century** - Introduction of silver Mexican Piaster.
**17th Century** - Silver by weight used as money.
**18th Century** - Unit of account: Tical, divided into 4 Salung, 8 Fuang, 64 Att, 16 Biche, 36 Rengui, 6,400 Cowries, or into 16 Song Pais, 32 Pais, 64 Clam.
Multiples - Catty of 20 Tael, 80 Tical, 512,000 Cowries. (10 Tael of Thailand equal to 8 Tael of China).
Specie monies:
    In gold - Tical, equal to 10 silver Tical
    In silver - Tical Salung (Mayon), Fuang, Song Pai

In lead - Rengui
Mexican Piaster had exchange rate of 8 Salung.
**19th Century** - Adoption of independent˜silver money. - See *Tical.*
**1928** (April 15th) - Adoption of gold standard with substitution of Baht for Tical. - See *Baht.*


# THALER


Silver money and unit of account created in Bohemia. Circulated in Germanic countries.

Origin of name - Abbreviation of Joachimsthaler, coin manufactured in Joachimsthal, town in Bohemia. From German *Thal* (valley) pertaining to valley of Joachim.

Variations of name - French, Taller, Daller; Scandinavian, Daler; Netherlands, Daalder and Daler; Polish, Talar; Italian, Tallero; Ethiopian, Talari or Ber; Spanish, Dollera and Dolera; English, Dollar.

**I.** - **German** silver money and unit of account from 16th to 19th Century.

**1519** - On south slope of Harz Mountains, the Count Schlick, proprietors of silver mines of Joachimsthal, imitated Saxony which minted heavy silver coins called Guldengroschen, and minted silver coins called Joachimsthalers, or generally Thalers (35 grams of pure silver), worth one gold Florin (Gulden).

**1542** - Modified fineness: Thaler of 35 grams 937 fine, or 32.8 grams fine silver.

**1549** - Thaler lowered to 31.5 grams fine. Minting was, in principle, reserved for Holy Roman Empire and forbidden for individual states.

**1551** - Weight lowered from 35 to 33 grams 752 fine, or 24.8 grams fine silver. Exchange rate: 66 Kreuzer.

**1555** - Became unit of account in Northern States for 24 Silbergroschen or 32 Mariengroschen.

**1559** - Thaler of 29.5 grams 925 fine, or 27.3 grams fine, then raised to 35 grams 889 fine, or 31.1 grams fine silver.

**1566** - Became money of Holy Roman Empire (Reich) under name Reichsthaler. Exchange rate: 68 Kreuzer. Reichsguldiner, created in 1524, took name Guldenthaler, because it was worth 1 Florin (Gulden) or 60 Kreuzer. - See *Reichsthaler.*

**1585** - Exchange rate of Guldenthaler raised from 60 to 64 Kreuzer by tradesmen assembled at Frankfurt.

**Early 17th Century** - Guldenthaler at 90 Kreuzer.

**1619-1622** (Thirty Years War) - Guldenthaler rose progressively from 96 to 510 Kreuzer.

**1623** (December 14th) - Imperial edict lowering Guldenthaler to 80 Kreuzer. Thaler of account divided into 30 Groschen or 360 Pfennig in countries of East (Saxony); into 3 Mark, 49 Schilling or 576 Pfennig in Northern regions (Hamburg). In Southern regions (Austria, Bavaria, Swabia, Franconia, Rhineland), where accounts were kept in Florins (Gulden) and Kreuzer, Thaler corresponded to 1.5 Florins (Gulden) or 90 Kreuzer.

**1665** - Exchange rate of Guldenthaler raised to 90 Kreuzer in Bavaria, Swabia and Franconia.

**1667** - Decisions of Conference of Zinna (among electoral Saxony, Brandenburg, Brunswick, Lüneburg): end to minting of Thaler. Issue of coins corresponding to 1/6, 1/3, 2/3 Thaler.

The 2/3 Thaler coin of 14.8 grams fine silver was worth 16 Gute Groschen or 24 Mariengroschen in Thaler accounting system, 1 Florin (Gulden) or 60 Kreuzer in Florin (Gulden) accounting system, 2 Mark or 32 Schilling in Mark accounting system.

Southern Regions (Austria, Bavaria, Swabia, Franconia) refused to abide by these decisions.

**1669** - Condemnation of decisions of Zinna by Emperor Leopold I. Repeated in 1676.

**1690** - Decisions of Conference of Leipzig (among electoral Saxony, Brandenburg, Brunswick, Lüneburg): Thaler of account (Current Thaler, equal to 19.48 grams of silver, consisted of 24 Gute Groschen or 288 Pfennig.

**1693** - Extension of decisions of Leipzig to entire Holy Roman Empire (except Hamburg and Lübeck). De facto maintenance of earlier systems of Thaler accounting in East, Florins (Gulden) in South and West, Mark in North.

**1736** - Thaler of account, equivalent to 17.12 grams of silver, consisted of 2 Florins (Gulden).

**1751** - In Prussia (system of Frederick II), Thaler equivalent to 16.7 grams of silver. Corresponded to 1.75 Florins (Gulden).

**1753** - Agreement of Vienna making monetary system of Holy Roman Empire uniform (except Prussia and Hanover); Thaler of account equal to 17.54 grams of silver. Value lowered to 1.5 Florins (Gulden).

In Austria and Bavaria, silver Thaler (28.06 grams 833 fine) had exchange rate of 2 Florins (Gulden).

As unit of account, Thaler (called Ecu in France) divided into 90 Kreuzer or 360 Pfennig in Frankfurt; 24 Gute Groschen or 288 Pfennig in Brandenburg, Saxony, Thuringia, Lüneburg; 78 Albus or 936 Pfennig in Cologne; 54 Petermännchen in Treve; 36 Mariengroschen, 288 Pfennig or 360 Schwaren in Bremen, Oldenburg; 30 Silbergroschen or 360 Denars in Silesia; 28 Schilling or 336 Pfennig in Münster; 21 Schilling or 252 Pfennig in Osnabrück; 48 Schilling or 576 Pfennig in Mecklenburg.

Reichsthaler and Speciesthaler sometimes used as unit of account.

Thaler was silver money in Silesia (for 30 Silbergroschen), Hanover and Brunswick (for 36 Mariengroschen).

**1765** - Minting of Maria Theresia Thaler. - See *Maria Theresia Thaler.*

**19th Century** - Variations of Thaler used before unification of 1857:

As unit of account in Hanover, Saxony, Anhalt, Frankfurt (equivalent to 17.5 grams of silver); in Baden (15.8 grams); in Bavaria, Hesse, Saxe-Coburg (14.6 grams); in Bremen and in Oldenburg (17.6 grams).

As specie monies in silver in Baden (18.1 grams 875 fine, or 15.8 grams fine, with exchange rate of 100 Kreuzer), in electoral Hesse (21.2 grams 750 fine, or 15.9 grams fine), in Lübeck and Mecklenburg (27.5 grams 750 fine, or 20.6 grams fine, with exchange rate of 3 Mark), in Prussia (22.3 grams 750 fine, or 16.7 grams fine).

**1838** (July 30th) - Convention of Dresden, attempting to join German monetary systems to silver standard base: equivalents fixed between units of account: 1 Thaler = 1.75 Florins (Gulden). Creation of common silver coin (Vereinsmünze) worth 2 Thaler or 3.50 Florins (Gulden).
Thaler remained unit of account in Prussia, Saxony and various states in North.

**1857** (January 24th) - Austro-German Monetary Convention making silver Thaler monetary unit of North German Confederation. Definition: 18.52 grams 900 fine, or 16.67 grams fine.
Equivalent to 1.50 Austrian Florins (Gulden) or 1.75 Florins (Gulden) of South German states. Divided into 30 Silbergroschen.
Not participating in agreement: Hamburg, Bremen, Lübeck, Holstein.

**1867** (January 13th) - Treaty of Berlin: Austria withdrew from Germanic Monetary Union.

**1871** (December 4th) - Law creating coins of 10 and 20 Mark in gold, suspending minting of silver monies and authorizing their withdrawal: 10 new Mark replaced 3.33 Thaler.

**1873** (July 12th) - Law establishing gold standard. Progressive withdrawal from circulation of Thaler, which kept exchange rate of 3 Mark.

**1876** (January 1st) - Activation of new system of accounting in Mark.

**1879** (May 19th) - Suspension of withdrawal from circulation of Thaler.

**1907** (October 1st) - Final demonetization of Thaler.

**II.** - In **Swiss** cantons, until 1850, Thaler was silver money often called Ecu. In Basel, unit of account divided into 108 Kreuzer, 270 Rappen or 540 Pfennig.

**III.** - Silver money issued in **Hungary** in 16th Century. Called Egisthaler in 18th Century.

**IV.** - In **Poland,** silver money from 16th to 18th Century, called Talar. First appearance in 1578 Groschen 28.24 grams 875 fine, or 24.7 grams fine. Ended Albus career at Pfennig grams fine. Exchange rate: 4 Florins Zloty. Minted again in Pfennig by Grand Duchy of Warsaw. Schilling Schilling
Gold money of 17th and 18th Century, under name of Talar Zloty (gold Thaler). - See *Zloty.*

**V.** - For **Scandinavian** countries, see *Daler.*

**VI.** - For **Netherlands,** see *Daalder* and *Rijksdaalder.*

**VII.** - For **Italian** states, see *Tallero.*

**VIII.** - For **Spain,** see *Dollera.*

**IX.** - For **United States,** see *Dollar.*

**X.** - For **Ethiopia,** see *Maria Theresia Thaler* and *Talari.*


# THALER, MARIA THERESIA

See *Maria Theresia Thaler*

# TIAO

In **China**, 10 rolls of 100 Tsien. - See *Tsien.*
Variation of name - Diao.

# *TIBET*

Primitive money - Tea, in small, compressed, flat discs weighing about 20 Ticals.
Predecessor - See *India.*
**19th Century** - Use of Indian Rupee of 16 Annas or 192 Pie. Minting of some local
gold coins. Use of silver Tang Ka of 1.50 Sho Kang, 2 Chhi Ke or 6 Annas. - See
*Tang Ka.*
**20th Century** - Silver Rupee (6 Tang Ka), linked to Indian Rupee (see *Rupee India*)
and Srang (see *Sho Kang*). Worth about ¼ Rupee.
Simultaneous use of Chinese monies. - See *China.*
**1951** (May) - Taken over by Communist China. - See *Jen Min Piao.*

# TICAL

**I.** - Monetary unit of **Thailand** (Siam) until 1928. Sometimes called Bat, or Baht.
Bank of issue - Banque de l'Indochine, Chartered Bank of India, Hongkong and
Shanghai Banking Corporation. Since 1902, by State.
Predecessor - See *Thailand.*
**18th Century** - Tical was simultaneously a unit of account, gold money, and silver
money. Worth 8 Fuang or 6,400 Bias or Cowries (shells from Maldive Islands).
- See *Cowrie.*
**19th Century** - Tical coined in silver in 3 forms: 15.23 grams 928 fine, or 14.13 grams
fine silver; 15.29 grams 903 fine, or 13.81 grams fine silver (also called Piastre);
15 grams 900 fine, or 13.50 grams fine silver.
Multiples - Double Tical called Piastre, 4 Ticals made 1 Tael; 80 Ticals made 1
Catty.
Submultiples - Salung or Mayon (¼), Fuang (⅛), Song Pai (1/16), Pai or Phai
(1/32), Att or Clam (1/64), Lott (1/128).
**20th Century** - Tical divided into 4 Salung and 100 Att.
**1902** - Suspension of free minting of silver.
**1908** (November 11th) - Link to Pound Sterling:
1 Tical = 1/13 Pound Sterling
1 Tical = 563.26 milligrams of fine gold
**1917** (June) - Because of rise in value of silver bullion, embargo on silver shipments.
Reduction of fineness of divisionary coins.
**1919** (January 27th) - Suspension of convertibility.
**1919** (September 4th) - Revaluation of Tical:

1 Tical = ¹/₁₂ Pound Sterling = 20 Pence
1 Tical = 610 milligrams of fine gold
**1928** (April 15th) - Adoption of gold standard with substitution of Baht for Tical. - See *Baht*.
**II.** - Early unit of account in Kingdom of Pegu **(Burma)**. Divided into 16 Toques.


## TIERCELIN

Silver money in **Hainaut** in 14th Century. Worth ¹/₃ Plaisant or 5 Deniers.
Origin of name - From old French, *tiercier* (to divide into three).
Variation of name - Tiercele.


## TIKCHUNG

Monetary unit of **Bhutan**. Submultiple (¹/₂) of Rupee.
Origin of name - From Bhutanese words *Tigroo* (Rupee) and *Chungoo* (small).
Bank of issue - Reserve Bank of India. Coins minted in Alipore by Indian Government Mint.
Predecessor - See *Bhutan*.
**1967** - Tikchung minted in nickel as principal money. Freely exchanged at:
      1 Indian Rupee = 2 Tikchung
      1 Tikchung = 50.00 Indian Naye Paise
      1 Tikchung = 59.2445 milligrams of fine gold
      1 U.S. Dollar = 15.00 Tikchung
**1968** (May 28th) - Bank of Bhutan established with primary purpose of supporting Tikchung exchange rate.
**1969** - Exchange controls introduced, giving exchange priority to imports of petroleum products.


## TILLA

Gold coin minted in Russian and Chinese **Turkestan** in second half of 19th Century. Value: 21 to 28 Tanga. Weight varied from 4.25 to 4.75 grams.


## TIMMIN

**I.** - Unit of account used in **Smyrna** in 18th Century. Equivalent to ¹/₁₂ Piastre, or 3.33 Para, 10 Aspers.
Variations of name - Temine, Temin, Tenin, Temmin.
**II.** - Name given in **Turkey** to French silver coins of 5 Sols. Issued in 1641 bearing

imprint of Anna Maria Louisa d'Orleans. Valued by Turks for its beauty, and often used as jewelry.

**III.** - For **Algiers,** see *Muzuna.*


## TIMOR

In Eastern portion of island (Portuguese), monetary unit from 1895: Pataca equal to 100 Avos. - See *Pataca Macao.* Subsequently replaced by Timor Escudo at par with Portuguese Escudo. - See *Escudo Portugal.*

For western portion, see *Indonesia.*


## TING

Early **Chinese** name for silver ingots or shoes. - See *Sycee.* Word Ting generally referred to ingot weighing 50 Taels.

Variations of name - Yin Ting, Pao, Sycee.


## TLEMCEN

Kingdom of Barbary minted gold monies called Rubie (35 Aspers), Median (50 Aspers) and Dian or Zian (100 Aspers).


## TOGO

Early native money - See *Ivory Coast.*

**1885** - German Occupation and German monetary system. - See *Mark.* Circulation of several types of European coins introduced through trade.

**1914** - Allied Occupation.

**1920** (September 30th) - Territory divided between Britain and France. British Togoland followed monetary developments of Gold Coast. - See *Gold Coast.*

In French Togo, use of Franc. - See *Franc.*

**1920** (December 31st) - Banque de l'Afrique Occidentale authorized to issue banknotes in French Togo.

**1921** (May 20th) - Legal tender status given to Banque de l'Afrique Occidentale banknotes denominated in Francs.

**1922** (April 1st) - Banque de l'Afrique Occidentale opened Lomé branch which subsequently issued banknotes.

**1924** (July 27th) - British money admitted into public treasuries.

**1926** (March 8th) - Importation of foreign coins prohibited. Continued acceptance of British money by government offices.

**1931** (February 26th) - British money ceased to circulate.

**1939** - Control of exchange rates inside Franc-Zone. Togo participated in monetary system of French West Africa. - See *French West Africa.*

**1960** (April 27th) - French Togo became independent Republic of Togo. Monetary unit unchanged. - See *Franc CFA.*


## TOISON

See *Vlies.*


## TOKEN

**I.** - Copper coin issued by merchants of Australian Seas in **Australia** and **New Zealand** at beginning of colonization. Denominated in Pennies.

**II.** - Private coins authorized during three periods of history in **England** from 1601-1811 when royal coinage was inadequate.

**III.** - In early **United States,** coins privately minted in 1789 and 1794.


## TOLA

Weight used chiefly for gold and silver in **India.**

Origin of name - From Sanscrit *tuta* (a balance) or *tul* (to weigh or lift up).

**1833** - Weight of Farrukhábád Rupee altered and accepted as unit of general system of weights for government transactions under name of Tola:

    1 Tola = 180 troy grains = 11.664 grams


## TOLER

Copper bars or plates used as money in **Sweden** in 17th and 18th Centuries. - See *Platmynt.*


## TOMAN

**I.** - Early gold money of **Persia.**

**1587-1629** - Toman worth 10 Hor (Kran), 50 Abbasis, 80 Larins, 100 Mahmudis, 200 Shahis, 1,000 Dinars-Bisti, 2,000 Kazbegi, 10,000 Dinars. Toman represented 121 grams of fine silver. Silver often weighed by sacks of 50 Toman.

**Before 1879** - Minting of gold Toman (3.22 grams 900 fine), similar to French coin of 10 Francs. Minting of Double Toman (equal to Napoléon) and ½ Toman. Represented 41.4 grams of fine silver. Toman worth 10 Hor, then 10 Kran, or 200 Shahis, or 10,000 Dinars.

**1879** - Minting of gold Toman (2.877 grams 900 fine, or 2.59 grams fine), also called Ashrafi. Coin of ½ Toman called Penzozari; the ⅕ Toman, Dohozari. Issue of banknotes in Toman from 1 to 500.

**II.** - Unit of account in **Arabia** (Basra, Persian Gulf) in 18th Century. Toman counted as 100 Mahmudis, 1,000 Danims, or 10,000 Falus.
In Goumron, on Persian Gulf (Persian possession until 1800), Toman counted as 100 Mahmudis or 2,000 Gass.

## TONGA

**1900** (May 18th) - British Protectorate established. Introduction of British monetary system with subsequent issue by Tonga Treasury of currency notes denominated in Tonga Pounds. - See *Pound Tonga.*

## TONKIN

See *Indochina.*

## TOQUE

Unit of account during 18th Century in Kingdom of **Pegu (Burma).** Equal to ¹⁄₁₆ Tical.

## TORALO

Silver money used in **Turkey, Syria** and **Arabia** in 18th Century: 26.5 grams 585 fine, or 15.5 grams fine silver.

## TORNESE

**I.** - Early unit of account in **Naples:** ¹⁄₂₀₀ Ducato, ¹⁄₄₀ Tarin, ¹⁄₂₀ Carlino, ⅕ Cinquino, ½ Grano, or ⅕ Quartini, 3 Piccioli, 6 Cavalli or Denari. Silver/copper coin valued at ½ Grano.

**II.** - Copper money of Kingdom of **Two Sicilies** until 1860. Valued at ¹⁄₃₀₀ Ducato or ⅓ Grano.

Plural - Tornesi.

## TORNESELLO

I. - Silver/copper money of **Naples** minted by Charles II of Anjou at beginning of 14th Century. Corresponded to Denaro.
Origin of name - Italian diminutive of Tournois (small Tournois). - Cf. *Torneso, Tornez.*
II. - Copper coin issued in **Venice** in 1343 (Doge Andrea Dandolo), and destined for Venetian Colonies in Middle East. Resembled Soldino.

## TORNEZ

**Portuguese** coin minted in silver during reign of Diniz (1279-1325). Exchange rate: 7 Soldos.
Meio Tornez (½) minted in silver/copper under Fernando (1367-1383). Tornez discontinued during latter's reign.
Origin of name - From French Tournois. - Cf. *Tornese, Tornesello.*

## TOSTAO

Early silver money of **Portugal.**
Origin of name - Portuguese for Teston. - See *Teston.*
Predecessor - See *Portugal.*
**1499** - With influx of metals, creation of silver (10.3 grams) Tostao by Emanuel I, equivalent to ¼ Portuguez (gold coin) or 100 Reis.
**1538** (November 26th) - Decree suspending minting of Tostao.
**1557-1578** - Under Sebastian, issue of silver (9.7 grams) Tostao and ½ Tostao.
**1640** - With return of House of Braganza, new minting of Tostao and ½ Tostao.
**1722** - Silver Tostao worth ¹⁄₁₆ gold Escudo or 100 Reis. Gold Escudo, sometimes called gold Tostao, had exchange rate of 1,600 Reis.
**1835** (April 24th) - Edict reorganizing monetary system. Silver Tostao (2.5 grams 916 fine, or 2.3 grams fine) worth 100 Reis.
**1854** (July 29th) - In monetary system linked to gold standard with Milreis as unit of account, silver Tostao (still 2.5 grams 916 fine, or 2.3 grams fine) represented 100 Reis. Word Tostao remained in general use to designate 100 Reis or 10 Centavos.

## TOSTON

I. - In **Mexico,** silver coin equivalent to ½ Piaster or 4 Reales. Minted after 1535.
II. - In **Ecuador,** until 1871. Equivalent to ½ silver Peso or 4 Reales.
III. - In **Peru,** silver coin minted after 1821. Worth 4 Reales.

# TOURNOIS

**I.** - **French** system of accounting first used in Tours, then extended to entire royal domain.

**12th Century** - Livre of Tours (Livre Tournois) of 455.2 grams was unit of weight in Touraine.

**1204** - Extension of Tournois system to Normandy.

**13th Century** - Under Saint Louis, adoption of Tournois system for accounts of Kingdom, to detriment of Parisis accounting system:

1 Livre Tournois = 20 Sous Tournois = 240 Deniers Tournois

However, coexistence of Tournois and Parisis systems until Louis XIV. - See *Livre Tournois.*

**1295** - Maille Blanche called Petit Tournois. Denier Tournois of silver carried name Petit Tournois (1.11 grams, then 1.08 in 1344; 1.16 grams of which 0.17 was silver in 1360; 1.16 grams, of which 0.19 then 0.29 was silver in 1361; 1.27 grams, of which 0.21 was silver in 1365.

**1610-1643** - Under Louis XIII, last minting of Denier Tournois.

**II.** - **Portuguese** silver coin. - See *Tornez.*

**III.** - For **Italy**, see *Tornese, Tornesello.*

# TRADE DOLLAR

Silver coin minted for export purposes by **United States.** Patterned after coins of international repute: Mexican Piaster and Maria Theresia Thaler.

Predecessor - See *Dollar.*

**1873** (February 12th) - As counterpart to proclamation of gold standard for domestic use, creation of Trade Dollar for international use, especially in Asia (in order to compete with Mexican Piaster in Far East).

1 Trade Dollar = 27.215 grams of silver 900 fine = 24.493 grams fine silver

**1873** (July) - Placed into circulation with free minting.

**1876** (July 22nd) - Law revoking Trade Dollar's domestic legal tender status formerly limited to 5 U.S. Dollars.

**1885** - In Indochina, minting of "Piastres de Commerce" based on Trade Dollar. - See *Piastre Indochina.*

**1887** (March 3rd) - Withdrawal from circulation of Trade Dollars in United States.

# TRAM

Submultiple ($\frac{1}{2}$) of Tahégan, silver money of **Armenia** from 12th to 14th Century.

## *TRANSJORDAN*

Monetary developments parallel to those in Palestine. - See *Palestine.*
**1946** (June 17th) - Renamed Hashimite Kingdom of Jordan. - See *Jordan.*


## TRESEL

Silver coin of 3 Deniers used in some **Swiss** cantons in 14th and 15th Centuries.


## TRESIN

Silver/copper coin minted in **France** during English Occupation in 15th Century.
**1423** - Minting of Tresin: 1.63 grams 252 fine, or 0.41 grams fine silver. Exchange rate:
3 Deniers Tournois.


## TRIENS

**I. - Roman** money worth 1/3 As, or 4 ounces. Used until 9th Century by Franks,
Lombards, Visigoths, Suevi, Anglo-Saxons, Frisians. . .
Origin of name - From *tres* and *As.*
Variations of name - Tremissis, Trimisium.
**II. - Roman** gold money, worth 1/3 Solidus in monetary system of Constantine. Issued
by Empire, then by German invaders.
**III. - Byzantine** gold money worth 1/3 Bezant (Solidus).


## *TRIESTE*

Roman monies (see *Rome*), then Carolingian monetary system (see *Livre* and *Lira*).
**13th Century** - Bishopric of Trieste issued Denier. Later, monetary systems of Venice
(see *Venice*) and Austria (see *Austria*).
**18th Century** - Two units of account: Lira of 20 Soldi or 240 Denari (or 12 Crazie);
Florin (Fiorino) of 60 Crazie (Kreuzer).
Specie monies minted by Austria:
In gold - Ducat or Zecchino (Sequin)
In silver - Talaro (Reichsthaler), Fiorino (Guilder)
In copper - Soldo
**19th Century** - Austrian monies.
**1918** - Introduction of Italian monetary system with Lira (see *Italy*).
**1945** - Free City of Trieste (Zone A) remained within Lira Zone with circulation of

Italian monies. - See *Lira Italy.* In Zone B, circulation of Yugoslav monies. - See *Dinar Yugoslavia.*

## TRILLINA

Silver/copper coin of **Milan** issued under reign of Giovanni Maria Visconti (1402-1412) and in circulation until mid-17th Century. Worth 1/3 Testone.

## *TRINIDAD AND TOBAGO*

**17th Century** - Spanish Colony with Spanish money in circulation.

**18th Century** - Introduction of some English and Portuguese coins, counter-marked Spanish Piasters predominant.

**1802** - Trinidad ceded to Great Britain. British monetary system in use. British gold, silver and copper coins became predominant.

**1889** - Trinidad and Tobago were joined.

**1935** - British West Indies Dollar began to circulate in form of government currency notes. British currency remained legal tender. - See *Dollar British West Indies.*

**1951** (August 31st) - Unified currency of Currency Board of British Caribbean Territories (Eastern Group) began circulating as legal tender along with British Pound Sterling. Coins in circulation were British.

**1956** (October 1st) - Subsidiary coins based on BWI Dollar came into circulation.

**1962** (August 31st) - Trinidad and Tobago became independent state of Commonwealth and withdrew from British Caribbean Currency Board.

**1964** - Central Bank of Trinidad and Tobago began operations. Issued new monetary unit, Trinidad Tobago Dollar, at par with BWI Dollar. - See *Dollar Trinidad* and *Tobago.*

**1965** (October 6th) - Monetary unit of East Caribbean Currency Authority, East Caribbean Dollar, allowed to circulate freely, but not legal tender. - See *Dollar East Caribbean.*

**1965** (December 31st) - BWI Dollar ceased to be legal tender.

## *TRIPOLI*

See *Libya.*

## *TRUCIAL STATES*

**1892** - "Exclusive Agreement", sheikdoms of Shargah, Ras al Khaimah, Umm ul Qawain, Ajman, Dubai, and Abu Dhabi became British protectorates, henceforth referred to as Trucial States. For money in circulation, see *Rupee India.*

**1952** - Sheikdom of Fujairah recognized as new Trucial State.
**1959** - New currency in circulation. - See *Rupee Persian Gulf.*
**1966** (June 16th) - Gulf Rupee replaced by Saudi Riyal, except in Abu Dhabi. - See *Riyal Saudi Arabia* and *Abu Dhabi.*
**1966** (September) - Saudi Riyal replaced by Qatar/Dubai Riyal. - See *Riyal Qatar/-Dubai.*
**1969** (October 22nd) - Trucial States became part of Federation of Arab Emirates. - See *Federation of Arab Emirates.*

## TSCHETWERTAK

I. - Silver coin of **Russia** introduced by Peter I in early 18th Century. Worth 25 Kopeks or ¼ Ruble.

II. - Silver coin of **Poland** struck in 1842 and later, with same value as in Russia.

## TSIEN

In **China,** money of copper, zinc, iron, or alloy of copper (60% to 66%) and lead (33% to 40%), used for two milleniums.
Weight and type varied according to time and province. Round coins marked on one side, generally pierced with 1 or 4 holes, and often tied together in rolls of 100 or 1,000. Ten rolls of 100 formed Tiao. 1 Bundle of 1,000 formed a Kuan.
Variations of name - Ch'ien, Sapèque, Cash, Li, Tsen (in Manchuria), Cholk (in Russia). - See *Cash.*

**About 200 B.C.** - Minting of Tsien, round, punctured copper coins, then minting of Chia Tsien, in form of fruit of elm tree.

**118 B.C.** - Under Han Dynasty, issue of Tsien weighing 5 Chus (or 2.8 grams), called Wu Chu.

**1st and 2nd Centuries A.D.** - New issue of Tsien of 5 Chus by Han dynasty.

**221** - In Kingdom of Wei (Northern China), copper Tsien withdrawn from circulation. Replaced by cereal grains and cloth, then restored after several years.

**238** - In Kingdom of Wu (South of Blue River), minting of Tsien of 15 Chus (9 grams). Demonetized in 246. Copper money fell into disfavor (debasement of small monies, exorbitant exchange rate for large coins).

**3rd Century** - Substitution of iron Tsien for copper Tsien.

**5th Century** - Minting of lightened Tsien.

**6th Century** - After depreciation of iron Tsien and return to commodity money (silks, millet, salt), reappearance of copper Tsien.

**540** - Issue of red copper Tsien.

**561** - Issue of large coins (Pu Ch'uan) worth 5 Tsien of 5 Chus.

**574** - Issue of large coins (Won Ring Ta Pu) worth 10 Tsien of 5 Chus. Quickly depreciated.

**589** - Wen-ti issued Tsien of 5 Chus (2.50 grams of copper) in unified China. Numerous private mintings of low quality.

**621** - T'ang Dynasty issued Yuan Pao, copper coin of 3.8 grams. Multiple: bundle of 1,000 coins called Kuan.

**758** - Minting of large coins (Kien Yuan Chong Pao) weighing 5 grams and equal to 10 Yuan Pao.

**759** - Minting of larger coins (Chong Louen Tsien) weighing 6 grams and equal to 50 Yuan Pao, then lowered to 30, and finally to 3 in 763.

**806** - Issue of checks (Fei Tsien or flying Tsien).

**924** - Embargo on exports of copper Tsien.

**960** - Under Sung dynasty, issue of copper Tsien (Tung Pao and Yuan Pao). In certain provinces poor in copper, minting of iron Tsien which depreciated.

**About 990** - Issue, at first private, of paper banknotes (Kiao tze) which, in 1105, became Tsien Yin (banknotes to "withdraw Tsien"). - See *Kiao tze.*

**1046** - Issue, in Shansi, of large copper and iron coins (K'ing Li Chong Pao), worth 10, then 2 small Tsien of copper.

**11th Century** - In Shansi, minting of Tsien from tin alloy.

**1106** - Withdrawal from circulation of Tsien Yin.

**1158** - Kin Dynasty minted copper Tsien.

**1197** - First minting of silver coins similar to Tsien (Tch'eng An Pao Huo). Rapidly counterfeited, and demonetized in 1200.

**1204** - Return to minting of copper Tsien.

**14th Century** - Ming Dynasty resumed minting of copper Tsien, called Ta Chong T'ont Pao Tsien, then Hong Wu T'ont Pao Tsien, of various weights.·

**1394** - Use of Tsien forbidden in order to support paper money.

**1425** - Return to Tsien for several centuries.

**16th to 19th Century** - Circulation of Tsien, only money coined in China: Tsien, or Sapèque, was coin of about 4 grams of copper and lead, 10 of which were equal to 1 Cash, 100 to 1 Mas, 1,000 to 1 Tael.

**20th Century** - Variable exchange rate in relation to silver Chinese Dollar: from 130 Tsien per silver Dollar in 1913, to 550 in 1936.

**1935** (November 3rd) - Monetary reform (see *Dollar China*) involving minting by Shanghai Mint of copper coins of ½ and 1 Cent and nickel coins of 5, 10 and 20 Cents. Stabilization of Tsien on basis of:

1 Chinese Dollar = 300 Tsien

# TSJAO

Submultiple (¹/₁₀) of Jen Min Piao, monetary unit of **China.** Also called Mao. Divided into 10 Fyng. - See *Jen Min Piao.*

# TUG

Monetary unit of **Tuva** in 1935. Equal to Ruble. - See *Tuva* and *Mongolia.*


# TUGHRIK

Monetary unit of **Mongolian People's Republic (Outer Mongolia).** Divided into 100
   Mongos.
Variations of name - Tougrie, Turik, Tukrik, Tugrik.
Bank of issue - By Siberian Trading Bank, then by Mongolbank (Commercial and
   Industrial Bank of Mongolia) since 1924. Name later changed to State Bank of
   Mongolian People's Republic.
Predecessor - See *China.*
**1915** (March) - Adoption of Tughrik, silver coin linked to Ruble, as monetary unit.
   Russian money also in circulation:
      1 Tughrik = 1 Ruble
      1 U.S. Dollar = 1.943 Tughriks
   Depreciation of Tughrik parallel to Ruble. - See *Ruble.*
**1924** - Commercial and Industrial Bank of Mongolia became monetary authority.
**1926** - Minting of silver Tughrik in Leningrad weighing 20 grams 900 fine, 50 Mongos
   of 10 grams 900 fine, and 20, 15 and 10 Mongos 500 fine.
**1941** - Tughrik banknotes in denominations of 1, 2, 5, 10, 25, 50 and 100 printed in
   Russian and Mongolian. Since 1955, only in Russian.
**1961** (January 1st) - Soviet monetary reform, which Mongolian People's Republic did
   not follow, created new rates:
      1 Tughrik = 22.50 Kopeks
      1 U.S. Dollar = 4.00 Tughriks (official)
      1 U.S. Dollar = 6.00 Tughriks (tourist rate)
**1970** (March) - Black market rate of Tughrik reached 30.00 per U.S. Dollar.


# *TUNISIA*

Successive monies of Carthage, Rome, Vandals, Byzantines, Arabs, Turks and local
   dynasties. Mixed circulation of Spanish, Turkish, Italian, Maltese, French and
   native coins.
**18th Century** - Unit of account: Piastre of 52 Aspers or 624 Burbes.
   Specie monies:
         In gold - Sultanine or Sequin (100 Aspers)
         In silver - Nasarra (52 Aspers), Double (24 Aspers)
         In copper - Burbe (1/12 Asper)
**19th Century** - Unit of account: Piastre of 16 Kharubs or 40 Para.
   Specie monies (minted in 1864):
         Gold coins of 100 to 5 Piastres (1 Piastre = 175.5 milligrams

of fine gold: Boumia, Boukhamsin, Boukoufa, Boukhama, Bouachera)
Silver coins of 2 and 1 Piastre (1 Piastre = 2.787 grams of fine silver)
Bronze coins of 1/4 to 1/32 Piastre. 1/16 Piastre called Kharub.
See *Piastre Tunisia.*

**1881** - French Occupation, and introduction of French Franc.

**1891** (July 1st) - Decree of Bey made Franc official monetary unit of Tunisia. Withdrawal of all other specie monies. - See *Franc Tunisia.*

**1958** (November 1st) - Creation of new unit to replace Tunisian Franc. - See *Dinar Tunisia.*

## TURIN

See *Piedmont.*

## TURKESTAN

Circulation of silver Tanga and copper Pul. Minting of gold Tilla. Gradual introduction of Russian monies.

## TURKEY

Before arrival of Turks, see *Greece, Rome* and *Byzantium.*

**12th Century** - In Antioch and Edessa, Crusaders minted bronze Follis.

**13th Century** - Trebizond issued concave silver Aspers and copper coins.

**14th Century** - After arrival of Ottoman Turks, rapid introduction of European monies, particularly gold Venetian Zecchini (Sequins) and silver Spanish Piasters.
In system of accounting of "States of Great Lord", basic unit was Piastre: Juik counted as 2 Beutel, 1,000 Piastres, 12,000 Timmins, 40,000 Paras, 100,000 Minas, or 120,000 Aspers.
Specie monies:
In gold - Sequin, copied from Venetian Zecchino, named Funduk, Sultanine, Altun (Ashrafi), or Sherify (see *Funduk*); Zer-mahbub; Toghrali.
In silver - Piastre or Ghrush; Utuzlik; Onlik; Beshlik; Para or Medino

**1811** - Minting of gold coin of 30,000 Piastres called Beutel.

**1844** - Adoption of Piastre of 40 Paras as monetary unit. - See *Piastre Turkey.*

**1845** - Minting of gold coin of 100 Piastres, called Medjidie, weighing 7.2166 grams 916 2/3 fine, or 6.6152 grams fine gold.

**1881** (January 6th) - Theoretical adoption of gold standard, and creation of new monetary unit. - See *Lira Turkey*.
Issue of silver coin called Medjidie, equal to 20 Piastres (Kurus), and variety of low grade silver coins called Metalliks. - See *Altilik* and *Beshlik*.

## TUSCANY

Monies of Rome (See *Rome*), then Florence (see *Florence*).

**1737** - Grand Duchy of Tuscany passed from Medicis to House of Lorraine-Austria. Four systems of accounting competed in Florence:
Gold system: Scudo d'Oro counted as 7.5 Lire, 20 Soldi d'Oro, 90 Crazie or 240 Denari d'Oro.
Ducat system: Ducato (or Ducatone, Scudo Corrente, or Piastra) counted as 7 Lire, 20 Soldi di Ducato, 84 Crazie or 240 Denari di Lira.
Pezza system: Pezza (or Livornino) counted as 5.75 Lire, 20 Soldi di Pezza, 69 Crazie or 240 Denari di Pezza.
Lira system: Testone (or Doppia Lira) counted as 2 Lire, 3 Paoli (or Giuli), 24 Crazie, 40 Soldi di Lira, 120 Quattrini or 480 Denari di Lira.
Specie monies:
    In gold - Double Doppia, Doppia, Ruspone, Zecchino
    In silver - Francescone (then Leopoldino), Franciscus,
            Ducato (or Piastra), Tallero (or Lanternina),
            Pezza (or Livornino), Quilo
    In silver/copper - Piastrino, Testone, Cavallotto, Lira, Paolo,
            Crazia
    In copper - Soldo, Duetto, Quattrino

**1801** - French Occupation. - See *Franc*.

**1826** - Monetary unit: Lira della Moneta Buona, of 20 Soldi or 240 Denari. However, Tuscany continued to keep accounts in Paoli of 40 Quattrini or 160 Denari.
Specie monies:
    In gold - Leopoldino d'Oro (32,000 Denari), Ruspone (9,600
            Denari), Zecchino (3,200 Denari)
    In silver - Leopoldino or Francescone (1,600 Denari); Fiorino
            (400 Denari), Lira (240 Denari), Paolo (160
            Denari), Crazia (20 Denari), Soldo (12 Denari)
    In copper - Quattrino (4 Denari), Picciolo (1 Denaro)

**1859** - Annexation to Italy. - See *Italy* and *Lira Italy*.

## TUVA

Widespread use of Tug (1935) and Aksa (1936), equal to Ruble. - See *Mongolia*.

## *TWO SICILIES*

Greek monies (see *Greece*), then Roman (see *Rome*).

**6th to 16th Century** - See *Sicily*.

**16th to 19th Century** - Unit of account: Oncia of 2.5 Scudi, 5 Fiorini, 30 Tari, 60 Carlini, 450 Ponti, 600 Grani, or 3,600 Piccioli.

Specie money:

In gold - Oncia

In silver - Scudo di Sicilia, Carlino

Also see *Naples*.

**Until 1860** - Use of Ducato of 100 Grani, 300 Tornesi, or 1,000 Cavalli.

**1860** - After unification, see *Italy* and *Lira Italy*.

## *UBANGI-SHARI*

See *French Equatorial Africa* and *Central African Republic.*

## *UGANDA*

**19th Century** - Arab traders introduced cowrie shells for ivory and slave dealings. Cowrie became an official submultiple of Penny, introduced by Imperial British East Africa Company:

1 Penny = 50 Cowries

**1897** - Use of Rupee minted by Imperial British East Africa Company. - See *Rupee East Africa.*

**1922** (January 1st) - Introduction of East African Shilling, equal to British Shilling. - See *Shilling East Africa.*

**1966** (August 15th) - Uganda Shilling replaced East African Shilling at par. - See *Shilling Uganda.*

**1967** (September 14th) - East African Shilling ceased to be legal tender.

## UKKIA

Silver coin minted in **Morocco** in 19th Century before monetary reform of 1881. Worth ¹/₁₀ Miscal, 4 Muzuna or 24 Falus.

Variations of name - Oukia, Ukie, Ounce.

**After 1881** - Minted in Paris according to new monetary system of Moulay-Hassan: coin of 10 Ukkias called Real Hassani (29.12 grams 909 fine, or 26.47 grams fine gold); coins of 1 and 5 Ukkias, the former 835 fine.

## *UKRAINE*

Predecessors - See *Russia* and *Ruble.*

**1919** - Use of Ruble of 2 Grivenki (Grivennik), 100 Kopeks, or 200 Chagiv.

**1923** - Ruble was called Carbovanez and consisted of 2 Grivenki.

**After 1923** - Return to Russian monetary system.

**1942 to 1944** - Under German Occupation, issue of special money called Carbovanez. - See *Carbovanez.*

**1944** - Return to Russian monetary system.

## UNCIA

In early **Rome,** a bar, usually bronze, representing ¹/₁₂ As and weighing one ounce. Semi-Uncia was of half the weight and value.

## UNICORN

Gold money issued in **Scotland** in 15th Century under James III. Weight: 3.82 grams.

## UNION LATINE

Name given to coins minted as result of monetary agreements, called Latin Monetary Union, or imitating type decreed by these agreements.

**1865** (December 23rd) - Agreement of Paris, composed of France, Belgium, Italy, and Switzerland determining type of their gold coins (100, 50, 20, 10 and 5 Francs 900 fine) and of silver (5 Francs 900 fine with divisionary coins 835 fine).

**1868** (September 26th) - Adherence of Greece.

**1874** (January 31st) - Because of decline in price of silver, agreement limiting minting of coins of 5 Francs 900 fine.

**1878** (November 5th) - Agreement suspending minting of silver coins of 5 Francs (already suspended in Belgium, December 18, 1873; in France, August 5, 1876).

**Until 1914** - Following coins were accepted by government offices in France without limitation as to quantity: French, Belgian, Greek, Italian, and Swiss gold coins; Spanish coins of 10 Pesetas (with effigy of Alphonso XII) and of 20 Pesetas (effigy of Alphonso XIII); Austrian coins of 4 and 8 Guilders; coins of Monaco of 20 and 100 Francs; Russian coins of ¹/₂ Imperial and Imperial struck in 1886 and following years.

**1921** (December 9th) - Agreement stipulating that each member nation would take back its silver coins.

**1925** (December 26th) - Denunciation of Latin Monetary Union by Belgium.

**1926** (December 31st) - Demonetization of gold coins of Union by Switzerland.

**1927** - Exchange of correspondence among France, Italy and Greece for liquidation of Union.

**1948** - Regulation of free gold market in Paris. Dealings in French and Swiss coins of 20 Francs, and coins of Latin Monetary Union of 20 Francs. Included in latter group were coins minted in Austria (8 Guilders, 20 Francs, but not 20 Koronas), Belgium, Bulgaria, Greece, Hungary, Italy, Monaco, Romania, Sardinia, Serbia, Russia (5 Ruble Alexander III and 7.5 Ruble Nicholas II).

## UNITE

Type of Sovereign minted in 1603 by James I to celebrate reunion of **England** and

Scotland. Weight: 10.4 grams 833 fine, or 8.66 grams fine gold. As unit of account, 20 Shillings.

## UNITED ARAB REPUBLIC

See *Egypt* and *Pound Egypt.*

## UNITED KINGDOM

See *England.*

## UNITED STATES

**Before European colonization** - Indian tribes used strands of two kinds of shells called Wampum as money. - See *Wampum.*
On Pacific Coast, monetary use of strings of shells in form of teeth or disks.
On prairies, monetary use of buffalo and bearskins.
**17th Century** - English settlers minted silver tokens worth 1 Shilling, 6 and 3 Pence.
**1652** - Regular mintings of Shillings and Pence. Use of English monies. - See *Pound.*
**1719** - In Louisiana, introduction of banknotes of John Law, then copper coins of 9 Deniers (1721) and playing card money (1735). - See *Canada.*
Depreciation of card money. Partial reimbursement by means of bills of exchange, ordered by Royal Declaration of April 27, 1744.
**1776** - Independence. - See *Dollar.*

## UPPER SENEGAL AND NIGER

See *French Sudan.*

## UPPER VOLTA

**Early history** - See *French Sudan.*
**1947** (September 4th) - Established as separate Colony and member of French West Africa.
- See *French West Africa.*
**1960** (August 5th) - Independent republic. Retained CFA Franc as monetary unit. - See *Franc CFA.*

## *URUGUAY*

**16th to 19th Century** - Circulation of Spanish and Mexican Piasters. - See *Spanish America.*

**1821** - Brazilian Occupation.

**1828** - Independent Uruguay retained Spanish monetary system, Piaster (or Peso) of 8 Reales.

**1854** - Minting in silver of Peso Fuerte (heavy Piaster), or Doubloon, divided into 10 Reales of 100 Reis or Centavos. Continued prevalence of the earlier Piasters or Patagons.

**1840 and 1957** - Minting of copper Centavos.

**1862** (June 23rd) - Creation of Uruguayan Peso, defined in terms of gold. - See *Peso Uruguay.*

## *U.S.S.R.*

Predecessors - See *Russia* and *Ruble.*

**1917** - Soviets inherited Ruble from Russia. Defined in 1897 as 774.234 milligrams of fine gold. Inconvertible since 1914.

**1922** - In full inflation, creation of Chervonets, equal to 10 gold Rubles. - See *Chervonets.*

**1924** - Stabilization of Ruble. - See *Ruble.*

## UTA

Early unit of account used in **Java,** equal to ¹⁄₁₀ Bahar, or 10 Catties, 100 Laxsan, 1,000 Peccoes, 25,000 Tayell, 50,000 Sata, 250,000 Mas, 1 million Cash, or 10 million Candareens.

## UTUZLIK

Silver coin of **Ottoman Empire.** Value: 30 Paras. Weighed about 19.9 grams 583 fine, or 11.6 grams fine silver. Coin of 2 Utuzlik called Altmishlik.

Origin of name - Turkish *utuz* (thirty).

Variations of name - Solota, Iselotta, Slota, Zolota, Zolotah, Otuzlik.

## VACQUETTE

Silver/copper Liard struck by Vicomtes de Béarn in early 15th Century and copied by Henry IV in 1608 for **Navarre.** Bore imprint of two Béarnaise cows.
Origin of name - Little cow (French).
Variation of name - Baquette.

## VARIDIMOVENTY

In **Madagascar,** early native submultiple (1/144) of Ariary. - See *Ariary.*

## VARIFITOVENTY

In **Madagascar,** early native submultiple (1/96) of Ariary. - See *Ariary.*

## *VATICAN*

Predecessors - See *Rome* and *Papal States.*
**1929** (June 7th) - Monetary independence in principle. Creation of Vatican Lira equal to Italian Lira. - See *Lira Vatican.*
Italian money retained legal tender status in Vatican territory. Vatican money accepted as legal tender in Italy.

## VENEZOLANO

Unit of account and monetary unit of **Venezuela** from 1857 to 1887. Divided into 10 Decimos and 100 Centavos or Centimos. Sometimes confused with Bolívar.
Origin of name - From Venezuela.
Predecessor - See *Venezuela.*
**1857** (March 23rd) - Adoption of Venezolano, similar to gold 5 Franc coin:
    1 Venezolano = 1,451.62 milligrams of fine gold
    Venezolano corresponded to silver Peso (22.5 milligrams fine silver), divided into 10 Reales.
**1871** (May 11th) - Monetary law copied after system of Latin Monetary Union: minting of gold Venezolano (1.612 grams 900 fine) and of Venezolano de Plata or Peso (25 grams of silver 900 fine). Other gold coins: Bolívar (20 Venezolanos), Doubloon (10), Escudo (5). Other silver coins: 1/2 Venezolano (50 Centavos), Decimo (10 Centavos), Ventesimo (5 Centavos).
**1880** - Venezolano sometimes called Bolívar, especially after issue of postage stamps. As unit of account, Venezolano sometimes worth 5 Bolívares.
**1887** - Adoption of money defined in gold, equal to Franc. - See *Bolívar.*

## VENEZUELA

**16th to 19th Century** - Circulation of Spanish and Mexican Piasters of silver.

**1810** - Independent Venezuela minted ¼ Real in copper.

**1819-1829** - Part of Greater Colombia retained the Spanish monetary system. - See *Colombia.*

**1821** - In Caracas, Spanish minted copper Cuartinos.

**1830** - After separation from Greater Colombia, Venezuela used old as well as foreign monies indiscriminately. Minting of copper Centavos.

**1857** (March 23rd) - Creation of Venezolano, gold unit worth 1 silver Peso. - See *Venezolano.*

**1871** (May 11th) - Monetary law suggested by system of Latin Monetary Union, with minting of gold coins (Bolívar, Doubloon, Escudo, Venezolano) and silver coins (Peso, Decimo, Ventesimo).

**1887** - Bolívar, defined in gold and equal to Franc, became national money. - See *Bolívar.*

## VENICE

Monies of Rome (see *Rome*), then introduction of Carolingian system of accounting (Livre of 20 Sols or 240 Deniers) which gave rise to Lira. - See *Lira di Piccioli* and *Lira di Grossi.*

**9th Century** - Minting of Carolingian Denier.

**1192** - Minting of silver Grosso. - See *Grosso.*

**1284** - Minting of gold Zecchino, or Ducato. - See *Zecchino.*

**14th Century** - Issue of Soldino and Tornesello.

**15th Century** - Minting of Grossone.

**1462** - First copper money, called Picciolo.

**1472** - First coining of silver Lira and Testone.

**1521** - First minting of Osella.

**1535** - Creation of gold Scudo.

**1561** - Minting of heavier silver coin: Ducato (Ducat), which became Scudo (Ecu) in 1578.
- See *Ducato* and *Scudo.*

**1587** - Systematic issue of bank money by Bank of Venice·which, dating from 12th Century, had already issued certificates of deposits. This paper, freely convertible, carried premium of 9%, then 20%, over specie money. Three suspensions of payments: in 1691, 1719 and 1739.

**18th Century** - Two units of account: Ducato of 24 Grossi or 288 Grossetti; Lira of 20 Soldi or 240 Denari. Ducato worth 6.2 Lire, 24 Grossi, 124 Soldi, 288 Grossetti, or 1,488 Denari. Moreover, Bank of Venice used Lira Grossa worth 10 Ducati or 62 Lire for its records.
Specie monies:

In gold - Double Doppia, Zecchino
In silver - Scudo, Ducaton, Ducato Effettivo
In silver/copper - Osella, Lirazza, Lira
In copper - Soldo, Bagattino

**1806** (March 21st) - Introduction of French monetary system denominated in Lira and Soldo.

**1807** (January 24th) - Legal tender status given in France to all monies of Kingdom of Italy.

**1815** - Cession to Austria. Venetian Lombardy used Fiorino (Guilder) of 100 Soldi (also called Gulden of 100 Kreuzer).

**1866** - Annexation to Italy. - See *Italy* and *Lira Italy.*

## VENTEIN

Early **Spanish** gold coin created June 22, 1742. Equal to ¼ Pistole.
Origin of name - Corruption of Vintem.

## VENTESIMO

Silver coin minted in **Venezuela** according to law of May 11, 1871: 1.25 grams 845 fine. Worth 1/20 Venezolano or 5 Centavos.

## VEREINSMUENZE

**German** silver money from 1838 to 1871.

**1838** (July 30th) - Monetary agreement among Prussia, Bavaria, Saxony, Württemberg, Baden, Hesse. . .to mint common silver coin, called Vereinsmünze (money of agreement), of 33.4 grams. Exchange rate: 2 Thaler or 3.5 Gulden.

**1857** (January 24th) - Germanic Monetary Union among all German states (except Hamburg, Bremen, Lübeck) and Austria. Minting of common silver coin, called Vereinsthaler (Thaler of agreement), equal to Prussian Thaler. Became Thaler of Northern States: 16.7 grams (or 1/2 Vereinsmünze).

**1871-1873** - Elimination of Vereinsmünze with adoption of monetary system based on Mark - See *Mark.*

## VICTORIATUS

**Roman** silver coin, minted first in Illyria. Complemented local Drachma.
Origin of name - Latin *Victoriatus,* from *victoria.* Celebrated victory of 228 B.C. over pirates of Illyria.
Plural - Victoriati.

**End of 3rd Century B.C.** - Appearance of Victoriatus. Soon circulated in Southern Italy and Sicily (and Marseilles). Weight 3.40 grams of silver. Equal to ¾ Denarius or 1 Drachma of Illyria.

**End of 2nd Century B.C.** - Disappearance of Victoriatus, debased to 2.90 grams. Name then applied to Quinarius, or ½ Denarius.

## VIERCHEN

Money of **Prussia** (Teutonic Order) in 14th Century. Equivalent to 4 Pfennig.

Origin of name - Diminutive of *vier* (four).

## VIERLANDER

Silver money issued in the **Netherlands** by Philip the Good (decree of October 21,1433). Rate of exchange: 2 Grooten. Minting of submultiples (½, ¼ and ⅛).

Origin of name - From Flemish *vier* (four) and *land* (country). Money common to 4 States (Flanders, Holland, Brabant, Hainaut).

## VIERLING

Name given to ¼ Pfennig or ¼ Denier in feudal **Germany.**

Origin of name - German *vier* (four).

**After 12th Century** - Issued in Cologne. Circulated through Holy Roman Empire in 13th Century:
$$1 \text{ Vierling } = ½ \text{ Hälbling}$$

## *VIET NAM*

Predecessor - See *Indochina.*

**1949** (March 8th) - Viet Nam recognized as independent associated state within French Union. Currency remained Indochinese Piastre.
$$1 \text{ U.S. Dollar } = 17 \text{ French Francs}$$
$$1 \text{ U.S.Dollar } = 20.59 \text{ Piastres}$$

**1951** (December 31st) - Banknote issue transferred to Institut d'Emission Quadripartite, functioning as Central Bank.

**1953** (May 11th) - Devaluation of Piastre:
$$1 \text{ Piastre } = 10 \text{ French Francs}$$
$$1 \text{ Piastre } = 25.391 \text{ milligrams of fine gold}$$
$$1 \text{ U.S. Dollar } = 35.00 \text{ Piastres}$$

**1954** (July 20th) - Geneva Accord partitioned Indochina. - See also *Cambodia* and

*Laos.* Viet Nam divided into North and South. For North, use of Dong. - See *Piastre Dong Viet* and *Dong.* For South, see *Piastre Viet Nam.*

**1954** (December 29th) - Viet Nam recognized as independent nation.

**1955** (January 1st) - Banque Nationale du Viet Nam (National Bank of Viet Nam) established as Central Bank and note-issuing authority.

**1955** (September 30th to October 31st) - Exchange of banknotes of Banque de l'Indochine and Institut d'Emission Quadripartite for those of Banque Nationale du Viet Nam at par.
Cambodian and Laos currency also ceased to be legal tender.

**1956** (January 1st) - Viet Nam left Franc-Zone.

**1959** (May 21st) - France no longer considered Viet Nam as member of Franc-Zone.

## VINTEM

**I.** - Early silver coin of **Portugal** issued under reign of Emanuel (1495-1521). Corresponded to Real.

**18th Century** - Struck in copper for Portuguese Colonies and valued at 20 Reis. Multiples to 12 Vintems.

**II.** - In **Brazil,** silver money introduced at end of the 17th Century for 20 Reis. Coins of 2 and 4 Vintem, worth 40 and 80 Reis. 16 Vintem made 1 Patacao (Pataca).

## VISLINO

Silver money issued in **Ragusa** in 1725 for 60 Grossetti.

## VLIES

Money of **Netherlands** struck by Philip the Hansome.

Origin of name - From Order of Golden Fleece. Chain of order appears on both sides of coin.

Variation of name - Toison.

**I.** - In fine gold (Toison d'or). Gouden Vlies minted in 1499 in Brabant.

**II.** - In silver (Toison d'Argent). Zilveren Vlies minted in 1496 in Holland and copied in Brabant. Exchange rate: 6 Grooten.

# VRENELI

Name given to **Swiss** gold coin of 20 Francs similar to type of Latin Monetary Union
and Napoléon.

Weight: 6.451 grams 900 fine, or 5.806 grams fine gold.

·Origin of name - Diminutive of Verena, name of young girl pictured on coin.

## WADÓ KAIHO

First money minted in **Japan** in 708 A.D. In form of copper coin patterned after Chinese Tsien, first of twelve ancient Sen (Jin Ni Zene). Initial weight: 7.9 grams. Used for small payments during feudal period. Eventually gave rise to Sen, or Zeni. - See *Sen.*

## *WALLIS AND FUTUNA ISLANDS*

Predecessor - See *New Caledonia.*
**1959** - Separate French territory. Monetary unit CFP Franc. - See *Franc CFP.*

## WAMPUM

Joining together of two sea shells, one white, the other violet. Used as money by Indian tribes in territories which were to become **Canada** and **United States.**
Cut into small cylinders or into spheres and strung together, these shells were valued according to their color.
**17th and 18th Centuries** - Wampum was used for transactions between Indians and settlers. Exchange ratio fixed in certain British Colonies: ½ Crown (or 2 Shillings 6 Pence) = 180 white Wampum = 360 purple Wampum.
Abundance of glass paste imitations of Wampum, manufactured in Europe, ruined their credit worthiness.

## WEN

Early **Chinese** monetary unit equivalent to $1/1,000$ Kuan. Circulated as copper coin (Tsien), or as banknotes (Pao Ch'ao).

## *WEST IRIAN*

Predecessor - See *New Guinea.*
**1963** (May 1st) - Became Province of Indonesia with separate monetary unit. - See *Rupiah Irian Barat.*

## *WESTERN SAMOA*

**1899** - Treaty of Berlin gave Germany authority over area then called German Samoan Islands. Use of German monetary system. - See *Germany.*

**1914** (August 29th) - Occupation by New Zealand military forces. Commercial transactions in New Zealand Pounds.

**1920** (December 17th) - Became New Zealand mandate. Use of Samoan Treasury notes issued under authority of New Zealand Government. Currency denominated in Samoan Pounds. - See *Pound Western Samoa.*

**1962** (January 1st) - Became independent republic. Monetary unit unchanged.

**1967** (July 10th) - Currency decimalization, and adoption of Tala to replace Samoan Pound. - See *Tala.*
Minting of independent coinage to replace New Zealand subsidiary coinage in circulation.

## WINDWARD ISLANDS

Consists of Grenada, St. Vincent, St. Lucia, and Dominica.

**Until 19th Century** - See *British West Indies.*

**19th Century** - Use of Spanish Piasters that were counter-marked and fragmented. British gold, silver, and copper coins began to replace other specie monies.

**Early 20th Century** - U.S. gold coins circulated along with British Sterling as legal tender. Barclay's Bank and Royal Bank of Canada issued banknotes denominated in 5 U.S. Dollars.

**1935** - British West Indies Dollar introduced in form of Trinidad and Tobago government currency notes. - See *Dollar British West Indies.*

**1951** (August 1st) - Unified currency of Currency Board of British Caribbean Territories (Eastern Group) began circulating as legal tender along with Pound Sterling.

**1965** (October 6th) - BWI Dollar replaced by East Caribbean Dollar as monetary unit. - See *Dollar East Caribbean.*

## WITTEN

Money of **North Germany** and **Denmark** from 14th to 18th Century.

Origin of name - Gothic *hweits* (white), from which came German *weiss*, English *white.* Originally designated silver money. - Cf. *Hvid, Albus, Blanc, Blanco.*

**I.** - Silver money of **Pomerania** in 14th Century.

**II.** - Unit of account and copper money of **Prussian Frisia** (Emden) in 18th Century. Worth 1/540 Reichsthaler, 1/200 Gulden, 1/20 Schaap, 1/10 Stuyver. In silver/copper: Oertchen (2.5 Witten), Syffert (5), Schaap (20), Flinderke (30).

**III.** - Unit of account in **Denmark** in 18th Century. - See *Hvid.*

## WON

**I.** - Money of **Korea** from 1905 to 1910 identical to Japanese Yen (750 milligrams of fine gold). Divided into 100 Cheun. Coins of 5, 10, and 20 Won in gold (4.16 grams, 8.3 grams and 16.6 grams 900 fine) were minted, also.

**1910-1945** - Japanese Occupation. Issue of Yen of Bank of Korea (Chosen), linked to Yen. - See *Yen*.

**1945** (August) - Korea divided at 38th parallel into North Korea and South Korea.

**II.** - Money of **North Korea** since August 1945. Divided into 100 Cheun.

Bank of issue - Central Bank of the Democratic People's Republic of North Korea, established in October 1946.

**1945** (August 8th) - Soviet Occupation of territory north of 38th parallel. Return to Won.

**1958** - Won linked to Ruble:
　　　　1 Ruble = 30.00 Won
On cross rate basis:
　　　　1 U.S. Dollar = 120.00 Won

**1959** (February) - Currency reform:
　　　　100 old Won = 1 new Won
　　　　1 Ruble = 0.30 Won
　　　　1 U.S. Dollar = 1.20 Won

**1961** (January 1st) - Soviet monetary reform with creation of hard Ruble:
　　　　1 hard Ruble = 1.34 Won
　　　　1 U.S. Dollar = 1.20 Won

**III.** - Money of **South Korea,** from 1945 to 1953 and from 1962. Divided into 100 Chon (or Mon), 500 Poon or 1,000 Rin.

Bank of issue - Bank of Chosen until June 1950, then Bank of Korea.

Variation of name - Wen.

**1945** (October) - U.S. Occupation:
　　　　1 U.S. Dollar = 15.00 Won
Mixed circulation of U.S. Dollars and Military Scrip.

**1947** (July 15th) - Rate raised:
　　　　1 U.S. Dollar = 50.00 Won

**1948** (October 1st) - Official exchange rate:
　　　　1 U.S. Dollar = 450.00 Won

**1949** (June 14th) - Dual rate established:
　　　　1 U.S. Dollar = 450.00 Won (official rate for government
　　　　　　　　　　transactions)
　　　　1 U.S. Dollar = 900.00 Won (all other transactions)

**1950** (May 1st) - Official exchange rate:
　　　　1 U.S. Dollar = 1,800.00 Won

**1950** (November 1st) - After invasion by North Korea, official exchange rate:
　　　　1 U.S. Dollar = 2,500.00 Won

**1951** (April 1st) - Exchange rate raised:
　　　　1 U.S. Dollar = 6,000.00 Won

**1953** - Prior to monetary reform and issue of new money, Won on black market fell to 30,000 per U.S. Dollar.

**1953** (February 15th) - Issue of new money, with exchange of banknotes. - See *Hwan.*

**1962** (June 10th) - Hwan replaced by Won:
   1 Won = 10 Hwan
All transactions at banking rate composed of:
   1 U.S. Dollar = 125.00 Won (fixed basic rate)
   1 U.S. Dollar =     5.00 Won (certificate rate)
   1 U.S. Dollar = 130.00 Won (banking rate)
Certificate rate could be varied. Certificates themselves no longer issued.
Export subsidies ranged from 5 to 25 Won per U.S. Dollar depending upon category, resulting in de facto multiple rate system.

**1963** (January 1st) - Range of export subsidies widened to 5-60 Won per U.S. Dollar.

**1963** (November 12th) - Aid imports subject to levy of 50 Won per U.S. Dollar.

**1964** (May 3rd) - Simplification of currency structure resulting in fluctuating rate based on Exchange Certificate system. No market for Exchange Certificate developed, and all transactions took place at:
   1 U.S. Dollar = 255.00 Won

**1964** (December 19th) - Range of export subsidies reduced to 3-25 Won per U.S. Dollar.

**1965** (March 22nd) - Exchange Certificate Market created with fluctuating rate not permitted to appreciate beyond 255.00 Won per U.S. Dollar. Export subsidies abolished.

**1965** (July) - Won on black market hit new low of 425.00 per U.S. Dollar.

**1967** (January 30th) - Foreign exchange operations of Bank of Korea taken over by Foreign Exchange Bank of Korea. Name later changed to Korea Exchange Bank.

**1967** (December 31st) - Bank of Korea buying and selling rates:
   1 U.S. Dollar = 274.50/274.90 Won

**1968** (December 31st) - Bank of Korea buying and selling rates:
   1 U.S. Dollar = 281.20/281.70 Won

**1969** (December 31st) - Bank of Korea buying and selling rates:
   1 U.S. Dollar = 304.00/304.90 Won

**1970** (June) - Central Bank announced that in the future, level of exchange rate would depend upon changes in domestic wholesale prices, tantamount to "crawling" devaluation system.

## XERAPHIN

In **Portuguese India** (Goa, Din, Ceilao, Basslin), silver coin dating back to about 1498.

Origin of name - Derived from Arabic Ashrafi.

Variations of name - Serafin, Seraphin, Xerafine, Xerafin, Xarife, Xarafin, Zeraphin, Cherafin.

**16th Century** - Xeraphin valued at 300 Portuguese Reis.

**17th Century** - Xeraphin equal to $1/12$ Santo Thomé or 5 Tangas, 25 Vintems, 375 Bazaruccos.

**18th Century** - Xeraphin referred to as Pardao. - See *Pardao*.

## XIQUIPILI

Axe money of Aztecs of **Mexico.**

Origin of name - Mexican equivalent of the number 8,000.

        20 Cacao Beans = 1 Olotl

        20 Olotl = 1 Zontle

        20 Zontle = 1 Xiquipili

## XU

Submultiple ($1/100$) of Piastre Dong Viet, money of **North Viet Nam.**

## YAP MONEY

Popular name for stone discs used by primitive tribes in **Caroline Islands.** - See *Caroline Islands.*

Origin of name - Used on Yap Island.

Native name - Fei.

## *YEMEN*

Predecessor - See *Arabia.*

**1923** - Minting of silver Thaler copying Maria Theresia Thaler, but with Arabic inscription. Called Imadi or Riyal. - See *Imadi.*
Simultaneous circulation of Indian Rupee. - See *Rupee India.*

**1964** (February) - Creation of Yemen Riyal as monetary unit of Yemen. - See *Riyal Yemen.*

## YEN

Monetary unit of **Japan.** Divided into 100 Sen, 1,000 Rin or 10,000 Mon.

Bank of issue - From 1872 to 1882, by all "National" Banks (numbering 954 in 1883), then by Nippon Ginko (Bank of Japan), transformed into State Bank in 1942. Special banks of issue for Korea and Formosa (Taiwan).

Predecessor - See *Japan.*

**1869** - Minting of first silver Yen: 26.96 grams 900 fine.

**1871** (June) - Monetary reform without elimination of silver Yen. Linking of Yen to gold Dollar:
    1 Yen = 1,504.656 milligrams of fine gold
    1 U.S. Dollar = 1 Yen
Minting of coins of 1 Yen in gold: 1,666 milligrams 900 fine.

**1884** - Adoption of silver standard:
    1 Yen = 25.12 grams of silver
Piece of 1 Yen minted on basis of 26.9 grams 900 fine.

**1897** (October) - Return to gold standard:
    1 Yen = 750 milligrams of fine gold
Minting of gold coins on this basis. Early gold coins had exchange rate double their nominal value.
Progressive increase of monetary gold stock and banknotes issued by Bank of Japan.

**1917** - Embargo on gold shipments. But Yen carried premium over U.S. Dollar (6% in 1918).

**1927** (April) - Financial panic, banking crisis, moratorium of 21 days. Yen was at discount of 9%.

**1930** (January 11th) - Lifting of embargo on gold. Restoration of 1897 parity.

**1931** (December 13th) - Suspension of gold standard. Progressive depreciation of Yen (60% in 1933).

**1932** (July 1st) - Foreign exchange controls.

**1933** - Maintenance of exchange rate in relation to Pound Sterling:
> 1 Yen = 14 Pence

**1934** (April) - Price of gold domestically:
> 1 Yen = 338.9 milligrams of fine gold

**1935** (January) - Price of gold domestically:
> 1 Yen = 322.6 milligrams of fine gold

**1936** (May) - Price of gold domestically:
> 1 Yen = 285.7 milligrams of fine gold

**1937** (July) - New valuation of monetary gold stock of Bank of Japan, acknowledging devaluation of 62%:
> 1 Yen = 285.714 milligrams of fine gold

**1938** (April 30th) - Price of gold domestically:
> 1 Yen = 259 milligrams of fine gold

**1939** (September) - Yen abandoned link to Pound Sterling.

**1939** (October) - Pegging of exchange rate in relation to U.S. Dollar:
> 1 U.S. Dollar = 4.267 Yen

**1941** (June 1st) - Stability in relation to Pound Sterling:
> 1 Yen = 14 Pence

**1941** (December 29th) - Decree rendering Yen independent from British and U.S. currency:
> 1 Yen = 1.705 Reichsmark

**1932-1944** - Expansion of Japanese monetary system in Asia and Pacific (Manchukuo, Mongolia, China, Philippines, Netherlands East Indies. . .) by creation of satellite currency linked to Yen. Rivals of Chinese Dollar (Dollar Hua Hsing, Yuan Nanking). Issue of military Yen. - See *Gumpyo.*

**1945** (August) - American Occupation. Use of foreign exchange prohibited. Military exchange rate:
> 1 U.S. Dollar = 15.00 Yen

**1946** (February) - Yen on black market fell to 875.00 per U.S. Dollar. Subsequent improvement.

**1946** (March 2nd) - After inflation, exchange of all banknotes for new issue (1 for 1). Limited to 100 Yen per person.
Remaining balances deposited in blocked accounts. Closing of foreign exchange markets (March 9th).

**1947** (March 12th) - Military exchange rate raised:
> 1 U.S. Dollar = 50.00 Yen

Accelerated inflation.

**1948** (July 5th) - Military exchange rate raised:
> 1 U.S. Dollar = 270.00 Yen

**1949** (April 25th) - Abolition of military exchange rates. Adoption of basic exchange rate for all transactions:
> 1 U.S. Dollar = 360.00 Yen

**1951** - Various Non-Resident Accounts established. Some were transferable, others blocked, and some difficult to transfer. Among latter were Movie Yen, resulting from receipts from film rentals, creating rate of about 445.00 per U.S. Dollar.

**1953** (May 11th) - Parity registered with International Monetary Fund:
      1 Yen = 2.46853 milligrams of fine gold
      1 U.S. Dollar = 360.00 Yen

## YEN CH'AO

Paper money issued in **China** in 11th and 12th Centuries, representing salt. Administration of Finances issued vouchers to salt vendors certifying that salt was paid for. These vouchers circulated as money, convertible into salt at offices of Administration, or into copper monies (Tsien) at banks. Banknote denominations varied according to whether "cover" was in coarse or fine salt.

**1102** - Salt vouchers continued to circulate even when vendors took delivery of salt.

**1126** - Collapse of system after invasion of Shansi Province.

## YIGIRMLIK

Silver coin in **Turkey** from 17th to 19th Centuries: 9.5 grams in 1691, then 2.65 grams in 1810. Value: 20 Para.

Origin of name - From Turkish *yigirmi* (twenty).

Variation of name - Yarimlik, Yigirmishlik, Yirmilik.

## YIN CH'AO

Paper money in form of banknotes (Ch'ao) of redemption (Yin), issued in **China** in 14th Century.

**1308** - Issue of Yin Ch'ao; exact name was Tche Ta Yin Ch'ao. Small banknotes denominated in weights of silver of 2 Liang (74.6 grams) to 2 Li (0.746 grams).

**About 1315** - Withdrawal of these banknotes.

## YUAN

**Chinese** name for Chinese Dollar, its variations and its derivatives. - See *Dollar China, Gold Yuan, Yuan Manchukuo, Dollar Canton, Dollar North China, Yuan Nanking, Yuan Hua Hsing, Jen Min Pao.*

## YUAN MANCHUKUO

Monetary unit of **Manchukuo** (Manchuria) while occupied by Japanese. Divided into 10 Chiao, 100 Fen, or 1,000 Li.

Bank of issue - Central Bank of Manchukuo created by law on June 11, 1932, nationalized in 1942.

Variation of name - Yan or Dollar Manchukuo.

**1932** (June 11th) - Silver standard, without effective mintings of silver coins:
1 Yuan Manchukuo = 23.91 grams of fine silver
Fluctuations in value of banknotes according to price of silver bullion.

**1934** (October) - **1935** (December 1st) - Rise in price of silver bullion and subsequent Chinese monetary reform (see *Dollar China*). Silver standard abandoned. Institution of foreign exchange controls. Link established with Japanese monetary system:
1 Yuan Manchukuo = 1 Yen = 14 Pence

**1940** (February) - All foreign exchange acquired by Manchukuo surrendered to Japan, which in turn furnished foreign exchange necessary for imports.

**1944** - Return to China. - See *Dollar China*.

## YUAN MONGOLIA

Monetary unit of **Inner Mongolia** from 1936 to 1945.

Variation of name - Yuan Mengku.

**1936** - Creation of Yuan of Central Bank of Inner Mongolia at par with Japanese Yen and Yuan Manchukuo.

**1940** - Theoretically linked to Yuan Manchukuo. In fact, depreciated parallel to Chinese Dollar. Establishment of foreign exchange controls.

**1945** - Return to Chinese sphere of influence. - See *Dollar China*.

## YUAN NANKING

Money issued by Japanese from 1941 to 1945 in occupied **China.**

**1940** - Creation of Central Reserve Bank of China in Nanking.

**1941** (January 6th) - Beginning of note issue to replace banknotes denominated in Chinese Dollars and in Hua Hsing Dollars:
1 Yuan Nanking = 1 Chinese Dollar

**1941** (December) - Following start of war between Japan and United States:
1 Yuan Nanking = 1/4 military Yen (Gumpyo) = 1 Chinese Dollar

**1942** (March 7th) - Exchange rate lowered to:
1 Yuan Nanking = 1/5 military Yen (Gumpyo) = 0.80 Chinese Dollar

**1942** (May 31st) - Withdrawal of Chinese Dollar from certain provinces (including Shanghai) occupied by Japanese. Conversion on basis of:

1 Chinese Dollar = 2 Yuan Nanking

Introduction of Yuan Nanking as only legal money in neighboring provinces.

**1942** (December 1st) - Severe penalties against holders and hoarders of Chinese Dollars in Kiangsu, Chekiang, Anhwei, Shanghai and Nanking.

**1943** (January 25th) - Same measures in Canton.

**1943** (February 14th) - Same measures in Hankow.

**1943** (March) - Consolidation of exchange rates at 0.18 Yen per Yuan, introduced in May 1942. Simultaneous circulation of Gumpyo and Yuan Nanking.

**1944** (April 30th) - Suppression of Gumpyo in zone of Yuan Nanking. Substitution of Yuan Nanking for Dollar North China in province of Hwei Hai.

**1945** - Gradual demonetization of Yuan Nanking. Reintroduction of Chinese Dollar in Shanghai and Nanking.

**1945** (October) - Exchange rate:

1 Chinese Dollar = 200 Yuan Nanking

See *Dollar China.*

## YUAN PAO

Ancient copper money of **China** first issued by T'ang Dynasty. Original submultiple ($1/_{1.000}$) of Kuan. Later, unit of account. Replaced by Wen.

**621** - Initial minting of copper coin weighing 3.8 grams.

**8th Century** - Weight of coin reduced.

**804** - Coin disappeared from circulation. Remained unit of account.

## *YUGOSLAVIA*

Predecessors - See *Ragusa* and *Serbia.*

**1918** - Yugoslavia adopted Serbian monetary unit. - See *Dinar Serbia.*

**1919** - In Fiume, local adoption of Crown (Corona) of 100 Centesimi.

**1921 to 1922** - In Dalmatia, use of Crown (Corona) of 100 Centesimi.

**1941 to 1944** - Division into Serbia and Croatia. - See *Dinar Serbia* and *Kuna.*

**1945** - Reestablishment of unified Yugoslavia. - See *Dinar Yugoslavia.*

## ZAIRE

Monetary unit of **Congo Democratic Repbulic.** Divided into 100 Makuta (singular: Likuta) and 10,000 Sengi.

Origin of name - From early name of Congo River.

Bank of issue - Banque Nationale du Congo (National Bank of Congo).

Predecessor - See *Franc Congo.*

**1967** (July 23rd) - New currency, Zaire, replaced Congo Franc:
      1 Zaire = 1,000 Congo Francs
      1 Zaire = 1,777.34 milligrams of fine gold
      1 Zaire = 2.00 U.S. Dollars

**1970** (December) - Zaire hit low of 1.32 U.S. Dollars on black market.


## *ZAMBIA*

Predecessor - See *Federation of Rhodesia and Nyasaland.*

**1964** (August 7th) - Bank of Zambia established as Central Bank with note-issuing authority.

**1964** (October 24th) - Northern Rhodesia renamed Zambia.

**1964** (November 16th) - Zambia issued own currency. - See *Pound Zambia.*

**1968** (January 16th) - New unit replaced Zambian Pound. - See *Kwacha Zambia.*


## *ZANZIBAR*

**8th to 15th Century -** Use of Arab and Persian specie monies.

**16th and 17th Centuries -** Introduction of Portuguese specie money.

**18th Century -** Reintroduction of Arab monies following expulsion of Portuguese.

**Early 19th Century -** Free trade with India resulted in adoption of British Indian Rupee, sometimes called Rupee of Mombasa, divided into 16 Annas or 192 Pie. - See *Rupee East Africa.* Circulation of British Sovereigns worth 15 Rupees and French Napoléons worth 12 Rupees. Local minting of bronze Pesetas worth about 1/4 Anna.

**1908 -** Government accounts kept in Rupees and Cents. Private accounts kept in Rupees, Annas and Pice.

**1936** (January 1st) - East African Shilling replaced Rupee. - See *Shilling East Africa.*

**1936** (April 6th) - Rupee ceased to be legal tender.

**1964** (October 29th) - Newly formed United Republic of Tanganyika and Zanzibar renamed Tanzania. Monetary unit unchanged. - See *Tanzania.*

# ZECCHINO

Gold money of Venice, then of various Italian states. Also called Ducat (see *Ducato* ).
Origin of name - Italian *Zecca* (mint).
Variations of name - Chechin, Chequin, Chekin, Chickino, Sequin.
Plural - Zecchini.
**I.** - With reappearance of gold in West, minting in **Venice** (1284) of gold Ducat, called Zecchino. Weighed 3.56 grams; equal to Fiorino (Guilder) of Florence.
**1491** - Weight of Zecchino lowered to 3.53 grams.
**1570** - Weight of Zecchino lowered and maintained at 3.49 grams.
Successive exchange rates for Zecchino in Lira and Soldi:

| | | | |
|---|---|---|---|
| 1284 | 2 Lire 8 Soldi | 1520 | 6 Lire 16 Soldi |
| 1324 | 3 Lire 2 Soldi | 1521 | 7 Lire 10 Soldi |
| 1350 | 4 Lire 16 Soldi | 1562 | 8 Lire |
| 1399 | 4 Lire 13 Soldi | 1594 | 10 Lire |
| 1417 | 5 Lire | 1638 | 15 Lire |
| 1429 | 4 Lire 4 Soldi | 1687 | 17 Lire |
| 1443 | 5 Lire 14 Soldi | 1739 | 22 Lire |
| 1472 | 6 Lire 4 Soldi | | |

Double Zecchino (weighing a little less than twice the Zecchino) was called Doppia (Double).
**II** - Gold money of Grand Duchy of **Tuscany,** called Zecchino Gigliato. Contained 3.5 grams of fine gold, as did Fiorino of Florence, its ancestor. Bore imprint of Fiorino.
**18th Century** - Until 1859, exchange rate was 13.33 Lire, 8 Fiorini, 20 Paoli, 800 Quattrini or 3,200 Denari.
Triple gold Zecchino called Ruspone.
**III.** - Gold monies used in various **Italian** states until 19th Century. Type nearly identical with Venetian Zecchino:
In Genoa, exchange rate in 18th Century: 13 Lire 10 Soldi
In Rome, exchange rate: 20.5 Paoli
In Turin (Piedmont-Savoy), exchange rate: 9 Lire 15 Soldi 6 Denari
In Bologna, exchange rate: 10 Lire 5 Soldi
In Trieste, Zecchino (or Ducat) minted by Austria. Exchange rate: 4 Guilders 10 Crazie
In Milan (Lombardy), Zecchino minted by Austria. Exchange rate: 14 Lire 10 Soldi
In Papal States, gold coin (3.4 grams fine) minted during 15th-18th Century. Called Ducat (Ducato di Camera).
In Malta, gold money minted from 16th to 18th Century.
**IV.** - Gold money minted in Venetian domains of **Near East** (Rhodes, Chios). In Rhodes in 14th Century, Zecchino worth 6.66 Bezants, 10 Gigliati, 20 Aspers, 160 Carats or 320 Deniers.

V. - For **Turkey, Egypt** and **Barbary** States, see *Sequin.*

## ZEHNER

I. - Silver money created in 1524 by Charles V (Degree of Essling), as a money of **Holy Roman Empire.** Worth 1/10 Florin (Gulden). Retained in monetary system of 1551, worth 10 Kreuzer.

Origin of name - German *zehn* (ten).

II. - Later applied to any coin representing 1/10 of a standard unit.

- In **Southern Germany** during 16th Century, name referred to 10 Kreuzer.
- In **Austria,** referred to 10 Kreuzer.
- In **Swiss** cantons, referred to 10 Batzen.

## ZEMBI

Former unit of account in **Sierre Leone,** equal to 1/2.000 Macuta.

## ZENI

See *Sen.*

## ZER-MAHBUB

In **Ottoman Empire** and **Egypt,** gold coin in 18th and 19th Centuries.

Origin of name - From Turkish *zer mahbub* (beloved gold).

Variations of name - Zar-Mahbub, Zermaboud, Zermabouck, Zermahbud.

Submultiple - Nisfiah, (1/2 Zer-Mahbub).

**1703 -** First minting: 2.6 grams of gold.

**1769 -** Exchange rate raised to 120 Paras.

**1781 -** Weight lowered from 2.4 to 2.1 grams.

**1835 -** Weight lowered to 1.6 grams.

**1844 -** Last minting.

## ZIAN

Gold money of Kingdom of **Tlemcen,** later of Kingdom of **Algiers,** in 18th Century. Minted in Tlemcen. Value: 100 Aspers.

Variation of name - Dian.

Submultiple - Median (50 Aspers).

# ZIANGI

Silver Rupee of **Mogul** States.

# ZLOTY

Monetary unit of **Poland.** Divided into 100 Grosze.

Origin of name - Polish word meaning gold. Same root as Russian *Zoloto,* German *gold,* Dutch *gulden,* English *gold.* Indo-European *ghel* (shining).

Bank of issue - Bank Polski (Bank of Poland, created January 25, 1924, liquidated in October 1940. Then by Bank Emisyjny w Polsce of Government-General, and in January 1945, by Narodowy Bank Polski (National Bank of Poland).

Predecessors - See *Poland, Florin Zloty, Marka.*

Plural - Zlote.

**1922** (September 26th) - Creation of new Zloty as unit of account.

**1924** (January 11th) - Full powers accorded by Diet to government to establish new monetary system.

**1924** (April 14th) - After collapse of Marka, issue of Zloty:
    1 Zloty = 1,800,000 Marka

**1924** (April 23rd) - Gold definition of Zloty at par with Franc Germinal:
    1 Zloty = 1 Franc Germinal
    1 Zloty = 290.322 milligrams of fine gold
    1 U.S. Dollar = 5.18 Zlote

**1925** - Forced parity. Rapid depreciation (53% by May 1926).

**1927** (October 13th) - Stabilization by Pilsudski, acknowledging devaluation of 41.88%. Convertibility into gold for sums above 20,000 Zlote:
    1 Zloty = 168.792 milligrams of fine gold
    1 U.S. Dollar = 8.91 Zlote

**1933** - Adherence to Gold Bloc.

**1933-1934** - Poland did not align to devaluation of U.S. Dollar.

**1935** - Zloty stabilized at
    1 U.S. Dollar = 5.30 Zlote

**1936** (April 26th) - Forced parity. Foreign exchange controls established.

**1939** (October) - Invasion of Poland. Substitution of new monies for Zloty in annexed territories:
    Zone annexed to Germany: 1 Reichsmark = 2 Zlote
    Zone annexed to Lithuania: 1 Litas = 2 Zlote
    Zone annexed to U.S.S.R.: 1 Ruble = 1 Zloty
In Government-General under German control, maintenance of Zloty on basis of 1 Reichsmark = 2 Zlote.

**1940** (May 20th) - Government-General exchanged at par banknotes of Bank Polski against banknotes of new Bank Emisyjny w Polsce in Cracow, denominated in Zloty and backed by general mortgage on landed properties.

**1941** (September) - In territories annexed by U.S.S.R., later occupied by Germans:

1 Reichsmark = 10.00 Rubles = 2.00 Zlote

**1944** (October) - Lublin Committee created new Zloty.

**1944** (December) - In Poland reoccupied by Russians:
    1 Ruble = 1 Lublin Zloty

**1945** (March) - Elimination of Reichsmark, Ruble and Zloty Cracow.
General reintroduction of Zloty at rate of:
    1 Zloty = 1 Zloty Cracow = 2 Reichsmark

**1945** (September) - Official parity:
    1 U.S. Dollar = 5.30 Zlote
Adoption of system of premiums, raising U.S. Dollar to 100.00 Zlote.

**1946** (April) - New official parity:
    1 U.S. Dollar = 102.00 Zlote

**1947** (July) - For foreign tourists in Poland and for transportation expenses:
    1 U.S. Dollar = 250.00 Zlote

**1948** (January) - Premium of 300.00 Zlote per U.S. Dollar for financial transfers, resulting in rate of:
    1 U.S. Dollar = 402.00 Zlote

**1950** (March) - Poland withdrew from International Monetary Fund, which had never registered parity of Zloty.

**1950** (October 28th) - Alignment to Ruble, and exchange of banknotes:
Banknotes, debts, credits: 100 old Zlote for 1 new Zloty
Salaries, prices, deposits: 100 old Zlote for 3 new Zlote
New definitions:
    1 Zloty = 222.168 milligrams of fine gold
    1 Ruble = 1 Zloty
    1 U.S. Dollar = 4.00 Zlote

**1954-1956** - Zloty on black market deteriorated from 24.00 to 135.00 per U.S. Dollar, premium of 3,275% for Greenback.

**1957** (February 11th) - Partial devaluation establishing Capitalistic tourist and/or support rate:
    1 U.S. Dollar = 24.00 Zlote

**1957** (May 1st) - Zloty devalued against Ruble:
    1 Ruble = 1.50 Zlote

**1958** (January) - Zloty fell to low of 185.00 per U.S. Dollar on black market, discount of 98% from official rate.

**1959** (August) - Zloty improved from previous low, but still at discount of 96%.

**1961** (January 1st) - Soviet monetary reform:
    1 New Ruble = 4.44 Zlote (official)
    1 New Ruble = 14.99 Zlote (Ruble Area noncommercial
             and tourist and/or support rate)
In addition, State Store (PKO) unit existed, redeemable at three times tourist rate (72.00 Zlote) either in banknotes or in imported luxury goods.

**1961** (June) - Zloty recovered in black market to 68.00 per U.S. Dollar, discount of 94%.

**1962** - De facto devaluation, as official rate became practically inoperative. Replaced by tourist variety. Old official rate (1950), now called Valuta Zloty, used only for statistical purposes.

**1963** (April 1st) - Ruble Area monetary realignment:
1 Ruble = 15.31 Zlote (Ruble Area noncommercial and tourist and/or support rate)

**1965** (June) - De facto devaluation. Government travel agency, Orbis, introduced "bonuscupon" valid for Western tourists. Enabled them to change any amount of hard currency, exceeding U.S. $20.00 (later adjusted to U.S. $50.00) or equivalent, at 40.00 Zlote per U.S. Dollar.

**1962-1969 -** Zloty in black market fluctuated between 89.00 and 149.00 per U.S. Dollar. Latter rate resulted in Dollar premium of 521% over tourist rate and 3,625% over inoperative official rate.

**1970** (December) - Zloty in black market dropped to low of 180.00 per U.S. Dollar, premium of 4,400% for Greenback over inoperative official rate.


## ZWANZIGER

Silver money in **Tyrol,** under monetary system of Holy Roman Empire, (decree of July 28, 1551). Value: 20 Berner, or Kreuzer.

Origin of name - German *zwanzig* (twenty).


## ZWEI DRITTEL

Silver coin of various **German** states (Cologne, Prussia, Prussian Frisia, Saxony) equivalent to Gulden or 2/3 Thaler.

Origin of name - German *Zwei* (two), *Drittel* (third).
Fine silver content: 14.8 grams (old Zwei Drittel of Germany), 12.7 grams (Zwei Drittel of Brandenburg, minted from 1689 to 1700), about 13 grams (Zwei Drittel of Brunswick, Hanover, Celle, Lüneburg, Saxony).


## ZWEIER

Divisionary copper money of **Holy Roman Empire.** Defined in 1680 by Diet of Regensburg. Worth 2 Pfennig or 1/2 Kreuzer.

Origin of name - German *Zwei* (two).

# Bibliography

*Annual Report of the Bank of International Settlements.* 40 vols. Basel: Bank of International Settlements, 1931-1970.

*Annual Report of the Director of the Mint: Department of the Treasury,* Document No. 3250. Washington, D.C.: GPO, 1970.

*Annual Report on Exchange Restrictions.* 21 vols. Washington, D.C.: International Monetary Fund, 1950-1970.

*Bankers' Almanac and Year Book 1969-1970.* London: Thomas Skinner and Company, 1970.

Bureau of Foreign and Domestic Commerce, U.S. Department of Commerce. *Handbook of Foreign Currency and Exchange.* Washington, D.C.: GPO, 1930.

Carson, R. A. G. *Coins of the World.* New York: Harper and Row, 1962.

Cavaignac, Eugène. *L'Economie Grecque.* Paris: Plon, 1951.

*Change des Monnaies Etrangères.* Ed. J. F. De Villefaigne. 10th ed. Paris: Change, 1963.

Despaux, Albert. *Les Dévaluations Monétaires dans l'Histoire.* Paris: Rivière, 1936.

*Dictionary of Numismatic Names.* Ed. Albert R. Frey. New York: American Numismatic Society, 1917.

*Dictionary of the World's Currencies and Foreign Exchanges.* Ed. William F. Spalding. London: Sir Isaac Pitman and Sons, Ltd., 1928.

Friedberg, Robert. *Gold Coins of the World.* New York: Coin and Currency Institute, 1958.

Gonnard, René. *Histoire des Doctrines Monétaires dans ses Rapports avec l'Histoire des Monnaies.* Paris: Sirey, 1935.

*International Financial Statistics.* 24 vols. Washington: International Monetary Fund, 1948-1971.

*La Zone Franc.* 13 vols. Paris: Secrétariat du Comité Monétaire de la Zone Franc, 1958-1970.

Lacour-Gayet, Jacques. *Le Commerce Extra-Européen jusqu'aux Temps Modernes: l'Histoire du Commerce,* vol. 3. Paris: Spid, 1953.

Mazard, Jean. *Histoire Monétaire et Numismatique des Colonies et de l'Union Française.* Paris: Emile Bourgey, 1953.

Mertens, Jacques. *La Naissance et le Développement de L'Etalon-Or.* Paris: Presses Universitaires, 1944.

Petrov, Vladimir. *Money and Conquest: Allied Occupation Currencies in World War II.* Baltimore: The Johns Hopkins Press, 1967.

Pick, Albert. *Papiergeld.* Braunschweig: Klinkhardt und Biermann, 1967.

Pick, Franz. *Black Market Yearbooks.* New York: Pick Publishing Corporation, 1951-1955.

*Pick's Currency Yearbook.* Ed. Franz Pick. 15 vols. New York: Pick Publishing Corporation, 1955-1970.

*Pick's World Currency Report.* Ed. Franz Pick. 26 vols. New York: Pick Publishing Corporation, 1945-1970.

Sanner, Pierre. *La Monnaie et le Crédit dans les Territoires d'Outre-Mer.* Paris: Ministère de la France d'Outre-Mer, 1950.

*Statesman's Year-Book.* Ed. S. H. Steinberg, et. al. 106 vols. London: MacMillan and Company, Ltd., 1864-1969.

*Statistical Year-Books of the League of Nations.* Geneva: League of Nations, 1926-1944.

*Survey of African Economics.* 2 vols. Washington: International Monetary Fund. 1968-1969.

Tate, William. *Modern Cambist.* 28th ed. London: Bankers Publishing Company, 1929.

*United Nations Statistical Yearbook.* 21 vols. New York: United Nations, 1949-1969.

Vasanne, Jacques. *L'Argent-Métal.* Paris: Gembloux, 1939.

*Wörterbuch der Münzkunde.* Ed. Friedrich von Schrötter. 2nd ed. Berlin: Walter De Grayter und Company, 1970.

# NOTES